PENSÉES

Translation edited by
Pierre Zoberman, with an introduction
by David Wetsel and notes by David Wetsel
and Pierre Zoberman

Translated by
Pierre Force, John Gallucci, Nicholas Hammond,
Erec Koch, Francis Mariner, Michael Moriarty,
Richard Parish, Richard Scholar,
Paul Scott, David Wetsel

In collaboration with
Peter Bayley, Gary Ferguson,
John D. Lyons

Blaise Pascal

PENSÉES

Mon pere s'est servi de ce corps
Qu'il droit pour son ouvrage
dus ce à circle

portrai de Mr pascal fait par mon pere

THE CATHOLIC UNIVERSITY OF AMERICA PRESS

Washington, D.C.

Originally published as *Blaise Pascal, Pensées opuscules et lettres*
éd. Phillippe Sellier (Paris: Classiques Garnier, 2010).

Translation Copyright © 2022
The Catholic University of America Press
All rights reserved

Cataloging-in-Publication Data is available
from the Library of Congress
ISBN: 978-0-8132-3345-1

CONTENTS

THE LIFE OF MONSIEUR PASCAL
BY HIS SISTER GILBERTE

PENSÉES

THE PROJECT OF JUNE 1658

Contents

Contents

EXCHANGE WITH M. DE SACY ON EPICTETUS AND MONTAIGNE

GENERAL EDITOR'S PREFACE

Translating a text like Pascal's *Pensées* involves a slow process, both intellectual and material. The following pages briefly outline some of the dilemmas that arose throughout the completion of the project and the principles underlying the choices that resulted in the English version published here. Some of these dilemmas and choices are simply a question of formatting. Others involve cultural, linguistic choices, when Pascal's usage (or more generally the period's) differs from our own. In addition there arose the question of which translations to adopt—when such translations existed—for texts from which Pascal quotes. Even though these editorial decisions are mainly concerned with translation issues, such questions are not divorced, as the last paragraph of this preface will explicitly show, from larger, intellectual, philosophical, or ideological problems.[1]

The Text

Philippe Sellier's groundbreaking edition of Pascal's *Pensées*, the first to use the most accurate original manuscript of the text, the so-called "Second Copy,"[2] first appeared in 1976. In 2000, Dr. Wetsel approached his publisher, The Catholic University of America Press, then directed by David McGonagle, and Nicholas Hammond of Cambridge University, with the idea of producing a collaborative English translation of the most recent Sellier edition of the *Pensées*.

To assist in the translation, Wetsel and Hammond (coeditors at the time), recruited a British and American team of Pascal scholars to translate sections of the text falling within their special areas of research: Pierre Force, John Gallucci, Erec Koch, Michael Moriarty, Richard Parish, and Paul Scott. The translation, to be based upon Sellier's then-current edition of the text,[3] would

1. For a discussion of the broader significance of the work itself, see the introduction. Punctual references are given in the following footnotes.

2. For a discussion of the significance of the "Second Copy", see introduction.

3. Blaise Pascal, *Pensées*, ed. Philippe Sellier (Paris: Classiques Garnier, 1999). As will be explained below, the present translation is actually based on the 2010 edition.

include two auxiliary texts: *The Life of Monsieur Pascal* and the *Exchange with Monsieur de Sacy*. Wetsel and Hammond invited Frank Mariner and Richard Scholar to translate these two texts, on which they had long worked.

To assist the translators, the coeditors asked Peter Bayley, Gary Ferguson, John D. Lyons, and myself to serve as "readers" of their initial translations. In 2010, Dr. Wetsel fell ill and Nicholas Hammond was called away from the project by his university. Having been one of the original "readers," I was able to take over as general editor and complete the editorial project, quite unfinished at the departure of the original coeditors. Wetsel later returned to the project to write a new introduction, based on Philippe Sellier's various editions of the *Pensées*, and make a most substantial contribution to the scholarly notes. The completed project was undertaken under the aegis of Dr. Trevor Lipscombe, the present director of The Catholic University of America Press.

Though some time has elapsed since Sellier's edition was first published, and two subsequent translations have already appeared,[4] there is still a need for a new translation that is at once convenient and scholarly. Because this is the only translation of Sellier's edition published with Philippe Sellier's approval, it has benefited from direct input from him. Since his first celebrated edition of the *Pensées* first appeared, Sellier has published a new edition with additional texts by Pascal and more scholarly material, from which this volume has benefited as well.[5] In addition to the *Pensées* proper, this translation includes *The Life of Monsieur Pascal*, by Pascal's sister Gilberte Périer, as well as the *Exchange with M. de Sacy*, which sheds light on Pascal's use of Epictetus and Montaigne, among other points.

While this translation rigorously follows Pascal's original composition of the *Pensées*, it aims to provide an English-speaking audience, not necessarily familiar with either French or Latin, with an easily accessible version of Pascal's *Pensées* in the Sellier edition, the most rigorous and certainly the most apt to provide an idea as to the state of Pascal's project when it was interrupted, and its posthumous evolution.[6] Therefore, this edition translates into English all of Pascal's Latin quotations, except in cases where the text hinges on the specific Latin terms used. Where original terms are kept, our edition offers explanations, when necessary.[7]

---

4. One by Honor Levi (Blaise Pascal, *Pensées and Other Writings* [Oxford: Oxford University Press, 1995]), the other by Roger Ariew (Blaise Pascal, *Pensées* [Indianapolis: Hackett, 2005]).

5. Blaise Pascal, *Pensées, opuscules et lettres*, ed. Philippe Sellier (Paris: Classiques Garnier, 2010). On the significance of Sellier's work, see the introduction of this edition.

6. Though what exactly Pascal's project *was*, and *how* the finished work might have looked are questions with no definitive answers—and this is probably one of the strongest appeals of the text.

7. See, below, the section on the use of italics.

At the same time, the footnotes, inspired by Sellier's original notes,[8] help to put Pascal's fragments in context, especially where theological controversies are concerned. Beyond providing necessary references, these footnotes begin to resolve some of the text's difficulties and provide some totally new insights. Chapter XXI ("The Rabbinical Tradition"), for instance, elucidates, as no other edition in French or in English has ever done before, some of Pascal's allusions and misconceptions about Judaism. Thus, readers receive not only an easily accessible edition of Pascal's text, but also a rigorous up-to-date apparatus of notes on the text.

French Words

Although the aim of this translation was to eliminate passages and words in foreign languages (Latin, but also French), it has been necessary to keep a few words in French, when no equivalent was available or when they were consubstantial with what they referred to. The very title of the work, the *Pensées*, is only one example. Not only is the title emblematic,[9] but it would be difficult to express the nature of the work with any single English word.

In several other cases, the polysemy of a word makes it difficult to find an equivalent. In chapter XIV, fr. 210,[10] for instance, the translation of *libertinage* by *libertinism* would not have been satisfactory. Some terms, though essential to Pascal's arguments, are translated by different English words (*esprit*, rendered by "mind," "intellect," etc.; or *misère*, rendered by "wretchedness," "misery," etc.). Sometimes, finding an English equivalent for a given word would have taken the proportion of a commentary. It is the case, for instance, with *liasse*, which refers to Pascal's dossiers, sometimes described as bundles. Pascal's method for preparing his apology (described in the introduction) entailed sewing together sheets of various sizes and shapes on which were written fragments pertaining to a common topic. Hence the choice to keep "Table-*Liasse*" for the first grouping. For the sake of convenience, however, notes referring to a specific *liasse* take the following format: "See ch. X, p. y or n. z." Titles given by Pascal appear after the chapter number. Those supplied by Philippe Sellier are given in square brackets.

Similarly, some terms referring to the status, character, and behavior of

---

8. The footnotes received direct input from Sellier, through personal conversations with David Wetsel, who acted as footnote editor, and through messages to the general editor.

9. Though, ironically, it is not Pascal's.

10. The abbreviation "fr." stands for "fragment," referring to an individual, numbered fragment of the *Pensées*.

the social elites are so determined by their cultural context that they are not translatable in any useful way. *Honnêteté*, the overall quality of polite society, and *honnête homme* or the collective *honnêtes gens*, the terms used to refer to the members of the elite, have been left in French, in italics.[11]

Other terms, like *finesse*, a kind of subtlety, can occasionally appear. But Pascal's use of *fin* is so ubiquitous in some parts of the *Pensées* that it is necessary to find an equivalent in English, even if some of the nuances are lost. The issue arises with particular acuity in chapter XLII, which opposes two kinds of mind, the geometric mind and the mind characterized by *finesse*. The latter is able to perceive very subtle truths, but without the argumentative acumen proper to the geometric mind—hence the choice of *intuitive* over *subtle*.

The case of chapter V, "*Ennui*," is slightly different, as the word exists in English. The French word covers a range of meanings that go from ennui to psychological torture (as in Racine's *Bérénice*: "*Dans l'Orient désert quel devint mon ennui!*"—in the desolate Orient, how dreadfully I suffered) to a general spleen—all meanings present in Pascal. The English *ennui*, however, seems best fitted to denote the existential *malaise* that results from the contradictions inherent in the human condition as outlined by Pascal.

Italics

French words not translated appear in italics in the text. Aside from their normal uses (when quoting book titles and inserting words in a language other than English), italics are used in several specific ways in the body of the text as well as footnotes, which readers should be aware of from the outset.

Suppressed Passages

As explained in the introduction, the writing of what was supposed to become Pascal's planned apology of the Christian religion was a process that involved a lot of second (or even third and fourth) thoughts. Passages crossed out by Pascal, but still legible on the strips of paper that constituted the *liasses*, are printed in italics between parentheses. It is a convention in nearly all French editions, and this translation accordingly has maintained it.

---

11. The behavior and qualities involved in *honnêteté* are severed from the innate *qualité* that characterized traditional nobility. They evolved as part of the accession of non-aristocratic individuals and groups to the upper echelons, and can be traced, among others, to Castiglione's *Courtesan*. Symptomatically, Nicolas Faret, who wrote the statutes for the French Academy, is also the author of a volume providing guidelines for success when one was not born in the nobility, *L'Honnête Homme, ou l'art de plaire à la cour* [The *Honnête Homme* or the art to please at court (1634)]. When used in the collective, the word *gens* [people] is substituted for *hommes* [men]: an *honnête homme, honnêtes gens*.

Scripture

Pascal quotes extensively from the Bible, from both the Jewish and the Christian canons. Some of the last sections are in fact collections of more or less literal quotations from Isaiah, Jeremiah, the Gospels, Letters, etc. Such passages appear normally in italics in the French original, and, in order to indicate that they are meant by Pascal as quotations (even if he does not always follow the most widespread versions or simply quotes from memory) the translation has been kept in italics.

In addition, italics are used in footnotes, when quoting biblical sources to show which part of the text Pascal quoted, often with variations.

Other Style and Layout Features

Fragments' titles are printed where they appear on the documents in Pascal's hand, which is a specific feature of Sellier's edition. And, so as not to obscure their function as titles, they are centered, even when they were in the margin in the original document (fr. 222) or when their length might be misleading (fr. 615).

The pen lines and blanks of the autograph documents are indicated. The rare passages underlined by Pascal are in small capitals. The punctuation has been updated—Pascal himself used little punctuation and the copyist already supplied much of it.

Texts Quoted by Pascal

Pascal's thought process is constantly predicated upon a discussion with others, most often in the form of a commentary on one or several passages quoted, or sometimes simply alluded to. The method was already present, though with a more ironic, albeit bitter, bent, in the *Provincial Letters*. In the *Pensées* as well as in his polemical contribution to the defense of Port-Royal and those we have come to know as Jansenists, he addresses the Jesuits.[12] There are, however, two main sources for which an edition of reference had to be chosen: on the one hand, as noted above, Pascal makes extensive references to the Bible; on the other hand, he is almost constantly engaged in a controversy with Montaigne, who serves both as support for some of his remarks on the lack of

---

12. See for instance, the various fragments in the last section, "Fragments Not Recorded in the Second Copy" (see the introduction for the significance of the Second Copy), fr. 747, with the opening address, "Reverend Father," directed at Father Annat.

rationality in people's behavior and as the prominent target for rebuttal. Montaigne plays a central role, in particular, in the *Exchange with Monsieur de Sacy*, but the *Essays* are present throughout the *Pensées*, whether explicitly or implicitly. Sellier very usefully adduces the actual passages of Montaigne's *Essays* in the Villey edition.[13] To provide the English-speaking reader with an equivalent access to Montaigne's writings, we used Donald Frame's translation.[14]

Scripture involves a more complex process of choice, with no decision totally satisfactory. Early on in the project, it was agreed to use the Douay-Rheims translation (DR) of the Vulgate, which was the text ordinarily used by Pascal himself. This version is chronologically relevant and was produced in an apologetic perspective. It is germane to Pascal's own choices, and gives a near equivalent of what seventeenth-century translations might feel like to a modern French reader. In Pascal's text, quotations are not always accurate or complete. Sometimes a note will supply what is missing, but when Pascal's text is self-sufficient (for example, when the reference is provided in the text), it is occasionally left as is. In the rare occurrences where another version of the Bible is used (for instance, when Pascal uses a different text), it is clearly indicated. Unless otherwise indicated, the numbering of books will follow the modern usage (even though DR, which is the version of reference, does not follow that order): for instance, the four books of Kings that are two in modern usage and, most notoriously, the numbering of the Psalms. In the "Prophecies" chapters (LIV–LX), Pascal excerpts biblical texts, but from memory, and the translation follows Pascal's reconstruction, not the original DR text. Most importantly, Pascal occasionally uses the Vatable Bible, which he explicitly mentions in chapter XXXI, fr. 437.[15] Vatable's Latin text may differ from the Vulgate, and the translation reflects such variations.[16]

Cultural and Ideological Perspectives

Choosing the Douay-Rheims Bible helps keep some of the flavor of Pascal's original text, as does retaining more arcane denomination such as Pascal's

---

13. Michel de Montaigne, *Les Essais*, Édition Villey-Saulnier (Paris: PUF, 1924; Nouvelle édition, 1965).

14. Michel de Montaigne, *The Complete Works: Essays, Travel Journals, Letters*, trans. Donald M. Frame, introduction by Stuart Hampshire (London: Everyman's Library, 1948). Pascal used the *Essays* as a thesaurus for citations from ancient writers, and though this translation gives many references to the available editions and translations for the original sources, it is not meant to be exhaustive, and in some cases it only indicates the author, title, and, when applicable, section of the work Pascal refers to.

15. On Vatable, see ch. XXXI (Miracles [2]), n. 76.

16. For specific examples, see fr. 653, 697.

word *Pyrrhonians*, rather than *skeptics* (especially since Pyrrhonism is a particular brand of skepticism). More generally, any translation involves making choices, especially with regard to cultural realities and relevance, some of which are more clearly ideological than others. Current trends in translation reflect changes in the way the relationship between the original text and its translation, between source and target language, is apprehended. Way beyond Walter Benjamin's reflections on the tangential relationship between original and translated text, and on the dialectic between freedom of language and faithfulness to the work,[17] greater freedom has been granted the translator; or, rather, ethical imperatives have been emerging, requiring translations in a sense to *correct* ideological biases.[18] The issue arises in Pascal, who ubiquitously delves into the human condition. As was then the practice, he mostly uses *l'homme* or *les hommes* ("man"/"men"), when ostensibly referring to humankind as a whole. Translators in the project were split in their choices, some using the gendered pair "man"/"men", others preferring such gender-neutral or inclusive terms as "humankind" or the plural "human beings", thus reflecting current practices in academia, and in broader contexts. It was indeed tempting to accept the claim to universality for *l'homme/les hommes* at face value. And in fact in some cases, such terms as "humankind" were retained for the final text. Yet, choosing systematically to remove the "mark of gender"[19] would have altered significantly the philosophical and ideological implications of Pascal's writings—even though it might have heightened the cultural relevance of the text by removing usages that have become problematic, at least for some readers, in the society of today. Hence the decision to limit the use of non-gendered translations to cases in which the universal value is unquestionable.[20] Here again, the underlying motive is to keep the translation as close as possible to the cultural context and implications of the *Pensées*. In that respect, the issue of "man"/"men" versus "humankind" is emblematic of the overall outlook at the origin of the final translation as it appears in this volume.

17. See Walter Benjamin, "The Task of the Translator," in *Selected Writings*, vol. 1, *1913–1926*, ed. Marcus Bullock and Michael W. Jennings (Cambridge, Mass.: Harvard University Press, 1996); 253–63, at 262–63.

18. See, for instance, Christopher Larkosh, ed., *Re-engendering Translation: Transcultural Practice, Gender/Sexuality and the Politics of Alterity* (Manchester: St Jerome Publishing, 2011).

19. "The Mark of Gender" is the title of an essay by Monique Wittig, published in *The Straight Mind, and Other Essays* (Boston: Beacon Press, 1992), 76–89.

20. For an analysis of the issue, and of the final choice, see Pierre Zoberman, "'Homme' peut-il vouloir dire 'femme'? Gender and Translation in Seventeenth-Century French Moral Literature," in *The Gender and Queer Politics of Translation: Literary, Historical and Cultural Approaches*, ed. William Spurlin, a special issue of *Comparative Literature Studies* 51, no. 2 (May 2014): 231–52.

ACKNOWLEDGMENTS

This translation has benefited from a generous grant from the Florence Gould Foundation, which helped launch the project. It is here most gratefully acknowledged.

The commitment of The Catholic University of America Press has also been an instrumental factor in the completion of the project. I am most happy to express my heartfelt appreciation to David McGonagle, The Catholic University of America Press's former director, under whose auspices the project was begun, and whose enthusiastic support helped provide the collaborative tools necessary at the inception. My deepest thanks also go to the current director, Trevor Lipscombe, who helped bring it to completion, and I would like to acknowledge the whole editorial team for their work on the volume.

Dominique Descotes (Professor Emeritus at Université Clermont-Auvergne) was extremely helpful in locating illustrations, and Pierre Force (Professor, Columbia University) was always ready to share his knowledge of Pascal's life and work when last-minute queries came up.

I also want to express my gratitude to Gary Ferguson (the Douglas Huntly Gordon Distinguished Professor of French at the University of Virginia) who briefly acted as co-editor, and on whose help and support I could always rely.

Finally, I want to thank my husband, Joseph Shesko, for his invaluable help in editing the manuscript.

Pierre Zoberman

∽

I wish to thank the following:

Professor Philippe Sellier, for his constant encouragement, consultation, new annotations, and many readings of the manuscript

Editions Classiques Garnier

Rabbi Harold Jaye, for his notes in the chapter "The Rabbinical Tradition"

Sorbonne Université

Gonville and Caius College, Cambridge University

St. Catherine's College, Oxford University

Arizona State University

University of Chicago Divinity School

The late Professor Jean Mesnard

Professor Gerard Ferryrolles

The Catholic University of America

Professor Frederic Canovas, Arizona State University

Professor Peter Bayley, Cambridge University

The late Professor Anthony Pugh, University of New Brunswick

National Endowment for the Humanities

Professor Gary Ferguson, University of Virginia

Professor Hugh Berryman

Reverend John Livingstone

St. George's Anglican Church, Paris

Societé des Amis de Port-Royal

Centre des Etudes Blaise Pascal

Society for Early Modern French Studies (formerly, Society for Seventeenth-Century French Studies, UK)

North American Society for Seventeenth-Century French Literature

David Wetsel

INTRODUCTION

David Wetsel[1]

What are Pascal's *Pensées*? Why are they so relatively unknown to the English reader? Why has their meaning eluded so many English readers for nearly three hundred years? Why has the most authentic text not been available in an English translation? Why has the reader unable to read French been offered so little scholarly help?

The *Pensées* take the form of some eight hundred fragments, of which about 80 percent were destined for a work that Pascal never lived to complete. Philippe Sellier has called the unfinished work a kind of defense and illustration of the Catholic vision of the world,[2] inspired by the writings of the early Church Fathers. Sellier, throughout his scholarly writings and everywhere within this edition itself, calls Pascal's great enterprise an "Apology for the Christian Religion." However, he is quick to point out that "Apology" and "*Pensées*" are not synonymous.[3]

Pascal, Philippe Sellier observes, nowhere uses the term "apology," which had a different meaning in the seventeenth century.[4] However, Sellier finds this title "indispensable for designating, within the heart of the *Pensées*" that 80 percent of the texts would with certainty have figured in Pascal's unfinished work.[5] Moreover, he insists that his is the first edition of the *Pensées* completely animated by the idea that the unfinished work would have been an Apology for the Christian Religion.

Sellier does not deny similar observations by his predecessors. When Pascal's fragments were first published, in the "Édition de Port Royal" in 1670,

---

1. Parts of this introduction have appeared in W. D. Wetsel, "Blaise Pascal," chapter 10 in *The History of Western Philosophy of Religion*, ed. Graham Oppy, vol. 3, *Early Modern Philosophy of Religion* (Acumen Publishing, 2009), 127–40.

2. Pascal, *Pensées*, ed. Sellier (2010), 29. Sellier clearly refers to, and parodies, Du Bellay's 1549's *La Défense et illustration de la langue française* [The defense and illustration of the French language], which constituted an important landmark in the claim to greatness and superiority of the Kingdom of France.

3. Pascal, *Pensées*, ed. Sellier (2010), 29.

4. Pascal, *Pensées*, ed. Sellier (2010), 28.

5. Pascal, *Pensées*, ed. Sellier (2010), 29.

Pascal's friends and relatives most certainly realized that he intended to write a defense of Christianity.[6] This perception was conveniently abandoned in the Age of Enlightenment, which, disinterested in or hostile to Pascal's religious perspectives, preferred to see the work as a collection of philosophical "thoughts." Such a reading persisted until the beginning of the twentieth century, when the second great editor of the *Pensées*, Leon Brunschvicg—the first editor to return to the original autograph of the work—would attempt his own arrangement of the fragments to stress Pascal's intention to defend Christianity. In the 1940s, Louis Lafuma, who for the first time used the First Copy,[7] also recognized the apologetic nature of Pascal's work.

However, as Sellier sees it, these editors saw but through a glass darkly, because they did not know what to do with that 20 percent of the fragments that would not have figured in Pascal's apology at all. Sellier rightfully claims that his is the first edition of the *Pensées* that clearly recognizes and works from the premise that 80 percent of its fragments, and perhaps some religious writings not figuring in the text to date,[8] would have been used by Pascal to write an apology for the Christian religion.

If French readers have often found themselves confused by competing views concerning the real nature and composition of the *Pensées*, English readers have found themselves in a far worse situation. They have all too often had trouble gaining a general (and adequate) understanding of the work, because available English translations have too often been based upon corrupt French texts, often mutilated and anthologized by their translators.[9] Furthermore, the complicated genesis and editorial history of the *Pensées* have never been adequately explained to English readers.

Even those generations of readers who grew up on the venerable Krailsheimer Penguin edition of the *Pensées*, based upon a translation of the Lafuma edition, have been denied a text that is completely accurate, because the Lafuma edition itself is based upon the inferior First Copy. Sellier's successive editions are the first to make use of the superior Second Copy of Pascal's original autograph, which was made at the instigation of Pascal's own family.[10]

6. For example, see below, *The Life of Monsieur Pascal*, §40: "And it was this circumstance that prompted the great ambition he had to work at refuting the strongest of the atheists' principal arguments. He had carefully studied them and had employed all of his intellectual capabilities in the search for all the ways to bring them around. This is the task to which he devoted himself entirely; and his final year of work was entirely employed in the compilation of diverse thoughts on this subject."

7. Blaise Pascal, *Œuvres complètes*, ed. Louis Lafuma (Paris: Seuil, 1963).

8. Pascal, *Pensées*, ed. Sellier (2010), 29–30.

9. As in the case of Levi's translation of the Sellier edition. See below, "Why the Present Translation?" and n. 117.

10. See below, the section titled, "A Brief History of Pascal's Text."

Now, for the first time, English readers will be able to read one of the greatest works of French literature, in the Sellier edition, upon which this new translation is based.

A universe in and of themselves, Pascal's *Pensées* have proved an enduring masterpiece since their publication in 1670. These fragments have fascinated the most diverse minds. As an anti-humanist enterprise, they triggered vehement reactions among the *philosophes* of the eighteenth century. Voltaire never ceased trying to marginalize Pascal. Condorcet accused him of depriving man of the courage to become happier. The Enlightenment could never accept Pascal's insistence that a duality of good and evil plagues humankind. Romanticism, by contrast, enthusiastically embraced Pascal as a contemporary. Chateaubriand celebrated his frightening genius. Sainte-Beuve accorded him the lion's share of his masterpiece of nineteenth-century criticism, his monumental *Port-Royal* (1837–67).

Even during the positivist period, Pascal's prestige remained intact. Many writers read him, from Nietzsche to Zola to Baudelaire to Valéry. With the collapse of humanism, undermined by the atrocities of the twentieth century, and the advent of psychoanalysis, the *Pensées* met with renewed interest. Writers like François Mauriac and Julien Green were faithful readers. Existentialism celebrated Pascal as one of its most striking precursors. A modern taste for dense, concise, and fragmentary writing won Pascal new admirers.

A work has rarely reverberated in so many directions. Pascal's texts engage multiple philosophies and works of art. Much has been written on Pascal's engagement with Montaigne's text, and on the connections between Pascal's work and those of Kant, Kierkegaard, and Nietzsche. The *Pensées* constitute perhaps the best introduction to that Augustinian Christianity which so marked Western religious culture for more than a thousand years. For Sellier, the *Pensées* invite a meditation on the self-awareness that constitutes one of the capital definitions of culture. In the field of sociology, Pierre Bourdieu, in his *Méditations pascaliennes* (1997), constructs an anthropological theory of realism derived from Pascal. Charles Taylor repeatedly notes that Pascal was the first thinker to explore human incompleteness and imperfection in terms that remain relevant today. Historians set on tracing the very idea of the self cannot ignore Pascal's acute meditations, which provide a powerful counterbalance to Descartes's more familiar confidence in the possibility of attaining certain knowledge. The modern Continental tradition, with its interest in the key notion of the *subject*, was fascinated by Pascal's influence on Freud's irreverent disciple, Jacques Lacan. His work is also the ultimate source of Althusser's theory of ideology. While fueling much theoretical literary speculation,

Pascal's nearly unprecedented contribution to Christian philosophy has often been neglected and unexplored in the English-speaking world. [11]

Pascal's Life

Blaise Pascal (1623–62) was a towering intellectual figure in seventeenth-century France, perhaps the last of the universal geniuses in European history. His discoveries and ideas still have great influence in the modern intellectual and scientific realms. A true polymath, he made contributions in physics, mathematics, philosophy, and theology. It was he who established experimentally that the weight of the earth's atmosphere varies according to altitude, and he who first gave theoretical embodiment to the idea of the vacuum. His ideas also gave rise to the concept of the calculator or computer and to inexpensive public transportation for the poor.

Pascal was born in Clermont-Ferrand on June 19, 1623, the second of three children. His mother died when he was three years old. As he was a sickly child, his father—an accomplished mathematician and lawyer—decided to educate him at home. When the family moved to Paris in 1631, Etienne Pascal frequented the intellectual circle of Father Mersenne and continued to tutor his son in Latin, Greek, mathematics, and science. After Etienne was named a principal tax collector in Rouen in 1639, Blaise, then sixteen, published a treatise on conic geometry and invented a primitive calculating machine (in 1642).

Pascal had a significant religious experience in 1646, when two disciples of Jean Duvergier de Hauranne, the Abbé de Saint-Cyran, came to care for Pascal's father during an illness. Pascal was "converted" to their Augustinian doctrine of abandonment of the world and submission to God and won over his family. His younger sister Jacqueline would later, over her father's objections, undertake a religious vocation with the nuns at Port-Royal. Pascal's first conversion, however, did not have an immediate effect on his scientific work. One reason was that he became seriously ill in 1647 and returned to Paris, where his physicians advised him to find diversions from his work. In January 1648, Pascal made a spiritual retreat at Port-Royal with the *solitaires* (as they were known because they withdrew from the world to lead a more spiritual life in solitude) in the quasi-monastic community they had established near the convent at Port-Royal-des-Champs.

11. See Nicholas Hammond, ed., *The Cambridge Companion to Pascal* (Cambridge: Cambridge University Press, 2003), which has been the authoritative guide in English to almost every aspect of Pascal's scientific and theological endeavors. Each of the fourteen essays is written by the most eminent English or American specialist on the subject. Hammond's edition is probably the most essential companion when one is reading the *Pensées* and Pascal's other works.

Six years later (and eight years after his conversion of 1646), in 1654, Pascal had a second profound mystical experience. He had become intimately associated with Port-Royal, where his sister had become a nun in 1652 and where Saint-Cyran (1581–1643) had been a spiritual director. And this association no doubt played a role in bringing about the intense religious experience that Pascal records in his *Mémorial* (fr. 742). The experience marked Pascal indelibly for the rest of his life, as is evidenced by the fact that the *Mémorial* was found after his death sewn into the lining of his coat. In 1658, one of the many further retreats that Pascal undertook at Port-Royal led to the *Exchange with M. de Sacy on Epictetus and Montaigne.*[12]

In 1657 he composed his *Provincial Letters*, his contribution to the pamphlet literature in the controversies between the so-called Jansenists and the Jesuits on grace and predestination. The choice of the epistolary genre and the success of the letters thrust a recondite dispute into the non-specialist arena of public opinion by means of a series of installments containing satires on the opponents of the Jansenists. To understand Pascal's *Provincial Letters* requires knowledge of the major contours of the neo-Augustinian doctrine advanced by Port-Royal.[13]

The Jesuits, who found this renewed version of Augustinianism too harsh and its view of salvation too narrow, began to manufacture a kind of caricature of the "Jansenists," a name that the neo-Augustinians rejected. As the slanders spread (for example, that the Jansenists did not believe in transubstantiation), Pascal's associates at Port-Royal asked him to mount an attack on the heretical doctrines of the Jesuits. The polemical campaign he undertook emerged as his *Provincial Letters*. Though they contain theological disputes that are now almost never debated in modern Catholic theology, the *Letters* remain a masterpiece of satire and irony in the French language. Though they were born of a religious polemic, the *Letters* have become a work central to French literature.

Despite the second spiritual experience recorded by the *Mémorial*, and his involvement in religious polemics, Pascal continued to maintain contact with his secular friends and attempted to win them over to Catholic belief. With two of his friends in mind—Antoine Gombauld, known as the Chevalier de Méré (1607–84), and Damien Miton (1618–80)—Pascal undertook writing an apology for the Christian religion. Méré and Miton were leading young intellectuals in Parisian society whose views of life simply ignored or bypassed religion entirely. They were not active atheists but a new type of what in the nineteenth-century would come to be called *agnostics*. Pascal realized that

---

12. See the "Exchange with M. de Sacy on Epictetus and Montaigne," in this volume.
13. On the theological aspects of the controversy, see the section below, "Port-Royal and Jansenism." See also the section, "Predestination."

their indifference was a much greater danger to Christianity than classical skepticism or traditional traditional scholarly disbelief. It was with that kind of indifference in mind that, as preparation for writing his Apology for the Christian Religion (the notes for which have been known as the *Pensées* from the first edition onward), Pascal began to collect an extensive set of notes, which he organized during the last years of his life, a life cut short by a recurrence of the illness that had befallen him in 1647.

Readers who delve into Pascal's life and what has been written about it will find multiple references to Pascal's several "conversions." They should not imagine that Pascal himself was converted from a skeptic to a Christian. From childhood, the apologist was already an ardent believer. Pascal's elder sister Gilberte, in her *Life of Monsieur Pascal* (1684), veers so close to hagiography that the scenes she describes must not always be taken literally.[14] When scholars speak of Pascal's "worldly period," readers should not imagine that Pascal abandoned his religious fervor and became a figure in Parisian society. His foray into gambling, for instance, came from his desire both to test his theory of probability and to observe such agnostics as Miton and Méré.

Pascal's younger sister Jacqueline died in October 1661, adding to his grief over the Sorbonne's condemnation of Jansenius's *Augustinus*, the work that defined the theology of Port-Royal. Pascal alone refused to accept the edict, to which the major theologians and most of the nuns of Port-Royal acquiesced in order to avoid suppression of the monastery. Pressure from his friends to accept the censure only served to agitate Pascal and advance the decline of his health. Remarkably, Pascal's severe illness did not prevent him from helping, in March of the very year of his death (1662), to design and inaugurate a carriage system for the poor from what would become the Place de la Bastille to the Luxembourg Gardens.

Although the last months of Pascal's life were marked by bitter grief and severe illness, his faith, devotion to God, and care for his neighbors only grew more steadfast. Pascal's remarkable mystical experience of 1654, recorded in the *Mémorial* (fr. 913), had deepened his private spirituality. The healing of his niece with a relic of the crown of thorns in 1656 had strengthened his resolve to write an apology.[15] His gradual sale of all his belongings, furniture,

---

14. On *The Life of Monsieur Pascal* as a variant of the *legend* literary genre, see the introduction to *The Life of Monsieur Pascal.*

15. Port-Royal possessed what they believed to be a splinter of the relic of the "Crown of Thorns" imposed on Christ during his Passion (John 19:2). This supposed relic came into the possession of Louis IX, who built the Sainte-Chapelle in Paris (1248) to house it. According to tradition, it had been broken up into smaller relics. Pascal's niece, Marguerite Périer, was believed by those at Port-Royal to have been miraculously cured of a dangerous fistula of the eye by the application of the relic on March 24, 1656. On this episode, see below, *The Life of Monsieur Pascal*, §38.

and books at the end of his life represented a literal response to Jesus' admonition in Mark 10:21,[16] as did his taking in an impoverished family afflicted with smallpox. Even his sister Gilberte thought he had gone too far, and, on June 29, 1662, Pascal, again seriously ill, had to move to his sister Gilberte's house. Having received the last rites, he died two days later on August 19, 1662, at the age of 39. His last words were: "May God never abandon me."[17]

The Intellectual Universe of the *Pensées*

How, asks Philippe Sellier, can we hope to conduct a dialogue concerning human history even with the most cultivated intellectuals of the Classical Age? The literary scholar must turn ethnologist to penetrate the mental universe of writers who date the Creation of the world in the year 4004 BCE and are convinced that they can establish the very day Abel was killed by Cain. Though the contemporaries of Louis XIV were starting to conceive of infinite space, how erroneous remained their notions of time and history! How impossible it is to understand adequately a Pascal or a Bossuet without entering into their essentially biblical understanding of the world and of history! Scripture not only stands at the center of their mental universe; it encloses and limits it.[18] Pascal, while not abandoning science, places theology far higher in the hierarchy of knowledge than scientific truth:

> I find it wise not to inquire too deeply into the opinion of Copernicus, but this /
>
> Everything in life depends on knowing whether the soul is mortal or immortal. (fr. 196)

In late sixteenth-century France, there arose among writers and artists a revived focus on fallen man, which had been only temporarily eclipsed by the Renaissance. Haunted by the inconstancy of the world, this sensibility took as its emblems mythological beings such as Circe and Proteus and the physical world of motion, clouds, and moving waters. Obsessed by death, those artists dwelt upon light versus darkness. While some baroque writers and painters viewed the universe from the perspective of the stability of God, many others

16. "Go, sell whatever thou hast, and give to the poor, and thou shalt have treasure in heaven; and come, follow me."

17. See, below, *The Life of Monsieur Pascal*, §88. For the best concise biography of Pascal in English, see Erec R. Koch, "Blaise Pascal," in *Seventeenth-Century French Writers*, ed. Françoise Jaouën, Dictionary of Literary Biography 268 (Detroit: Gale, 2003), 272–89.

18. Philippe Sellier, *Avant-propos* in David Wetsel, *Pascal and Disbelief: Catechesis and Conversion in the "Pensées"* (Washington, D.C.: The Catholic University of America Press, 1995), xi–xiii.

beheld the cosmic flux and the human psyche with bewilderment and horror. In this impermanence, they perceived the painful absence of God and the inheritance of some primordial human flaw. Pascal was among the last of those writers obsessed with time and life as rivers careening in a silent universe and in impenetrable darkness. Fallen man and original sin regained the preeminence they had held before the Renaissance but with the difference of now being permeated with a desperate skepticism.[19]

The great philosophical schools of antiquity, in renewed form, began once again to express this *tragic* perspective. The Skeptics (or "Pyrrhonians," as Pascal called them) began once again to speculate that the very principles underlying human knowledge were suspect and uncertain. Montaigne had embraced this uncertainty, as would La Mothe Le Vayer. Descartes would postulate the hypothesis of an evil genius who could lead the human mind into irreversible doubt. As contemptuous as Pascal was of the "philosophers," who he thought had returned to idolatry, he had certain esteem for the Skeptics. He would make use of their poisonous remedy of doubt to shock his unbelievers into a realization of the naiveté of their rationalism.

While affirming a universal but insufficient sense of what Wordsworth would call "something far more deeply interfused,"[20] Pascal rejected philosophical proofs of Divinity. The philosophers of antiquity, like their modern counterpart Descartes, had managed to perceive some kind of presence of Divinity in the universe. Yet, because they remained ignorant of the Fall, even these exceptional thinkers arrived only at deism and failed to find the Christian God. Thus, Pascal rejected any kind of philosophical proof of the truth of Christianity:

This is why I will not undertake to prove by reasons drawn from nature either the existence of God, or the Trinity, or the immortality of the soul, or anything of that sort. [...] Without Jesus Christ such knowledge is useless and vain. [...] The God of the Christians is not a God who is merely the author of geometrical truths and the order of the elements. (fr. 690)

"All human beings seek to be happy," Pascal observed in fragment 181. But no one has ever achieved it in this world. Pascal insisted that original sin has totally corrupted the human heart. "Custom is a second nature that destroys the first" (fr. 159). Natural law is inscribed in the human heart. Yet, human fragility resulting from the Fall has engendered the relativity of morality throughout the world.

19. Philippe Sellier, introduction to Pascal, *Pensées*, ed. Sellier (2010), 45–46.
20. Wordsworth, *Tintern Abbey*, 1.88.

This anthropology, which originates with Saint Augustine, was received doctrine prior to the advent of that humanism which Pascal so excoriates. Pascal's stroke of genius was to turn to another human faculty, the heart. For Pascal, the human heart constituted a locus that was immediate, yet at the same time indemonstrable. Imagination and reason could not be more foreign to it. From a theological perspective, the heart is man's only faculty capable of perceiving the infinite and the absolute.[21] Yet the Fall perverted not only the human will but the human heart itself. Now only *amour-propre* (the love of oneself, usually translated as *self-love*) remains in what Pascal sees as the tyranny of the self. Nothing is more foreign to the modern sensibility than Pascal's admonition that the *moi* (the ego, the self) is only worthy of hate and destruction (see fr. 494).

Borrowing Saint Augustine's expression, Pascal qualifies humanity as nothing less than a "mass of perdition." God chooses to extend a free and inscrutable mercy only to a small number of the "elect," who are saved by the unfailing grace of the redemption wrought by Jesus Christ. For Pascal, this Augustinian interpretation of grace, as adumbrated by Jansenius, stands at the very center of the Catholic faith. "Nothing," Pascal insists, "shocks us more harshly than this doctrine" (fr. 164). Yet humanism's attempt to dilute man's corruption serves only to lead him to eternal perdition.[22]

Port-Royal and Jansenism

"In the beginning were the Arnaulds," writes Philippe Sellier;[23] and, indeed, they were. By the end of the sixteenth century, the ancient Cistercian foundation (1204) of Port-Royal had fallen into a worldly decadence. In 1602, at the age of eleven, Angélique Arnaud was elected as abbess. In 1609, inspired by the Council of Trent, she reformed the monastery in an austere manner in conformity with the founding principles of Cistercian spirituality.

In 1626 the sisters, fleeing the unhealthy marshes surrounding Port-Royal-des-Champs, migrated to Paris and settled in the Faubourg St.-Jacques. Re-

21. Sellier, preface to Pascal, *Pensées*, ed. Sellier (2010), 50.

22. Given Pascal's strict adherence to Augustinianism, the modern reader will be relieved to find Pascal parting company with Saint Augustine on a weighty matter. Saint Augustine justified the recourse to force, torture, and constraint should persuasion fail to produce recantation in instances of heresy. His *Letter to Vincent* (*Epistle* 93) had been published in 1573 to justify the Saint Bartholomew's Day Massacre. It was released again in 1686 after the revocation of the Edict of Nantes. Pascal, by contrast, finds violence as a means of conversion "terror rather than religion" (fr. 203). Pascal may well have been the first theologian of early modernity to reject force in religious matters.

23. Philippe Sellier, introduction to Antony McKenna, *Dictionnaire de Port-Royal* (Paris: Honoré Champion, 2004), 15.

nouncing the ancient privileges granted by the popes, the new abbey placed itself under the jurisdiction of the archbishop of Paris. In 1636 the Abbé de Saint-Cyran[24] became the spiritual director of the convent. He gathered around him Antoine Singlin,[25] the two brothers of Mère Angélique—Arnauld d'Andilly and Antoine ("the great") Arnauld,[26]—Le Maistre de Sacy,[27] Pierre Nicole, Claude Lancelot,[28] and others, who, seeking solitude and study, would withdraw to the grounds surrounding Port-Royal-des-Champs.

During the same period when Port-Royal was thus evolving, some of the faculty of the Sorbonne had again advanced the notion of a Gallican Church, a French Church in many ways immune from the interference of the Roman See. The kings of France had long been fervent supporters of this idea. The Jesuits, on the other hand, had taken a fourth vow of obedience to the Holy Father, as per their *Constitutions*. The aims of the Society of Jesus coincided almost perfectly with those of the Council of Trent (1545–63). The Jesuits sought to open the Church onto the world. Many of the reforms of

24. Duvergier de Hauranne was always known as Saint-Cyran, the title of the monastery of which he was the titular but absent abbot.

25. Antoine Singlin (1607–64) was a preeminent preacher at both Port-Royals. He became Pascal's confessor and spiritual director after his "second conversion."

26. Robert d'Andilly Arnaud (c.1589–1674) shocked his worldly friends by abandoning a significant political career in 1648 to join the solitaires at Port-Royal-des-Champs, where he served as horticulturist.

Antoine Arnauld (1612–94), known as the "great Arnauld" because of his immense role in defending Port-Royal, had been a leading intellectual figure in Parisian society before he entered into association with Saint-Cyran and Port-Royal. He retired to Port-Royal the day after he was ordained in 1641. After the controversy over his treatise *De la fréquente communion* [On frequent Communion] (see n. 31, below), he anonymously published his *Apologie de Monsieur Jansenius* [A Defense of M. Jansenius], a manifesto of "Jansenist" theology. From 1644 onwards he became the acknowledged leader of the Augustinians and wrote extensively on their behalf. Pascal sought to justify Arnauld's positions in the first of his *Provincial Letters*. Nonetheless, he was censored and degraded by the Sorbonne and remained in deep retirement until the "Peace of the Church" in 1668. When the Jansenist controversy broke out again in 1679, Arnauld fled to the Netherlands, where he continued to write in favor of Gallicanism and against the Jesuits and the Protestants until his death in 1694.

27. Also written as Lemaistre de Sacy (1613–84). Sacy was a translator and exegete who produced a monumental French Bible that retained its prestige well into the nineteenth century. As recounted in the *Entretien avec M. de Sacy* [Exchange with M. de Sacy], Sacy became the most sought-after spiritual director at Port-Royal. Nicolas Fontaine, the chronicler of the history of Port-Royal, recounts how Sacy ministered to the solitaires. "[His] ordinary practice in his exchanges with people was to tailor his conversation to suit his interlocutor. If he were seeing Monsieur Champaigne, for example, he would talk to him about painting; if he were seeing Monsieur Hamon, he would discuss medicine.... Everything served him as a means of moving straight to God—and of making others move in the same direction." (See below, Nicholas Fontaine, *Exchange with M. de Sacy*, §3).

28. Pierre Nicole (1625–95), theologian and controversialist, often collaborated with Le Grand Arnaud in defending the doctrines advanced by the Augustinians. His later writings often constitute a defense of Catholic doctrine against criticism by the Protestants.

Claude Lancelot (1616–95) taught at the Little Schools and authored many of the texts used there (see below, n. 40). His *Chronologia Sacra*, later appended to the 1702 edition of the Sacy Bible, dates the history of the world according to biblical genealogies.

the Council of Trent and advances by the Jesuits seemed to the Jansenists to contravene the dogmas formulated at the end of the patristic period by Saint Augustine.

Had Saint-Cyran never served as the spiritual director of the nuns at Port-Royal, would the term "Jansenist" (and the name of Pascal himself) ever have come to be associated with that ancient monastery? Saint-Cyran and the Flemish theologian Cornelius Jansen had been fellow students at the University of Louvain in what is now Belgium. Their mutual passion, carried on in a subsequent correspondence over many years, had focused on how the Catholic Church could be restored to the theology of the Church Fathers, particularly that of Saint Augustine. Saint-Cyran and Jansen both viewed the Council of Trent (1545–63) as semi-heretical and the very source of what they thought was the human-centered course of the Counter-Reformation.

At the same time, the Protestant reformers, and in particular Calvin, had so emphasized man's fallen state and the doctrine of predestination that the Society of Jesus (Jesuits) tried to moderate the teachings of Saint Augustine that had inspired the reformers. The Jesuits, the great missionaries to the world outside Europe, could hardly hope to win converts to a religion teaching the salvation of so very few.

Cornelius Jansen (1570–1638)—usually referred to by the Latin form of his name, Jansenius—had undertaken, but never finished before his death, a great treatise on the works of Saint Augustine, particularly those on grace and predestination. Saint Augustine had formulated these ideas to refute the teaching on the salvific value of good works advanced by the monk Pelagius.[29] The neo-Augustinians at Port-Royal, inspired by Jansenius, came to view the Church as in perilous danger of falling once again into Pelagianism.[30] They thought that Pelagianism had been revived by the Jesuits' teachings on grace as exemplified in works of the sixteenth-century Jesuit Molina. The teachings ascribed to Pelagius in the quotation that follows could not have been more

29. Pelagius (c. 411) denied original sin, insisted on the naturalness of concupiscence and ascribed the existence and universality of sin to the bad example of Adam. He regarded the moral strength of man's will and his good works as sufficient in themselves to attain salvation. The value of Christ's redemption was limited mainly to instruction and example. Man retains the ability to conquer sin through good works and to gain eternal life even without the aid of grace. Saint Augustine, in 412, wrote *On Nature and Grace*, in which he violently attacked Pelagius and insisted on the historical origin of original sin, the necessity of infant baptism and the impossibility of a life without sin.

30. See Leszek Kolakowski, *God Owes Us Nothing: A Brief Remark on Pascal's Religion and on the Spirit of Jansenism* (Chicago: University of Chicago Press, 1995), a remarkable analysis and history of Augustinianism and Pelagianism from their inception to the contemporary Catholic Church, which Kolakowski views as semi-Pelagian. He argues that Augustinianism never really penetrated Catholic doctrine and practice in any lasting way.

alien to orthodox Christian doctrine, and in particularly that of Saint Augustine and Jansenius:

Adam's sin harmed only him, not the human race and was never inherited. Children just born are in the same state as Adam before his Fall. The whole human race neither dies through Adam's sin or death, nor rises again through the resurrection of Christ. Even before the advent of Christ there were men who were without sin.[31]

What were the doctrinal and spiritual issues distinguishing Port-Royal, the *Solitaires*, and the larger circle of Jansenist sympathizers from mainstream Catholicism? Why did they provoke such an explosive reaction on the part of the ecclesiastical authorities?

From the reform of the monastery by Mère Angélique in 1609 onwards, the sisters were increasingly held to a rigorous standard of austerity that rejected any kind of pleasure and the world itself. Their spiritual directors, Saint-Cyran and Antoine Singlin, continually preached the harsh teachings found in Saint Augustine's later writings. They insisted that a lack of explicit faith in Jesus Christ excluded the possibility of the salvation of unbaptized infants. It also precluded the rescue from damnation of ancient pre-Christian philosophers like Plato, a hope cherished by humanist theologians since ancient Christian times. Because of their lack of explicit faith in the person of Christ, the great masses of the "pagans" were doomed to perdition. Saint Cyprian of Carthage (258 CE) rigorously held this position, writing: "Outside of the Church, no salvation."

Port-Royal's absolute insistence on Saint Augustine's doctrine of predestination provoked great hostility among the humanists, the ecclesiastical authorities, and the Jesuits. As would Pascal, the Augustinians saw the entire human race, without exception, as a "mass of perdition," condemned to hell. They held that only the inscrutable will of God, transcending his own justice to exercise unfathomable mercy, extended his grace to the elect.

Unfortunately for the Jansenists, the greatest Protestant reformers—Calvin and Luther—had interpreted this doctrine of Saint Augustine in the same way. They too reached the conclusion that God's grace was given only to the elect. Thus, the door was open for the enemies of Port-Royal to accuse the Jansenist theologians of crypto-Protestantism.

In 1639, Saint-Cyran had been arrested by Richelieu's order and cast into

31. Joseph Lataste, "Port-Royal," in vol. 12 of *The Catholic Encyclopedia* (New York: Robert Appleton Company, 1911), http://www.newadvent.org/cathen/12295a.htm. Much of the information in the following paragraphs is gleaned from this article.

prison, from which he was not set free until 1643, just a few months before his death. In 1640, Arnauld's work, *De la fréquente communion* [On Frequent Communion],[32] gave rise to violent controversy. Port-Royal found itself the epicenter of opposition to Catholic humanism. Partisans of this renewed Augustinian teaching turned toward Port-Royal for support. Saint-Cyran's mantle passed to Antoine ("le grand") Arnauld, a theologian at the Sorbonne. Arnauld began to defend the Augustinian revival and specifically the teachings of Jansenius. The Jesuits mocked him by labeling his followers as Jansenists, an appellation they never accepted.

In what for us might seem a highly technical theological quarrel, the faculty of the Sorbonne condemned five specific propositions that were said they found in the *Augustinus*. Arnauld argued that, as a matter of "fact," these propositions that were said to be found in Jansenius's treatise at all. However, Bossuet considered the five propositions to be "the soul of the book." Ultimately, each of the propositions was condemned by the Sorbonne, the French bishops, and two papal bulls.[33]

From that time began the persecution of Port-Royal, which was only exacerbated by Pascal's *Provincial Letters*.[34] Port-Royal refused to subscribe to the formulary drawn up by the Assembly of the Clergy in 1657. The novices were driven out of the abbey, and the confessors expelled. In vain, the Archbishop of Paris, Hardouin de Péréfixe, endeavored to bring the recalcitrants to reason. "They are as pure as angels," said the archbishop, "but proud as demons." The obstinate were finally dispersed and sent to different communities, before being reunited with the non-signing community at Port-Royal-des-Champs. The sisters who had signed the formulary were given the house at Port-Royal in Paris. Henceforth the two convents became independent of, and hostile towards, one another. In 1666, Le Maistre de Sacy was imprisoned in the Bastille.[35]

In September 1668, the Jansenist prelates signed what was called "The Peace of the Church" with the Holy See. But the controversy once again flared

---

32. Arnauld's treatise was satirically labeled "On Infrequent Communion" by his enemies, because it insisted that one might avail oneself of the sacrament only after an extensive preparation of confession, fasting, and intense self-reflection.

33. In 1649, the faculty of theology of Paris had drawn up a list of five propositions summing up five erroneous assertions in the *Augustinus*. On May 31, 1653, Pope Innocent X had condemned those five propositions in his bull, *Cum occasione*. Pope Alexander VII, in his bull *Ad sanctam*, of October 16, 1656, again condemned the five propositions in the meaning and intention of Jansenius.

34. *Les Provinciales ou Les Lettres écrites par Louis de Montalte à un provincial de ses amis et aux RR. PP.* [*Révérends Pères*] *jésuites*, known in English as *The Provincial Letters*. See Robert J. Nelson, *Pascal: Adversary and Advocate* (Cambridge, Mass.: Harvard University Press, 1981), a study of Pascal's polemical role in the Jansenist controversies.

35. On Sacy, see above, n. 26, and, in this translation, *Exchange with M. de Sacy.*

up within a year. In 1679, at the death of Madame de Longueville, a cousin of the king who had protected Port-Royal, Arnauld had to flee to the Netherlands. Louis XIV, who had long hated the so-called Jansenists, resolved to destroy them entirely. In 1704, Port-Royal-des-Champs was suppressed by Pope Clement IX.

In 1709 the last twenty-five nuns were expelled. Finally, in 1711, to blot out all traces of the center of revolt, the buildings of Port-Royal were razed, the site of the chapel turned into a marsh, and the bones of the nuns dating back to the twelfth century dispersed.

However, the writings issued and inspired by Port-Royal remained hugely influential within seventeenth-century French literature. Le Maistre de Sacy's monumental translation of the Bible into French sometimes parallels the magnificence of the Authorized Version in English. Saint-Cyran's and Mère Angélique's *Lettres spirituelles* [Spiritual letters], Arnauld's *De la fréquente communion* [On frequent Communion] and *De la Nécessité de la foi en Jésus-Christ* [The necessity of faith in Jesus Christ] (written in 1642, published in 1701), and Le Nain de Tillemont's ecclesiastical history remain among the great spiritual classics of their time.[36] Two of the greatest writers in all of French literature were intimately connected to Port-Royal: Jean Racine, estranged from and ultimately reunited with the abbey, had been its pupil in the *petites écoles*.[37] Pascal was its most distinguished champion. Among others, Boileau remained united in heart with Port-Royal in his *Épître sur l'amour de Dieu*.[38] Mme. de Sévigné was passionately devoted to Nicole's *Essays*.[39] La Rochefoucauld's pessimism is closely related to the Jansenist emphasis on man's fallen state.

Another great legacy of Port-Royal was the pedagogy developed in the *petites écoles*,[40] which were founded by the "Messieurs" who had settled near Port-Royal-des-Champs (and differed from the Solitaires only insofar as they had not severed their ties with the world as radically). They eschewed the older Scholastic methods. Their principle was that knowledge and learning are not an end in themselves, but a means. The "Messieurs" adopted an openly rationalistic pedagogy. They endeavored to cultivate the intellect and to limit traditional learning by rote. Breaking with the traditions of the Jesuits, who taught in

36. Le Nain de Tillemont, *Mémoires pour servir à l'histoire ecclésiastique des six premiers siècles*, 1693–1712.

37. Racine had been buried at Port-Royal. When the remains of the nuns were dispersed, Racine's widow succeeded in convincing Louis XIV to allow her to inter his remains at Saint-Étienne-du-Mont, where they rest next to those of Blaise Pascal.

38. Epistle on the Love of God, the twelfth of his Epistles, written in 1695.

39. *Essais de morale*, 1671.

40. See the entry "Les Petites Écoles de Port-Royal" in McKenna's *Dictionnaire de Port Royal*, 819–20. See also Nicholas Hammond, *Fragmentary Voices: Memory and Education at Port-Royal* (Tübingen: Gunter Narr, 2004).

Latin, their instruction was in French. Their introduction to ancient Greek, of which they were unrivalled teachers, was almost unprecedented. They discouraged rivalry among the pupils and wrote innovative manuals for teaching: the *Grammar*, edited by Arnauld and Lancelot; the *Logic* of Arnauld and Nicole; the *Jardin des racines grecques* [Garden of Greek roots] of Lancelot.[41]

Pascal's Christ

Jesus Christ is the purpose of everything and the center towards which all things gravitate. He who knows him knows the reason for all things. (fr. 690)

To penetrate to the heart of Pascal's Christocentrism, one can do no better than to consult Pascal himself. For Pascal, Christ is not only the meaning of the Christian religion, he is the meaning and purpose of everything that exists. "Without Jesus Christ, the world would not continue to exist. It would either be destroyed or be like a living hell" (fr. 690).

Most people know deism best from the model of Voltaire's Clockmaker God. "When His Highness [the Sultan] sends a ship to Egypt, is he concerned whether the mice that happen to be aboard are comfortable or not?"[42] Looking at deism is an excellent way of understanding the primordial role of Jesus Christ in Pascal's theology. Deism is not atheism. It is the perception of that magnificent Intelligence who created everything from galaxies to quarks. But subsequently, this Intelligence removed himself from the universe. In a sense, the deist God has become the physical laws he created. Many thought that deism might well be a path to Christianity itself, since its core meaning is a belief in a supreme being. Pascal could not disagree more strenuously.

Pascal believed that Christianity abhors deism almost as much as it does atheism (fr. 690). Voltaire's hidden deist God is certainly not Pascal's. The deists' God absolutely never intervenes, or has never intervened, in his Creation. Should he do so, Voltaire's God would violate the very physical laws he created. He is eminently worthy of the praise, thanksgiving, and worship given him by the subjects of Voltaire's Eldorado in *Candide*. But he can neither answer prayers nor violate his eternal laws by performing miracles.

The Christian God, on the other hand, answers prayers, is the source of miracles, and rescues men from the stain of the Fall in the person of Je-

41. A. Arnauld and Cl. Lancelot, *Grammaire générale et raisonnée* (known as the *Grammaire de Port-Royal*), published in 1660 [The Port-Royal Grammar: General and rational grammar]; A. Arnauld and P. Nicole, *La Logique, ou l'art de penser. Logique de Port-Royal*, published in 1662 [Logic, or the art of thinking, being the Port-Royal logic]; Lancelot, *Le Jardin des racines grecques* (1660).

42. Voltaire, *Candide* (Paris: Larousse, 2002), ch. 30, 186 (translation courtesy of the Editor).

sus Christ. Pascal's Christ reveals himself to the worthy and merciful in the Eucharist, in the Gospels, and in the conversion of sinners. The unique and unprecedented intervention of God in human affairs was his holy Incarnation in Jesus Christ. The Incarnation is, in a sense, Christianity itself. For Pascal, deism blasphemes the Incarnation. It is a doctrine worthy only of the most violent abhorrence on the part of the believing Christian (see fr. 690).

Belief and adoration of God the Father is "useless and vain" without the personal knowledge, worship, and experience of Jesus Christ (fr. 690). He is, as the Greek Orthodox liturgy puts it, "God Himself in human vesture." He has taken on human flesh to live that very suffering human beings endure. He has emptied himself on the cross to save the entire world from the legacy of original sin. It is revealing to compare Pascal's conception of an incarnate God with the deists' objections to the anthropomorphic God of the Old Testament. The *Quatrains of the Deist*, a forbidden manuscript by an unknown author, seems to have been secretly passed from hand to hand among the erudite atheists. Qualifying the Christians as *bigots*, this deist poem condemns the notion of hell as severely as it does the Christian anthropomorphic God:

> 'Tis no less terrible to deny
> A Divinity, than to believe him capable
> Of taking pleasure and finding joy
> In making us suffer unending punishment.[43]

From all accounts, the two afternoons Pascal spent with Descartes in September of 1647 did not go well. In a statement attributed to Pascal by Marguerite Périer, Pascal taxes Descartes with outright deism:

I cannot forgive Descartes: in his whole philosophy he would like to do without God; but he could not prevent himself from allowing Him, with a flick of the finger, to set the world in motion; after that he had no more use for God.[44]

In Descartes's celebrated proof of God's existence, in his third *Meditation*, he seeks to prove the existence of what amounts to a deist God. The proof itself, in Pascal's view, is irrelevant with regard to the Incarnation, Jesus Christ, or the Fall. Pascal, by contrast, repeatedly defines Christianity itself in terms of Christ's reversal of the effects of Adam's sin. His emphasis is essentially Pauline: "The Christian faith serves almost wholly to establish these two things: the corruption of nature and the redemption wrought by Jesus Christ" (fr. 681). "Faith consists entirely of Jesus Christ and Adam" (fr. 258).

---

43. See Wetsel, *Pascal and Disbelief*, 106 (translation by David Wetsel).
44. Lafuma edition of the *Pensées*: Pascal, *Œuvres complètes*, ed. Lafuma, fr. 1001, p. 640.

One of the most beautiful passages invoking Pascal's Christ stands outside the Copies but is included in this translation as fragment 749. At Port-Royal, devotions evoking episodes in the life of Christ were a common spiritual exercise. "The Mystery of Jesus" evokes Jesus' agony in the garden just before his arrest and passion. While the disciples sleep, Jesus anticipates the salvation of the world. He prays to know the will of the Father. For Pascal, the reality of Christ's agony will always be as present as his presence in the Eucharist. "Jesus will be in agony until the end of the world" (fr. 749).

In the *Mémorial*, Pascal evokes Christ as the "God of Abraham, God of Isaac, God of Jacob," as the God of scripture, "not of philosophers and scholars." While experiencing "tears of joy," he confesses that he has renounced, fled, and crucified Jesus. He promises that his only endeavor for the rest of his life will be the renunciation of everything but Jesus Christ. In the *Mémorial*, Pascal anticipates the last words he would ever speak. "May I not be eternally separated from him" (fr. 742).

The *Mémorial* actually allows present-day readers to understand how Pascal's Christocentrism is an integral part of a unified experience of faith. Pascal writes "Fire" on the parchment—Fire: God's revelation of himself in the burning bush (Exodus 3:1–6); the descent of tongues of fire on the apostles at Pentecost in the coming of the Holy Ghost (Acts 2:1–4); the fire from heaven that blinded Paul on the road to Damascus (Acts 9:3–9). Perhaps only in the writings of such great mystics as Saint John of the Cross might we find the sheer power of Pascal's experience of this presence.

The Mystery of the Jewish People

Another key element in Pascal's worldview is his conception of the role of the Jewish people in God's design: for Pascal, the Jews' rejection of Christ and the fact that the Jewish people has endured since the creation of the world mainly serve as unwitting proofs of the truth of Christianity. Though Pascal repeatedly speaks of the Jewish people in the present tense, he seems to know little of post-Exilic Jewish history. Did he know about the many expulsions (and occasional recalls) of the Jews from France in the late Middle Ages? Did he know that Henry II had issued a call for Marrano merchants to settle in his territories in 1550?[45] Had he any idea that by his time there were 50,000 Jews in France, four-fifths of whom were in the eastern and northern provinces of Alsace and Lorraine? In France proper there were colonies of Spanish and Portu-

---

45. *Marrano* was the derogatory term used for the Spanish and Portuguese Jews converted to Christianity by intimidation in Spain after the Alhambra decree (1492) and in Portugal in 1496.

guese Jews in Bordeaux, Bayonne, and Marseilles. They came as Marranos and gradually returned to Judaism, but, many being wealthy, they largely escaped harm.[46] A small number had found their way to Paris, where the well-to-do, so-called Portuguese Jews were tolerated by the police, while the poorer Alsatians or Germans were subjected to periodic expulsions. "In Paris [...] Jews enjoyed no legally recognized status whatever; it was only by sufferance of police bribery that the city's eight hundred Sephardic Jews managed to remain."[47]

We can say with almost complete certainty that Pascal never encountered a single Jewish person, much less a Jewish rabbinical scholar. Nor, excellent Hebrew scholar that he was, did Joseph de Voisin, translator of the Talmudic passages transcribed by Pascal in titled chapter XXI of the *Pensées*. Such consultations would have to await the research of Richard Simon a couple of decades later.[48]

Pascal nowhere indicates that he knows anything about the horrors so long suffered by the Jewish people during the Christian era. He speaks of their reprobation, suffering, and wandering. But he simply passes over in silence the mass exterminations to which the Jewish people had been subjected. Or did he not know about them? He disagrees strongly with Saint Augustine's affirmation of the legitimate use of torture in the matter of the forced conversions of the Donatists.[49] But he fails to acknowledge the many instances over history when violence was used against the Jews and they were forced to conversion.

How do we explain such a gaping lacuna in Pascal's knowledge of the post-Exilic history of the Jews? He does not seem to make much of the virulent anti-Jewish polemics in the writings of the Church Fathers. Nor does he ever really focus on the destruction of the Second Temple in 72 CE. The latter seems odd in light of the tremendous significance that had been attached to the catastrophe in the entire Christian apologetic tradition.

Pascal's sources for the absolutely central role the Jewish people play in the Apology seem to have been limited to the scriptures themselves, to Saint Augustine, and to other apologists like Grotius. His scant references to Josephus suggest that he never read his *History of the Jews* from one end to the other. With regard to the Talmud, he consulted only the thirteenth-century

46. Max Margolis and Alexander Marx, *A History of the Jewish People* (Philadelphia: Jewish Publication Society, 1967), p. 608.

47. Howard M. Sachar, *The Course of Modern Jewish History* (Cleveland: World Publishing, 1958), p. 54.

48. See Jean Steinmann, *Richard Simon et les origines de l'exégèse biblique* (Paris: Desclée de Brouwer, 1959). The first Biblical scholar to advance the Documentary Theory concerning the origin of the Pentateuch, Simon also translated Leon de Modena's *Cérémonies et coutumes qui s'observent aujourd'hui parmi les juifs* [Ceremonies and Customs Observed Today among the Jews] (1674).

49. See n. 21, above. See also fr. 203: "to try to plant [religion] in the mind and heart by force and threats is planting not religion, but terror, *terrorem potius quam religionem* [terror rather than religion].

Dominican Raymond Martin's *Pugio fidei Adversus Mauros et Judæos* in the edition by Joseph de Voisin.[50]

Pascal's reading of the omnipresent role of the Jews in divine history leaves the impression of something curiously personal about it. He appears particularly struck by the historical permanence of the Jewish people. "The encounter with this people astounds me and seems worthy of my attention" (fr. 694). "The Jewish people immediately attract my attention by a number of wonderful and singular qualities apparent in them. [...] This people is not only remarkable by virtue of its antiquity; it is also singular owing to the manner in which it has survived and has continued unbroken" (fr. 691).[51]

As Philippe Sellier sees it, the apologist focuses on what he sees as the three greatest aspects of Israel:

Its historical transcendence. Pascal underlines the antiquity of the Jews, the intransigence of their monotheism, the greatness of their Law, their adherence to their own people, their passage through the worst trials and hardships, their messianic message. Constantly menaced with annihilation, the Jews survived in order to carry with them those sealed Old Testament prophecies in which Christianity is announced. Dispersed throughout the world at their reprobation, the Jews possessed those very prophecies proving the authenticity of both Testaments. However, unlike most Christian thinkers, Pascal does not believe that the conversion of the Jews *en masse* will take place before the end of time.

Its apologetic mission. Inspired by Saint Augustine, Pascal holds that with the exception of that small number of "saints"—the Christians of the Old Law—the Jews were from the beginning abandoned to *self-love*—that historical image of damnation. God chose this "carnal" people with whom to hide His pure Revelation. Erroneously supposing that this revelation spoke of wealth and prosperity, this most covetous and materialistic of all peoples guarded their Scriptures with their very lives. In order to assure that the Jewish people would love and later testify to the historicity of this revelation, God multiplied their victories and pleasures. Thus their true treasure became safer as their hearts became more and more corrupt.

A theological category, the Judaic. Even though Pascal appears to reject the charge of Deicide, he has no soft spot in his heart for this people. Apart from its

---

50. *The Dagger of the Faith against the Muslims and the Jews* (c. 1280). It remained in manuscript form until 1651, when it was edited and published by Joseph de Voisin. Raymond Martin (also known as Ramon Marti) was one of eight Dominican friars chosen in 1250 by his order to make a study of several Oriental languages with the purpose of carrying out missions to Muslims and Jews in Arab-occupied Spain. Martin was widely read in Hebrew literature, quoting not only from Talmudic and Midrashic works, but from Rashi, Abraham ibn Ezra, and Maimonides.

51. Like almost all writers of his time, Pascal assumes that the Jewish people constituted the original population of the world.

saints (Abraham, Moses, David, Isaiah), he sees them as motivated by cupidity and blinded to the truth. If the pagan lives in ignorance of the true God, the Jewish people represent a whole different category of human beings. Had their hearts been fixed on heavenly things, the Jews would have understood that God's promises were "spiritual," not "literal." Throughout the Old Testament, God scattered entirely comprehensible passages announcing that His messages were couched in a hidden, spiritual language, a language which would confound most of them. Failing to understand the true meaning of these texts which they guarded so zealously, the Jews came to be the irreproachable hostile witnesses to the truth of Christianity.[52]

Pascal's Rhetoric of Conversion

How are Pascal's Christocentrism and his views on the role of the Jewish people in God's history made an effective tool? Pascal seems aware of his own rhetorical innovations in the realm of apologetics.[53] "Let it not be said that I have said nothing new: the disposition of the material is new" (fr. 575). His claim was not lost on his sister Gilberte:

He possessed a natural eloquence that gave him the marvelous ability to say precisely what he set out to say; but he added to that rules [...] that he employed so advantageously that he mastered his own style [...], and his discourse achieved the desired effect. [...] As soon as the *Provincial Letters* appeared, it was clear to one and all that he was their author, despite the care he had always taken to conceal this, even from those closest to him.[54]

Voltaire would later complain of Pascal's "despotic and contemptuous tone" in the *Pensées*. Indeed, Pascal's imagination is haunted by a contemptuous vision of human "concupiscence." "The rivers of Babylon flow, and fall, and sweep all away" (fr. 748). "We should think of ourselves as prisoners," Pascal writes to Gilberte, "clinging to the image of a liberator who will tell us how to be free."[55] Pascal regards the human race, observes Philippe Sellier, as "a bes-

52. Sellier, introduction to *Pensées* (2010), p. 63–65.

53. Erec Koch has written the seminal work in English on Pascal's rhetoric from the perspective of a variety of critical approaches. See Koch, *Pascal and Rhetoric: Figural and Persuasive Language in the Scientific Treatises, the "Provinciales," and the "Pensées"* (Charlottesville, Va.: Rookwood Press, 1997). See, as well, Hugh M. Davidson, *The Origins of Certainty: Means and Meanings in Pascal's "Pensées"* (Chicago: University of Chicago Press, 1979).

54. Gilberte Périer, *The Life of Monsieur Pascal*, §37.

55. Blaise and Jacqueline Pascal, Letter to Gilberte Périer, 1 April 1648. In Pascal, *Pensées* ed. Sellier (2010), 658 (translation by David Wetsel).

tiary of ants and worms."[56] "How empty and full of filth is the human heart!" (fr. 171). Yet the potential, unknown to the skeptic, of an ascent of man's soul out of the darkness of the unconscious and toward divine light, brings with it an intuition of the reality of God.

In the dossier "Beginning" (XIII), Pascal contemplates exploiting invective: against the pagan religions, against Islam, and against those delving into physical science at the expense of seeking God. Pascal's vehement attacks never weaken. The Gospel of Saint Matthew, Pascal reflects, teaches us that the Kingdom of God is under attack. "We must resign ourselves to the burden of this struggle for the remainder of our lives [. . .]. Jesus Christ comes to bring a sword, not peace."[57]

Often, however, Pascal modulates his negative rhetoric into genuine sympathy for the seeking unbelievers. In "Beginning," he sets down a different attitude with regard to those who are making at least a tentative effort to seek the truth: "Pity for the atheists who are searching. Are they not unhappy enough as it is?" (fr. 188). Pascal expresses an even greater sympathy for the true seekers. "I can feel only compassion for those who sincerely bemoan their doubt,[58] who regard it as the worst of misfortunes, who spare no effort to escape it, and who seek to make this search their principal and most serious endeavor" (fr. 681). Yet invective remains warranted in the case of those confirmed atheists who think seeking God is a vain enterprise: "Leave the invective for the ones who brag about it" (fr. 188).

In the same section, Pascal organizes a tripartite division of the whole of humanity, which will come to shape the entire Apology:

There are but three types of people: those who serve God, having found him; those who spare no effort to seek him, having failed to find him; those who live without seeking him, having failed to find him. The first are reasonable and happy; the last are insane and unhappy; those in the middle are unhappy and reasonable. (fr. 192)

In what would have been the preface to the Apology, this tripartite division of the whole of humanity is transformed into a duality excluding the hardened unbelievers and envisaging only those who can be qualified as "reasonable":

56. Sellier, preface to Pascal, *Pensées*, ed. Sellier (2010), 71.

57. See Blaise Pascal, "Letter II to Charlotte de Roannez (24 September 1656)," in which Pascal quotes Matthew 11:12 and 10:34. In Pascal, *Œuvres complètes*, ed. Lafuma, 266 (translation by David Wetsel).

58. Pascal's use of the French verb *gémir* ("to groan" or "to moan") with "*dans leur doute*" (literally, "those who sincerely moan in their doubt") recalls the more traditional usage of "*gémir sous*," echoed in the entry for *gémir* in Cotgrave's *A Dictionarie of the French and English Tongues* (London: Adam Islip, 1611): "To grone; sigh, sob, mourne, complaint grieuously, as those opprest, or ouercharged [overcharged]."

those who serve God with all their heart because they know him, and those who search for him with all their heart because they do not know him. (fr. 681)

Pascal then turns the tables on the seeker. He reveals that "the poor in spirit" effectively believe without knowing anything of theology or having ever read the two Testaments:

[These] have a truly holy inner disposition and [...] everything they hear about our religion is in accordance with it. [...] They wish to love only God; they wish to hate only themselves. [...] It is God Himself who inclines them to believe. (frs. 413, 414)

Pascal ends the outline of his chapters with a warning to those who have become seekers. They should not imagine that true conversion means a two-way conversation with God:

True conversion consists in annihilating oneself in the face of that universal Being [...]. It consists in understanding that [...] without a mediator there can be no communication with him. (fr. 410)

What a distance there is from knowing God to loving him. (fr. 409)

In saving the elect, God transcends his own hidden nature in order to reveal himself to those who seek him with all their hearts. Those whose hearts are fixed on temporal things will never penetrate the veil under which God has hidden his revelation. Those who seek God sincerely must, somehow, already have been touched by grace. Otherwise they would not be seeking God. As Christ tells the seeker, in what Sellier calls the "prosopopœia" known as the *Mystery of Jesus*: "You would not be seeking me, if you had not already found me" (fr. 751).[59]

The Preface to the Apology

Most scholars now agree that the first twenty-eight titled *liasses* represent Pascal's tentative outline for his Apology. The first, "Order," contains key fragments indicating the shape of the entire Apology. Fragment 40 outlines the principal parts of the anticipated project:

---

59. For a more extensive overview of Pascal's theology, see Jan Miel, *Pascal and Theology* (Baltimore: Johns Hopkins University Press, 1970).

First part: Wretchedness of man without God.
Second part: Happiness of man with God.

Fragment 45 shows that highly polished fragment 681, long ignored because it does not figure in the Original Collection, is in fact the preface to the entire Apology. Pascal first confronts the skeptics and atheists head on. They argue that they see no evidence of God's hand in human affairs. This raises the "problem of evil." Pascal then informs them that their observation is in perfect accord with Christian doctrine. Scripture teaches that God is indeed a hidden God, a *Deus absconditus*.

Pascal insists that the question whether the human soul is immortal is the enigma that should preoccupy every human being. The skeptics' lack of interest in this question must have a "supernatural cause." Those who neglect the question altogether are "monstrous." They are not even motivated to investigate the question most relevant to their own self-interest:

You do not need to possess a very lofty soul to realize that this life is the source of no true or lasting satisfaction, that all our pleasures are but vanity, that our sufferings are infinite, and that finally death, which threatens us at every moment, will in but a few years infallibly present us with the horrible necessity of being forever either annihilated or unhappy. (fr. 681)

Pascal follows this analysis with a series of portraits of skeptics, hardened unbelievers, and those feigning disbelief. Because of the random nature of seventeenth-century citation marks, many editors and readers have seen Pascal himself expressing a profound skepticism, which in fact belongs to the skeptics whose portraits he is painting. "The eternal silence of these infinite spaces frightens me" (fr. 233) has over and over been read by critics as an expression of Pascal's own fear. In fact, Pascal places it in the mouth of the skeptic.

Those who refuse to undertake a search for God are probably predestined to the damnation they merit. Believers must summon up all the charity required by Christianity in order to pity them. As long as they are still in this world, however, the unbelievers remain capable of receiving the grace that alone can save them. God's will is inscrutable. In the twinkling of an eye, the unbeliever could be enlightened by grace. Likewise, the believer might well fall into the very blindness of the unbelievers (see fr. 681).

The Wager

In the fragment "Order," Pascal makes it clear that the preface was to be immediately followed by the fragment that has come to be called "The Wager."[60] Pascal himself designates it as a "Discourse on the Machine" (fr. 680). It is designed to remove obstacles to belief and to prepare the "machine" to search for God via reason. In the light of Cartesian philosophy, the "machine" is obviously the physical human body. For Pascal, training the body to act as if the mind believed—praying, genuflecting, taking holy water, having masses said—serves to "prepare the machine" so that the passions may be suppressed by bodily humiliation and the obstacles to belief dissolved. The creation of this prelude to faith by the "mechanical" movements of the body is a theory that Pascal links to the Cartesian idea of mechanism (fr. 680).

No discourse in the whole of the *Pensées* is more famous—or more misinterpreted and abused—than this long fragment (fr. 680). Voltaire, in his *Philosophical Letters*, insists that given the gravity of the subject, the notion of winning or losing is "indecent and puerile."[61] This "Discourse on the Machine" has been traditionally and erroneously taken to be Pascal's ultimate argument for the existence of God. It is not. Rather, it is an invitation to practice the Christian life while awaiting the grace that will lead to conversion.

"The Wager" in no way points toward any proof whatsoever of the Christian God. Proofs of his existence can be found only in sacred history and holy tradition. In fragment 702, Pascal insists that no canonical writer ever used nature to prove God's existence. In fragment 690, which sketches the preface to part 2 of the Apology, Pascal reiterates that he will not undertake to prove either the existence of God or the immortality of the soul by natural reason. Not only would such arguments not convince the hardened atheists, but "without Jesus Christ, such knowledge is useless and vain" (fr. 690).

If a man were convinced that numerical proportions were immaterial and eternal truths dependent on a first truth in which they subsist and which we call God, I should not consider that he had made much progress towards salvation.

The God of the Christians is not a God who is merely the author of geomet-

---

60. Helpful discussions of "The Wager" in English include Jeff Jordan, *Pascal's Wager: Pragmatic Arguments and Belief in God* (Oxford: Oxford University Press, 2006); Michael Moriarty, "Pascal: The Wager and Problems of Order," in Hammond and Moriarty, ed., *Evocations of Eloquence*; Anthony Pugh, *The Composition of Pascal's Apologia* (Toronto: University of Toronto Press, 1984); Leszek Kolakowski, *God Owes Us Nothing*.

61. Voltaire, *Lettres philosophiques* [Philosophical letters], Letter 28 ("Sur les pensées de M. Pascal" [On M. Pascal's *Pensées*], remark V (Amsterdam: E. Lucas, 1734), 306.

rical truths and the order of the elements [...]. The God of Christians is a God of love and consolation. He is a God who fills the heart and soul of those he possesses. He is a God who makes them inwardly aware of their wretchedness and of his infinite mercy; who unites himself with them in the depths of their soul; who fills it with humility, with joy, with trust, with love; who renders them incapable of any other end but him. (fr. 690)

The wager that God exists entails only two possible consequences: (1) being wrong but never knowing it because consciousness is annihilated by death; or (2) being right and having the possibility of an eternity of life and happiness. Pascal omits a third possibility: being right but ultimately being sentenced to hell.

Pascal then turns to the consequences in this life for those who wager on God's existence. They will be "loyal, virtuous, humble, grateful, kind, [friends] sincere and true" (fr. 680). Repressing carnal passions will remove the "obstacles to belief" that make one act mechanically, as does an animal. By training oneself to adopt reflexes of religious significance, one opens oneself to the possibility of receiving God's grace.

The reader might assume that Pascal's text appears straightforward in the Original Collection. But the pages on which the text appears are very nearly indecipherable, even by those few scholars who can read Pascal's handwriting. Fragments are partly written from top to bottom, with many lines and passages struck through. Other fragments appear in the margins, with many lines and crosses indicating where they were to be inserted. Parts of the discourse are written at the top of pages turned upside down. Moreover, Pascal's handwriting (often blurred by ink smears) makes the "Wager" perhaps the most difficult fragment in the *Pensées* to transcribe.[62] Indeed, it will never be possible to establish a definitive text of this renowned discourse.

Anthropology and Theology: The Enigma of the Human Condition

When Philippe Sellier took up the Second Copy, he found that, with the exception of the preface and the "Discourse on the Machine," the first set of titled chapters follows the schema found in the chapter "Order." Chapters I–X present the enigma of the fallen condition of humanity from an almost entirely anthropological perspective. Chapters XV–XXIII, on the other hand, serve

---

62. For an idea of what the autograph notes look like, the reader should look at the plates in ch. XLV, "Discourse on the machine," fr. 680, n. 2.

to document the reason behind human corruption and demonstrate how it has been vanquished through Christ's redeeming sacrifice.

Bossuet could not understand why the visible activity of providence could not be perceived by unbelievers. Pascal's perspective is strictly Augustinian:

One understands nothing of the works of God unless one takes as a first principle that his *intention* was to blind some and enlighten others. (fr. 264, emphasis added)

How is it possible to write an apology inviting conversion within the framework of the severe Augustinian doctrine of predestination? Why attempt to convert those who seem predestined to damnation? Pascal's answer is that the initiative leading to conversion is God's alone. If God does not grant the unbeliever a passion for truth, any presentation of proofs will be futile. Arguments will be heard without interest or even mocked. On the other hand, if someone expresses an interest in finding God, it is because God has granted it. As soon as the apologist meets a person aware of his condition and passionate about truth, he issues him an invitation to subject himself to the possibility of grace.

Pascal's sister Gilberte was fond of saying that when he conferred with "atheists," her brother never began by preaching theology or scripture. If they were sincere in the pursuit of truth, Pascal commenced by starting to build up his case that the human condition amounts to a disastrous enigma. In the "anthropological" chapters, Pascal rarely mentions theology or religion. Rather, he draws from the skepticism of Montaigne to provoke ever-increasing doubt on the part of the unbeliever that the tragedy of the human condition can ever be explained by philosophy, nature, or human experience. Pascal's mentor at Port-Royal, Le Maistre de Sacy, is profoundly shocked, in the *Exchange with M. de Sacy*, by Pascal's plan to make use of Montaigne's dangerous skepticism. Only once he learns how Montaigne will figure in Pascal's apologetic itinerary does he describe Pascal as an extremely gifted physician who knows how to manipulate fatal poisons in order to effect miraculous cures.[63]

The essential source of Pascal's anthropological analysis is, of course, Saint Augustine. The "anthropological" chapters reach their climax in the chapter, "The Sovereign Good" (XI). Without exception, human beings fail, and have always failed, in their attempt to attain happiness. Only the Christian doctrine of the Fall can explain why happiness has always eluded humankind:

What, then, do this avidity and this impotence cry out to us, but that there once was in man true happiness, of which there now remains only an empty mark and

---

63. See the *Exchange with M. de Sacy*, §54.

trace, [...] [an] infinite abyss [that] can be filled only by something infinite and immutable, that is to say by God himself? (fr. 181)

Having transited from knowledge of humanity to that of God in chapters XV–XVI, Pascal turns to Islam as the perfect example of a false religion. In the next chapter, he urges the unbelievers to at least *wish* that Christianity were true. God is in an unfathomable way hidden from the seeker. But he has left signs in sacred history for those who truly seek him. The seeker must learn how to unlock holy scripture.

All of the arguments build toward an ultimate and decisive argument. The fulfillment of the Old Testament prophecies in the New Testament validates the whole of holy scripture as historically true. The Fall and the redemption are the only true keys to the enigma of the human condition. Only they can point the way to how the human dilemma may be transcended.

The last two hundred years of biblical scholarship have voided many of Pascal's exegetical arguments. Together with the fact that these chapters are far less complete and far more enigmatic than the "anthropological" chapters, readers and scholars alike have tended to ignore them.

However, Pascal's diagnosis of a flawed human condition is no less chilling and powerful for modern readers than it was for those of Pascal's own time. Even the theory of the Fall outlined in the chapter "A.P.R." is an impressive metaphor. But the thesis of evolution has rendered the Fall impossible to interpret literally. It never occurred to Pascal—or any other Christian thinker of the Classical period—that the Fall could possibly be anything other than historical fact. Rescuing original sin from historicity has largely been ignored by modern theologians. Only a few such as Ricœur and Tillich have even entertained the question.[64]

No scientist in the Classical period ever even suspected that the world was far older than the six thousand years calculated from the scriptural genealogies. The deep abyss of time escaped the intuition of everyone. The model Pascal so carefully follows is that of Saint Paul and the writers of the four Gospels, amended and hallowed by fifteen hundred years of Christian exegesis and commentary. If anything, Pascal follows the more stringent exegetes at Port-Royal, who were returning to the Hebrew and Greek texts. Both as traditional exegesis formulated in an exceptional literary form and as a revelation of Pascal's mode of thought, these exegetical chapters are vital to understanding the Apology as a whole.

---

64. See Henri Blocher, *Original Sin: Illuminating the Riddle* (Grand Rapids, Mich.: Eerdmans, 1999).

Pascal's Exegetical Proofs

The first eighteen *liasses* of the Apology, while unceasingly calling the unbeliever to wake up to conscious lucidity, multiply allusions to the Christian revelation. Proceeding by repetition, and by what Philippe Sellier calls ever-increasing "incantations," Pascal has striven to persuade his interlocutor that Christianity is a powerful and deep synthesis, a vision of the world that deserves his respect. The unbeliever must at least admit that Christianity is "venerable" because it perfectly describes man and his dilemma. Pascal affirms, without yet proving, the transcendence of Christian revelation. By this point, the apologist has made the unbeliever, as anticipated in the itinerary filed in "Order" (fr. 46), at least *wish* that Christianity were true. Only then, by appealing to the proofs found in scripture, can he "show that it *is* true" (fr. 46). Hence his call to exegesis of the text of scripture.

Unlike modern biblical scholars, who stress the historicity of Jesus, Pascal depicts a Christ who remains hidden in his Incarnation and in his "secret" resurrection (fr. 339). Christ remained hidden in the person of Jesus of Nazareth, as he continues to be hidden in the Gospels, the poor, and the Blessed Sacrament of the Altar. Yet, for those who had the eyes to see him, he was "humble, patient, holy, holy, holy to God,[65] terrifying to demons, and without any sin. With what great pomp and in what prodigious magnificence he came to the eyes of the heart, which perceive wisdom!" (fr. 339).

No chapter in the entire *Pensées* requires a greater expertise in that scriptural exegesis Pascal inherited from the ancient Christian tradition than the *liasse* "Prophecies" (XXV). It is replete with notes that refer to lengthy passages in the book of Daniel. Pascal sketches the argument in which the ninth book of Daniel predicts almost the very year of Christ's death on the cross:

> The prophets, having given various signs that were all to come to pass at the coming of the Messiah, all these signs had to appear at the same time. Thus the fourth kingdom would have to come when Daniel's seventy weeks ended and the scepter had to be removed from Judah. (fr. 371)

Pascal's nearly impenetrable argument is clearly elucidated in Le Maistre de Sacy's preface to his monumental translation of the Bible into French. Sacy first explains that the "four monarchies" spoken of in the Book of Daniel are those of the Chaldeans, the Persians, the Greeks, and the Romans. The "weeks" alluded to by the prophecy are "weeks of years as in Leviticus." Sacy

---

65. "Holy, holy, holy," the three-fold "Sanctus" of the Roman Mass.

therefore multiplies seven times seventy to arrive at the number "490." He then subtracts four years, since Daniel 9:12 specifies that the Messiah will be put to death "in the middle of this last week."

Following the dictates of traditional exegesis, Sacy explains that Daniel 9 must be interpreted as requiring that the number "486" be added to the date "when the order went out for the rebuilding of Jerusalem" after the Babylonian captivity. Consulting his colleague Claude Lancelot's *Holy Chronology*, Sacy finds that Artaxerxes issued this edict in the "Year of the World" 3,547, that is, 3,547 years after the Creation. Adding "486" to "3,547," Sacy arrives at the "Year of the World" 4,033. Taking 4,000 as the traditional date of Christ's birth, Sacy concludes that Daniel 9:24–27 predicts that the Messiah would be put to death in the year 33 CE.[66]

The duality of meaning in the ancient scriptures—literal and figurative— was perceived only by the "saints" of the Old Testament. This dual sense of the Old Testament represents one of God's most profound mysteries. Pascal sees the prophecies of the First Dispensation, fulfilled in the New Testament, as the ultimate proof of the truth of Christianity.

As the unique author of the Pentateuch, "Moses was the first to teach the Trinity,[67] original sin, the Messiah" (fr. 346). The prophets exercise their divine authority by the prediction of "literal figures." These accomplished prophecies, such as the date and the manner of the arrival of the Messiah, represent an "enduring miracle" for those who have the eyes to recognize it. The prophecies constitute "the greatest proof of Jesus Christ" (fr. 368). The Old Testament predicts the end of the pagan religions. That monotheism to which Plato was only able to convert a few intellectuals remained in the possession of the Jews alone until the advent of Christ:

The rich abandon their wealth. Sons and daughters abandon the luxury of their parents' houses for the austerity of the desert [...]. No heathen had worshipped the God of the Jews. At the time foretold [...] the temples [of the heathen] are destroyed, and even kings submit to the cross.[68] (fr. 370)

The second half of the chapters organized in 1658 have the ultimate aim of proving the Fall. However, proving the historicity of the Fall means first demonstrating the authenticity of Genesis. Hence the "Proofs of Moses"

66. See David Wetsel, "Pascal and Holy Writ" in Hammond, ed., *The Cambridge Companion to Pascal*, 178–80.

67. See the visit of the Three Strangers to Abraham (Gn 18:2).

68. This is a reference to the first cenobites who established themselves in the deserts of Egypt at the beginning of the third century CE. Pascal moves the Church at the conversion of the Emperor Constantine and the first monastic establishments back to apostolic times.

(XXIII). Because of the longevity of the Patriarchs, Moses was only four generations removed from Adam:

Shem, who saw Lamech, who saw Adam, also saw Jacob, who saw those who saw Moses. Therefore the Flood and the Creation are true. This evidence is conclusive among certain people who understand the matter properly. (fr. 327)

Not even a generation later, Richard Simon would anticipate the fundamentals of the Documentary Theory concerning the Pentateuch in his *Histoire critique du Vieux Testament* [Critical history of the Old Testament] (1678). The treatise was immediately placed on the Roman Index. Only in 1948 would the Pontifical Biblical Commission authorize Catholic scholars to make use of that Documentary Theory, confirmed by Wellhausen's (1844–1918) later discovery that the two accounts of the Creation represent two narrative traditions—the "Yahwistic" (Genesis 2:4) and the "Priestly" (Genesis 1).

Pascal's use of a biblical exegesis as old as Christianity itself stands light-years away from modern biblical criticism. Yet Pascal's literal understanding of Genesis was shared by every scholar of his time. All orthodox exegetes believed that the scriptural canon was closed with the death of the last apostle. They held that even things in the Bible that are literally false remain sublimely true spiritually. And they considered scripture's anthropomorphic description of God but a consequence of the limitations of human language.

Pascal admits that scripture appears to contain much that is obscure and incomprehensible. But the Bible also contains things of striking clarity and prophecies that were manifestly fulfilled. He held that the ancient exegetical tradition of assigning sacred and spiritual meanings even to those obscurities was completely justified (fr. 251).

None but a few erudite atheists suspected that the Bible's account of the Fall was at best mythical. For the more radical, but unknown, author of *The Three Impostors*, Moses, like Jesus and Mohammed, had only the intent of seducing men into political submission.[69] From Voltaire to Marx, it would take quite some time for this view to gain popularity.

The Contours of Disbelief

Given his apologetic itinerary, it is surprising that Pascal uses the word "atheist" only five times in the course of the *Pensées*.

---

69. See Wetsel, *Pascal and Disbelief*, 89.

Atheists should be perfectly clear in what they say. Now, it is not perfectly clear that the soul is but matter. (fr. 193)

The *atheists'* objection.
"But we have no light." (fr. 277)

Atheists. What reason have they to say that one cannot rise from the dead? (fr. 444)

Atheism or *deism*, two things that the Christian religion abhors almost equally. (fr. 690)

Jean Mesnard has never ceased to remind us that Pascal intentionally excludes the names of notorious erudite atheists and their theories from his Apology in order to trivialize them. Pascal refuses to be distracted by the philosophical tenets of their scholarly disbelief. The atheists would only listen and attempt to debunk those philosophical and rational proofs that in fact play no role at all in his Apology. Pascal's sister Gilberte Périer speaks of his desire to refute the principles and the strongest reasoning of the atheists. "He had carefully studied them and had employed all of his intellectual capabilities in the search for all the ways to bring them around. This is the task to which he devoted himself entirely; and his final year of work was entirely employed in the compilation of diverse thoughts on this subject."[70]

Nowhere in the *Pensées* do we find Pascal refuting the "principles and the strongest reasoning" of the atheists. Why, then, if Pascal purposely avoids refuting the principles and arguments of the atheists, should we take a brief look at these principles and those who espoused them?

Pascal's project takes place in a larger cultural universe whose contours we must explore. Those who seek must have at least heard of the arguments advanced by the professional atheists. In the preface, Pascal's last portrait of the unbelievers presents those who only "feign" disbelief. Their arguments have, without a doubt, been derived from conversations with (and perhaps the writings of) the hardened atheists. However, those who only "feign" disbelief present a perfectly ridiculous façade:

---

70. See *The Life of M. Pascal* in this translation, §40. For a recent, extended discussion of the figure of the *libertin* in the *Pensées*, see Antony McKenna, *Pascal et son libertin*, Littérature, libertinage et spiritualité 6 (Paris: Classiques Garnier, 2017). In view of the following paragraphs, it is important to note that McKenna argues that Pintard (and Mesnard, who follows him) was mistaken and that Pascal's arguments aim to refute Gassendist unbelief: he seeks to argue from the same empiricist premises as the "libertins érudits" such as Gassendi (and Molière).

However, experience has shown me so great a number of such men that it would be surprising, if we did not know that the majority of them [....] are people who have *heard* that the worldly manners of polite society require them to display such extravagance. They call it "throwing off the yoke." (fr. 681; emphasis added)[71]

What exactly do those people repeat? They proclaim that the soul is only a puff of "wind or smoke." They assert that God never watches over human affairs. But the hardened atheists laugh at them and with great satire assert that such talk would convert *them* to Christianity (fr. 681).[72]

Pascal cites the name of a single notorious atheist: Des Barreaux. A flamboyant libertine, former lover of Théophile de Viau, and a notorious seducer of Parisian youth, Des Barreaux had written that our senses are all extinguished the moment we die and that we must recognize that we are but "brute beasts."[73]

How could Des Barreaux profess such blasphemy when the penalties were so severe? A lackey uttering the slightest blasphemy could have his tongue cut. But atheists among the nobility escaped punishment. "The real atheists," René Pintard reminds us, "continued to sound their spurs on the paving stones of the Place Royale."[74] Those Pascal pictures as feigning atheism probably had not spent much time reading such erudite disbelievers as La Mothe Le Vayer (1588–1672) or Gabriel Naudé (1600–1653).[75] These scholars had to be far more cautious because they set their theories down on paper. Their books were published under pseudonyms, with false dates and places of publication.

But what of Montaigne, who occupies a very strategic position in the *Pensées*? He is evoked by name only about fifteen times in the *Pensées*, but Pascal's text is replete with citations, references and echoes of his *Essays*. Though Montaigne might be viewed as a believing, though not fervent, Catholic, Pascal foregrounds and makes use of Montaigne's skepticism in the first part of the Apology to deride reason. But he is horrified by Montaigne's rejection of any significant interest in the fate of the soul and his "pagan" and nonchalant

---

71. Matthew 11:30: "My yoke is easy and my burden light."

72. See fr. 662: *You will convert me.* This is obviously a note set down in preparation for the writing of the preface. It sounds like part of a repartee Pascal may have overheard.

73. Cited by G. Couton, ed., *L'Édition de Port-Royal* (Saint-Étienne: Université de la région Rhône-Alpes, 1971), introduction, 18.

74. René Pintard, *Le Libertinage érudit dans la première moitié du XVIIe siècle* [Scholarly disbelief in the first half of the 17th century] (Geneva: Slatkin Reprints, 1983), 24–26.

75. See Wetsel, "La Mothe Le Vayer," in Jaouën, ed., *Seventeenth-Century French Writers*, 220–26. For an extensive account of the theories of La Mothe Le Vayer and Gabriel Naude, see Wetsel, *Pascal and Disbelief*, 66–81; see pages 182–86 for discussions of Pascal's vision of *honnêteté* and such figures of the *honnête hommes* as Miton and Méré, discussed below and other aspects of Pascal's attitude toward atheism and the atheists.

attitude toward death. He is particularly revolted by Montaigne's "foolish project in painting himself" (fr. 644).

Montaigne's *Essays* constituted the Bible of those "men of the world" (literally "honest men" or "decent people"—*honnêtes gens*)[76] like Miton and Méré, whom Pascal is trying to rescue from skepticism. Pascal is trying to urge them to join the "seekers." These men of the world do not understand that man's ego is the most vicious product of the Fall:

The self is hateful. You, Miton, cover it up, but that does not mean that you remove it. [...] I hate the self [...] because it makes itself the center of all things, I will always hate it. (fr. 494)

What more alien concept to modern thought than the notion of extinguishing the self and one's individuality in the hope of experiencing the will of God and the Beatific Vision? We seek to rehabilitate the ego. Pascal insists that it must be destroyed.

Predestination

At the core of Pascal's critique lies a staunch endorsement of the Augustinian view of predestination. How are modern Christians to understand the principle that God intends to damn certain people, regardless of their good works, pure lives, and total devotion to him? Or, how can we conceive of how God can extend his grace to the most heinous of sinners? Yet, Pascal makes our acceptance of the doctrine of predestination an absolute prerequisite for us to accede to his Apology:

One understands nothing of the works of God unless one takes as a first principle that his intention was to blind some and enlighten others. (fr. 264)

Pascal admits that God's actions are completely inscrutable and even seemingly horrifying to any purely human sense of morality. "What is more contrary to the rules of our miserable justice than damning for all eternity a child, incapable of will, for a sin in which he seems to have had so little part that it was committed six thousand years before he existed" (fr. 164).

Yet only the Fall, "this most incomprehensible of all mysteries," can account for the present human condition. Had the whole of Creation not fallen with Adam, we should have never known suffering, evil, or even death. "*The knot of our condition takes its twists and turns in this abyss, so that man is more in-*

---

76. On the *honnête homme*, see the section on "French Words" in the editor's preface.

conceivable without this mystery than this mystery is inconceivable to man" (fr. 164, emphasis added).

When Pascal looks into the human heart his reaction is far more than simply pessimistic. "How empty and full of filth is the human heart" (fr. 171). When Pascal imagines his own interior, Sellier reminds us, he represents it as a shadowy space whose bottom is a swamp of filth, where sprouts a network of deeply rooted and grotesque vegetation. Such is the hideous *depth of man* (fr. 244), an abyss of concupiscence (fr. 751). Whereas Saint Augustine had encountered God in the depths of his own soul, Pascal insists upon hatred of self.[77]

The long history of the doctrine of predestination is far too complicated to address here. But because Jansenius, Port-Royal, and Pascal all considered Saint Augustine the ultimate arbiter in theology, we must very briefly look into Saint Augustine's definition of predestination. Augustine developed the doctrine on the basis of Saint Paul's teaching, especially in Romans 8:28–30. For him, as for Pascal, the mystery of predestination consists in the inaccessibility of the reasons for the divine choice to the human mind.

Nevertheless, this choice is made in perfect justice. It is the vocation not only to grace, but also to glory. It depends not on human acceptance but on the eternal decree of God and is therefore infallible without, however, violating free will. Evil enters into the plan of predestination insofar as it is permitted by God in view of a greater good. For Augustine, it is impossible to contest the theology of predestination without contesting that of scripture itself, particularly the Letter to the Romans and the opening of the Letter to the Colossians.

The debate over predestination continued for well over a thousand years. During the time of Pascal, Calvin made predestination the corner-stone of his theological system. Rejecting, like the Jansenists, the universal saving will of God, he maintained that Christ's atoning death was offered for the elect alone. Calvin added the further teaching of the positive reprobation of the damned, to whom salvation has been denied from all eternity without any fault on their part.

The Jesuits attacked by Pascal argued that predestination is but a consequence of God's omniscience. God has simply known from all eternity those whose evil lives would result in their damnation. Pascal, however, vigorously denounced this argument as semi-Pelagian.

Even today, the controversy continues. Following the text of the Latin Mass promulgated by Vatican II, Pope Benedict XVI has insisted that the prayer of consecration in English read that the sacrifice of the Mass is offered, not for "all," but for "many."

77. Pascal, *Pensées*, ed. Sellier (2010), 233n1.

Philippe Sellier insists that Augustine's doctrines of grace and predestination, though never adumbrated in detail, underlie and inform the entire Apology without exception. Pascal evokes over and over a human condition in which man has been "abandoned" by God and "left" to deviate from truth. Human beings, condemned to death and punishment, must be "healed." Only Christianity alerts them to the unique, efficacious "remedy" for their condition. This vocabulary, along with that of many other passages in the *Pensées* too often read as "profane," comes directly from Augustine's writings on grace and predestination.[78]

Again and again, Pascal speaks of the "two states" of man: his state of innocence before Adam's sin and his current corrupt condition. The apologist constantly evokes our two "natures," the vestiges of our "first nature." Yet, in our "second nature," we still retain the ability to conceive of the infinite and of a paradise lost. This terminology of the two states, in complete conformity with Saint Augustine, comes particularly from Jansenius. His *Augustinus* rests upon two pillars: the state of innocent nature, and the state of fallen nature, *De statu naturae lapsae*.[79]

The twin doctrines of predestination and free will totally escape the confines of human reason. Pascal underlines this with particular clarity. "Nothing goes against our reason more than to say that the sin of the first man should implicate in its guilt those who being so remote from the source, seem incapable of having any part in it" (fr. 164). Those theologians who attempt to attenuate and tone down the doctrine of predestination will please most people because they appeal to common sense. Yet to dilute the doctrine of predestination is to attenuate God's *own* freedom to choose his elect.

How, asks Philippe Sellier, is Pascal, particularly in a work meant to draw people closer to God, capable of adhering to such a harsh doctrine? He does so by yielding completely to divine revelation and by refusing to limit divine freedom. Human reason dissolves into complete incomprehension in the face of the infinite and the eternal. But only revelation is truly reasonable. And it is the only valid guide ever evoked in the Apology for the Christian Religion.

One may hesitate in the face of the severity of the theology of the Augustinians of Port-Royal. But one can only admire, says Sellier, their prodigious effort to take seriously the whole of sacred scripture as still understood in the seventeenth century and before the advent of modern biblical exegesis.[80]

Christ's grace cannot be merited. This conviction illuminates the entire

---

78. Sellier, introduction to Pascal, *Pensées*, ed. Sellier (2010), 55–56.
79. Sellier, introduction to Pascal, *Pensées*, ed. Sellier (2010), 56.
80. Sellier, introduction to Pascal, *Pensées*, ed. Sellier (2010), 56.

reasoning behind the *Pensées*. Any apology is only an instrument. Only God can render its proofs intelligible, enlighten a seeker, and open his heart—and this, only if and when he chooses. Grace is never definitively acquired. No one can be sure of persevering in faith since God's grace may inscrutably be withdrawn at any moment. Hence Pascal's own fear of abandonment, a fear so present in the *Mémorial* (fr. 742).[81]

The Three Orders

Fragment 339, in the "Proofs of Jesus Christ" (XXIV), examines the "ego" from another perspective. Pascal sets up a tripartite hierarchy of the degrees of being that animate human beings. According to Jean Mesnard, this hierarchy reflects a deep structure in Pascal's conception of the world and in the *Pensées* themselves.[82]

For Pascal, thought is the one attribute that man must have in order to be a human being. "I can indeed conceive of a man without hands, feet, and head [...]. But I cannot conceive of man without thought [...]. He would be a stone or a brute beast" (fr. 143). "All our dignity consists in thinking" (fr. 232). Pascal advances this idea most memorably in his passage about man as a thinking reed:

Man is nothing but a reed, the weakest thing in nature, but he is a thinking reed. The whole universe does not have to marshal its forces to crush him—a vapor, a drop of water is enough to kill him. But even if the whole universe were to crush him, man would still be nobler than that which is killing him, since he knows he is dying and the power the universe has over him. The universe has no knowledge of it. (fr. 231)

Pascal divides being into ascending orders based upon the extent to which a man can perceive true reality. Inanimate things and beings incapable of thought are excluded from this hierarchy. To put it most simply, the three orders are the flesh, the intellect, and the heart, corresponding to different orders of being in the world.

The carnal order is *concupiscence*, a legacy of the Fall. Pascal focuses on the carnal desire for power (*libido dominandi*). Exemplars of this order are kings, the rich, and military heroes. Their power is totally terrestrial. They are blind to the next level of consciousness, the order of the intellect.

---

81. Sellier, introduction to Pascal, *Pensées*, ed. Sellier (2010), 57.

82. Jean Mesnard, "Le thème des trois ordres dans l'argumentation des *Pensées*," in *La Culture du XVIIe siècle: Enquêtes et synthèses* (Paris: PUF, 1992), 484.

Human consciousness in the second order is far superior to that of the carnal order. "From all bodies put together, we could not succeed in producing a single tiny thought" (fr. 339). The model of intellectual consciousness is Archimedes. He fought no battles, but he bequeathed his ideas and inventions to other minds. Intellectual genius has its own kind of "empire," "greatness," and "luster." It has no need of carnal "greatness," etc.

Intellectual consciousness is nonetheless another kind of *concupiscence*, the curiosity to know (*libido sciendi*). There is an infinite distance between the orders of the carnal and that of the intellect. But this distance only prefigures the "infinitely more infinite" distance in the ascent to the supernatural consciousness of charity (fr. 339).[83] God's holy wisdom remains invisible both to carnal and intellectual perception.

Because of the limitations of human languages, the words "empire," "greatness," "luster," and the like, that describe the attributes of the three orders take on entirely different meanings in each of the three orders. Their true meaning changes drastically with the ascent to the reality of truth:

Saints have their dominion, their radiance, their victory, and their luster and have no need of carnal or intellectual greatness. Such greatness stands in no relationship to them because it adds nothing to them nor takes anything away from them. [...] God is enough for them. (fr. 339)

Those who could perceive holiness were not deceived by the apparent lowliness of Christ's incarnation. For those who could perceive true reality because their hearts were conscious of holy wisdom, Christ did come in great "pomp" and "prodigious magnificence." Christ possessed or wrote nothing. He never reigned or advanced any intellectual theories. But he was "humble, patient, and holy, holy, holy to God." "With what great pomp and in what prodigious magnificence he came to the eyes of the heart, which perceive wisdom" (fr. 339).

It is indeed ridiculous to be scandalized by the lowliness of Jesus Christ, as if this lowliness were of the same order as the greatness that he came to reveal. Let us consider this kind of greatness in his life, in his passion, in his obscurity, in his death, in the choosing of those who were his own, in their abandonment of him, in his secret[84] resurrection. (fr. 339)

---

83. "Charity" is taken in the sense of the Authorized Version's use of the word "charity" and now is most often translated as "love."

84. See fr. 331: "Jesus Christ in such a state of obscurity (in the world's understanding of obscurity), that historians, who were only writing of the important affairs of kingdoms, hardly noticed him." God remains hidden even in human vesture.

According to Jean Mesnard, Pascal understands human nature as composed of only three elements: body, mind, and will. In the celebrated fragment, "The Disproportion of Man" (fr. 230), Mesnard finds Pascal elaborating a parallel tripartite depiction of man's relationship to finitude and the infinite. The first constitutes a contrast between the infinitely immense and the infinitely miniscule. In the realm of the mind, the infinitely small represents the principles of human reason. The infinitely immense represents the infinite consequences of the thoughts produced by this very reason. The third proposes the almost impossible conception of man as constituted by both mind and matter.[85]

The word *carnal* in the "Three Orders" applies both to Jews and Christians. The spiritual Jews were the "Christians of the Old Law." They realized that the Old Testament anticipated the New. The carnal Jews expected a "great temporal prince" (fr. 319) who would bless them with material riches: in other words, a carnal Messiah. Carnal Christians are "Jews of the new law [...] [and] think that the Messiah has dispensed them from loving God. True Jews and true Christians worship a Messiah who makes them love God" (fr. 318).

Pascal and Modernity

Why should the modern reader be fascinated by a Christian apology written more than three hundred and fifty years ago? The answer partially lies in the text's demonstration that the question of the fate of the soul after death—and more broadly, of the meaning of human life—never loses its power over the human imagination. The appeal of the text to modern readers is even stronger because Pascal's premature death left the text in fragmentary form. This fragmentary state and the fragmented strategy of writing are of fundamental interest to modern literary critics. Indeed, they might be tempted to consider it fortunate that Pascal never lived to complete his Apology.

The finished Apology would obviously have been devoid of fragmentary writing. Nor would it have constituted that immense puzzle which has long intrigued readers and scholars alike. Who can say precisely what form the finished Apology would have taken? Might Pascal's multiple references to "letters" in the chapter "Order" suggest that the Apology might have taken a form not unlike that of the *Provincial Letters*?

---

85. Jean Mesnard, "Le thème des trois ordres dans l'argumentation des *Pensées*," in *La Culture du XVIIe siècle*, 470.

Letter urging the search for God. (fr. 38)

A *letter* of exhortation to a friend to bring him to search. (fr. 39)

Letter showing the usefulness of proofs. (fr. 41)

In the *letter* concerning injustice [...]. (fr. 43)

After the *letter* that one must seek God, write the *letter* about removing obstacles [to belief], which is the discourse on the machine, about preparing the machine and searching by means of reason.[86] (fr. 45)

Many modern literary critics seek to understand Pascal's approach as having the effect of deconstructing traditional notions of totality. The publication of Lucien Goldmann's *The Hidden God: A Study of the Tragic Vision in the "Pensées" of Pascal and in the Theatre of Racine*[87] initiated a wave of criticism stressing the paradoxical nature of Pascal's text. Goldmann's Marxist approach underscores an irreconcilable set of contradictions in the fragments of the *Pensées*, which makes any synthesis or reconciliation impossible.

For Goldmann, there can be no discussion of the fragments as notes for a future Apology. The seminal study of the dialectical nature of the *Pensées*, Goldmann's book argues that the theological resolution of the human enigma is no resolution at all. The tragic implications of the *hidden God* dictate the inevitability of fragmentary form:

Seeking the "true" itinerary of the *Pensées* seems to me the anti-Pascalian project *par excellence* [...]; for a tragic work, there is a single valid order, that of the fragment, which has sought, but failed to find order. It cannot succeed in approaching it.[88]

Erec Koch suggests that more recent critical studies of Pascal's dialectics do not move much further beyond Goldmann.[89] Turning from an understanding of Pascal's ideas to the language of the text itself, these critical studies essentially argue that this language fails to mediate any real understanding of

---

86. The notation "Order by dialogues" in fragment 38 suggests yet another possible format.

87. Lucien Goldmann, *Le Dieu caché. Étude sur la vision tragique dans les "Pensées" de Pascal et le théâtre de Racine* (Paris: Gallimard, 1955). Translated by Philip Thody as *The Hidden God: A Study of Tragic Vision in the Pensées of Pascal and the Tragedies of Racine* (London: Routledge, 1964).

88. Goldmann, *Le Dieu caché*, 220.

89. Erec R. Koch, "Blaise Pascal," in Jaouën, ed., *Seventeenth-Century French Writers*, 287. For a highly original and innovative approach from a modernist reading of the *Pensées*, see Nicholas Hammond's *Playing with Truth: Language and the Human Condition in Pascal's Pensées* (Oxford: Oxford University Press, 1994).

Pascal's enterprise. In her *Discourses of the Fall*,[90] Sara Melzer posits the incapacity of Pascal's language to speak the truth.

Religious Challenges to the Modern Reader

Few things could be more alien to modern liberal religious thought than the religious universe in which Pascal lived. How foreign to us is that practice of extreme mortification of the body undertaken to free the soul from self-love! Not as foreign as burning heretics, but still very unlike what we usually encounter in contemporary Christianity. When reading the *Pensées*, we might do well to remember that their author wore a cilice, a hair shirt, under his clothing (as well as an iron belt with sharp points, as his sister avers in her *Life*), fasted to the point of harming his already poor health, and probably practiced self-flagellation. Contemporary accounts suggest that Pascal was rarely absent from any kind of liturgical event he heard about and that he continually consulted an "Almanac" detailing every religious service taking place in Paris.[91] What might be qualified today as religious fanaticism bordering on mental illness, was, in Pascal's France, viewed as a particularly laudable practice of devotion.

Only by attempting to penetrate this religious universe can we hope to understand what Pascal means when he tells us that we must hate the *moi*,[92] that very consciousness which makes us unique human beings. Modern psychology, on the contrary, tells us that we must love our "selves" in order to achieve our true potential. Catholic practice today, with the exception of such severe religious orders as the Trappists, requires nothing more from the faithful than to fast for an hour before Mass and perform an act of self-denial on Fridays during Lent. Long gone is the Eucharistic fast from midnight and abstinence from meat during the whole of Lent. Indeed, modern Catholic preaching often emphasizes the good mental hygiene of loving one's self. Joseph Ratzinger, later Pope Benedict XVI, memorably described self-hatred as a distortion of repentance:

---

90. Sara E. Melzer, *Discourses of the Fall: A Study of Pascal's "Pensées"* (Berkley: University of California Press, 1986).

91. These Almanacs, which detail every ceremony of every church in Paris for every day of the year, may be consulted at the National Archives in Paris. Unfortunately, those coinciding with Pascal's possible use of them are not extant.

92. The *ego* in psychoanalytical terms.

Christian love presupposes faith in the Creator. It must include acceptance of myself as His creature and love of the Creator's creation in me; it must lead to the freedom to accept myself as well as any other member of the Body of Christ. [...] The same is true of repentance. It is a way of saying Yes and is distorted into its opposite when it becomes hatred of self.[93]

Even the editors of the first edition of the *Pensées*, the "Port-Royal Edition," were taken aback by Pascal's assertion that "the self [*moi*] is hateful" (fr. 494). They placed the following caveat right before this fragment. "The word *moi* which the author uses in the following thought signifies only *l'amour-propre*,"[94] in other words an excess love of oneself that results in egotism.

Philippe Sellier mentions a reference to Pascal in the *Logic of Port-Royal* that reveals a far more radical use of the word *moi* as practiced by Pascal himself:

The late M. Pascal, who knew as much of true rhetoric as any one ever did, carried this rule so far as to maintain that well-bred man ought to avoid mentioning himself, and even to avoid using the words "I" and "me"; and he was accustomed to say, on this subject, that Christian piety annihilated the human me, and that human civility concealed and suppressed it.[95]

In "Conclusion," the last of those titled *liasses* that reveal the order of the Apology, Pascal tells the unbelievers that true conversion to Christianity inevitably means nothing less than self-annihilation (fr. 410). Pascal elsewhere asserts that one key proof that Christianity is the only true religion is that it is the only religion that has ever proposed hating the self. "No other religion has ever emphasized self-hatred" (fr. 253). Are we to conclude that Pascal considered the self so abominable that it must be completely extirpated?

I think we must. Pascal's Augustinian perspective could not be more different than that of modern Christian thinking. The "self," that ego which defines personhood, is nothing less than that "evil leaven" (fr. 309) which is the residual infection from original sin. Just as yeast causes dough to rise, the ego instituted by the Fall gives rise to sin in every human being without exception.

93. Joseph Ratzinger, *"In the Beginning…" A Catholic Understanding of the Story of Creation and Fall*, trans. Boniface Ramsey, OP (Grand Rapids, Mich.: Eerdmans, 1990), 95.

94. *Pensées de M. Pascal sur la religion et de quelques autres sujets* (Paris: Guillaume Desprez, 1670; 2nd ed., 1678), 279. On this point, and the following reference to the *Logic of Port-Royal*, see Sellier, in *Pensées* (2010), 411n2.

95. Antoine Arnauld et Pierre Nicole, *The Logic or the Art of Thinking: Being the Port-Royal Logic*, trans. Th. Spencer Baynes (Edinburgh: Sutherland and Knox, 1850), 268 ("well-bred man" stands for the French *honnête homme*). See *Pensées*, ed. Sellier (2010), 411n2. (The reference is to III, 20, not III, 19, as the note indicates.)

The hardened unbelievers in fragment 410 could not have a more erroneous notion of what true conversion entails. Their flippant attitude toward miracles is ironic on their part and plainly offensive to Pascal:

"If I had witnessed a miracle," they say, "I would convert." How can they be sure they would undertake that which they know nothing about? They imagine that this conversion consists in the worship of God as an exchange or a conversation, such as they picture it. (fr. 410)

The atheists posit a conversion in which they can negotiate with God, promising to perform charitable acts in return for some material reward. But, as noted before, one does not attempt "conversation" with Pascal's God:

True conversion consists in *annihilating oneself* [s'anéantir] in the face of that universal Being whom we have angered so many times and who may legitimately send you to hell at any moment. It consists in recognizing that we can do nothing without him and that we have deserved from him nothing but the withdrawal of his grace. It consists in understanding that there is an invincible opposition between God and us, and that without a mediator there can be no communication with him. (fr. 410, emphasis added)

The very possibility of communication between God and humanity was inexorably broken off by Adam's sin. God can legitimately damn us because we are infected with that sin instigated by our first parents. Original sin is like some fatal genetic defect that has been passed on to every human being who has ever lived or will ever live. Of course, underlying this doctrine is the supposition that Adam was the biological father of the entire human race, something that few, if anyone, in the Classical period ever doubted. Reason alone is incapable of penetrating this mystery of the perpetual transmission of original sin because it too, like the whole of creation, was irremediably corrupted in the Fall. Moreover, God has intentionally hidden this mystery from human reason:

Nothing goes against our reason more than to say that the sin of the first man should implicate in its guilt those who, being so remote from the source, seem incapable of having any part in it. This transmission seems to us not only impossible, it even appears very unjust. For what is more contrary to the rules of our miserable justice than damning for all eternity a[n unbaptized] child, incapable of will, for a sin in which he seems to have had so little part that it was committed six thousand years before he existed. Certainly nothing shocks us more harshly than this doctrine. And yet without this most incomprehensible of all mysteries, we are incomprehensible to ourselves. The knot of our condition takes its twists and turns in this abyss. (fr. 164)

From the perspective of Augustinian theology, God has the right to damn the entire human race, irrespective of our actions. Indeed, according to Pascal's reading of the doctrine of predestination, God actually *intends* to damn some and save others, regardless of their practice of Christianity or lack of it. Fragment 264 bears repeating: "One understands nothing of the works of God unless one takes as a first principle that his *intention* was to blind some and enlighten others" (emphasis added).

The doctrine of predestination might seem to us a terrible cruelty on the part of a supposedly loving God. But, from an Augustinian point of view, salvation is meaningless without damnation. God's total freedom depends upon his damnation of that *mass of perdition* constituted by all humanity. The entire human race merits damnation because of its participation in original sin. The elect are saved only by an inexplicable supererogation of his mercy. Olivier Tonneau directs us to Jansenius's *Discourse concerning the Reformation of the Interior Man*. Jansenius proposes what indeed may seem to us an inhumane and incomprehensible explanation for the reprobation and damnation of the many. God does not abandon them out of cruelty or indifference, but because their rejection is an indispensable element in the salvation of the elect. The damnation of almost all of humanity serves to remind the elect that they too could be rejected at any moment and that their election depends entirely on God's "efficacious" and inscrutable grace.[96]

Though Pascal sometimes allows his adversaries to speak, he never gives their names. Only the name of a single interlocutor appears in the entire text of the *Pensées*. Therefore "Damien Miton," whose name is mentioned three times, is of great interest, because he is the single interlocutor Pascal identifies by name.[97] Miton, along with his friend the Chevalier de Méré, might very well number among the relatively few men indifferent or hostile to religion whom Pascal, living within the austere religious cocoon of Port-Royal and his family, actually ever met in the flesh.[98]

Indifference to religion is, of course, one of the great themes of the Apology. In fragment 494, Miton prescribes *honnêteté*, a code of civility in society, as a remedy for the human condition.[99] Miton agrees with Pascal that "all hu-

---

96. See Olivier Tonneau, "The Science of the Cross: The Jansenist Doctrine of Predestination and Their Pedagogy of Conversion," in Hammond and Moriarty, ed., *Evocations of Eloquence*, 126.

97. In fragments 494, 529b, and 433.

98. Born into a rather modest bourgeois family in 1618, Miton acquired a considerable fortune, which he mainly spent on gambling. A friend of La Fontaine's, he was considered an important arbiter of taste. His *bons mots* on *l'honnêteté* were collected and published after his death in 1690. Méré (1607–84), a far more hardened *libertin* than Miton, appears to be the one who put two problems on probability—for the purposes of gambling—to Pascal in 1653.

99. Jean Lafond remarks that Miton's theory of *honnêteté* addresses an ideal essentially foreign to that

man beings seek to be happy" (fr. 181). He also agrees with Pascal that all men have been corrupted; but he has no idea why. Nor can he, ostensibly ignorant of the consequences of original sin, understand why men cannot transcend the human condition. "Miton sees clearly that nature is corrupt and that men are the reverse of what *honnêteté* prescribes. But he does not know why they cannot fly higher" (fr. 529b). Another fragment, also filed among the *liasses* Pascal set aside in 1658, seems to confirm that Pascal is attempting to move Miton into the category of those who sincerely seek God: "Reproach Miton for not lifting a finger" (fr. 433).

Nothing suggests that Damien Miton was an aggressive atheist. None of his writings contain the impieties of the *libertins*. And after all, such active disbelief would have been at odds with Miton's own portrait of the *honnête homme*:

The *honnête homme* [...] is not motivated by self-interest. His conduct is always moderate, and he never lives a dissolute life [...]. The *honnête homme* attaches great importance to the intellect, but he attaches even more importance to reason [...]. He wants to know all things but he is not upset at knowing nothing. He says nor does anything which is not agreeable and reasonable, and which does not tend to the greater happiness of all men.[100]

Miton is Pascal's direct interlocutor in fragment 494. Does the fragment echo an actual conversation with Miton? In any event, the fragment, long ignored, is one key to the question of to whom the Apology was to have been addressed. Pascal first refutes Miton's prescription for transcending the human condition. *Honnêteté* can only attempt to disguise the *moi*, that "evil leaven" planted in all generations of human beings by original sin. It has no power to extirpate it. "The self [*moi*] is hateful. You, Miton, cover it up, but that does not mean that you remove it: you are, therefore, still hateful" (fr. 494).

How are we to understand exactly what Pascal means by that *moi* which is so hateful? Is not the ego best defined by Carl Gustav Jung as a tiny island of consciousness floating on the vast sea of unconsciousness? Does Pascal mean that extirpating the *moi* completely destroys human consciousness and individuality? Is the purified soul that remains in the elect then absorbed into the Beatific Vision? Probably not. Such a theory is tantamount, Sellier objects,

---

of Méré. "The most unexpected and original thing in Miton's reflections on *l'honnêteté* is the attention he pays to the condition of the poor, something all too rare in the Seventeenth Century." Jean Lafond, ed., *Moralistes du XVIIe Siecle* (Paris: Laffont, 1992), 84 (translation by David Wetsel).

100. Damien Miton, "Pensées sur l'honnêteté," in Lafond, ed., *Moralistes*, 86 (translation by David Wetsel).

to Buddhism.[101] Christian theology has always preserved individuality after death. Saint Paul tells us that we shall be "changed," not destroyed.[102]

In the preface to the Apology (fr. 681) Pascal qualifies not bothering to attempt to ascertain the fate of the soul after death as "monstrous." Yet nowhere in the *Pensées* does he give the seeker even a clue as to what fate awaits the soul in heaven or hell. He never attempts to motivate the seeker by describing the joys of heaven or the torments of hell. Nor does he ever invoke the Pauline doctrine of the last judgment, a significant leitmotiv in Jesus' teachings in the Gospels. We are left wondering whether predestination results in election or reprobation immediately after death, or at the last judgment after a long sleep. Medieval Catholicism had so obscured the doctrine that the tares and the wheat must be allowed to grow together until the harvest, that the great mass of the faithful were obsessed with immediately trying to free souls from purgatory and assumed that at least the saints and maybe others were already in heaven. Pascal gives us no indication as to where he stands on these doctrinal matters.

The doctrine of predestination is inexorably linked to that of justification. For Pascal, the elect have been justified by Christ's salvific work on the cross. That great multitude of the damned are not justified, by the express intention of God, irrespective of their actions. *Amour-propre* has invaded the "self," body and soul. All human beings are infected with original sin. All *deserve* damnation. In saving the elect, God is not acting contrary to justice. Rather, in his inscrutable wisdom, he is showing mercy to a very few elect, even though they by right deserve damnation. Trying to render the *moi* lovable is an attribute of those predestined to damnation. One must hate the *moi* because of its intrinsic self-centeredness. Pascal is certain of his position:

If I hate the *moi* [self] because it is *unjust* [and] makes itself the center of all things, I will always hate it.

In a word, the self has two qualities: it is *unjust* in itself, in that it makes itself the center of all things; it [...] would like to be the tyrant of all others. (fr. 494, emphasis added)

The only documentation of Pascal's relations with Miton is the three fragments we have just examined. But perhaps Pascal's admonitions to Miton did finally bear fruit. According to the Jesuit René Rapin, Miton returned to the practice of Christianity.[103] However, this was towards the end of his life, af-

---

101. Philippe Sellier, private conversation with David Wetsel.
102. 1 Corinthians 15:51.
103. Lafond, ed., *Moralistes*, 83. Lafond's introduction to Miton's *Pensées sur l'honnêteté* remains the

ter he had been paralyzed and estranged from his children for twenty years. Ironically, Miton's suffering might be considered a kind of involuntary mortification of the "self" to which Pascal had admonished him to strive thirty-five years previously.

A thorny and never-resolved question remains: To whom would the finished Apology be addressed? Few scholars now doubt that Pascal planned on writing an apology for the Christian religion using a great many of the fragments we read as the *Pensées*. I have advanced the idea that Pascal's work would have been aimed, not at the atheists as his sister thought, but at the interlocutor whose presence we feel in the preface to the Apology. I have called him the "seeker" because of Pascal's many modulations of the verb "to seek" in the preface as he invokes his interlocutor. Looking at the Apology as a whole, Jean Mesnard has always pronounced the "seeker" a serious Christian by the end of the Apology.

The Apology has at least one other purpose. The apologist means to assure not only the "seeker," but also the "bad Christians" and even the believers that Christianity is both historically and empirically true. Rising above the question of authorial intent, might we speculate that the true aim of the Apology is reassurance to those who already believe? The "Jesus Seminar," an attempt to ascertain which words in the Gospels Jesus actually spoke, is a scandal to most Christian theologians of our time. But one participant in the "Jesus Seminar" offers us an entirely new perspective on Christian apologetics. Robert J. Miller argues that apologetics nearly always fails when addressed to "outsiders": "Informed, intelligent, sincere and spiritual people are almost never persuaded by apologetics to change their core beliefs [...] . If the purpose of apologetics is to convince outsiders to adopt new beliefs, then apologies are almost always abject failures."[104]

However, there is another, more promising way to evaluate the apologetic genre: we can determine its audience, not by whom it *seems* to be aimed at, but by who *actually* reads apologetic works:

We can determine an apology's purpose, not by what the author seems to intend, but by how it actually functions. If we proceed like this, we reach two important findings: (1) the audience for an apology is insiders; (2) its function is to support what the audience already believes. This is nothing new to apologists, who know full well that their audiences are insiders.[105]

---

best scholarly treatment of Miton's relations with Pascal. In English, see Henry A. Grubbs, *Damien Miton (1618–1690) "Bourgeois honnête homme"* (Princeton, N.J.: Princeton University Press, 1932).

104. Robert J. Miller, *The Jesus Seminar and Its Critics* (Santa Rosa, Calif.: Polebridge Press, 1999), 96.
105. Miller, *The Jesus Seminar*, 97.

This radical understanding of apologetics, completely alien to traditional approaches to the *Pensées*, opens up a new vein of questions we can ask about Pascal's unfinished Apology. We could hardly argue, given Pascal's portrait of his "seeker," that he knew full well that his audience would be "insiders." Or could we? Is the "seeker" really an "outsider?" Or is he an "insider," baptized and brought up as a Catholic, who has become indifferent to religion? Is he not an "insider," if only because he is now seeking to find out whether his religion is true or not? Does he not figure within what we might call a hermeneutic circle of belief constituted by the Apology itself?

Christians do in fact convert to other religions and to other versions of Christianity.[106] But do they do so as a result of reading an apology? Is their "core belief" really changed? Did the apologetic works of the early Church Fathers, on which Sellier believes Pascal intended to model his Apology, really play a major role in the great conversions to Christianity in the third century? Does Pascal really know that his Apology is really addressed to "insiders?" Can we posit an Apology that functions otherwise than Pascal intended?

Pascal's blast against the hardened *libertins* in fragment 410 is essentially rhetorical. They are the last who would heed his call to self-annihilation. Nor does Pascal really expect Miton to come to agree that the *moi* is hateful. Rather, these most severe of all admonitions in the *Pensées* might be directed to the great majority of nominal Christians. They might really be held up as a call to conversion on the part of those conventional or lukewarm Christians who have not yet experienced the kind of intense inner conversion that Pascal records in the *Mémorial*. The Apology might best be approached, at least by the modern reader of the *Pensées*, as a call to inner conversion and a reassurance to "insiders" that Christianity can rationally be proved to be both venerable and true?

A Brief History of Pascal's Text[107]

According to Gérard Ferreyrolles, the actual papers constituting Pascal's fragments can be read from three perspectives. First of all, one may consider the actual form and status of the papers themselves. There are identifiable complete sheets, most often cut up into pieces. Other papers register complete

---

106. One can only imagine Pascal's dismay at seeing Christians today converting to Islam—a religion that he considered to be ultimately diabolical—or to Buddhism—whose atheistic philosophy he could never have entertained.

107. Anthony Pugh gives an exhaustive account of the history of the texts. See Pugh, *The Composition of Pascal's Apologia*.

fragments, fragments that sometimes cover several parchment sheets. From a second perspective, the fragments may be viewed from the degree of their elaboration and completion. Some, elliptic and enigmatic, register but a single word or two. Others appear very nearly complete. A third perspective concerns which fragments prefigure Pascal's actual Apology and which represent notes for Pascal's other works, private meditations, and so on.[108]

Toward the beginning of the eighteenth century, the autograph papers constituting the *Pensées* ended up in the hands of Pascal's second nephew, Louis Périer. Périer had the laudable aim of preserving these fragile papers for posterity by pasting them into large parchment sheets, which he bound together and deposited in 1711 at the monastery of Saint-Germain-des-Prés. Seeking to make use of as few parchment sheets as possible, he destroyed the order and form of Pascal's writings by cutting them up into pieces whose shape would most conveniently fit on the large pages of his album, known as the *Recueil original des Pensées*, the Original Collection.

For the text, the Original Collection remains the gold standard with reference to which all editions must be corrected. For the most part, it is in Pascal's own hand. Those texts dictated to a secretary were reviewed and corrected by Pascal himself. However, Louis Périer's mutilation of the order of the autograph renders it almost useless as a guide to the order in which Pascal left it upon his death. Thus, the order and form in which Pascal left his papers seemed lost forever.

In addition, by 1711 and the Original Collection, the *Pensées* had already been published for forty-one years in the "Port Royal Edition,"[109] organized by the Duke of Roannez and Pascal's associates at Port-Royal. These first editors thought it essential to rearrange many of Pascal's fragments into an order that they thought would reflect Pascal's ultimate work. They also thought it necessary to polish and sometimes reword Pascal's text in accordance with the dictates of classical style.

This 1670 edition, reissued in 1678, became the basis of all subsequent editions of the *Pensées*—and that of all English translations of the *Pensées*—until the middle of the nineteenth century. For nearly three hundred years, scholars and editors assumed that the original order and disposition of Pascal's text had been lost forever.

However, two long-forgotten copies of Pascal's papers in *opus interruptum*

---

108. Gérard Ferreyrolles, introduction to Pascal, *Pensées: Presentation et notes par Gérard Ferreyrolles* (Paris: Bordas, 1991), 16–18.

109. Blaise Pascal, *Pensées de M. Pascal sur la religion et de quelques autres sujets* (Paris: Guillaume Desprez, 1670; second complete edition, 1678). Facsimile edition by Georges Couton and Jean Jehasse (Saint-Étienne: Centre interuniversitaire d'Éditions et Rééditions, 1971)

had been commissioned by his family. In the preface to the "Port-Royal Edition," Pascal's nephew Etienne Périer states that Pascal's papers had all been found by his family immediately following his death, threaded "into diverse bundles":

Since we knew Monsieur Pascal's intention to work on religion, after he died we took great care in collecting all his writings on the subject. We found them all threaded together in diverse bundles, without any order or sequence [...]. Moreover, everything was so incomplete and so poorly written that deciphering them was extraordinarily difficult. *The first thing we did was to have them copied just as they were, and in the same disorder in which we found them.*[110]

This reference to the copies remained neglected for almost three centuries. Their actual existence was finally established by Zacharie Tourneur in 1938. He also identified more than two hundred needle marks in the Original Collection. Most had disappeared when Louis Périer trimmed the margins of many fragments with scissors. According to a practice that was common in the sixteenth and seventeenth centuries, Pascal filed his notes into separate *liasses*[111] by sewing them together using a needle and thick thread.

Pascal did not usually write on various kinds of small slips of paper. He usually wrote on large sheets folded in two, or on half-sheets. He marked the separation between his notes with a stroke of the pen. Thus, when Pascal decided to sort them into stacks to be sewn together (*liasses*), he was able to cut up the sheets by using these marks of separation.

We still possess these two remarkable copies, transcribed around 1662–63, and now in the collections of the Bibliothèque Nationale, the French National Library.[112] The contents of the two documents are much the same, with a few differences.[113] But why does the Second Copy clearly constitute the most reliable text? Why does the Sellier edition mark an enormous step forward in Pascalian studies?

110. Etienne Périer, "Préface à l'Édition de Port-Royal," in Pascal, *Œuvres complètes*, ed. Lafuma, 498 (translation by David Wetsel, emphasis added).

111. Given the fact that no English term (some have used the infelicitous "bundles") really describes Pascal's sewn-together dossiers, we have chosen to retain the French word *liasse(s)*, universally used by French Pascal scholars. See the section "French Words" in the editor's preface.

112. The First Copy (C1) is now ms. 9203 in the French Manuscripts collection (Bibliothèque nationale de France, ms. français 9203, "Pensées sur la religion, par Blaise PASCAL"), and the Second Copy (C2) is ms. 12449 (Bibliothèque nationale de France, ms. français 12449, "Pensées sur la religion, par Blaise Pascal").

113. C2 has 61 dossiers, while C1 has only 60. More importantly, the sequencing of the dossiers differs in part. The text of C1 has been altered by corrections in many different hands (Arnauld, Nicole, Étienne Périer), to the extent that it is sometimes impossible to tell the difference between the original copy and the additions, which editors have sometimes published as being by Pascal. C2, on the contrary, is intact. The corrections are in a single hand, that of Étienne Périer. Their purpose is only to repair errors of transcription.

In the First Copy, each of Pascal's bundles was transcribed in a separate notebook. These notebooks long had an autonomous existence. They formed the basis of the Port-Royal edition of the *Pensées* (1670) and they appear to have circulated among Pascal's family and friends. The corrections by Arnauld and Nicole, Pascal's friends at Port-Royal, never appear together in the same notebook. Obviously, they divided up the work. And the notebooks of the First Copy were bound together only years later.

By contrast, in the Second Copy, Pascal's fragments flow across the notebooks, preserving Pascal's original order. The copyist transcribed these notebooks without leaving a single blank page. Thus, the order of the Second Copy was determined from the start. And the Second Copy offers us the best possible order of Pascal's *Pensées*, preserving the arrangement of Pascal's papers as he left them.[114]

The Second Copy is apparently the text that the Périers had transcribed for their own use. Étienne Périer appears to have constantly improved it, often on the basis of the autograph. Philippe Sellier is the first editor to use the Second Copy, correcting it when necessary by consulting the Original Collection. Thus, his various editions constitute an enormous advance in Pascalian studies.

The Chapters Subsequent to the Project of 1658

While the first half of the Pensées has a relative unity, the second half consists of notes on a great variety of topics—religion, miracles, style, political power, the nature of poetic language, and so on—that contain *inter alia* references to Montaigne, Descartes, and the Bible. Some of the most important fragments of the entire work are to be found in these latter sections. A fundamental problem in the interpretation of the *Pensées* is the relationship between these fragments and Pascal's overall apologetic endeavor. Philippe Sellier believes that these chapters (with the exception of chapters XXXVI–LXI) were set aside by Pascal in June of 1658.

We can be almost certain that chapters XXX–XXXII (frs. 419–50), entitled "Miracles," though included in all modern editions of the *Pensées*, would not have figured in the Apology at all. These fragments appear to be notes for a never written *Treatise on Miracles*. In the aftermath of the miracle wrought with the relic of the sacred thorn at Port-Royal, Pascal appears to have con-

---

114. C2 is strikingly well organized. The copyist started by transcribing *liasses* I–XLI. The originals of dossier XXX have been lost. *Liasses* I–XXXV were probably put together around 1658.

templated an Apology based upon miracles. However, Pascal seems to have realized early on that such a work would hardly have been capable of leading unbelievers to Christianity.

On the other hand, we can be reasonably sure which chapters would have been placed in the Apology. The "Letter Urging the Search for God" (fr. 681) would have been placed at the very beginning of the Apology as a preface. Philippe Sellier qualifies it as an overture, containing all the major leitmotivs of the Apology. Jean Mesnard calls fragment 681 the most finished, complete, and one of the most beautiful of all the fragments.[115] The editors of the Port-Royal edition placed it at the very beginning of their edition. But why did Pascal himself never insert this chapter in front of the titled *liasses*?

This preface (fr. 681) is enigmatic from another perspective. It is absent from the Original Collection. It exists only because it was transcribed from the autograph into the First and Second Copies. Given its primordial importance, how did it disappear from the Original Collection? Where would a second highly finished fragment (fr. 690) have been incorporated into the project of 1658? Perhaps it would have been used in the preface to the second part of the Apology.

A number of series of independent chapters consist principally of long lists of notes and documentation. They represent a great challenge for the reader. Take, for example, the long documentary chapters (LIV–LX) dealing with Old Testament prophecies of Christ's coming and events in the New Testament. Essentially, long passages mainly from the books of the Old Testament named after prophets are copied out in French and in Latin. Obviously they are related to the chapter "Prophecies" (XXV). But it is by no means certain that more than a few of these fragments themselves would have been incorporated into that chapter. The many long citations from the Old Testament copied out by Pascal would have weighed down the chapter and obscured the coherence of his argument.

Another five chapters concerning "The State of the Jews" (XLVIII–LII) include one chapter (L) that lists a long series of scriptural references. But the other chapters contain rather finished discourses, which appear likely to have been added to chapters XX–XXIII: "That the Law was Figurative"; "The Rabbinical Tradition"; "Perpetuity"; "Proofs of Moses." Chapters XXXVI–XLIV, the last of the miscellaneous chapters (written between July of 1658 and July of 1662), appear to have been set aside by Pascal for an eventual sorting out.

---

115. Jean Mesnard, *Les Pensées de Pascal* [Pascal's *Pensées*] (Paris: S.E.D.E.S, 1976), 340.

Why the Present Translation?

The great majority of available English translations follow the First Copy, including the most widely used translation, the venerable Krailshimer Penguin edition.[116] As explained above, the First Copy is clearly inferior to the Second. The Lafuma French text of the First Copy used by Krailshimer and others contain a great many mis-readings and mis-transcriptions.

The mis-transcriptions inherent in the First Copy resulted from the erroneous copying of Pascal's autograph in 1662–63. Disconcertingly, the edition figuring in the prestigious Pléiade collection prepared by Michel Le Guern has largely borrowed Lafuma's text,[117] further propagating many mis-readings. A translation of any of these editions would hardly seem to be warranted. Krailshimer uses Lafuma. Le Guern uses Lafuma. How would such a translation of Lafuma be new?

Though an earlier version of Philippe Sellier's edition has been translated into English—in 1995, by Honor Levi, and in 2005, by Roger Ariew[118]—this translation is the first to be published with the approval of Ph. Sellier. Moreover, it is the only one to benefit from the wealth of scholarly material with which Philippe Sellier has recently enriched his edition. These include comprehensive critical footnotes, a magisterial preface upon which we have based this introduction, a rich chronology, and a bibliography of critical works in many languages. Sellier has also included other texts to assist the reader in understanding the historical and biographical contexts of the *Pensées*: Gilberte Périer's *The Life of Monsieur Pascal*, and in the 2010 edition, Nicolas Fontaine's *Exchange with Monsieur de Sacy*.

Sellier admits that Pascal never used the word "apology," but observes that the title *Pensées* is hardly a synonym for Pascal's projected Apology. However, he maintains that only the title Apology adequately describes those fragments meant to constitute a "Defense and Illustration of Catholic theology and spirituality."[119] Testimonies from Pascal's entourage, as well as numerous passages from the text itself, lead one to situate the great majority of the fragments within a literary and theological genre almost as old as Christianity itself.

---

116. Blaise Pascal, *Pensées*, trans. A. J. Krailshimer (London: Penguin, [1995] 2004).

117. Blaise Pascal, *Œuvres complètes*, ed. Michel Le Guern, 2 vols., Bibliothèque de la Pléiade (Paris: Gallimard, 1998–2000)

118. Blaise Pascal, *Pensées*, trans. Roger Ariew (Indianapolis: Hackett, 2005). Blaise Pascal, *Pensées and Other Writings*, trans. Honor Levi (Oxford: Oxford University Press, 1995). This last is closer to an anthology, as it leaves out individual fragments and even entire chapters.

119. Sellier, introduction to Pascal, *Pensées*, ed. Sellier (2010), 29. On this phrase, "defense and illustration," see n. 1, above.

The genre is found as early as the second century in Christian writers known as the "apologists." Sellier views the Apology as what theologians now call "fundamental theology," that is, "a deep reflection on the path to the Absolute":

The two leading lights in this tradition are Cardinal Newman (1801–90) and Pascal himself. The fact that the former entitled his most celebrated book the *Apologia pro Vita Sua* (1865) demonstrates that this very old Christian term—which goes back to the New Testament (*First Letter of Peter*, III, 15)—has not been discredited along with the superannuated genre of traditional Christian apologetics.[120]

A Reader's Guide to the *Pensées*

We have insisted on the importance of producing a translation based upon Philippe Sellier's now-authoritative edition of the *Pensées*. In France, Sellier's edition is almost universally accepted by Pascal scholars. It is used in nearly all advanced university courses on French seventeenth-century literature. However, the order of the fragments in Sellier's (or any other) scholarly edition may well not be the most coherent way of reading the *Pensées* for the great majority of our English readers.

Using his own text, Philippe Sellier has put together yet another edition of the *Pensées* designed for those whom Virginia Woolf so felicitously calls the "common reader."[121] Not necessarily a novice, the "common reader" is often well-read and familiar with the basic works of Western literature. Even for such a sophisticated reader, reading our translation in the scholarly order we follow might well prove a daunting task.

Following this introduction, the reader will find the order of chapters as arranged by Philippe Sellier in his "Reader's Edition." Starting with the preface (XLVI), readers should then proceed to the "Discourse on the Machine" (the "Wager") (XLV). At this point, they should then read the titled chapters in the order of Sellier's reconstruction. Into this order, Sellier has interpolated those chapters related to these major titled chapters.

For those readers who have never read the *Pensées* or who have read only extracts, we cannot recommend strongly enough following the order of the concordance below. Those who already know the *Pensées* will find Sellier's reconstruction of Pascal's apologetic itinerary provocative and illuminating.

---

120. Sellier, introduction to Pascal, *Pensées*, ed. Sellier (2010), 29. How different, Sellier observes, are the *Pensées* from those other apologetic works of the seventeenth through the nineteenth centuries.

121. Blaise Pascal, *Pensées: Edition établie d'après l'ordre pascalien*, ed. Philippe Sellier (Paris: Agora, 2003).

The Sellier "Reader's Edition"

To use this guide, the reader should approach Sellier's chapters by following the order of the numbers in Roman numerals on the right side. (Roman numerals are used to refer to Pascal's chapters as presented in this translation. The numbers in Arabic numerals represent fragments not transcribed in the Second Copy.)

THOUGHTS ON MIRACLES

FRAGMENTS NOT RECORDED IN THE SECOND COPY

BIBLIOGRAPHY

1. Complete Works of Pascal in French

Brunschvicg Edition

Pascal, Blaise. *Œuvres complètes.* Edited by Léon Brunschvicg, Pierre Boutroux, and Félix Gazier. 14 vols. Paris: Hachette, 1904–14. (The *Pensées* occupy the last three volumes.)

Lafuma Edition

Pascal, Blaise. *Œuvres complètes.* Edited by Louis Lafuma. Paris: Seuil, 1963.

Le Guern Edition

Pascal, Blaise. *Œuvres complètes.* Edited by Michel Le Guern. 2 vols. Bibliothèque de la Pléiade. Paris: Gallimard, 1998–2000. (Essentially follows the Lafuma edition; the *Pensées* are in volume 2.)

Mesnard Edition

Pascal, Blaise. *Œuvres complètes: Édition du tricentenaire.* Edited by Jean Mesnard. 4 vols. Paris: Desclée de Brouwer, 1991.

2. Photographic Reproductions of the Original *Pensées* Manuscripts

Pascal, Blaise. *Le Recueil Original des Pensées.* Brunschvicg's photo copy of ms. 1905. Bibliothèque Nationale, Paris. (Photographic reproduction of the Original Collection by Brunschvicg in 1905 [reprinted by Slatkine Reprints, 1960].)
———. *Les Manuscrits des Pensées de Pascal.* Lafuma's photo copy of ms. 1962. Bibliothèque Nationale, Paris. Copies 1 and 2 of the *Pensées*. (Photographic reproduction of the Original Collection. Photographs are rearranged according to the numbering of Lafuma's own edition.)

3. First Edition in French

"Édition de Port-Royal"

Pascal, Blaise. *Pensées de M. Pascal sur la religion et sur quelques autres sujets.* Paris: Guillaume Desprez, 1670. (Second complete edition 1678.)
———. *Pensées de M. Pascal sur la religion et sur quelques autres sujets: l'édition de Port-Royal*

(*1670*) *et ses compléments* (*1678–1776*) facsimile edition, with a preface by Georges Couton and Jean Jehasse. Saint-Étienne: Éd. de l'Université de Saint-Étienne, 1971.

———. *Pensées sur la religion et sur quelques autres sujets.* Edited by Jean-Robert Armogathe and David Blot. Paris: Honore Champion, 2011. (This modern edition compares the text to the First and Second Copies [Lafuma and Sellier] and to other modern editions.)

4. Concordance

Davidson, H. M. *A Concordance to Pascal's Pensées.* Ithaca: Cornell University Press, 1975. (This monumental index cites every occurrence of any given word in the *Pensées*.)

5. Modern French Editions of the *Pensées*

Pascal, Blaise. *Pensées.* Edited by Léon Brunschvicg. Paris: Livre de Poche, 1974.

———. *Pensées sur la religion et sur quelques autres sujets.* Edited by Louis Lafuma. Paris: Luxembourg, 1951.

———. *Les Pensées de Pascal.* Edited by Francis Kaplan. Paris: Cerf, 1982.

———. *Pensées.* Edited by Michel Le Guern. 2 vols. Paris: Gallimard, 2004.

———. *Pensées.* Edited by Philippe Sellier. Paris: Classiques Garnier, 1999.

———. *Pensées: Edition établie d'après l'ordre pascalien.* Edited by Philippe Sellier. Paris: Agora, 2003. (Reader's edition arranged according to evidence in the text itself.)

———. *Les Pensées, les Provinciales et opuscules philosophiques.* Edited by Philippe Sellier and Gérard Ferreyrolles. Paris: Livre de Poche, 2004.

———. *Pensées, opuscules et lettres.* Edited by Philippe Sellier. Paris: Classiques Garnier, 2010. (The original text on which this translation is based.)

6. Essential French Commentaries

Gouhier, Henri. *Blaise Pascal: Conversion et apologétique.* Paris: Librairie Philosophique Vrin, 1986.

McKenna, Antony. *De Pascal à Voltaire: Le Rôle des Pensées dans l'histoire des idées entre 1670 et 1734.* Oxford: The Voltaire Foundation at the Taylor Institute, 1990.

———. *Pascal et son libertin.* Littérature, libertinage et spiritualité 6. Paris: Classiques Garnier, 2017.

Mesnard, Jean. *Les Pensées de Pascal.* Paris: S.E.D.E.S, 1976.

———. *La Culture du XVIIe siècle: enquêtes et synthèses.* Paris: PUF, 1991.

Sellier, Philippe. *Pascal et la liturgie.* Paris: French and European Publications, 1965.

———. *Pascal et saint Augustin.* Paris: Armand Colin, 1970.

———. *Essais sur l'imaginaire classsique. Pascal. Racine.* Paris: Champion, 2006.

———. *Port Royal et la littérature. Pascal.* Tome 1. Paris: Champion, 2010.

———. *Port Royal et la littérature: le siecle de Saint Augustin.* Tome 2. Paris: Champion, 2012.

———. *Port Royal et la littérature. De Cassien à Pascal.* Tome 3. Paris: Champion, 2019.

7. Principal Modern Complete English
Translations of the *Pensées*

Ariew Edition

Pascal, Blaise. *Pensées*. Translated by Roger Ariew. Indianapolis: Hackett, 2005. (Unauthorized translation of the Sellier edition.)

Krailsheimer Edition

Pascal, Blaise. *Pensées*. Translated by A. J. Krailsheimer. Rev. ed. London: Penguin Books, 2004. (Translation of the Lafuma edition.)

Levi Edition

Pascal, Blaise. *Pensées and Other Writings*. Translated by Honor Levi. Oxford: Oxford University Press, 1995. (In spite of its title, this unauthorized translation based on the Sellier edition is actually truncated and omits entire chapters and a great many fragments.)

8. Other Complete Modern English Translations

Cohen, J. M., trans. *The Pensées*. Baltimore: Penguin Books, 1961.

Paul, C. Kegan, trans. *The Thoughts of Blaise Pascal*. Whitefish, Mont.: Kessinger, 2012. First published 1901 by George Bell & Sons (London).

Stewart, H. F., trans. *Pascal's Pensées*. New York: Pantheon, 1950.

Taylor, Isaac, trans. *Thoughts on Religion and Philosophy by Blaise Pascal*. London: Harper, 1995.

Trotter, W. F., trans. *Pascal's Pensées*. Introduction by T.S. Eliot. New York: Everyman's Library, 1932.

———. *Pascal's Pensées and the Provincial Letters*. New York: Modern Library, 1941.

———. *Pensées. Pascal's Thoughts on God, Religion, and Wagers*. n.p.: Suzeteo Enterprises, 2010.

———. *Pensées*. Introduction by T.S. Eliot. New York: Create Space Independent, 2012.

Thayer, Elisabeth B., trans. *Pensées*. New York: Washington Square Press, 1965.

Turnell, Martin, trans. *Pensées*. London: Harvill Press, 1962, repr. 1971.

Warrington, John, trans. *Pensées*. London: J. M. Dent, 1973.

9. Selected English Anthologies of the *Pensées*

Appelbaum, Stanley, ed. and trans. *Selected "Pensées" and Provincial Letters: Bilingual Edition*. Mineola, N.Y.: Dover, 2004.

Mauriac, François, ed. *The Living Thoughts of Blaise Pascal*. New Delhi: Rupa & Co., 2002.

Popkin, Richard H., ed. and trans. *Pascal: Selections*. New York: Macmillan, 1989.

Stewart, H. F. *The Heart of Pascal: Being His Meditations and Prayers, Notes for His Anti-Jesuit Campaign, Remarks on Language and Style, etc.: Drawn from the Pensées*. Cambridge: Cambridge University Press, 1945.

———, ed. *Pascal's Apology for Religion: Extracts from the Pensées*. Cambridge: Cambridge

University Press, 2013. (New edition of the 1942 companion to the title above. The French text is elegantly annotated in English by the editor.)

Trotter, W. F., ed. *Blaise Pascal: Foundations of the Christian Religion*. Foundations of Faith 6. Orlando, Fla.: Relevant Books, 2006.

Van De Weyer, Robert, ed. *Selected Readings from Blaise Pascal*. Grand Rapids, Mich.: Revell, 1991.

10. English Translations of the *Pensées* 1688–1905

All the English translations prior to 1850 appear to be based upon increasingly corrupt versions of the Édition de Port-Royal. Faugère, whose text was translated in 1850 by Pearce, was among the first French editors to consult the Recueil Original [autograph ms.]. Trotter's translation of 1904 is based on an early edition of Brunschvicg, the first French editor to produce an edition entirely based on the Recueil Original, albeit completely rearranging Pascal's autograph manuscript according to his theories of how the Apology was to have been organized.

1688

Pascal, Blaise. *Monsieur Pascal's Thoughts, Meditations and Prayers Touching Matters Moral and Divine*. Translated by Joseph Walker. London: Printed for Jacob Tonson.

1704

———. *Pensées: Thoughts upon Religion*. Translated by Basil Kennet. London: W. B. for A. & J. Churchill.

1727

———. *Pensées: Thoughts upon Religion*. Translated by Basil Kennet. 2nd ed. London.

1739

———. *Pensées: Thoughts on religion, and other curious subjects*. Translated by Basil Kennet. 4th ed. Dublin: re-printed by and for George Faulkner.

1806

———. *Pensées: Thoughts on Religion*. Translated by Thomas Chevalier. 2nd ed. London: Samuel Bagster.

1850

———. *Pensées: Thoughts on Religion, and Evidences of Christianity (newly translated and arranged, with large additions from original MSS.)*. Translated by M. P. Faugère. London: Longman, Brown, Green, and Longmans.

1887

———. *Pensées: The Thoughts, Letters, and Opuscules of Blaise Pascal*. Translated by O. W. Wight. Boston: Houghton, Mifflin and Company.

1889
———. *Pensées: The Thoughts of Blaise Pascal.* Translated by C. Kegan Paul.

1891
———. *Pensées: Thoughts on Religion and Other Subjects.* Translated by Basil Kennet. Sir John Lubbock's Hundred Books 47.

1898
———. *Pensées: Thoughts of Pascal.* Translated by C. S. Jerram. The Library of Devotion.

1904
———. *Pensées: The Thoughts of Blaise Pascal.* Translated by W. F. Trotter.

1905
———. *Pensées: Thoughts on Religion and Philosophy.* Translated by Isaac Taylor.

11. Critical Scholarship in English

Adamson, Donald. *Blaise Pascal: Mathematician, Physicist and Thinker about God.* New York, Saint Martin's Press, 1995.

Bartha, Paul, and Lawrence Pasternack, eds. *Pascal's Wager.* Cambridge: Cambridge University Press, 2018.

Bloom, Harold. *Blaise Pascal.* New York: Chelsea House, 1989.

Broome, J. H. *Pascal.* London: Edward Arnold, 1965.

Canovas, Frédéric, and David Wetsel, eds. *Pascal/ New Trends in Pascal Studies: Actes du 33ᵉ Congrès de la North American Society for Seventeenth-Century French Literature, Arizona State University (Tempe).* Vol 1. Bibio 17 143. Tübingen: Gunter Narr Verlag, 2002.

Caws, Mary Ann. *Blaise Pascal: Miracles and Reason.* Renaissance Lives. Chicago: University of Chicago Press, 2017.

Cruickshank, John. *Pascal, Pensées.* London: Grant & Cutler, 1983.

Davidson, Hugh M. *The Origins of Certainty: Means and Meanings in Pascal's Pensées.* Chicago: University of Chicago Press, 1979.

———. *Pascal and the Arts of the Mind.* Cambridge: Cambridge University Press, 1993.

Elster, Jon. "Pascal and Decision Theory." In Hammond, *The Cambridge Companion to Pascal,* 53–74.

Force, Pierre. "Innovation as Spiritual Exercise: Montaigne and Pascal." *Journal of the History of Ideas* 66, no. 1 (2005): 17–35.

———. "Pascal and Philosophical Method." In Hammond, *The Cambridge Companion to Pascal,* 216–34.

———. "Géométrie, finesse et premiers principes chez Pascal." *Romance Quarterly* 50, no. 2 (2003): 121–30.

———. "Invention, disposition et mémoire dans les *Pensées* de Pascal." *Dix-septième siècle* 181 (1993): 701–16.

Goldmann, Lucien. *The Hidden God: A Study of Tragic Vision in the Pensées of Pascal and the Tragedies of Racine.* Translated by Philip Thody. London: Routledge, 1964. Originally published as *Le Dieu caché: Étude sur la vision tragique dans les "Pensées" de Pascal et le théâtre de Racine* (Paris: Gallimard, 1955).

Hammond, Nicholas, ed. *The Cambridge Companion to Pascal*. Cambridge: Cambridge University Press, 2003.

———. *Playing with Truth: Language and the Human Condition in Pascal's "Pensées"*. Oxford: Oxford University Press, 1994.

———. *Fragmentary Voices: Memory and Education at Port-Royal*. Tübingen: Gunter Narr, 2004.

Hammond, Nicholas, and Michael Moriarty, eds. *Evocations of Eloquence: Rhetoric, Literature and Religion in Early Modern France; Essays in Honour of Peter Bayley*. Oxford: Peter Lang, 2012.

Hazelton, Roger. *Blaise Pascal: The Genius of His Thought*. Philadelphia: Westminster Press, 1974.

Hunter, Graeme. *Pascal the Philosopher: An Introduction*. Toronto: University of Toronto Press, 2013.

Jaouën, Françoise, ed. *Seventeenth-Century French Writers*. Dictionary of Literary Biography 268. Detroit: Gale, 2003.

Jordan, Jeff. *Pascal's Wager: Pragmatic Arguments and Belief in God*. Oxford: Oxford University Press, 2006.

Koch, Erec R. "Blaise Pascal." In Jaouën, *Seventeenth-Century French Writers*, 272–89.

———. *Pascal and Rhetoric: Figural and Persuasive Language in the Scientific Treatises, the Provinciales, and the Pensées*. Charlottesville: Rookwood Press, 1997.

Lyons, John D. *The Phantom of Chance: From Fortune to Randomness in Seventeenth-Century French Literature*. Edinburgh: Edinburgh University Press, 2012.

Kolakowski, Leszek. *God Owes Us Nothing: A Brief Remark on Pascal's Religion and on the Spirit of Jansenism*. Chicago: University of Chicago Press, 1995.

Mariner, Francis. "Family Perspectives in Gilberte Périer's *Vie de Monsieur Pascal*." In Canovas and Wetsel, *Pascal/ New Trends in Pascal Studies*, 203–17.

Melzer, Sara E. *Discourses of the Fall: A Study of Pascal's Pensées*. Berkeley: University of California Press, 1986.

Miel, Jan. *Pascal and Theology*. Baltimore: Johns Hopkins University Press, 1970.

Moriarty, Michael. *Early Modern French Thought: The Age of Suspicion*. Oxford: Oxford University Press, 2003.

———. "Grace and Religious Belief in Pascal." In Hammond, *The Cambridge Companion to Pascal*, 144–61.

———. "Pascal: The Wager and Problems of Order." In Hammond and Moriarty, *Evocations of Eloquence*, 99–115.

Muggeridge, Malcolm. *A Third Testament: A Modern Pilgrim Explores the Spiritual Wanderings of Augustine, Blake, Pascal, Tolstoy, Bonhoeffer, Kierkegaard, and Dostoevsky*. Maryknoll: Orbis Books, 2004.

Natoli, Charles M. *Fire in the Dark: Essays on Pascal's Pensées and Provinciales*. Rochester: University of Rochester Press, 2005.

Nelson, Robert J. *Pascal: Adversary and Advocate*. Cambridge, Mass.: Harvard University Press, 1981.

Norman, Buford. *Portraits of Thought: Knowledge, Methods and Styles in Pascal*. Columbus: Ohio University Press, 1989.

Parish, Richard. "*Mais qui parle?* Voice and Persona in the *Pensées.*" *Seventeenth-Century French Studies* 8 (1986): 233–40.

———. *Catholic Particularity in French Seventeenth-Century Writing.* Oxford: Oxford University Press, 2011.

———. "*État présent*: Blaise Pascal." *French Studies* 71, no. 4 (2017): 539–50.

Parker, Thomas. *Volition, Rhetoric, and Emotion in the Work of Pascal.* New York: Routledge, 2008.

Probes, Christine McCall. "In Commemoration of the 350th Anniversary of Pascal's *Lettres Provinciales*: 'L'Amour de Dieu,' Rhetorical Strategies of the Controversy." *Papers on French Seventeenth Century Literature* 36, no. 71 (December 2009): 529–40.

Pugh, Anthony. *The Composition of Pascal's Apologia.* Toronto: University of Toronto Press, 1984.

———. "Imagination and the Unity of the *Pensées.*" In Canovas and Wetsel, *Pascal/ New Trends in Pascal Studies,* 65–73.

Rogers, Ben. *Pascal.* New York: Routledge, 1999.

Sellier, Philippe. "Sur les fleuves de Babylone: The Fluidity of the World and the Search for Permanence in the *Pensées.*" In *Meaning, Structure and History in the "Pensées" of Pascal,* edited by David Wetsel, 33–44. Biblio 17. Tübingen: Papers on French Seventeenth-Century Literature, 1990.

Scholar, Richard, ed. *Pascal, Entretien avec Sacy.* Arles: Actes Sud, 2003.

Steinmann, Jean. *Pascal.* Translated by Martin Turnell. New York: Harcourt, Brace & World, 1965.

Topliss, Patrica. *The Rhetoric of Pascal: A Study of His Art of Persuasion in the "Provinciales" and the "Pensées."* Leicester: Leicester University Press, 1966.

Tonneau, Olivier. "The Science of the Cross: The Jansenist Doctrine of Predestination and Their Pedagogy of Conversion." In Hammond and Moriarty, *Evocations of Eloquence,* 117–31.

Wetsel, David. *L'Écriture et le Reste: The Pensées of Pascal in the Exegetical Tradition of Port-Royal.* Columbus: Ohio State University Press, 1981.

———. "Histoire de la Chine: Pascal and the Challenge to Biblical Time." *The Journal of Religion* 69, no. 2 (1989): 199–219.

———. *Pascal and Disbelief: Catechesis and Conversion in the "Pensées".* With an *avant-propos* by Philippe Sellier. Washington, D.C.: The Catholic University of America Press, 1995.

———. "Pascal and Holy Writ." In Hammond, *The Cambridge Companion to Pascal,* 162–81.

———. "Self-Annihilation, Self-Hatred and Original Sin in Pascal's *Pensées.*" In Hammond and Moriarty, *Evocations of Eloquence,* 87–98.

Wood, William. *Blaise Pascal on Duplicity, Sin and the Fall: The Secret Instinct.* Oxford: Oxford University Press, 2013.

THE LIFE
OF MONSIEUR
PASCAL

BY HIS SISTER
GILBERTE

INTRODUCTION

Gilberte Périer wrote this *Life* at the request of family and friends shortly after her brother's death in the final months of 1662. Manuscript copies circulated soon thereafter, but publication was not at first envisioned, though the author's husband, Florin Périer, made use of this impressive narrative as early as 1663 in his preface to Pascal's *Treatises on the Equilibrium of Liquids*. In 1669, Gilberte's son Etienne would rely on this *Life* in writing the preface for the first edition of the *Pensées*. Only in 1684, and without Gilberte's knowledge, would *La Vie de Monsieur Pascal* be published in Amsterdam by Abraham Wolfgang.[1] In December of the same year, in the *Nouvelles de la République des Lettres*, Pierre Bayle characterized Gilberte's biography in these terms: "One hundred volumes of sermons do not measure up to such a life, and are much less effective in disarming the impious [...]. They can no longer say that it is only inferior minds that possess piety, for piety of the most highly developed sort has been revealed to them in one of the greatest geometers, in one of the most subtle metaphysicians, and in one of the most penetrating minds that has ever existed in the world."

The Success of a Literary Genre

Over the years, the authoritative historical documentation provided in Gilberte's biography has continued to play an important role in Pascal studies. This superior individual and accomplished writer followed the lead of Jansenist historians and hagiographers in keeping "everything historical" in her narrative. This circumstance is all the more surprising when one considers the fact that *The Life Monsieur Pascal* belongs to a literary genre that has given rise to all sorts of fanciful extravagances. The genre in question is, of course, the legend. Nonetheless, in the precise sense as defined in literary analysis, legend refers only to a type of narrative, with no particular aspersions cast on its historical value. The legend is a short narrative, in verse or prose, recounting the life of an exemplary Christian, written for the purpose of being recited in pub-

---

1. Henceforward referred to as *The Life of Monsieur Pascal*, or simply the *Life*.

lic. Legend, from the Latin *legenda*, is "what is to be read" on the feast day of a saint, generally in a liturgical setting. In the course of the growth and development characterizing the life of any literary form, the legend naturally evolved: certain cuts were made, a specific order adopted, and emphasis shifted to particular narrative sequences. The historical development of the genre cannot be adequately explained by the influence of the second sophistic, that is, the renewal of interest in rhetoric, beginning in the second century and continuing through the fifth century, in which period the legend first developed. The facility with which the narrative grammar and syntax of the legend have been assimilated by the least well-read of narrators across all periods argues in favor of the more direct influence of oral tradition and Christian references—the Life of Christ and the Lives of Saints repeatedly heard over time.

It was Christianity that affirmed the unique and irreplaceable character of every human being, created in the image of God, and so prompted, after the development of autobiography, the expansion of the legend. Pleasure was taken in examining the lives of those who had followed the path of Christ: first, the lives of the martyrs, soon after, the lives of monks and nuns, and finally, the lives of ordinary lay people. Quite naturally, the stress fell, especially when martyrs were concerned, on the "final days," the crowning glory of an existence and the embodiment of its truth. As the narrative is intended to be the truthful account of a life, it opens and closes with precise dates: moreover, the first sequence always insists on anchoring the story in historical fact (the country, the city, the family, and the date of birth of the hero). Between this record of the historical circumstances surrounding the birth and death, three complementary ensembles stand out: the time for choices (childhood and adolescence, natural dispositions, education); the fervent expression of faith and the conversion experience; and the manner of living and the sayings. What all this amounts to is an evangelical X-ray of a life. For this reason, we do not read about the physical attributes of the heroes or the tangible results of their acts—publishing books, for example—which are unimportant when viewed from the perspective of sainthood. Minor failings are also omitted, as the overriding ambition is to trace out the unbroken arc of an existence. Declining to engage in the meaningless transcription of scattered facts, the legend aspires to impart understanding of the suprareality of a life.

The structure of the *Life* conforms in every way to the characteristic structure of the legend. In this respect, Gilberte is influenced by two factors: on the one hand, by the important moments and teachings from the Gospel (conversion, the perfect life, the passion, and death); and, on the other hand, by the narrative model slowly engraved in her mind, over time, through oral tradition and the reading of hundreds of Lives of Saints. Thus, in the absence of any external evidence, it is really unnecessary to assume that Gilberte should have had recourse to any sort of narrative "grid" or model.

The division of *The Life of Monsieur Pascal* into its principal, constitutive components is greatly facilitated by the clean breaks established by the transitions, which are a testimony to Gilberte's accomplishments as a writer (see table on page 6).

Cursory inspection of the narrative organization reveals two notable characteristics of this text in particular and, more generally, of the literary genre of the legend. In the first place, there is the rule concerning the decreasing speed of the narrative. The legend hastens to arrive at the comprehensive presentation of the high point in an existence, a sort of climax, which is clearly dated here (the final nine years), but which is often chronologically vague. The legend subsequently lingers over the final moments. Gilberte devotes fifty-four of the eighty-eight paragraphs in the *Life* to the years 1654 to 1662. Such an imbalance should not be attributed to the fact that these were the years during which work was proceeding on the *Lettres Provinciales* [Provincial letters] and the *Pensées*, since Gilberte hardly speaks at all of her brother's literary works.

In the second place, the autonomy of the principal sequences and the groupings they impose is also notable. The legend brings considerable pressure to bear on the small disorders inherent in historical reality. Gilberte's text provides a striking example of this at the articulation between parts 2 and 3. At the end of part 2, Pascal ends his career as a scientist after conducting the experiments on the vacuum (§21). At the beginning of part 3, the young Pascal has turned over a new leaf: he has understood that "the Christian religion obliges us to live only for God," and this realization "brought to an end all intellectual endeavors" (§22). This notwithstanding, the experiments on the vacuum conducted in Rouen are chronologically situated after this first "conversion." And it should also be noted that Pascal's genuine, but gradual, renunciation of the sciences would only be complete in 1659. In those places where the existence conforms only gradually over time to preliminary, intuitive perceptions of the truth, the legend neglects to mention the backward steps, the hesitations, and even the slow pace of the progress being made. The legend considers that there is a time for everything: a time for self-development, a time for choosing God, and a time for living and dying as a saint. This forceful influence of the genre explains the haze surrounding the "worldly" period and the omission of the disputes over Etienne Pascal's estate. What Gilberte and the legend "see" is that the 1646 conversion constitutes a decisive turning point. For this reason, the author does not even bother to verify the dates—

I	Historical introduction: §1 (first and second sentences) The historical record of the birth

II	The time for choices: §1 (the third sentence)–§21 Childhood, natural dispositions, education, stories of early success (twenty-one paragraphs for twenty-three years)

III	Faith and the two "conversions" (1646 to 1654): §22–§34 the important turning point of 1646 (§22); the submission and use of reason (§23–§25); the Saint-Ange Affair (§26–§29); the conversion of the entire family (§30); the good use of illness (§31–§32); the second "conversion" (§33–§34).

IV	"The manner of living he led up until his death": §35–§74 (as formulated in §34), or "The rules governing the conduct of his life" (as formulated in §35, §43) The "two principal maxims" (§35–§50): introduction (§35); digression on the defender of the faith (§36–§41), probably prompted by the mention of the iron, disciplinary belt (§42); austerities associated with the "two maxims" (§42–§50): the iron, disciplinary belt (§42); voluntary, self-deprivation (§43), even in illness (§44–§47); indifference to ailments and treatments (§48–§50). The self-portrait (§51–§70): "I love poverty" (§51–§56); "assisting the wretched" (§58, prompting the development on purity in §57); a "tenderness" without attachment (§59–§64); "I remain loyal" (§59); "I do not return wrongs" (§66–§67); Citation of the self-portrait written in his own hand on a small piece of paper (§68–§70). The "simplicity" of a great mind (§71–§74)

V	The "final illness": §75–§88

dates which, in any event, belong to the life of the man who was, and to a period of his life that is henceforth without relevance. This lack of concern is even more noteworthy when we examine the following articulation between parts 3 and 4 where, to mark the conclusion of the "conversion," Gilberte takes the trouble to find the date of a change of residence. If she considers this definitive change of neighborhoods important, it is because it symbolizes the definitive change brought about in her brother's life. She reconstitutes history in the same way that the prophets of Israel deciphered the meaning of events. From such a viewpoint, a seemingly unimportant event, such as a change of neighborhood, can be more significant than a great discovery. These clean breaks between the different stages of the itinerary are even more clear-cut in the majority of the Lives of Saints. Indeed, Gilberte introduces repeats, somewhat in the style of a fugue, concerning her brother's simplicity (§24, later reprised in §71–§74) or his illness (§30–§32, §44–§47, later reprised in §75–§88).

Individuality at Risk?

Predestined to relate the story of a life in its full intensity, the legend has much too often extinguished originality in an ocean of goodness. Of the legend's five constitutive "units," four more successfully resist the drowning in pious generalities: the historical introduction, the time for choices, faith and the two "conversions," and the final illness. This is truly where Gilberte excels in capturing her brother's presence on the page, just as she will later excel in bringing her sister to life, from her birth up until her entry into the Port-Royal convent, in her *Life of Jacqueline Pascal*.[2] Throughout these four sequences, what predominates is the rapid and exhilarating succession of verbs conjugated in the past historic; indeed, these are singular events produced only once. We witness the staging of genuine, small-scale scenes indebted at once to the folktale (the interdictions / the transgressions) and to theater, as in the discovery of Euclid's thirty-second proposition (§10–§13). The final illness is gripping in the concrete detail concerning the suffering, the treatments, the doctors' alarming prognoses, and the preparations for the end. Between midnight and one o'clock in the morning, Pascal is at the gates of death; Father Beurrier, summoned in haste, believed him to be in a coma, which prompts Gilberte to furnish this detailed account: "The parish priest then entered the room with the Blessed Sacrament and announced to him: 'Here is Our Lord whom

2. *La Vie de Jacqueline Pascal* in Blaise Pascal, *Œuvres complètes*, ed. Jean Mesnard (Paris: Desclée de Brouwer, 1964), 1:652–71.

I bring to you [...].' These words had the effect of awakening him; and as the parish priest came closer to give him communion, he made an effort and, on his own, half raised himself to receive it with more reverence [...]" (§88). Such an achievement is all the more remarkable given that the legend—and Gilberte's text in particular—customarily employs the plainest, if not also the most uniform, of writing styles. There is no place for anything that could enliven the discourse: no rhetorical questions, no exclamatory phrases, no apostrophes, no anacolutha, no bold juxtapositions of words, no hypotyposes.

The narrative "unit" that represents the greatest threat to singularity is the inevitable, and sometimes interminable, exposition of the virtues. A haze comes to envelop the narrative: spatio-temporal references become rare; we take note of the relentless erasure of proper names, particularly those of individuals. Despite the fact that this lengthy dissection of the virtues takes up a full half of *The Life of Monsieur Pascal*, the name of Port-Royal is not pronounced a single time, not even in the evocation of the miracle of the holy thorn (§38–§39). Indeed, with respect to Jacqueline, it is only stated that she became a nun "in a quite saintly and austere convent" (§30). This periphrasis is not the consequence of some hypothetical precautionary measure; it is merely an example of one of the most common literary practices associated with legendary narratives. This explains why the Duke of Roannez is raised to the status of "this person, recognized for his piety as well as for the preeminent qualities of his mind and the elevated station of his birth" (§45); he is, in sum, an individual who excels in each of the three categories that so compellingly pertain to Pascal's case. But we will also catch fleeting glimpses of "a very pretty, young girl" (§48), of "a quite virtuous and enlightened individual" (§72), and of "a good man" (§77). In this respect, the legend often appears to be motivated by two conflicting goals: anchoring the narrative in historical facts that will never be repeated a second time (the beginning and the end of the narrative); and skipping over the ephemeral surface of the world (particularly in the middle section of the narrative). It is this second goal that presides over the seamless transitioning of the legend to a colorless ending, reminiscent of the dénouement of *The Princess of Cleves*.[3]

The exaggerated character of the periphrastic substitutions for proper names quite naturally leads us to a second procedure, which also results in the elimination of all nuances: the use of hyperbole. Admittedly, this rhetorical figure appears to have been an ingrained trait characterizing the writing of the

---

3. "Her life, which was not long, furnished inimitable examples of virtue." So reads the celebrated concluding sentence of Marie Madeleine de Lafayette's 1678 novel, *The Princess of Clèves*, ed. and trans. John D. Lyons (New York: W. W. Norton, 1994), 108.

entire Pascal family; but understanding hyperbole as a characteristic attribute of the genre itself will shed more light on Gilberte's text. *The Life of Monsieur Pascal* delights in employing the customary vocabulary of hyperbole: *always, never, nothing, everything, quite, extremely*, etc. Indeed, we encounter the Pascal who, beginning in 1646, "did nothing else for the rest of his life other than meditate on divine law day and night" (§24); and the Pascal who "never had any interest in public renown" (§16); and the Pascal who "had a particular love for all the divine offices, especially for the minor liturgical offices" (§72). All of this is not without consequence for the interpretation of certain statements made by Gilberte: statements, for example, concerning Pascal's "total" renunciation of the sciences after 1646 or his "complete" exhaustion in the four final years (§44). Those characteristic conventions of the legend that feature prominently in the praise accorded the various virtues are conspicuous throughout the text. For example, should we not attribute Gilberte's jubilant celebration of the two traits characterizing her brother's genius to her propensity to employ hyperbole? Pascal is presented from the first as a solitary inventor who works alone (§10, §12, §14, §15, §17); and what is even more striking, he invents by amusing himself. Concerning this effortlessness, the sister cites countless examples: "during his hours free from study," he invented mathematics (§10); it was for this reason that his father "gave him Euclid's *Elements* to read during his hours free from study," for he only studied geometry during "his hours free from study" (§14, §15); as for the invention of the arithmetic machine, he arrived at it "without difficulty"; what tired him was having to explain his invention to the artisans (§19); finally, concerning the solution of the *roulette*, "he discovered it without really thinking about it" while he was suffering from a toothache (§21, §45). Although we may smile at this arrangement of the facts, it provides a hint—which it would be ill advised to discount—of the impact that Pascal had on others. Numerous passages attest to the liveliness of his intellectual capabilities, which are always qualified as "singular" or "surprising" (§11, §13, etc.). Irrespective of the endeavor to which Pascal applies himself, he breaks new ground, whether it is in mathematics, physics, religious controversy, rhetoric, or fundamental theology. The hyperbolic staging literally translates the intensity of a personality outside the norm. In sum, for today's readers, *The Life of Monsieur Pascal* can be recommended as a true-to-life legend and as a consummate achievement of this literary genre.

Note on the Present Edition

The *Life* was first published in 1684 in a 49-page brochure, accompanied by a Latin epitaph for Pascal, beginning on the verso of page 49 and continuing onto the following page. The complete title reads: *La Vie de M. Pascal écrite par Madame Périer sa sœur, femme de M. Périer conseiller de la Cour des Aydes de Clermont* [The life of Monsieur Pascal written by Madame Périer, his sister, wife of Monsieur Périer, magistrate in the Tax Court of Clermont]. An engraved bust of Pascal appears at the beginning of the brochure.

The text published in Amsterdam by Abraham Wolfgang (*W*) follows the text of a manuscript now lost (*Wº*). For a critical edition of the text, we also have at our disposal five manuscript copies, all belonging to the same "family" or branch. In 1898, one of these manuscript copies was published in the *Revue d'Histoire Littéraire de la France* by Augustin Gazier who underscored the need of referring to this manuscript to correct diverse errors in the published text (*W*). In 1964, in the first volume of his edition of the complete works of Pascal, Jean Mesnard published critical editions of two different versions of the *Life*. There exists, in fact, a longer version of Gilberte's narrative that has come down to us through a single manuscript of mediocre quality. The additions notably concern the presentation of fragments from the *Pensées* as they appear in the so-called Port-Royal edition (1670, 1678), suggesting that at one time some consideration had been given to employing the *Life* as the preface to this publication. Can we attribute this reworking of the text to Gilberte? There is room for doubt here. Moreover, as this second version could not have been written earlier than 1669, the superiority of the 1662 version cannot be seriously questioned. For this earlier version, Jean Mesnard chose the best of the five available manuscripts as the basis for his critical edition, the so-called Haumont Manuscript, which he corrected against the other manuscripts or the published version.

Careful study reveals, however, the paradoxical status of the published text (*W*). There is no doubt that the typesetter as well as the copyists committed numerous errors: typographical errors, eye-skips to the same word, repetitions, inaccurate transcriptions, etc.[4] Moreover, the copyist made numerous "corrections" and stylistic "improvements" even before submitting the manuscript to the typesetter.[5] The paradox is that these shortcomings are not serious enough to compromise the authority of the published text, many of whose variants—on subtle textual points—are identical to those encountered

---

4. For a discussion of some of these errors, see Pascal, *Pensées*, ed. Sellier (2010), 142.

5. For a discussion of these "corrections" and "improvements" see Pascal, *Pensées*, ed. Sellier (2010), 142.

in the Haumont Manuscript. What can this mean other than that Manuscript *W*ᵒ was of superior quality, and that we should endeavor to arrive at a text that is as close to it as possible? For this reason, the present edition is based on the 1684 brochure, as amended on those points where the authority of the manuscripts is irrefutable or highly credible. For paragraph divisions, I have,[6] with the consent of Jean Mesnard, retained those of the Haumont Manuscript, which are not always without problems (see, for example, §69). The motivation behind this uniform numbering of paragraphs is to avoid the proliferation of numbering schemes that has on occasion interfered with the reading of the *Pensées*.

6. That is, Philippe Sellier, the author of the original version of this introduction to *The Life of Monsieur Pascal* in French.

THE LIFE OF
MONSIEUR PASCAL

[1] My brother was born in Clermont on the nineteenth of June in the year 1623. My father, Etienne Pascal, was a magistrate in the *Cour des Aides*,[1] and my mother's name was Antoinette Begon. As soon as my brother was of an age when others could converse with him, he gave every indication of possessing an extraordinary mind by the small remarks he made, which were quite appropriate, but even more so by the questions he asked on the nature of things, which surprised everyone. This beginning, which showed great promise, was never belied, for as he grew older, he continued to develop his powers of reasoning, so that he was always far above his age.

[2] After my mother had died as early as 1626 when my brother was only three years old, my father, finding himself alone, applied himself more diligently to caring for his family; and as he had no other son than this one, this distinction of only son and the great signs of intelligence that he perceived in the child, created so great an affection for him that he could not bring himself to entrust his education to anyone else; and he resolved at that time to educate him himself, and he did so, my brother never having attended school and never having had any teacher other than my father.

[3] In the year 1631, my father retired to Paris, taking us all along with him, and established residency there. My brother, who was only eight years old at the time, profited greatly from this move, given the commitment that my father had made to educate him; for without a doubt, he would not have been able to devote as much care to his education had he remained in the provinces where the duties of his office and the constant company at home would have greatly distracted him. But as he was at complete liberty in Paris, he applied himself to it wholeheartedly, and achieved all the success that could be expected from the devotion of a father as intelligent and as loving as one could be.

[4] His principal maxim in this education was always to keep the child ahead of his work. It was for this reason that he did not wish to begin teaching

---

1. The *Cour des Aides* is a tax court.

him Latin until he was twelve years old so that he could learn it with greater ease.

[5] During this period, my father did not let him remain unoccupied, for he conversed with him about everything that he considered within his reach. He brought him to a general understanding of what languages were; he explained to him how they had been shown in grammars to be governed by certain rules; that these rules moreover had exceptions that had been duly noted; and that because of this, they had found a way for languages to be understood from one country to another. This general idea sorted things out in his mind, and made him see the reason for the rules of grammar, so that when he came to study it, he knew why he was doing it, and he applied himself precisely to studying those things requiring the most attention.

[6] After these lessons, my father would make him acquire other knowledge; he often spoke to him of the extraordinary effects of nature, such as gunpowder and other things, which are surprising when one considers them. My brother took great pleasure in these discussions, but he wanted to know the reason for all these things; and as they were not all known, he was not satisfied when my father could not explain them to him or when he would give him one of those inadequate explanations that were customarily put forward to hide ignorance: for he always possessed a wonderfully clear mind, capable of discerning falsehood, and it may be said that, in all things, truth was always the sole objective behind his intellectual inquiries since nothing other than its attainment could ever satisfy him. Thus, from childhood, he could only accept that which had the unmistakable appearance of truth; so that when he was not given proper reasons, he searched them out himself; and once he had applied himself to something, he would not let go of it until he had found some reason capable of satisfying him.

[7] On one particular occasion, among others, someone at the table happened inadvertently to strike a faience dish with his knife; he noticed that this produced a loud sound, but that as soon as a hand was put on it, it stopped. He immediately wanted to know the reason for this, and this experiment led him to conduct many others on sounds; he discovered so many things that at the age of eleven, he wrote them up into a treatise that was found to be very well reasoned.

[8] His extraordinary aptitude for geometry first appeared when he was only twelve years old, through an encounter so out of the ordinary that I believe it is worth describing in some detail.

[9] My father was quite knowledgeable about mathematics and, for this reason, frequented those accomplished in this science, who were often re-

ceived in his home; but as he intended to instruct my brother in languages and as he knew that mathematics is something that fully occupies and satisfies the mind, he did not want my brother to have any knowledge of it, for fear that it lead him to neglect Latin and the other languages he wanted him to master. For this reason, he put under lock and key all books treating the subject and refrained, in his presence, from speaking about it with his friends. But these precautions did not prevent the child's curiosity from being piqued, for he would often beg my father to teach him mathematics; but he refused to do so, and offered it up as a reward, promising that he would teach it to him as soon as he had learned Latin and Greek.

[10] Sensing this resistance, my brother asked him one day what this science was and what it treated. My father explained to him that, in general, it was the method of drawing accurate figures and determining their proportional relations to each other; and at the same time he forbade him to speak about it anymore or even to think about it ever again. But this exceptional mind could not be confined within such bounds, once it had grasped the simple idea that mathematics was the infallible method of drawing perfectly proportioned figures; so he began to dream about it on his own; and as he would find himself alone, during his hours free from study, in a room where he was used to entertaining himself, he would use charcoal to draw figures on the tiled floor, endeavoring to discover, for example, the way of drawing a perfectly round circle or a triangle whose sides and angles were equal, or other similar things. He made all these discoveries on his own; then he sought to determine the proportional relations of the figures to each other. But as my father had taken such great care to conceal all these things from him, he did not even know the names, so that he was obliged to create his own terminology, calling a circle *a round*, a line *a bar*, and so forth. After arriving at these definitions, he formulated axioms, and then completed perfectly rigorous demonstrations; and as one thing leads to another in such things, he made such significant progress in his study that he had arrived at the thirty-second proposition in Euclid's first book.[2]

[11] While he was so engaged, my father came into the room where my brother was without being heard by him. My father found him so concentrated that a long time passed before my brother noticed his presence. It would be difficult to say who was the more surprised: the son, on seeing the father, because of the latter's express prohibition, or the father, on seeing the son in the middle of all these things. But the father's surprise was even greater, when after he had asked him what he was doing, my brother told him that he was

2. "The sum of the angles in a triangle is equal to two right angles."

looking for something, which was the thirty-second theorem of Euclid's first book. My father asked what had led him to think about investigating this: he replied that it was because he had found some other thing; upon which my father asked him the same question again, and he told him about yet another demonstration that he had completed; and so finally, working backwards in this way, and always using the terms *rounds* and *bars* to explain himself, he arrived at his definitions and axioms.

[12] My father was so awed by the breadth and force of this genius that he left without saying a word, and went to see Monsieur Le Pailleur, a close friend, who was also very learned. Once he had come in, he stood there without moving, like a man in a daze; and seeing this and noticing also that he was shedding tears, Monsieur Le Pailleur was quite concerned, and begged him not to conceal from him any longer the cause of his displeasure. My father told him: "I do not cry for sorrow, but for joy. You are aware of all the precautions that I had taken to prevent my son from acquiring knowledge of mathematics, for fear of turning him away from his other studies; but just see what he has done." After that, he showed him all he had accomplished, about which it could be said that he had, in a sense, invented mathematics.

[13] Monsieur Le Pailleur was not less surprised than my father had been, and he told him that he did not consider it right to hold this mind captive any longer and persist in concealing this knowledge from him; and that he should be allowed to examine the books without being held back any longer.

[14] Finding this reasonable, my father gave him Euclid's *Elements* to read during his hours free from study. He read and understood it on his own, without ever having need of any explanation; and at the same time that he was reading it, he would produce work of his own, and he made such progress that he regularly attended the conferences that were held every week, where all those who were clever in Paris met to present their own works or to examine those of others.

[15] My brother held his own there both with respect to evaluating the work of others and to producing his own; for he was one of those who most often brought in new things. They would often examine in these meetings propositions sent from Italy, Germany, and other foreign countries, and they would solicit his opinion on everything with more care than anyone else's; for he had such penetrating insight that on occasion it happened that he discovered errors that others had not noticed at all. Nonetheless, he only devoted to the study of geometry his hours free from study; for he was learning Latin following the rules that my father had expressly set down for him. But as he discovered in this science the truth for which he had always been so earnest-

ly searching, he was so pleased by this that he brought to it the full force of his intellectual capabilities; so that he had only to apply himself to make such progress that at the age of sixteen, he wrote a *Treatise on Conic Sections*, which was acknowledged as such a great intellectual accomplishment that it was said that not since Archimedes had anything of this substance been seen.

[16] All those who were learned were of the opinion that it should be published without delay, because they said that although it was a work, which would always be praiseworthy, if it were published when he, who had written it, was only sixteen years old, this circumstance would do much to enhance its beauty. But as my brother had never had any interest in public renown, he did not take that into account; and thus this work was never published.

[17] During all this time, he continued studying Latin, and he also studied Greek; and in addition to that, during and after meals, my father would converse with him sometimes about logic, at other times about physics or the other branches of philosophy; and this is all that he learned about them, never having been at school nor having had any other teacher for these subjects as for all the others.

[18] My father took pleasure, as one can imagine, in the great progress that my brother achieved in all these fields of learning, but he did not notice that these strenuous and continuous intellectual exertions at so tender an age could significantly affect his health; and in fact, it did begin to deteriorate when he reached the age of eighteen. But as the ailments he experienced at that time were not of great severity, they did not prevent him from continuing his usual occupations; indeed, it was during this time, at the age of nineteen, that he invented the arithmetic machine, which not only performed all sorts of calculations without pen or counters, but also without needing to know a single rule of arithmetic, and with infallible accuracy.

[19] This work was regarded as something new in nature, for it reduced to a machine a science residing entirely in the mind and provided the means of performing any calculation with complete accuracy and with no need for intellectual effort. This work greatly tired him, but neither for the idea nor for the invention of the mechanism, which he arrived at without difficulty, but for having to convey all these things to the artisans. So that he spent two years working on it to bring it to its current perfection.

[20] But this fatigue and the fragile state of his health that had persisted for several years brought on ailments, which did not leave him from that moment on; indeed, he told us on several occasions that from the age of eighteen he had not spent a single day without pain. But as his ailments were not always of the same uniform severity, as soon as he experienced some relief, his mind immediately endeavored to search out something new.

[21] It was on one of these occasions at the age of twenty-three, after he had seen Torricelli's experiment, that he conceived and subsequently carried out those new experiments that have been named the experiments concerning the vacuum, which clearly establish that all the effects attributed until then to *horror vacui* are caused by the heaviness of air. This endeavor was the last for which he would expend his intellectual efforts in the human sciences; and although he afterwards invented the cycloid, this does not contradict what I have said, for he discovered it without really thinking about it, and in a way that clearly establishes that he had not expressly set out to do so, as I will explain when the time comes.

[22] Immediately after these experiments, before he was twenty-four years old, Divine Providence caused an event to come about obliging him to read certain works of piety; God so enlightened him through this reading that he perfectly understood that the Christian religion obliges us to live only for God and to have no object other than him; and this truth appeared so obvious, so necessary, and so useful to him that it brought to an end all intellectual endeavors: and from that time, he renounced all other knowledge in order to devote himself exclusively to the one thing that Jesus Christ calls necessary.[3]

[23] He had, until then, been preserved, through God's particular grace, from all the vices of youth; and what is even more uncommon for a mind of this caliber and temperament, he had never been inclined toward libertinism so far as religion was concerned, having always confined his curiosity to natural phenomena; and he told me on several occasions that he joined this debt to all the others he owed my father, who, having himself great respect for religion, had instilled it in him from childhood and had given him these maxims: that whatever is the object of faith cannot be the object of reason and much less submit to it.

[24] These maxims, which were often repeated by a father for whom he had great esteem and in whom he saw great learning accompanied by clear and powerful reasoning, made such a great impression on his mind that, notwithstanding the speeches that he heard the libertines make, he was not at all moved; and even though he was quite young, he was of the opinion that they subscribed to the erroneous principle that human reason is above all things, and that they did not understand the nature of faith. And thus this mind so great, so vast, so filled with curiosity and so bent on discovering the cause and reason for everything, was at the same time submissive like a child in ev-

---

3. As she contemplates the complete biographical trajectory, Gilberte is struck by the importance of the 1646 "conversion." Pascal's work on the vacuum, however, occurs shortly after this transformation of his heart. Given the sheer quantity of her brother's theological works, she also forgets to mention his return to science in the first six months of 1654.

erything concerning religion; and this simplicity ruled him his entire life; so that from the very moment he resolved to pursue no other study than that of religion, he never applied himself to investigating speculative theological questions, and he applied the full capabilities of his mind to knowing and practicing the perfection of Christian morality, to which he dedicated all the talents that God had given him; and he did nothing else for the rest of his life other than meditate on divine law day and night.

[25] But even though he did not undertake a particular study of scholasticism, he was not unaware of decisions taken by the Church against heresies that were born of subtleties in the mind; and it was against these sorts of intellectual inquiry that he was most heated, and God provided him an opportunity at that time to reveal the zeal he had for religion.

[26] At the time he was in Rouen, where my father was employed in the king's service, and, at the same time, a man there was also teaching a new philosophy, which attracted the attention of all the intellectually curious. Having been urged by two young men counted among his friends to go with them to meet him, my brother did so; but they were quite surprised during their conversation with this man that, in expounding the principles of his philosophy, he drew conclusions on doctrinal points that were contrary to decisions taken by the Church.

[27] He proved, through his reasoning, that the body of Jesus Christ was not formed of the blood of the Blessed Virgin, but of an expressly created substance, and that the body of the Virgin, etc.,[4] and several other similar things. They attempted to persuade him of his error, but he remained firm in his beliefs. So that after discussing among themselves the danger of allowing a man of such mistaken beliefs to instruct young people, they resolved first to warn him and subsequently to denounce him, should he resist the advice that they would give him.

[28] Things came to pass in this way, for he disregarded their advice, so that they believed it to be their duty to denounce him to Monsieur du Bellay,[5] who, at the time, through delegation of the archbishop, was performing episcopal duties in the diocese of Rouen. Monsieur du Bellay sent for this man and questioned him, but was deceived by an equivocal confession of faith, written and signed by his hand, not bothering any further with a complaint of such importance that had been presented to him by three young men.

4. "That the body of the Virgin. . ." This phrase was omitted from the 1684 brochure, but can be found in the five manuscripts; it is, in fact, one of the theses of Jacques Forton, sieur de Saint-Ange, that the body of the Virgin had not been formed of the blood of her parents, etc.

5. The famous Jean-Pierre Camus (1584–1652), formerly bishop of Bellay, was at the time assisting the archbishop of Rouen.

[29] Nonetheless, as soon as they examined this confession of faith, they recognized the deficiencies; this obliged them to travel to Gaillon to see Monsignor the Archbishop of Rouen who, after examining all these matters, found them so important that he wrote an official letter to his council and gave explicit instructions to Monsieur du Bellay to have this man completely retract all the points on which he was accused, and to receive nothing from him except through the intermediary of those who had denounced him. Everything was carried out in this way; and he appeared before Monsignor the Archbishop's council, and renounced all his beliefs; and it could be said that he did so sincerely, for he never expressed any animosity against those who had brought up this affair. This leads one to believe that perhaps he had himself been misled by the false conclusions that he had drawn from his false beliefs. It is thus quite certain that they had no intention of damaging his reputation and no goal other than to have him recognize his errors and prevent him from misleading young people who would not have been able to distinguish truth from falsehood in questions of such subtlety.

[30] And so this affair came to a quiet close, and as my brother continued, more and more, to search out ways to please God, this love for Christian perfection became so impassioned that by the time he was twenty-four years old, it had spread through the entire household. Even my father saw no shame in submitting to his son's teachings, and embraced at that time a more rigorous manner of living that he continued to perfect through the continuous practice of virtue up until his death, which was Christian in all respects. And my sister, who had quite extraordinary intellectual capabilities, and had acquired in childhood a reputation that few girls attain, was so moved by my brother's words that she resolved to renounce all the advantages that she had until then affectioned in order to give herself over entirely to God, as she has done since, by becoming a nun in a very saintly and austere convent,[6] where she made such good use of the perfections that God had bestowed upon her, that she was found worthy of the most difficult tasks, of which she always acquitted herself with all imaginable devotion; and she died there in saintly fashion on the 4th of October in the year 1661 at the age of thirty-six.

[31] At the same time, my brother, whom God had employed to bring about all these good works, never stopped suffering from illness that became ever more debilitating as it progressed. But as he now knew no other science than perfection,[7] he discovered a great difference between this science and the others that had occupied his mind until then; for although his ailments

6. Port-Royal.
7. That is, Christian perfection.

had retarded his progress in these other sciences, this one, on the contrary, profited from these same ailments by the admirable patience with which he suffered through them. To demonstrate this, I will limit myself to citing one example.

[32] He had, among other ailments, the inability to swallow liquids unless they were warm. Moreover, he could only do so drop by drop. But as he had, in addition to that, unbearable pain in the head, burning intestinal pain, and many other ailments, the doctors prescribed a purge every other day for three months. He had to take all these medicines and to do so he had to warm them and swallow them drop by drop, a veritable torture, and quite painful for those around him, but he never complained about it.

[33] The continuation of these treatments, with the many others that he was required to follow, brought him some relief, but not perfect health. This led the doctors to believe that, in order completely to reestablish his health, he had to abandon all intellectual exertion and search out, as much as possible, opportunities for diversion. My brother had some difficulty in accepting this advice because he saw the danger in it; but he finally agreed to follow it as he believed himself obliged to do all that he possibly could to reestablish his health, and he convinced himself that sensible diversion could do him no harm; and so he entered the world. And through God's grace, he was always preserved from worldly vice; but as God was calling him to higher perfection, he had no wish to leave him there, and to that end, he employed my sister, just as he had previously employed my brother, when he wanted to have my sister withdraw from her engagements in the world.

[34] She was at the time a nun, and she led such a saintly life that she edified the entire community. Being in this state, she was pained to see that the person, to whom she was indebted after God for the many graces she enjoyed, was not in possession of these same graces; and as my brother saw her frequently, she was often able to speak to him about it. And in the end, she did it so forcefully and at the same time so softly that she persuaded him, as he had previously persuaded her, to quit unconditionally the world and all worldly commerce; so that he resolved to eliminate all that was purposeless in his life, even at the risk of endangering his health, for he believed that salvation was to be preferred over all else. At the time he was thirty years old, constantly ill, and from then on he embraced the manner of living that he led up until his death.

[35] To arrive at this goal and break with all his usual routines, he moved to a different neighborhood, and remained for a time in the country; and on his return he expressed so firmly his desire to leave the world that the world finally left him. He founded the rules governing the conduct of his life in this

retreat on two principal maxims, which were to renounce all pleasure and all that was superfluous; and this was the practice that he followed for the rest of his life. To succeed in this, he began at that time, and continued thereafter, to refrain as much as he could from employing the services of his servants. He made his own bed, he went to the kitchen to retrieve his dinner, he carried it to his room, and he brought it back afterwards; and eventually, he only employed his servants to cook meals, to go into town, and for other tasks that he truly could not do himself.

[36] All his time was occupied in prayer and in reading holy scripture. He took immense pleasure in this, and he said that holy scripture was not a science of the mind, but a science of the heart, and that it was only intelligible to those who possessed a truthful heart, and that all the others found there nothing but obscurity. It was in this spirit that he read scripture, refusing to call upon his intellectual capabilities; and he applied himself to it so diligently that he came to know it all by heart; so that one could not cite it inaccurately in his presence. For whenever one would speak to him about it, he would unerringly say: "That is not in holy scripture," or "That is in holy scripture," and he would then indicate the precise reference. He also read all the commentaries with great care, for that respect for religion, in which he had been raised in his youth, was transformed into fervent and demonstrable love for all the truths of faith, whether for those truths concerning the submission of intellect or those concerning the practice of moral precepts towards which all of religion is directed; and this love led him to work incessantly at destroying all that was contrary to these truths.

[37] He possessed a natural eloquence that gave him the marvelous ability to say precisely what he set out to say; but he added to that rules that had not been thought of before, and that he employed so advantageously that he mastered his own style; so that, not only did he say all that he wished to say, but he said it in the desired manner, and his discourse achieved the desired effect. And this manner of writing, at once natural, sincere, and forceful was so uniquely his that, as soon as the *Provincial Letters* appeared, it was clear to one and all that he was their author, despite the care he had always taken to conceal this, even from those closest to him.

[38] It was at this time that it pleased God to cure my daughter of a lachrymal fistula, which had made such progress in three and a half years that the pus not only came out of the eye, but also from the nose and mouth. And this abscess was of such a malignant quality that the most adept surgeons in Paris judged it incurable. This notwithstanding, she was cured instantaneously after the abscess was touched by a holy thorn. This authentic miracle was

acknowledged by all, having been confirmed by quite reputable doctors and the most adept surgeons in France, and authorized by a solemn judgment of the Church.

[39] My brother was profoundly touched by this grace, which he regarded as one bestowed on himself, since it concerned a person who, in addition to being a close relation, was also his spiritual daughter in baptism; and his consolation was immense to see that God had shown himself so clearly in a time when faith seemed extinguished in most everyone's heart.[8] The joy that he felt was so great that he was entirely possessed by it; and his mind was so caught up in it that God inspired in him a multitude of wonderful thoughts on miracles, which, giving him new insights on religion, intensified the love and respect that he had always had for it.

[40] And it was this circumstance that prompted the great ambition he had to work at refuting the strongest of the atheists' principal arguments. He had carefully studied them and had employed all of his intellectual capabilities in the search for all the ways to bring them around. This is the task to which he devoted himself entirely; and his final year of work was entirely employed in the compilation of diverse thoughts on this subject. But God, who had inspired this ambition and all these thoughts, did not permit him to bring it to full fruition for reasons unknown to us.

[41] Nonetheless, the great care he took to distance himself from the world did not prevent him from receiving individuals of great intellect and high station who, thinking about their own withdrawal from the world, would often ask him for advice and then follow it to the letter; other individuals, who had serious doubts on matters of faith and knew that he possessed great insight on the subject, also came to see him and always went away satisfied. Indeed, all these individuals, who are presently living a Christian life, still affirm today that it is his advice, counsel, and enlightened guidance to which they are indebted for all the good work they do.

[42] These conversations, in which he frequently found himself engaged, though they were all entered into for charitable reasons, did not fail to instill

---

8. Starting with the nuns of Port-Royal, who understood little of the quarrel, refusal to sign the formulary stating that the heretical propositions attributed to Jansenius were in fact to be found in his *Augustinius*, the monastery came under intense scrutiny and persecution. Those nuns at Port-Royal-des-Champs who refused to sign the formulary (those at the convent in Paris did sign) were removed to other orders. The order was prohibited from taking in new novices and was later suppressed entirely. Ultimately, in 1711, under the direct orders of Louis, the monastery was demolished. Not a stone was left standing and the graves of the nuns going back to the Middle Ages desecrated, their bones being thrown into a common pit. Such was the hatred of Louis XIV and his Jesuit confessors of everything the so-called "Jansenists" stood for. Only the bones of Racine, whose widow appealed directly to the King, were spared and interred in the church of Saint Etienne-du-Mont, next to those of Blaise Pascal.

in him the fear that there might be some danger in them. But as he believed that he could not, in good conscience, withhold the assistance that these individuals requested of him, he found a solution for this. On those occasions, he would retrieve an iron belt with many sharp points and wear it directly on the unprotected skin; and when stray, frivolous thoughts would arise or when he would take pleasure in the place where he happened to be or in something similar, he would jab himself with his elbow to increase the biting pain of the points and, in this way, would remind himself of his commitments. This practice seemed to him so useful that he continued it up until his death, and even in the final moments of his life when he was in constant pain; for not being able to write or read, he was obliged to remain unoccupied, without anything to do, or sometimes to take a walk. And he was in constant fear that this lack of activity should turn him away from his commitments. We did not learn about any of these things until after his death from a person of great virtue, who had great confidence in him, and to whom my brother had been obliged to speak about it for reasons relating to this particular person.

[43] This rigorous discipline that he exercised over himself was drawn from that important maxim of renouncing all pleasure, on which he had founded the rules governing the conduct of his life at the beginning of his retreat. Nor did he fail to practice scrupulously the other maxim that obligated him to renounce all that was superfluous. For he so strictly cut back on all that was nonessential that he was reduced, little by little, to dispensing with tapestries in his room because he did not think that they were necessary; and moreover he did not feel obliged by decorum since the only people who came to see him were those to whom he was continually recommending cutting back on the superfluous; so that they were not surprised by the fact that he himself lived in the same manner that he counseled others to live.

[44] That is how he spent five years of his life, from age thirty to thirty-five, working incessantly for God, for his fellowman, or for himself, while endeavoring to achieve ever greater perfection in himself; and it might arguably be said that this was all the time that he really lived, for the four years that God accorded him afterwards were years of continuous languor. It was not exactly an illness that newly came upon him, but an intensification of those serious ailments to which he had been subject since childhood. But they attacked him at the time so violently that he eventually succumbed to them; and during all that time, he was not able to work a single instant on that important work that he had undertaken on behalf of religion, nor assist, through conversation or in writing, those individuals who approached him for advice; for the pain was so great that he could not oblige them, though he had a great desire to do so.

[45] This return of his ailments began with a toothache completely depriving him of sleep. One night, during one of his sleepless vigils, a thought happened to come to him unexpectedly concerning the problem of the cycloid. This thought was followed by another and this second thought by yet another; finally, a multitude of thoughts succeeded one another and revealed to him, in spite of himself, the solution to all these things, which surprised him. But as he had long ago renounced all such learning, he did not even bother to write it down. Nonetheless, he chanced to speak about it to a person to whom he owed all manner of deference, out of respect and gratitude for the friendship with which he honored him; this person,[9] recognized for his piety as well as for the preeminent qualities of his mind and the high station of his birth, conceived of a use for it that would only promote the glory of God, and considered it appropriate that he should make use of it in the way he did, and subsequently to have it published.

[46] It was only then that he wrote it down, but he wrote with unusual speed, finishing it in eighteen days; for as the printers worked, he would furnish two of them at the same time with two different treatises, even though there were never any other copies other than those prepared for the publication; which came but six months after his discovery.

[47] Meanwhile, his ailments persisted, not giving him a single moment of relief, and reduced him, as I have said, to the state of no longer being able to work or to see practically anyone. But while they prevented him from serving the public and private individuals, they were not at all unhelpful for himself; and he endured them with such equanimity and patience that there is every reason to believe that God intended, in this way, to make him such as he desired him to be when he would appear before him; for during his long illness, he never turned away from his commitments, and always kept in mind those two important maxims to renounce all pleasure and all that was superfluous. He practiced these maxims in the throes of his pain by exercising continuous vigilance over the senses, categorically refusing them all that was pleasurable; and when necessity obliged him to do something that might please the senses, he had a marvelous ability to turn his mind away from it so as not to take part in it at all.

[48] For example, as his continuing ailments obliged him to eat lightly and with care, he took great care not to notice the taste of what he ate; and we observed that, however much trouble we took to provide him with agreeable tasting viands, because of his susceptibility to nausea, never did he say: "Here is something that is good." And even when he was served something new that

---

9. The Duke of Roannez (see "Fragments Not Recorded in the Second Copy," fr. 804 and n. 2).

was in season, if he was asked after the meal if he had found it to his liking, he simply said: "You should have told me about it beforehand, for presently I no longer have any memory of it, and I must confess that I did not pay attention to it." And when someone happened to praise the quality of a dish in his presence, he could not put up with it, qualifying it as an expression of sensuality, even if it was only the most ordinary of fare; because he said that it was an indication that one was eating to please the palate, which was always blameworthy.

[49] To avoid falling into this evil, he never allowed anyone to make any sauces or tasty preparations for him, not even with oranges or verjuice, or with anything that might excite the appetite, even though he naturally liked all these things. And to keep himself within these strict limits, he had taken the trouble, at the beginning of his retreat, to note what was required to satisfy the needs of his stomach and, from that time, he had settled on what it was he would eat; so that however great his appetite, he never went beyond those limits; and however great his distaste for his fare, he always forced himself to eat it; and when he was asked the reason why he placed such constraints on himself, he replied that it was the needs of the stomach that should be satisfied and not those of our appetite.

[50] Mortification of the senses extended not only to depriving them of anything capable of pleasing them, but also not refusing them, for this reason, anything that could be cause for displeasure, whether in his food or in his medicines. He took clear soups for four full years without voicing the least aversion for them; and he took everything that was prescribed for his health without the least difficulty however disagreeable; and when I expressed surprise that he did not voice the least repugnance in taking them, he chided me in bemused fashion, and stated that he himself could not understand how people could express repugnance in taking a medicine voluntarily after having been forewarned that it was unpleasant, adding that it was only violence or surprise that ought to induce such a reaction. It was in this fashion that he worked incessantly for the mortification of his senses.

[51] He had such a great love of poverty that it was always present in his thoughts; so that whenever he considered doing something or whenever someone asked for his advice, the first thought that came to mind was to determine if it provided the opportunity to practice poverty. One of the things on which he examined himself the most was the fanciful desire to excel in everything: to employ, for example, the best workmen for everything, and other similar things. Nor could he tolerate people who aspired tirelessly to have every convenience, such as having everything close at hand and a thousand

other things that people do without a second thought because they do not believe there is harm in it. But he did not judge things in the same way, and he would often tell us that there was nothing more capable of extinguishing the spirit of poverty than the curious pursuit of convenience, and of that decorum which leads to our wanting always to have the best and the best made of everything; and he would tell us that as for workmen, one should always choose the poorest and the most worthy, and not opt for that excellence which is never necessary or useful in any circumstance. He would sometimes exclaim: "If my heart were as impoverished as my mind, I would be quite happy; for I am truly convinced that poverty is a great means to realize one's salvation."

[52] This love that he had for poverty moved him to love the poor with such great tenderness that he could never refrain from giving alms, although he had to do so from his own living expenses as he had only limited means and was obliged to incur expenses exceeding his income because of his illness. But when others tried to point this out to him after he had made a consequential charitable gift, he would become angry and say: "One thing that I have noticed is that however poor we are, we always leave something behind when we die." In this way, he stopped all discussion; and sometimes he would go so far that he was reduced to borrowing money on interest after he had given everything that he had to the poor, since he did not want to inconvenience his friends after he had done this.

[53] As soon as the public carriage system had been set up, he told me that he wanted to ask for a 1000-franc advance on his share from the lenders with whom they were dealing; and as they were of his acquaintance, he wondered if an agreement could not be reached with them to send this sum to the poor of Blois; and when I told him that the venture was too uncertain to allow for that and he would have to wait another year, he immediately responded that he did not see that as a significant obstacle since if they lost their investment, he would reimburse them from his own funds, and that he could not contemplate waiting another year as the need was too pressing to defer this charitable assistance. But as no agreement was reached with these individuals, he could not carry through on this resolve, through which he made us see the truth of what he had told us so often, that he only desired wealth in order to assist the poor, since when God created the expectation of his coming into some wealth, he began to distribute it in advance, and even before he was assured of obtaining it.

[54] His charity toward the poor had always been very great, but at the end of his life it was so greatly increased that I could give him no greater pleasure than conversing with him about it. He had been exhorting me quite insis-

tently for four years to devote myself to the service of the poor, and to inspire my children to do the same. And when I would tell him that I was concerned it might turn me away from caring for my family, he would tell me that it was only for lack of firm resolution, and that as there are diverse levels of commitment in the practice of this virtue, it could be practiced in such a way so as not to compromise household duties in the least. He would say that it was a general spiritual calling addressed, without exception, to all Christians, and that no particular sign was required to know whether one had been called, because it was, without a doubt, on the response to that calling that Jesus Christ would base his judgment of the world; and that when one considers that the mere omission of this virtue is cause for damnation, this thought alone should suffice, had we faith, to inspire us to part with all we possess. Moreover, he would tell us that frequenting the poor was extremely useful, for in continually seeing the misery and afflictions that overwhelm them, and seeing that even in acute stages of illnesses, they are without the most basic necessities, that after seeing all this, one would have to be, indeed, quite cold hearted not to deprive oneself voluntarily of unnecessary conveniences and superfluous adornments.

[55] All this talk inspired us, and would sometimes move us to propose plans to find resources to fund a general scheme providing for all these needs; but he did not approve of this, and he would say that we are not called upon to fulfill general obligations, but particular ones, and he believed that the manner most agreeable to God was to serve the poor in the spirit of poverty, that is, each in accordance with his means, without filling one's mind with those grand schemes inspired by that excellence whose pursuit he criticized in all things. It was not that he was against the establishment of public hospitals; on the contrary, he had great love for them as his last will attests; but he would say that these grand ventures were reserved for those individuals whom God had predestined to that purpose and whom he had led there in quasi visible fashion; but that it was not a general vocation that was expected of all of us as was the individual assistance ministered daily to the poor.

[56] These are part of the teachings he gave us to inspire practice of that virtue which held such an important place in his heart. It is a small sampling revealing to us the profound greatness of his charity.

[57] His purity was not of a lesser quality, and he had such great respect for this virtue that he was constantly on guard to prevent its being compromised either in himself or in others; and it is scarcely believable how scrupulous he was on this point. I myself even felt somewhat intimidated here; for he often found fault in remarks I made that seemed to me entirely innocent until he made me see the deficiencies that I would never have been aware of

without his observations. If I sometimes happened to say that I had seen a beautiful woman, he would become angry and he would tell me that such remarks should never be made in the presence of lackeys and young people as I could not know what thoughts my remarks might arouse in them. Nor could he suffer the caresses that I received from my children, and he told me that they should be forced to break with that habit, and that it could only harm them; and that tenderness could be shown to them in thousands of other ways. Those were the instructions that he gave me on the subject, and such was his vigilance for the safeguarding of purity in himself and in others.

[58] An event, which occurred about three months before his death, is tangible proof of this, and demonstrates at the same time the profound greatness of his charity. As he was coming home one day from mass at Saint Sulpice, he was approached by a very pretty young girl about fifteen years old, who asked him for alms. He was upset to see this person exposed to such obvious danger. He asked her who she was and what had obliged her to ask for alms; and having learned that she was from the country, that her father had died, and that her mother had fallen ill and been taken that very day to the *Hôtel-Dieu*,[10] he believed that God had sent her to him at that precise moment because she was in need. So that, within the hour, he took her to a seminary where he placed her in the hands of a good priest, gave him money and asked him to look after her and to find her a situation where she would receive guidance because of her very young age, and where she would find safety. And to assist him in this endeavor, he informed him that he would send him a woman the following day to buy her clothes and everything that she would need to enable her to enter service with a mistress. The next day he sent a woman who collaborated so well with this good priest that after they had provided her with new clothes, they succeeded in finding a position for her in a very good household. And when this good priest asked this woman the name of the person who had performed this great act of charity, she informed him that she had not been given permission to tell him that; but that she would, from time to time, come to see him and continue to assist him in meeting the needs of this young girl. Upon which he said to her: "May I ask that you obtain his permission to tell me his name. I promise you that I will never speak about it during his lifetime. But if God provides that he should die before me, I would have the great consolation of publicizing this action; for I find it so worthy of praise that I cannot suffer its being relegated to oblivion." Thus, on the basis of this single encounter, this good priest, without knowing my brother, was able to judge the full extent of his charity and love of purity.

10. The oldest hospital in Paris.

[59] He had great tenderness for us, but this affection did not go so far as attachment, and he gave quite tangible proof of this at my sister's death, which preceded his own death by ten months. For when he received this news, he said nothing other than: "May God also grant us the grace to die so well!" And from that time, he was always in a state of admirable submission to the orders of Divine Providence, never making any other observation on this than the extraordinary grace that God had granted my sister during her lifetime, and the circumstances surrounding her death; this led him to say continually: "Blessed are those who die, provided that they die in the Lord!" And when he saw that I was in a state of constant grieving over this loss, which I felt so deeply, he became angry and told me that it was not at all appropriate, and that one should not have such feelings concerning the death of the righteous; and that one should, on the contrary, praise God for having rewarded her so soon for the small services that she had rendered him.

[60] In this way he made clear that he had no attachment to those whom he loved; for were he capable of having such an attachment, it would have undoubtedly been to my sister, for she was, without doubt, the person he most loved in the world.

[61] But he did not stop there; for not only did he not feel any attachment to others, he did not wish others to feel any attachment to him. I am not speaking of those criminal or dangerous attachments that are common and crude, and generally acknowledged as such, but of the most innocent of friendships; and this was one of the things on which he monitored himself most carefully so as not to encourage it and even prevent it in others. And as I was not aware of this, I was quite surprised by the reproaches that he would sometimes express to me, and I told my sister about it, complaining that my brother did not love me and seemed to be displeased with me in those very moments when I was most affectionately attending to his infirmities. My sister told me that I was mistaken on that account and that she knew on the contrary that he had as great an affection for me as I could have hoped for.

[62] In this way my sister set my mind to rest, and I scarcely had to wait to receive confirmation of this; for whenever I would happen to need my brother's assistance in a particular circumstance, he would embrace it with such devotion and affection that I had no reason to doubt he loved me greatly; so that I came to attribute the cold manner with which he responded to my assiduous efforts to unburden him to the sorrow occasioned by his illness; and this mystery was not resolved for me until the very day of his death, when a person, among those most highly esteemed for their great intellect and piety, with whom he had extensive discussions concerning the practice of virtue,

informed me that my brother had given him this teaching among others that he should never suffer being loved by anyone with attachment; and that this was a fault on which people did not examine themselves adequately because they did not understand all the ramifications, and failed to realize that by encouraging and tolerating such attachments, they were taking possession of a heart that should be God's alone, which amounted to stealing from him the one thing in the world that was most precious to him.

[63] We subsequently discovered that this principle was rooted deeply in his heart; for to keep it always foremost in his thoughts, he wrote it down, in his own hand, on a small, separate piece of paper using these words: "It is unjust for anyone to become attached to me, although this might be done both pleasurably and voluntarily. I would be deceiving those in whom I aroused such a desire, for I am not the final end of anyone and I do not have what is needed to satisfy anyone. Am I not close to death? And so the object of their attachment will die. Therefore, as I would be guilty in leading others to believe a falsehood, even if I insinuated it gently and they believed it with pleasure and thereby gave me pleasure, I am guilty as well if I make myself loved and attract people to become attached to me. I must warn those who might be willing to accept a lie that they must not believe it, whatever advantage I might gain from it, and so too they must not become attached to me, for they must spend their life and their efforts in pleasing God or in searching for him."[11]

[64] It was in this way that he would instruct himself, and he practiced his own teachings so rigorously that I myself had misinterpreted his conduct. Through these indications we have of his spiritual practice, which came to our knowledge only by chance, we can perceive some of the insight that God gave him into the perfection of a Christian life.

[65] He had such great zeal for God's divine order that he could not suffer its being violated in any way at all. This is what made him so fervent in his support of the respect due the king, and led him to resist all overtures during the public disturbances in Paris;[12] and afterwards, he always labeled as mere pretexts all the reasons that were put forward to excuse this rebellion; and he stated that in a state established as a republic like Venice it would be exceedingly wrong to participate in efforts to impose a king and suppress the freedom of a people on whom God had bestowed it; but that in a state where royal

---

11. *Pensées,* fr. 15.

12. A reference to the Fronde, a heterogeneous uprising on a large scale (1648–53), which reflected the sometimes conflicting discontents (and interests) of the princes of the blood, the nobility, the members of the parliamentary milieus; it highlighted Mazarin's unpopularity and so impressed the young Louis XIV that he never forgot that troubled period and took measures to strip the parliamentary institutions and the nobility of any power to resist the royal authority.

authority is established, to violate the respect that is its due would be a form of sacrilege; for it is not only an image of God's divine authority, it also partakes of that very authority, against which one cannot rebel without manifestly expressing opposition to God's divine order; and for this reason, the magnitude of the fault cannot be overemphasized, since it is always accompanied by civil war, which is the greatest sin that can be committed against the interests and well-being of one's neighbors. And he observed this maxim so faithfully that he refused certain significant advantages at that time so as not to go against it. He would frequently say that he felt the same great estrangement from this sin as he did from murder and highway robbery; and that, in a word, there was nothing more contrary to his nature and nothing that tempted him less.

[66] Those were the sentiments that he held on the respect due the king. Accordingly, he could not come to agreement with anyone who opposed these views. And what proves that his conduct was not motivated by temperament or by attachment to his beliefs, is that he used admirable gentleness in dealing with those who committed wrongs against his own person; so that he never treated these individuals differently from anyone else, and he so completely forgot about wrongs that only concerned his own person that it was difficult to have him remember them; and to achieve that, one had to describe the particular circumstances. And when people would sometimes express their admiration over this, he would say: "Do not be so surprised by this, it is not a mark of virtue but of true forgetfulness; I just do not remember at all." Nonetheless, as can be plainly seen here, it is certain that wrongs concerning only his individual person had no great effect on him since he so easily forgot them; for he had such an excellent memory that he often said that he had never forgotten anything that he had wanted to remember.

[67] He practiced this gentleness in his sufferance of disobliging behavior up until the end; for shortly before his death, having been treated badly in dealings that deeply mattered to him by someone who was greatly indebted to him, and having at the same time been rendered a kind service by this person, my brother thanked him so profusely and with such politeness that he reached a point of excess. This did not occur, however, because of a memory lapse, since it all transpired at the same time; but quite simply because he felt no resentment at all for wrongs that only concerned his person.

[68] All these traits and dispositions that I have described in some detail are best seen in the summary self-portrait that he wrote, as follows, in his own hand, on a small piece of paper: "I love poverty, because Jesus Christ loved it.[13] I love wealth, because it gives me the means to help the destitute. I keep

13. The autograph fragment (Pascal, *Pensées*, ed. Sellier [2010], 759) reads "…because he loved it."

faith with everybody. I do not return ill to those who do ill to me, but I wish them a condition similar to mine, in which one receives neither good nor ill at the hands of men. I try to be fair, true, sincere and loyal to all men. And I have a heartfelt affection for those with whom God has united me more closely. And whether I am alone, or in the sight of men, I keep God in mind in all my actions, since it is he who will judge them and since I have dedicated them all to him.

[69] "These are my feelings. And I bless my Redeemer every day of my life, since it was he who placed them in me and he who, out of a man full of weakness, wretchedness, concupiscence, pride, and ambition, has made a man free from all these ills by the power of his grace, to which all glory is due, since I find in myself only wretchedness and error."

[70] Thus, he painted his own portrait so as to have continually before his eyes the path along which God was leading him that he might never stray from it.

[71] His extraordinary insight conjoined with his exceptional intellectual capabilities did not preclude a wonderful simplicity that appeared throughout the remainder of his life and that made him so scrupulous in his observance of all religious practices.

[72] He had a particular love for all the divine offices, especially for the minor liturgical devotions as they were made up of Psalm 119 in which he found so many wonderful things that he experienced special delight in reciting it. And when he would converse with his friends about the beauty of this psalm, he would be so elated that he seemed to be in an ecstatic state; and this meditative practice made him so aware of all the different ways through which we aspire to honor God that he did not neglect a single one of them. When he would be sent *billets*[14] every month, as is customary in many places, he would receive them with wonderful reverence and he would recite the lesson every day; and as he was unable to work in the last four years of his life, his principal diversion was to visit churches where relics were displayed or where there were certain religious ceremonies; and for that purpose, he had a spiritual almanac that informed him of the places where he would find certain devotional ceremonies; and he did all of this with such devotion and simplicity that those who saw him were surprised by it. This prompted a well-turned remark by someone quite virtuous and enlightened, that God's grace makes itself known

---

Gilberte provides here the concrete reference for the allusive pronoun. In her personal transcription of the autograph fragment, she also eliminates the break between the second and third paragraph occurring after the phrase: "Voilà quels sont mes sentiments" (§69).

14. Religious houses sent out circulars or *billets* proposing a meditation on one of the mysteries concerning the life of Christ or one of the great truths of Christianity.

in great minds through small things, and in ordinary minds through great things.

[73] This extraordinary simplicity appeared as soon as one spoke to him about God or about himself. Indeed, the day before his death, a priest[15] of great learning and great virtue came to see him, as he had requested, and after spending an hour with him came away so edified that he told me: "Be consoled, for if God calls him, you will have reason to praise him for the grace that he has accorded him. I had always admired many wonderful things in him, but I had never noticed the extraordinary simplicity that I have just seen. That is an unsurpassable quality in a mind such as his, and I would desire with all my heart to be in his place."

[74] The parish priest of Saint-Étienne,[16] who saw him throughout his illness, noticed the same thing, and frequently said: "He is a child. He is as humble and as submissive as a child." It was because of this same simplicity that others were at complete liberty to point out his faults, and he would always take into account, without resistance, the remarks that were made. The extreme vivaciousness of his mind would sometimes make him so impatient that it was difficult to satisfy him; but when it was brought to his attention, or when he himself noticed that he had upset someone because of his impatience, he would immediately mend relations through manners so gentle and kind acts so numerous that he never lost anyone's friendship over such matters.

[75] I endeavor here, as much as I can, to be brief; otherwise I should have a great deal to say on each of the particular points that I have raised. But as I have no wish to provide a more extensive account, I come now to his final illness.

[76] It began with an unusually pronounced lack of appetite, which came upon him two months before his death. His doctor advised him to refrain from eating solid food and to purge. While he was in this state, he performed a notable act of charity.

[77] He had in his house a trustworthy man, with his wife and his entire family to whom he had given a room and whom he supplied with firewood. He did all of this out of charity, for he did not require any service from them, beyond the fact that he was not alone in his home. This good man had a son who fell ill at the time from smallpox, and as my brother was in need of my assistance, he feared that I might be apprehensive about going to his home because

15. The priest in question was Monsieur de Sainte-Marthe, as we learn from Gilberte in a letter dated 1665. It was at Pascal's request that the confessor of Port-Royal came to visit him.

16. A footnote in the margins of the 1684 brochure reads: "It is Monsieur Beurrier, who subsequently became abbot of Sainte-Geneviève." See *La Vie de M. Pascal, escrite par Mme Perier, sa sœur, femme de M. Perier, conseiller de la Cour des aydes de Clermont* (Amsterdam: Abraham Wolfgang, 1684).

of my children. This obliged him to think about putting some distance between himself and this sick child; but as he feared the child might be in some danger were he to be transported elsewhere in such a state, he preferred moving out himself, even though he was doing quite poorly, stating: "There is less danger for me in changing my living quarters, and for this reason, I should be the one who leaves." Thus, he left his home on June 29th to come stay with us, and he never went home again; for three days after that, he began to have very violent attacks of colic, which prevented him from sleeping at all. But as he had great fortitude and great courage, he endured the pain with remarkable patience. He did not fail to get out of bed every day and take his medicine himself as he was not willing to suffer others providing him the least assistance. The doctors, who were treating him, were aware of the severity of his pain; but as he had a strong and steady pulse and was without fever, they were convinced there was no danger, and even used these words: "there is not the slightest hint of danger."

[78] Not withstanding these words, and realizing that the persistent pain and the sleepless nights were weakening him, on the fourth day of the colic, and even before becoming bedridden, he sent for the parish priest and made his confession. This caused a stir among his friends and led several of them, in a frightened state of apprehension, to come see him; and the doctors themselves were so surprised by this that they could not keep themselves from saying so, stating that it was a sign of fear that they had not expected from him. When my brother saw all the emotion his conduct had created, he was distressed by it and said to me: "I would have liked to take communion; but as I see that others are surprised by my confession, I fear that they would be even more surprised; this is why it is better to wait." And as the parish priest was of the same opinion, he did not take communion.

[79] Meanwhile his illness continued to progress; and as the parish priest came to see him from time to time on pastoral visits, he did not let pass a single one of these opportunities without making his confession; but he did not say anything about it for fear of frightening others, for the doctors continued to provide assurances that there was no danger in his illness. Indeed, as there was a slight abatement in his pain, he was sometimes capable of getting up out of bed in his room. Yet, the pain never left him entirely, and it even sometimes returned, and he also lost a lot of weight, which did not however cause the doctors concern; but irrespective of what they would say, he always said that he was in danger, and he did not fail to make his confession on every occasion the parish priest came to see him.

[80] He even drew up his last will and testament at this time, in which the poor were not forgotten, and he struggled painfully with himself not to leave

them more, for he told me that if Monsieur Périer had been in Paris and had given his consent, he would have disposed of all of his fortune in favor of the poor. Indeed, he had nothing on his mind and in his heart other than the poor, and he would sometimes say to me: "How did it come about that I never did anything for the poor, though I have always had such great love for them?" I told him: "It is that you never had enough of a fortune to be of any great help to them." He responded: "As I had no money to give them, I should have given them my time and effort; it is in this that I have failed, and if the doctors are correct, and if God provides for my recovery from this illness, I am resolved to have no employ or occupation for the rest of my life other than serving the poor." Those were his sentiments when God took him.

[81] During his illness, he joined to this fervent charity a patience so wonderful that he edified and surprised all those who were around him. He would say to those who were pained over his condition that he himself was not at all concerned about it, and that he was even afraid of being cured; and when they would ask the reason for this, he would say: "It is that I know the dangers of good health and the advantages of illness." He would also say, in the throes of acute pain, when others were pained to see him suffering: "Do not feel sorry for me; illness is a natural state for Christians because in it one is as one should always be, suffering from misfortune, divested of all possessions, deprived of all pleasure of the senses, free from all the passions that burden the full course of a lifetime, released from ambition and greed, and continually anticipating death. Is this not the way that Christians should spend their lives? And is it not a great joy when one finds oneself, of necessity, in that state where one should be, and when one has nothing to do other than to submit humbly and peacefully? This is why I ask nothing of you other than to implore God to grant me this grace." It was in this frame of mind that he bore his pain.

[82] He very much wanted to take communion, but the doctors were against it, stating the he could not do so while fasting unless it was during the night, which they advised against unless it were necessary, and that to receive communion as the Viaticum there had to be a danger of dying; as this was not the case, they could not give him their consent. This opposition upset him, but he was obliged to concede on this.

[83] But as the colic persisted, he was ordered to drink waters, which did much to relieve the pain; but on the sixth day of the waters, which was the fourteenth of August, he experienced extreme dizziness accompanied by severe head pain, and although the doctors were not surprised by this, and assured him that it was only the vapor of the waters, he did not fail to make his confession, and he asked with incredible insistence that he be allowed to take

communion, and that, in the name of God, they find a way to put aside the objections that they had been raising until then; and he was so insistent on this, that a person, who happened to be present, reproached him for being so anxious, and told him that he should concur with the sentiments of his friends; that he was in better health; that he was nearly cured of his colic; and that as he was suffering from no more than a vapor from the waters, it was not appropriate for him to have the Holy Sacrament brought; and that it was better to defer receiving communion until he could do so in a church. He responded to this: "Others do not feel my pain; they will realize they are mistaken; the pain in my head is something quite out of the ordinary."

[84] Yet, as he saw great opposition to his wishes, he dared not speak of it anymore; but he told me: "As they do not wish to grant me this request, I would like to compensate for this by doing some good work, and as I cannot enter into spiritual communion with the head,[17] I would enter into such union with the limbs,[18] and for that purpose, I have been thinking about taking in a poor person in ill health who would receive the same care as myself and for whom a servant would be expressly hired, so that in the end, there would not be the slightest difference between him and me, thus, in the shame I feel at having an abundant supply of everything I need, I would have the consolation of knowing that there is a poor person who is being as well cared for as myself. For when I consider that while I am so well off, there are great numbers of the poor who are sicker than I and who lack the most basic necessities, that brings on pain that I cannot bear; so I beg you to ask the parish priest to send a sick person for my purposes."

[85] I immediately sent this request to the parish priest who replied that there was no one whose condition permitted him to be moved, but that as soon as my brother was well, he would give him the means of practicing his charity by entrusting to his care an old man whom he would look after for the rest of his life. For the parish priest had no doubt at the time that he would be cured.

[86] When he realized that he could not have a poor person with him in his home, he then begged me to grant him the favor of being transported to the Incurables,[19] for he had a great desire to die in the company of the poor. I told him that the doctors did not find it advisable to move him in his present

---

17. Jesus Christ.

18. The Furetière clarifies Pascal's reference: "*Membre* [limb or member] is used figuratively, in the moral sense, to describe mystical and political bodies. The poor, the faithful are the *limbs* of Jesus Christ; He is persecuted every day in his *limbs*" (translation by Francis Mariner). Antoine Furetière, *Dictionnaire universel, contenant généralement tous les mots françois tant vieux que modernes, et les termes de toutes les sciences et des arts* (La Haye, A., et R. Leers, 1690.

19. A Parisian hospice for the destitute.

state, which upset him greatly; and he made me promise that if there were some improvement in his condition, I would give him this satisfaction.

[87] Meanwhile, the pain in his head continued to progress, and he suffered through it as he did with all of his ailments, that is, without complaining. On one occasion, on the seventeenth of August, in the throes of severe pain, he asked me to summon the doctors; but at the same time he brought up personal scruples and said to me: "I fear that there is too much probing betrayed in this request." I did not fail, however, to act on it; and the doctors directed him to drink some whey, and assured him once again that there was no danger and that it was only his migraine combined with the vapor of the waters. But not withstanding what they said, he never believed them, and asked me to have a priest spend the night at his side; and I myself found him in such a poor state that, without saying anything to anyone, I gave orders to prepare the candles and everything else that was needed to have him take communion the following morning.

[88] These preparations were not unnecessary but they were needed earlier than we had thought: for around midnight he had such a violent fit of convulsions that, when it had stopped, we believed he was dead, and we had the extreme displeasure, along with all the others, of seeing him die without the sacraments after he had requested them so often and so insistently. But God, who wished to reward so fervent and just a desire, miraculously suspended this fit of convulsions and restored all of his reasoning capabilities just as they had been when he was in perfect health. The parish priest then entered the room with the Holy Sacrament and announced to him: "Here is Our Lord whom I bring you, here is he whom you have so greatly desired." These words had the effect of awakening him; and as the parish priest came closer to give him communion, he made an effort, and, on his own, half raised himself to receive it with more reverence; and after the parish priest had asked the customary questions on the principal mysteries of faith, he clearly responded: "Yes, Monsieur, I believe all that, and with all my heart." And then he received the Holy Viaticum and Extreme Unction with such tender sentiments that he shed tears. He responded to all questions and thanked the parish priest; and when the priest blessed him with the holy chalice, he said: "May God never abandon me!" which were the last words he spoke. For the moment after he had offered up his thanks for this grace, the convulsions took hold of him once again, never leaving him after that, nor permitting him a single moment of clear thinking. They persisted until his death, which came twenty-four hours later, on the nineteenth of August, at one o'clock in the morning, at the age of thirty-nine years and two months.

PENSÉES

The Project
of June 1658

1^1

Order	A.P.R.
	Beginning
Vanity	Submission and Use of Reason
	Excellence
Wretchedness	Transition
	Nature Is Corrupt*[2]
Ennui	Falsity of Other Religions
	Religion Lovable
(*Sound Opinions of the People*)	Foundation
	Figurative Law
Reasons for Effects	Rabbinical Tradition
	Perpetuity
Greatness	Proofs of Moses
	Proofs of Jesus Christ
Contradictions	Prophecies
Diversion	Figures
	Christian Morality
Philosophers	Conclusion
The Sovereign Good	

1. Both Copies open with this list of twenty-nine *liasse* titles. Neither is in Pascal's own handwriting. Though preserving the original order in which the titled dossiers were first discovered, it is hardly a table of contents. "Beginning" is found in the middle of the list. "Transition" is not in its proper place, etc.

2. The copyist, finding no *liasse* corresponding to this title, signaled his perplexity with an asterisk.

[I The Table-*Liasse* of June 1658]¹

2

To be indifferent to the point of despising the things that concern us and to become indifferent to the one thing that concerns us the most.

3

Maccabees from the time they have had no more prophets. Masorah since the coming of Jesus Christ.²

4

But it was not enough that the prophecies [of Christ] should exist, they needed to be disseminated throughout the world and preserved throughout the ages.

And so that his coming should not be taken as resulting from chance, it was necessary for it to be foretold.

_____

It is much more glorious for the Messiah that they [the Jews] should be the spectators and even the instruments of his glory, in addition to the fact that God reserved them for this role.

5

*The bewitching of vanity.*³

So that passion not be harmful, let us act as if there was only a week of life.⁴

1. The reader who has never read the *Pensées* might do well to delay reading this chapter of seemingly unrelated fragments and move on to "[II] Order."
2. The Masorah, the work of the Masoretes, the Jewish scholars who sought to defend the authentic text of the Old Testament by adding annotations. Since written Hebrew is constituted by only consonants, the Masoretes facilitated its reading by inventing a system of vowel-points placed above the sacred text. From the sixth to the twelfth centuries, they worked on the shores of Lake Tiberius. See also fragments 325 and 328. In fragment 736 the notation is reproduced exactly.
3. Wisdom 4:12.
4. See frs.191, 324, and 358.

6
Order

I would be much more afraid of being mistaken on finding that the Christian religion is true than I would of being mistaken in believing it to be true.

7

How the two Testaments consider Jesus Christ: the Old as what it looks forward to, the New as its model, both as their center.

8

Why did Jesus Christ not come in a manifest way instead of providing proof through forerunning prophecies?

———

Why did he have himself foretold through figures?

9
Perpetuity

Let us consider that, since the beginning of the world, the Messiah has been expected or worshipped without interruption; that there were men who said that God had revealed to them that a Redeemer would be born who would save his people; that Abraham then came and said that he had had the revelation that the Redeemer would be born of him through a son he would have; that Jacob declared that of his twelve children he would be born of the line of Judah; that Moses and the prophets then came and announced the time and manner of his coming, saying that their law existed only in expectation of the Messiah's law, that until then it would be permanent but that the other law would last for all eternity; and so that either their law or the Messiah's law, of which it was the promise, would always be on the earth, that in effect it has always endured, and that finally Jesus Christ came in exactly the circumstances foretold. This is to be marveled at.

10

If this was so clearly foretold to the Jews, how could they fail to believe, or why were they not wiped out for resisting something so clear?

I reply. First, it was foretold both that they would not believe something so clear and that they would not be wiped out. And nothing serves the Messiah's glory more, for it was not sufficient that there be prophets, they needed to be kept free of any suspicion. Now, etc.

11

Figures

God, wanting to create for himself a holy people whom he would keep apart from all other nations, deliver from its enemies, and bring to a place of rest, promised to do it and foretold through his prophets the time and manner of his coming. And in the meantime, in order to strengthen the hope of his elect throughout the ages, he granted them an image of it, never leaving them without assurances of his power and of his will to save them. For in the creation of man, Adam was the witness of it as he was the guardian of the promise of the Savior who was to be born of woman, at a time when men were still so close to the time of Creation that they could not have forgotten their Creation and their Fall. When those who had seen Adam were no longer in the world, God sent Noah and saved him and drowned the whole earth through a miracle, which was a clear sign both of his power to save the world and of his will to do so as well as to bring forth from the seed of woman the one whom he had promised.

This miracle was enough to strengthen the hope of men.

As the memory of the Flood was still so fresh amongst men when Noah was still alive, God made his promises to Abraham. And when Shem was still alive,[5] God sent Moses, etc.

12

Man's true nature, his true good, true virtue, and true religion are things that cannot be known separately.

13

Instead of complaining that God has hidden himself, you will give him thanks for revealing himself as much as he has. And you will thank him yet again for not revealing himself to those proud wise men unworthy of knowing so holy a God.

———

Two kinds of people know him: those whose heart is humbled and who rejoice in their lowliness, whatever their degree of intelligence, whether high or low, or those who are intelligent enough to see the truth, whatever objections they may have against it.

---

5. Shem was Noah's oldest son.

14

When we wish to think of God, is there nothing that distracts us or tempts us to turn our thoughts in another direction? All this is bad and born with us.

15[6]

It is unjust for anyone to become attached to me, although this might be done both pleasurably and voluntarily. I would be deceiving those in whom I aroused such a desire, for I am not the final end of anyone and I do not have what is needed to satisfy anyone. Am I not close to death? And so the object of their attachment will die. Therefore, as I would be guilty in leading others to believe a falsehood, even if I insinuated it gently and they believed it with pleasure and thereby gave me pleasure, I am guilty as well if I make myself loved and attract people to become attached to me. I must warn those who might be willing to accept a lie that they must not believe it, whatever advantage I might gain from it, and so too they must not become attached to me, for they must spend their life and their efforts in pleasing God or in searching for him.

16

Man's true nature being lost, anything becomes his nature. Just as man's true good being lost, anything becomes his true good.

17

The philosophers did not prescribe feelings in conformity with the two states of man.

They inspired impulses of pure greatness, and that is not man's true state.

They inspired impulses of pure lowliness, and that is not man's true state.

Impulses of lowliness, not of nature but of penitence, are needed, not for us to remain in that state but to move on to greatness. Impulses of greatness, not of merit but of grace, are needed, but only after we have passed through lowliness.

18

If man is not made for God, why is he happy in God alone?

If man is made for God, why is he so contrary to God?

---

6. Pascal kept the original of this text with him, to serve as a reminder to maintain a certain reserve in his relationships with others, including members of his family. See Gilberte Périer's *The Life of M. Pascal*, §§59–63.

19

Man does not know at which level to place himself. He is clearly lost and fallen from his true place without being able to find it again. He searches for it everywhere, anxiously but in vain, in impenetrable darkness.

20

We desire truth and find only uncertainty within ourselves.

We seek happiness and find only wretchedness and death.

We are incapable of not desiring truth and happiness and yet we are incapable of either certainty or happiness.

This desire has been left in us as much to punish us as to make us perceive from where we have fallen.

21

Proofs of religion

Christian morality/Doctrine/Miracles/Prophecies/Figures[7]

22

Wretchedness

Solomon and Job knew and spoke best of man's wretchedness.[8] One was the happiest and the other the unhappiest of men. One knew the vanity of pleasures through experience, the other knew the reality of suffering.

23

All those contradictions that seemed to steer me furthest from the knowledge of any religion are what led me most quickly to the true religion.

24

I reprove equally those who choose to praise man, those who choose to blame him and those who choose to amuse themselves, and I can approve only of those who search in anguish.[9]

---

7. This much older list constitutes Pascal's preoccupations in 1656–57. See the list of "Proofs" in fr. 717.

8. In the seventeenth century, Solomon was still thought to be the author of Ecclesiastes, which deplores the vanity of human existence.

9. The central theme of the preface to the Apology adumbrated in fr. 681.

25
Instinct, reason

We have an incapacity to prove that dogmatism cannot ever overcome.
We have an idea of the truth that Pyrrhonism[10] cannot ever overcome.

26

The Stoics say: "Turn inward, stay within yourself. There you will find your rest."—And that is not true.

The others say: "Go outside and look for happiness in some kind of diversion." And that is not true. Illnesses ensue.

Happiness is neither outside nor within ourselves. It is in God and both outside and within ourselves.

27

A *Letter* on the folly of human knowledge and philosophy.[11]
This *Letter* to come before *Diversion*.
Happy he who has been able [to know the origin of things].[12]
Happy to wonder at nothing.[13]
Two hundred and eighty kinds of sovereign good in Montaigne.[14]

28

Falsity of those philosophers who did not discuss the immortality of the soul.
Falsity of their dilemma in Montaigne.[15]

---

10. *Pyrrhonism*: the traditional term to designate skepticism, derived from the name of the ancient philosopher Pyrrho (ca. 365–ca. 275 BCE).

11. After the immense success of the *Provincial Letters*, Pascal may have initially envisaged an apology consisting of a series of letters. In fr. 45, he notes: "After the *letter* that one must seek God [fr. 681], write the *letter* . . . which is the discourse of the machine" (fr. 680; emphasis added).

12. *Felix qui potuit*. Virgil's *Georgics*, II, 490. Pascal could have read this line in Montaigne's *Essays*: "happy who knows the origin of things" (III, 10, 949 [numbers refer to the book, chapter, and page within Montaigne's *Essays*]).

13. *Felix nihil admirari*. Horace's *Epistles*, I, VI, 1.7. See Montaigne, *Essays*, II, 12, "To wonder at nothing, that is [almost] all I know to make men happy and to keep them so."

14. Montaigne, *Essays*, II, 12. "There is no combat so violent among the philosophers, and so bitter, as that which arises over the question of the sovereign good of man, out of which, by Varro's reckoning, two hundred and eighty-eight sects were born."

15. Montaigne, *Essays*, II, 12: "The philosophers [. . .] always have this dilemma in their mouths to console us for our mortal condition: 'The soul is either mortal or immortal. If mortal it will be without pain; if immortal, it will go on improving.' They never touch the other branch: 'What if it goes on getting worse?' And they leave to the poets the threats of future punishments" (501).

29

This internal war of reason against the passions has caused those who wanted peace to split into two sects. One group wanted to renounce the passions and become gods, the other wanted to renounce reason and become brute beasts. Des Barreaux.[16] But neither group has been able to do it and so reason still remains to denounce the baseness and injustice of the passions, and to disturb the peace of those who abandon themselves to them, while the passions are still alive in those who wish to renounce them.

30

Greatness of man

We have such a lofty idea of man's soul that we cannot bear to be despised or not to be esteemed by a soul. And men's entire happiness consists in this esteem.

31

Men are so necessarily mad that it would be mad by another twist of madness not to be mad.

32

Anyone wishing to know fully the vanity of man need only consider the causes and effects of love. The cause is a *Je ne sais quoi*. Corneille.[17] And its effects are terrifying. This *Je ne sais quoi*, so trivial that it is not possible to recognize it, moves the whole earth, princes, armies, the entire world.

Cleopatra's nose: had it been shorter, the whole face of the earth would have changed.

16. Jacques Vallée des Barreaux (1599–1673). A flamboyant libertine and former lover of Théophile de Viau, who became known for his numerous homosexual affairs with younger men. A genuine atheist, des Barreaux had written that our senses are all extinguished at the moment of death and that we are but brutish beasts ("Et, par ma raison, je butte /À devenir bête brute" [and, by my reason, I am on the way to becoming a brutish beast], quoted by Gédéon Tallemant des Réaux, *Historiettes*, ed. Louis Monmerqué [Paris: Mercure de France, 1906], 179).

17. *Médée*, II.5, v. 635–36: "Souvent *je ne sais quoi qu'on ne peut exprimer* / Nous surprend, nous emporte et nous force d'aimer" [Often a certain *je ne sais quoi* that cannot be expressed / Catches us unawares, carries us away, and forces us to fall in love] (Corneille, *Œuvres complètes*, ed. André Stegmann, [Paris, Seuil, "Intégrale", 1961], 182; translation courtesy of the Editor). For an analysis of the *je ne sais quoi* in the Classical period, see Richard Scholar, *The "je ne sais quoi" in Early Modern Europe: Encounters with a Certain Something* (Oxford: Oxford University Press, 2005).

33
Wretchedness

The only thing that brings us consolation from our miseries is diversion, and yet that is the greatest of our miseries. For this above all is what prevents us from thinking of ourselves, and that imperceptibly brings about our downfall. Without it we would be in a state of *ennui*, and that *ennui* would drive us to search a more reliable means to escape it. But diversion amuses us and imperceptibly delivers us to death.

34
Agitation

When a soldier or a laborer etc. complains about his hard life, try leaving them with nothing to do.

35
Nature is corrupt

Without Jesus Christ, man can only be in a state of vice and wretchedness.
With Jesus Christ, man is free from vice and wretchedness.
In him lies all our virtue and happiness.
Apart from him there is only vice, wretchedness, error, darkness, death, despair.

36

Not only do we know God through Jesus Christ alone but we know ourselves through Jesus Christ alone. We know life and death through Jesus Christ alone. Apart from Jesus Christ we do not know the meaning of our life or our death or God or ourselves.

Thus without the scriptures, which have Jesus Christ as their sole object, we know nothing and see only darkness and confusion in God's nature and in nature itself.

[II] Order[1]

37

The psalms sung throughout the earth.[2]
Who bears witness to Mohammed? Himself.[3]
Jesus Christ considers his own witness to be nothing.[4]
The status of witnesses is such that they must exist always and everywhere and be wretched. He is alone.

38

Order

By dialogues[5]

"What should I do? I see nothing but darkness everywhere. Am I to believe that I am nothing? Am I to believe that I am God?"[6]

———

"All things change and follow on from each other."
"You are wrong, there is. . ."

———

"What then! Do you not say yourself that the sky and the birds prove God?"[7] No. "And your religion does not say this?" No. For while it is true in a

1. "Order" assembles the various notes that Pascal set down, at the time when he ordered his twenty-six provisional rubrics (chs. 3–28) of the Apology, to remind himself about the new ideas germinating in his mind. Chief among these are the major discourses that he would write: the "Letter urging the search for God" (681); the "Discourse on the machine" (680); "On corruption" (fr. 690). To these he adds another project, "The state of the Jews," which would result in several dossiers of notes.

2. The Jewish people, dispersed throughout the known world at the fall of the Temple, continued to sing, without realizing their true meaning, those Messianic Psalms predicting Christ. As hostile witnesses, their testimony served to prove the truth of Christianity.

3. See ch. XVII, frs. 235–42. This line continues the reasoning of the preceding one. The Jews bear witness to Christ. Mohammed has no witnesses besides himself.

4. See John 5:31.

5. The paper on which this fragment is written appears to date from a time, perhaps quite earlier, during which Pascal was considering the various forms in which his Apology could be cast. See above, ch. I, n. 11.

6. See the tableau depicting the hardened skeptic in par. 12 of the "Letter urging the search for God" (681): "I know not who put me into the world. . . ."

7. The traditional cosmological proof of God's existence.

sense for a few souls whom God chose to enlighten, it is nonetheless false for the majority.

———

Letter urging the search for God.[8]

And then have him search for him amongst philosophers, Pyrrhonists,[9] and dogmatists, who will disconcert the person who is searching.

39
Order

A letter of exhortation to a friend to bring him to search.[10] And he will reply: "But what use will it be for me to search? I see no result." And then reply to him: "Do not despair." And he would reply that he would be happy to discover some light, but that according to that very religion if he were to believe in this way, it would be of no use to him, and so he would just as soon not search at all. And on that point reply to him: "The machine."[11]

40

First part: Wretchedness of man without God.
Second part: Happiness of man with God.

———

or

First part: Nature is corrupt, as proved by nature itself.
Second part: There is a Redeemer, as proved by the scriptures.[12]

41

Letter showing the usefulness of proofs. Through the machine.[13]

Faith is different from proof. One is human; the other is a gift from God. *The just man liveth by faith.*[14] It is this kind of faith that God himself puts into

8. The same letter as the one in fr. 39 "exhorting a friend to seek," which will ultimately constitute the preface to the Apology set down in fr. 681.

9. Skeptics. See introduction, "The Intellectual Universe of the *Pensées*," and ch. I, fr. 25, n. 10.

10. This will result in the highly-finished preface constituted by fr. 681. See the introduction, in particular, the section "The Chapters Subsequent to the Project of 1658." Pascal here refers to the same "letter" anticipated in fr. 45: "the letter that one must seek God." See introduction, " Pascal's Rhetoric of Conversion" and "The Preface to the Apology." The friend was probably the would-be *honnête homme*, Damien Miton. See introduction, "The Contours of Disbelief," and fr. 494.

11. The discourse sketched in fr. 680, commonly called "The Wager." Influenced by Descartes's insistence upon the role of habit in human existence, Pascal is convinced that the human body and part of the human mind are mechanisms.

12. Pascal's formulation, in two equivalent aphorisms, of the broad outline of the Apology.

13. In fragment 680, "Discourse on the Machine." See introduction, "The Wager."

14. Romans 1:17.

our hearts, and proof is often the instrument of it. *Faith* [...] *cometh by hearing.*[15] But this faith resides in our hearts and makes us say not "I know" but "I believe."

42
Order

See what is clear and indisputable about the whole state of the Jews.

43

In the letter concerning injustice can be included,

The joke about elder brothers who have everything. "My friend, you were born on this side of the mountain. It is therefore just that your elder brother should have everything."

"Why are you killing me?"[16]

44

The miseries of human life have subverted all this. Since they have seen this, they have taken to diversion.

45

Order. After the letter that one must seek God,[17] write the letter about removing obstacles, which is the discourse on the machine, about preparing the machine and searching by means of reason.[18]

46
Order

Men despise religion. They detest it and are afraid that it might be true. To cure this, it is necessary to start by showing that religion is not at all contrary to reason. Venerable, inspire respect for it. Next, make it worthy of love, make good people wish[19] that it were true, and then show that it is true.

Worthy of respect, because it has fully understood man.

Worthy of love, because it promises the true good.

---

15. Romans 10:19.

16. See the completed version of this thought in fr. 84. Law and custom are relative. What is right in one country is wrong in another.

17. I.e., fr. 681.

18. I.e., fr. 680.

19. Once Pascal's interlocutor comes to "wish" Christianity *were* true, his fatal indifference is overcome, and he has taken the most crucial step toward belief. He is on his way to becoming the "seeker" commended in par. 5 of the preface to the Apology (fr. 681).

[III] Vanity

47

Two similar faces, neither of which provokes laughter on its own, provoke laughter when seen together because of their similarity.

48

True Christians observe these follies nonetheless, not because they respect such follies but because of God's order that for mankind's punishment has made them subject to these follies. *"For every creature was made subject to vanity. The creature shall be delivered."*[1] Thus Saint Thomas explains the passage in Saint James[2] about showing preference to the rich that unless they do it in view of God, they are going against the order of religion.

49

Perseus king of Macedonia, Paulus Aemilius
Perseus was reproached for not killing himself.[3]

50

Vanity

That something as obvious as the vanity of the world should be so little known and that people should find it strange and surprising to be told that it is foolish to seek honors, that is astounding.

---

1. Romans 8:20–21: "*For the creation was subjected to futility*, not of its own will but by the will of him who subjected it in hope; Because *the creature* also itself *shall be delivered* from the servitude of corruption."
2. The second chapter of the Epistle of James cautions the Christian communities not to reserve the best seats at liturgical gatherings for the rich.
3. See Montaigne, *Essays*, I, 20, 72: "Aemilius Paulus replied to the messenger sent to him by that miserable king of Macedonia, his prisoner, to beg him not to lead him in his triumphal procession: 'let him make that request of himself'." See fr. 149.

51

Inconstancy and peculiarity

To live by one's work alone and to reign over the most powerful state in the world are two very different things. They are combined in the person of the Grand Turk.[4]

52

751. The shape of a cowl can make twenty-five thousand monks take up arms.[5]

53

He has four lackeys.[6]

54

He lives across the water.[7]

55

If one is too young, one does not judge well, too old likewise.

If one thinks too little, if one thinks too much about things, one becomes obstinate and fixated.

———

If one looks at one's work again just after finishing it, one is still completely preoccupied with it, if too long afterwards one can no longer engage with it.

———

It is the same with paintings that are viewed from too far away or too close. There is only one indivisible point that is the true place. All others are too near, too far, too high, or too low. Perspective determines it in painting. But in truth and morality, who will determine it?

56

The power of flies: they win battles, prevent our souls from acting, and eat our bodies.[8]

---

4. One of the many fables still current, though long discredited, concerning the Grand Turk. He was supposed not to have disdained manual work. See G. Postel's *On the Republic of the Turks,* 1560.

5. On page 751 of the *Essays,* 1652 edition, Pascal found Montaigne commenting on the vanity of most human preoccupations. Pascal adds an allusion to the endless quarrels of the Friars Minor as to what should be the shape of their hoods. At Port-Royal, these disputes were compared to those surrounding the Five Propositions.

6. See fr. 123.

7. See fr. 94.

8. Flies, i.e., bees. See Montaigne, *Essays,* II, 12, 424: "In recent memory, when the Portuguese were

57
Vanity of science

The knowledge of physical things will not console me for the ignorance of morality in times of affliction, but the knowledge of moral philosophy will always console me for the ignorance of physical sciences.

58
Man's condition

Inconstancy, *ennui*, anxiety.

59

The habit of seeing kings accompanied by guards, drummers, officers, and all those things that incline the machine towards respect and fear means that their faces, even when sometimes alone and without this entourage, impose respect and fear in their subjects, because in our mind we do not separate the person from the retinue that we normally see with him. And the world, which does not know that this effect is the result of this habit, believes that it comes from some natural force. Hence the words "The sign of divinity is imprinted on his face," etc.

60

The power of kings is founded upon reason and the people's folly, but much more upon folly. The greatest and most important thing in the world has weakness as its foundation. And this foundation is wonderfully reliable, for there is nothing more reliable than that the people will always be weak. Whatever is founded upon sound reason has a truly unstable foundation, like the esteem for wisdom.

61

It is not man's nature to go always in one direction. It has its comings and goings.

Fever has its chills and high temperatures. And cold indicates how high a fever runs as effectively as heat does.

---

besieging the town of Tamly in the territory of Xiatine, the inhabitants of the town carried upon the walls a large quantity of hives, in which they are rich, and with fire drove the bees so fiercely upon their enemies that they were put to rout, being unable to withstand the assaults and stings."

It is the same with men's inventions over the centuries. It is the same with the goodness and wickedness of the world in general.

"Often the great choose for a change to roam."[9]

62

Weakness

All men's occupations revolve around acquiring wealth, and it is impossible for them to obtain a title to show that they own it justly, for they can only draw on human imagination. Nor do they have the strength to possess it with surety.

It is the same with knowledge, for illness carries it off.

We are incapable of both truth and goodness.

63

A fierce race to whom life without arms was not life.[10]

They prefer death to peace, others prefer death to war.

Any opinion can be preferable to life, the love of which seems so strong and natural.[11]

64

To steer a ship you do not choose the traveler who is from the best family.[12]

65

In towns which we are passing through, we do not worry about being held in high esteem. But when we have to spend a little time there, we do worry about it. How much time is necessary? A time proportionate to our vain and paltry life span.

66

Vanity

Marks of respect mean "Inconvenience yourself."[13]

---

9. Horace, *Odes*, III, 29, 13, as transmitted by Montaigne, *Essays*, I, 42. Montaigne cites further, "A simple meal, a poor man's humble home, No purple, no display—These waft their cares away" (235).

10. The inhabitants of certain Spanish towns, having been forbidden by Cato from bearing arms, killed themselves. Livy, *History of Rome*, I, 34, as cited by Montaigne in *Essays*, I, 14, 50.

11. See Montaigne, *Essays*, I, 14, 41: "Any opinion is strong enough to make people espouse it at the price of life."

12. See fr. 786.

13. See fr. 115.

67

What astonishes me most is to see that not everybody is astonished by his own weakness. We act seriously and everybody follows his vocation not because it is indeed good to follow it since it is fashionable to do so, but as if each person knew for certain where justice and reason lie. We find ourselves disappointed at every moment, and through a laughable humility we think that it is our fault and not that of the skill that we always boast of having. But it is good that there be so many people of this kind in the world who are not Pyrrhonists,[14] to the glory of Pyrrhonism, in order to demonstrate that man is truly capable of the most extravagant opinions, since he is capable of believing that he is not inevitably in this natural weakness and of believing, on the contrary, that he possesses natural wisdom.

Nothing strengthens Pyrrhonism more than that there are people who are not Pyrrhonists. If everyone were a Pyrrhonist, they would be wrong.

68

This sect gains strength more from its enemies than from its friends, since man's weakness is much more apparent in those who are not aware of it than in those who are aware of it.

69

Heel of a shoe[15]

Oh how well fashioned that is! What a skillful worker this is! What a brave soldier he is! This is the origin of all our preferences and of our choice of conditions. How impressively that person drinks! How little that person drinks! And this is what makes people sober and drunkards, soldiers, cowards, etc.

70

Whoever does not see the vanity of the world is truly vain himself.

But then, who does not see it, apart from young people who are wholly engrossed in noise, diversion, and thoughts of the future?

But take away their diversion, and you will see them shrivel up with *ennui*.

Then they feel their nothingness without understanding it, for it is to be truly miserable to be unbearably overcome by sadness as soon as one is reduced to reflecting upon oneself without any form of diversion.

---

14. The Skeptics of antiquity. Pascal almost without exception uses this appellation. See ch. I, fr. 25, n. 10.

15. This enigmatic title, evoking the profession of shoemaker, makes more sense if read alongside Pascal's reflections on professions in fragments 71 and 162. See also frs. 527 and 97.

71

Professions

So great is the sweetness of reputation that whatever object we associate it with, even death, we love it.

72

Too much and too little wine. Give him none, he cannot find the truth. Give him too much, likewise.

73

Men spend their time running after a ball and a hare.[16] It is the pastime even of kings.

74

What vanity there is in painting, which attracts admiration for its resemblance to original things we do not admire in the first place![17]

75

When reading too rapidly or too slowly, we understand nothing.

76

How many kingdoms know nothing of us!

77

It takes little to console us because it takes little to distress us.[18]

78

Imagination[19]

It is man's dominant faculty, the mistress of error and falsehood, all the more deceptive because it is not consistently so; for it would be an infallible

---

16. See fr. 168. The image of the ball and hare as signifying diversion appears also in fragment 453.

17. As does Saint Augustine (*On Christian Doctrine,* II, 25, no. 39), Pascal imagines no other dogma of painting than the perfect resemblance of the model and the picture. See Boileau: "There is no serpent or hideous monster that, imitated by art, could not please the eye" (*Art poétique,* 1674, III, 1–2, in Boileau, *Œuvres,* ed. Sylvain Menant, vol. 2, *Épîtres, art poétique, œuvres diverses* [Paris: Garnier-Flammarion, 1969], 98; translation by Pierre Zoberman).

18. See Montaigne, *Essays,* III, 4, p. 770: "It takes little to divert and distract us, for it takes little to hold us."

19. As Sellier observes, this entire celebrated fragment "teems with reminiscences of the *Essays,* often used with great liberty." Pascal, *Pensées,* ed. Sellier (2010), 181.

standard of truth if it were an infallible standard of deception. But, since most frequently it is false, it gives no indication of its real quality, making no distinction between true and false. I am not speaking of mad people here but of the wisest people, amongst whom imagination is most entitled to persuade. As loudly as reason may protest, it cannot set the price for things.[20]

This arrogant power, the enemy of reason, which relishes controlling and dominating it, so as to show its power in all things, has established a second nature within man. It has its happy and unhappy people, its healthy and sick, its rich and poor. It makes reason believe, doubt, and deny. It both numbs and arouses the senses. It has its own madmen and wise men. And nothing annoys us more than to see that it fills its hosts with a fuller and more complete satisfaction than does reason. Those who imagine themselves to be intelligent are far more self-confident than the prudent can reasonably be. The former look upon people with a sense of superiority, and argue boldly and confidently, the latter argue timorously and diffidently. And their cheerful demeanor often holds sway over their listeners' opinions, such is the favor that those who think themselves wise enjoy with their judges, who are of the same ilk.[21]

Imagination cannot make the mad wise, but it does make them happy, contrary to reason,[22] which can only make its friends miserable. The one covers them with glory, the other with shame.

What dispenses reputation, what bestows respect and veneration upon people, works, laws, and the great if not this faculty of imagination? How insufficient are all the riches of the earth without its approval.

Would you not say that this magistrate whose venerable old age commands respect from everyone is governed by pure and sublime reason, that he judges things by their nature without paying heed to those vain circumstances[23] which make an impression only on the imagination of the weak? Watch him go to hear a sermon, armed with a pious zeal and strengthening the solidity of his reason with the ardor of his charity. There he is, ready to listen to the sermon with an exemplary respect. But if, when the preacher appears, nature has endowed him with a hoarse voice or strange facial features, and his barber

---

20. See Montaigne, *Essays*, I, 14, 51: "our opinion gives value to things."

21. Pascal seems to be thinking of a passage in Montaigne's *Essays*, III, 8, 870–71: "Moreover, nothing vexes me so much in stupidity as the fact that it is better pleased with itself than any reason can reasonably be. It is unfortunate that wisdom forbids you to be satisfied with yourself and trust yourself, and always sends you away discontented and diffident, whereas opinionatedness and heedlessness fill their hosts with rejoicing and assurance. It is for the most incompetent to look at other men over their shoulders, always returning from the combat full of glory and cheer. And besides, this arrogance of language and gaiety of countenance usually give them the victory in the eyes of the audience, which is generally weak and incapable of judging and discerning clearly where the real advantages lie."

22. Pascal attributes to imagination what Montaigne applied to fortune in his *Essays*, III, 8, 864.

23. Montaigne uses the same term, "circumstances," [*circonstances*] in his *Essays*, III, 8.

has shaved him poorly, if by accident he is all besmirched into the bargain, whatever great truths he may be proclaiming, I wager that our senator will not keep his grave demeanor for long.

Take the greatest philosopher in the world, standing on a plank wider than necessary: if he is above a precipice, even though his reason persuades him of his safety, his imagination will prevail.[24] Many people would be unable to bear the thought without turning pale and breaking into a sweat.[25]

I do not intend to make a list of all the effects of imagination. Who does not know that the sight of cats or rats, the crushing of a piece of coal, and so on, unhinge our reason? Tone of voice influences the wisest of us and can change the impact of a speech or poem. Love or hatred alters the face of justice. And how much more just does a lawyer who has been well paid in advance find the case he is arguing! How much stronger do his bold gestures make the case appear to the judges who are taken in by this show! Laughable reason, swayed in every direction by a breeze![26] I could adduce almost all the actions of men, who are hardly ever moved by anything other than the jolts of imagination. For reason has had to give way, and even the wisest kind of reason takes for its principles those which human imagination has rashly introduced in all areas. (*We must, since it so pleases, work all day for goods known to be imaginary. And when sleep has refreshed us from the exertions of our reason, we must straightaway bolt out of bed in order to chase after illusions and submit to the impressions of this mistress of the world.*)

Our magistrates have fully understood this mystery. Their red robes, the ermine in which they wrap themselves like furry cats, the palaces in which they deliver their verdicts, the fleurs-de-lis, all of these august paraphernalia are very necessary. And if physicians did not have cassocks and slippers and learned scholars did not have square caps and gowns that are four times too big, they would never have hoodwinked the world, which finds such a solemn display irresistible. If they possessed true justice and if physicians mastered the true art of healing, they would have no use for square caps. The majesty of these sciences would command respect in itself. But since their knowledge is purely imaginary, they have no choice but to have recourse to these vain instruments that strike the imagination, with which they are dealing. And by this means they indeed gain respect.

Men of war alone do not dress up in this way, because their role is ef-

---

24. A reworking of Montaigne in the *Essays*, II, 12 (see p. 546).

25. See Montaigne, *Essays*, I, 21, 82: "We drip with sweat, we tremble, we turn pale and turn red at the blows of our imagination; reclining in our leather beds we feel our bodies agitated by their impact, sometime to the point of expiring."

26. Many of the images in this paragraph come from Montaigne's *Essays*, II, 12.

fectively more essential. They impose themselves through force, the others through disguise.

That is why our kings have not sought out such disguises. They have not masked themselves in extraordinary outfits in order to appear like kings, but they have surrounded themselves with guards and halberdiers. These armed troops whose hands and strength are dedicated to them alone, the trumpeters and drummers who march before them, and these legions that surround them make the most resolute people tremble.[27] They do not have the trappings alone, they have power. One would have to possess truly refined reason to view the Grand Turk like any other man,[28] surrounded as he is in his imposing Seraglio by forty thousand janissaries.[29]

The mere sight of a lawyer in his robes and cap is enough for us to form an advantageous opinion of his capabilities.

Imagination orders everything. It establishes beauty, justice, and happiness, which is everything in the eyes of the world.

I would dearly like to see the book in Italian that I know only by its title, which alone is worth as much as many books, *On opinion, queen of the world*.[30] Without knowing this work, I embrace it, except for any evil it may contain.

Such, more or less, are the effects of this deceptive faculty, which seems to be given to us for the express purpose of leading us into necessary error—for which we have many other sources.

Long-established impressions are not the only ones capable of deceiving us; the charms of novelty have the same power. Hence all the disputes between men, who blame one another either for following false impressions derived from their childhood or for rashly chasing after new ones.[31] Who maintains the proper balance? Let him come forward and prove it. There is no principle, however natural it may have been, even since childhood, that cannot be shown to be a false impression either of education or of the senses.

"Because, some say, you have believed from childhood that a chest was empty when you saw nothing in it, you believed that it was possible for a vacuum to exist. It is an illusion of your senses, reinforced by custom, that must be corrected by science."[32]—Others say, "Because you were taught at University

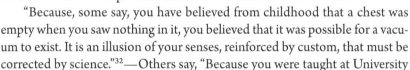

27. See fr. 59.
28. See fr. 51.
29. The Janissaries were infantry units that formed the Ottoman Sultan's household troops and bodyguards. The force was created by the Sultan Murad I from male children of conquered countries in the fourteenth century, and was finally abolished by Sultan Mahmud II in 1826.
30. No work with this title has been identified.
31. See Descartes, *Principes de la philosophie* [Principles of philosophy] (Paris: Vrin, 1993), I, 71–72.
32. Another evocation of Descartes, *Principles of Philosophy*, II, 17–18.

that there is no vacuum, your common sense, which was able to understand it clearly before this bad impression, has been corrupted. This you need to correct by returning to your first nature." Which has therefore deceived us? The senses or education?

We have another source of error: illnesses. They ruin our judgment and our senses. If serious illnesses grievously distort them, I have no doubt that minor ones make a proportionate impression.[33]

Our own self-interest is another wonderful instrument for blinding ourselves agreeably. The most just man in the world cannot be allowed to be a judge in his own case. I know some people who, in order to avoid the pitfall of self-love, have been as unjust as possible, in the other direction. The surest way to lose a perfectly just case was to have it recommended to them by their close relatives. Justice and truth are such subtle points that our instruments are too blunt to touch them with precision. If they manage to do so, they flatten out the point and press round about it more on the false than on the true.

(*Man is thus so felicitously made that he has no reliable principle of the true and several excellent ones of the false. Let us now see how many.*

But the most laughable cause of his errors is the war that rages between the senses and reason.)

Man is nothing but a subject full of natural error that cannot be remedied without grace. [Nothing] can show him the truth. Everything deceives him.[34]—That should be the start of the chapter on deceptive powers[35]—These two principles of truth, reason and the senses, apart from the fact that each lacks sincerity, deceive each other. The senses deceive reason through false appearances, and this same trickery that they bring to the soul they receive from it in their turn. The soul turns the tables on them. The soul's passions cloud the senses and make false impressions on them. They compete in lying and deceiving one another.[36]

But apart from this error, which results from chance and from the lack of understanding between these heterogeneous faculties . . .

---

33. Montaigne uses similar imagery in *Essays*, II, 12, the "Apology for Raymond Sebond."

34. Pascal condenses a paragraph of Montaigne's "Apology for Raymond Sebond" (*Essays*, II, 12, 504). After an evocation of Babel, Montaigne writes: "All that we undertake without his assistance, all that we see without the lamp of his grace, is only vanity and folly. The very essence of truth, which is uniform and constant, we corrupt and adulterate by our weakness, when fortune gives us possession of it."

35. A note in the margin, indicating a change of title or a development within the chapter "Vanity."

36. This paragraph is similarly influenced by Montaigne. See *Essays*, II, 12, 347–48: "The same deception that the senses convey to our understanding they receive in their turn. Ours at times takes a little revenge; they compete in lying and deceiving each other. [. . .] Our senses are not only altered, but often completely stupefied by the passions of the soul. [. . .] Thus, both the inside and the outside of man are full of weakness and falsehood."

79
Vanity

The cause and effects of love.
Cleopatra.[37]

80

We never hold to the present time. We anticipate the future, in our view always too slow in coming, as if to hasten its course, or we recall the past, in our view always too fleeting, in order to halt it. We are so imprudent that we wander through times that are not ours and give no thought to the only one that does belong to us; and we are so vain that we ponder those times that are nothing and let slip away without reflection the only one that abides. This is because the present generally hurts us. We hide it from view because it causes us pain, and if it gives us pleasure we regret its passing. We try to sustain it with the future and are concerned with ordering things that are not within our power for a time that we have no assurance of ever reaching.

Let each one of us examine his thoughts, he will find them completely occupied by either the past or the future. We hardly ever think of the present, and if we do, it is only to take some insight from it to make preparations for the future. The present is never our end. The past and present are our means, the future alone is our end. Thus, we never live but hope to live, and, while always preparing ourselves to be happy, it is inevitable that we should never be so.

81

The mind of this sovereign judge of the world is not so independent that it is not liable to be disturbed by the first din that occurs in his vicinity. It does not take the noise of a cannon to disturb his thoughts. All it takes is the sound of a weathercock or a pulley. Do not be surprised if he is not reasoning well at the moment: a fly is buzzing around his ears. This is quite enough to render him incapable of good counsel. If you want him to be able to find the truth, chase away that creature which is thwarting his reason and paralyzing this mighty intellect which governs cities and kingdoms.

What a preposterous god this is! *Oh most ridiculous of heroes!*[38]

---

37. This note indicates where fr. 32, provisionally filed in the table-*liasse*, was to have been inserted.

38. *O ridicolossimo heroe!* An address to the *commedia dell'arte* figure Scaramouch in the dedicatory piece to a book on buffoonery (1657). All professions, including scholars, whom the Italian farcical character represents here, are but comical roles on the great stage of the world.

82

It seems to me that Caesar was too old to amuse himself by going off to conquer the world. This pastime was fitting enough for Augustus or Alexander. They were young people, and as such, difficult to stop. But Caesar ought to have been more mature.[39]

83

The Swiss take affront at being called *gentlemen*,[40] and prove their lowly origins so as to be considered fit for high office.[41]

84

"Why are you killing me?" "What! Do you not live on the other side of the water? My friend, if you lived on this side, I would be a murderer, and it would be unjust to kill you in this way. But since you live on the other side, I am a hero, and it is just."

85

Good sense

They are forced to say: "You are not acting in good faith, we are not asleep," etc. How I love to see this proud reason humbled and craven! For this is not the language of a man whose rights are being disputed and who defends them weapons in hand. Such a man does not waste time protesting that people are not acting in good faith; rather, he punishes such bad faith with force.

---

39. Pascal reverses Montaigne's judgment, in his essay on Caesar (*Essays*, II, 34, 678). Caesar more carefully thought out his conquests than did Alexander the Great, because he was of a riper age. Alexander "was occupied in war in the flower and first ardor of his youth, whereas Caesar took to it when he was already mature and well advanced in years."

40. Noble by birth.

41. In certain Swiss cantons (Basel, Zurich), the nobility were in the minority and suspected of collusion with the Hapsburgs. This apparent paradox shows the arbitrariness, hence the vanity, of concrete sociopolitical distinction. See fr. 668.

[IV] Wretchedness

86

Baseness of man, going so far as to submit to the beasts, even so far as to adore them.

87

Inconstancy

Things have diverse qualities and the soul has diverse impulses, for nothing that offers itself to the soul is straightforward, and the soul never offers itself in a straightforward way to anything. This is why we laugh and cry at the same thing.[1]

88

Inconstancy

We think we are playing on an ordinary organ when we play on man. Men are in truth organs, but strange, changing, variable ones (*whose pipes are not arranged according to regular scales. Those who know only how to play an ordinary organ*) would not produce harmonious chords on these. You need to know where the keys are.[2]

89

We are so unfortunate that we can only take pleasure in something on condition that we become angry if it turns out badly, as indeed thousands of things can and do at every moment. Whoever would find the secret of rejoicing in the good without being angered by the contrary evil would have found the point. It is perpetual motion.

---

1. "How we cry and laugh for the same thing," the title of Montaigne's essay 38 in book I, 208, of *Essays*.
2. In "On the inconstancy of our actions" (*Essays*, II, 1, 292), Montaigne has recourse to the metaphor of the spinet to show "a harmony of perfectly accordant sounds," which represents the life of Cato the Younger, as opposed to that of the majority of men.

90

It is not good to be too free.

———

It is not good to have all that is necessary.

91

Tyranny[3]

Tyranny is wishing to have by one means something that can only be had by another. We have different duties to different merits: a duty of love to love-liness, a duty of fear to force, a duty of credence to knowledge.

We are obliged to fulfill these duties. It is unjust to deny them and unjust to ask for others.

Therefore, these statements are false and tyrannical: "I am handsome, therefore I should be feared. I am strong, therefore I should be loved. I am..." And it is similarly false and tyrannical to say: "He is not strong, therefore I will not hold him in esteem. He is not clever, therefore I will not fear him."

92

Tyranny consists in the desire for universal domination outside its order.[4]

Different jurisdictions—of the strong, of the handsome, of lofty minds, of the pious: each one is master in his sphere and nowhere else, and on occasion comes into contact with the others. The strong and the handsome struggle for domination to no purpose, for the mastery of each is distinct. They do not understand one another. And their error lies in wishing to rule everywhere. Nothing has that power, not even sheer force. It is of no effect in the realm of the learned. It has dominion only over external actions.

93

When it is a question of deciding whether one should engage in war and kill so many men, condemning so many Spaniards to death,[5] it is a single man who decides, and what is more, somebody who is an interested party. It ought to be a neutral third party.

---

3. See fr. 203: "*Terror rather than religion.*" Pascal rejects Saint Augustine's approval of torture and forced conversion in the case of the Donatist heretics who would not listen to reason. Augustine's *Letter to Vincent* was republished in 1573 to justify the Saint Bartholomew's Day massacre and again in 1686 after the revocation of the Edict of Nantes. See also fr. 490. Sellier considers Pascal to be the first modern religious writer to reject the use of force in religious matters. See Philippe Sellier, "De la tyrannie" [On tyranny], in *Port-Royal et la littérature* [Port-Royal and literature], vol. 1, *Pascal* (Paris: Champion, 1999), 231–38.

4. See introduction, "The Three Orders."

5. France and Spain were at war between 1635 and 1659.

94[6]

On what will man base the organization of the world that he wants to govern? Will it be on the whim of each individual? What confusion! Will it be on justice? He is ignorant of it. Certainly, if it were known to him, he would not have established this maxim, which is the most general of all those known to mankind: that everybody should follow the customs of his own country. The brilliance of true equity would have drawn all peoples into its thrall. And legislators would not have taken the whims and fancies of the Persians and Germans as their model,[7] rather than this invariable justice. We would see it solidly established across all the nations of the world and in all ages, whereas we cannot find anything just or unjust that does not change character with the climate. Three degrees of latitude overturn the whole of jurisprudence. A meridian determines the truth. Within a few years of being enacted, fundamental laws change. The law has its phases, and Saturn's entry into Leo marks the origin of such and such a crime.[8] Fine justice, indeed, that is bounded by a river! Truth on this side of the Pyrenees, error beyond.[9]

They admit that justice is not to be found in these customs but rather resides in the natural laws common to all countries. Doubtless they would maintain this stubbornly if the rashness of chance, which introduced all human laws, had hit upon even one that was universal. But the funny thing is that men's whims have become so diverse that there is none (*that is general*).[10]

Theft, incest, infanticide, and parricide: everything has had its place amongst virtuous actions. Can there be anything more laughable than for a man to have the right to kill me because he lives on the other side of the water and his prince has a quarrel with mine, even though I have none with him?

Undoubtedly there are natural laws, but this fine corrupt reason has cor-

6. Obsessed, as was Saint Augustine, with the weakness of fallen man, the apologist can but delight in the attacks in the *Essays* on the very notion of universal reason and justice. No other "*pensée*" is closer to Montaigne. Using mostly his own words, Pascal takes up, almost theme by theme, three pages of essay II, 12, 531ff.

7. Montaigne, *Essays*, II, 12, 530: "If it is from ourselves that we derive the ruling of our conduct, into what confusion do we cast ourselves? For the most plausible advice that our reason gives us in the matter is generally for each man to obey the laws of his country, which is the advice of Socrates, inspired, he says, by divine counsel. And what does reason mean by that, unless that our duty has no rule but an accidental one? Truth must have one face, the same and universal. If man knew any rectitude and justice that had body and real existence, he would not tie it down to the condition of the customs of this country or that. It would not be from the fancy of the Persians or the Indians that virtue would take its form."

8. The planet Saturn had entered the constellation of Leo on August, 12, 1654.

9. Montaigne, *Essays*, II, 12, 530. "What am I to make of a virtue that I saw in credit yesterday, that will be discredited tomorrow, and that becomes a crime on the other side of the river? What of a truth that is bounded by the mountains and is falsehood to the world that lives beyond?"

10. See, again, Montaigne, *Essays*, II, 12, 532. "The murder of infants, the murder of fathers, sharing of wives, traffic in robberies, license for all sorts of sensual pleasure, nothing in short is so extreme that it is not accepted by the usage of some nation."

rupted everything. "Nothing is ours anymore; what I call ours is a product of art."[11] There are crimes committed as a result of decrees of the Senate and of popular votes.[12] As formerly we suffered from vices; so now we suffer from laws.[13]

The result of this confusion is that one says that the essence of justice lies in the authority of the legislator, another in the convenience of the sovereign, yet another in current custom.[14] And the last is the safest. Nothing, according to reason alone, is just in itself, everything shifts with time. Custom makes up the whole of equity, for the sole reason that it is accepted. This is the mysterious basis of its authority. Whoever tries to trace it back to its origin obliterates it. Nothing is so faulty as those laws that redress previous faults. Whoever obeys them because they are just is obeying what he imagines to be justice but not the essence of the law. It is utterly self-contained, a law and nothing more.[15] Anyone who endeavors to examine the motive behind it will find it to be so weak and frivolous that, if he is not accustomed to contemplating the wonders of the human imagination, he will marvel that in one century it has garnered so much pomp and esteem. The art of sedition, of revolution is to shake established customs by probing their very sources in order to show their lack of authority and justice. It is said that we must return to the fundamental and original laws of the state that an unjust custom has abolished. This is a game in which one is certain to lose everything; on these scales nothing will be just. Nevertheless, the people are quick to lend their ears to such arguments. They shake off the yoke as soon as they recognize it,[16] and the great take advantage of this, to the ruin of the people and of those inquisitive examiners of established customs.[17] That is why the wisest of legislators said that

---

11. Cicero, *On the Ends of Good and Evil,* V, 2. Cited by Montaigne, *Essays,* II, 12, 532.

12. Seneca, *Letters,* 95. Cited by Montaigne, *Essays,* III, 1, 732. The same citation figures in frs. 675 and 796.

13. Tacitus, *Annals,* III, 25. Cited in Montaigne, *Essays,* III, 13, 993.

14. Montaigne, *Essays,* II, 12, 531: "Protagoras and Aristotle assigned no other essence to the justice of the laws than the authority and judgment of the lawgiver; and said that apart from that, the good and the honest lost their qualities and remained empty names of indifferent things. Thrasymachus, in Plato, thinks that there is no other right than the advantage of the superior."

15. Montaigne, *Essays,* III, 13, 999–1000: "All this reminds me of [. . .] what the Cyrenaics hold, that there is nothing just in itself, that customs and laws shape justice [. . .]. Now, laws remain in credit not because they are just, but because they are laws. That is the mystic foundation of their authority [. . .]. There is nothing as grossly and widely and ordinarily faulty as the laws. Whoever obeys them because they are just, does not obey them for just the reason he should."

16. See fr. 681, par. 21.

17. Montaigne, *Essays,* II, 12, 388. "For the common herd, [. . .] once they have been given the temerity to despise and judge the opinions that they had held in extreme reverence, [. . .] will soon after cast easily into like uncertainty all the other parts of their belief, which had no more authority or foundation in them than those that have been shaken; and they shake off as a tyrannical yoke all the impressions they had once received from the authority of the laws or the reverence of ancient usage." See also *Essays* I, 23, 105: "Those who give the first shock to a state are apt to be the first ones swallowed up in its ruin."

for men's own good they must often be tricked. And another good politician: *"Since he does not know the truth whereby he may be free, it is convenient for him to be deceived."*[18] He must not have an inkling of the truth of this usurpation. It was once introduced without reason, it has become reasonable. It must be made to appear as authentic and eternal, and its origins must be hidden if we do not wish it to come to a swift end.

95

Justice

Just as fashion defines charm, so too does it define justice.

96

Would anyone who had the king of England, the king of Poland, and the queen of Sweden as friends have expected to find himself without a place of retreat or refuge in the world?[19]

97

Reputation

Admiration spoils everything already in childhood. Oh how well said that is, oh how well he has done, how wise he is, etc. The Port-Royal children, who are not given this spur of envy and reputation, fall into a state of idleness.[20]

98

Mine, yours

"This dog is mine," those poor children were saying. "That is my place in the sun." Therein lies the beginning and image of the usurpation of the whole earth.[21]

---

18. Montaigne, *Essays*, II, 12, 485. "Since he seeks the *truth whereby he may be free*, let us believe that *it is expedient for him to be deceived*." Montaigne evokes Varro and the Roman high-priest Scaevola, admirers of religious and political impostures stigmatized by Saint Augustine in *The City of God*, (IV, 27), the source of the citation. Cited by Pascal from memory.

19. Charles I of England was beheaded in 1649. John II Casimir of Poland was overthrown by the Swedes for a few months in 1656. Queen Christina of Sweden abdicated in 1654. The *Gazette* of September 16, 1656 reported the fall of Warsaw at the hands of the Swedes, the flight of the King of Poland, and the arrival of Queen Christina in Paris. If, on the other hand "the King of England" refers instead to the future Charles II, then in exile with the Stuart Court at Saint-Germain-en-Laye, this fragment could have been written in the first months of 1658. The autograph in the Original Collection contains a title crossed out by and not registered by the Copies: "*Trois hôtes*" [Three Hosts].

20. See the introduction, "Port-Royal and Jansenism," for an account of the "Little Schools" established by the "solitaires" at Port-Royal-des-Champs. See also Nicholas Hammond, *Fragmentary Voices: Memory and Education at Port-Royal* (Tübingen: Gunter Narr, 2004).

21. This *pensée* echoes countless texts against private property by the Fathers of the Church. The

99

Diversity

Theology is a science, but at the same time how many sciences does it consist of? Man is a substance,[22] but if he is dissected, is he the head, the heart, the stomach, the veins, each vein, each part of each vein, the blood, each humor in the blood?

Viewed from afar, a town or the countryside is a town and the countryside, but as one approaches, they become houses, trees, tiles, leaves, blades of grass, ants, ants' legs, *ad infinitum*. All that is encapsulated in the noun *countryside*.[23]

100

Injustice

It is dangerous to tell the people that the laws of the land are not just, for they obey them only because they believe them to be just. That is why they must be told at the same time that laws should be obeyed because they are laws, just as one's superiors should be obeyed not because they are just but because they are superior. Thus all sedition is forestalled, if the people can be made to understand this—and that it is precisely the definition of justice.[24]

101

Injustice

Jurisdiction is not established for the sake of the judge but for the sake of the judged.[25] It is dangerous to tell the people this. But the people have too much faith in you; that will not harm them and can serve your purposes. It therefore must be spread widely. "Feed my sheep, not yours."[26] You owe me pasture.

---

entire earth, they admonished, belongs to the human community. From today's perspective, this calls to mind Rousseau's *Discourse on the Origins and Foundations of Inequality among Men* (first published in 1755). Yet here, Sellier observes, the *pensée* reverses "for" and "against." The inequality of property is folly, just as "equality of wealth is just" (fr. 116). However, attacking such "follies" means unleashing civil war. Throughout his writings, Sellier notes, Pascal is hostile to revolution, but seems open to progressive reform.

22. An Aristotelian term opposing intangible "substance" to "accidents," such as quantity.

23. See Montaigne, *Essays*, I, 46, 243: "Whatever variety of herbs there may be, the whole thing is included under the name of salad."

24. See fr. 94.

25. The sentence is a quasi-citation from the *Essays* (III, 6, 836). Montaigne goes on: "A superior is never appointed for his own benefit, but for the benefit of the inferior, and a doctor for the sick not for himself."

26. John 21:17. Having asked Peter, "Simon, son of John, lovest thou me?" Jesus said to him, "Feed my sheep." Pascal comments: "not yours."

102

When I think about the short span of my life swallowed up in the eternity that precedes and follows it, *as the remembrance of a guest of one day that passeth by,*[27] the small space that I fill and even that I see, engulfed in the infinite immensity of spaces that I do not know and that do not know me, I become afraid and I am amazed to see myself here rather than there, for there is no reason why here rather than there, why at present rather than then. Who put me here? Upon whose order and direction have this place and this time been assigned to me?

103

Wretchedness

Job and Solomon.[28]

104

If our condition were truly happy, there would be no need to divert ourselves from thinking about it.

105

Contradiction

Pride, counterbalancing all miseries. Either he hides his miseries or if he reveals them he glories in knowing them.

106

It is necessary to know oneself.[29] Even if it should not serve to find truth, at least it serves to regulate one's life. And there is nothing more just than that.

107

The awareness of the falsity of present pleasures and the ignorance of the vanity of absent pleasures are the cause of inconstancy.

27. Wisdom 5:15. "For the hope of the wicked is as dust, which is blown away with the wind, and as a thin froth which is dispersed by the storm: and a smoke that is scattered abroad by the wind: and *as the remembrance of a guest of one day that passeth by.*"

28. This notation marks the place where fr. 22, provisionally filed in the table-*liasse*, was to have been inserted.

29. The immortal words of the Delphic oracle, taken up by Socrates and passed on by Plato.

108

Injustice

They[30] have found no other way to satisfy their concupiscence without doing wrong to others.

109

Job and Solomon.[31]

110

Ecclesiastes shows that man without God is in a state of complete ignorance of inevitable unhappiness. For to want and to be unable is to be unhappy. Now, man wants to be happy and assured of some truth, and yet he can neither know nor desire not to know. He cannot even doubt.

111[32]

13[33]—(*Is the soul then still too noble a subject for its limited insight? Let us then bring it down to matter. Let us see whether it knows of what stuff its own body, to which it gives breath, is made, as well as the other bodies, which it contemplates and moves about at will.*

What did they know about it, those great dogmatists, who are ignorant of nothing?

393[34]

Of these opinions.[35]

---

30. They: the "*honnêtes gens*" of fr. 681.

31. See above, ch. IV, n. 28. Pascal's second reminder to himself where to place fr. 22.

32. The copyist correctly placed this entire crossed out fragment outside of the rubric "Wretchedness," a *liasse* to which it does not belong. The disposition of the fragment in the autograph sheets in the Original Collection demonstrates the difficulty of making sense of Pascal's working habits. Pascal had already written "The Laws" (fr. 92) on the front leaves of two sheets, finishing it at the top of the reverse side of the second sheet. Then, in the space remaining on this sheet, he wrote fr. 111 from the beginning through the words "grasp the truth." Having no more space on this reverse side, he continued fr. 111 to its end at the number "399," on the blank reverse side of the first sheet. When it came time to order his papers, Pascal had to choose which text to sacrifice. He kept what is fr. 94, "The Laws," in the *liasse* "Wretchedness." He struck out all his other notes, which now constitute fr. 111. However, he filed a note (fr. 27) in the table-*liasse* to remind himself that he would take up fr. 111 again in a projected letter on the "Folly of Human Science and Philosophy" (27). This "Letter," according to fr. 27, was to have been placed just before the chapter "Diversion."

33. Perhaps the vestige of part 13 of a "Discourse on Man," of which certain passages were used in the classification of June 1658. Fr. 229 is titled "H. [*Homme:* man] 5"; fr. 230, entitled "H. Disproportion of Man," is followed by the number 9; fr. 231 bears the title "H.3."

34. Page reference to the 1652 edition of the *Essays*. The struck notes condense pages 488, 491, 496ff.

35. Montaigne, having enumerated in essay II, 12, the infinitely varied opinions of philosophers on the subject of the soul, concludes with a sentence from Cicero's *Tusculum Disputations* (1, 11): "*Of these opinions, let some god decide which is true*" (493).

That would no doubt be sufficient if reason were reasonable. Reason is quite reasonable enough to admit that it has still not found anything certain, but it has not yet given up hope of doing so. On the contrary, it remains as fervent as ever in this search and is confident of possessing the strength needed to conquer.

We must therefore bring it to the end, and after examining its powers through their effects, let us know them in themselves. Let us see if reason has any strength and holds with which to grasp the truth.

13—But perhaps this subject goes beyond reason's reach. Let us then examine what it has managed to contrive over those things of which it has control. If there is one thing where in its own interests it should have applied itself most serious-ly, it is in searching for the sovereign good. Let us then see where these strong and clear-sighted souls have placed it and if they are in agreement.

One says that the sovereign good is in virtue, another locates it in carnal plea-sure, another in following nature, another in truth, "Happy he who has been able to know the origin of things,"³⁶ another in blissful ignorance, another in indolence,³⁷ others in resisting appearances, another in being in awe of nothing, "To wonder at nothing, that is [almost] all I know to make men happy and to keep them so,"³⁸ and the good old Pyrrhonists in their state of ataraxia,³⁹ doubt and continual sus-pension of belief, and other yet wiser people, that it cannot be found, not even in our wishes. So much for our efforts!⁴⁰

Transpose after the laws *Next article*	*Yet, we need to see whether this fine philosophy has not obtained something certain through such long and sustained toil. Perhaps at the very least the soul will have self-knowledge. Let us listen to the know-alls of the world on this subject.* *What have they thought about its substance?* 395 *Have they had any more luck in assigning it a place?* 395 *What have they found out about its origins, duration and departure?* 399)*

36. Virgil, *Georgics*, II, 490. Quoted in Montaigne, *Essays*, III, 10, 949. See fr. 27.

37. The Stoic ideal of impassiveness.

38. Montaigne, *Essays*, II, 12, 529. See fr. 27.

39. The Stoic precept that suspending judgment frees one from anguish.

40. This paragraph enumerates some of the "two hundred and eighty kinds of sovereign good" (see fr. 27) thought up by philosophers, according to Varro (Montaigne, *Essays*, II, 12, 527–29).

[V] *Ennui* and the Essential
Qualities of Man[1]

112
Pride

Most often curiosity is nothing other than vanity. We only wish to know in order to be able to talk about it. Otherwise, we would not travel by sea without ever saying anything about it, and for the sole pleasure of seeing things without the hope of ever discussing them.

113
Description of man
Dependence, desire for independence, needs.

114

The pangs we feel in leaving activities to which we have become attached! A man lives pleasurably in his household. Let him see a woman who appeals to him, or enjoy himself gambling for five or six days, how miserable he is when he returns to his previous activity. Nothing is more common than that.

---

1. Neither "ennui" nor any single English word would adequately translate the word *ennui*, a psychological state characterized by varying degrees of unhappiness, anxiety, vexation, weariness, despair, unease, disquiet, or ennui itself. Nicholas Hammond observes that all studies of the evolution of the word *ennui* recognize "the original and central importance which Pascal brought to it." See his analysis of Pascal's use of the term in his *Playing with Truth: Language and the Human Condition in Pascal's "Pensées"* (Oxford: Oxford University Press, 1994), 103–16.

[VI] Reasons for Effects[1]

115

Respect means: "Inconvenience yourself."

This is pointless in appearance, but in fact it is perfectly sound, because it means, "I would certainly inconvenience myself if you needed me to, since here I am doing it even though you gain nothing by my doing so." Besides, respect serves to distinguish the nobility. If respect meant that one could sit in an armchair, everybody would get respect, and there would be no distinction.[2] But when you are inconvenienced, you see the distinctions very clearly.

116

The only universal rules are the laws of the land in ordinary matters, and the majority in everything else. Why? Because the majority has force on its side.

This is why kings, who have force from another source, do not go by the majority advice of their ministers.

Indeed, equality of wealth is just, but since force could not be made to obey justice, justice was made to obey force. Unable to strengthen justice, we justified force, so that justice and force go together, and there be peace, which is the supreme good.

Wisdom returns us to the condition of children. *Unless you become as little children.*[3]

---

1. Pascal presents "effect" as a paradox, an apparent absurdity, mocked by the "half-clever" (*demi-habiles*). Yet behind this absurdity, sharper minds (*les habiles*) discern a kind of wisdom. Custom, for instance, is often essential for the maintenance of an orderly society. Yet even the most brilliant minds fail to perceive that only the Fall can explain the reason behind the paradox of the human condition. See frs. 238 and 708.

2. In the *ancien régime*, there were strict rules governing who was entitled to sit in the presence of whom, and the kind of chair in which they might sit.

3. Matthew 18:3, where Jesus says: "*unless you* be converted, and *become as little children*, you shall not enter into the kingdom of heaven."

117

The world is a good judge of things, because of its natural ignorance, which is the true condition of man. In knowledge there are always two extremes that meet. The first is sheer natural ignorance, the state of all human beings at birth. The other extreme is reached by great minds who, having gone through all that human beings can know, find that they know nothing, and find themselves back in the same ignorance from which they started. But this is a learned ignorance, which knows itself. Those in the middle, who have gone beyond natural ignorance, but have not yet attained the other kind, have a smattering of this self-satisfied knowledge, and put on knowing airs. These cause all the trouble in the world and they judge poorly of everything. The people[4] and the clever ones are the way of the world. These despise it and are despised in their turn. They judge everything poorly and the world judges well.[5]

118

(*Descartes.*

We have to say in general "Everything happens as a result of shape and movement," because it is true. But saying which shapes and what movements, and setting up the machine—that is ridiculous, because it is useless and uncertain and tedious.[6] And even if it were all true, we do not think philosophy is worth an hour's trouble.)

119

Ultimate law, ultimate injustice.[7]

———

Going by the majority is the best way, because it is visible and it has force on its side to make it obeyed. But this is the opinion of the less clever.

If it had been possible, we would have placed force in the hands of justice, but since force cannot be handled at will, because it is a material quality, whereas justice is a spiritual quality and we can do what we like with that, we have placed justice in the hands of force. Thus we call just what we are bound to follow.

———

4. I.e., the masses.

5. In *Essays*, I, 54, 275–76, Montaigne had conceded: "There is an abecedarian ignorance that comes before knowledge, and another, doctoral ignorance, that comes after knowledge. [...] The half-breeds, who have disdained the first seat, ignorance of letters, and have not been able to reach the other—their rear end between two saddles, like me and so many others—are dangerous, inept, and importunate: these men trouble the world."

6. A critique of Descartes's physics in his *Treatise on the Passions*, which Pascal finds replete with extravagant ideas.

7. See Terence, *Heautontimoroumenos* [*The Self-Tormentor*]: "Ius summum saepe summast malitia" (act IV, sc. V, l. 796). Quoted by Pierre Charron, *De la sagesse* [Of wisdom] (Rouen: Vve Durant, 1623), I, 37, 5.

[Hence] comes the right of the sword, for the sword confers a genuine right.

———

Otherwise, we would have violence on one side, and justice on the other. The end of the twelfth *Provincial Letter*.[8]

———

Hence comes the *Fronde*'s injustice: it tries to assert its supposed justice against force.[9]

———

This is not how things work in the Church, for there is authentic justice and no violence.

120

On True Law.[10] We do not have it any more. If we did have it, we would not choose for our rule of justice that everyone follow the customs of his country.

This is where, unable to find what is just, we have found what is strong, etc.

121

The chancellor looks dignified and wears a lot of ornaments, because his position is false. Not so the king: he has force. He has no use for imagination. Judges, physicians, etc., have nothing but imagination.

122

It is the effect of force, not of custom, because those capable of invention are few. The greater number want only to follow, and they deny inventors the fame they seek through their inventions. And if they persist in seeking it and in despising those who invent nothing, the latter will give them ridiculous names: they would give them thrashings if they could. So one had better not pride oneself on one's inventive subtlety or keep one's satisfaction to oneself.

---

8. At the end of the twelfth *Provincial Letter* Pascal notes that violence can never weaken truth but that truth can never subdue violence.

9. *Fronde*: the civil unrest that shook France from 1648 to 1653. The parliaments (high courts) and the highest nobility, along with the people, in a paradoxical, confused, and unstable combination of interests, revolted against Cardinal Mazarin, the power behind the regency of Anne of Austria, mother of Louis XIV. Forced to go into hiding, the future king resolved to crush the powers behind the insurrection during his own reign.

10. "We have no solid and exact image *of true law* and genuine justice; we use the shadow and reflections of it." Cicero, *De officiis* [On duties], III, xvii, 69. Cited in Montaigne, *Essays* III, 1, 732.

123

Reasons for effects

This is extraordinary: I am being told I should not honor a man dressed in brocade, with a train of seven or eight lackeys. What! He will have me horse-whipped if I do not salute him. These clothes of his are a kind of force. It is just the same with a horse in a fancy harness compared to another. Montaigne is silly not to see the difference, and to marvel that anyone see any, and to ask why. WHENCE, INDEED, he says, etc.[11]

124

Reasons for effects.

Gradation. The people honor those who are of high birth. The half-clever despise them, saying that birth is not an advantage that belongs to the person, but depends on chance. The clever honor them, not with the same view as the people, but from a deeper perspective. The devout, who have more zeal than knowledge, despise them, despite the considerations that lead the clever to honor them, because they judge according to a new light that comes from piety. But perfect Christians honor them according to yet another, superior light.

So opinions follow one another, pro and con, according to the lights one has.

125

Reasons for effects

We must have a deeper perspective, and judge everything that way, yet speaking all the time as the people do.[12]

126

Reasons for effects

So it is true to say that the whole world is in the grip of illusion, for although the people's opinions are sound, they are not so in their heads. For they think the truth lies where it does not. The truth is certainly in their opinions, but not in the way they imagine it is. It is true that we should honor noblemen, but not because birth is in essence an advantage, and so on.

---

11. Pascal echoes a passage from Montaigne, *Essays*, I, 42, 229–30: "It is a wonder that, ourselves excepted, nothing is evaluated except by its own qualities. We praise a horse because it is vigorous and skillful [...] not for his harness [...]. Why do we not likewise judge a man by what is his own? He has a great retinue, a beautiful palace, so much influence, so much income: all that is around him, not in him."

12. See Montaigne, *Essays*, I, 23, 104.

127

Reasons for effects

Continual reversal between pro and con.

Thus we have shown that man is vain on account of his esteem for things that are not essential. And all these opinions have been undone.

Then we have shown that all these opinions are very sound, and so that, since all these vain ideas are in fact very well founded, the people are not so vain as it is claimed. Thus we have undone the opinion that undid the opinion of the people.

But now we have to undo this last proposition and show that it always remains true that the people are vain, even though their opinions are sound, because they do not perceive the truth where it lies, and, since they locate it where it does not lie, their opinions are still utterly false and utterly unsound.

128

The people's opinions are sound

The greatest of all evils is civil war.

But one is certain to have it, if one means to give everyone what they deserve, because everyone will claim to be deserving. The evil that is to be feared from a fool who comes to his position by right of birth is neither so great nor so certain.

129

The people's opinions are sound

To be finely dressed is not all that vain, for it shows that you have a lot of people working for you. You show, with your hair, that you have a personal servant, and a perfumer, etc. And with the collar, the stitching, the lace, etc. Now it is not a matter of externals, or of mere trappings, to have several arms.

The more arms you have, the stronger you are. To be finely dressed is a show of strength.

130

Reasons for effects

Man's weakness is the reason for setting up so many sorts of beauty, like being a good lute-player. [Not being able to play the lute] is an evil only because of our weakness.

131

Reasons for effects

Concupiscence and force are the source of all our actions: concupiscence causes voluntary ones, force, involuntary ones.[13]

132

How is it that we are not annoyed by a person with a limp, but we are by a person whose mind is lame.[14] Because the person with a limp acknowledges that we can walk straight, and the person whose mind is lame says that we are the ones who are lame. Otherwise, we would feel pity, not anger.

Epictetus asks the question much more forcefully: why are we not angry with someone who says that we have a headache, but we are with someone who says that we are not reasoning right or that we are not choosing right?[15]

The reason is that we are quite certain we do not have a headache, and that we do not have a limp, but we are not quite so certain that we are choosing the truth. So that, since the only certainty we have here comes from our seeing it in our full purview, when someone else sees the opposite in their full purview, it leaves us hanging and astounds us; and this is even more so when a thousand other people laugh at our choice, because we then have to put our own lights before those of so many others. It's a bold and difficult step. There is never any such conflict of perception when it comes to limping.

The way man is constituted, if you keep on telling him he is a fool, he believes it. And by keeping on telling himself, he makes himself believe it. For man carries on an inner conversation with himself, which it is vital to regulate properly. *Evil communications corrupt good manners.*[16] We must keep silent as much as we can, and talk to ourselves only of God, who we know is the truth. That is how one persuades oneself of it.

13. A fundamental Augustinian thesis. The will of fallen man is but concupiscence. It can be flattered or constrained by those more powerful.

14. Montaigne, *Essays*, III, 8, 861. "Why can we encounter someone with a crooked and malformed body without being moved, when we cannot bear encountering an ill-ordered mind without getting angry?"

15. See Epictetus, *Discourses*, IV, 6.

16. 1 Corinthians 15:33: "Be not seduced: *Evil communications corrupt good manners.*"

133

Reasons for effects

Epictetus,[17] the people who say, "You have a headache."

It is not the same. We are sure about health, but not about justice. And in fact his idea of justice was idiotic.

And yet he thought he could prove it by saying "It is either in our power, or it is not."

But he failed to realize that it is not in our power to regulate the heart, and he was wrong to conclude that it is, since there were Christians then.

134

The people have very sound opinions. For instance:

1. In choosing diversion, the hunt, rather than the catching of the prey. The half-clever pour scorn on this, and gloatingly show how foolish the world is on that score. But, for a reason they fail to penetrate, it is quite right.[18]

2. In distinguishing between human beings on the basis of external criteria, like noble birth or property. Here again people gloatingly show how unreasonable that is. But it is very reasonable. Cannibals laugh at the idea of a child king.[19]

3. In taking offence at receiving a slap on the face, or desiring reputation so much.

But that is highly desirable because of the other essential goods that are linked to it. And a man who receives a slap in the face without being stirred is overwhelmed with insults and hardship.[20]

4. In working for an uncertain gain, taking to the sea, crossing a plank bridge.

135

Justice force.

It is just that what is just be followed. It is necessary that what is strongest be followed.

Justice without force is powerless. Force without justice is tyrannical.

---

17. See the introduction to *Exchange with M. de Sacy*, in this translation.

18. See fr. 168.

19. Montaigne, *Essays*, I, 31. In "On Cannibals," Montaigne recounts the astonishment of the Brazilian natives at Rouen when they saw big bearded men, strong and armed, "obeying a child king."

20. A sarcastic analysis of the logic of corruption, as found in so many of Pascal's political reflections. Among the nobility, to be slapped was an inadmissible affront that only a duel could resolve. Intrinsically, however, dueling is an irrational sin. See the seventh *Provincial Letter*.

Justice without force is contradicted because there are always evildoers. Force without justice is indicted. So justice and force have to be joined together, and for that either what is just made strong, or what is strong made just.

Justice is open to dispute. Force is very recognizable, and beyond dispute. So it proved impossible to deliver force into the hands of justice, because force contradicted justice, and asserted it was unjust, and claimed to have justice on its side.

So, unable to make what is just strong, we have made what is strong just.

136

Nobility is such a great advantage, giving a nobleman, as soon as he turns eighteen, the prospects, reputation, and respect that another's merit might have earned him by the age of fifty! It is thirty years spared—and with no effort.

[VII] Greatness

137

If an animal did by reason what it does by instinct, and if it spoke by reason what it speaks by instinct about hunting or warning its mates that its prey has been caught or lost, it would also speak about things that affect it more strongly, like saying: "Gnaw this rope that is hurting me and is out of my reach."

138
Greatness

Reasons for effects mark the greatness of man, who has extracted such a fine order from concupiscence.[1]

139

The parrot which cleans its beak even though it is spotless.

140

What is it that feels pleasure within us? Is it the hand, the arm, the flesh, the blood? We shall see that it must be something immaterial.

141
Against Pyrrhonism

(*It is therefore a strange thing that these things cannot be defined without obscuring them.*) We assume that everyone conceives of things in the same way. But this assumption is quite unwarranted, because we have no proof of it. I see indeed how words are used on the same occasions and how each time that two men see a body change position they both express the view of the same object by using the same words, each one saying that it has moved. And so from

---

1. By manipulating men's concupiscence—by flattering them, rewarding them, decorating them—those holding power manage to constitute a paradoxical, yet precarious, form of "order." See fr. 150.

this conformity of use we derive a powerful conjecture about the conformity of ideas. But this is not convincing, at least not ultimately, although there is enough to wager that it is the case, since it is well known that the same consequences are often derived from different suppositions.

This is enough at least to cloud the issue. Not that this extinguishes completely the natural light which makes us certain of such things. Members of the Academy[2] would have wagered in favor of it, but that dims the light and troubles the dogmatists, to the glory of the Pyrrhonists' cabal, who depend upon such ambiguous ambiguity, remaining in a certain doubtful obscurity from which neither our doubts can remove all light nor our natural light banish all the darkness.

142

We know the truth not only through reason but also through the heart. It is through the heart that we know first principles, and reasoning which plays no part in this knowledge attempts in vain to fight against them. The Pyrrhonists, who have no other object than this, are uselessly preoccupied with it. We know that we are not dreaming, however powerless we may be to prove it through reason. This powerlessness proves nothing other than the weakness of our reason, and not the uncertainty of all our knowledge, as they claim.

For knowledge of first principles, like space, time, movement, numbers, is as sure as any knowledge that our reasoning gives us. And it is on these kinds of knowledge of the heart and of instinct that reason must rely and base all its arguments. The heart senses that there are three dimensions in space and that numbers are infinite, and reason then demonstrates that there are no two square numbers of which one is double the other. Principles are sensed, propositions proved, and both with certainty, although by different routes. It is as useless and ridiculous for reason to demand of the heart proof of first principles in order to agree as it would be ridiculous for the heart to demand of reason a sense of all the propositions that it is demonstrating in order to accept them.

This powerlessness must therefore be used only in the humbling of reason, which would be the judge of everything, but not in assailing our certainty. As if reason alone were capable of teaching us! May it please God that, on the contrary, we never had need of it and that we knew all things through instinct and intuition! But nature has refused us this benefit. On the contrary, it has given us very little knowledge of this kind. All other kinds of knowledge can only be acquired through reasoning.

2. Plato's school of philosophy.

And that is why those to whom God has given religion through a sense of the heart are truly happy and quite rightly convinced. But we can only give religion to those who do not already have it through reasoning, until God gives it to them through an intuition of the heart. Without this faith is only human and useless for salvation.[3]

143

I can indeed conceive of a man without hands, feet, or head, for experience alone teaches us that the head is more necessary than the feet. But I cannot conceive of man without thought. He would be a stone or a brute beast.

144

Instinct and reason, signs of two natures.

145

Thinking reed

It is not in space that I must search for my dignity but in the regulation of my thought. I will have no advantage in owning land. Through space, the universe enfolds me and engulfs me like a speck; through thought, I enfold it.

146

The greatness of man is great in that he knows himself to be wretched. A tree does not know that it is wretched.

It is therefore to be wretched to know oneself to be wretched, but it is to be great to *know* that one is wretched.

147

The immateriality of the soul. Philosophers who have managed to control their passions: what material substance could have done it?

---

3. See fr. 690, par. 25: "Even if a man were convinced that numerical proportions were immaterial and eternal truths dependent on a first truth [...] which we call God, I should not consider that he had made much progress towards salvation." The "reasoning" Pascal envisages is not that of those cosmological proofs of traditional apologetics, or indeed of his own so-called "Wager" (fr. 680). These lead only to the God of Deism.

148

All those miseries prove his greatness.
They are the miseries of a great lord, of a dispossessed king.[4]

149

The greatness of man

The greatness of man is so visible that it is even inferred from his wretchedness. For what is nature to the animals we call wretchedness in man.[5] From which we recognize that, as his nature is today the same as that of the animals, he has fallen from a better nature that once belonged to him.

For who thinks he is unhappy not to be king other than a dispossessed king? Was Paulus Aemilius thought to be unhappy not to be consul? On the contrary, everybody thought that he was happy to have been consul because his condition did not include being consul. But Perseus was thought to be so unhappy not to be king any longer because his condition was to be a king forever, that it was thought strange that he was able to bear life.[6] Who thinks himself unhappy to have only one mouth? And who would not think he is unhappy to have only one eye? It has perhaps never occurred to anybody to be distressed at not having three eyes, but one is inconsolable to have none.

150

Greatness of man in his very concupiscence, for he has been able to derive an admirable system from it and has made an image of charity from it.

---

4. "Pascal is haunted," Sellier remarks, "by the royal figures of man: royalty of the mind, royalty of the saints.... Fallen man is a King Lear, blind, wandering, deprived of mind. The poem of this fallen king is the *Book of Ecclesiastes.* Yet the Saints will reign over the forecourt of the celestial Jerusalem." Pascal, *Pensées,* ed. Sellier (2010), 215n1; the reference is to fr. 748.

5. "We": the Augustinian theologians. As had Jansenius, Pascal prioritizes the great principle of Saint Augustine: "Man's vice is a beast's nature." See *On the Grace of Christ and on Original Sin,* bk 2, ch. 46, trans. Peter Holmes and Robert Ernest Wallis, rev. Benjamin B. Warfield, from Nicene and Post-Nicene Fathers, 1st ser., vol. 5, ed. Philip Schaff (Buffalo, N.Y.: Christian Literature Publishing Co., 1887); rev & ed. for New Advent by Kevin Knight, http://www.newadvent.org/fathers/15062.htm.

6. See fr. 49.

[VIII] Contradictions[1]

151

After showing the baseness and greatness of man.

Let man now assess his own true worth. Let him love himself, for there is in him a nature capable of good; but let him not for that reason love the baseness that also forms a part of him. Let him despise himself, because that capacity is empty; but let him not despise such a natural capacity for that reason. Let him love himself and hate himself: he has the capacity within himself to know the truth and to be happy, but he has no truth that is either constant or satisfying.

I would therefore like to help man desire to find some truth and be ready and free from passions in order to follow the truth wherever he finds it, knowing how much his consciousness is clouded by the passions. I would have him hate within himself concupiscence, which is self-determining, so that it does not blind him in making his choice and does not stop him when he has chosen.

152

We are so presumptuous that we would like to be known throughout the world, and even by people who will come after we are dead. And we are so vain that the esteem of five or six people around us keeps us amused and contented.

153

It is dangerous to let man see too clearly how much he is on a level with the beasts without showing him his greatness. And it is also dangerous to let

---

1. In this *liasse*, Pascal draws a profound pessimism about man from the depths of the *Essays*. Yet, at the same time, he insists on man's "greatness": his aspirations to the infinite; his awareness of himself and particularly of his own misery. Man is a web of contradictions, incomprehensible to himself. He is plunged into either despair or presumption. Progressively, Pascal continues to set the stage for the unique resolution of these contradictions. This will be Christianity's revelation of the paradox of God as both "True Man" and "True God."

him see too clearly his greatness without his baseness. It is even more danger-ous to leave him in ignorance of both, but it is a great advantage to represent both to him.

154

Man must not think that he is equal to either the beasts or the angels, nor should he remain in ignorance about both. Rather, he should know about both.[2]

155

A.P.R.[3] Greatness and wretchedness

With wretchedness being deduced from greatness and greatness from wretchedness, some have concluded for wretchedness all the more since they have used greatness to prove it, while others have concluded for greatness with all the more vehemence since they have concluded it from wretchedness itself. Everything that some have been able to say shows greatness has only served as an argument for others to conclude for wretchedness, since the higher one falls, the more wretched one is. And the others say the opposite. They fol-lowed one another in a never-ending circle, since it is certain that according to what lights they have, people will find both greatness and wretchedness in man. In a word, man knows that he is wretched. He is therefore wretched, because he is so. But he is truly great, because he knows it.

156

Contradiction, scorn for our very being, to die for nothing, hatred of our being.[4]

2. See frs. 453 and 557. Among the philosophers, the Epicureans saw only man's misery and proposed only a terrestrial ideal. The Stoics, seeing only his greatness, went so far as to propose that he could become a "companion to God." That neither saw both sides of the equation is the centerpiece of the *Exchange with M. de Sacy*.

3. See ch. XII, n. 1. This fragment may be an addition to the discourse that Pascal intended to present "At Port-Royal," which was later misfiled in this *liasse*. Or perhaps, having written it, he decided it was not all that relevant to the outline of his Apology, so he detached it and filed it here.

4. A note taken while reading Montaigne, *Essays*, II, 3, 308–9: "As for the opinion that disdains our life, it is ridiculous. For after all, life is our being, it is our all. Things that have a nobler and richer being may ac-cuse ours; but it is against nature that we despise ourselves and care nothing about ourselves. It is a malady peculiar to man, and not seen in any other creature, to hate and disdain himself. It is by a similar vanity that we wish to be something other than we are. The object of such a desire does not really affect us inasmuch as the desire contradicts and hinders itself within. [...] The security, the freedom from pain and suffering, the exemption from the ills of this life, which we purchase at the price of death, bring us no advantage. To no purpose does the man avoid war who cannot enjoy peace, and to no purpose does the man flee from trouble who does not have what it takes to relish repose."

157

Contradictions

Man is naturally credulous, incredulous, fearful, and bold.

158

What are our natural principles if not our accustomed principles? And in children, those that they have received from the custom of their fathers, like hunting in animals?[5]

A different custom will provide other natural principles. We see this through experience. And if there are natural principles that cannot be erased by custom, there are also some principles born of custom and against nature that cannot be erased by nature or a second custom. It depends on disposition.

159

Fathers fear that children's natural love might be erased. What, then, is this nature that is liable to be erased?

Custom is a second nature that destroys the first. [6]

But what is nature? Why is not custom natural?

I greatly fear that this nature is itself nothing more than a first custom, just as custom is a second nature.[7]

160

Man's nature can be considered in two ways: the first with respect to its end, and in that case he is great and incomparable; the second with respect to the masses, as we judge the nature of horses or dogs by the masses, seeing in them the ability to run AND THE INSTINCT TO KEEP AT BAY;[8] and thus man is abject and vile.[9] And these are the two routes that give rise to such diverse judgments on him and that make philosophers engage in so many disputes.

For one denies the other's supposition. One says: "He <u>cannot have been</u>

---

5. Montaigne, *Essays*, I, 23, 100: "The laws of conscience, which we say are born of nature, are born of custom. Each man, holding in inward veneration the opinions and the behavior approved and accepted around him, cannot break loose from them without remorse, or apply himself to them without self-satisfaction. [...] And the common notions that we find in credit around us and infused into our soul by our fathers' seed, these seem to be the universal and natural ones."

6. Montaigne, *Essays*, III, 10, 938: "Habit is a second nature, and no less powerful."

7. See Michael Moriarty, *Early Modern French Thought: The Age of Suspicion* (Oxford: Oxford University Press, 2003), 126–29, for a subtle reading of this and other fragments on custom.

8. *The instinct to keep at bay*, e.g., by barking.

9. "Man is abject and vile": a formula inspired by the conclusion of Montaigne's "Apology for Raymond Sebond." *Essays*, II, 12, 555. See fr. 453.

born for such an end, for his actions completely contradict it."[10] The other says: "He strays from his end when he performs these base actions."[11]

161

Two things teach man about his complete nature: instinct and experience.

162

Profession
Thoughts

All is one, all is diverse. How many natures are there in man's nature! How many professions, and by what chance! Ordinarily everyone chooses what he has heard praised. A well fashioned heel.[12]

163

If he exalts himself, I abase him
If he abases himself, I exalt him
And contradict him always
Until he comprehends
That he is an incomprehensible monster.

164

The main strengths of the Pyrrhonists (I will omit the lesser ones) are that we have no certainty of the truth of these principles—except by faith and revelation—other than that we sense them naturally within us. Now, this natural sense is not convincing proof of their truth, since, as we have no certainty beyond faith whether man was created by a good God, a wicked demon,[13] or simply by chance, we cannot know whether these principles are given to us as true, false, or uncertain, according to our origin.

Moreover, no one has any assurance—outside of faith—whether he is awake or asleep; given that during sleep we believe ourselves to be as wide awake as when we are awake.[14] We think we see space, figures, and move-

---

10. The Pyrrhonist, i.e., the skeptic. See the introduction, and ch. I, n. 10, of this translation.

11. The dogmatist. See ch. XVII, n. 14.

12. See fr. 69.

13. Descartes, *Meditations on First Philosophy*, I: "I shall then suppose, not that God who is supremely good and the fountain of truth, but some evil genius [...] has employed his whole energies in deceiving me." In *The Philosophical Works of Descartes*, trans. Elizabeth S. Haldane and G. R. T. Ross (Cambridge: Cambridge University Press, 1911), 1:148; consulted online: https://yale.learningu.org/download/041e9642-df02-4eed-a895-70e472df2ca4/H2665_Descartes%27%20Meditations.pdf.

14. Descartes, *Metaphysical Meditations*, I: "How often has it happened to me that in the night I dreamt

ments. We sense time elapsing, we even measure it, and ultimately we behave in the same way as when we are awake. With half our life spent asleep, either by our own acknowledgment or in whatever way it may appear, we have no idea of the truth, so that all our feelings are mere illusions. Who knows whether the other half of our life where we think we are awake is not another kind of sleep slightly different from the first from which we awake when we think we are sleeping?[15] (*As we often dream that we are dreaming, piling one dream upon another, it is also quite possible that the half of life where we think we are awake is itself only a dream, on which all other dreams are grafted, and we only wake from it at death. During life we possess the principles of truth and goodness as little as during natural sleep, and all the passing of time and the bodies that we sense as well as the different thoughts that disturb us are perhaps only illusions similar to the passing of time and the vain specters of our dreams.*)

Those are the main strengths on each side. I will leave the lesser ones, like the Pyrrhonists' arguments against the impressions made by custom, education, different countries' ways of life, and other similar things, which, although for the most part they carry along with them ordinary men who put forth dogmatic discourses on nothing but such vain foundations, are blown away by the slightest breath uttered by the Pyrrhonists. You only have to see their books, and if you are not sufficiently persuaded, you soon will be and perhaps overly so.

I will stop at the dogmatists' single strong point, which is that if we are speaking sincerely and in good faith, we cannot doubt natural principles.

Against which the Pyrrhonists in one word oppose the uncertainty of our origins, which includes the uncertainty of our nature. To which the dogmatists have not yet found a reply since the world has been in existence.

And so there is open warfare between men, where each one must take sides, of necessity aligning himself with either dogmatism or Pyrrhonism, for anyone who thinks he can remain neutral will be the ultimate Pyrrhonist. This

---

that I found myself in this particular place, that I was dressed and seated near the fire, whilst in reality I was lying undressed in bed!" In *The Philosophical Works of Descartes*, trans. Haldane and Ross, 1:145–46.

15. Montaigne, *Essays*, II, 12, 548: "Those who have compared our life to a dream were perhaps more right than they thought. When we dream, our soul lives, acts, exercises all her faculties, neither more nor less than when she is awake [...]. Sleeping we are awake, and waking asleep. [...] Since our reason and our soul accept the fancies and opinions which arise in it while sleeping, and authorize the actions of our dreams with the same approbation as they do those of the day, why do we not consider the possibility that our thinking, our acting, may be another sort of dreaming, and our waking another kind of sleep?" This is a commonplace motif used, for example, in Calderon's *Life is a Dream* (c. 1633). After this sentence, Pascal struck out the following passage, which C2 does not retain: "*And who doubts that if we dreamed in the company of others and the dreams happened to agree—something common enough—but we were alone in our waking hours, we would think that things were reversed?*"

neutrality forms the essence of this clique. Whoever is not against them is their greatest ally. They are not even for themselves; they are neutral, indifferent, suspending belief with regard to everything, themselves included.

What then shall man do in such a state? Shall he doubt everything? Shall he doubt whether he is awake, whether he is being pinched, whether he is being burnt? Shall he doubt whether he doubts? Shall he doubt whether he exists? It is not possible to go this far, and I state it as fact that there has never been a truly perfect Pyrrhonist. Nature comes to the aid of impotent reason and prevents it from straying so fantastically.

Shall he say on the contrary that he possesses the truth with certainty when at the slightest urging he is unable to show any proof of it and is forced to let go of his grip?

What a chimera then is man! What a novel sight, what a monster, what chaos, what a subject of contradictions, what a prodigy, the judge of all things, a feeble earthworm, the repository of truth, a sewer of uncertainty and error, the glory and refuse of the universe!

Who can unravel such a muddle? (*Certainly this is beyond dogmatism and Pyrrhonism and all human philosophy. Man is beyond man. Let us therefore grant the Pyrrhonists what they have so crowed about, that the truth is neither within our grasp nor within our sights, that it does not reside on earth but inhabits heaven, lodged within God's bosom, and it is possible to know it only to the extent that it pleases God to reveal it. Let us therefore learn about our true nature from the uncreated and incarnate truth.*

It is impossible to be a Pyrrhonist without stifling nature, and it is impossible to be a dogmatist without renouncing reason.) Nature confounds the Pyrrhonists and reason confounds the dogmatists. Oh man, what will become of you, you who search for your true condition through your natural reason? You can neither escape one of these sects nor survive in either.

Know then, you proud creature, what a paradox you are to yourself! Humble yourself, impotent reason! Be quiet, feeble nature! Learn that man is infinitely beyond man, and hear from your Master your true condition about which you know nothing.

Listen to God.

(*Is it not as clear as day that man's condition is dual? Certainly.*) For, clearly, if man had never been corrupted, he would confidently enjoy truth and happiness in his innocence. And if man had never been anything other than corrupt, he would have no idea of either truth or beatitude. But, unhappy that we are, and more so than if there were no greatness in our condition, we have an idea of happiness and are unable to reach it, we sense an image of the truth and possess only falsehood, we are incapable both of absolute ignorance and of certain knowledge, so manifest it is that we were once in a degree of perfection from which we are unhappily fallen.

How astonishing, however, that the mystery that is the furthest removed from our knowledge, that of the transmission of sin, should be something without which we cannot have any knowledge of ourselves!

For there is no doubt that nothing goes against our reason more than to say that the sin of the first man should implicate in its guilt those who being so remote from the source, seem incapable of having any part in it. This transmission seems to us not only impossible, it even appears very unjust. For what is more contrary to the rules of our miserable justice than damning for all eternity a child, incapable of will, for a sin in which he seems to have had so little part that it was committed six thousand years before he existed.[16] Certainly nothing shocks us more harshly than this doctrine. And yet without this most incomprehensible of all mysteries, we are incomprehensible to ourselves. The knot of our condition takes its twists and turns in this abyss, so that man is more inconceivable without this mystery than this mystery is inconceivable to man.

(*Hence it appears that God, in order to reserve for himself alone the right to teach us about ourselves, wanting to make the difficulty of our beings unintelligible to ourselves, hid the knot in a place so high, or, to put it more aptly, so low, that we were completely incapable of reaching it.*[17] *It is therefore not through the presumptuous commotion of our reason but rather through the simple submission of reason that we can truly know ourselves.*

These foundations, which were solidly established upon the inviolable authority of religion, make us know that there are two truths of faith that are equally assured: one is that man, in the state of creation or in a state of grace, is raised above the whole of nature, as if like God, partaking in divinity; the other is that in his corrupt and sinful state he is fallen from this state and placed at the same level as beasts. Both of these propositions are equally solid and certain.

The scriptures manifestly declare these truths to us when in various places they announce: My delights were to be with the children of men.[18] And it shall come to pass after this, that I will pour out my spirit upon all flesh.[19] *Etc. And they*

---

16. See the introduction, "Predestination."

17. A fundamental doctrine of neo-Augustinianism and a principal leitmotiv of the *Pensées*. The *Deus absconditus* has purposely hidden revelation from man so that the non-elect may never find it. He has left clues in scripture for the "seeker" to discern.

18. Divine Wisdom speaking in Proverbs 8:31.

19. Joel 2:28.

say in other places: You are gods.[20] All flesh is grass.[21] And man is compared to senseless beasts, and is become like to them.[22] I said in my heart concerning the sons of men—Eccl. 3.[23]

   Hence it is clear to see that, through grace, man is made like God and partakes in his divinity and that, without grace, he is deemed similar to brute beasts.)[24]

   20. Psalm 81:6. *"You are gods* and all of you the sons of the most High."

   21. Isaiah 40:6.

   22. Psalm 48:13: "*And man* when he was in honor did not understand; he *is compared to senseless beasts, and is become like to them.*"

   23. Ecclesiastes 3:18: "*I said in my heart concerning the sons of men,* that God would prove them, and show them to be like beasts."

   24. The gift of grace is what separates the elect from the damned and the seeker from the rest of humanity.

[IX] Diversion[1]

165

"If man were happy, he would be the more so for being less diverted, like the saints and God."—"Yes. But to enjoy diversion, is that not to be happy?"—"No, because it comes from elsewhere, from outside, and as a result can be troubled by many different circumstances and thus become a source of affliction."

166

Notwithstanding these miseries, he wants to be happy, and only to be happy, and is unable not to want to be happy. But how will he go about it? To do it effectively, he would have to make himself immortal. But, not being able to achieve this, he has decided to stop thinking about it.

As they have been unable to find a remedy against death, wretchedness, and ignorance, men, in order to make themselves happy, have decided not to think about them.[2]

167

I sense that I might never have existed because the self consists in my thought. And so I who am thinking would never have existed if my mother had been killed before I was invested with a soul. And so I am not a necessary being. By the same token, I am neither eternal nor infinite. But I see clearly that in nature there is a necessary, eternal, and infinite Being.[3]

---

1. Pascal's source is not so much Montaigne's essay "On Diversion" (III, 4) as Augustine's *On Free Will* (II, 19, 53). Fallen man turns away from God to perishable things. The opposition between listening to God and "diversion" is a central theme of neo-Augustinianism.

2. See Montaigne, *Essays*, I, 20, 69: "The goal of our career is death. It is the necessary object of our aim. If it frightens us, how is it possible to go a step forward without feverishness? The remedy of the common herd is not to think about it. But from what brutish stupidity can come so gross a blindness!"

3. Pascal, who judges all metaphysical proofs of the existence of God useless, here evokes the Augustinian notion of consciousness of self as granting access to such eternal truths as those of mathematics. See the beginning of "The Wager" (fr. 680).

168

Diversion

When sometimes I have applied myself to contemplating the diverse activities of men and the dangers and the troubles that they expose themselves to at court or in battle, giving rise to so many quarrels, or passions, or rash and often nefarious enterprises and so forth, I have often said that all human unhappiness comes from one thing alone, the inability to remain quietly in a room. If a man who is wealthy enough to lead an easy existence knew how to find pleasure in remaining at home, he would not leave home to venture onto the seas or besiege a fortress. The only reason why one pays such a high price for a commission in the army is because one would find it unbearable to remain in town. And the only reason why one goes out in search of company and the diversion offered by gambling is because one cannot find pleasure in staying at home. And so on.

But after thinking about it more closely, now that I knew the cause of all our unhappiness, I wanted to discover the reason for it; I found that there is one quite effective reason, which lies in the natural unhappiness of our weak and mortal condition, so wretched that nothing can console us when we think about it more closely.

Whatever station in life we imagine, in which we gather all the wealth that can belong to us, royalty is the finest position on earth. But let us imagine a king, surrounded by all the advantages pertaining to his rank. If he has no diversions and is left to consider and reflect upon his condition, this languid happiness will not sustain him. He is bound to fall into thinking about the threats posed by possible revolts, and in the end by death and disease, which are inevitable. As a result, if he is without what is called diversion, he is unhappy, more unhappy in fact than the least of his subjects who finds diversion in gambling.

That is why gambling and women's company, war and high office are so sought after. It is not that there is in effect any happiness in these, nor that we imagine true bliss to reside in the money that can be won through gambling or in a hare we are chasing—we would not want it if it were offered to us. We seek neither that easy, peaceful existence that might make us think of our unhappy condition nor the dangers of war nor the toil of office, but rather the agitation that stops us from thinking about it and diverts us.—That is why we prefer the hunt to the catch.[4]

---

4. Montaigne, *Essays*, II, 12, 459: "It must not be thought strange if people despairing of the capture have yet taken pleasure in the chase."

That is why men so love hustle and bustle. That is why prison is such a terrible punishment. That is why finding pleasure in solitude is so incomprehensible. And, ultimately, the greatest source of felicity in being a king comes from the fact that people try constantly to divert kings and provide them with all kinds of pleasure.—The king is surrounded by people whose only thought is to divert him and prevent him from thinking about himself; for, king though he be, he is unhappy if ever he thinks about himself.

This is all that men have been able to devise to make themselves happy. Those would-be philosophers who believe that the world is quite unreasonable for spending the whole day chasing after a hare that they would not have wanted to buy hardly know our nature. This hare would not protect us from the vision of death and the miseries which distract us from it, but hunting it does.

A. And so, when they are faced with the reproach that what they search for so ardently could not possibly satisfy them, if they replied (as they ought to do if they thought of it carefully) that in doing so they are searching only for some violent and impetuous pastime to distract them from thinking about themselves and that it is for this reason alone that they choose an attractive object that entices and attracts them so ardently, they would leave their adversaries at a loss for an answer.... But they do not reply this, because they do not know themselves. They do not know that they are seeking only the hunt and not the catch. They imagine that if they managed to secure that one office they would gladly rest, and they fail to perceive the insatiable nature of cupidity. They believe that they are sincerely seeking rest when in effect they are seeking only agitation. They have one secret instinct driving them to seek external diversion and occupation, which comes from a sense of their continual wretchedness; and yet they have another secret instinct, which is a vestige of the greatness of our original nature, making them recognize that happiness can effectively be found only in rest and not in restlessness. As a result of these two opposing instincts, a blurred purpose takes shape within them, hidden from their view in the depths of their soul, making them both aim for rest through agitation and imagine that the satisfaction they do not feel will fall to their lot, if, in overcoming the few difficulties they can envision, they can thereby open the door to rest.

Our whole life flows by like this: we seek rest by fighting against a few obstacles, and yet if they are overcome, rest becomes intolerable through the *ennui* that it generates. We have to go out in urgent search of agitation. For we think either of miseries that beset us or of those that threaten us. And even were we well shielded on all sides from such worries, *ennui* would nonetheless rise, of its own authority, from the bottom of our hearts, where it is naturally rooted, and fill our minds with its venom.

The advice that Pyrrhus[5] was given to take the rest that he was ever seeking through much travail met with many a difficulty.[6]

Dancing: one must think carefully where one puts one's feet.

A nobleman sincerely believes that hunting is a great pleasure, a royal pleasure. But his huntsman is not of this opinion.

———

B. Thus man is so unhappy that he could become bored without any reason for *ennui*, by the very nature of his temperament; and he is so vacuous that, even if he had a thousand and one reasons for being bored, the slightest thing, like hitting a billiard ball with a cue, is enough to divert him.

———

C. But, you will say, what is his object in all this? Just so that tomorrow he can boast to his friends that he played better than someone else. Similarly, others sweat in their study in order to show learned men that they have solved an algebra problem that had not been solved until now. And so many others expose themselves to the greatest dangers so as to boast afterwards about a fortress they have seized, just as foolishly, if you ask me.[7] Then there are the others who kill themselves taking note of all these things, not to become wiser, but simply to show that they know such things. These people are the most foolish of the bunch, since they are foolish with knowledge of what they are doing, while it is conceivable that the others would no longer be so foolish if they had such knowledge.

———

A man spends his life without *ennui*, by gambling a little every day. But give him every morning the money that he can win each day, on condition that he not gamble, and you will make him unhappy. It might be said that he

5. Pyrrhus, king of Epirus (300 BCE), failed to conquer Italy and Greece any more than briefly and at great cost. Hence the term "Pyrrhic Victory."

6. See Montaigne, *Essays,* I, 42, 237–38: "When King Pyrrhus was undertaking his expedition into Italy, Cyneas, his wise counselor, wanting to make him feel the vanity of his expedition, asked him: 'Well, Sire, to what purpose are you setting up this great enterprise?' 'To make myself master of Italy, [...]. 'And then [...] when that is done?' 'I shall pass over into Gaul and Spain' [...]. 'And after that?' 'I shall go and subdue Africa; and finally, when I have brought the world under my subjection, I shall rest and live content and at my ease.' 'In God's name, Sire, [...] 'tell me what keeps you from being in that condition right now, if that is what you want. Why don't you settle down at this very moment in the state you say you aspire to, and spare yourself all the intervening toil and risks?'"

7. Montaigne, *Essays,* III, 4 ("On Diversion"), 773: "If you ask that man 'What interest have you in this siege?' He will say: 'The interest of example and of common obedience to the prince. I aspire to no profit whatever from it and as for glory I know how small a share of it can concern a private person like myself.' [...] Yet see him on the next day, all changed, all boiling and red with rage at his post in the line of attack: it is the gleam of so rough steel, and the fire and racket of our cannon and drums that have injected this new rigor and hatred in his veins."

is seeking the enjoyment of gambling and not the gain. Then, make him gamble for no stakes at all, and he will not become excited but rather bored by it. It is therefore not amusement alone that he seeks. A languid and passionless amusement will bore him. Rather, he needs to become excited and thus deceives himself by imagining that he would be happy to win what he would not want if it were given to him on condition of not gambling, in order that he make up an object for his passion and that, thereupon, he excite his desire, his anger, his fear for the object that he has invented, like children who are frightened by a face that they have painted.[8]

How is it that a man, who only a few months previously lost his only son and who overwhelmed by law-suits and quarrels, was so distressed only this morning, no longer even thinks about it now? Do not be surprised by it: he is completely taken up with the direction a wild boar, which has been ardently chased by the dogs for six hours, will take. Nothing more is needed. If man, however filled with sadness he may be, can be prevailed upon to indulge in some diversion, he will be happy for the time that the diversion lasts. And if man, however happy he may be, is not diverted and occupied by some passion or amusement that prevents ennui from spreading, he will soon be glum and unhappy. Without diversion, there is no joy. With diversion, there is no sadness. And this is also what makes up the happiness of people of high rank; they have a number of people diverting them and they have the power to maintain themselves in this state.

D. If you think of it, what is it to be superintendent, chancellor, or chief justice other than to be of such status as to have a great number of people in the morning coming from all parts so as not to leave them a single hour in the day where they might be able to think about themselves? And when they are in disgrace and banished to their country houses, where they lack neither wealth nor servants to assist them with their every need, they nonetheless feel wretched and abandoned, because nobody prevents them from thinking about themselves.

169

Diversion

Is not the kingly dignity sufficiently great in itself to make the person who possesses it happy simply through seeing what he is? Will he need to be divert-

---

8. Montaigne, *Essays*, II, 12, 479: "It is a pity that we fool ourselves with our own monkey tricks and inventions—'They fear their own imaginings' (Lucan)—like children who take fright at that very face that they have smeared and blackened for their playmates."

ed from such a thought like ordinary people? I see clearly that you make a man happy if you divert him from the view of his domestic troubles by filling his entire thoughts with a care for dancing well, but will it be the same for a king, and will he be happier attending to his vain amusements than to the sight of his greatness? And what more satisfying object could be offered to his mind? Would it not therefore impede his joy to fill his mind with thoughts of measuring his steps to the rhythm of a melody or skillfully throwing a javelin, instead of leaving him to enjoy in peace the contemplation of that majestic glory that surrounds him? Let us put it to the test. Let us leave a king completely alone, without anything to satisfy his senses, without any care to occupy his mind, and without company, to think about himself totally at leisure, and we shall see that a king without diversion is a man full of miseries. And so this is carefully avoided, with no end of people always beside the persons of kings, making sure that diversion follows affairs of state and watching over their leisure hours to provide them with pleasures and games so that there is no empty moment. In other words, they are surrounded by people who take exceptional care to ensure that the king is never alone and in a state to think about himself, knowing full well that, king though he be, he will be wretched if he thinks about it.

In all this, I am not talking about Christian kings as Christians but only as kings.

170
Diversion

It is easier to bear death without thinking about it than the thought of death even when one is not facing it.

171
Diversion

From childhood onward, men are put in charge of the care of their honor, property, and friends, and even with the care of their friends' property and honor. They are overwhelmed with responsibilities, learning languages, and exercises, and are given to understand that they can never be happy unless their and their friends' health, honor, and fortune are in good shape and that a single missing element will make them unhappy. So they are given burdens and responsibilities that agitate them from the break of day. That, you may say, is a strange way of making them happy. What better way to make them unhappy? What do you mean, what better way? All one need do is take away these cares from them, for then they would look at themselves and think about what they are, where they come from, and where they are going. And so they cannot be too occupied or distracted, and that is why, after having been given so many responsibilities, if they have any time for relaxation, they are advised to spend it diverting themselves, gambling, and keeping themselves fully occupied.

How empty and full of filth is the human heart.[9]

9. Sellier reminds us that Pascal not only dismisses the Platonists' pursuit of eternal truths in the mind, but even Saint Augustine's search for God in his own soul. Few theologians have ever evoked a more negative vision of the human interior than did the neo-Augustinians of Port Royal. And among them, Pascal's vision is perhaps the most sinister of all. "When he looks into his heart, Pascal sees only an 'abyss of pride, of curiosity, and concupiscence' (fr. 751). Whereas Augustine encountered God in the enchanted depths of his own soul, Pascal insists on self-hatred (fr. 494). God may be found only 'outside.'" Sellier, in Pascal, Pensées, ed. Sellier (2010), 233n1. See the section "Predestination," in the introduction to this translation.

[X] Philosophers[1]

172

Even had Epictetus seen the way perfectly well, he announces to mankind: "You are following the wrong way." He shows that there is another way, but he does not lead us to it. The way is wanting what God wants. Jesus Christ alone leads to it. *Via, Veritas. The way, the truth.*

173

The vices of Zeno himself.[2]

174
Philosophers

What a fine thing to cry out to a man who does not know himself that he needs to find God by himself! And what a fine thing to say it to a man who does know himself!

175
Philosophers

Believing that God alone is worthy of being loved and admired, they wished to be loved and admired by all men. But they are unaware of their corrupt state. If they are filled with feelings of love and admiration for God and they find their principal joy in it and thereby consider themselves to be good people, then well and good. But if they find themselves opposed to this, having no inclination other than to establish themselves in men's esteem, if their only perfection lies in trying to make men, without forcing them, find happiness in loving them, then I say that this perfection is horrible. What! They have known God and have not made it their sole desire for men to love him, but

---

1. Pascal nearly always uses the terms *philosophers* and *philosophy* in a pejorative sense. Human reason alone being incapable of reaching true moral and metaphysical truths, man's only option is to turn to that Divine Wisdom who speaks in scripture. Sellier often observes that Pascal is more theologian than philosopher.

2. Zeno of Citium (333–261 BCE), founder of Stoicism and advocate of free love. See Montaigne, *Essays*, I, 26, and III, 10.

instead have made it their desire for men not to search beyond them! They wanted to be the object of men's desire for happiness.

176
Philosophers

We are full of things that propel us outwards.

Our instinct makes us sense that we must seek happiness outside ourselves. Our passions drive us outwards even were there no objects in view to excite them. Outward objects in themselves tempt and call out to us, even when we are not thinking of them. And so the philosophers may well say: "Go within yourselves, there you will find your good."[3] They are not believed. And those who do believe them are the most empty-headed and stupid of people.

177

What the Stoics propose is so difficult and so useless!

The Stoics assert: All those not at the highest pinnacle of wisdom are equally mad and iniquitous,[4] like those who are in two inches of water.[5]

178

The three kinds of concupiscence have formed three sects,[6] and the philosophers have done nothing other than to follow one of these three kinds.

179
Stoics

They conclude that you can always do what you sometimes do and that, since the desire for reputation makes people who have it do something well, then the others will be able to do it as well.

These are feverish whims that health cannot imitate.

Epictetus concludes that, given the fact that there are steadfast Christians, everybody can be so.[7]

---

3. See fr. 26. When Pascal looks inside himself, he finds only "pride, curiosity, and concupiscence" (fr. 751). He insists on self-hatred (fr. 405). God can only be found "outside" the human mind and heart: in Christ, scripture, the Eucharist, and the poor. (See Pascal's "Letter 4 to Charlotte de Roannez," in Pascal, Œuvres complètes, ed. Lafuma, 267). In the human interior, there is only that evil leaven that is the product of the Fall (fr. 309).

4. See Montaigne, Essays, II, 2, 296.

5. An image taken from P. Charron's De la sagesse, III, 37.

6. Epicureanism, the product of sensuality; Cartesianism, that of intellect; Stoicism, that of pride.

7. Epictetus, Discourses, IV, 7, 6.

[XI] The Sovereign Good[1]

180

Dispute over the sovereign good

*Be satisfied with yourself
and the goods that are born from you.*[2]

There is a contradiction here, because they advise suicide in the end.
Oh, what a happy life, from which you free yourself like the plague!

181

Part Two

**Man without faith can know
neither the true good, nor righteousness.**

All human beings seek to be happy. There is no exception to this, however different the means they employ. They all aim for this goal. The reason why one man goes off to fight a war and another does not is this same desire in both of them, though it is accompanied by different perspectives. The will does not make a single move that is not directed toward this object. It is the motive of all human beings' every action, including those who hang themselves.[3]

And yet, in all the years that have gone by, no one, without the faith, has ever arrived at this point at which they are all continually aiming. They all complain: rulers, subjects, aristocrats, commoners, the old, the young, the strong, the weak, the learned, the ignorant, the healthy, the sick, from every country, every period, people of all ages, and all conditions.

An experience so long, so continuous, and so universal should be a con-

---

1. The title and first fragment come from the *Augustinus* (II, 8) of Jansenius, in which the ideas of Seneca are repeatedly subjected to ironic attack. Jansenius himself paraphrases a passage from Letter 155 of Saint Augustine. See Jansenius, *Augustinus seu doctrina Sancti Augustini de humanæ naturæ sanitate, ægritudine, medicinâ adversùs Pelagianos et Massilienses* (Louvain: Jacob Zeger, 1640).

2. Seneca, *Letters to Lucilius*, XX, 8.

3. Following Jansenius and Saint Augustine, Pascal subjects to irony the Stoic precept that while man can find happiness in his own virtue, suicide is nonetheless a moral alternative.

vincing proof of our utter inability to attain the good by our own efforts. But we learn little from example. No two situations are ever so alike that there is not some tiny difference, on the basis of which we expect that this time our expectations will not be disappointed as they were the time before. And so, since the present never satisfies us, experience deludes us, and leads us from one misfortune to another until death, the supreme and eternal misfortune.

What, then, do this avidity and this impotence cry out to us, but that there once was in man true happiness, of which there now remains only an empty mark and trace, a gap that he tries, to no avail, to fill with everything around him, seeking in absent things the help he cannot get from those that are present, a help however that they are totally incapable of providing because this infinite abyss can be filled only by something infinite and immutable, that is to say by God himself?[4]

He alone is man's true good. And since he has forsaken him, it is a strange thing that there is nothing in nature that has not been able to take his place: stars, sky, earth, elements, plants, cabbages, leeks, animals, insects, calves, snakes, fever, plague, war, famine, vices, adultery, incest. And since man lost the true good, anything can appear to him equally so, even his own destruction, although that is so contrary to God, reason, and nature all together.[5]

Some seek the sovereign good in authority, others in curiosities and the sciences, others in sensual pleasures.

Others, who in effect have come closer to it, have reflected that this universal good desired by all men cannot reside in any of the particular things that can be possessed only by a single individual, and that, when they are shared, cause more grief to the possessor on account of the part he does not have than satisfaction in the enjoyment of what belongs to him. They have realized that the true good must be such that everyone can possess it undiminished and without envy at the same time, and that no one can lose it against his will. Their reason is that, because this desire is natural to man, since it exists necessarily in all of us and we cannot not have it, they conclude from this. . .

---

4. Man innately senses some "paradise lost" because the Fall has left in him an "empty mark and trace" of what he once possessed. The search for man's pre-lapsarian happiness is at the root of all of human activity, however foolish.

5. Pascal's enumeration of this multiplicity of human follies cascades polemically into his conclusion that men seek to fill the void left by the Fall in absurd ways. He seeks to embrace, both vertically and horizontally, the entirety of human experience. "Calves" alludes to the Golden Calf of Exodus 32; the "serpents" to the tempter of Eve and to the "fiery serpents" of Numbers 21. Because they are nonsensical, "cabbages," "leeks," and "insects" serve to reinforce Pascal's conclusion that man's search for God in any created thing is as ridiculous as seeking happiness in a cabbage. Coincidentally, in a text written in the early 1650s, *Voyage to the Moon*, the *libertin* Cyrano de Bergerac has one of his characters discuss the soul of a cabbage.

[XII] A.P.R.[1]

182

APR Beginning
After having explained the incomprehensibility.[2]

The greatness and wretchedness of man, in their various forms, are so clearly visible that the true religion must necessarily teach us both that there is some great source of greatness in man and there is some great source of wretchedness.

Moreover, it must account for these astonishing contradictions.

It must show man, if it is to make him happy, that there is a God, that we are obliged to love him, that our true happiness is to live in him, and our only misfortune to be separated from him. It must acknowledge that we are full of darkness, which prevents us from knowing and loving him, and that therefore, since our duties oblige us to love God and our concupiscence turns us away from him, we are full of injustice. It must account for our own resistance to God and to our own good. It must teach us the remedies for our powerlessness and the means to obtain these remedies. Now examine all the religions of the world on this point, and see if there is another one, apart from Christianity, that fulfills all these requirements.

Will the philosophers do so, when the only good they can offer us is the

---

1. Sellier describes this chapter as a discourse "shrouded in mystery." The title also appears in the *Liasse* Table (fr. 1). For most scholars the letters have long signified "At Port-Royal." Pascal had used PR to signify Port-Royal in fr. 97. The prefaces written by Nicolas Filleau de La Chaise and Etienne Périer for the 1670 edition of the *Pensées* evoke a presentation to the Messieurs at Port-Royal in which Pascal outlined his project for an Apology for the Christian Religion. "A.P.R." is the only chapter title in those of the project of June 1658 that bears no connection to the contents of its chapter. The periods after the letters were added by the copyist of C2 as a chapter title. Pascal himself writes "APR" both times he uses it in his text.

2. God's will is inscrutable. Why he must damn some people for his absolute freedom to be preserved is inherently incomprehensible. "One understands nothing of the works of God unless one takes as a first principle that his *intention* was to blind some and enlighten others" (fr. 264, emphasis added). See ch. VIII ("Contradictions"), fr. 164, par. 15: "For what is more contrary to the rules of our miserable justice than damning for all eternity a child, incapable of will, for a sin in which he seems to have had so little part that it was committed six thousand years before he existed. [...] And yet without this most incomprehensible of all mysteries, we are incomprehensible to ourselves."

good within us? Is that the true good? Have they found a remedy for our ills? Is it really curing man's presumption to set him on an equal footing with God?[3] As for the other philosophers who reduce us to the level of beasts[4] and the Mohammedans, who, even in eternity, offer us no good apart from earthly pleasures—have they brought us the remedy for our concupiscence?[5]

What religion, then, will teach us how to cure pride and concupiscence? What religion, finally, will teach us our good, our duties; the weaknesses that turn us away from them, the cause of these weaknesses, the remedies that can cure them, and how to obtain these remedies? Every other religion has failed in this. Let us see what God's wisdom can achieve.[6]

"Do not," it says, "O men, expect either truth or consolation from men. I am the one who created you, and I alone can teach you who you are.

"But you are no longer in the state in which I created you. I created man holy, innocent, and perfect. I filled him with light and intelligence. I gave him a share in my glory and in my wonders. In those days, man's eyes could see the majesty of God. He was not yet plunged in the darkness that blinds him, or in the mortality and the ills that afflict him. But he could not bear so exalted a glory without falling into presumption, he wanted to be centered on himself and independent of my help. He withdrew from my domination, and since he set himself up as my equal in desiring to find his happiness in himself, I abandoned him, and left him to himself. By stirring up revolt among the creatures that were subordinate to him, I made them his enemies, so that nowadays man has become like the animals, and is so remote from me that he retains only the faintest idea of his author; so obscured or murky has all his knowledge become. The senses, acting independently of reason, and often in control of reason, have dragged him away to search for pleasure. All created things torment or tempt him and dominate him, either subjugating him by their power, or seducing him by their charms, a more terrible and more damaging form of domination.[7]

3. The Stoics, who in Pascal's definition of them in the *Exchange with M. de Sacy,* claimed to be able to "become holy, a friend and companion to God" because they believed that an element of "the soul is a portion of the divine substance." See *Exchange with M. de Sacy,* §§12–13.

4. The Epicureans maintained that man lacks any capacity to rise above his condition as an animal.

5. According to the Qur'an (Sura 2), the paradise of the Muslims will be a lush garden in which "men will encounter beautiful virgins." Du Ryer had translated the Qur'an into French in 1647 (*L'Alcoran de Mahomet;* Paris: A. de Sommaville), but Pascal's source is more likely Montaigne's *Essays,* II, 12, 467: "[...] Mohammed promises his followers a paradise tapestried, adorned with gold and precious stones, peopled with wenches of surpassing beauty, with rare wines and foods."

6. From this point onward, Pascal's text becomes a prosopopoeia of God's wisdom (the term appears explicitly as a heading later on). See below, n. 9.

7. This Augustinian genealogy of human wretchedness is probably derived from Jansenius's *Oratio de interioris hominis reformation* [Discourse on the reformation of the inner man] (Antwerp: Hieronymus Ver-

"This is the state in which men are today. They retain some faint instinctive sense of the happiness of their former nature, and they are plunged into the wretchedness of their blindness and their concupiscence, which has become their second nature.

"From this fundamental truth I am disclosing to you, you may recognize the cause of all the contradictions that have baffled all men and have driven them to adopt such different views. Now, observe all the impulses toward greatness and glory that the experience of so many miseries has been unable to extinguish, and consider whether there can be any other explanation but that they derive from another nature."

APR For tomorrow[8]

Prosopopoeia[9]

"It is in vain, O men, that you seek in yourselves a remedy for your wretchedness. All your insights can never go beyond recognizing that it is not in yourselves that you can find either the truth or the good.

"The philosophers have promised you this; yet they have failed to achieve it.

"They do not know what your true good is, or what your true state is. (*I alone can teach you both what your true good is and* [*what your true state is*]. *I disclose these things to those who will listen to me, and they are revealed unambiguously in the Books I have placed in the hands of men. But I did not wish that this knowledge be so open. I show men what can make them happy. Why do you refuse to hear me?*

"*Do not look for satisfaction on this earth; do not hope for anything from human beings. Your good is in God alone, and the supreme happiness consists in knowing God and being united with him forever in eternity. Your duty is to love him with all your heart. He created you.*) How could the philosophers have given you remedies for your ills, which they did not even know? Your most grievous diseases are pride, which draws you away from God, and concupiscence, which ties you to the earth, and all the philosophers have achieved is to preserve at least one of these diseases. If they have given you God as an object, it was only to train you in arrogance. They caused you to think you were like him

---

dussius, 1628). Translated from Latin as *Discours de la reformation de l'homme interieur* by Arnaud d'Andilly (Paris: veuve Jean Camusat, 1642).

8. This second notation of "APR" in the context of "for tomorrow" seems to reinforce the thesis that Pascal planned a discourse to be given the next day for the Messieurs of Port-Royal. The same notation appears at the end of the chapter. See above, n. 1.

9. This rhetorical figure is borrowed from the Book of Proverbs (chs. 1 and 8), in which Divine Wisdom addresses herself directly to men.

and akin to him in nature. And those who realized the futility of this aspiration threw you down into the other abyss, giving you to understand that your nature was similar to that of animals and encouraging you to seek for your good in concupiscence, which is the lot of animals.

"This is not the way to be cured of your iniquities, which these wise men did not even recognize. I alone can make you understand who you are." Etc.[10]

(*"I do not ask you to believe blindly."*)[11]

Adam. Jesus Christ.[12]

> If you are united to God, it is by grace, not by nature.

If you are brought low, it is by repentance, not by nature.[13]

Thus there is a twofold capacity:

You are not in the state in which you were created.

Once these two states have been disclosed it is impossible for you not to recognize them.

Keep track of your impulses, observe yourselves, and see if you do not find within you the living traits of these two natures.

Could so many contradictions be found in a simple subject?

---

10. The testimony of Divine Wisdom temporarily breaks off at this point and does not resume until the sentence following Pascal's last line of division with the sentence beginning "I do not intend . . ."

11. The copyist faithfully transcribes this sentence struck by Pascal and here printed in italics. It is obviously an initial version of the first part of the sentence that reopens the discourse of Divine Wisdom: "I do not intend for you to subject your belief . . ." The texts separated by Pascal's lines of division down to the rubric "Incomprehensible" represent Pascal's notes to himself concerning how he will complete the testimony of Divine Wisdom. With the exception of "You are not in the state of your creation," it is unclear which fragments addressed to a second person would have been placed *verbatim* in the mouth of Divine Wisdom. The first, fourth, and last notations, though relevant to the discourse, obviously represent only Pascal's notes to himself, which were not destined to be included in the discourse itself.

12. According to Saint Paul (Romans 5:14, cited in fr. 489), Adam is the figure of "the one who is to come" and Christ "the new Adam." In fr. 258, Pascal reiterates this opposition as a principal organizing theme of the Apology: "Faith consists entirely in Jesus Christ and Adam." This adumbration had already been set down as representing parts 1 and 2 of the Apology in chapter II, "Order," fr. 40.

13. See fr. 17.

Incomprehensible[14]

That something is incomprehensible does not prevent its existing.[15] Infinite number, an infinite space equal to a finite one.[16]

Unbelievable that God should unite himself to us. This reflection derives purely from the view of our baseness. But if you really hold it sincerely, follow it as far as I have done and recognize that we are in fact so low that we are incapable by ourselves of knowing whether his mercy cannot make us capable of union with him. For I would like to know on what grounds this animal, which recognizes itself as so weak, has the right to measure the mercy of God, and to set whatever limits to it its fancy suggests. It has so little knowledge of what God is that it does not know what it is itself. And disturbed by the perception of its own state, it dares to say that God cannot make it capable of sharing in him. But I would like to ask it whether God requests anything else of it except to love him and know him, and why it thinks that God cannot make himself knowable and lovable to it, since it is naturally capable of love and knowledge. There is no doubt that it knows at least that it exists and that it loves something. Therefore, if it can see anything in the darkness in which it lives and if it finds something to love among the things of this earth, why, if God reveals to it some rays of his essence, should it not be capable of knowing him and loving him in the way in which God chooses to share himself with us? There is therefore, without doubt, some unbearable presumption in arguments of this kind, although they appear to be based on what looks like humility. Such humility is neither sincere nor reasonable unless it leads us to acknowledge that, not knowing by ourselves who we are, we can learn it from God alone.

—————

"I do not intend you to subject your belief to me without reason, and I do not mean to subjugate you by tyranny.[17] But at the same time I do not mean to account for everything to you. And in order to reconcile these con-

14. The following two notes separated by a line obviously do not form part of the discourse of Divine Wisdom. In the first sentence, Pascal first imagines directly addressing the unbeliever. Then, speaking of him in the third person, Pascal meditates upon the questions he will put to him in order to advance his submission to the will to believe.

15. Saint Augustine, *The City of God,* XXI, 5, no. 1: "it cannot be concluded that a thing has not been or shall not be because it cannot be reconciled to reason," trans. Marcus Dods, from Nicene and Post-Nicene Fathers, 1st ser., vol. 2, ed. Philip Schaff (Buffalo, N.Y.: Christian Literature Publishing Co., 1887); rev. & ed. for New Advent by Kevin Knight, http://www.newadvent.org/fathers/120121.htm.

16. See fr. 680, par. 3. Since space is divisible to infinity, an infinite space and a finite space will both contain an infinity of parts.

17. Pascal has defined tyranny in ch. IV ("Wretchedness"). See frs. 91 and 92.

traditions, I intend to show you clearly, by convincing proofs, divine marks in myself that will convince you of who I am, and to gain authority by miracles and proofs you cannot reject. I want you then to believe the things I teach you, when you can find no other motive for rejecting them than the fact that you cannot know by yourselves whether they are true or not."

God wished to redeem humankind, and to make salvation available to those who seek him. But men make themselves so unworthy that it is only just that God should refuse some, on account of their hardened hearts, what he grants to others by a mercy that they do not deserve.[18]

If he had wished to overcome the obstinacy of the most hardened, he could have done so by revealing himself to them so manifestly that they could not have doubted the truth of his essence, just as he will appear at the last day, with such a crash of thunder and such an upheaval of nature that the resurrected dead and the most blind will see him.

But this is not how he chose to appear in his coming of gentleness,[19] because since so many men make themselves unworthy of his clemency, he decided to leave them deprived of the good they do not want. It would not, therefore, have been just for him to appear in a manner manifestly divine and absolutely capable of convincing all men. But it would not have been just either for him to come in so concealed a manner that he could not have been recognized by those seeking him sincerely. To these, he wanted to make himself fully recognizable. And therefore, wishing to appear openly to those who were seeking him with all their heart, and yet hidden from those who flee him with all their heart, he has tempered[20]

[A.P.R. for tomorrow. 2[21]

tempered the knowledge they could have of him, such that he gave signs of himself that were visible to those who seek him and not to those who do not seek him.

There is enough light for those who desire only to see and enough darkness for those of the contrary disposition.]

18. Because of original sin, not a single human being merits the gift of grace. All are destined to damnation. God merely leaves the great majority of men in the state they already merit. His mercy in saving the elect is inscrutable.

19. In his incarnation as Jesus of Nazareth.

20. "Tempered," in the sense of "moderated" or "altered." The sentence breaks off here. The copyist transcribes what follows in brackets as explained below.

21. Pascal wrote what follows the word "tempered" on the reverse side of a second sheet, as indicated by the number "2." Pascal then transferred the passage to fragment 274, reflecting that this evocation of the *Deus absconditus* would find a more appropriate context in the chapter "Foundations." Ever scrupulous, the copyist inserted it here at the end of "A.P.R." to complete the meaning of the sentence. However, in the margin of Copy 2, he inserts a note: "This passage is to be found in the chapter 'Foundations of Religion.'"

[XIII] Beginning[1]

183

Unbelievers who profess to be guided by reason ought to be remarkably strong in reason.

So what do they[2] say?

"Do we not see," they say, "animals dying and living just like human beings, and Turks[3] just like Christians? They have their ceremonies, their prophets, their teachers, their saints, their monks, just the same as we do", etc...[4]

Is that contrary to scripture? Does scripture not say exactly that?[5]

If you do not much care whether you know the truth or not, that kind of argument is enough to buy you peace of mind. But if you desire with all your heart to discover it, then you have to look more closely into the matter. That would be good enough for a philosophical debate, but here everything is at stake...

And yet, after a piece of cursory thinking like that, we amuse ourselves, etc. Let us enquire of this religion itself whether it does not account for this obscurity. Perhaps it will reveal the explanation.

1. Sellier, unlike most editors, sees this chapter as Pascal's initial and perhaps quite early assembly of particular notes (scattered among his as yet unclassified fragments) in view of the writing of the two "letters" opening the Apology: the "Letter Encouraging the Search for God" (fr. 681) and the "Letter Removing Obstacles" (fr. 680). However, several of Pascal's most striking metaphors in this fragmentary chapter do not make their way into the discourses constituted by frs. 680–81. The title itself is, in effect, explained by fr. 194, which anticipates the opening of the preface. It reappears as the first word of fr. 196.

2. "They": the erudite, as opposed to the great majority of the *libertins*.

3. "Turk" does not merely refer to the subjects of the Ottoman Empire. In the seventeenth century, "Turk" was the universal word referring to all Muslims.

4. This argument had been used in the objections to Christianity by such scholarly unbelievers as François de La Mothe Le Vayer and Gabriel Naudé. Their source may well have been Du Ryer's translation of the Qur'an (1647).

5. See Ecclesiastes 3:18–19: "God would prove them [the sons of men], and show them to be like beasts. Therefore the death of man and of beasts is one, and the condition of them both is equal: as man dieth, so they also die: all things breathe alike, and man hath nothing more than beast: all things are subject to vanity."

184

It is ridiculous for us to be content with the society of our fellow-creatures, who are wretched as we are, helpless as we are. They will not help us. We shall die alone.

We must then act as if we were alone. If we did, would we build magnificent houses, etc.? No, we would search for the truth without hesitation. And if we refuse to, we show ourselves to esteem men's esteem more than the search for truth.

185

Between us and hell or heaven, there is only the interval of life, the most fragile thing in the world.

186

What are you promising me in the end but ten years—since ten years is what is at stake—ten years of self-love, of trying hard to please without success, not counting the inevitable suffering?

187

The odds

We must live differently in the world, depending on these different suppositions.

If we could exist here forever.

If it is certain that we shall not be here for long and uncertain if we shall be here in an hour's time.

The latter is the one that applies to us.

Heart.

Instinct.

Principles.

188

Pity for the atheists who are searching. Are they not unhappy enough as it is? Leave the invective for the ones who brag about it.

insult?   *? Searching / atheism*

189

Atheism: a proof of strength of mind
but only up to a point.

190

Based on the odds, you have to take the trouble to search for the truth, because if you die and do not worship the true source of everything, you are doomed. "But," you say, "If he had wanted me to worship him, he would have left me some signs of his will." But that is just what he has done; only you are overlooking them. So look for them. It is worth the effort.

191

If you ought to give up a week of your life, you ought to give up a hundred years.

192

There are but three types of people: those who serve God, having found him; those who spare no effort to seek him, having failed to find him; those who live without seeking him, having failed to find him. The first are reasonable and happy; the last are insane and unhappy; those in the middle are unhappy and reasonable.[6]

193

Atheists should be perfectly clear in what they say. Now, it is not perfectly clear that the soul is but matter.

194

Begin with sympathy for the unbelievers. They are unhappy enough in their condition.

It would be right to rail against them only if that would do them good. But it does them harm.

195

A man in a dungeon, not knowing if his sentence has been passed, with only an hour to find out, time enough, if he knows it has been passed, to get it revoked: it is unnatural for him to spend that hour not finding out if the sentence has been passed, but playing piquet.[7]

6. Nowhere in the *Pensées* does Pascal so clearly classify human beings from the perspective of neo-Augustinian theology. This major theme runs right through the entire planned Apology. In fr. 681, par. 10, these three categories are reduced to two: those who serve God because they have found him and those who seek God because they have not found him.

7. A trick-taking game of cards for two players.

Therefore it is beyond nature that man etc. It is the hand of God weighing heavy upon him.[8]

So not only is the zeal of those who search for him a proof of God, so is the blindness of those who do not search.

196
Beginning

Dungeon.

———

I find it wise not to inquire too deeply into the opinion of Copernicus,[9] but this

———

Everything in life depends on knowing whether the soul is mortal or immortal.

197

The final act is bloody, however decorous the rest of the play is. In the end, earth is thrown on your head, and that is it forever. [10]

198

We cheerfully rush over the precipice after covering our eyes to hide it from view.

---

8. The weighty hand of God resides in the theology of predestination, in God's inscrutable freedom to damn and to save at will. The Fall has so distorted human reason that it can no longer distinguish the inessential from the all-important. Hence man's indifference to his eternal fate. See fr. 681, pars. 3–9.

9. In the eighteenth *Provincial Letter*, Pascal had taken up the defense of Galileo. Presumably he accepts Copernicus's theory as well. Yet from the perspective of eternity even the greatest scientific advance pales to insignificance in the face of the question of the fate of the immortal soul.

10. Montaigne, *Essays*, I, 19, 65–66: "this [...] happiness of our life [...] should never be attributed to a man until he has been seen to play the last act of his comedy, and beyond doubt the hardest. In everything else there may be sham [...]. But in the last scene, between death and ourselves, there is no more pretending." Pascal, like Montaigne, uses "comedy" to mean "play," a normal usage at the time.

[XIV] Submission and Use of Reason, in Which True Christianity Consists[1]

199

How I hate this nonsense, not believing in the Eucharist, and so forth. If the Gospel is true, if Jesus Christ is God, where is the difficulty?[2]

200

I would not be a Christian without the miracles, says Saint Augustine.[3]

201

Submission

We have (*to have these three qualities: Pyrrhonist, geometer, Christian. Docile. Doubt. And they all go together*) to know when to doubt, when to assert, when to submit. Anyone who does not do so does not understand the power of reason. There are people who go against these three principles, either by asserting everything as if it were self-demonstrative, for lack of knowledge about demonstration or by doubting everything, for lack of knowledge of when to submit; or by submitting in everything, for lack of knowledge of when to make a judgment.[4]

---

1. Sellier has often characterized this *liasse* as essentially a "critique of pure reason." Reason's authority extends only to those physical phenomena that may be assessed empirically. Only six fragments in this *liasse* (201, 204–205, 213–14, and 220) appear to bear any relationship to the chapter's title. Fragments 202 and 211 would seem to belong respectively to the chapters on prophecy and on Jesus Christ. Fragments 199, 206, 212, and 215 have distinct affiliations with fragments in chapter XXVIII, "Conclusion."

2. This extemporaneous and perhaps somewhat indignant notation might best be read in the context of chapter XXVIII, "Conclusion."

3. Augustine, *The City of God*, XXII, 7. The "miracles" of which Saint Augustine speaks are the Resurrection and the Ascension. The fragment might be a residual trace of Pascal's original intention to use miracles as the basis of an apology.

4. In his *Preface to the Treatise on Vacuum*, Pascal elaborates a dichotomy between science and theology, opposing "reason" to "authority." Whereas theology inhabits a realm of closed revelation whose bounds are traced by the closed canon of the Bible, the natural sciences are open-ended. Geometry and physics are enriched by ongoing scientific investigation and are subject only to experiment and reason. It would be

202

"They received the word with all eagerness, searching the scriptures, whether these things were so."[5]

203

The way of God, who disposes all things with gentleness, is to plant religion in the mind by way of reasoning and in the heart by way of grace. But to try to plant it in the mind and heart by force and threats is planting not religion, but terror, *Terror rather than religion.*[6]

204

If everything is subjected to reason, our religion will have nothing mysterious or supernatural about it.

If we flout the principles of reason, our religion will be absurd and ridiculous.

205

St Augustine.[7] Reason would never submit if it did not judge that there are occasions when it should submit.

It is therefore right for it to submit when it judges that it ought to do so.

206

One of the humiliations of the damned will be to see themselves condemned by their own reason, in the name of which they claimed to condemn the Christian religion.

---

inappropriate, indeed folly, to subject the sciences to any kind of theological authority. The letters relevant to the treatise are translated by Richard H. Popkin in his *Pascal: Selections* (New York: Macmillan, 1989), under the title "The Great Experiment," 42–48.

5. Acts 1:11. "Now these were more noble than those in Thessalonica, who *received the word with all eagerness,* daily *searching the scriptures, whether these things were so.*" Saint Paul cites the example of the Jews of the synagogue at Berea, who diligently studied the Old Testament prophecies in an attempt to evaluate the apostles' claim that Jesus was the Messiah.

6. In his unfortunately celebrated *Letter to Vincent* (*Epistle* 93), Saint Augustine, reacting to the failure of reason and instruction in bringing the Donatist heretics to orthodoxy, had ended up by justifying a recourse to torture and violence. Pascal rejects Augustine's conclusion as "terror," not religion. Saint Augustine's text had been promulgated in 1653 to justify the Massacre of Saint Bartholomew's Day, as it would be in 1686 after the revocation of the Edict of Nantes. For Sellier, Pascal is the first modern Christian theologian to reject the use of force and physical violence in matters of religion.

7. See Augustine, *Letters*, 120, I, no. 3, on the relationship between reason and faith.

207

Those who do not love the truth appeal to the pretext that it can be challenged, and that there are many who deny it, and so their error derives only from their not loving truth or charity. So their excuse is in vain.

208

Contradiction is a poor mark of truth.
Many things that are certain are contradicted.
Many that are false go without being contradicted.
Contradiction is not a mark of falsity, nor is its absence a mark of truth.

209

See the two kinds of people in the "Perpetuity" section.

210

There are few true Christians. I mean even as far as faith goes. There are plenty who believe, but out of superstition. There are plenty who do not believe, because of *libertinage*.[8] There are few in the middle ground.

I do not include in this those whose character and conduct show true piety and all those who believe from a feeling from the heart.

211

Jesus Christ performed miracles and so did the apostles after him, and the earliest saints, in great numbers. This was because the prophecies were not yet fulfilled, and the miracles were in fulfillment of them, so that miracles were the only proof. It was foretold that the Messiah would convert the nations: how could this prophecy be fulfilled if the nations had not been converted? And how could the nations have been converted to belief in the Messiah, without seeing this final effect of the prophecies that prove him? So before he died, was raised from the dead, and converted the nations, not everything was yet fulfilled, and thus miracles were needed throughout that time. But now they are no longer needed to confute the Jews and the impious, for the fulfilled prophecies are a continuing miracle.[9]

8. See the preface, "French Words," and the introduction, "The Contours of Disbelief," in this translation. The word "libertinage" has multiple meanings in the *Pensées*: "hardened atheism"; "scholarly disbelief"; "convinced skepticism"; "agnosticism" (though this latter word was not coined until the nineteenth century); "atheism which has led to disordered morals or manners"; "complete indifference to religion"; "active or aggressive impiety"; "active aversion to Christianity"; "disparaging belief."

9. This affirmation shows that the dossiers on miracles (chapters XXX, XXXI, and XXXII) would

212

Piety is not the same as superstition.

To carry piety to the point of superstition is to destroy it.

Heretics criticize us for this superstitious submission. This is doing what they reproach us for.

Impiety not to believe in the Eucharist just because we cannot see it.

Superstition to believe propositions, etc.[10]

Faith, etc.

213

Nothing is so much in accordance with reason as this disavowal of reason.

214

Two excesses

To exclude reason, to admit only reason.

215

It would not have been a sin not to believe in Jesus Christ without the miracles.[11]

216

See whether I lie.[12]

---

have had no place in the Apology. Pascal realized that the rarity and limitations of post-apostolic miracles was too shaky a ground on which to build an Apology for the Christian Religion. Here, we find him forging the idea that the Old Testament prophecies accomplished in the New Testament constitute a "continuing miracle."

10. Pascal situates the proper use of intelligence somewhere between the passion with which the Protestants reject the doctrine of the Eucharist and the servility of those who submit to the pope in matters in which he does not solemnly express the faith of the universal Church. In 1653, the pope was right to condemn the five heretical propositions on grace, supposedly advanced by Jansenius in his *Augustinus* (1640). However, to proclaim that the propositions were actually present in the book was an abuse of his authority. This, the "Jansenists" argued, was a *de facto* question, to be resolved by an actual examination of the *Augustinus*. To submit to authority in a matter of empirical fact would be erroneous, and would, as Pascal notes, give the impression of confirming Protestant claims about Catholic "superstition."

11. John 15:24: "If I had not done among them the works that no other man hath done, they would not have sin; but now they have both seen and hated both me and my Father."

12. Job 6:28: "Give ear, and *see whether I lie.*"

217

Faith certainly says what the senses do not say, but it does not say the contrary of what they see. It is above them, not contrary to them.[13]

218

You are taking unfair advantage of the people's belief in the Church so as to mislead them.[14]

219

It is no uncommon thing to have to criticize the world for being too docile. It is a natural vice, like unbelief, and no less pernicious. Superstition.

220

Reason's ultimate step is to acknowledge that there are an infinity of things that are beyond its grasp. It is nothing but weak unless it can go far enough to recognize this.

———

But if natural things are beyond its grasp, what shall we say of supernatural ones?

13. An explicit echo of Aquinas's Eucharistic *Pange lingua*, a hymn principally sung on Holy Thursday, Corpus Christi, and at the Benediction of the Blessed Sacrament. *Sing my tongue the mystery telling, of the Glorious Body sing*. Port-Royal had become a monastery of the Holy Sacrament. Eucharist liturgies like the procession of the Blessed Sacrament profoundly affected Pascal. Christ hidden in the Holy Sacrament parallels the doctrine of the *Deus absconditus*.

14. This recalls a passage from the seventeenth *Provincial Letter* of January 1657 condemning the decadence of the Jesuits.

[XV] Excellence of This Manner of Proving God[1]

221

God through Jesus Christ.

We know God only through Jesus Christ. Without this mediator, all communication with God is cut off; through Jesus Christ we know God. All those who claimed to know God and to prove him without Jesus Christ had only ineffectual proofs. But to prove Jesus Christ we have the prophecies, which are solid and tangible proofs. And these prophecies having been fulfilled and proven true by the event, they show the certainty of these truths and hence, the proof of the divinity of Jesus Christ. In him and through him therefore we know God. Apart from this and without scripture, without original sin, without a mediator who was necessary, who was promised and has come, we cannot prove God absolutely nor can we teach proper doctrine or proper morality. But through Jesus Christ and in Jesus Christ, we can prove God and teach morality and doctrine. Jesus Christ is therefore mankind's true God.

But, at the same time, we know our wretchedness, for this God is none other than the healer of our wretchedness. And so we can truly know God only by knowing our iniquities. Therefore those who have known God without knowing their wretchedness have not glorified him but have glorified themselves. *For [the world] by wisdom, knew not God, it pleased God, by the foolishness of our preaching, to save them.*[2]

---

1. This short *liasse* synthesizes all the major elements of the Apology. Christ as the mediator between man and God is directly linked to the themes of the Fall, "wretchedness," and the Old Testament prophecies. Pascal rejects all metaphysical proofs, not just the ontological and cosmological proofs of God's existence employed by Aquinas and Descartes, but even the geometrical proof of his own "Wager" (fr. 680). Man's fallen state has rendered human reason incapable of seizing and retaining such abstract proofs (fr. 222). More importantly, without Jesus Christ, they are "useless" and "sterile." A man persuaded only of God's existence, Pascal will insist, has "advanced very little toward his salvation" (fr. 690, par. 25). The truly "excellent" proofs of Christ will be those constituted by the "solid and palpable" Old Testament prophecies.

2. After an allusion (the word "glorified") to Paul's Letter to the Romans 1:21, Pascal cites most of 1 Corinthians 1:21: "*For* seeing that in the wisdom of God the world, *by wisdom, knew not God, it pleased God, by the foolishness of our preaching, to save them* that believe."

222

Preface.[3]   The metaphysical proofs of God are so far removed from men's reasoning and so involved, that they have little effect. And even should this be useful to some, it would be effective only during the time that they see this demonstration. But an hour later, they are afraid they have made a mistake.

_____

Pride made them lose what their intellectual thirst for knowledge had found.[4]

223

This[5] is what the knowledge of God leads to when it is reached without Jesus Christ, namely, to communicate without a mediator with a God who has been known without a mediator.

Whereas those who have known God through a mediator know their wretchedness.

224

It is not only impossible but useless to know God without Jesus Christ. They did not get further away but closer. They did not lower themselves but *the better one is, the worse one becomes, if one ascribes to oneself that by which one is good.*[6]

225

Knowing God without knowing one's wretchedness brings pride.

Knowing one's wretchedness without knowing God brings despair.

The knowledge of Jesus Christ creates a middle ground, because therein we find both God and our wretchedness.[7]

3. A note anticipating the preface to the second part of the Apology. Preliminary versions might be fragments 644 and 690.

4. Augustine, *Sermons* 141, 1–2. Saint Augustine refers to the followers of Neoplatonic thought, to whom he repeatedly applies the two verses of Romans 1:20–21, cited in ch. XV, n. 2, above.

5. The antecedent of "this" is "pride" (*superbia*) in the citation from Saint Augustine just above in fragment 222. Fragment 223 was separated from fragment 222 in the Original Collection by Louis Périer only in 1711 by an accidental stroke of the scissors.

6. Saint Bernard, *Sermons on the Canticle*, 84 ("On seeking God"). "The more excellent a man is, the more vile does he become, if one attributes to himself that which makes him excellent." *St. Bernard's Sermons on the Canticle of Canticles*, translated from the original Latin by a priest of Mount Mulleray (Dublin: Browne & Nolan, 1920), 2:497.

7. Augustine, Sermon 142, no. 1. "The reading of the Divine Scriptures elevates us and spares us from being broken by despair. Conversely, it fills us with fear, so that we not be dissipated in the clouds of pride. But to establish ourselves in the middle way (*viam mediam*), which is true and straight, with despair on the left and presumption on the right, so to speak, that would be extremely difficult for us if Christ had not said unto us: '*I am the Way, the Truth, and the Life*' [John 15:6]." (Translation by Pierre Zoberman.) See frs. 172 and 384.

[XVI] Transition from the Knowledge of Man to God

226

Preconceptions as a source of error.

It is a deplorable thing to see all mankind deliberating only about means and not about the end. Everyone thinks about how to discharge one's occupation, but as for choosing an occupation or a country, we leave it up to chance.[1]

It is a pitiful thing to see all those Turks, heretics, and unbelievers following in their fathers' footsteps, for the sole reason that they have been taught to believe that it is the best way. That is what determines everyone to a particular occupation: locksmith, soldier, and so forth.

This is why savages would have no use for Provence.[2]

227

Why is my knowledge limited? Why is my size? Why is my lifespan limited to a hundred years rather than a thousand? What reason was there for nature's making it such for me, and choosing this midpoint within infinity, rather than another, when there is no reason to choose one rather than the other, nothing more tempting than anything else?

228

(*Since it is impossible to be universal by knowing everything that can be known about everything, we should know a little about everything. For it is far nobler to know something about everything than to know everything about one thing. This is the noblest kind of universality. If it were possible to have both, so much the better.*

---

1. Compare to the reflection on custom in fr. 527, a commonplace of Pyrrhonist skepticism, much emphasized by Montaigne.

2. Adapted from a remark added in the 1595 edition of Montaigne's *Essays* (I, 23, 101): "It is by the mediation of custom that every man is content with the place where nature has planted him, and the savages of Scotland have no concern with Touraine, nor the Scythians with Thessaly."

But if one has to choose, this is the one to choose. And the world senses this and does so, because the world is often a good judge.[3]

———

My fancy causes me to hate someone who croaks while speaking and someone who pants while eating.[4]

———

Fancy carries great weight. What is there to be learned from that? To let ourselves be swept along by this weight because it is natural? No, but to stand up to it.

Nothing more fully shows the vanity of man than to consider the causes and effects of love, because they can change the whole universe. Cleopatra's nose.)[5]

229
H 5[6]

When I see the blindness and the wretchedness of man, when I gaze at the whole silent universe, and at man without light abandoned to himself and as if lost in this remote corner of the universe without knowing who put him there, what he came there to do, and what will become of him when he dies, incapable of any knowledge, I am seized with horror, like a man transported in his sleep onto a hideous desert island who wakes up without knowing where he is and without means to escape. Whereupon I marvel that anyone can contemplate this wretched state without despair. I see other people around me whose nature is similar to my own; I ask them if they have more knowledge than I do. They say they do not. Whereupon these wretched deluded creatures, looking around them and seeing a few attractive objects, have devoted themselves to these and become attached to them. As for me, I have never been able to form any attachment to them, and considering how much more likely it is that there is something other than what I see, I have investigated whether this God has perhaps left some trace of himself.

3. Pascal comments on Montaigne, *Essays*, I, 26, 129: "a little of everything, and nothing thoroughly, French style." Montaigne's remark anticipates, and Pascal's comment echoes, the *honnête homme* ideal: to be able to talk about everything in a conversation, yet without being a specialist in any domain. "*Le vrai honnête homme est celui qui ne se pique de rien*" [He is truly an *honnête homme* who does not claim to be versed in anything], writes La Rochefoucauld in his *Réflexions ou sentences et maxims morales* [Reflections or sentences and moral maxims], *Maximes et réflexions diverses*, ed. Jacques Truchet (Paris: Garnier-Flammarion, 1977), no. 203, 62. Translation by Pierre Zoberman.

4. "Fancy" (*fantaisie*) is closely linked to "imagination" (see fr. 78), the source of irrational inclinations and aversions and false judgments. Although a person's manners or characteristics may be disagreeable, they are not rational grounds for hatred. Pascal echoes Montaigne's *Essays*, II, 12, 547: "many, on hearing someone chewing nearby, or someone talking who has the passages of his nose or throat stopped up, are moved to the point of anger and hate."

5. See frs. 32 and 79.

6. H likely stands for *homme*, and the numbers probably refer to subdivisions of a projected discourse on Man: see frs. 230, 231, 111.

I see several religions contradicting each other, and therefore all false except one. Each of them asks to be believed on its own authority and threatens those who do not believe. I do not therefore believe them for that. Anyone can say that. Anyone can call himself a prophet. But I see the Christian religion in which I find prophecies, and this is not within everyone's abilities.

230

H Disproportion of man

9—(*This is where natural knowledge leads us. If it is not true, there is no truth in man, and if it is, it is a powerful source of humiliation for him, since it means he has to lower himself in one way or another.*

And since he cannot go on existing without believing it, I would like him, before engaging in any deeper exploration of nature, just once to take the time to consider it seriously; to take a good look at himself as well, and to judge whether he has any proportion with it, by comparing these two objects.)

Let man then contemplate the whole of nature in all its exalted majesty, let him look away from the lowly objects that surround him, let him gaze at this dazzling light set there like an eternal lamp to illumine the universe, let the earth appear to him as a mere speck compared to the vast orbit this star describes, and let him wonder at the thought that this vast orbit itself is only a tiny point compared to that of the stars rolling in the firmament.[7] But if our sight can go no further, let our imagination reach beyond. It will grow tired of conceiving before nature tires of supplying objects for it. This whole visible world is but an imperceptible speck in the ample bosom of nature: no idea can represent it even faintly. Try as we may to expand our conceptions beyond all imaginable space, we bring forth only atoms, compared to the reality of things. It is an infinite sphere whose center is everywhere, and whose circumference is nowhere.[8] Indeed, it is the greatest perceptible mark of God's omnipotence that our imagination should lose itself in that thought.

Let man, coming back to himself, appraise what he is, compared to all that is: let him consider himself as lost in this remote corner of nature. Let him learn, from this tiny cell in which he is lodged—I mean, the universe—to value the earth, its kingdoms, its cities, and himself at their true price.[9]

---

7. Here Pascal's perspective is geocentric, i.e., the sun orbiting the earth. The heliocentric model had been advanced by Copernicus and asserted by Galileo, who had been condemned by the Church for holding it. Though Pascal had defended Galileo, he did not want his seeker to get embroiled in the controversy. See fr. 196: "I find it wise not to inquire too deeply into the opinion of Copernicus, but this—Everything in life depends on knowing whether the soul is mortal or immortal."

8. Applied to God, this metaphor recalls Empedocles (fifth century BCE).

9. See Montaigne, *Essays*, I, 26, 141: "This great world, which some multiply further as being only a

What is a man in the infinite?

But to present him with another and no less remarkable source of wonder, let him examine the most delicate things he knows: let him consider a mite, the tiny body of which contains incomparably tinier parts, legs with their joints, veins in the legs, blood in the veins, humors in the blood, drops in the humors, vapors in the drops; let him divide these last things up further until his imaginative power is quite exhausted, so that the final object he can arrive at now is the subject of our discussion. Perhaps he will think that he has reached the extreme of minuteness in nature.

I mean to show him a further abyss within it. I want to make him see not only the visible universe, but the immensity in nature we can conceive within the confines of this diminutive atom. Let him see within it an infinity of universes, each one with its own firmament, its own planets, its own earth, in the same proportions as the visible world; with animals on the earth, and finally mites, again, in which he will find the same as he found in the first ones, and so on and so forth, without end or interruption. Let him lose himself in these wonders, as astounding in their minuteness as the others were in their immensity. For who can help but marvel at the thought that our body, which just now was imperceptible in a universe itself imperceptible within the totality of all that exists, is now a colossus, a world, or rather a totality when compared to the nothingness to which we can never attain?

Whoever considers himself in this way will be frightened by himself, and, when he considers himself as suspended in the mass allotted him by nature between the two abysses of the infinite and of nothingness, will tremble at the sight of these wonders; and I think that his curiosity will give way to wonderment, leaving him more disposed to contemplate these things in silence than to presume to investigate them. For what, after all, is man within nature? A nothingness when compared to the infinite, a totality when compared to nothingness, a mid-point between nothing and everything, at an infinite distance from being able to understand these two extremes: the ultimate end of things and their ultimate origin are irrecoverably hidden in impenetrable secrecy (*what can he then understand? he is*) equally incapable of seeing the nothingness out of which he was drawn and the infinite, in which he is swallowed up.

What then shall he do, beyond glimpsing [some] appearance of the in-

---

species under one genus, is the mirror in which we must look at ourselves to recognize ourselves from the proper angle." See also *Essays*, II, 12, 473: "You see only the order and government of this little cave you dwell in, at least if you do see it. His divinity has infinite jurisdiction beyond; this part is nothing in comparison with the whole." Whereas in fr. 78, imagination sets a price on things, thus defeating any rational attempt on the part of reason to "set a price for things," imagination here is envisioned as a means for man to grasp his real situation in the universe.

termediate realm of things, eternally despairing to know either their ultimate origin or their end? All things have emerged from nothing and are expanded to infinity. Who can follow this extraordinary process? He who made these wonders comprehends them. No one else can.

Having failed to consider these two infinities, men have rashly embarked on the investigation of nature, as if they were in any way proportionate to it.

It is strange that they have tried to understand the ultimate origin of things, so as to move on from there to the knowledge of everything with a presumption as infinite as their object. For there is no doubt that one cannot form this project without either infinite presumption or an infinite capacity, like that of nature.

When we have more knowledge, we understand that since nature has engraved its image and that of its author in all things, they almost all partake in the twofold infinity. This is how we see that all the sciences are infinite in the domain they investigate. For who can doubt that geometry, say, has an infinite infinity of propositions to expound? They are infinite also in the multiplicity and the fineness of their first principles. For anyone can see that what are put forward as the ultimate principles do not stand up by themselves, but are based on others, which in turn are based on others, so that there is never an ultimate principle.

But we treat the ones that appear ultimate to our reason as we do with material things, where we speak of an "indivisible point," meaning a point beyond which our sense-perception cannot register, even though by its nature it is infinitely divisible.[10]

Of these two infinites of the sciences, that of infinite greatness is far more perceptible, and this is why few people have ventured to claim they know everything. "I will speak of everything," said Democritus.[11] (*But beside the fact that it means nothing simply to speak of it, without proof and knowledge, it is none the less impossible to do so, since the infinite multitude of things is so hidden from us that all we can express in words and thoughts is only an invisible outline of it. Hence it appears how foolish, futile, and ignorant it is to call a book, as some people have, "De omni scibili."*[12])

(*One can see at first glance that arithmetic alone provides a numberless supply of properties, as does every science.*)

10. Knowledge is patterned on the material universe. The process of expanding knowledge, e.g., by deduction in geometry, is akin to the movement outwards towards the infinitely great. In the search for foundations, we go further and further back; this is akin to the movement towards the infinitely small.

11. Attributed to Democritus by Montaigne (*Essays*, II, 12, 438): "Of like impudence is this promise of the book of Democritus, 'I am going to speak of all things.'"

12. "About everything that can be known": fragment of the title of a thesis that Pico della Mirandola, the Florentine Renaissance philosopher, undertook to defend in 1486.

But the infinity of smallness is far less visible. This is where the philosophers *have* hoped they would reach it. This is where they have all fallen short. This is the source of such common titles as: *On the Principles of Things, On the Principles of Philosophy,*[13] and so forth, just as pretentious in reality, although less so in appearance, as this other one, *De omni scibili,*[14] which is blatantly excessive.

We believe ourselves far more able by nature to reach the center of things than to embrace their circumference, and the visible extent of the world visibly exceeds us. But since we exceed little things, we believe ourselves much more capable of mastering them; and yet no less capacity is needed to reach all the way to nothingness than to the whole. It has to be infinite in both cases. And it seems to me that if someone were able to grasp the ultimate principles of things, they could also attain to the knowledge of the infinite. One depends on the other and one leads to the other. The extremes meet and come together by their very remoteness: they coincide in God and in God alone.

Let us, then, recognize our extent. We are something, and we are not everything. What being we have prevents us from knowing the first principles, which arise from nothingness. And the smallness of our being hides from us the sight of the infinite.[15]

Our intellect occupies the same position in the order of intelligible things as our body in the extension of nature.

Limited as we are in every respect, this condition of holding the mid-point between two extremes pervades all our powers. Our senses perceive nothing extreme. Too much noise deafens us, too much light dazzles us, too near and too far both make it impossible to see. Too long a speech, too short a speech are equally obscure. Too much truth stuns us. I know people who cannot grasp that if you subtract four from zero, you are left with zero.[16] The first principles are too obvious for us.[17] Too much pleasure is burdensome;[18] harmonies in excess are unpleasant in music and favors in excess vex us. We want to be able

13. The treatise *On the Principles of Things* was attributed to Duns Scotus (late thirteenth century); the second treatise is Descartes's *Principes de la philosophie* (1644).

14. See above, ch. XVI, n. 12.

15. The idea of man as participating both in being and in nothingness is set out in Descartes's *Meditations on First Philosophy,* IV: "I notice that there is present in my thought not only a real and positive idea of God, or rather of a supremely perfect being, but also, so to speak, a certain negative idea of nothingness, or of what is infinitely removed from every kind of perfection. And I see that I am, as it were, a mean between God and nothingness, that is, [...] placed between the supreme Being and not-being." René Descartes, *Discourse on Method and Meditations,* trans. Laurence J. Lafleur (Indianapolis: Bobbs-Merrill, 1960), 110.

16. The concept of negative numbers was not fully recognized by European mathematicians until the eighteenth century.

17. See Aristotle, *Metaphysics,* II, I, 3 (993b).

18. See Montaigne, *Essays,* III, 10, 934: "Even sensual pleasure is painful in its depth."

to pay back the debt with interest. *Benefits are agreeable as long as they seem returnable; but if they go much beyond that, they are repaid with hatred instead of gratitude.*[19] We can perceive neither extreme heat nor extreme cold, excessive qualities are our enemies, not perceptible by us. Beyond a certain point we do not perceive them, we suffer them. Too young, too old an age obstructs the mind; too much or too little education, likewise.[20] In short, all extreme things are for us as if they did not exist, and we do not exist in relation to them, they elude us, or we them.[21]

This is our true condition. This is what makes us incapable either of knowing with certainty or of being utterly ignorant. We are drifting in the middle of a vast sea, always uncertain, always directionless, driven from one shore toward the other and back again.[22] Whenever we set our sights on a landing where we may moor ourselves and regain our footing, it gives way and slips away from us. And if we pursue it, it eludes our grasp, slides away from us, and flees in an eternal flight. Nothing stands still for us, this is the condition that is natural to us and yet the most contrary to our inclination. We are consumed with the desire to find some firm ground, and at last a solid base on which to erect a tower reaching upwards to the infinite, but the whole foundation cracks, and the earth opens up to reveal the abyss.[23]

Let us then not seek for certainty and stability. Our reason is always deceived by the inconstancy of appearances. Nothing can fix the finite between the two infinites that encompass and elude it.

This being once properly understood, I think we will remain at rest, each in whatever condition nature has placed us.

Since this middle realm allotted to us is always distant from the two extremes, what does it matter if one person has a little more understanding of

19. Tacitus, *Annals*, IV.18, cited in Montaigne, *Essays*, III, 8, 872.

20. See frs. 55, 72, 75, and Montaigne, *Essays*, II, 12, 453: "If it is a boy that judges, he does not know what it is about; if it is a scholar, he is prejudiced."

21. See Pierre Charron, *Discours chrétiens* [Christian discourses], I, in *De la sagesse.*

22. See Montaigne, *Essays*, II, 12, 469–70: "Reason does nothing but go astray in everything, and especially when it meddles with divine things. [...] We see daily how, when it strays however little from the beaten path and deviates or wanders from the way traced and trodden by the Church, immediately it is lost, it grows embarrassed and entangled, whirling round and floating in that vast, troubled, and undulating sea of his opinions, unbridled and aimless."

23. See fr. 796, par. 12. Man's attempt to oppose the solidity of stone to the flux of the perishable appears to Pascal to be a general obsession of human beings. The image of knowledge as requiring (but currently lacking) an underlying foundation is mobilized by Montaigne (*Essays*, II, 12, cf. *supra*); Descartes reworks it, comparing his own activity to that of one who finds and builds on solid foundations (see the *Discourse on Method*, part II, passim). Pascal takes it up yet again, turning it against Descartes, but also drawing on the scriptural image of the tower of Babel (Genesis 11:1–9). "Pascal himself," observes Sellier, "is haunted both by the fear of falling (the precipice, the abyss, the gulf) and by an intense *"rêverie de la tour"* [tower fantasy]. See Pascal, *Pensées*, ed. Sellier (2010), 266.

things than another? If he does, and if he can see them from a somewhat higher perspective, is he not still infinitely distant from the end? And is not the length of our life equally tiny when compared to eternity, even if one person's lasts ten years longer than another's?

In view of these two infinites, all finite quantities are equal, and I cannot see why we should attach our imagination to one rather than another.[24] Simply comparing ourselves with finite quantities is a source of pain.

If man were to study himself first and foremost,[25] he would see how incapable he is of going further. How could it be possible for a part to know the whole? But perhaps he will aspire to know at least the parts to which he is proportionate. But the parts of the world are all so interrelated and interconnected, that I think it impossible to know one without the other, and without the whole.

Man, for example, has a relationship with everything in his experience. He needs space to contain him, time in order to endure, movement in order to live, elements of which he is composed, heat and food in order to nourish him, air in order to breathe. He sees the light, he perceives bodies, in short, he forms an alliance with everything.[26] Thus, to know man, we have to know why it is that he needs air in order to continue to exist, and to know air, we have to know how it is related to man's life, etc.

Flame cannot continue to exist without air. So to know one of them we must know the other.

Thus since all things both cause and are caused, both help and are helped, mediately and immediately, and since they all hold to one another by a natural and imperceptible bound linking those furthest and most different from one another, I hold it impossible to know the parts without knowing the whole, and no less impossible to know the whole without knowing the parts severally.

(*The eternity of things in themselves or in God must yet again stun our short span.*

The fixed and constant immutability of nature, in comparison with the constant change taking place in us, should have the same effect.)

And what sets the seal on our utter inability to know things is that they are simple in themselves, whereas we are composed of two natures, opposed and different in kind, namely of soul and body. For it is impossible that the part of

---

24. It is the imagination, the habitual and generally delusive source of our value judgments, that permits us to think, e.g., that a life of seventy years is intrinsically more valuable than one of sixty.

25. See frs. 106, 566.

26. The word "*alliance*" is borrowed from Montaigne's translation of Raymond Sebond's *Natural Theology.*

us that reasons should be other than spiritual.²⁷ And even if one were to claim that we are purely bodily, that would exclude us all the more from the knowledge of things, since there is nothing so inconceivable as to say that matter knows itself. It is impossible for us to know how it could know itself.

And thus if we [are] simple, material, we cannot know anything at all. And if we are composed of mind and matter, we cannot have a perfect knowledge of simple things (*since the entity that is active in this knowledge is in part spiritual. And how could we have a clear knowledge of spiritual things, when we have a body that weighs us down and pulls us toward the earth?*²⁸), whether spiritual or corporeal.

This is why nearly all philosophers confuse the ideas of things and speak of corporeal things in spiritual terms and of spiritual things in bodily terms. For they will boldly assert that bodies have a downward tendency, that they aspire to the center, that they flee from destruction, that they fear a vacuum, that they have inclinations, sympathies, antipathies—all things that pertain to minds alone.²⁹ And when they are speaking of minds, they consider them as occupying a particular place, and credit them with movement from one place to another—things that pertain to bodies alone.³⁰

Instead of receiving the ideas of these things in a pure state, we taint them with our own qualities, and stamp our own composite nature upon all the simple things we envision.

Who would not think, from the way we make out everything to be a composite of mind and body, that this combination is something we thoroughly understand? But there is nothing we understand less. Man is, to himself, the most prodigious object in nature, for he cannot conceive what body is, and even less what mind is, and less than anything can he conceive how a body can be united to a mind. That is the utmost of his difficulties, and yet it is his own

27. Here as elsewhere, Pascal seems to accept the dualist theory of Descartes whereby mind and body are radically distinct substances. But he singles out reasoning as the index of the soul's immateriality, whereas Descartes regards thought or consciousness in general as a sufficient proof. In any case, Descartes, as a dualist, may be exempted from the subsequent criticism of "nearly all philosophers."

28. This is a biblical verse cherished by Saint Augustine. Wisdom 9:15: "For the corruptible body is a load upon the soul, and the earthly habitation presseth down the mind that museth upon many things." Sellier explains, "This entire reflection on the use of metaphors is inspired by Saint Augustine, always attentive to the figurative language men use when speaking of God (*True Religion*, ch. 33, etc.), and the polemics on the 'horror of the vacuum.' See fr. 795." Pascal, *Pensées*, ed. Sellier (2010), 268n1.

29. Pascal criticizes the language of orthodox Aristotelian physics. A similar critique of the Aristotelian confusion of physical and spiritual properties had already been voiced by Descartes in his *Sixièmes réponses* [Sixth replies], in *Œuvres de Descartes*, ed. Charles Adam and Paul Tannery, vol. 7, *Meditationes de prima philosophia* [Meditations on first philosophy] (Paris: Cerf, 1904), 440–42.

30. In Aristotelian theory, movement, being peculiar to living creatures, must be a function of the soul that endows them with life.

being. *The way in which spirits combine with bodies cannot be grasped by man; yet that combination is what a man is.*[31]

(*These are some of the causes that render man so helpless when it comes to knowing nature. Nature is infinite in two ways, he is finite and limited. Nature endures and maintains itself perpetually in its being; he passes away and is mortal. Individual things are corrupted and changed from moment to moment; he sees them only as they pass. They have their beginning and their end, and he can conceive neither the one nor the other. They are simple, and he is composed of two different natures.*)

Finally, to seal the proof of our weakness, I shall finish by these two considerations.

231
H 3

Man is nothing but a reed, the weakest thing in nature, but he is a thinking reed. The whole universe does not have to marshal its forces to crush him—a vapor, a drop of water is enough to kill him. But even if the whole universe were to crush him, man would still be nobler than that which is killing him, since he knows he is dying and the power the universe has over him. The universe has no knowledge of it.

232

And so all our dignity consists in thinking. That is where we should look in order to raise ourselves, and not to space or duration, which we can never fill.

Let us, then, strive to think well. That is the principle of all moral conduct.

233

The eternal silence of these infinite spaces frightens me.[32]

234

Take heart: it is not from yourself that you should be expecting it; but, on the contrary, it is by expecting nothing from yourself that you must expect it.

31. Pascal cites, with slight variations, a passage from Saint Augustine, *City of God*, XXI, 10, which he may have come across, already slightly altered, in Montaigne, *Essays*, II, 12, 489.

32. A Romantic tradition, turning Pascal into a kind of brooding Hamlet and his *Pensées* into his intimate spiritual journal, placed this highly memorable aphorism into the mouth of Pascal himself. Nothing could be farther from the perspective of an Apology. This terrified cry is that of the skeptic, awakened by the apologist from his profound torpor. He is the same skeptic permitted to testify in the overture to the Apology, fr. 681, par. 13: "I see nothing but infinity on every side, surrounding me like an atom and like a shadow that lasts but an instant and returns no more."

[XVII] Nature is Corrupt[1] and
Falsity of Other Religions

235
Falsity of other religions

Mohammed without authority.[2]

His reasons must have been very powerful in that case, having nothing but their own strength.

So what does he say? That you must believe him.

236
Falsity of other religions

They[3] do not have any witnesses. These[4] do.

God challenges other religions to produce such signs. *Isaiah* 43:9–44:8.[5]

237

If there is a single principle behind everything. A single purpose for everything. Everything by him, everything for him. Then the true religion must teach us to worship only him and to love only him. But since we find ourselves powerless to worship what we do not know or to love anything other than ourselves, the religion that instructs [us] of these duties must also instruct us of this powerlessness. And teach us the remedies as well. It teaches us that by

---

1. The copyist, surveying the inventory of the *liasses* constituted by fr. 1, could find no *liasse* corresponding to the title "Nature is corrupt." He indicated his perplexity by placing an asterisk next to the title. Pascal appears to have filed the fragments belonging to two chapters, but closely linked in his mind, in the same *liasse*. Eleven fragments, particularly fr. 240, anticipate the major discourse, "On corruption" (fr. 690). Of the nineteen *pensées*, six fragments attack Islam, one paganism, and another the scriptures of other religions.

2. He has no prophecies (fr. 241), nor witnesses (fr. 37), nor miracles (fr. 352).

3. Other religions.

4. Christians.

5. Pascal had translated these texts into French from the Latin Vulgate in fr. 735

one man[6] all was lost and the link broken between God and us, and that by one man[7] the link has been restored.

We are born so contrary to this love of God, and it is so necessary, that we must have been born guilty or God would be unjust.[8]

238

They have seen the thing, but they have not seen the cause.[9]

239

Against Mohammed

The Qur'an is no more by Mohammed than the Gospel is by Saint Matthew,[10] for it is quoted by several authors, century after century. Even its enemies, Celsus and Porphyry, never denied that.[11]

The Qur'an says that Saint Matthew was a good man. So he was a false prophet, either in calling wicked men good, or in not agreeing with what they said about Jesus Christ.

---

6. Adam.

7. Jesus Christ.

8. A fundamental affirmation of Augustinianism. The present state of man is so hideous that it would be blasphemous to hold that God had created him as he is now. This world of blindness, hate, suffering, and death could not possibly be the work of a God who is good incarnate. According to Saint Augustine, the evidence of reality (*rerum evidentia*), reinforcing scripture, serves to prove man's corruption. Augustine, *Against Julian*, IV, 16, no. 78. See Pascal, *Pensées*, ed. Sellier (2010), 271.

9. Augustine, *Against Julian*, IV, 12, no. 60. Saint Augustine had used this aphorism, in the singular, to refer to Cicero. In Book III of his *Republic*, Cicero presents man as the product of a perverse Mother Nature—fragile, naked, and wretched—yet inhabited by a spark of the divine. However, while correctly diagnosing the duality of our true state, Cicero could not fathom the reason for it. He could not, because he knew nothing of original sin. Pascal pluralizes the subject of Augustine's sentence in Latin so as to include all the philosophers of antiquity. See Pascal, *Pensées*, ed. Sellier (2010), 271n2.

10. This elliptical sentence probably means that attributing the Gospel of Matthew to Saint Matthew is at least, if not more, certain than attributing the Qur'an to Mohammed.

11. According to Grotius's *The Truth of Religion* (II, 5), Celsus and Porphyry both acknowledge Saint Matthew as the author of the first Gospel. Celsus was a second-century Greek philosopher whose *The True Word* (c. 177) was the first comprehensive pagan attack on Christianity. Porphyry (c. 234–c. 305 CE) was a Greek Neoplatonic philosopher and author of *Against the Christians*. His *Introduction* remained the standard textbook on logic throughout the Middle Ages. The following remark, which shows Pascal's way of arguing, is interesting from the perspective of the history of the translation of the *Pensées*. Translators seem to have been unable to accept Pascal's hypothesis: the implication that Matthew might have been a wicked man—though naturally Pascal does not believe it—appears to be too difficult to accept. The phrase gets turned around and translated as though Pascal meant to blame Mohammed for calling good men wicked. However, Pascal's reasoning is that Mohammed cannot be a true prophet and not follow the doctrine upheld by a man he claims is good.

240

Without this divine knowledge what could men have done other than re-joice in the inner awareness they retain of their past greatness, or despair in the light of their present weakness? For, without seeing the whole truth, they have been unable to attain perfect virtue, with some considering nature as in-corrupt, and others as irreparable, they have been unable to flee either pride or sloth, which are the two sources of all vice, since they can do nothing other than give in to it through cowardice or escape from it through pride. For if they were aware of the excellence of man, they are ignorant of his corruption, so that they certainly avoided sloth, but gave in to arrogance, and if they recog-nized the infirmity of nature they are ignorant of its dignity, so that they could certainly avoid vanity, but only by casting themselves into despair.

Hence the various sects of Stoics[12] and Epicureans,[13] Dogmatists,[14] and Academicians,[15] etc.

The Christian religion alone has been able to cure men of these two vic-es, not by using one to eliminate the other through the wisdom of the world, but by eliminating both through the simplicity of the Gospel. For it teaches the righteous, whom it elevates to the point of participation in the Godhead itself,[16] that in that sublime state they still carry the source of all corruption that renders them, throughout their lives, subject to error, wretchedness, death and sin, and it cries out to the most impious that they are capable of the grace of their Redeemer. Thus, by leading those whom it justifies to tremble and consoling those it condemns, it tempers fear with hope so precisely, by this

12. Founded in Athens by Zeno in the early third century BCE, Stoicism taught that a person of moral perfection would not suffer such emotions as joy, grief, pleasure, or pain. The later Roman Stoics taught calm acceptance of all that was the divine will or decreed by nature. Seneca and Epictetus, whose philoso-phy Pascal critiques in the *Exchange with M. Sacy*, maintained that since virtue is sufficient for happiness, the sage was immune to misfortune.

13. Epicurus (341–270 BCE), whose atomist materialism led him to attack divine intervention in hu-man affairs, believed what he called "pleasure" to be the greatest good. But the way to attain such pleasure, defined as the absence of pain, was to live modestly and to gain knowledge of one's desires. It could not be more different from the modern definition of "hedonism." Originally a challenge to Platonism, it later be-came the main opponent of Stoicism. It was resurrected in the seventeenth century in a Christianized form by the atomist Pierre Gassendi, whose circle Pascal's father frequented. See introduction to the *Exchange with M. de Sacy*.

14. *Dogmatist* is the term used by Sextus Empiricus (160–210 CE) for those philosophies—Stoicism, Epicureanism, Aristotelianism—that claim to reveal the reality behind appearances. It is picked up in this sense by Montaigne in the "Apology for Raymond Sebond," which is probably Pascal's immediate source for this term.

15. Platonists. Plato's Academy underwent numerous transformations after his death. At one stage, its dominant doctrine was a form of Skepticism, which unlike "Pyrrhonism" (the term Pascal nearly always uses to designate Skepticism), admitted that some beliefs were more probable than others.

16. 2 Peter 1:4: "that by these you may be made partakers of the divine nature."

double capacity for grace and for sin that is common to all men, that it casts man down infinitely lower than could simple reason, but without causing him to despair, and it raises him up infinitely higher than could natural pride, but without inflating him, showing clearly as a result that since it alone is free of error and of vice, it alone is enabled both to instruct and to correct mankind.

Who then can refuse to believe and to worship this heavenly enlightenment? For is it not clearer than day that we are aware within ourselves of the indelible marks of excellence, and is it not just as true that we experience at every moment the effects of our pitiable condition?

What then does this chaos and this monstrous confusion cry out to us, other than the truth of these two states, and with such a powerful voice that it is impossible to resist?

241

Difference between Jesus Christ and Mohammed

Mohammed not foretold. Jesus Christ foretold.

Mohammed by killing. Jesus Christ by having his own killed.

Mohammed by forbidding people to read,[17] the apostles by commanding people to read.[18]

242

In the end, there is such a contrast that if Mohammed took the path of succeeding in human terms, Jesus Christ took that of perishing in human terms, so that instead of concluding that since Mohammed was successful Jesus Christ could just as well have been so too, we must conclude that since Mohammed was successful, Jesus Christ had to perish.

243

All men naturally hate one another. People have done what they could with concupiscence so as to subjugate it to the public good. But that is just pretence and a false image of charity. Because deep down it is no more than hatred.

---

17. Grotius, *The Truth of the Christian Religion*, VI, 2: "The vulgar are prohibited reading these books they account sacred." See *The Truth of the Christian Religion*, ed. Le Clerc, trans. John Clarke (Oxford: Baxter, 1818), 232.

18. See Romans 15:4, 1 Peter 1:19, 1 Timothy 4:13.

244

People have used concupiscence to establish and derive admirable rules of social order, morality, and justice.

But at the core, this evil core of man, this EVIL LEAVEN[19] is only covered up, it is not removed.

245

Jesus Christ is a God whom we can approach without pride, and before whom we can humble ourselves without despair.

246

More deserving of blows than of kisses, I am fearless because I love.[20]

247

The true religion must be marked by the obligation to love its God. That is only right, and yet none has commanded it. Ours has done so.

It must also have understood concupiscence and powerlessness. Ours has done so.

It must have provided remedies. One is prayer. No religion has asked of God that he should be loved and followed.

248

Once everything about human nature has been grasped, it is necessary, for a religion to be true, for it to have understood our nature. It must have understood greatness and smallness, and the reason for the one and for the other. What religion has understood it, other than Christianity?

19. As often, when emphasizing the pathetic (in the rhetorical sense) dimension of his assertions, Pascal leaves the phrase in Latin: "*figmentum malum.*" In fragment 494, Pascal's friend Miton proposes that a code of general civility (*honnêteté*) could put an end to human strife. Pascal replies that the "self"—infected by that *figmentum malum* (fr. 309) resulting from the Fall—is "hateful." "You, Miton," Pascal replies, "cover it up, but you do not remove it for all that." In fragment 309 of the chapter "The Rabbinical Tradition," Pascal cites Genesis 8:21: "the imagination of man's heart is evil from his youth." Pascal erroneously concludes that this "evil leaven," referred to in the Talmud, speaks to "an ample tradition of original sin according to the Jews." Judaism never even entertained such ideas as the Fall, original sin, or the transmission of human corruption. Such ideas are completely alien, not only to the Talmud, but to the entire Jewish tradition. See ch. XXI, n. 1. On Miton, see introduction, nn. 97 and 98.

20. Saint Bernard, *Sermons on the Canticle*, 84, vol. 2, p. 500: "And doest Thou run to be caressed by thy Bridegroom from Whom thou hast deserved nothing but hard stripes? . . . 'I have no fears because I love.'"

249

The true religion teaches us our duties, our powerlessness, pride and concupiscence, and the remedies, humility and mortification.

250

There are clear and demonstrative figures, but there are others that seem somewhat far-fetched, and that only serve as proof to those who are already convinced. These are like the "Revelationists."[21] But the difference between us is that they have no irrefutable figures, so that there is nothing more unjust than when they point out that theirs are as securely grounded as some of ours. Because they have none that are as demonstrative as some of ours. So the sides are not evenly matched. We must not equate and confuse these things just because they seem similar in one respect, whereas they are so different in another. It is the things that are clear when they are divine that justify the respect due to the things that are obscure.

251

It is not by what is obscure in Mohammed, which can be passed off as having a mysterious meaning that I want him to be judged, but by what is clear: by his paradise[22] and such like. He is ridiculous in that respect. And that is why it is wrong to see what is obscure in him as being mysterious, given that what is clear is ridiculous. The same is not true of scripture. I fully accept that there are obscure things that are just as strange as those of Mohammed, but there are things that are admirably clear and prophecies that are visibly fulfilled. So the sides are not evenly matched. We must not confuse and equate things that are alike only because of their obscurity and not their clarity, which earns respect for the things that are obscure.

---

21. The Edition of Port-Royal (1670) interpolates an explanation of this term into the text: "those who ground prophecies, which they interpret according to their fancy, in the Book of Revelation." See fr. 478. The Revelationist phenomenon persisted in various forms throughout history and is far from dead today.

22. As described in Sura 2 of the Qur'an. As noted above, Pascal's source is more likely either Montaigne or Grotius than Du Ryer's 1647 translation (see fr. 182, n. 5). In *Essays* II, 12, Montaigne observes: "Mohammed promises to his followers a paradise tapestried, adorned with gold and precious stones, peopled with wenches of surpassing beauty, with rare wines and foods" (167). In *The Truth of the Christian Religion,* Grotius mentions, among other stories, "that of getting rid of banquets in the other life by sweat; and that of a company of women's [*sic*] being appointed to every one, for sensual pleasures" (VI, 10, 240).

252

Other religions, such as pagan ones, are more popular, because they are superficial, but they do not cater to clever people. A purely intellectual religion would be better suited to clever people, but it would be of no use to the masses. The Christian religion alone is well-suited to all, being a mixture of the outer surface and the inner depth. It elevates the masses inwardly, and humbles the proud outwardly, and is not perfect without both levels, since the masses must understand the spirit of the letter and clever people must subject their spirit to the letter.

253

No other religion has ever emphasized self-hatred.[23] So no other religion can appeal to those who hate themselves, and who are seeking a being truly worthy of love. But such people, if they had not already heard of the religion of a humiliated God, would embrace it instantly.

---

23. See William Cenkner, ed., *Evil and the Response of World Religion* (St. Paul, Minn.: Paragon House, 1997), for an evaluation of the notion of self-hatred in the Christian, Jewish, Islamic, Asian, and African traditions. Might Buddhism, for instance, countenance self-hatred as a path to the immolation of the self? For a synthesis of this key theme in the *Pensées*, see David Wetsel, "Self-Annihilation, Self-Hatred and Original Sin in Pascal's *Pensées*," in *Evocations of Eloquence*, ed. N. Hammond and M. Moriarty, 87–98.

[XVIII] Make Religion Lovable[1]

254

Jesus Christ for all.

Moses for a people.

The Jews blessed in Abraham, *I will bless them that bless thee*, but all nations blessed in his seed.[2]

It is a small thing that, etc., Isaiah.[3]

A light to enlighten the Gentiles.[4]

He hath not dealt so with any other nation, said David, in speaking of the law. But in speaking of Jesus Christ one must say *He hath dealt so with every nation; It is a small thing that*, etc. Isaiah.[5]

The quality of being universal belongs therefore to Jesus Christ. The Church itself offers sacrifice[6] only for the faithful. Jesus Christ offered the sacrifice of the cross for all.

1. The two notes Pascal filed in this *liasse* themselves offer no real clue as to the purpose of the chapter. The title, however, is a primordial theme of the Apology, as revealed in fragment 46. The entire Apology hinges on banishing apathy and making those who seek *"wish* that [Christianity] were true" (fr. 46, emphasis added). After the "anthropological" chapters, the unbeliever was to have come to view the Christian religion as "venerable" because it alone describes the duality of man's state, and as "worthy of love" because it alone promises the "true good." Wishing Christianity "were true" then opens the door to the unbeliever's willingness to consider Pascal's historical proofs showing that Christianity *is* "true." Had Christianity not been rendered potentially "lovable," the seeker would perhaps not have been willing to take up Pascal's historical demonstrations, which begin in the very next chapter, "Foundations."

2. Genesis 12:3 and 22:18.

3. Isaiah 49:6: *"It is a small thing* that thou shouldst be my servant to raise up the tribes of Jacob, and to convert the dregs of Israel. Behold, I have given thee to be the light of the Gentiles, that thou mayst be my salvation even to the farthest part of the earth." Over and over, Pascal uses the phrase to evoke the universal vocation of Israel, a vocation only accomplished by Christianity.

4. Luke 2:32. Pascal knows this verse by heart from the *Nunc dimittis* recited every night at compline: "Now thou dost dismiss thy servant, O Lord, according to thy word in peace; Because my eyes have seen thy salvation, Which thou hast prepared before the face of all peoples: A light to the revelation of the Gentiles, and the glory of thy people Israel." It had been revealed to old Simeon that he should not die before seeing the Messiah. He comes into the Temple just as Jesus is brought there by his parents and, holding him up, rejoices that he has seen the Lord.

5. See above, ch. XVII, n. 3.

6. The holy sacrifice of the Mass, offered only for "many." To the consternation of many liberal Catholics, Pope Benedict XVI has mandated that the use of "all" in the English version of the Mass be changed to "many," the correct translation of the official Latin text of the liturgy promulgated by Vatican II. Pascal's position is in fact the one always held by the Catholic tradition.

255

The carnal Jews and the heathen have their miseries and the Christians too. There is no redeemer for the heathen, as they do not even hope for one. There is no redeemer for the Jews, they hope for him in vain. There is a redeemer only for Christians.

See "Perpetuity"

[XIX] Foundations of Religion and
Reply to Objections

256

We must transfer what we have said about the nature of symbols from the chapter on "Figurative Types" to the chapter on "Foundations": why Jesus Christ's first coming was foretold; why the manner of his coming was foretold obscurely."[1]

257

Unbelievers—the most credulous. They believe in Vespasian's miracles[2] in order not to believe in those of Moses.

258

Just as Jesus Christ remained unknown among men, so does his truth among common opinions without external difference. So does the Eucharist among common bread.

Faith consists entirely of Jesus Christ and Adam; and Christian morality consists entirely of concupiscence and grace.

259

What can they say against the resurrection and against a virgin giving birth? Is it more difficult than to produce a man or an animal than to reproduce them? And if they had never seen a particular kind of animal, would they be able to say whether they could be produced without one another?[3]

---

1. See fr. 287. See also fr. 339: "in his obscurity . . . in his secret resurrection." See the introduction, "The Three Orders."

2. Montaigne's *Essays*, III, 8: "[Tacitus] says [*Histories* IV, 81] that Vespasian, by the favor of the god Serapis, cured a blind woman in Alexandria by anointing her eyes with his saliva, and I know not what other miracle" (875).

3. Opposition to miracles is based not on reason but on the prejudices of custom. Augustine, *City of God*, XXII, 4 and 8. See fr. 444.

260

What do the prophets say of Jesus Christ? That he will manifestly be God? No. But that he is *a God who is truly hidden*,[4] that he will be unrecognized, that no one will think that it is him, that he will be a stumbling block on which many will trip, etc.[5]

Let no one then blame us any more for lack of clarity, since we profess it. But—they say—there are obscurities, and without these, we would not have been stubborn about Jesus Christ. But that is one of the explicit goals of the prophets. *Harden* [their heart].[6]

261

What men were able to discover by their greatest insights, this religion would teach its children.[7]

262

That something is incomprehensible does not prevent it from existing.[8]

263

(*If one wishes to say that man is too insignificant to deserve communication with God, one must be great indeed to judge the matter.*)[9]

264

One understands nothing of the works of God unless one takes as a first principle that his intention was to blind some and enlighten others.[10]

265

Jesus Christ does not say that he is not from Nazareth in order to leave the wicked in blindness, nor does he say that he is not the son of Joseph.[11]

---

4. Isaiah 45:15: "Verily thou art a hidden God." The principal "foundation" on which the entire Apology rests. In the very first paragraph of the preface to the Apology (681), Pascal evokes this doctrine to ironically agree with his adversaries' contention that they see no evidence of God's presence in the world.

5. Isaiah 50:3 and 8:14. See fr. 734.

6. Isaiah 6:10.

7. See fr. 370.

8. See fr. 182.

9. See fr. 182.

10. Following Jansenius, this fragment, a corollary of the doctrine of predestination, might well be thought of as the founding principle of the entire theology inherent in Pascal's Apology. Few things could be more shocking to the modern theological sensibility than the notion that God, in order to preserve his absolute and total freedom, must *necessarily* damn some men.

11. John 6:41–42; 7:41–44.

266

God wants to dispose the will more than the mind. A perfect clarity would be useful to the mind and detrimental to the will.

Humble that pride.

267

Jesus Christ has come to blind those who see clearly and give sight to the blind, to cure the sick, and to let the healthy die, to call to penitence and justify the sinners, and to leave the righteous in their sins, to fill the indigent and *leave the rich empty*.[12]

268

To blind, to enlighten

Saint Augustine, Montaigne, Sebond.[13]

There is enough real clarity to enlighten the elect and enough obscurity to humble them. There is enough obscurity to blind the reprobate and enough clarity to condemn them and deny them any excuse.

———

The genealogy of Jesus Christ in the Old Testament is mingled among so many useless ones that it does not stand out. If Moses[14] had kept a record of Jesus Christ's ancestors only, that would have been too obvious. If he had not written down that of Jesus Christ, it would not have been sufficiently visible. But when all is considered, the reader who looks closely sees that of Jesus Christ distinguished rightfully by Thamar, Ruth, etc.[15]

———

Those who ordered these sacrifices[16] knew they were useless, and those

12. The antepenultimate verse of the *Magnificat* (Luke 1:46–55) sung daily at the office of vespers. Like the RSV, the DR version has: "sent away." The verb "to leave" belongs to the vocabulary of Augustinian theology. All of humanity, past, present, and to come, was corrupted in the Fall. Apart from those few "elect" whom he chooses to save out of his inscrutable and supererogatory mercy, God simply "leaves" that "mass of perdition" constituted by most of the human race in the state of damnation that it chose in Adam's Fall. God does not actively damn them. He only "leaves" them to the punishment they merit. See Pascal, *Pensées*, ed. Sellier (2010), 281n2.

13. In his "Apology for Raymond Sebond" (*Essays*, II, 12, 504), Montaigne cites with approval the following sentence from Augustine's *City of God* (11, 22): "The very concealment of what is useful is either an exercise in humility or an attrition of pride."

14. Until the advent of the Documentary Theory of Richard Simon in the generation after Pascal, no one ever doubted that Moses was the sole author of the Pentateuch.

15. The Old Testament abounds in genealogies. But there is one of them whose links give way to important developments: Tamar (Genesis 38); Ruth, to whom a whole book is devoted. These two women figure in the genealogy of Jesus in Matthew 1:3–5. See Pascal, *Pensées*, ed. Sellier (2010), 281n1.

16. The sacrifice of animals prescribed by Mosaic Law. On the "figurative" nature of these sacrifices, see frs. 289–91.

who have declared that these sacrifices were useless practiced them nonetheless.

_____

If God had permitted one single religion only, it would have been recognized too easily. But let anyone look at it closely, one indeed recognizes the true one within this confusion.

_____

Principle: Moses was an able man. If therefore he followed his thought, he ought not to have written anything down that would be directly opposed to this thought.

All the passages that clearly seem to be weaknesses are therefore strengths. For example, the two genealogies of Saint Matthew and Saint Luke.[17] What is clearer than that this was not done in concert?

269

If Jesus Christ had come only to sanctify, all of scripture and everything else would emphasize the point, and it would be very easy to convince unbelievers. If Jesus Christ had come only to blind, all his actions would be confusing, and we would have no way to convince the unbeliever. But as he came to be a *sanctuary and a stumbling stone*, as Isaiah says,[18] we cannot convince the unfaithful and they cannot convince us—but we do convince them by this very fact, since we say that in all of his conduct there is no conviction on either side.

270

Figures

God wanting to deprive his followers of earthly possessions and to show that it was not a sign of impotence, he created the Jewish people.[19]

271

Man is not worthy of God, but he is not incapable of being made worthy of him.

It is unworthy of God to join himself to man, wretched as he is; but it is not unworthy of God to lead him out of his wretchedness.

_____

17. Matthew 1:1–16 and Luke 3:23–38. These two genealogies differ, Matthew giving Jesus' dynastic line, Luke his natural line. The fact that they do differ, like the differing accounts of the four Gospels (fr. 349), renders the possibility of a conspiracy unlikely and confirms the historicity of scripture.

18. Isaiah 8:14.

19. See frs. 301 and 306.

272
Proof

Prophecy with fulfillment.
What preceded Jesus Christ and what followed.

273[20]

Source of contradictions.
A God humbled to the point of dying on the cross. In Jesus Christ, two natures.[21] Two comings.[22] Two states of man's nature. A Messiah triumphing over death by his death.

274
APR for Tomorrow[23]

[Wanting to appear openly to those who search for him with all their heart, and to remain hidden from those who flee him with all their heart, God has] tempered[24] knowledge of himself in such a way that he has given signs of himself that are visible to those who search for him, but not to those who do not search for him.

There is enough light for those who truly wish to see, and enough obscurity for those who have the opposite disposition.

275

On God wanting to conceal himself.
If there were only one religion, God would be plainly revealed in it.
If there were martyrs in only our religion—likewise.

———

God being hidden in this way, any religion that fails to say that God is hidden is not true. And any religion that does not give the reason for this is

---

20. See fr. 285.
21. True man and True God.
22. The humble birth of Jesus Christ; his return in glory at the end of time.
23. See ch. XII, "A.P.R." (fr. 182, n. 1), to which this fragment appears to belong. If Pascal did intend, as reported by Filleau de la Chaise in the preface to the 1670 edition of the *Pensées*, to outline his proposed Apology for the solitaires at Port-Royal, he here meditates upon an idea absolutely central to his larger argument. All men deserve damnation. But in his inscrutable mercy, God has *moderated* his unapproachable hidden nature in order to save the elect who seek him. Paradoxically, those "signs of himself" hidden in scripture remain impenetrable to those who fail to seek him with their whole heart. Pascal's entire preface to the Apology (fr. 681) might be seen as germinating from this fertile fragment.
24. See ch. XII, n. 21.

not a religion that enlightens. Ours achieves all of this. TRUTH YOU ARE A HIDDEN GOD.[25]

276

The heathen religion has no foundation (*today. It is said that it once did through the oracles who spoke. But of what sort are the books that assure us of this? Are they so worthy of faith by virtue of their authors? Are they conserved with so much care that one can be assured that they are not corrupted?*)

The Mohammedan religion has the Qur'an and Mohammed as its foundation. But this prophet, who was supposed to be the world's last hope, was he foretold? And what sign has he that any man who wants to call himself a prophet does not also have? What miracles does he say that he has performed himself? According to his own tradition, what mystery has he taught? What morality and what happiness?[26]

The Jewish religion must be viewed differently in the tradition of their saints and in the tradition of the people. Its morality and happiness are ridiculous in the tradition of the common people,[27] but it is admirable in their saints' tradition. Its foundation can be admired. It is the most ancient and the most authentic book in the world. Unlike Mohammed who, in order to make his book endure, forbade that it be read, Moses ordered everyone to read his own book in order to make it endure.[28] And likewise with any religion, for in its holy books and in the casuists Christianity is indeed different.[29]

Our religion is so divine that another divine religion only has its foundation.

277

The atheists' objection

"But we have no light."[30]

---

25. Isaiah 45:15: God has hidden himself under the veil of nature, under that of humanity in his Incarnation, and underneath the literal text of scripture. "Finally, wanting to accomplish the promise he made to his apostles to remain with them until his coming again, he chose to hide himself in the most strange and obscure secret of all, under the elements of the Eucharist." Pascal, Letter 4 to Charlotte de Roannez.

26. See fr. 251.

27. Pascal refers to those he will call the "carnal Jews" (frs. 318, 321, etc.), who love only earthly things.

28. Deuteronomy 31:11.

29. The casuists were theologians who specialized in resolving cases of conscience. In his *Provincial Letters* Pascal denounces the casuists in the Society of Jesus, who, lax in their interpretations of morality, appeal to those "carnal Christians" (fr. 319) whose love of earthly things parallels that of the mass of the "carnal Jews" in the Old Covenant.

30. Ironically, this objection testifies to the truth of the Augustinian doctrine of the "hidden God." Pascal turns this objection against the atheists in the first paragraph of the preface to the Apology (fr. 681).

[XX] That the Law Was Figurative[1]

278
Figure

The Jewish and Egyptian peoples visibly foretold by these two individuals whom Moses met: the Egyptian attacking the Jew, Moses avenging him and killing the Egyptian, and the Jew being ungrateful.[2]

279
Figuratives

Make all things according to the pattern which was shewn thee on the mount.[3] In relation to which Saint Paul says the Jews have painted the things of heaven.[4]

280
Figure

Prophets prophesied with the help of figures: of a belt, of burned beard, and hair,[5] etc.

1. Pascal's ultimate proof of the truth of Christianity will be the "prophecies" (fr. 368). But in order to interpret them, one must understand their figurative nature, which is a result of God's having hidden himself in scripture. The notion of *figure* as well as the *figurative* interpretation must be understood in the perspective of Christian typology.

2. Exodus 2:11–14. Saint Augustine saw in "these characters [...] *figures* foreshadowing something that would happen in the future" (*Against Faustus*, XXII, 70). The episode, Pascal believes, foretells not only the liberation of Israel from their Egyptian captivity, but its subsequent ingratitude to God, from its worship of the golden calf to its rejection of Jesus Christ. See fr. 692.

3. This is Exodus 25:40, in which God showed Moses the *pattern* of the tabernacle he was to build. Pascal's citation is from the Letter to the Hebrews 8:45.

4. Hebrews 8:2–3: "[In Heaven, Jesus Christ is] a minister of the holies, and of the true tabernacle, which the Lord hath pitched, and not man" while the cult rendered to God by the high priests on earth consists in figures and shadows of the things of heaven.

5. A belt refers to Jeremiah 13:11: "For as the girdle sticketh close to the loins of a man, so have I brought close to me all of the house of Israel." "Burned beard and hair" refers to Daniel 3:94, and specifically the three Jews cast into the fiery furnace by Nebuchadnezzar: "the fire had no power on their bodies, and [...] not a hair of their head had been singed."

281

Figuratives Key to the cipher.[6]

True adorers. Here is the Lamb of God who taketh away the sin of the world.[7]

282

Figurative things

These words: sword, shield, *O thou most mighty.*[8]

283

Whoever wishes to give the meaning of scripture without drawing it from scripture is an enemy of scripture. Augustine, *On Christian Doctrine.*[9]

284

Two errors: 1. Taking everything literally. 2. Taking everything spiritually.

285

Figures

Jesus Christ opened up their minds to the understanding of scriptures.[10]

Here are two great revelations: 1. *All things happened to them in figure.*[11] *Israelite, indeed,*[12] *Free indeed,*[13] *True bread from heaven.*[14]

2. A God humbled even unto death on a cross. Christ had to suffer in

---

6. The Old Testament is a "cipher" (fr. 307), an encrypted text, whose key is the New Testament.

7. John 4:23: "But the hour cometh, and now is, when the *true adorers* shall adore the Father in spirit and in truth." John 1:29: "John [the Baptist] saw Jesus coming to him and and he saith: Behold *the Lamb of God, behold him who taketh away the sin of the world.*" In the Mass, the verse is recited by the priest when he elevates the Host just before Communion.

8. Psalm 45:3: "Gird thy *sword* upon thy thigh, *O thou most mighty.*" See fr. 493.

9. Augustine, *On Christian Doctrine*, III, 28, no. 39. This is a gloss Pascal had found in a marginal note in the *Triumphs of the Christian Religion*, I, 7, a work of apologetics published by the Franciscan Jean Boucher, in 1628.

10. This is an allusion to the road to Emmaus (Luke 24:26 and 32), when Jesus appears unrecognized by his disciples, and explains to them the Old Testament prophecies of the Messiah. The disciples recognize him only in the breaking of the bread, an allusion to the Eucharist.

11. 1 Corinthians 10:11.

12. John 1:47: "Jesus saw Nathanael coming to him: and he saith of him: Behold an Israelite indeed, in whom there is no guile."

13. John 8:36: "If therefore the son shall make you free, you will be *free indeed.*"

14. John 6:32: "Moses gave you not bread from heaven, but my Father giveth you *the true bread from heaven,*" i.e., the Eucharist.

order to come into his glory. That he would triumph over death through his death.[15] Two comings.[16]

286

Speak against the excessively figurative.

287

In order to make the Messiah knowable to the good and unknowable to the wicked, God has had him foretold in this manner. If the manner of the Messiah's birth had been foretold clearly, there would have been no obscurity, not even for the wicked. If the time had been foretold obscurely, there would have been obscurity even for the good, (*because the goodness of their hearts*) could not have made them understand for instance that ם means six hundred years.[17] But the time was foretold clearly and the way figuratively.

Thus the wicked, seeing the promised goods as material err in spite of clear predictions about time, and the good do not err.

That is because the understanding of the promised goods is dependent upon the heart that calls good what it loves, but the understanding of the promised time does not depend upon the heart. Thus the clear prediction of time and the obscure prediction of the goods confuse only the wicked.

288

Carnal Jews understood neither the greatness nor the humbling of the Messiah who was foretold in their prophecies. They failed to recognize him in his predicted greatness, as when he says that the Messiah will be David's Lord, even though he is his son,[18] and that he was before Abraham [was] and he has seen him.[19] They did not believe he was great to the point of being eternal, and

---

15. Philippians 2:8; Luke 24:26. The liturgical preface of Easter, particularly Easter Monday: "through his death he has destroyed our death."

16. These are the Incarnation and the Last Judgment. See fragment 303.

17. The letter [ם] (*mem*) is a letter in the Hebrew alphabet. Its form is open [מ] at the beginning or in the body of a word; it is closed [ם] at the end of a word. During the rabbinical period, when the alphabetical system was used to represent numbers, the closed *mem* was assigned the numeral value of six hundred. The verse in question is Isaiah 9:6 ("For a child is born to us, and a son is given to us, and and the government is upon his shoulder: and his name shall be called [...] the Prince of Peace."). In the *Pugio fidei*, a medieval apology written by the Dominican Raymond Martin (see ch. XXI, n. 2), Pascal had read that because of the form of the *mem* the Messiah was to be born of a virgin six hundred years after the prophecy. Yet, as anticipated by the preceding fragment (286), Pascal finds such a figure is too excessive to be useful in the Apology.

18. Matthew 22:45. "If David then calls him Lord, how is he his son?"

19. John 8:56. "Abraham your father rejoiced that he might see my day: he saw it, and was glad."

they failed to recognize him as well in his humbling and in his death. The Messiah, they said, remains eternally, and this one says he will die.[20] They thought he was neither mortal nor eternal, and they only sought carnal greatness in him.

289
Contradiction

You cannot compose a good physiognomy without reconciling all our contrarieties, and it is not enough to reconcile a sequence of congruent qualities without reconciling the contrary ones. In order to understand the meaning of an author, one must reconcile all the contrary passages.

Thus in order to understand scripture, one must have one meaning that reconciles all contrary passages. It is not enough to have one that fits several congruent passages; one must have one that reconciles even the contrary passages.

Every author has one meaning that can be reconciled with all contrary passages, or he has no meaning at all. One cannot say that about scripture and the prophets, they clearly had too much good sense. One must therefore look for one that will reconcile all contrarieties.

The true meaning therefore is not that of the Jews, but in Jesus Christ all the contradictions are reconciled.

The Jews cannot reconcile the cessation of kingship and principality that Hosea foretold with Jacob's prophecy.

If one takes the law, the sacrifices, and the kingdom as realities, one cannot reconcile all the passages. Therefore, they must necessarily be figures. One cannot even reconcile passages in a single author, or even a single book, or sometimes a single chapter, which is a clear indication of the meaning of the author. As when Ezekiel, chapter 20, says that they will live according to God's commandments and they will not.[21]

290

It was forbidden to sacrifice outside Jerusalem, which was the place God had chosen, and it was forbidden to eat the tithe elsewhere.[22] Deuteronomy 12:5, etc. Deuteronomy 14:23, etc.; 15:20; 16:2–7 and 11–15.

---

20. John 12:34. "The multitude answered him: We have heard out of the law, that Christ abideth for ever; and how sayest thou: The Son of man must be lifted up? Who is this Son of man?"

21. Ezekiel 20:11 and 25.

22. The law required that the Hebrews dedicate one tenth of their crops to God and eat it in his honor. Orthodox Jews continue to give one tenth of their income to charity. In modern Israel, many Jews continue the practice of agricultural tithing. There are also less literal interpretations of this prescription (for instance, giving through volunteer work).

Hosea predicted that he would be without king, without prince, without sacrifice, etc., without idols. This has now been accomplished, since no legitimate sacrifice can be made outside Jerusalem.

Figure

If the law and the sacrifices are the truth, they must please God and not displease him. If they are figures, they must please and displease.

Now in all of scripture they please and displease. It is said that the law will be changed, that the sacrifice will be changed, that they will be without king, without princes, and without sacrifices, that a new covenant will be made, that the law will be renewed, that the precepts they received are not good, that their sacrifices are abominable, that God did not ask for them.

It is said on the contrary that the law will last forever, that the alliance will be eternal, that the sacrifice will be eternal, that the scepter will never leave their midst since it must not leave until the eternal king arrives.

Do all these passages[23] indicate that they refer to reality? No. Do they indicate that they are figurative? No, they indicate that it is one or the other. But since the former exclude reality, they indicate that everything is figurative.

All the passages together cannot be construed as referring to reality. All can be construed as figurative. Therefore, they must be construed not as referring to reality but as figurative.

The Lamb was slain from the foundation of the world.[24] *The continual sacrifice.*[25]

291

A portrait implies absence and presence, pleasure and displeasure. Reality excludes absence and displeasure.

———

Figures

In order to find out if the law and the sacrifices are real or figurative, we must see if the prophets, when speaking about those things, had their sights and minds set on them in such a way that they saw nothing but the old alliance. Or if they saw them as the painted image of something else. Because in a portrait one sees the thing that is figured. In order to do this, it suffices to examine what they say.

23. See fr. 294.
24. Revelation 13:8.
25. "*The continual sacrifice*" [i.e., in the Temple] shall be taken away, and the abomination . . . set up." Daniel 12:11.

When they say that it will be eternal, do they mean the covenant they also mention as destined to be changed? The same goes for the sacrifices, etc.

The cipher has two meanings. When one intercepts an important letter that reads clearly and nonetheless says that its meaning is veiled and obscured, that it is hidden in such a way that one will see the letter without seeing it and one will hear it without hearing it, what should one conclude other than the fact that it is a cipher with a double meaning? Even more so if manifest contradictions are found in the literal meaning. The prophets have said clearly that Israel would always be loved by God and that the law would be eternal. They have also said that their meaning would be misunderstood and that it was hidden.

How estimable are those who unveil the cipher for us and teach us to apprehend the hidden meaning, especially when the principles they follow are completely natural and clear. This is what Jesus Christ and the apostles did. They have lifted the seal. They have torn open the veil and uncovered the spirit. In order to do this they have taught us that man's enemies are his passions, that the redeemer would be spiritual and his kingdom a spiritual one, that there would be two comings, one in misery in order to put down man's pride, and one in glory to lift man up from his humiliation, that Jesus Christ would be God and man.

292

The time of the first coming [is] foretold, the time of the second one [is] not, because the first one had to be hidden and the second one had to be spectacular, and so manifest that even his enemies would have to recognize him. But since he had to come in an obscure way, and known only to those who would interrogate scripture...

293

What could the Jews do, being his enemies?

If they accept him, they prove him by their acceptance, because those in charge of waiting for the Messiah accept him, and if they reject him they prove him by renouncing him.[26]

---

26. On the one hand, this rejection was predicted. Yet this very hostility of the Jews renders them "irreproachable witnesses" of the Old Testament prophecies with which they have been entrusted (fr. 734)

294

Contrarieties.

The scepter until the Messiah. *Without king or prince.*[27]

Law eternal, changed.[28]

Eternal alliance, new alliance.[29]

Good law, *bad precepts. Ezekiel* 20.[30]

295

The Jews were accustomed to great and spectacular miracles. Having seen the great feats of the Red Sea and the land of Canaan as a sample of the great things from their Messiah, they were expecting something even more spectacular, of which the feats of Moses were only a foretaste.

296

A figure implies absence and presence, pleasure and displeasure.

———

Cipher with double meaning. One is clear and says that the meaning is hidden.

297

One might think that when the prophets predicted that the scepter would not depart from Judah until the eternal king,[31] they were speaking to flatter the people and their prophecy would be invalidated by Herod.[32] But in order to show that they did not mean it in this way, and that, on the contrary, they knew very well that the temporal kingdom was to end, they say that they will be without king and without prince, and for a long time. Hosea.[33]

---

27. In Genesis 49:10, Jacob, just before his death, prophesies: "The sceptre shall not be taken away from Juda, nor a ruler from his thigh, till he come that is to be sent." And yet Hosea 3:4 predicts: "For the children of Israel will shall sit many days *without king,* and *without prince,* and without sacrifice, and without altar."

28. Leviticus 7:34 speaks of a "law that will always be observed." Many of the biblical passages that Pascal collected in fragment 693 predict that the law "must change with the Messiah" (fr. 305).

29. In Genesis 17:7 God promised Abraham an "perpetual covenant." Yet in Jeremiah 31:31 he announces a "new covenant."

30. The excellence of law is celebrated in all of Deuteronomy. Yet Pascal read in Ezekiel, 20:25: "I also gave them statutes that were not good, and judgments, in which they shall not live."

31. See fr. 294.

32. Herod the Great was the first foreign-born king of the Jews. See fr. 693.

33. See n. 27 above.

298

Figures

Once one has uncovered the secret, it is impossible not to see it. Read the Old Testament in this way and see if the sacrifices were true, if Abraham's lineage was the true cause of God's friendship, if the Promised Land was the authentic place of rest? No. Therefore, those were figures.

See as well all the mandated ceremonies and all the commandments that are not aimed at charity; you will see that they are figures of charity.

Therefore, all the sacrifices and ceremonies were either figures or rubbish. Now, some of the things said clearly are too lofty to be thought of as rubbish.

Find out if the prophets had their sight circumscribed by the Old Testament or if they saw other things in it.

299

The letter kills.[34]
All things happened in figure.
Christ had to suffer.[35]
A God humiliated. This is the cipher Saint Paul gives us.

Circumcision of the heart, true fasting, true sacrifice, true temple. The prophets indicated that all of it had to be spiritual.[36]
Not the food that perishes, but the food that does not perish.[37]

You shall be free indeed.[38] Therefore the other freedom is but a figure of freedom.

I am the true bread from heaven.[39]

300

When David predicts that the Messiah will deliver his people from their enemies, one may think carnally that he is referring to the Egyptians. In that

---

34. 2 Corinthians 3:6: "For the letter killeth, but the spirit quickeneth."

35. Acts 17:3. Paul "declar[es] and insinuat[es]" to the Jews of Thessalonica understand "that the Christ was to suffer."

36. See fr. 693.

37. John 6:27. After the feeding of the multitudes, Jesus urges his disciples to seek "not [...] the meat which perisheth, but [...] that which endureth unto life everlasting" An allusion by the evangelist to the Eucharist.

38. John 8:36: "If therefore the son shall make you free, you shall be *free indeed.*" See above, n. 13.

39. John 6:32.

case, I cannot show that the prophecy has been realized. On the other hand, one may think that he is referring to iniquities, because in truth the Egyptians are not enemies but iniquities are.

The word enemy is therefore ambiguous. But if he says elsewhere, as he does, that he will deliver his people from their sins,[40] as Isaiah and others do,[41] the ambiguity is lifted, and the double meaning of enemies is reduced to a single meaning: iniquities. Because if what he had in mind was the sins, he could refer to them as enemies, but if he was thinking of the enemies, he could not call them iniquities.

Now Moses and David and Isaiah used the same terms. Therefore, how could one deny that they all had the same meaning, and that David's meaning, which is clearly iniquities when he says enemies, is the same as Moses's meaning when he says enemies?

<hr>

Daniel 9 prays for the deliverance of the people from the bondage of their enemies. But he had their sins in mind, and in order to make it clear he says that Gabriel came to him to say that his prayers had been heard and that he had only seventy weeks to wait. After this time the people would be freed from iniquity, sin would end, and the liberator, the saint among saints, would bring ETERNAL justice, not a legal one, but an eternal one.

<hr>

Some see clearly that man has no enemy other than the concupiscence that diverts him from God, and not [armies] and no good other than God, and not a rich soil. As to those who believe that the good of man is in his flesh and his ills in what takes him away from the pleasures of the senses, let them have them to their heart's content, and let them die in them. But for those who seek God with all their heart, who find displeasure only in being deprived of the sight of him, whose desire is set on possessing him and whose enemies are those who take them away from him, who are sad to be surrounded and ruled by such enemies, there is consolation. I have happy news: they have a liberator. I will present him to them. I will show that there is a God for them. I will not present him to the others. I will show that a Messiah was foretold who will bring deliverance from enemies, and that one has come to bring deliverance from iniquities, not enemies.

40. Psalm 130:8.
41. Isaiah 43:25: "I am he who blots out your transgressions for my own sake, and I will not remember your sins."

301
Figures

The Jews had grown old with such earthly thoughts: God loved their father Abraham, his flesh and his descendants; for that reason he had multiplied them and distinguished them from all other peoples without tolerating any mixing. When they languished in Egypt, he led them out with great signs of his favor; he fed them with the manna in the desert; he took them to a very fertile land; he gave them kings and a well-built temple to make animal sacrifices and through the bloodshed they would be purified; he would send them the Messiah to make them masters of the world. And he foretold the time of his coming.

The world having grown old in those carnal errors, Jesus Christ came at the time foretold, but not with the expected splendor. Thus, they did not think it was he.[42] After his death, Saint Paul came to teach men that all those things had happened in a way that had figurative meaning;[43] the kingdom of God did not consist in flesh but in spirit;[44] the enemies of men were not the Babylonians but their own passions; God did not like handmade temples[45] but a pure and humbled heart. The circumcision of the body was useless, but that of the heart was needed;[46] Moses had not given them the bread from heaven,[47] etc.

———

However, because God did not want to reveal those things to a people that was unworthy of them, and because he wanted nonetheless to put them forward so that they might be believed, he predicted the time clearly, and the events themselves clearly at times, but mostly in a figurative way. Thus those who liked the figurative would stop at it (I do not say rightly) and those who liked what is figured would see that.

———

All that does not pertain to charity is a figure.[48]

———

42. This is an allusion to the song of the Suffering Servant (Isaiah 53:3–4): "Despised, and the most abject of men [...] and his look was as it were hidden and despised."

43. 1 Corinthians 10:11.

44. Romans 8:8.

45.Hebrews 9:24: "For Jesus is not entered into the holies made with hands, the patterns of the true: but into heaven itself."

46. Romans 2:28–29.

47. John 6:32: "Moses gave you not bread from heaven, but my Father giveth you the true bread from heaven. For the bread of God is that which cometh down from heaven."

48. Augustine, *Catechizing Beginners*, 26, no. 50: "In everything he will hear in the Canonical Books, all that cannot be related to the love of eternity, of truth, of holiness, or to the love of one's neighbor must be construed as having been done or said figuratively."

The unique purpose of scripture is charity.[49]

———

All that does not pertain to the one good is a figure of it. Since there is but one goal, all that does not pertain to it explicitly is a figure.

———

This is how God diversifies the one principle of charity in order to satisfy our curiosity, which seeks diversity, with a diversity that always leads us to the one thing alone that is necessary to us. Because *one thing alone is necessary,*[50] and we like diversity. Thus God satisfies one and the other with those diversities that lead to the only thing that is necessary.

———

The Jews were so fond of figurative things, and they waited for them so intently that they failed to recognize reality when it came at the time and in the manner it was foretold.

———

Rabbis see the breasts of the spouse as a figure,[51] as well as everything that does not represent the single desire they have for temporal goods.

———

And Christians see the Eucharist itself as a figure of the glory for which they aim.

302

All Jesus Christ did was to teach men that they were in love with themselves, that they were enslaved, blind, ill, unhappy, and sinful, that he had to free, enlighten, beatify, and heal them, that the way to do it was to hate oneself and to follow him through misery and death on the cross.[52]

303

Figures

When God's word, which is true, is false literally, it is true spiritually. "Sit thou at my right hand."[53] This is false literally, therefore it is true spiritually.

In expressions like these, one speaks of God in human terms. It only means that God's intention will be the same as the intention men have when they seat someone to their right. It is therefore a sign of God's intention, not of his way of carrying it out.

---

49. Augustine, *On Christian Doctrine,* III, 10, nn. 15–16: "Scripture prescribes nothing, if not charity."
50. Luke 10:42.
51. This is the spouse to the beloved in the Song of Songs 4:5: "Your two breasts [are] like two young roes that are twins, which feed among the lilies."
52. Pascal adapts and freely translates a passage from Saint Augustine's *The Merits of Sinners,* I, 26, no. 39.
53. DR, Psalm 109:1; RSV: Psalm 110:1: "The Lord says to my Lord, Sit at my right hand."

Thus when he says: *The Lord smelled a sweet savor and he will reward you with the fatness of the earth*,[54] it signifies the intention of a man who would give a fertile land in reward because he has welcomed a gift of pleasing odors. God will have the same intention for you because you had for him the intention one has in giving perfume. Similarly, *The wrath [of the Lord] is kindled*,[55] jealous God,[56] etc. The things of God being inexpressible, this is the only way they can be described. And the Church continues to use such expressions. *Because he hath strengthened the bolts*, etc.[57]

It is not allowed to ascribe a meaning to scripture unless this meaning has been revealed by scripture itself. Thus there is no revelation saying that ם in Isaiah means six hundred.[58] Nothing says that the defective צ or ה would point to mysteries.[59] It is therefore not legitimate to say that. And even less to say that it is the way of the philosophical stone.[60] On the other hand, we say that the literal sense is not the true sense because the prophets themselves said it.

304

Those who find it hard to believe look for a reason in the fact that the Jews do not believe: "If things were so clear, they say, why would they not believe?" And they would almost want them to believe, so that they may not be deterred by the example of their refusal. But this very refusal is the foundation of our belief.[61] We would be much less inclined if they were with us. In that case, we would have much more of an excuse.

It is amazing that the Jews should have been made so fond of predictions and so opposed to their accomplishment.

54. Pascal quotes freely from Genesis 8:21 and 27:27–28.

55. Isaiah 5:25: "therefore *is the wrath* of the Lord *kindled* against his people."

56. Exodus 20:5: "I am the Lord thy God, mighty, jealous." (RSV: "I the Lord your God am a *jealous God*.")

57. Psalm 147:12–13. "Praise the Lord, O Jerusalem: praise thy God, O Sion. *Because he hath strengthened the bolts* of thy gates, he hath blessed thy children within thee."

58. See n. 17, above.

59. See n. 17, above. The letter [צ] (*tsade*) and the letter [ה] (*he*) are, as is *mem*, letters in the Hebrew alphabet. *Tsade*, like *mem*, is written differently according to its place in the word. *Mem* has a closed and open form. *Tsade* has initial and final forms. *He* may or may not be written. In the latter case, it is called "defective" (*deficiens*). Raymond Martin, the thirteenth-century Dominican whose *Dagger of the Faith against the Muslims and the Jews* Pascal read in the edition of Joseph de Voisin (1651), had thought these variants contained hidden meanings. Pascal disagrees. Here he fulfills the agenda he proposes in fr. 286: "Speak against excessive figurative language."

60. This is the philosopher's stone (*lapis philosophorum*), a legendary alchemical substance, supposedly capable of turning base metals into gold and achieving immortality. It was sought after by alchemists like Sir Isaac Newton and Nicolas Flamel. The stone was the central symbol of the mystical terminology of alchemy, symbolizing perfection, theophany, and the Christ.

61. See n. 26, above.

305
Proof of the two Testaments together

In order to prove them both at once, we only need to see if the prophecies of one are accomplished in the other.

In order to examine the prophecies, we must understand them.

Because if we believe they have only one meaning, then it is certain that the Messiah did not come. But if they have two meanings, it is certain that he came in Jesus Christ.

The whole question therefore is whether they have two meanings.

That Scripture has two meanings,

given by Jesus Christ and the apostles,

and here are the proofs.

1. Proofs by scripture itself.

2. Proofs by the rabbis. Moses Maimonides says it has two proven faces.[62] And also that prophets prophesied only about Jesus Christ.

3. Proofs by the Kabala.[63]

4. Proofs by the mystical interpretation that the rabbis themselves give to scripture.

5. Proofs by the principles of the rabbis themselves that there are two meanings.

That there are two comings of the Messiah: glorious or wretched according to their merit.

That the prophets have prophesied only about the Messiah.

[That] the law is not eternal, but must change with the Messiah.

That at that time one will no longer remember the Red Sea.

That Jews and Gentiles will mingle.[64]

306
Figures

Isaiah 51,[65] the Red Sea as an image of redemption.

---

62. Moses Maimonides (1135–1204) was a renowned Jewish theologian, philosopher, and physician, author of a *Commentary on the Mishnah,* and of the *Guide to the Perplexed.*

63. This is the oral law, which Moses received on Mt. Sinai when he also received the Torah. Transmitted orally down to the present day, it has come to designate a great number of mystical Jewish writings.

64. Pascal had added here and then crossed out: "6. Proofs by the key given us by Jesus Christ and the apostles."

65. Isaiah 51:10–11.

But that you may know that the Son of Man hath power to forgive sins, I say to thee, Arise.[66]

Because God wanted to show that he could endow a holy people with invisible holiness and fill them with eternal glory, he did things that are visible. Nature being an image of grace, he did in the good things of nature what he was about to do in the good things of grace, so that people would conclude that he was able to do what was invisible, since he was doing what was visible.

Therefore he saved the people from the Flood, he made them descend from Abraham, and he redeemed them from their enemies and found a place of rest for them.

God's aim was not to save them from the Flood and to have an entire people descend from Abraham just to bring them to a fertile land.

And even grace itself is but a figure of glory because it is not the ultimate end. It has been figured by the law and is itself a figure of [glory], but it is its figure and its principle or cause.

———

The ordinary life of men is similar to that of saints. They all look for satisfaction, and they differ only in how they define it. They call enemies those who stand in the way, etc. Thus God has shown the power he has to accord good things that are invisible by the power he has on good things that are visible.

307

Two people tell silly tales. One sees a double meaning according to the Kabala;[67] the other has only the plain meaning. If someone who does not share in the secret hears them both in this way, he will reach the same conclusion about both. However, if they continue speaking and if one says things that are angelic while the other keeps saying things that are ordinary and common, he will conclude that one was speaking mysteriously while the other was not, since one has shown sufficiently that he is incapable of such silliness and capable of being mysterious, while the other is incapable of mystery and capable of silliness.

———

The *Old Testament* is a cipher.

66. Mark 2:10–11: *But that you may know that the Son of man hath power* on earth *to forgive sins,* (he saith to the sick of the palsy,) *I say to thee: Arise.*
67. See above, n. 63.

[XXI] The Rabbinical Tradition[1]

308
Chronology of the rabbinic sages

The page numbers are from the book *The Dagger* [*of Faith Against the Muslims and the Jews*].[2]

p. 27.

R. Hakadosh.[3]
author of the *Mishnah*,[4] or oral law,

Commentaries on the *Mishnah* Tosefta[7]

or second law, year 200.[5]
one is the *Sifra*[6]
(which is a commentary on the Mishna)
Baraitot[8]
Talmud hierosol[9]

year 340

---

1. In this chapter, Pascal seeks to find evidence of original sin in Judaism, the Old Testament, and particularly in the rabbinical commentaries. Whatever Pascal (and Raymond Martin, the author of *The Dagger of Faith*) derived from their selective references to individual rabbinic sages, Judaism completely rejects the notion of original and hereditary sin and the subsequent corruption of the flesh. See Kauffman Kohler, *Jewish Theology: Systematically and Historically Considered* (New York: Ktav, 1968), 220–25. No French edition, including Sellier's, has ever offered more than scant notes to help the reader decipher Pascal's arcane notes. We want to express our thanks here to Rabbi Dr. Harold Jaye of Brandeis University and Temple B'nai Darom in Ocala, Florida, who wrote the notes below, which have greatly elucidated this heretofore inaccessible (even in the French editions) *liasse*.

2. For the most part, Pascal borrows the observations of Joseph de Voisin, editor of *The Dagger of Faith against the Muslims and the Jews*. Written in the thirteenth century by the Spanish Dominican Raymond Martin, this treatise had remained in manuscript form until Voisin's edition in 1651. Pascal's sources are for the most part chapters XIII and XVII of Voisin's preface.

3. Rabbenu Hakadosh, "Our holy Rabbi." This is the honorific title of Rabbi Judah Hanasi ("The Prince"), who lived from 135–c. 193, and was editor of the Mishnah. See Hermann L. Strack, *Introduction to the Talmud and Midrash* (Minneapolis, Minn.: Fortress Press, 1996).

4. *Mishnah*: the code of Jewish oral law (derived from the written law, i.e., the Old Testament) in six "orders" (volumes) and further subdivided into sixty-three tractates each treating of a specific matter of either civil, criminal, or ritual law.

5. The approximate year of the editing of the Mishnah.

6. *Sifra*: a halakhic (tannaitic) midrash [interpretive commentary] on Leviticus.

7. *Tosefta*: "Addition," a collection of oral laws, the remnants of earlier compilations made by Rabbi Akiba, Rabbi Meir, and others. It is not adopted in the *Mishnah* of Rabbi Judah the Prince.

8. The plural of *baraita*, an extraneous teaching of the oral law quoted in the *Gemara*. It is not included in the *Mishnah* of Judah the Prince, but is quoted from lost collections of oral law or from the *Tosefta*, *Mekhilta*, *Sifra*, or *Sifre*.

9. *Talmud Yerushalmi* [Talmud of Jerusalem]: the Talmud edited in the fourth and fifth centuries in Palestine. The *Talmud Bavli* (*Babylonian Talmud*) was edited between 200 and 500 CE.

Bereishit Rabbah by R. Hoshayah Rabbah,[10]
commentary on the *Mishnah,*
Bereishith Rabbah,[11] *Bar Meishoni*
are subtle, pleasant, historical, and theological discourses. This same author wrote the books called *Rabot.*[12]

———

A hundred years after the *Talmud of Jerusalem,* the *Babylonian Talmud* was written by R. Ashi[13] with the universal consent of all the Jews, who are necessarily required to follow everything in it: 440.[14]

The addition by R. Ashi is called the *Gemara,* that is, a commentary on the *Mishnah.*

And the *Talmud* includes both the *Mishnah* and the *Gemara.*

309[15]

Concerning original sin

Ample tradition of original sin according to the Jews.[16]

On the saying from Genesis 8: *the composition of the human heart is evil from his childhood.*[17]

Masechet Sukkah:[18] the evil leaven has seven names in scripture. It is called evil, foreskin, unclean, enemy, scandal, heart of stone, north wind: all this signifies the wickedness that is hidden and imprinted in the heart of man. *Midrash Tehillim*[19] says the same thing, and also that God will deliver man's good nature from his evil one.

This wickedness renews itself every day against man, as is written in Psalm 37:[20] *The wicked watcheth the just man, and seeketh to put him to death, but the Lord will not leave him.*

10. Rabbi Hoshaya Rabbah, the *Amora* [teacher quoted in the *Gemara*] to whom tradition assigns the authorship of the Genesis *Rabbah,* in third-century Palestine.

11. *Bereshith Rabbah:* expository midrash on Genesis assigned by tradition to Rabbi Hoshaya Rabbah (third-century Palestine); this midrash forms a haggadic commentary on the whole of Genesis.

12. *Rabot:* homiletic *midrashim* on several biblical books.

13. Rav Ashi was head of the rabbinical academy at Sura in Babylonia (c. 427 CE).

14. The approximate date of the editing of Babylonian Talmud.

15. In this fragment Pascal notes examples from *Pugio fidei* [The dagger of faith], III, 2, 16, 463–67, which he believes record a tradition of original sin in Judaism. See note 1, above. Had Pascal met any rabbis, as would Richard Simon a generation later, he would have learned that the rabbinical commentators never entertained any such interpretation concerning original sin. It is highly unlikely that there were any rabbis in Paris during his time, the Jews having been expelled long before. Sellier estimates that there were perhaps only five hundred Jews in Paris at the time, most of whom practiced their religion in secret.

16. See ch. XXI, nn. 1 and 15, above.

17. Genesis 8:21: "the imagination and thought *of man's heart* are prone to *evil from his* youth."

18. *Masechet Sukkah:* The Mishnaic tractate dealing with the Festival of Tabernacles; in the order *Moed* (Festivals).

19. *Midrash Tehillim:* Haggadic midrash on the Psalms.

20. Psalm 37:32–33. Pascal sums up v. 33 ("*the Lord will not leave* in his hands; nor condemn him when

This wickedness tempts the heart of man in this life and will accuse him in the next.

All of this is found in the Talmud.

Midrash Tehillim on Psalm 4: *Stand in awe and you shall not sin.*[21] Stand in awe and strike fear into your concupiscence and it will not lead you into sin. And on Psalm 36:[22] *The unbeliever hath said in his heart. Let the fear of God not be before me.* That is to say, the natural wickedness of man has said that to him.

Midrash el Kohelet:[23] *Better the poor and wise child than the old and foolish king who knows not how to foresee the future.* The child is virtue, and the king is man's wickedness. It is called king because all the members obey it, and old because it is in the heart of man from childhood to old age, and foolish because it leads man down the road of perdition that he does not foresee.

The same thing is in *Midrash Tehillim.*[24]

Bereishith Rabbah[25] on Psalm 35:[26] *Lord, all my bones will bless you because you deliver the poor from the tyrant.* And is there a greater tyrant than the evil leaven?

And on Proverbs 25:[27] *If thy enemy be hungry, give him to eat.* In other words, if the evil leaven is hungry, give him the bread of wisdom of which it is spoken in Proverbs 9.[28] And if he is thirsty, give him it the water of which it is spoken in Isaiah 55.[29]

Midrash Tehillim says the same thing and that scripture in that passage, speaking of our enemy, means the evil leaven, and that by giving him this bread and water, we shall heap fiery coals upon his head.

Midrash el Kohelet[30] on Ecclesiastes 9:[31] *A great king besieged a little city.* This great king is the evil leaven; the great bulwarks surrounding it are temptations. And a poor wise man has been found to deliver it: namely, virtue.

---

he shall be judged"). Here Pascal exceptionally retains the Hebrew numbering of the Psalms, used in all Protestant Bibles since the Authorized Version and in modern Catholic translations. Almost everywhere else Pascal uses the unfamiliar numbering of the Psalms in the Vulgate, which the Council of Trent had declared the only correct and authorized text of scripture and the very words of God.

21. Psalm 4:5: "Be angry and sin not."

22. Psalm 36:1. "The unjust *hath said* within himself, that he would sin: there is no *fear of God before* his eyes." (RSV: "Transgression speaks to the wicked deep in their hearts; there is no fear of God before their eyes.")

23. *Midrash el Kohelet:* Haggadic midrash on Ecclesiastes.

24. See above, ch. XXI, n. 19.

25. See above, ch. XXI, n. 11.

26. Psalm 35:10.

27. Proverbs 25:21.

28. Proverbs 9:5.

29. Isaiah 55:1.

30. See above, ch. XXI, n. 23.

31. Ecclesiastes 9:13–18.

And on Psalm 41:[32] *Blessed is he that understandeth concerning the poor.*

And on Psalm 78:[33] *The spirit goeth and returneth not.* This has led some to contrive to go astray and argue erroneously against the immortality of the soul, but its meaning is that this spirit is the evil leaven that accompanies man until death and will not return at the resurrection.

And on Psalm 103.[34] The same thing.

And on Psalm 16.[35]

310

Principles of the Rabbis. Two Messiahs.[36]

---

32. Psalm 41:2 (DR); Psalm 41:1 (RSV): "Blessed be he who considers the poor."

33. Psalm 78:39: "a wind that *goeth and returneth not*" (RSV: "a wind that passes and comes not again").

34. Psalm 103:15–16.

35. Psalm 16:10. See *The Dagger of Faith*, III, 2, 16.

36. "Two messiahs." Either the messiah son of Joseph and messiah son of David or the pre-existing heavenly messiah and the earthly messiah. See *Jewish Encyclopedia*, s.v. Messiah, and especially the section "Messiah ben Joseph," https://jewishencyclopedia.com/.

[XXII] Perpetuity[1]

311

From a single statement of David, or Moses, such as "God will circumcise their hearts,"[2] we can understand their way of thinking. All their other expressions may be ambiguous and may cast doubt on whether they are philosophers or Christians, but in the end a single statement of this kind should determine all the others, just as a single statement of Epictetus determines all the others to the opposite meaning.[3] Ambiguity lasts until this point, but not afterward.

312

States would perish if their laws did not often give way in times of necessity.[4] But religion has never tolerated or practiced this. So either these compromises or miracles are needed.

There is nothing strange in trying to preserve oneself by giving way, but this is not, strictly speaking, preservation. Moreover, all states wholly perish in the end; none has endured a thousand years. But the fact that this religion has always been preserved and is inflexible... this is divine.

313

Perpetuity

This religion, which consists in the belief that man has fallen from a state of glory and of communication with God and has plunged into a state of sorrow, penitence, and estrangement from God, but that after this life we will be

---

1. Like nearly everyone until the late nineteenth century, Pascal believed that human history consisted only of six thousand years. From this perspective, the ancient saints going back as far as Adam were able to penetrate the veil of the Old Testament and announce Christ. Therefore, the true religion has always existed on the earth, while the false ones have succeeded one another and perished one by one.

2. Deuteronomy 30:6.

3. Epictetus (55–135 CE) was a Greek Stoic philosopher who taught that fate being out of our control, we can only accept what happens dispassionately through rigorous self-discipline. Suffering, he argued, comes from trying to control that which we cannot. See the introduction to the *Exchange with M. de Sacy*, in this edition.

4. Montaigne, *Essays*, I, 23, 107: "Yet it is true that Fortune, always reserving her authority above our reasonings, sometimes presents us with such a necessity that the laws must needs give some place to it."

restored by a Messiah who was to come, has always existed upon the earth. All things have passed, but this one, for which all things are, has endured.

In the first age of the world, men were given to all kinds of debauchery, and yet there were saints, such as Enoch, Lamech, and others who patiently waited for the Christ promised from the beginning of the world. Noah witnessed human wickedness at its highest degree and had the merit in his own person to save the world through the hope for the Messiah, whom he prefigured. Abraham was surrounded by idolaters when God made known to him the mystery of the Messiah whom he hailed from afar. In the time of Isaac and Jacob, abomination was spread across the world, but these saints lived in their faith. And Jacob, when he was dying and blessing his children, cried out in a rapture that caused him to interrupt what he was saying: *I will look for the Savior that you promised, O Lord. Salutare tuum expectabo, Domine.*[5]

The Egyptians were infected with idolatry and magic. Even the people of God were led astray by their example. Yet Moses and others saw him whom they did not see, and worshipped him in consideration of the eternal gifts that he was preparing for them.

The Greeks and Romans subsequently erected their false deities. The poets created a hundred different theologies. The philosophers divided into a thousand different sects. And yet, in the heart of Judea, there were always chosen men foretelling the coming of this Messiah who was known only to them.[6] He came at last in the fullness of time, and since then we have witnessed the birth of so many schisms and heresies, so many states overthrown, so many changes in all things; yet this Church, which worships him who has always been worshipped, has endured without interruption. It is wonderful, incomparable, and altogether divine that this religion, which has always endured, has continually been under attack. A thousand times she has been on the verge of universal destruction, and every time she has been in this state, God has raised her up by extraordinary strokes of his power. What is astonishing is that she has been preserved without yielding or bending to the will of tyrants, for it would not be strange for a state to endure when its laws are sometimes made to yield to necessity.[7] But for that, SEE THE CIRCLE IN MONTAIGNE.[8]

---

5. Genesis 49:18: "*I will look for thy salvation, O Lord.*" Pascal quotes in French and repeats the phrase in Latin for emphasis.

6. Psalm 75:2 (RSV 76:1): "In Judea God is known: his name is great in Israel." This fragment is a mosaic of biblical reminiscences: John 8:56; Hebrews 11:13 and 23–27.

7. Pascal reiterates how the Jewish people, in the obscure heart of Judah, resisted any outside influences and retained their belief in monotheism and their hope for the Messiah while the entire world surrounding them was given over to idolatry and false philosophies. Threatened a thousand times with annihilation, only the intervention of something as incomparable as divine protection could have permitted the Jewish people to maintain their law, beliefs, and hopes.

8. Pascal refers to his mark in his edition of the *Essays*, signaling the text used in fr. 312. See fr. 322.

314

Perpetuity

The Messiah has always been believed in. The tradition of Adam was still fresh in Noah and in Moses.[9] The prophets have foretold him ever since, while always foretelling other things, which, being accomplished from time to time in the sight of men, showed the truth of their mission, and consequently that of their promises concerning the Messiah. Jesus Christ performed miracles, as did the apostles, converting all the heathen. In this way, with the fulfillment of all the prophecies, the Messiah has been proved for all time.

315

The six ages, the six fathers of the six ages, the six wonders at the arrival of the six ages, the six dawns at the start of the six ages.[10]

316

The only religion contrary to nature,[11] to common sense, and to our pleasures, is the only one that has always existed.

317

If the ancient Church was in error, the Church has fallen. If the Church should be in error today, it is not the same thing, because it has always the higher principle of the ancient Church's tradition of faith. And so this submission and conformity to the ancient Church prevail and correct everything. But the ancient Church did not presuppose the future Church and did not consider it, as we presuppose and consider the ancient Church.[12]

---

9. See frs. 322, 327. Because of the longevity of the patriarchs, only five generations separated Moses from Adam.

10. Pascal summarizes Saint Augustine's *Genesis against the Manicheans,* I, 23. The history of the world is to be divided into six ages, recapitulating the six days of Creation. Each age, with an evening and a morning, is revealed by a stupendous event: Adam to the Flood; Noah to Babel; Abraham to Saul; David to the deportation to Babylon; purification through exile to the rejection of the Messiah; Jesus humbled to Jesus glorified. The seventh age will be that of the eternal beatitude of those who love God.

11. Our second nature, our fallen state.

12. The Church of the first centuries could fall into heresies like Arianism because it had no holy tradition upon which to rely. That very tradition, however, subsequently constituted over the centuries by such Doctors of the Church as Saint Augustine, guarantees that the Church of today cannot err. The Arians were followers of the anti-Trinitarian presbyter Arius (250–336 CE), who taught that God the Father and the Son did not exist together eternally and that the pre-incarnate Jesus was a divine being created by (and therefore inferior to) God the Father.

318

Two sorts of men in each religion[13]

Among the pagans, animal worshippers, and others who worship one God in natural religion.

Among the Jews, the carnal and the spiritual, who were the Christians of the old law.

Among Christians, coarse men, who are the Jews of the new law.

Carnal Jews awaited a carnal Messiah and coarse Christians think that the Messiah has dispensed them from loving God. True Jews and true Christians worship a Messiah who makes them love God.

319

Whoever judges the religion of the Jews through the coarse men will misunderstand it. It is to be seen in the holy books and in the tradition of prophets, who made it clear enough that they did not interpret the law literally. Thus, our religion is divine in the Gospels, in the apostles, and in tradition, but it is absurd in those who misuse it.

According to carnal Jews, the Messiah was to be a great temporal prince. According to carnal Christians, Jesus Christ came to dispense us from loving God, and to give us sacraments that are efficacious without our participation.[14] Neither of these is the Christian, or the Jewish, religion.

True Jews and true Christians have always awaited a Messiah who would make them love God and, through this love, triumph over their enemies.[15]

320

Moses, Deuteronomy 30, promises that God will circumcise their heart to make them capable of loving him.

---

13. See "The Mystery of the Jewish people," in the introduction of this edition. The notion that the Old Testament patriarchs and prophets were "Christian by anticipation" is not new. It is particularly elucidated in the preface to Le Maistre de Sacy's translation of the Old Testament. Like Sacy, Pascal opposes "carnal Christians" to "spiritual Jews." Nowhere in Pascal's writings about the Jews, Sellier maintains, is there any hint of the vicious notion of "Deicide." Rather, we might qualify Pascal's position as a kind of "anti-Judaism," which is derived essentially from Saint Augustine. See Sellier's introduction to *Pensées* (2010), 64. Sellier's exculpation should be tempered, however, in view of such fragments as 342, where Pascal justifies the Jews' constant wretchedness: "It is a surprising thing and one worthy of particular attention to see this Jewish people survive for so many years and to see it always wretched, since it is necessary as a proof of Jesus Christ both that it survive in order to authenticate him, and that it be wretched because they crucified him."

14. See the tenth *Provincial Letter*.

15. I.e., their sins. See fr. 300.

321

Carnal Jews hold the middle place between Christians and heathen. Heathen do not know God and only love earthly things. Jews know the true God and love only earthly things. Christians know the true God and do not love earthly things. Jews and heathen love the same objects. Jews and Christians know the same God.

There were two kinds of Jews: the first only had heathen sensibilities; the others had Christian sensibilities.

[XXIII] Proofs of Moses[1]

322
Another circle[2]

The longevity of the patriarchs, rather than causing the loss of past events, served, on the contrary, to preserve them. For the reason why we are sometimes insufficiently well-informed about the history of our ancestors is that we have hardly ever lived with them, and they often died before we reached the age of reason. Now, when men lived for such a long time, children lived for a long time with their fathers. They spent a long time conversing with them. And what else would they have talked about except the history of their ancestors? For all history was reduced to that, since they had no studies, sciences, or arts, which make up a good deal of daily conversation. So we see that in those days peoples took particular care to preserve their genealogies.[3]

323

This religion, so great in miracles; holy, pure, irreproachable, learned, and mighty witnesses; martyrs; established kings (David), Isaiah a prince of the royal blood; this religion so great in learning, after having displayed all its miracles and all its wisdom, it rejects it all and says that it has neither wisdom nor signs, only the cross and folly.[4]

For those who, by these signs and this wisdom, have earned your belief and have proved their good character to you, declare to you that none of all this can change us and enable us to know and love God, other than the virtue

---

1. Given the importance of the first books of the Bible in his arguments, Pascal opens this dossier to establish the historicity of the Pentateuch, still universally thought in his time to be written by Moses alone. Pascal sees in Moses a historian who is almost a contemporary of what he writes concerning the origins of the world in the fifteenth century before Christ.

2. See the end of fr. 313. Here Pascal signals another passage he circled in his copy of Montaigne's *Essays* (II, 18, 612: "What a satisfaction it would be to me to hear someone tell me, in this way, of the habits, the face, the expression, the favorite remarks, and the fortunes of my ancestors!"), which inspired the fragment which follows.

3. See below, ch. XXIII, n. 5.

4. 1 Corinthians 1:18.

contained in the folly of the cross, without wisdom or signs, and certainly not the signs without this virtue. Thus our religion is foolish if you examine the efficacious cause, but wise if you examine the wisdom that prepares for it.

324
Proofs of Moses

Why should Moses make men's lives so long, with so few generations?

Because it is not the length of years, but the multitude of generations that makes things obscure.

For truth is only corrupted as men change.[5]

And yet he puts two of the most memorable things ever imagined, namely, the Creation and the Flood, so close that you can touch them.[6]

If we must give up eight days, we ought to give up our whole life.
Proofs of Moses.

325

As long as there were prophets to uphold the law, the people were negligent. But after there were no more prophets, zeal has prevailed.

326

Josephus[7] hides his nation's shame.
Moses hides neither his own shame nor ... [8]
Who will grant me that all the people might prophesy? [9]
He was weary of the people.[10]

5. Until Moses composed the Pentateuch, the transmission of the accounts of such essential historical events as the Creation, the Fall, the Flood, and the lives of the patriarchs was oral and would have been subject to alteration had not only five generations separated Moses from the Creation (fr. 327). Modern Biblical scholarship has established that the longevity of the patriarchs was used figuratively as a mark of homage and honor.

6. See fr. 327.

7. The historian Flavius Josephus (37–c.100 CE), a Hellenized Jew, author of the *Jewish Wars* and the treatise *Against Apion*, recounts in his twenty-volume *Antiquities of the Jews*, the history of the world from a Jewish perspective for an ostensibly Greco-Roman audience.

8. [... *nor that of his nation*]. The Pentateuch was not invented by the Jews. Had it been, would Moses have retained such self-incriminating episodes as their worship of the golden calf? Unlike Moses, Josephus passes over the incident in silence.

9. Numbers 11:29. Moses, seeing that only two Israelites were prophesying, proclaims: "O *that all the people might prophesy*, and that the Lord would give them his spirit!" Pascal follows the text of the Vatable Bible.

10. Numbers 11:14: "I am not able alone to bear this entire people, because it is too heavy for me." It is not clear how these two scriptural citations figure in Pascal's argument.

327

Shem, who saw Lamech, who saw Adam, also saw Jacob, who saw those who saw Moses. Therefore the Flood and the Creation are true. This evidence is conclusive among certain people who understand the matter properly.[11]

328

Zeal of the Jewish people to its law, especially after there were no more prophets.[12]

---

11. See fr. 741: "This proof suffices to convince reasonable people of the truth of the Flood and the Creation. The providence of God, seeing that the Creation was beginning to fade into the distance, provided a historian who may be described as contemporary." The argument concerning the longevity of the patriarchs had been used by the entire exegetical tradition Pascal inherited. However, in arguing that only five generations (during the two thousand years reckoned by contemporary chronologists) stood between Moses and Adam, Pascal exceeds anything any previous exegete had dared conclude.

12. The zeal with which the Jews remained attached to the law of Moses, argues Pascal's mentor Le Maistre de Sacy, assured their survival. "Their reprobation became more useful to the Church than would have been their conversion." Dispersed throughout the world, the Jew served as irreproachable witnesses to the historicity of the Old Testament and as promulgators of its prophecies of Christ.

[XXIV] Proofs of Jesus Christ[1]

329

Order—Against the objection that scripture has no order.

The heart has its own order, as does the mind, which goes by principle and demonstration.[2] The order of the heart is different. You do not prove that you should be loved by giving an ordered account of the causes of love. That would be absurd.

Jesus Christ, Saint Paul have the order of charity,[3] not of the mind, because they wanted to inspire, not to instruct.

The same is true of Saint Augustine. This order consists principally of a digression on each point that relates to the conclusion, without ever losing sight of it.

330

The Gospel only speaks of the virginity of the Virgin before the birth of Jesus Christ. Everything in relation to Jesus Christ.[4]

331

Jesus Christ in such a state of obscurity (in the world's understanding of obscurity) that historians,[5] who were only writing of the important affairs of kingdoms, hardly noticed him.

1. Pascal's proofs of the veracity of Jesus Christ take several forms. The prophetic fragments anticipate the following chapter, "Prophecies," which will constitute the greatest proof of Christ. Pascal also undertakes an exegesis of those New Testament citations that speak to Christ's divinity and examines the person of Jesus in the context of the "Three Orders." See the introduction, "The Three Orders."

2. Pascal further explains the order of the mind in "The Three Orders" and in the treatise *On the art of persuasion*. See Nicholas Hammond, "Pascal's *Pensées* and the Art of Persuasion" in *The Cambridge Companion to Pascal*, 235–52.

3. Again, see "The Three Orders," in the introduction of this edition.

4. Pascal is alluding to the tradition of the perpetual virginity of Mary. Here, however, he appeals not to holy tradition, but only to the text of the New Testament itself.

5. Historical references to Jesus are slim. In his *Annals* Tacitus mentions a *Christos* as being convicted by Pontius Pilate during the reign of Tiberius. Suetonius mentions the *Christians* as being persecuted by

332
Holiness

I will pour out my spirit.[6] All peoples were in a state of faithlessness and concupiscence, all the earth was afire with love. Princes left their splendor behind, young girls suffered martyrdom. Where did this power come from? It was because the Messiah had arrived. These were the effects and the marks of his coming.

333

Combinations[7] of miracles.

334

An artisan who speaks of riches, a solicitor who speaks of war, of royalty, etc. But the rich man speaks well of riches, the king speaks dispassionately of a great gift he has just made, and God speaks well of God.[8]

335
Proofs of Jesus Christ

Why the *Book of Ruth* has been preserved.
Why the story of Thamar.[9]

336
Proofs of Jesus Christ

They were not really captives since they were assured of being delivered in seventy years' time. But now they are captives without any hope.[10]

Nero. More disputed are those passages in the *Antiquities of the Jews* of Josephus (end of first century CE), which recount his career as "the brother of James the Just."

6. Joel 2:28. "*I will pour out my spirit* upon all flesh, and your sons and your daughters shall prophesy."

7. Having rejected miracles as the basis of his Apology, Pascal here insists upon *combinations* of miracles taken together.

8. The simplicity of the style of the Gospels speaks to the divinity of Jesus. The quintessential study of this fragment is Sellier's, "Rhétorique et apologie: Dieu parle bien de Dieu" [Rhetoric and apology: God speaks well of God], in *Port-Royal et la littérature. Pascal*, 2nd ed. (Paris: Champion, 2010).

9. See fr. 268. According to the Gospels (Matthew 1:1–16; Luke 3:23–38), only two accurate genealogies of Jesus run through the innumerable and confusing genealogies of the Old Testament. Thus the unexpected importance of Tamar in Genesis 38 and of Ruth, to whom an entire book is denoted.

10. See fr. 345. Jeremiah 25 11–12, prophesies that the captivity of the Jews in Babylon will last seventy years. However, once their Temple was destroyed forever in 70 CE, the Jews had no hope of being liberated from their oppression. Because they had been blinded to serve as hostile witnesses to the historicity of the Old Testament, they had no hope of enlightenment.

God promised them that even if he dispersed them to the ends of the earth, nonetheless if they were faithful to his law he would bring them back together again. They are very faithful to it, and yet remain oppressed.[11]

337

The Jews, by testing to ascertain whether he was God, showed that he was man.

338

The Church has had as much difficulty in showing that Jesus Christ was man, against those that denied it, as in showing that he was God. And the appearances were just as great on both sides.[12]

339[13]

The infinite distance between bodies and minds is a figure of the infinitely more infinite distance between minds and charity, for charity is supernatural.

None of the splendor of greatness has any luster for people who are engaged in the pursuits of the mind.

The greatness of people who pursue the life of the mind is invisible to kings, to the rich, to captains, to all these princes of the flesh.

The greatness of wisdom, which is nothing if not of God, is invisible to people of the flesh and to those of the mind. They are three different orders. By their nature.

11. Deuteronomy 28:1–5. See "the Mystery of the Jewish People," in the introduction of this edition.

12. Pascal evokes the heresies of the Gnostics, the Nestorians, the Monophysites, and others, who advanced the proposition that Jesus had less than full humanity. Nestorius taught the disunion of Christ's divine and human natures. Condemned at the Council of Ephesus (431 CE), his doctrine provoked a reverse heresy, Monophysitism, according to which Jesus had but a single divine nature. Both heresies were finally repudiated by the Council of Chalcedon (451 CE), which established the doctrine that Christ was both "true man" and "true God" and confirmed the Virgin Mary's status as *Theotokos* ("Mother of God").

13. The definitive analysis of what scholars call "The Three Orders," which begins here, is that of Jean Mesnard, "Le Thème des trois ordres dans l'organisation des *Pensées*" [The Theme of the three orders in the organization of the *Pensées*] in *La Culture du XVIIe siecle* [The culture of the seventeenth century] (Paris: PUF, 1992), 462–84. The fragment is explained more fully under the rubric "The Three Orders" in our introduction. One of the several tripartite paradigms in the *Pensées* (see frs. 192 and 681), it is an indispensable key to the entire Apology. Christ stands in an order (that of sanctity and charity) that is totally separate from, and cannot be breached by, the orders of power and intellect. "From all physical bodies and minds, it would be impossible to bring forth the slightest impulse of charity." Sellier views the fragment as one of the most magnificent "poems" in the entire *Pensées*. Fr. 761 probably represents a second version of the fragment.

Geniuses have their dominion, their radiance, their greatness, their victory, and their allure, and have no need of carnal greatness, with which they have no affinity. They are seen not with the eyes but with the mind. That is enough.

Saints have their dominion, their radiance, their victory, and their luster, and have no need of carnal or intellectual greatness. Such greatness stands in no relationship to them because it adds nothing to them nor takes anything away from them. They are recognized by God and by the angels, and not by inquisitive bodies and minds. God is enough for them.

Archimedes[14] without any allure would enjoy the same veneration. He fought no battles visible to the eyes, but he gave his discoveries to the minds of all mankind. How brilliantly he shone for such minds!

Jesus Christ with no possessions, and with no outward manifestation of learning, is in his own order of holiness. He did not make any discoveries, he did not reign, but he was humble, patient, holy, holy, holy[15] to God, terrifying to demons, and without any sin. With what great pomp and in what prodigious magnificence he came to the eyes of the heart, which perceive wisdom!

It would have been pointless for Archimedes to play the prince in his books on geometry, even though he was one.[16]

It would have been pointless for Our Lord Jesus Christ,[17] in order to reveal his brilliance in his reign of holiness, to come as a king. But he truly came with the brilliance of his own order.

It is indeed ridiculous to be scandalized by the lowliness of Jesus Christ, as if this lowliness were of the same order as the greatness that he came to reveal.

Let us consider this kind of greatness in his life, in his passion, in his obscurity,[18] in his death, in the choosing of those who were his own,[19] in their

---

14. Archimedes of Syracuse, c. 287–c. 212 BCE), was a Greek mathematician, physicist, inventor, and astronomer. Although few details of his life are known, he is regarded as one of the leading scientists of antiquity. References to Archimedes's lever are ubiquitous in seventeenth-century French texts—including panegyrics of Louis XIV, where the Sun-King is presented as the fixed point of balance, capable of setting the universe in motion.

15. This is a liturgical echo of the thrice-holy *Sanctus* in the preface to the canon of the Mass, the prayer of consecration.

16. Plutarch (*Marcellus*, 14) makes Archimedes a relative of King Hieron, the tyrant of Syracuse.

17. An echo of the liturgical formula.

18. See above, ch. XXIV, n. 5.

19. Of his apostles and followers, such as Mary Magdalene, the first witness to his Resurrection.

abandonment of him, in his secret resurrection,[20] and in all the rest. We shall see that it is so great that we will have no reason to be scandalized by lowliness, which is nowhere to be found in it.

————

But there are some people who can only be impressed by carnal greatness, as if there were no such thing as intellectual greatness. And others who are only impressed by manifestations of intellectual greatness, as if there were none that were infinitely higher, in the realm of wisdom.

————

All bodies, the firmament, the stars, the earth and its kingdoms, are not worth the least of minds. For the mind knows all these things, and itself, yet bodies know nothing.

————

All bodies and all minds put together and all their output are not worth the least impulse of charity. That is of an infinitely higher order.

————

From all bodies put together, we could not succeed in producing a single tiny thought; that is impossible and of another order. From all bodies and minds we cannot produce a single impulse of true charity; this is impossible and of another, supernatural, order.

340
Proofs of Jesus Christ

Jesus Christ said great things so simply that he seems as though he had given no thought to them, and yet so clearly that we easily see what he thought about them. Such clarity combined with such spontaneity is remarkable.

341
Proofs of Jesus Christ

The hypothesis that the apostles were impostors is quite absurd. Take it to its logical conclusion, and imagine these twelve men meeting after the death of Jesus Christ to hatch a plot saying that he had risen from the dead! In so doing they would have been at odds with all the authorities. Men's hearts are strangely attracted by fickleness, by change, by promises, by possessions. To however small a degree any one of these men might have repudiated his story

20. A response to the objection implicit in fr. 331. Whereas traditional apology had stressed, and continues to stress, the very public witness to the Risen Christ, Pascal, ever attentive to the theme of the *Deus absconditus,* implies that only the elect were accorded the privilege. Just as God had hidden himself in Christ's humanity, so he remains just as hidden in Christ's Resurrection.

on account of these attractions, to say nothing of the fear of imprisonment, torture and death, all of them would have been lost.

That is the logical conclusion!

342

It is a surprising thing and one worthy of particular attention to see this Jewish people survive for so many years and to see it always wretched, since it is necessary as a proof of Jesus Christ both that it survive in order to authenticate him, and that it be wretched because they crucified him. And although it is contradictory to be both wretched and to survive, it nonetheless still survives in spite of its wretchedness.

343

Read the prophecies.
See what has been accomplished,
Collect what is left to be accomplished.[21]

344

Canonical writers

The heretics, in the early days of the Church, serve to authenticate the canonical writers.[22]

345

When Nebuchadnezzar led his people away, in order that it should not be believed that the scepter had been taken from Judah, they were told beforehand that they would not be there for long and yet that they would be there, and that they would be restored.[23]

———

They were always consoled by the prophets, their kings endured.

But the second destruction[24] carries no promise of restoration, with no prophets, no king, no consolation, no expectations, because the scepter is taken away forever.

21. Saint Augustine, *Letter* 137, 4, no. 16. *City of God*, VII, 32; X, 32.

22. Pascal is thinking of the Gnostics, the Manicheans, and the Priscillianists, who by contesting the received canon of the scriptures led the Church to firmly close the canon.

23. See fr. 336.

24. This is the second destruction of the Temple in Jerusalem by the armies of Titus in 70 CE. The first had been committed by Nebuchadnezzar in 587 BCE.

346

Moses was the first to teach the Trinity,[25] original sin, the Messiah.

David a great witness.

King, good, forgiving, pure soul, good mind, powerful, he prophesies,[26] and his miracle happens. That is infinite.

He only had to say that he was himself the Messiah, if he had been vain enough, because the prophecies concerning him are clearer than those concerning Jesus Christ.

And the same is true of Saint John.[27]

347

Who taught the evangelists the qualities of a perfectly heroic soul so as to allow them to depict one so perfectly in Jesus Christ? Why do they make him weak in his agony? Do they not know how to depict constancy in death? Yes. Because the same Saint Luke depicts the death of Saint Stephen[28] as stronger than that of Jesus Christ.

So they make him capable of fear, before dying becomes inevitable, and thereafter completely strong.

But when they make him so troubled, it is when he is troubling to himself.[29] And when men trouble him, he is utterly strong.

348

The commitment of the Jews to their law and their temple. Josephus and Philo Judæus, *Embassy to Caius*.[30]

What other people has such commitment? They certainly needed it.[31]

---

25. Moses, author of the Pentateuch, recounts the visit of the Three Strangers to Abraham in Genesis 18. Augustinian teaching always presents the Old Testament saints as beholding from afar and as through a veil, the whole of revelation to come.

26. David prophesies of his victory over Goliath, 1 Samuel 17:36–37 and 46–47.

27. Saint John the Baptist.

28. Acts 7:58–59.

29. See fr. 749, the "Mystery of Jesus," Pascal's meditation on the Agony in the Garden.

30. The Greek philosopher of Jewish origin, Philo of Alexandria (15 BCE–50 CE), in his *Embassy to Caius* [*Ad Caium*] (14ff) recounts the vigorous objection mounted by the Jews against the emperor Caius Caligula, who wanted to erect a statue of himself in the Jewish Temple in Jerusalem. On Philo, see below, ch. XXIX, fr. 417, n. 11.

31. In order for the prophecies contained in the scriptures to be preserved accurately and in their entirety.

(*Figures*)

Jesus Christ foretold with respect to the time and the state of the world. The leader drawn out from the thigh,[32] and the fourth monarchy.[33]

_____

How fortunate we are to have such light in such darkness!

_____

How beautiful it is to see with the eyes of faith Darius and Cyrus, Alexander, the Romans, Pompey and Herod acting without knowing it for the glory of the Gospel![34]

349
The apparent discrepancies between the Gospels.[35]

350
The Synagogue preceded the Church; the Jews, Christians. The prophets foretold the Christians; Saint John, Jesus Christ.

351
Macrobius.[36] Innocents killed by Herod.[37]

352
Any man can do what Mohammed did, for he performed no miracles; his advent was not foretold. No man can do what Jesus Christ did.

32. Genesis 49:10: "Judah shall not want a branch from his stem, a prince drawn from his stock (*dux de femore ejus*), until the day when he comes who is to be sent to us, he, the hope of the nations."

33. See the prophecy of Daniel 2, translated in fragment 720. The four monarchies are presented in a different version in Daniel 7.

34. When viewed from the perspective of the prophecies, secular history takes on an entirely new meaning. Darius, Cyrus, Alexander, and the Romans are the "four monarchies" of Daniel 8:20–25, which must precede the arrival of the Messiah. Pompey, the conqueror of Jerusalem, and Herod act without suspecting it to accomplish the prophecy of the removal of the scepter from Judea, which must also come to pass before the Messiah can arrive. The powerful of this world are but pawns in the hands of Divine Providence. Like God himself, the history of salvation is hidden from human reason and can only be perceived by "the eyes of faith."

35. The discrepancies among the four Gospels testify to the fact that they were not fabricated in concert by the early Christians but come from different oral traditions. Still a major motif in modern Christian apologetics, this conclusion has been bolstered by a hundred and fifty years of New Testament research concerning the origins of the four texts and a hypothetical Q-text no longer extant.

36. Writing in the early fifth century CE, Macrobius was one of the last pagan writers of Ancient Rome. In his *Saturnalia*, a compendium of ancient Roman religious and antiquarian lore, he idolizes Rome's pagan past. See fr. 623.

37. Matthew 2:16.

353

The apostles were either deceived or deceivers. Both are difficult to believe, since it is not possible to imagine that a man has risen from the dead.

———

While Jesus Christ was with them, he could sustain them. But afterwards, if he did not appear to them, who made them act as they did?[38]

38. The great leitmotiv of Pauline preaching. If Christ's Resurrection is not true, Christians are the most unfortunate of all people.

[XXV] Prophecies[1]

354

The Jews and heathen ruined by Jesus Christ.
All the nations shall come and adore before him.[2]
It is but a small thing that, etc. Isaiah.[3]
Ask of me.[4]
And all kings shall adore him.[5]
Unjust witnesses.[6]
He shall give his cheek to to him that striketh him.[7]
They gave me gall for my food.[8]

355

That idolatry would be overthrown, that this Messiah would overturn all idols, and bring men into the religion of the true God.[9]

1. The Apology has been moving toward this chapter from the beginning of the historical *liasses.* "The prophecies are the greatest proof of Jesus Christ" (fr. 368). Pascal first invokes the monumental changes in both the religious and secular realms that speak to Christ's having changed the entire course of human history. Then he comes to what he sees as the ultimate demonstration of the truth of Christianity, the fulfillment of the Old Testament prophecies in the New Testament. Those unbelievers who have been sincerely seeking the truth and who have followed his arguments in good faith up until this point will be, he believes, convinced by this ultimate argument.

2. Psalm 85:9: "*All the nations* thou hast made *shall come and adore before* thee."

3. Isaiah 49:6: "*It is but a small thing that* thou shouldst be my servant to raise up the tribes of Jacob." Pascal returns again and again to this verse. *Parum est ut . . .* The election of the Jews was "but a small thing" from the perspective of the conversion of the masses of the Gentiles through the fulfillment of the prophecies accorded them but which they failed to understand.

4. Psalm 2:8: "*Ask of me,* and I will give thee the Gentiles for thy inheritance, and the utmost parts of the earth for thy possession."

5. Psalm 72:11:"*And all kings* of the earth *shall adore him.*"

6. Psalm 35:11: "*Unjust witnesses* rising up have laid to my charge things I knew not."

7. Lamentations 3:30.

8. Psalm 69:21: "And *they gave me gall for my food,* and in my thirst they gave me vinegar to drink." A prophecy of an episode in the crucifixion of Jesus. Modern scholars now see the process as the reverse of that traditional exegesis which Pascal invokes. The writers of the Gospels sought in the Old Testament prophecies with which to illustrate their narrative.

9. Ezekiel 30:13: "Thus saith the Lord God: I will also destroy the idols, and I will make an end of the idols of Memphis: and there shall be no more a prince of the land of Egypt: and I will cause a terror in the land of Egypt."

That the temples of idols would be cast down and that among all the nations throughout the world, a pure sacrifice would be offered up to him and not a sacrifice of beasts.[10]

356

That he would teach men the way of perfection.[11]

And never before or since has there come any man who taught anything even approaching such divine teaching.

357

That he would be king of the Jews and the Gentiles.[12] And here we see this king of the Jews and the Gentiles oppressed by both, who conspire to kill him, now ruling over both and destroying the religion of Moses in Jerusalem, its center, where he founds his first Church; and he destroys as well the worship of idols in Rome, its center, and establishes his principal Church there.[13]

358

What crowns all this is that it was foretold, so that it may never be said that it happened by chance.

Would not anyone who had only a week to live find that the best wager is to believe that all this is not a stroke of chance?

Now, if we were not in the grip of our passions, a week or a hundred years come to the same thing.

359

After many people had come before him, at last Jesus Christ came, saying: Here I am and now is the time. What the prophets said had to come in the fullness of time, I tell you that my apostles will bring it to pass. The Jews will be rejected; Jerusalem will soon be destroyed. The heathen will enter into the knowledge of God. (Celsus[14] ridiculed this). My apostles will bring this to pass after you have slain the heir of the vineyard.[15]

---

10. Malachi 1:11: "And there is offered to my name *a clean oblation.*" See *Hostiam puram, Hostiam sanctam, Hostiam immaculatam* in the canon of the Tridentine Mass.

11. Isaiah 2:3.

12. Psalm 72:11.

13. Pascal invokes the Petrine doctrine of the primacy of the Roman Church.

14. On Celsus and his attack on early Christianity, see above, ch. XVII, fr. 239, n. 11.

15. Mark 12:6.

And then the apostles said to the Jews: "You will be accursed." And to the heathen: "You will enter into the knowledge of God." And then this came to pass.

360

Then they shall teach no more every man his neighbor, saying: Know the Lord, FOR GOD SHALL MAKE HIMSELF KNOWN TO ALL.[16]

YOUR SONS SHALL PROPHESY. I will pour out my spirit and my fear IN YOUR HEART.[17]

This is all the same thing.

To prophesy is to speak of God, not by outward proofs, but from an inward and IMMEDIATE sense.

361

That Jesus Christ would be small in his beginning and would increase thereafter. The little stone of Daniel.[18]

Supposing I had never heard anything at all about the Messiah, nevertheless, after seeing such remarkable predictions about the course of the world fulfilled, I see that this is divine. And if I knew that these same books foretold a Messiah, I should feel certain that he would come, and seeing that these books set the time before the destruction of the second temple,[19] I would say that he had come.

362

Prophecies

The conversion of the Egyptians.

Isaiah 19:19:[20]

An altar in Egypt to the true God.[21]

---

16. Jeremiah 31:34.

17. Joel 2:28: "I *will pour out my spirit* upon all flesh: and *your sons* and your daughters *shall prophesy.*"

18. Daniel 2:34–5: "A stone was cut out of a mountain without hands: and it struck the statue upon the feet thereof that were of iron and of clay, and broke them in pieces."

19. In 70 CE.

20. "In that day there shall be an altar of the Lord in the midst of the land of Egypt."

21. The altars of the Egyptians had been to demonic gods. Those of the first (Coptic) Christians would be to "the true God."

363

At the time of the Messiah, this people follow two separate directions.

The spiritual ones embraced the Messiah. The fleshly ones remained to bear witness to him.

364

Prophecies

Had a single man written a book predicting the time and circumstances of the coming of Jesus Christ, and Jesus Christ had come in accordance with these prophecies, this would carry infinite weight.

But there is even more here. Here is a succession of men during four thousand years,[22] constantly and invariably following one after another to foretell this same coming. Here is an entire people proclaiming it. They have endured for four thousand years in order to give testimony as one to their certainty of it, from which they cannot be diverted by whatever threats and persecutions made against them. This is wholly on another scale.

365

Prophecies

The time foretold by the condition of the Jewish people, by the condition of the heathen people, by the condition of the temple, by the number of years.[23]

366

Hosea 3.[24]

_____

Isaiah 42, 48: *I foretold it of old* so that they might know it was I, 54, 60, 61, and the last chapter.[25]

_____

Jaddus to Alexander.[26]

22. It was universally believed in Pascal's time that the world was only four thousand years old at the coming of Christ.

23. See below, ch. XXV, n. 34.

24. Hosea 3:4–5: "For the children of Israel shall sit many days without king, and without prince, and without sacrifice, and without altar, and without ephod [sacred mantle] and without theraphim [images to consult]. And after this the children of Israel shall return, and shall seek the Lord their God, and David their king; and they shall fear the Lord, and his goodness in the last days."

25. When Pascal translates or summarizes those chapters from Isaiah (see frs. 294, 297, 735), he emphasizes two points: the mission of the Gospel to the Gentiles and the reprobation of the Jews.

26. An allusion to a passage in Flavius Josephus's *History of the Jews* (11, 8). According to Josephus, the high priest Jaddus contradicted Alexander the Great, who consequently worshipped the God of the Jews.

367

It takes boldness to predict the same thing in so many ways. The four idolatrous or pagan monarchies, the end of the kingdom of Judah, and the seventy weeks all had to come to pass at the same time. And all this before the second temple was destroyed.[27]

368

The prophecies are the greatest proof of Jesus Christ.[28] It is also for them that God made the most provision, because the event that fulfilled them is a miracle continuing from the birth of the Church to the end. Thus God raised up prophets in the course of one thousand six hundred years, and for four hundred years afterwards dispersed all of these prophecies with all the Jews, who carried them to every corner of the world.[29] Such was the preparation for the birth of Jesus Christ, and, since his Gospel was to be believed by the entire world, not only did there have to be prophecies to make men believe it, but these prophecies had to be spread throughout the world for the whole world to embrace it.

369

Herod believed to be the Messiah.[30] He had taken away the scepter from Judah. But he was not of Judah. This produced a considerable sect.

And Bar Kochba and another accepted by the Jews. And the rumor that was heard everywhere at that time. Suetonius, Tacitus, Josephus.[31]

---

27. See fr. 370. See below, ch. XXV, n. 34.

28. This sentence, often glossed over, is the key to the entire Apology. The prophecies of the Messiah in the Old Testament and their confirmation in the New Testament are the ultimate proof of Christ's unique salvific role as the son of God.

29. Pascal does not allude to the complete dispersal of the Jewish people by the Romans in 70 CE after the destruction of the Second Temple. Rather, he refers to the last four hundred years recounted by the Old Testament, beginning with their exile to Babylon. Contemporary chronologists, basing sacred history on the supposition that the world was about six thousand years old, placed the deportation to Babylon in the "year of the world" 3400, six hundred years before the birth of Christ. However, since chronologists differed on the date of Creation, Pascal's estimate of four hundred years would not have seemed unreasonable. Having read Josephus and Philo of Alexandria, Pascal would have also known of the existence of Jewish communities all over the Greek and Roman Empires. This dispersal of the Jews and their prophecies prepared the Gentiles to receive the Gospel.

30. See fr. 297. The prophets had predicted that the scepter would not leave Judea until the arrival of the Messiah. Herod the Great (74 BCE–4 BCE) proved the prophecy false, Pascal notes, by removing the scepter from Judea. He was declared by the Roman Senate "King of the Jews," but he was not born in Judea. Jesus encounters the "Herodians" several times. In Matthew 22:16, they ask him if it is lawful to give tribute unto Caesar. See also Mark 3:6, 8:15, and 12:13.

31. All the allusions in this paragraph come from Grotius's The Truth of the Christian Religion (1643), III, 2 and 4; V, 14, 17, 19. Bar Kochba led an uprising against the Roman occupation in 132 CE. He was pro-

What kind of man had the Messiah to be, since through him the scepter was to remain eternally in Judah, but at his coming the scepter had to be removed from Judah?

———

So that seeing they should not see and hearing they should not hear,[32] nothing could have been better devised.

Curse of the Jews against those who calculate the periods of time.[33]

370[34]

Predictions

That in the fourth monarchy,[35] before the destruction of the second temple,[36] before the dominion of the Jews was taken away,[37] in the seventieth week of Daniel,[38] while the second temple was standing, the heathen would be instructed and brought to the knowledge of the God worshipped by the Jews;

———

claimed King and Messiah. Grotius cites Suetonius's *Life of Claudius,* 25, and Tacitus's *Annals,* 15. Suetonius, Tacitus, and Josephus are the sole secular writers who ever allude to Christ. Traditional Christian apologists had accorded the references great importance. Pascal, both suspicious of secular sources and insisting upon the obscurity of the historical Jesus, accords them no importance. For Pascal, Jesus was as hidden in profane history as he is in the Eucharist. See fragment 339, in which he speaks of Christ's "secret resurrection."

32. Isaiah 6:9–10. The Jews were blinded to the meaning of the very prophecies that they dispersed throughout the world. See fr. 264: "One understands nothing of the works of God unless one takes as a first principle that his intention was to blind some and enlighten others."

33. Pascal inadvertently wrote "Curse of the *Greeks.*" According to Sellier, the correction "Jews" is justified by a discovery of Paul Ernst. Sellier, ed., *Pensées* (2010), 327. Pascal takes up a passage of the medieval *Pugio fide* (fr. 213), in which the rabbi Jonathan prohibits the Jews on pain of death from calculating the date of the Messiah's coming.

34. As it stands, the argument in fr. 370 is so abbreviated that it is well-nigh incomprehensible. Fortunately, we have the scriptural commentaries of Le Maistre de Sacy, translator of the Bible of Port-Royal, and probably Pascal's mentor in scriptural exegesis. Sacy's commentary on the second, eighth, and ninth books of Daniel greatly clarifies Pascal's argument. Sacy explains that the four monarchies in Daniel's dream are those of the Chaldeans, the Medes, the Persians, and the Greek and Roman empires. The "seventy weeks" predict the year of Christ's death. Daniel 9:24–27 adds parts of the prophecy neglected by Pascal. The calculation, some five hundred years before Christ's death, must begin at the commandment to rebuild Jerusalem after the Babylonian captivity. Christ will be put to death after "seven weeks, and threescore and two weeks" after the commandment to rebuild Jerusalem. Sacy explains that "weeks" means "weeks of years" as in Leviticus. Sacy multiplies seven times seventy, arriving at the number 490. These years must subsequently be adjusted since verse 27 predicts Christ's death "in the middle of this last week." Subtracting four years from 490 years, Sacy arrives at the number 486. Sacy learned from Lancelot's *Sacred Chronology* that the order to rebuild the temple takes place in "Year of the World" 4036. Adding the previous calculation from Daniel of 486 years, Sacy comes up with "Year of the World" 4036. Using the ancient date of Christ's birth as 6000 BCE, Sacy interprets Daniel 9 as predicting that Christ would be put to death in the year 36 CE. Sacy's commentaries accompanied his translations, and they can also be found in several editions. See Isaac-Louis Le Maistre de Sacy, *L'Histoire du Vieux et du Nouveau Testament, représentée avec des figures et des explications* . . . par le Sieur de, prieur de Sombreval [Le Maistre de Sacy], 3rd ed. (Paris: Le Petit, 1671), esp. 315–334.

35. Daniel 2, translated in fr. 720.

36. Haggai 2, translated in fr. 718.

37. Genesis 49, translated in fr. 719.

38. Daniel 9, translated in fr. 720.

that those who love him would be delivered from their enemies and filled with the fear and love of God.

And it came to pass that under the fourth monarchy, before the destruction of the second temple, etc. the multitude of the heathen worshipped God and led the life of angels.

———

Maidens dedicate their virginity and their life to God. Men renounce all pleasures. What Plato was not able to persuade a few chosen and highly educated men to accept, a secret force makes hundreds of thousands of ignorant men believe by the power of a few words.

The rich abandon their wealth. Sons and daughters abandon the luxury of their parents' houses for the austerity of the desert, etc.[39] See Philo Judæus.[40]

What is all this? It is what has been foretold so much earlier. For two thousand years no heathen had worshipped the God of the Jews.[41] At the time foretold, the multitudes of the heathen worship this one and only God. The temples are destroyed, and even kings submit to the cross. What is all this? It is the spirit of God spreading over the earth.

No heathen believed from the time of Moses to that of Jesus Christ, according to the rabbis themselves. And then after Christ, the multitude of the heathen believe in the books of Moses and observe their essence and their spirit, rejecting only what was of no use.[42]

371

The prophets, having given various signs that were all to come to pass at the coming of the Messiah, all these signs had to appear at the same time. Thus the fourth kingdom would have to come when Daniel's seventy weeks ended and the scepter had to be removed from Judah. And all this happened without any difficulty. And then the Messiah had to come. And then came Jesus Christ, calling himself the Messiah; and this again was without any difficulty. This bears the stamp of the truth of the prophecies.[43]

39. Pascal does not seem to realize that the first cenobites did not flee the world for the Egyptian desert until almost the fourth century and that the first Western religious foundations for women and for men were not established until the sixth century. He writes as if the monastic calling dated from the time of the apostolic Church.

40. In his treatise *On the Contemplative Life*, Philo of Alexandria, praised the *Jewish* sects such as the Essenes, who were devoted to austerity and withdrawal from the world. Pascal, like several of the Church Fathers, thinks that Philo's reference is to the early *Christian* ascetics.

41. Pascal appears to know nothing about the ancient tradition of the "righteous Gentiles."

42. "Multitude of the heathen." Pascal appears to move the time of Constantine back to the apostolic age.

43. See above, ch. XXV, n. 34. The long scriptural passages translated by Pascal in fragments 720, 718, and 719 suggest that he might have fleshed out this argument considerably.

372

We have no king but Caesar.[44] Therefore Jesus was the Messiah, since they had no longer any king, but a foreigner, and they did not want another.

373

Prophecies

The seventy weeks of Daniel are ambiguous with regard to when they begin because of the terms of the prophecy, and as regards their end because of the differences between chronologists. But all this difference only amounts to two hundred years.[45]

374

Prophecies

The scepter was uninterrupted by the Babylonian captivity because the return was prompt and foretold.[46]

375

Prophecies

The great Pan is dead.[47]

376

What can we feel but reverence for a man who clearly foretells things that come to pass, who declares his intention both to blind and to enlighten and who mingles obscurities with clear things that come to pass?

377

It is but a small thing. Isaiah.[48] Vocation of the Gentiles.

44. John 19:15. The coming of a foreign sovereign would signal the imminent arrival of the Messiah (Genesis 49:8–10).

45. The "seventy weeks" were to be calculated from "the commandment to rebuild Jerusalem." Is Pascal thinking of the edict of Cyrus (538 BCE) or those of Artaxerxes (458, 435 BCE)? Counting back through the genealogies of the Old Testament, pre-modern chronologists had attempted to establish the year of the Creation in modern notation. Ancient tradition held that Christ was born in the 4000th year of the Creation. The science of geology lay 150 years in the future. The abyss of Deep Time was never even suspected. Even Voltaire would later consider the world to be only about 25,000 years old. On this chronology, see above, ch. XXV, n. 34.

46. See fr. 345.

47. Plutarch, *The Cessation of Oracles*, 17. The theme of the silencing of the entire pantheon of pagan gods by the death of Christ on the cross was an apologetic mainstay beginning with Eusebius, if not before. Some sources place the oracle in the mouth of the prophetess at Delphi when consulted by Julian the Apostate.

48. Isaiah 49:6. See above n. 3 and fr. 254. The first dispensation, the election of the Jews, would appear but "a small thing" when viewed from the vocation of all the peoples of the earth.

378
Predictions

It has been foretold that, at the time of the Messiah, he would come to establish a new covenant that would make them forget the Exodus from Egypt—Jeremiah 23:5,[49] Isaiah 43:16 [50]—that he would implant his law, not externally, but in the heart; that he would put his fear, which had only been in outward things, in their inmost heart. Who cannot see the Christian law in all this?

379
Prophecies

That the Jews would reject Jesus Christ and that they would be rejected by God for that reason. That the chosen vine would yield only sour grapes. That the chosen people would be unfaithful, ungrateful, and unbelieving. *To a people that believeth not, and contradicteth me.*[51]

28:28: That God will strike them with blindness and that they would grope at midday like blind men.[52]

That a forerunner would come before him.[53]

380

The eternal reign of the line of David: 2 Chronicles.[54] By all the prophecies, and with an oath. And not fulfilled temporally. Jeremiah 33:20.[55]

---

49. "I will raise up to David a just branch: and a king shall reign [...] and shall execute judgment and justice in the earth."

50. Isaiah 43:16–19: "Thus saith the Lord, who made a way in the sea, and a path in the mighty waters. Who brought forth the chariot and the horse, the army and the strong: they lay down to sleep together, and they shall not rise again: they are broken as flax, and are extinct. Remember not former things, and look not on things of old. Behold I do new things, and now they shall spring forth, verily you shall know them: I will make a way in the wilderness, and rivers in the desert."

51. Isaiah 5:1–7, 65:3. The phrase, which Pascal writes in Latin for emphasis (*populum non credentem et contradicentem*) actually comes from Romans 10:21.

52. Deuteronomy 28:28–29: "The Lord strike thee with madness and blindness and fury of mind. And mayst thou grope at midday as the blind is wont to grope in the dark."

53. Malachi 3:1: "Behold I send my angel and he shall prepare the way before my face."

54. 2 Chronicles 7:18: "I will raise up the throne of thy kingdom, as I promised to David thy father, saying: There shall not fail thee a man of thy stock to be ruler in Israel."

55. "If ye can break my covenant of the day, and my covenant of the night, and that there should not be day and night in their season."

[XXVI] Particular Figures[1]

381
Particular figures
Law, double; Tables of the law, double; temple, double; captivity, double.

382

(Japhet begins the genealogy).[2]

———

Joseph[3] crosses his arms and prefers the younger.[4]

1. "In order to strengthen the case for the truth of the messianic prophecies, which are of infinite consequence to all humanity, God has prepared specific prophecies: a certain Jewish victory in battle, a certain event which came to pass [...]. The fulfillment of these 'particular prophecies' predisposed the Jewish people to believe in the messianic prophecies. The same distinction applies to figures. Some of them are only internal to Jewish history. The captivity in Egypt prefigures that in Babylonia, etc." Sellier, in Pascal, *Pensées*, ed. Sellier (2010), 332n1.

2. "According to Saint Augustine (*City of God*, XVI, 3), among the sons of Noah Sem prefigured the Jews and Japheth the Christians. By beginning his genealogy with Japheth, the younger, Moses predicted the rejection of the Jewish people (Genesis 10:2). Pascal struck this line, either because it was 'too great a figurative' or because it was a matter of a universal figure." Sellier, in Pascal, *Pensées*, ed. Sellier (2010), 332n2.

3. "Joseph": a mistake for *Jacob*.

4. See Genesis 48:13–14. "Pascal appears to have noted this down from reading Saint Augustine's *City of God* (XVI, 42). Pascal translated this citation in fr. 719. Ephraim, the younger son chosen by his father Jacob, in fact did prosper among the tribes of Israel." Sellier, in Pascal, *Pensées*, ed. Sellier (2010), 332n3.

[XXVII] Christian Morality[1]

383

Christianity is strange: it commands man to recognize that he is vile and even abominable, and it commands him to want to be like God. Without such a counterweight, this elevation would make him horribly vain, or this abasement would make him horribly abject.

384

Wretchedness persuades of despair.

Pride persuades of presumption.

The Incarnation shows man the greatness of his wretchedness by the greatness of the remedy that was required.

385

Neither an abasement that would make us incapable of good, nor saintliness exempt of evil.[2]

386

There is no doctrine more appropriate for man than the one that teaches him of his double capacity to receive and to lose grace because of the double peril to which he is always exposed of despair or of pride.

1. This *liasse* assembles notes that would apparently have demonstrated the superiority of Christian ethics and ideals. This "so divine morality" constitutes one of the principle "foundations" of the Christian religion. Christianity appears as a strange paradox, urging man to recognize his abominable nature yet to aspire to the divine. Unlike any religion that has ever existed, Christianity mandates not only loving God but hating the self.

2. See fr. 240.

387

Of all that which is on earth he[3] partakes only in the pains and not the pleasures. He loves those close to him, but his charity is not confined within those limits and extends to his enemies, and then to those of God.

388

What difference between a soldier and a Carthusian monk as regards obedience? For they are equally obedient and dependent, and in equally arduous exercises. But the soldier always hopes to become the master and never does, for captains and even princes are always slaves and dependent, but he always hopes, and always strives to come to that point, whereas the Carthusian monk takes a vow never to be anything but dependent. Thus they do not differ in their perpetual servitude, which always binds both, but in the hope that one always entertains and the other, never.

389

No one is as happy as a true Christian, nor as reasonable, as virtuous, as worthy of love.

390

With what little pride does a Christian believe himself united with God! With what little abjection does he see himself on a par with earthworms! What a beautiful way to face life and death, goods and ills.

391

The examples of the resolute deaths of Spartans[4] and others hardly move us. For what does that do for us?

But the example of the death of the martyrs moves us, for they are our members.[5] We have a common bond with them. Their resolution can shape ours, not only by their example, but because it has perhaps deserved ours.

There is nothing of this kind in the examples of the heathen. We have no bond with them. Just as one does not become rich by seeing a stranger who is rich, but by seeing that one's father or husband is.

---

3. He: the Christian.

4. The three hundred Spartans who made a last stand against a massive Persian army at the Battle of Thermopylae in 480 BCE.

5. In the unity of Christ's mystical body. See Romans 13:5 and 12:4–5.

392
Morality

Having made heaven and earth, which do not feel the happiness of their being, God decided to create beings who would know that happiness and who would compose a body of thinking members. For our members do not feel the happiness of their union, of their wonderful accord, of the nurturing care nature takes to direct the spirits[6] there and to make them grow and endure. How they would rejoice if they could feel it, if they could see it! But for that they would have to possess intelligence to know it, and good will to consent to that of the universal soul.[7] And if, having been granted intelligence, they used it to retain all nourishment for themselves without allowing it to pass to the other members, they would not only be unjust but also wretched, and they would hate themselves rather than loving themselves, since their beatitude as well as their duty consists in consenting to the conduct of the whole soul to which they belong, which loves them more than they love themselves.

393

Are you less a slave for being loved and flattered by your master? You are certainly well off, O slave, your master flatters you. But soon he will beat you.[8]

394

The individual will would never be satisfied, even if everything it wants were in its power. But we are satisfied from the moment that we renounce the will. Without it, we cannot be unhappy; with it, we cannot be happy.

395

They[9] give concupiscence a free hand and rein in scruples, whereas it should be the other way around.

396

It is superstitious to place one's hopes in formalities, but it is arrogant not to want to submit to them.

---

6. In Classical physiology, animal spirits were thought to be corpuscles inciting the movement of the members of the body.

7. The soul that rules the entire body.

8. See Augustine, *Enchiridion*, 29–30.

9. The morally laxist casuists.

397

Experience shows us an enormous difference between piety and goodness.[10]

398

Two kinds of men in every religion.
See "Perpetuity."[11]

399

Superstition, concupiscence.[12]

400

Not formalists

When Saint Peter and the apostles deliberate about abolishing circumcision, which required acting against the law of God, they do not consult the prophets but only the reception of the Holy Spirit in the person of the uncircumcised.[13]

They judge it more certain that God approves those whom he fills with his Spirit than that the law should be observed.

———

They knew that the end of the law was but the Holy Spirit and thus, since it was indeed received without circumcision, it was not NECESSARY.[14]

401

Members
Begin with this.

To regulate the love that we owe to ourselves, we must imagine a body full of thinking members, for we are members of the whole, and see how every member ought to love itself, etc.

———

10. Montaigne, *Essays*, III, 12, 988: "Practice makes us see an enormous distinction between piety and conscience."
11. See fr. 318.
12. The link between the two concepts is clarified in frs. 209, 255, 318, and 451.
13. Acts 15:5–11.
14. Acts 15.

Republic

The Christian Republic,[15] and even the Jewish one, had only God for its master, as Philo Judæus remarks, ON MONARCHY.[16]

When they fought it was for God alone, and their hope rested principally on God, they considered their cities only as belonging to God and kept them for God. 1 Paralipomenon 19:13.[17]

402

To ensure that the members are happy, they must have a will and must make it conform to the body.

403

You have to imagine a body full of thinking members!

404

To be a member is to have life, being, and movement only through the spirit of the body and for the body. The separated member, no longer seeing the body to which it belongs, has but a withering and dying being. However, it believes itself to be a whole and, seeing no body on which it depends, it believes that it depends only on itself and wants to make itself center and body of itself. But, possessing no principle of life in itself, it does nothing but go astray and is bewildered by the uncertainty of its being, since it does sense that it is not a body, and yet it does not see that it is a member of a body. At last, when it comes to know itself, it is as if it had returned home and it loves itself thereafter only for the body. It regrets its past straying ways.

By its nature, it could not love another object except for itself and in order to subjugate it, because everything loves itself above all else. But in loving the body it loves itself, because it has being only in it, by it, and for it. *But he who is joined to the Lord, is one spirit.*[18]

———

The body loves the hand, and the hand, if it had a will, should love itself in the same way as the soul loves it. All love that goes beyond is wrong.

But he, who is joined to the Lord, is one spirit. We love ourselves because

---

15. The "City of God," of which the Church on earth is but an image.

16. Philo, *The First Book of Monarchy.*

17. I.e., Chronicles. Joab says to his brother Abishai, in the moment when they marched against the Syrians and the Ammonites: "Be of good courage and let us behave ourselves manfully for our people, and for the cities of our God: and the Lord will do that which is good in his sight."

18. 1 Corinthians 6:17.

we are members of Jesus Christ. We love Jesus Christ because he is the body of which we are a member. All is one. The one is in the other. Like the three Persons.[19]

405

We must love only God and hate only ourselves.[20]

———

If the foot had never known that it belonged to the body and that there was a body on which it depended, if it only had knowledge and love of itself, and then came to learn that it belonged to a body on which it depended, what regret it would feel, what dismay over its past life, for having been useless to the body that imparted life to it, which would have destroyed it if it had separated itself from the member in the same way that the member had separated itself from the body! What entreaties it would make to be retained there! And with what humility would it allow itself to be governed by the will that ruled the body, to the point of consenting to be cut off if necessary! Otherwise it would lose its status as a member, for every member should be willing to perish for the body, for the sake of which alone everything exists.

406

If the feet and the hands had their own will, they could never be in their proper order, except by submitting their own will to the primary will that governs the whole body. Otherwise, they are in disorder and despair. But by wishing only what is good for the body, they bring about their own good.

407

Philosophers have consecrated vices by attributing them to God himself. Christians have consecrated virtues.

408

Two laws[21] suffice to govern the entire Christian republic better than all political laws.

19. Of the Trinity.
20. Augustine, *The City of God*, XIV, 28. On hatred of the self, see above, ch. XVII, fr. 253, n. 23.
21. Those that command the love of God and the love of others. See Matthew 22:37–39.

[XXVIII] Conclusion[1]

409

What a distance there is from knowing God to loving him.[2]

410

"If I had witnessed a miracle," they say, "I would convert." How can they be sure they would undertake that which they know nothing about? They imagine that this conversion consists in the worship of God as an exchange or a conversation, such as they picture it.[3] True conversion consists in annihilating oneself[4] in the face of that universal Being whom we have angered so many times and who may legitimately send you to hell at any moment.[5] It consists in recognizing that we can do nothing without him and that we have deserved from him nothing but the withdrawal of his grace. It consists in understanding that there is an invincible opposition between God and us, and that without a mediator[6] there can be no communication with him.

411

Miracles serve, not to convert, but to condemn. I, q. 113, a. 10, ad 2.[7]

---

1. These fragments appear to Sellier to be Pascal's prefatory notes for the writing of the conclusion of the second part of the Apology, "Knowledge of God."
2. The entire Apology can take the seeker no further than the knowledge of God that invites belief and to the threshold of learning to love God.
3. Pascal dismisses this impertinent claim on the part of the unbelievers with the rebuke that they have no notion whatsoever of what true "conversion" means. They suppose that worshipping God is like some kind of business transaction in which one's prayers are answered in return for performing certain acts of devotion or charity.
4. Pascal's metaphor of self-annihilation goes much further than the notion of self-hatred in frs. 405, 253 (and n. 23), and 494.
5. See Pascal's last words: "May God never abandon me." "Legitimately": because of the transmission of original sin.
6. Only Christ's salvific work on the cross makes communion with God possible. God reaches out to man, not the contrary.
7. Thomas Aquinas, *Summa theologica*, I, q. 113, a. 10, ad 2.

412

You should not be surprised to see simple people believe without reasoning about it: God fills them with love for him and hatred of themselves; he inclines their hearts to believe. We will never believe, with an effective belief and faith, unless God inclines our heart. And we will believe as soon as he does incline it.

And this is what David fully understood: *Incline my heart O God into,* etc.[8]

413

Those who believe without ever having read the Testaments do so because they have a truly holy inner disposition[9] and because everything they hear about our religion is in accordance with it. They sense that a God has created them. They wish to love only God; they wish to hate only themselves. They sense that they do not have the strength to do this by themselves, that they are incapable of going to God, and that, unless God comes to them, they are incapable of any communication with him, and they hear it said in our religion that we ought to love only God and to hate only ourselves, but that, all of us being corrupt and incapable of God, God made himself man in order to be at one with us. Nothing more is needed to convince men who have this disposition in their heart and who possess this understanding of their duty and of their incapacity.

414

Knowledge of God

Those whom we see to be Christians without knowledge of the prophecies and proofs judge of Christianity no less soundly than those who possess that knowledge. They judge with their hearts as the others judge with the mind. It is God himself who inclines them to believe, and thus they are most effectively convinced.

(*Someone might reply that unbelievers would say the same thing. But to that I reply that we possess proofs that God truly inclines those he loves to believe the Christian religion and that unbelievers have no proof at all of what they say. And so, while our propositions may seem similar as to their use of terms, they differ in that one lacks proof whereas the other is most soundly proved.*)[10]

---

8. Liturgical response drawn from Psalm 119:36. Pascal had a particular affection for this psalm, which his Parisian Breviary included in every daily devotion.

9. The "poor in spirit" have this "truly holy inner disposition" because Christ dwells in them, just as he does in the Gospels and in the Holy Eucharist.

10. Pascal realizes that the context of the "holy poor" is no place to again take up the objections of

I freely admit that one of those Christians who believe without proofs may not have the means of convincing an unbeliever who might say the same of himself. But those who know the proofs of religion will easily prove that this believer is truly inspired by God, even though he cannot prove it himself.

For since God said through his prophets (who are undoubtedly prophets) that in the reign of Jesus Christ he would pour out his spirit upon the nations, and that the sons, daughters, and children of the Church would prophesy,[11] there is no doubt that the spirit of God is upon them and not upon the others.

---

the atheists. He strikes these lines, going on to simply admit that those who do not need proofs in order to believe would not have the intellectual ability to refute an "unbeliever." Conversely, however, the intellectual believer, armed with the proofs of the Apology, will easily be able to prove the divine inspiration of the "poor in spirit."

11. Joel 2:28. See ch. XXIV, fr. 332, n. 6.

The Folders Set
Aside in 1658

[XXIX] Against the Fable of Esdras[1]

415
Against the Fable of Esdras

2 Maccabees 2[2]

_____

Josephus, *Antiquities*, 2, 1.[3] Cyrus[4] released the people on account of Isaiah's prophecy.

The Jews peacefully held possessions under Cyrus in Babylon. Hence they could well have had the law.

_____

In the entire story of Esdras, Josephus does not mention one word about this restoration. 4 Kings 17:27.[5]

---

1. The apocryphal "Fourth Book of Esdras" relates that the original Torah (Pentateuch) in the Tabernacle was lost when the Temple was burned at the time of the Babylonian exile and reconstituted by Esdras under divine inspiration (14, 22). Pascal insists on the historicity of the Pentateuch and dismisses this account as a "fable." The "Fourth Book of Esdras" was probably written as a consolation after the final destruction of the Second Temple in 70 CE. Pascal takes such great pains to refute this account because 4 Esdras was well known as an apocalyptic vision and as a liturgical source. Verses from 4 Esdras had been much integrated into the Roman Liturgy. The cherished *introitus* of the Requiem Mass is loosely based on chapter 2, 34–35: "Eternal rest grant unto them, O Lord, and may light perpetual shine upon them."

2. 2 Maccabees 2:5–7. Jeremiah himself hid "the tabernacle and the Ark [containing the original Torah received by Moses] and the altar of incense" in a "hollow cave" on the mountain Moses had ascended, blocking the door so that no one could find it. The hiding place was to remain unknown "until God gathered together the congregation of the people, and received them to mercy."

3. On Flavius Josephus, see ch. XXIII, n. 7.

4. "Cyrus the Great" (600–530 BCE) issued the edict in 538 BCE that allowed the Israelites to return home. He even ordered the rebuilding of the Temple of Jerusalem, returned the vessels that had been looted from the Temple, and committed funds from his treasury.

5. 4 Kings of the Vulgate is 2 Kings in the Authorized Version and in all modern translations. Ch. 17:27–28: "And the King of the Assyrians commanded, saying: Carry thither one of the priests whom you brought from thence captive, and let him go and dwell with them: and let him teach them the ordinances of the God of the land." Had the Torah perished in the fire that destroyed the temple, the returning priests would have no "ordinances" to teach concerning the true "God of Israel."

416

If the fable of Esdras is believable, then we must believe that scripture is holy scripture, for this fable is based only on the authority of those who tell that of the Seventy,[6] which shows that scripture is holy.

Therefore, if this story be true, we have our account; if not, we have it from elsewhere. Thus, those who would like to destroy the truth of our religion,[7] based on Moses, establish it with the same authority with which they attack it. So, through this providence it still endures.

417

On Esdras

Fable: the Books were burned with the temple. Disproved by Maccabees: JEREMIAH GAVE THEM THE LAW.[8]

Fable: That he recited all of it by heart.

Josephus and Esdras point out that HE READ THE BOOK.[9]

Baronius,[10] *Annals* 180: *Among the ancient Hebrews none can be found who maintains that the books were destroyed and restored by Esdras, except in the Esdras IV.*

Fable: that he changed the letters.

Philo[11] in his Life of Moses: *The language and characters in which the law was previously written remained so until the Seventy.*[12] Josephus says that the law was in Hebrew when the Seventy translated it.

---

6. Towards the end of the third century BCE, a group of Hellenized Jewish scholars in Alexandria took up the project of translating the Hebrew Bible into Greek. Legend has it that this translation was the work of seventy sages. Hence the title "Septuagint." The translation, cited in the Pauline Epistles, was made for the Alexandrian Jews who could not read Hebrew, at a time when Koine Greek was the *lingua franca* of the eastern Mediterranean.

7. Pascal seems to be referring to those erudite and scholarly atheists, who are not his usual adversaries in the Apology. See "Religious Challenges to the Modern Reader," in the introduction.

8. See n. 2 above.

9. Esdras 2:8, and 5:1–8. Josephus, *Jewish Antiquities*, book XI, ch. 5; see Josephus, *Jewish Antiquities, Volume IV*, trans. Ralph Marcus, The Loeb Classical Library (Cambridge: Harvard University Press, 1937).

10. Cesare Baronius (1538–1607) was an ecclesiastical historian, whose *Ecclesiastical Annals* offer a history of the Church organized by year; thus "*Annals* 180" refers to the year 180 after Jesus Christ.

11. Philo of Alexandria was the most important representative of Hellenistic Judaism. Rejecting a literal interpretation of the Hebrew Bible, he sought use allegory to harmonize Greek and Jewish philosophy.

12. Philo, *Life of Moses*, II; see *Philo Volume VI: On Abraham, on Joseph, on Moses*, trans. F. H. Colson, Loeb Classical Library (Cambridge: Harvard University Press, 1935). See also Josephus, *Jewish Antiquities*, XII; see Josephus, *Jewish Antiquities, Volume V*, trans. Marcus, 2, 14.

Under Antiochus[13] and Vespasian,[14] when they wanted to abolish the Books and there was no prophet, it could not be done. And under the Babylonians when there were no persecutions and there were so many prophets, would they have let them be burned?

———

Josephus mocks the Greeks who would not tolerate . . .

418

Tertullian:[15] *He could equally have restored it under the inspiration of the Holy Spirit after it had been destroyed by the violence of the cataclysm, just as, after the destruction of Jerusalem by the Babylonian attack, every document of Jewish literature is generally agreed to have been restored by Esdras.* Tertullian, book 1, *On the Apparel of Women*, ch. 3.

He says that Noah could just have as easily reconstructed from memory the book of Enoch,[16] lost in the Flood, as Esdras could have reconstructed the scriptures lost during the captivity.

The scriptures were destroyed when the people were the captives of Nebuchadnezzar. After seventy years the Jews returned to their country, and later, in the time of Artaxerxes, king of the Persians, Esdras, priest of the tribe of Levi, reconstructed from memory, through divine inspiration, all the sayings of the prophets of the past and restored to the people the law once given by Moses.[17]

He alleges this to prove that it is not incredible that the Seventy could have explained the holy scriptures with that uniformity we admire in them. Eusebius, *Ecclesiastical History*, book 5, ch. 8. And he took this from Saint Irenaeus,[18] book 3, ch. 25.

In his preface to the Psalms, Saint Hilary[19] says that it was Esdras who put the Psalms in order.

13. Antiochus was the king of Syria (d. 163 BCE) whose attempt to impose Greek culture on the Jews met with violent resistance.

14. Vespasian was the Roman emperor (d. 79 CE) who subjugated Judea during the Jewish rebellion of 66 CE.

15. Tertullian (160–225 CE) is an African Church Father and author of a long list of apologetic works. He is considered the Father of Latin Christianity and the founder of Western theology.

16. Excluded both from the Hebrew Bible and the Septuagint, the Book of Enoch is received as canonical only by the Ethiopian Orthodox Church and is extant only in their sacred language, Ge'ez. It is purportedly written by Noah's great-grandfather, Enoch, and describes his visits to heaven in the form of visions and recounts the fall of the angels.

17. This passage, which Pascal copied out in Greek from Eusebius's *Ecclesiastical History*, constitutes a part of the Latin text at the end of the fragment. The translation offered in the text is derived from Sellier's translation of the passage into French; see Pascal, *Pensées*, ed. Sellier (2010), 347n1.

18. Saint Irenaeus (c.130–c.200 CE), recognized by the Church as the first great Catholic theologian, established the authority of the episcopate, and that of the canon of scripture, the co-ordinate authority of all four Gospels, and the unity of the Father and the Son in revelation.

19. Saint Hilary of Poitiers (c. 325–67 CE) was known as the anti-Arian "Athanasius of the West" and

The origin of this tradition comes from the fourteenth chapter of the fourth book of Esdras.

———

God was glorified, and the scriptures were recognized as truly divine, for they all rendered the same things in the same words and the same phrases, from beginning to end, so that even the people today understood that the scriptures had been interpreted through God's inspiration. And it is not surprising that God accomplished this through them, for the scriptures were destroyed when the people were the captives of Nebuchadnezzar, after seventy years the Jews returned to their country, and later in the time of Artaxerxes, king of the Persians, Esdras, priest of the tribe of Levi, was inspired to reconstruct all the sayings of the previous prophets and to restore to the people the law once given by Moses.[20]

———

much later proclaimed "Doctor of the Church." His chief works were written against the Arians. His other works include commentaries on the Psalms and on Matthew, in which he closely followed Origen. On Arianism, see ch. XXII, fr. 317, n. 12.

20. This is Pascal's rendering in Latin of the passage from Eusebius, of which the last lines are copied out in Greek, above.

[XXX] Miracles[1] [1]

419

The main points that I have to raise with M. l'abbé de Saint-Cyran[2] are the following. But since I have no copy of them, would he please take the trouble to return this sheet with the answers that he will kindly provide.

1. Whether it is necessary, for an effect to be deemed miraculous, that it be beyond the power of men, demons, angels, and all created nature.

Theologians state that miracles are supernatural either in substance, quoad substantiam (*as when two bodies occupy the same space, or the same body occupies two different spaces, simultaneously*); *or that miracles surpass nature in the way that they are effected,* quoad modum (*as when they are brought about by means of things which have no natural power to effect them, such as when Jesus Christ cures the eyes of the blind man using mud; and Saint Peter's mother-in-law by bending over her; and the woman, suffering from a flow of blood, when she touches the hem of his robe*). *And most of the miracles that he performed in the Gospels are of this second kind. So too is the curing of a fever, or any other illness when it is performed in an instant or more completely than nature allows, through touching a relic or by invoking the name of God; so that the thinking of the person proposing these problems is correct and in conformity with all theologians, even with those of this day and age.*

---

1. *Liasses* XXX–XXXII, which Sellier entitles Miracles [1]–[3], would not have figured in the Apology at all. They go back to 1656–57, when Pascal considered the possibility of writing an apology based on miracles. The miraculous healing of Marguerite Périer, Pascal's niece and goddaughter, by the intervention of the "sacred thorn" inspired Pascal to reflect upon the nature of miracles. Examining the matter in the next three *liasses*, Pascal becomes aware not only of the rarity of contemporary miracles and the paucity of genuine eye witnesses, but also of their inability to impress, let alone convert, the hardened *libertins*. In the "Conclusion" (XXVII) of the titled *liasses*, the *libertins* jest: "'If I had witnessed a miracle,' they say, 'I would convert'" (fr. 410). Citing Aquinas, Pascal can only conclude: "Miracles serve, not to convert, but to condemn" (fr. 411). In the Apology, it will be the biblical prophecies and their fulfillment that will constitute an enduring miracle (fr. 368).

2. This dossier constitutes a consultation with Martin de Barcos, nephew of the famous Abbé de Saint-Cyran, the collaborator and friend of Jansenius. Pascal, who knows Saint Augustine by heart, knows little of Scholasticism. But he knows that the theology of the miracle is treated extensively in Saint Thomas Aquinas's *Summa theologiæ*. Pascal's questions were set down before their submission. Barcos's answers are in italics.

2. Whether it is not sufficient that it be beyond the natural power of the means that are used to perform it, by which I mean that every effect is miraculous, which exceeds the natural power of the means that are used to perform it. And so, I call it a miracle when an illness is cured through touching a holy relic; when a person possessed by a demon is cured by invoking the name of Jesus, etc., because these effects exceed the natural power of the words with which God is invoked and the natural power of a relic, which cannot cure the sick or drive out demons.

But to drive out demons by the art of the devil I do not call a miracle, because whenever the power of the devil is used to drive out the devil, the effect does not exceed the natural power of the means used for that purpose. I have therefore come to the conclusion that the true definition of a miracle is the one that I have just put forth.

Whatever the Devil is able to accomplish is not a miracle, any more than what an animal is able to accomplish, even though a man cannot accomplish it by his own powers.

3. Whether Saint Thomas is not opposed to this definition, and whether he is not of the opinion that an effect, in order to be miraculous, must exceed the power of all creation.

Saint Thomas is of the same opinion as the others, although he divides the second kind of miracle into two groups, namely into miracles that are quoad subjectum,[3] *and miracles that are* quoad ordinem naturae.[4] *He states that the first ones are those that nature can produce absolutely, but not in a particular subject: for example, nature can produce life, but not in a dead body. He states that the second ones are those that nature can produce in a subject, but not by a particular means, or so quickly, etc., for example when a fever or other illness, although not incurable, is cured in an instant and through a single touch.[5]*

4. Whether professed and known heretics can perform real miracles in order to confirm an error.

5. Whether professed and known heretics can perform miracles, such as curing illnesses that are not incurable; whether they can, for example, cure a fever in order to confirm an erroneous statement of doctrine. Father Lingendes preaches that they can.[6]

True miracles can never be performed by anyone, whether Catholic or heretic, saint or evildoer, in order to confirm an error, because God would be giving his seal

---

3. "As regards their subject."
4. "As regards the order of nature."
5. Aquinas, *Summa theologiæ,* I, q. 105, a. 8.
6. An allusion to a Lenten sermon preached by Fr. Claude de Lingendes "On the miracles of Christ," at the Church of Saint-Merri.

of approval to error as a false witness, or rather as a false judge, to confirm and approve error. This is certain and established.

6. Whether professed and known heretics can, by invoking the name of God or by using a holy relic, perform miracles that are beyond the power of all created nature.

They can do so for a truth to be confirmed, and there are historical examples of this.

7. Whether covert heretics who, while not separating themselves from the Church, are nonetheless in error, and who, in order to lead more easily the faithful into error and strengthen their own party, do not profess themselves to be against the Church, can, either by invoking the name of Jesus or by using a holy relic, perform miracles that are beyond anything in nature; or even whether they can perform some that are merely beyond the power of men, such as curing instantaneously illnesses that are not incurable.

Covert heretics have no more power to work miracles than professed heretics, since nothing is hidden from God who is the sole author and worker of miracles, of whatever kind they be, provided they are true miracles.

8. Whether miracles performed in the name of God, and by the intermediary of divine objects, are not signs of the true Church; and whether all Catholics have not maintained this as true against all heretics.

All Catholics are in agreement on this, and especially the Jesuit writers. One need only read Bellarmine.[7] Even in those cases in which heretics have performed miracles, something that has happened occasionally although rarely, these miracles were signs of the Church, because they were performed solely so that the truth that the Church teaches be confirmed, and not the heretics' error.

9. Whether it has ever happened that heretics have performed miracles; and of what nature are those they have performed.

There are very few certain ones; but those that are mentioned are miraculous only quoad modum, *that is to say they are natural effects of nature brought about miraculously and in a way that exceeds the natural order.*

10. Whether the man in the Gospels who drove out demons in the name of Jesus Christ and of whom Jesus Christ says: *He that is not against you, is for you,*[8] was a friend or enemy of Jesus Christ; and what the interpreters of the Gospels say about it. I ask this because Father Lingendes preached that this man was opposed to Jesus Christ.

The Gospels give ample evidence that he was not opposed to Jesus Christ; and the Church Fathers maintain this, as do almost all Jesuit writers.

7. Cardinal Robert Bellarmine (1542–1621) was a noted Jesuit polemicist.
8. Mark 9:38–40.

11. Whether the Antichrist will perform his signs in the name of Jesus Christ or in his own name.

Since he will come not in the name of Jesus Christ but in his own name, according to the Gospels, he will not perform miracles in the name of Jesus Christ but in his own name and against Jesus Christ in order to destroy faith and Christ's Church: because of this, they will not be true miracles.

12. Whether the oracles were miraculous.

The miracles of the pagans and idols were no more miraculous than the other works performed by the demons and magicians.

420

The second miracle can presuppose the first; the first cannot presuppose the second.

[XXXI] Miracles [2]

421

5. Miracles.[1]

Beginning

Miracles make the difference between doctrines, and doctrine makes the difference between miracles.

———

There are false ones and true ones. There needs to be a sign so that they be known, otherwise they would be useless.

Now they are not useless and on the contrary they are a foundation.

Now the rule we are given must be such that it not destroy the proof that true miracles give of the truth, which is the primary goal of miracles.

———

Moses gave two: that what was foretold does not come to pass, Deuteronomy 18.[2] And that they do not lead to idolatry, Deuteronomy 13.[3] And Jesus Christ [gave] one.[4]

———

If doctrine is the rule for miracles, miracles are useless for doctrine. If miracles are the rule. . .

Objection to the rule.

Distinction of the times, one rule during Moses, another rule at present.

———

1. The meaning of the number "5" has yet to be elucidated.
2. Deuteronomy 18:22. "Thou shalt have this sign: Whatsoever that same prophet foretelleth in the name of the Lord and it cometh not to pass: that thing the Lord hath not spoken, but the prophet hath forged it by the pride of his mind: and therefore thou shalt not fear him."
3. Deuteronomy 13:1–3: "If there rise in the midst of thee a prophet or one that saith he hath dreamed a dream, and he foretell a sign and a wonder, [a]nd that come to pass which he spoke, and he say to thee: Let us go and follow strange gods, which thou knowest not, and let us serve them: Thou shalt not hear the words of that prophet or dreamer: for the Lord your God trieth you, that it may appear whether you love him with all your heart, and with all your soul, or not."
4. Mark 9:38–40. John tells Jesus that they had seen a man who was not a disciple casting out devils in Jesus' name and that they had tried to stop him. Jesus replies that anyone working a miracle in his name is unlikely to speak evil of him. "He that is not against you is for you."

Any religion is false that, in its faith, does not worship one God as the principle of all things and that, in its morality, does not love one single God as object of all things.

422

Reason why one does not believe

John 12:37:
And whereas he had done so many miracles before them, they believed not in him. That the saying of Isaiah the prophet might be fulfilled: He hath blinded, etc. These things said Isaiah, when he saw his glory, and spoke of him.

———

The Jews require signs, and the Greeks seek after wisdom . . .
But we Christ crucified,[5]
But full of signs, and full of miracles.
While you, a Christ who is not crucified, and a religion without miracles and without wisdom . . .[6]

———

What makes us not believe in true miracles is lack of charity. *John: But you do not believe, because you are not of my sheep.*[7]
What makes us believe in false ones is lack of charity.
2 Thessalonians 2.[8]

Foundation of religion

It is miracles. What then! Does God speak against miracles, against the foundations of the faith that one has in him?

———

If there is a God, there had to be faith in God on earth. Now the miracles of Jesus Christ are not foretold by the Antichrist, but the miracles of the Antichrist are foretold by Jesus Christ. And so if Jesus Christ were not the Messiah, he would certainly have led people into error; but the Antichrist can certainly not lead them into error.

When Jesus Christ foretold the miracles of the Antichrist, did he believe that he was destroying faith in his own miracles?

———

5. 1 Corinthians 1:22–23: "For both *the Jews require signs, and the Greeks seek after wisdom*: But we preach *Christ crucified.*"
6. A text constituted by Pascal, opposing the new theologians to Saint Paul. "*While you* [corrupt theologians, you preach] *a Christ not crucified and a religion without sign nor wisdom.*"
7. John 10:26.
8. 2 Thessalonians 2:9–10. "Whose coming is according to the working of Satan, in all power, and signs, and lying wonders, and in all seduction of iniquity to them that perish; *because they receive not the love of the truth, that they might be saved.*"

There is no reason for believing in the Antichrist that is not a reason for believing in Jesus Christ. But there are some reasons to believe in Jesus Christ that are not reasons for believing in the other.

Moses foretold Jesus Christ[9] and commanded to follow him. Jesus Christ foretold the Antichrist and forbade following him.[10]

It was impossible in the time of Moses for one's belief to be reserved for the Antichrist, who was unknown to them. But it is indeed easy in the time of the Antichrist to believe in Jesus Christ who is already known.

423

The prophecies, the miracles themselves, and the proofs of our religion are not of such a nature that they can be said to be absolutely convincing, but they also are such that it cannot be said that to believe them is to be without reason. There is therefore evidence and obscurity, in order to enlighten some and create obscurity for others. But the evidence is such that it surpasses or at least equals the evidence of the opposite, so that it is not reason that may induce one not to follow it. And therefore it can only be concupiscence and the malice of the heart. And in this way, there is enough evidence to condemn yet not enough to convince, so that, in those who do follow our religion, it be manifest that it is grace and not reason that leads one to follow; and, that in those who flee our religion, it is concupiscence and not reason that leads them to flee it.

Disciples INDEED,[11] an Israelite INDEED,[12] free INDEED,[13] SUSTENANCE INDEED.[14]

I take for granted that one believes in miracles.

You[15] corrupt religion either in favor of your friends or against your enemies. You dispose of it at your pleasure.

424

If there were no false miracles, there would be certainty.

If there were no rule to distinguish between them, miracles would be useless and there would be no reason to believe.

Now, there is, humanly speaking, no human certitude, but there is reason.

9. Deuteronomy 18:15.
10. Pascal's gloss on Matthew 24:24 and Mark 13:21–22.
11. John 8:31. See fr. 654.
12. John 1:47.
13. John 8:36.
14. The Eucharist (John 6:56: "true bread from heaven"). See above, fr. 285.
15. *You*: the Jesuits, who contested the miracle that occurred at Port-Royal.

The Jews, who were called to subdue the nations and kings, were slaves to sin. And the Christians, whose vocation has been to serve and to be subjects, are free children.

Judges 13:23: *If the Lord had wanted to put us to death, he would not have shown us all these things.*[16]

Hezekiah, Sennacherib.[17]

Jeremiah: Hananiah, false prophet, dies in the seventh month.[18]

---

2 Maccabees 3. The temple, about to be pillaged, miraculously rescued.[19] *2 Maccabees* 15.[20]

---

3 Kings 17. The widow to Elijah, who had brought the child back to life: *By this I know that your words are true.*[21]

---

3 Kings 18. Elijah, with the prophets of Baal.[22]

Never in the dispute over the true God, over the truth of religion, has a miracle occurred on the side of error and not on the side of truth.

425

This is not the land of truth, it wanders unknown among men. God has covered it with a veil, which lets it go unrecognized by those who do not hear its voice. This place is open for blasphemy, even against the truths that are at least very apparent. If the truths of the Gospel are proclaimed, the opposite is proclaimed as well, and the issues become so confused that the people cannot

---

16. "*If the Lord had a mind to kill us, he would not* have received a holocaust and libations at our hands, neither would he *have shewed us all these things,* nor have told us the things that are to come."

17. Hezekiah, king of Judah, son and successor of Ahaz. During his reign Sennacherib, King of Assyria, sacked a number of cities in Judah. He laid siege to Jerusalem but, according to 2 Kings 19:35, the siege failed because "it came to pass that night, that an angel of the Lord came, and slew in the camp of the Assyrians a hundred and eighty-five thousand."

18. Jeremiah (28:14–17) correctly predicted that the false prophet Hananius would die within the year: "Therefore thus saith the Lord: Behold I will send thee away from off the face of the earth: this year shalt thou die: for thou hast spoken against the Lord. And Hananius the prophet died in that year, in the seventh month."

19. Heliodorus, who was going to seize the treasures of the Temple, was struck unconscious by three apparitions. He was subsequently converted.

20. God gave Judas Maccabeus victory over the blasphemer Nicanor in spite of his superior troops.

21. 1 Kings 17:24. "Now, *by this I know* that thou art a man of God, and the *word* of the Lord in thy mouth is *true.*"

22. 3 Kings 18:20, ff. Elijah confounds the prophets of Baal by making fire descend from the heavens on the offering.

distinguish among them. And they ask: "What do you have to make people believe you rather than others? What sign do you give? You have only words, and so do we. If you had miracles, that would be good." It is a truth that doctrine ought to be supported by miracles, and this is misused in order to blaspheme against doctrine. And if miracles do happen, it is said that miracles are insufficient without doctrine. And this is another truth they misuse in order to blaspheme against miracles.

Jesus Christ cured the man born blind and performed many miracles on the Sabbath day; in this way he blinded the Pharisees, who said that miracles had to be judged by doctrine.

We have Moses: but as to this man, we know not from whence he is.[23]

Herein is a wonderful thing, that you do not know from whence he is, and yet he works such miracles.[24]

Jesus Christ spoke neither against God, nor against Moses.

The Antichrist and the false prophets foretold by both Testaments will speak openly against God and against Jesus Christ.

He who is not against, he who would be a covert enemy—God would not allow that he perform miracles openly.

Never in a public dispute in which the two parties each say that they belong to God, to Jesus Christ, to the Church, do miracles occur on the side of the false Christians and not on the side of truth.

He hath the devil. John 10:21. *And the others said: Can the devil open the eyes of the blind?*[25]

The proofs that Jesus Christ and the Apostles draw from scripture are not demonstrative proofs. For they say only that Moses has said that a prophet would come, but they do not thereby prove that he is that prophet, and that was the whole question. These passages therefore serve only to show that they were not opposed to scripture and that it presents no contradiction, but not that there is agreement. But this is sufficient: exclusion of contradiction, with miracles.

---

23. John 9:29–30 describes Pharisees' reaction to Jesus' miracles: "*We* know that God spoke to *Moses: but as to this man, we know not from whence he is.*"

24. John 9:30: "The man answered, and said to them: Why, *herein is a wonderful thing that you know not from whence he is,* and he hath opened my eyes."

25. John 10:20–21: "And many of them said: *He hath the devil,* and is mad: why hear you him? *Others said:* These are not the words of one that hath a devil: *Can the devil open the eyes of the blind?*"

426

Jesus Christ says the scriptures bear witness to him.[26] But he does not show specifically in what.

———

Even the prophecies could not prove Jesus Christ during his lifetime. And therefore, one would not have been guilty for not believing in him before his death if miracles had not been sufficient without doctrine. Now, those who did not believe in him while he was still alive were sinners, as he himself says, and they had no excuse. It was therefore necessary that they be given a demonstration that they could resist. Now, they did not have scripture but only miracles. Therefore, miracles are sufficient when doctrine does not contradict them. And they must be believed.

———

John 7:40. Controversy among Jews, as among Christians today.[27]

Some believe in Jesus Christ, others do not believe in him because of the prophecies that said that he was to be born in Bethlehem. They ought to have taken more care to ascertain whether he was in fact not from there, as his miracles being convincing, they ought to have assured themselves thoroughly regarding the so-called contradictions between his doctrine and scripture. And this obscurity did not excuse them but blinded them. Thus, those who refuse to believe the miracles today because of a so-called contradiction, totally imaginary, have no excuse.

The people who believed in him on account of his miracles—the Pharisees say to them: *This people is cursed who does not know the law. But is there a prince or a Pharisee who did believe in him? For we know that no prophet comes out of Galilee. Nicodemus answered: Does our law judge a man before hearing him?*[28]

427

Our religion is wise and foolish. Wise, because it is the most learned and the most founded on miracles, prophecies, etc.; foolish, because it is not all this that makes us embrace it. This is indeed a cause for condemning those who do not embrace it but it does not make those who do embrace it believe. What makes them believe is the cross. *Lest the cross should be made void.*[29]

26. John 5:39. "Search the scriptures, for you think in them to have life everlasting; and the same are they that give testimony of me. And you will not come to me that you may have life."

27. The disputes between the Pharisees and the Sadducees parallel those between the adversaries and partisans of Port-Royal.

28. John 7:48–9; ("Hath any one of the rulers believed in him, or of the Pharisees? But this multitude, that knoweth not the law, are accursed.") 50–2: "*Nicodemus said to them,* (he that came to him by night, who was one of them:) *'Doth our law judge any man, unless it first hear him,* and know what he doth?' They answered, and said to him: 'Art thou also a Galilean? Search the scriptures, and see, that *out of Galilee a prophet riseth not.*'"

29. 1 Corinthians 1:17. Paul refuses to preach according to human wisdom so as not to empty the cross

And thus Saint Paul, who came in wisdom and signs, says that he came neither in wisdom nor in signs: for he came to convert. But those who come only to convince can say that they come in wisdom and signs.

———

There is quite a difference between not being for Jesus Christ and saying so, and not being for Jesus Christ and pretending to be for him. The first ones can perform miracles, not the latter. For it is clear of the former that they are against the truth, not of the latter. And thus the miracles are clearer.

———

It is so manifest that one must love one God alone that no miracles are required to prove it.

———

Fine state for the Church when she is no longer supported except by God.

428

There is a reciprocal duty between God and men. One must pardon this saying: *What could I have done?*[30] *Accuse me*, says God in Isaiah.[31]

God must accomplish his promises, etc.

Men owe it to God to accept the religion that he sends to them.

God owes it to men not to lead them into error.

Now, they would be led into error if miracle workers proclaimed a doctrine that should not appear visibly false in the light of common sense, and if a greater maker of miracles had not already warned against believing them.

Thus, if there were division in the Church, and if the Arians,[32] for example, who said they were founded in scripture like the Catholics, had performed miracles, and not the Catholics, one would have been led into error.

———

For just as a man who announces to us God's secrets is not worthy of being believed on his own authority and that is why the unbelievers doubt him; likewise, a man who, as a sign of the communication that he has with God, raises the dead, foretells the future, parts the seas, cures the sick—there is none so hardened who would not bow down to him, and the incredulity of Pharaoh and the Pharisees is the effect of a supernatural obstinacy.

———

———

of its saving power. "Christ sent me not to baptize, but to preach the gospel: not in wisdom of speech, *lest the cross* of Christ *should be made void.*"

30. Isaiah 5:4 : "*What is* there *that I ought to do* more to my vineyard, that I have not done to it?" God compares Israel to a vineyard that he carefully surrounded and protected.

31. Isaiah 1:18. This is an erroneous translation in the Vulgate. Authorized Version has: "Come now and let us reason together." Jerusalem Bible has: "Come now let us talk this over."

32. On the Arians, see ch. XXII, fr. 317, n. 12.

When, therefore, one sees miracles and a doctrine above suspicion altogether on one side, there is no difficulty. But when one sees miracles and a suspect doctrine on the same side, then one must see which is the clearer. Jesus Christ was suspect.

Bar-Jesus blinded.[33] God's might overcomes that of his enemies.

The Jewish exorcists beaten by the devils saying: *I know Jesus and Paul, but who are you?*[34]

Miracles are for doctrine, and not doctrine for miracles.

If miracles are true, will it be possible to persuade people of any doctrine? No. For that will not happen.
Though an angel . . .[35]

Rule

One must judge doctrine by miracles. One must judge miracles by doctrine. All of this is true, but it does not contradict itself.

For it is necessary to distinguish between the times.

How pleased you are in knowing general rules, thinking thereby to create confusion and render everything useless. You will be prevented from doing so, my Father.[36] The truth is one and firmly established.

It is impossible, from God's duty, that a man who hides his evil doctrine and lets only a good one show and who says that he conforms to God and to the Church, perform miracles in order to insinuate imperceptibly a false and subtle doctrine. This cannot be.

---

33. Acts 13:11. Paul strikes a Jewish sorcerer (Bar-Jesus) with blindness. "And now behold, the hand of the Lord is upon thee, and thou shalt be blind, not seeing the sun for a time."

34. Acts 19:13–16: "Now some also of the Jewish exorcists who went about, attempted to invoke over them that had evil spirits, the name of the Lord Jesus, saying: I conjure you by Jesus, whom Paul preacheth. And there were certain men, seven sons of Sceva, a Jew, a chief priest that did this. But the wicked spirit, answering, said to them: *Jesus I know, and Paul I know; but who are you?*"

35. Galatians 1:8. "But *though* we, or *an angel* from heaven, preach a gospel to you besides that which we have preached to you, let him be anathema." A celebrated text invoked against the Montanists, who claimed to have received private revelations.

36. Fr. François Annat, (1590–1670) was the Jesuit Provincial of Paris and confessor to Louis XIV. An ardent foe of Port-Royal, he was the author of the *Rabat-joie des Jansénistes* [Kill-joy of the Jansenists] (1666), an attack on the miracle of the healing of Pascal's niece Marguerite Périer at Port-Royal. Pascal addresses him in his last two *Provincial Letters.*

And still less that God, who knows the hearts of men, perform miracles in favor of such a one.[37]

429

Jesus Christ verified that he was the Messiah, never by verifying his doctrine through scripture or prophecies, but always through his miracles.

———

He proves by a miracle that he remits sins.[38]

———

Rejoice not in your miracles, says Jesus Christ, but in this, that your names are written in heaven.[39]

———

If they believe not Moses, neither will they believe one risen from the dead.[40]

———

Nicodemus recognizes by his miracles that his doctrine is of God: *Rabbi, we know that thou art come a teacher from God; for no man can do these signs which thou dost, unless God be with him. . . .*[41] He does not judge of miracles by doctrine, but of doctrine by miracles.

———

The Jews had a doctrine about God, as we have one about Jesus Christ, a doctrine confirmed by miracles, and a prohibition against believing in all miracle workers; and what is more, the commandment to have recourse to the high priests and to seek no further.[42] And therefore, all the reasons that we have for refusing to believe miracle workers, they had in regard to their prophets. And yet they were most guilty in their rejection of their prophets because of their miracles and because of Jesus Christ; and would not have been guilty if they had not seen the miracles. *If I had not done . . . they would not have sin.*[43]

Therefore, belief hangs entirely on miracles.

———

A prophecy is not called a miracle. As for example when Saint John speaks of the first miracle in Cana; and then of what Jesus Christ says to the Samari-

---

37. "Such a one" indicates "the man who hides his evil doctrine" in the preceding lines.

38. Mark 2:10–11. Cited in fr. 306. Jesus asks whether it is easier to say to the paralytic, "Your sins are forgiven" or to tell him to stand, pick up his stretcher, and walk. He then proves his authority to forgive sins by telling the paralytic to stand, pick up his stretcher, and walk: "And immediately he arose; and taking up his bed, went his way in the sight of all; so that all wondered and glorified God, saying: We never saw the like."

39. Luke 10:20: "But yet *rejoice not* in this, that spirits are subject unto you; *but* rejoice *in this, that your names are written in heaven."*

40. Luke 16:31.

41. John 3:2.

42. Deuteronomy 18:10-11 and 17:9.

43. John 15:24. "*If I had not done* among them the works that no other man hath done, *they would not have sin they would not have sin."*

tan woman when he uncovers her whole hidden life; and then cures the son of a lord. And Saint John calls that *the second sign.*[44]

430

By showing truth, one makes it believed. But by showing the ministers' injustice, one does not correct it. One assures one's conscience by showing falsehood, one does not assure one's purse by showing injustice.

———

Both miracles and truth are required, because it is necessary to convince the whole man, in body and in soul.

———

Charity is not a figurative precept. It is dreadful to say that Jesus Christ, who came to replace figures in order to set up the truth, came only to set up the figure of charity, in order to take away the existing reality that was there before.

If the light be darkness, what shall the darkness be?[45]

431

There is quite a difference between exposing to temptation and leading into error. God tempts but he does not lead into error. To expose to temptation is to provide occasions such that, while no necessity is imposed, if one does not love God, one will do a certain thing. To lead into error is to impose upon man the necessity of drawing a false conclusion and following it.

432

If thou be the Christ, tell us. . .[46]
The works that I do IN THE NAME OF MY FATHER,
They give testimony of me.
But you do not believe, because you are not of my sheep.
My sheep hear my voice.[47]

John 6:30: *What sign therefore dost thou shew, that we may see, and may believe thee?* They do not say: what doctrine do you preach?[48]

———

44. John 4:54. "This is again *the second miracle* that Jesus did, when he was come out of Judea into Galilee."

45. Matthew 6:23: "*If* then *the light* that is in thee, *be darkness: the darkness* itself how great *shall it be!*"

46. John 10:24. "The Jews therefore came round about him, and said to him: How long dost thou hold our souls in suspense? *If thou be the Christ, tell us* plainly."

47. John 10:25–27.

48. The last sentence is Pascal's commentary (in Latin in the original).

No man can do these signs which thou dost, unless God be with him [49]
2 Maccabees 14:15:
God protects his portion by evident signs.[50]

We want to see a sign, OUT OF THE HEAVEN, TO TEMPT *him.* Luke 11:16.
An evil generation seeketh a sign: and a sign shall not be given. . .[51]
And sighing deeply, he saith: Why doth this generation seek a sign? Mark 8:12.
It was asking for a sign with wicked intent.
Nor could he do.[52] And nevertheless he promises them the sign of Jonah,
the sign of his resurrection, the great and incomparable sign.

Unless you see signs, you believe not.[53] He does not blame them for not believing without miracles, but for not believing without seeing those miracles
themselves.

The Antichrist [whose coming is] *in signs and lying wonders,* says Saint
Paul, 2 Thessalonians 2. *According to the working of Satan. And in all seduction of
iniquity to them that perish because they receive not the love of the truth that they
might be saved. And for this cause God shall send them the operation of error, to
believe lying.* As in the passage of Moses: *The Lord thy God trieth you to know
whether you love him.*[54]

Behold I have told it to you, beforehand. Watch ye therefore.[55]

433

In the Old Testament: Any time you are turned away from God. In the
New: Any time you are turned away from Jesus Christ.

And with that, the occasions for excluding faith in miracles are identified.
No other exclusions should be allowed.

Does it then follow that they had the right to exclude all the prophets who

49. John 3:2. Cited in fr. 429.
50. 2 Maccabees 14:15: "the Jews [. . .] made supplication to him, who chose his people to keep them
forever, and who *protected his portion by evident signs.*"
51. Matthew 12:39. Having been asked for miracles, Jesus answers: "An *evil* and adulterous *generation
seeketh a sign: and a sign shall not be given* it, but the sign of Jonas the prophet."
52. Mark 6:5. Staying in Nazareth and rejected by his own people, Jesus "*could not do* any miracles
there."
53. John 4:48: "*Unless you see signs* and wonders, *you believe not.*"
54. Deuteronomy 13:3: "For the Lord *your God trieth you, that it may appear whether you love him* with
all your heart, and with all your soul."
55. Matthew 24:25 and 42.

came to them? No. They would have sinned in not excluding those who denied God, and would have sinned in excluding those who did not deny God.

———

Therefore, as soon as someone sees a miracle, one must either submit or have unusual signs to the contrary. One must ascertain whether they deny one God, or Jesus Christ, or the Church.

———

Reproach Miton[56] for not lifting a finger.
Since God will reproach him.

434

Though you will not believe me, at least believe the miracles;[57] he refers them as it were to the strongest proof.

———

It had been told to the Jews as well as to Christians that they should not always believe the prophets. But nevertheless, the Pharisees and scribes made much of his miracles and tried to show them to be false or to have been performed by the devil, since they had to be convinced if they recognized they came from God.

———

Today, we need not be troubled to make this distinction. Still, it is very easy to make. Those who deny neither God nor Jesus Christ perform no miracles that are not certain.

There is no man who doth a miracle in my name and can soon speak ill of me.[58]
But we do not have to make this distinction.

Behold a sacred relic, behold a thorn from the crown of the world's Savior, in which the prince of this world has no power, which performs miracles by the very power of this blood shed for us. Behold, God himself chooses this house[59] in order to make his power shine forth.

It is not men who perform these miracles by virtue of an unknown and doubtful power that requires us to make a difficult distinction: it is God him-

---

56. On Miton, see the introduction, nn. 97 and 98. "Not lifting a finger" (*se remuer*, lit. "get moving"): not even making an effort (to seek God).

57. John 10:38: "If I do not the works of my Father, believe me not. But if I do, *though you will not believe me, believe the* works."

58. Mark 9:38. The text that follows celebrates the miracle of the holy thorn, which occurred at Port-Royal on March 24, 1656. Pascal's niece, Marguerite Périer, had suffered from a suppurating lachrymal fistula for three years. She was instantaneously healed when a tiny splinter reputed to come from the crown of thorns, which Jesus was made to wear at his crucifixion, was applied to the wound. See n. 15 in the introduction, in the section on "Pascal's Life"; see also in this edition *The Life of Monsieur Pascal*, §38.

59. The Sisters' convent of Port-Royal in Paris, now the maternity hospital near the R.E.R. metro stop "Port-Royal."

self, it is an instrument of the passion of his only Son, who, existing in many places, chooses this one, and draws men from all quarters to receive this miraculous relief from their afflictions.

435

John 6:26: *not because you saw the miracles, but because you were filled.*[60]

Those who follow Jesus Christ because of his miracles honor his power in all the miracles it produces.

But those who, professing to follow him because of his miracles, follow him in fact only because he comforts them and satisfies them with worldly goods, dishonor his miracles, when miracles threaten their own comforts.

———

John 9. *This man is not of God, who keepeth not the Sabbath. Others said: How can a man that is a sinner perform such miracles?*[61] Which is the clearer?

This is the house of God, for he performed peculiar miracles in it. Others: This house is not of God, because in this house they do not believe that the five propositions are in Jansenius.[62] Which is the clearer?

What sayest thou? I say that he is a prophet. Unless this man were of God, he could do nothing.[63]

436

Contestations.

Abel, Cain.[64]

Moses, magicians.[65]

Elijah, false prophets.[66]

Jeremiah, Hananiah[67]

60. The complete verse reads: "Jesus answered them, and said: Amen, amen I say to you, you seek me, *not because you have seen* miracles, *but because you* did eat of the loaves, and *were filled.*"

61. John 9:16. "Some therefore of the Pharisees said: *This man is not of God, who keepeth not the Sabbath. But others* said: *How can a man that is a sinner do such* miracles? And there was a division among them."

62. By drawing a parallel between the controversies surrounding Jansenius's *Augustinus* (see, in the introduction of this edition, "Port-Royal and Jansenism") and the verse in John 9 cited above, Pascal creates a *pro domo* argument. Port-Royal held that the five propositions attributed to Jansenius and condemned by the Sorbonne were not to be found in the *Augustinus* at all.

63. John 9:17 and 33: "They say therefore to the blind man again: *What sayest thou* of him that hath opened thy eyes? And he said: *He is a prophet.*"

64. Genesis 4:4–5.

65. Exodus 8:16–19. The Egyptian sorcerers serving Pharaoh.

66. I Kings 18:20–39. See fr. 424.

67. Jeremiah 28. See fr. 424. Hananiah: a false prophet who angered the Lord by breaking the wooden yoke from around the neck of Jeremiah: As a punishment the Lord vowed an iron yoke be put upon the Hebrews in the form of servitude under Nebuchadnezzar, the King of Babylon.

Micah, false prophets.[68]
Jesus Christ, Pharisees.[69]
Saint Paul, Bar-Jesus.[70]
Apostles, exorcists.[71]
Christians and infidels.[72]
Catholics and heretics.[73]
Elijah, Enoch;[74] Antichrist.
The truth always prevails in miracles. The two crosses.[75]

437

Jeremiah 23:32: the *miracles* of the false prophets. In the Hebrew and Vatable[76] there are the *sleights-of-hand*.

Miracle does not always signify miracles. 1 Kings 14:15; *miracle* signifies *fear*, and so in the Hebrew.

Likewise in Job manifestly 33:7.

And again Isaiah 21:4. Jeremiah 44:22.

_____

Portentum signifies *image*: Jeremiah 50:38. And so in the Hebrew and Vatable.

_____

Isaiah 8:18. Jesus Christ says that he and his disciples will serve as a miracle.

_____

The Church has three kinds of enemies: the Jews, who have never been part of its body; the heretics, who have withdrawn from it; and bad Christians, who tear it apart from within. Ordinarily, these three different kinds of

_____

68. 1 Kings 22:6–38.
69. For example, in Luke 5:17–26 and John 9:16. See frs. 425 and 435.
70. Acts 13:6–12.
71. Acts 19:13–16. See fr. 428.
72. Infidels: non-Christians, more specifically Muslims.
73. I.e., Protestants.
74. Enoch: the father of Methuselah, and great-grandfather of Noah. Like Elijah he "walked with God," and was translated directly to heaven (Genesis 5:24). The Book of Enoch, accepted as canonical only by the Ethiopian Orthodox Church and surviving complete only in Ethiopia (see above, ch. XXIX, fr. 418, n. 16), embodies a series of revelations on such matters as the origin of evil, the angels and their destinies, and the nature of Gehenna (hell) and paradise.
75. The Feast of the Discovery (Book of Common Prayer: "Invention," May 1) of the True Cross (September 15) recalls how the mother of Constantine (Saint Helena), having excavated the site of Calvary, found two crosses. A number of miracles were required to ascertain which of the two crosses was the true cross carried by Christ.
76. François Vatable, early French Hebraist. Vatable's Bible is the first polyglot text in which the Latin, Greek, Hebrew, and Syriac texts stand in parallel columns (1586). In certain philological matters Pascal has recourse to the sixteenth-century translation of the Bible by Robert Estienne, with notes by Vatable.

adversaries assail it in diverse ways. But here, they are attacking it in one and the same way. Since all of them lack miracles, and as the Church has always had some miracles against them, they have all had the same interest in eluding them; and they all make use of this excuse: that one must not judge of doctrine by miracles, but miracles by doctrine. There were two parties among those who listened to Jesus Christ, the ones who followed his teaching because of his miracles, the others who said ...[77] There were two sides in Calvin's time.[78] There are now the Jesuits,[79] etc.

77. The apostles and the Pharisees.
78. The Protestants and the Catholics.
79. Who deny the miracle of the holy thorn at Port-Royal vs. the Augustinians, whose doctrines the miracle affirms.

[XXXII] Miracles [3]¹

438

Unjust persecutors of those whom God is visibly protecting.[2]

If they reproach you for your excesses—they speak like heretics.[3]

If they say that the grace of Jesus Christ discerns[4] us—they are heretical.

If miracles occur—then it's a sign of their heresy.[5]

It is said: Believe in the Church;[6] but it is not said: Believe in the miracles, because the second is natural and not the first. The one required a precept, not the other.

Ezekiel.
It is said: Behold God's people who speak thus.[7]

Ezekias.[8]

---

1. In this extensive *liasse* Pascal concludes his collection of notes and Biblical citations for his Apology based on miracles, which he soon abandoned. However, in this chapter we find a number of reflections and notes that will be carried over into his preparatory notes for the writing of his Apology for the Christian Religion.

2. *Persecutors*: the Jesuits. *Visibly*: by the signal evidence of the miracle of the holy thorn. See the sixteenth *Provincial Letter*.

3. While Pascal denounces the moral laxity of the Jesuits, the latter respond by accusing Port-Royal of using the same language against them as the Protestants.

4. A fundamental assertion of Saint Augustine and Saint Paul. Among all humanity, which abandoned God in the Fall, God chooses ("discerns") those he wants to save out of a supererogation of his mercy. His justice and his mercy dictate that all be left to their fate. But the ways of God are inscrutable. His gratuitous mercy, so to speak, saves those he distinguishes as the elect.

5. The rather curious thesis of Father Annat in the *Rabat-joie des Jansénistes* [Kill-joy of the Jansenists]. See above, ch. XXXI, fr. 428, n. 36.

6. Matthew 18:17: "And if he [the brother that offended the addressee] will not hear them [a few people gathered as witnesses]: tell the church. And if he will not hear the church, let him be to thee as the heathen and publican."

7. See fr. 470.

8. Ezekiel 22. The prophet's denunciation of Israel's disobedience and God's curse on them. See fr. 424.

The Synagogue was the figure, and so it did not perish, and was only a figure, and so has perished. It was a figure that contained the truth, and so it has endured until it no longer held the truth.

Reverend Father, *all these things happened in figure.*[9] Other religions perish, this one does not.[10]

Miracles are more important than you think. They have served as a foundation and will serve to the continuation of the Church until the Antichrist, until the end. The two witnesses.

<hr>

In the Old Testament and the New, miracles are performed by touching a face, by a greeting, or something useless except in its showing the need to submit to God's creatures.[11]

Figure for the sacraments.

439

All through time, either men have spoken of the true God, or the true God has spoken to men.

<hr>

Two foundations: the one internal, the other external; grace, miracles, both supernatural.

<hr>

The wretches who have forced us to speak of the core of religion.

<hr>

Montaigne against miracles.

<hr>

Montaigne for miracles.[12]

<hr>

Sinners purified without penitence, the righteous sanctified without charity, all Christians without the grace of Jesus Christ, God without power over men's will, predestination without mystery. A redeemer without certitude.[13]

<hr>

Miracles are no longer necessary because enough have already been recorded. But when tradition is no longer observed, when one refers to the pope only, when he is deceived,[14] and when having thus excluded the true source

<hr>

9. 1 Corinthians 10:11: "Now *all these things happened* to them *in figure.*" The same passage is quoted in frs. 285 and 299, in the *liasse* devoted to the figurative nature of the law.

10. A fundamental theme of the Apology formally set down in *liasses* XLIX, LI, and LII.

11. By "God's creatures" Pascal means "God's creation," an important theological distinction.

12. See fr. 440, n. 21, below.

13. Pascal here summarizes his indictment of the Jesuits' theology.

14. An allusion to the Papal Bull *Ad sacram* signed by Pope Alexander VII in October 1656, which declared that Jansenius's five propositions were indeed to be found in the *Augustinus.* See fr. 792.

of truth, which is tradition, and having prejudiced the pope, who is its depositary, truth is no longer free to manifest itself, then men no longer speak the truth, the truth itself must speak to men. This is what happened in the time of Arius.[15]

Miracles, under Diocletian.
And under Arius.

440

Perpetuity

Is your character founded on Escobar?[16]

———

You have reasons perhaps for not condemning them.
It is enough that you approve of what I tell you about it.

———

Would the pope be dishonored for receiving his insights from God and tradition? And is it not dishonoring him, to separate him from this holy union, etc.

———

Tertullian:[17] *The Church will never be reformed.*[18]

———

In order to turn a man into a saint, grace is indeed necessary. And who doubts this knows neither what a saint is, nor what a man is.

———

Heretics have always assailed these three signs,[19] which they do not have.
Perpetuity.
Molina.[20]
Novelty.

15. On Arius, see ch. XXII, fr. 317, n. 12. Pascal admired Saint Athanasius (295–373 CE), the greatest opponent of the Arian heresy. The Arians, armed with the support of Pope Liberius, almost carried the day and made Arius's anti-Trinitarianism (the Son inferior to the Father) the official doctrine of the Church as it would be of the barbarians converted by Arian missionaries. Pascal saw a parallel in the struggle of 1650–60.

16. Antonio Escobar de Mendoza, SJ, was a Spanish Jesuit (1589–1669) who advanced the doctrine of probabilism, one of the most ultra-laxist principles. No one, he held, is required to follow what is more perfect and certain. God demands only that we should act with such moral certainty as is to be found in probable opinion.

17. Tertullian (ca. 160–ca. 220 CE) was perhaps the earliest of the Latin Church Fathers and a very early Christian apologist who was the earliest extant Latin writer to use the term *Trinity.*

18. Tertullian, *On the Veiling of Virgins,* 1.

19. "Perpetuity, a moral life, miracles" (fr. 448).

20. Luis de Molina (1535–1600) was a Spanish Jesuit and a staunch defender of "human liberty" in the controversy over grace during the Renaissance. He attempted to reconcile the Augustinian doctrines of predestination and efficacious grace with the new ideals of the Renaissance concerning human free will.

Miracles

How I hate those who profess to doubt miracles!

Montaigne speaks appropriately of them in these two passages. In the one, we see how prudent he is.[21] Yet in the other, he nonetheless believes in them and mocks those who are incredulous.[22]

Whatever the case may be, the Church has no proof, if they[23] are right.

God has either confounded the false miracles, or he has foretold them. And through both of these means, he has raised himself above what is "supernatural with respect to us" and has raised us as well to that higher level.

The Church teaches and God inspires, both infallibly. The operation of the Church serves only to prepare for grace, or for condemnation. What it does is enough to condemn, not to inspire.

Every kingdom divided against itself...[24] For Jesus Christ was acting against the Devil and destroyed his empire over the heart, the figure of which is exorcism, in order to establish the kingdom of God. And so he adds: *But if I by the finger of God cast out devils; doubtless the kingdom of God is come upon you.*[25]

If the Devil favored the doctrine that destroys him, he would be divided, as Jesus Christ has said. If God favored the doctrine that destroys the Church, he would be divided: *When a strong man armed keepeth his court, those things are in peace which he possesseth.*[26]

441

Will *yes and no*[27] become part of faith itself as of moral doctrine, if it is so inseparable in actions?

21. "And, in truth, in such researches, a very prudent, attentive, and subtle inquirer is needed, impartial and unprejudiced [...]; in many things [...] surpassing our knowledge, it is my opinion that we should suspend our judgment just as much in the direction of rejecting as of accepting." Montaigne, *Essays*, III, 11, 958.

22. Montaigne ascribes a heightened credulity to "empty" minds, but goes on to state: "on the other hand, it is foolish presumption to go around disdaining and condemning as false whatever does not seem likely to us, which is an ordinary vice in those who think they have more than common ability; [...] reason has taught me that to condemn a thing thus, dogmatically, as false and impossible, is to assume the advantage of knowing the bounds and limits of God's will and of the power of our mother Nature, and that there is no more notable folly in the world than to reduce these things to the measure of our capacity and competence. If we call prodigies or miracles whatever our reason cannot reach, how many of these appear continually to our eyes!" Montaigne, *Essays*, I, 27, 160–61.

23. I.e., the Jesuits.

24. Luke 11:14–20. Having healed a man who was mute, Jesus is accused of having chased away demons with the help of Beelzebub. He answers: "*Every kingdom divided against itself* shall be brought to desolation."

25. Luke 11:20.

26. Luke 11:21.

27. "*Est et non est*," that is, "it is permitted" and "it is not permitted," are formulae that resume the "fantastic decisions" of the casuists.

(*Saint Hilary:*[28] *You wretches, who force us to speak of the miracles!*)

When Saint Xavier performs miracles.[29]

Unjust judges, do not make laws thus on the spur of the moment. Judge by well-established laws, and established by yourselves. *Woe to you that make wicked laws.*[30]

In order to weaken your adversaries, you take away the arms of the entire Church.

Continual miracles, false.

If they say that they submit to the pope—that's hypocrisy.

If they are ready to subscribe to all his constitutions—that is not enough.

If they say that our salvation depends on God—they are heretics.

If they say that one must not kill for an apple[31]—they are attacking Catholics' morality.

If miracles do take place among them, this is not a sign of their holiness, but instead a reason for suspecting them of heresy.

The way the Church has endured is because the truth has not been contested. Or if it was contested, there was the pope. And if not, there was the Church.

442
First objection: *Angel from heaven.*[32]

One must not judge of truth by miracles, but of miracle by truth.

Therefore miracles are useless.

But they are useful, and we must not be against truth.

Therefore what Father Lingendes said,[33] that God will not permit that a miracle could lead into error . . .

Whenever there is a dispute within the same Church, miracles will decide.

---

28. Saint Hilary was a third century Latin Church Father. Bishop of Poitiers, he was known as the "hammer against the Arians." Holding the highest rank among the Latin writers of his century before Saint Ambrose, he was designated by Saint Augustine as "the illustrious doctor of the churches." On the Arians see ch. XXII, fr. 317, n. 12.

29. Saint Francis Xavier (1506–52), the first and greatest Jesuit missionary to Asia, who penetrated as far as China and Japan, was said to have wrought many miracles during his journeys and by his intercession after his death. He was canonized in 1664. Pascal reminds the Jesuits that their co-founder too performed many miracles.

30. Isaiah 10:1: "*Woe to them that make wicked laws.*"

31. According to Pascal's fourteenth *Provincial Letter*, the Jesuit Lessius allowed one to kill "to keep an apple."

32. Galatians 1:8. See fr. 428.

33. During Lent, 1657. See fr. 419, n. 6.

Second objection:
But the Antichrist will perform signs.[34]

Pharaoh's magicians did not lead into error.[35]

Therefore, it is not possible to say to Jesus Christ about the Antichrist: You have led me into error. For the Antichrist will perform them against Jesus Christ, and so they cannot lead into error.

Either God will not allow false miracles, or he will bring on greater ones.

(*Since the beginning of the world, Jesus Christ has endured. This is more powerful than all the Antichrist's miracles.*)

If, within the same Church, there occurred a miracle on the side of those who err, people would be led into error.

Schism is visible, miracles are visible. But schism is more a sign of error than miracles are a sign of truth. Therefore, miracles cannot lead into error.

But outside of schism, error is not as visible as miracles are visible. Therefore, miracles would lead into error.

Where is thy God?[36] Miracles reveal him and are a bolt of lightning.
(*Men naturally roofers and of all trades, except in their room.*)[37]

443

The five propositions condemned, no miracle. For truth was not attacked. But the Sorbonne, the bull . . .[38]

It is impossible that those who love God with all their heart not recognize the Church, so evident is it.

It is impossible that those who do not love God be convinced of the Church.

---

34. 2 Thessalonians 2:9. See fr. 432.

35. Exodus 7.

36. Psalm 42:4: "My tears have been my bread day and night, whilst it is said to me daily: *Where is thy God?*"

37. These lines were added in the margin, perpendicular to the text, and then struck out. See frs. 168 (on the inability to remain at rest in one's room) and 527 (on the "choice" of one's profession).

38. As long as Pope Innocent X (1653) had only condemned the five propositions, which everyone judged heretical, there was no controversy about their truth. But when the Sorbonne censured Arnauld and Alexander VII (1656) and ruled that the five propositions were in the *Augustinus*, the very theology of Saint Augustine was put into question. God's answer was the miracle at Port-Royal.

Miracles have such power that God had to warn beforehand that they were not to be a reason for thinking against him. Clear as it may be that there is a God. Otherwise, they would have been capable of unsettling minds.

And therefore these passages, Deuteronomy 13, far from attempting to contradict the authority of miracles, more than anything reveal their power. And for the Antichrist likewise: *insomuch as to deceive (if possible) even the elect.*[39]

444
Atheists

What reason have they to say that one cannot rise from the dead? Which is more difficult: to be born or to rise again? For what has never existed to exist or for what has existed to exist again? Is it more difficult to come into being than to come back into it? Custom makes the one easy, the lack of custom makes the other impossible. The common people's way of judging!

———

Why cannot a virgin give birth? Does a hen not produce eggs without a rooster? What distinguishes them outwardly from the others, and who told us that the hen cannot create this seed just as the rooster does?

———

There is so much disproportion between the merit which he believes he has, and stupidity, that one could not believe that he is so mistaken.

———

After so many marks of piety, they[40] also suffer persecution, which is the best mark of piety.

445

It is right that they do acts of injustice, out of fear that the Molinists appear to have acted with justice. And so they must not be spared—they are worthy of committing them.

———

Pyrrhonian,[41] for stubborn.

———

Descartes—useless and uncertain.[42]

———

No one says courtier but those who are not; pedant, but a pedant; provincial, but a provincial. And I would wager that it was the printer who included it in the title for the *Letters to the Provincial.*[43]

39. Matthew 24:24.
40. The "Jansenists."
41. On Pyrrhonism (skepticism), see ch. 1 (table-*liasse*), n. 10.
42. See fr. 118 and n. 5.
43. In effect, this is what happened.

Thoughts

In all these I sought rest.[44]

If our condition were truly happy, we would not have to divert ourselves from thinking about it in order to make ourselves happy.

———

All the occupations of men are about pursuing some good. And they have neither the entitlement to possess it justly, nor the strength to possess it securely. Likewise: knowledge, pleasures. We have neither the truth nor the good.

———

Miracle

It is an effect that surpasses the natural power of the means used for it. And a non-miracle is an effect that does not surpass the natural power of the means used for it. Thus, those who cure by invoking the devil do not perform a miracle, for doing that does not surpass the natural power of the devil.[45] But...

446

Abraham, Gideon: signs beyond Revelation.[46]

The Jews blinded themselves in judging miracles by scripture.

God has never abandoned his true worshippers.[47]

I prefer to follow Jesus Christ above all others, because he has miracle, prophecy, doctrine, perpetuity, etc.

Donatists[48]: no miracle that forces one to say that it is the devil.

The more one particularizes God, Jesus Christ, the Church...[49]

---

44. This phrase is the beginning of several liturgical texts for the Feast of the Assumption, based on Ecclesiasticus 24:11, in which Divine Wisdom speaks: "And by my power I have trodden under my feet the hearts of all the high and low: and in all these I sought rest."

45. See fr. 419.

46. See Genesis 15:8–21 and Judges 6:36–40. See fr. 450.

47. See fr. 281.

48. During the persecution under Diocletian (305 CE), many in the established Church in North Africa had recanted. The Donatists declared their sacraments and ordinations void and formed a parallel schismatic church. By the time of Saint Augustine in the late fourth century, the sect remained of great importance. Augustine campaigned against them through his tenure as Bishop of Hippo. Augustine held, in accordance with all subsequent Church doctrine, that it was the office of priest, not the personal character of the incumbent, that gave validity to the celebration of the sacraments. As a testament to the importance Augustine attached to refuting this heresy, we have twenty-one of Augustine's extant letters as well as eight formal treatises bearing on the controversy.

49. Augustine blames the Donatists for "particularizing" the Church, i.e., restricting it to the small territory in Africa where they are. This entire fragment consists of notes taken by Pascal from Saint Augustine's *Letter against the Donatists*. Abraham received the promise of numberless descendants. Gideon, as

447
Blindness of scripture

Scripture, said the Jews, says that one does not know where the Christ would come from: John 7:27. And 12:34: *Scripture says that Christ abideth forever, and he says that he will die.* Thus says Saint John, *they believed not in him, whereas he had done so many miracles, that the saying of Isaias might be fulfilled:* HE HATH BLINDED THEIR EYES, etc.[50]

448

The three signs of religion: perpetuity, a moral life, miracles. They[51] destroy perpetuity by probability, moral life by their moral tenets, miracles by destroying either their truth or their significance. If one believes them, the Church will have no need of perpetuity, of holiness, of miracles.

––––––

Heretics deny them, or deny their significance. They, likewise. But one would have to be devoid of sincerity to deny them, or to have lost one's senses to deny their significance.

––––––

Religion is proportioned to all types of minds. The first do not see beyond its establishment[52]—and this religion is such that its establishment alone is enough to prove its truth. Others go all the way back to the apostles. The most learned go all the way back to the beginning of the world. Angels see religion more clearly still and from farther away.

––––––

My God, these sayings are such nonsense: Would God have made the world in order to damn it? Would he ask so much from people who are so weak? etc. Pyrrhonism is the remedy for this evil, and it will beat down such vanity.[53]

––––––

well, manifested the universal reach of the Gospels—a miracle afforded to Gideon announced the rejection of Israel. The Jews were blinded and thought revelation was for them alone. Even the Donatists had experienced miracles, but they were blinded and failed to understand their role in the conversion of the entire world. See Philippe Sellier, *Pascal et saint Augustin* (Paris: Armand Colin, 1970), 610.

50. John 12:34: "We have heard out of the law, *that Christ abideth for ever*; and how *sayest thou:* The Son of man *must be lifted up?* Who is this Son of man?" John 12:37–38, 12;40, invokes Isaiah 6:10: "*And whereas he had done so many miracles* before them, *they believed not in him: That the saying of Isaias* the prophet *might be fulfilled,* which he said: Lord, who hath believed our hearing? and to whom hath the arm of the Lord been revealed? [...] *He hath blinded their eyes.*"

51. The Jesuits.

52. See fr. 717.

53. See Montaigne, *Essays*, 2, 12. "The means I take to beat down this frenzy, and which seems fittest to me, is to crush and trample underfoot human arrogance and pride; to make them feel the inanity, the vanity and nothingness, of man, to wrest from their hands the puny weapons of their reason; to make them bow

SOFTENING MY HEART, Saint Paul: such is the Christian character.[54] ALBA HAS CHOSEN YOU, I NO LONGER KNOW YOU, Corneille:[55] such is the character of inhumanity. The character of humanity is the opposite.

Never has anyone become a martyr for miracles that one claims to have seen. As for those that the Turks believe by tradition, men's foolishness might go all the way to martyrdom perhaps, but not for those that have been seen.

The Jansenists resemble heretics in their reformation of moral behavior, but you[56] resemble them in your evil.

Those who wrote that in Latin speak in French.

The harm having been done by putting them into French, good had to be done by condemning them.[57]

There is one single heresy that is explained differently in the schools and in the world.

449

Miracles distinguish between things that are in doubt: between Jewish and heathen peoples, Jew and Christian; Catholic, heretical; slandered, slanderers; between the two crosses.[58]

But miracles would be useless to heretics, since the Church, authorized by the miracles that have laid the foundation for belief, tells us that they do not possess the true faith. There is no doubt at all that they are not of it, since the Church's first miracles exclude faith in theirs. Thus miracle is set against miracle. And the first and greatest ones on the side of the Church.

These sisters,[59] astonished at hearing that they are on the road to perdition, that their confessors are leading them to Geneva, planting in their mind

their heads and bite the ground beneath the authority and reverence of divine majesty" (397). See, in this volume, the *Exchange with M. de Sacy*, §37.

54. Acts 21:13 recounts Paul's response to his friends who try to keep him from departing for Jerusalem, where he will be arrested.

55. Corneille, *Horace*, II, iii, 502. Horace renounces his friendship with the Alban Curiace out of duty to Rome. See Pierre Corneille, *Œuvres completes*, ed. André Stegmann. (Paris: Seuil, 1963), 255.

56. The Jesuits.

57. The casuists' maxims were written in Latin, the language of the scholastics. In order to condemn them in the eyes of the faithful, Pascal had to translate them into French. The maxims themselves, not his use of them in the *Provinciales*, should be condemned.

58. The two crosses: Saint Helena identifies the true cross. See fr. 436, n. 76. As in fr. 348, above, Pascal uses the term *discern*.

59. The sisters of Port-Royal.

the idea that Jesus Christ is not in the Eucharist nor on the right hand of the Father[60]—they know all that to be false. They therefore offer themselves to God in this state: *See if there be in me the way of iniquity.*[61] Whereupon what happens? This place, said to be the Devil's temple—God makes it his own temple. It is said that the children must be removed from there—there God heals them. It is said that it is hell's arsenal—God makes it the sanctuary of his grace. Finally, they are threatened with all of heaven's fury and all its vengeance—and God fills them with his favors. One would have to have lost one's senses to conclude from this that they are therefore on the road to perdition.

We have without a doubt the same signs as Saint Athanasius.[62]

450

The insane idea that you have of your Society's importance has led you to establish these horrible methods. It is indeed obvious that this is what has led you to follow the path of slander, since you consider the slightest impostures as horrible faults in me, whereas you excuse them in yourselves, because you consider me as a private person and yourselves as Imago.[63]

It is clear to see that your praises are just instances of insanity from your insane visions, like the privilege of not being damned.[64]

Are you really giving courage to your children, when you condemn them while they are serving the Church?

———

To divert to other ends the weapons by which these people[65] would fight heresies is an artifice of the Devil.

———

You are bad political maneuverers.

———

60. These were charges of heresy leveled at the sisters of Port-Royal. Pascal had refuted these accusations in the sixteenth *Provincial Letter*. In spite of the fact that the sisters' order was known as the Daughters of the Holy Sacrament, the Jesuits constantly accused those at Port-Royal of not believing in the real presence of Christ in the Eucharist.

61. Psalm 139:24.

62. In his *Response à un escrit publié sur le sujet des miracles qu'il a pleu à Dieu de faire à Port-Royal depuis quelque temps par une sainte espine de la couronne de Nostre-Seigneur* [Response to a text made public on the subject of the miracles that it has pleased God to perform at Port-Royal lately by a holy thorn of the crown of your Lord] (1656), the Jesuit Du Cambout de Pontchâteau had written that God had showed himself on the side of the Catholics and not the Arians (see ch. XXII, fr. 317, n. 12) when Saint Anthony of the Desert came to Alexandria at the behest of Saint Athanasius to perform miracles.

63. In the *Imago primi sæculi Societatis Jesu* [Image of the first century of the Society of Jesus] (Antwerp, 1640), the Society of Jesus had taken a self-satisfied inventory of the first hundred years since their foundation.

64. In Pontchâteau's *Morale pratique des Jésuites* [Practical morals of the Jesuits] (1669), it is alleged that the Jesuits hold that "no Jesuit will be damned."

65. The theologians of Port-Royal.

Pyrrhonism.

Each thing here is in part true, in part false. Essential truth is not so: it is entirely pure and true. This mixture dishonors it and annihilates it. Nothing is purely true, and so nothing is true—in terms of what is purely true.

It will be objected that it is true that homicide is bad. Yes, for we indeed know evil and falsehood. But what then can be called good? Chastity? I say no—for the world would end. Marriage? no—continence has more value.[66] Not to kill? no—for the resulting disorders would be horrible and the wicked would kill all good people. To kill? no—for it destroys nature. We possess neither the true nor the good except in part and mingled with falsehood and evil.[67]

The story of the man born blind.[68]

What does Saint Paul say? Does he spend his time referring to the prophecies? No, but to his miracle.[69]

What does Jesus Christ say? Does he refer to the prophecies? No. His death had not fulfilled them. But he says: *If I had not done ... Believe the works.*[70]

Two supernatural foundations for our religion, itself wholly supernatural: the one visible, the other invisible.

Miracles with grace, miracles without grace.

The synagogue, which has been treated with love as a figure of the Church and with hatred because it was only its figure, has been restored when it was ready to succumb, when it was indeed with God, and so it is a figure.

66. See Montaigne, *Essays*, III, 1: "Let us choose the most necessary and useful action of human society; that will be marriage. Yet the council of saints finds the contrary was more honorable, and excludes from marriage the most venerable vocation of men, as we assign to stud those horses which are of least value" (740). In *De la sagesse*, Charron is more explicit: "The Apostle prefers the solitude of continence over marriage." The reference is to 1 Corinthians 7:1 and 8:26, 32ff.

67. See the title of Montaigne's chapter: "We taste nothing pure" (Montaigne, *Essays*, III, 20, 619ff.), and such passages as: "Of the pleasures and good things that we have, there is not one exempt of some mixture of pain and discomfort" (619). Pascal, however, is taking the statement from the ethical plane of pleasure and pain to the higher, moral one of the knowledge of good and evil.

68. John 9. See fr. 425.

69. 2 Corinthians 12:12: "Yet the signs of my apostleship have been wrought on you, in all patience, in signs, and wonders, and mighty deeds." Paul's conversion is itself a miracle. See Acts 9.

70. John 15:24: "*If I had not done* among them the works that no other man hath done, they would not have sin; but now they have both seen and hated both me and my Father"; and John 10:38: "But if I do, though you will not believe me, *believe the works*: that you may know and believe that the Father is in me, and I in the Father."

Miracles prove the power God has over hearts by the power that he wields over the body.

Never has the Church approved of a miracle among heretics.[71]

———

Miracles—religion's support. They distinguished the Jews. They distinguished the Christians, the saints, the innocent, the true believers.

———

A miracle among schismatics is not so much to be feared. For schism, which is more visible than a miracle, marks their error clearly. But whenever there is no schism and error is disputed, a miracle distinguishes.

———

If I had not done the works that no other man hath done . . .[72]

———

These wretches who have forced us to speak about miracles.

———

Abraham, Gideon.[73]
Confirm faith by miracles.

———

Judith:[74] God finally speaks at the ultimate stages of oppression.

———

If the cooling of charity leaves the Church almost without *true worshippers,*[75] miracles will rouse others. They are the final efforts of grace.

If a miracle happened among the Jesuits.

When a miracle fails to fulfill the expectations of those in whose presence it occurs, and there is disproportion between the state of their faith and the instrument of the miracle, then it must lead them to change, but, etc. Otherwise, you might as well say that if the Eucharist were to bring a dead person back to life, there would be as much reason to become a Calvinist as to remain a Catholic. But whenever it crowns one's expectation and those who hoped that God would bless the remedies see themselves healed without remedies . . . [76]

———

71. The miracle of the healing at Port-Royal by the application of the holy thorn was officially declared authentic by the Archbishopric of Paris on October 26, 1656.

72. John 15:24. "*If I had not done* among them the *works that no other man hath done,* they would not have sin." See frs. 429 and 450.

73. See n. 49, above.

74. In the biblical book bearing her name, Judith appears and promises to defeat the Assyrians, who are besieging Bethulia. Having fasted and prayed, she dresses in her finest garments and proceeds to the Assyrian camp, where she succeeds in killing Holofernes while he lies in a drunken stupor. The Assyrians panic when they discover this, and the Jews are able to rout and slaughter them. Thus God "finally speaks."

75. See frs. 281 and 446.

76. Pascal responds to the Jansenists' adversaries, who claimed that miracles were usually used to convert those who lacked the true faith.

The ungodly.   Never has a sign occurred from the Devil without a stronger
                sign from God.

                At least, without the occurrence having been foretold.

451

Probability. They have a few true principles, but they misuse them. And misusing true principles must be punished just as much as the introduction of a lie.

As if there were two hells, one for the sins against charity, the other against justice.

Aperitive virtue of a key, attractive virtue of a hook.[77]

Superstition and concupiscence.

Scruples, wrong desires, wrong fear.

Fear—not the fear that comes from believing in God, but from doubting whether he is or not. Proper fear comes from faith, the wrong kind of fear comes from doubt, the proper fear belonging to hope because it is born of faith and one hopes in the God whom one believes, the wrong kind belonging to despair because one fears the God in whom one has had no faith. Some fear losing him, the others fear finding him.

(*People who do not keep their word, who are without faith, without honor, without truth, double in heart, double in tongue and similar, as you were once blamed for being, to this amphibious animal in the fable who maintained itself in an ambiguous state between fish and bird.*)[78]

Whenever it is said that Jesus Christ did not die for all, you exploit a bad tendency in men who immediately apply this exception to themselves; and this furthers despair instead of turning them away from despair and furthering hope.

For thus one becomes accustomed to inner virtue through these outer habits.[79]

It matters to kings and princes to be esteemed for their piety. And for that, they must make confession to you.[80]

---

77. Pastiche of scholastic style and explication. If a key opens a door, it is said that it has an *aperitive* power. Aperitive, from the Latin *aperire*, to open.

78. See the end of the thirteenth *Provincial Letter*.

79. See fr. 680 and Pascal's idea of training the body (the "machine") to perform religious reflexes.

80. The Jesuits were the confessors to the court and Fr. Annat to Louis XIV himself. Using casuistry as a kind of jurisprudence, they were able to adjust to the new, absolutist monarchical system and the demands of the then modern model of sociability—which allowed the court elite and the King himself to think of themselves as deeply religious. Louis XIV, remarked Saint-Simon, thought of himself as the thirteenth apostle when he revoked the Edict of Nantes in 1685.

Port-Royal is indeed worth as much as Voltigerode.[81]

Just as your procedure is just from this perspective, so it is unjust if one considers Christian piety.

The figures for the totality of the redemption, that the sun shines for all for example, signify only a totality, but those that figure exclusions, the Jews who are chosen to the exclusion of the Gentiles, for example, signify exclusion.

Jesus Christ redeemer of all.[82] Yes—since he has offered as a human being who has redeemed all those who will want to come to him. Those who will die on the way—that is their misfortune. But for his part, he was offering them redemption. This argument avails in this example, in which the one who redeems and the one who prevents death are two, but not in Jesus Christ, who accomplishes both the one and the other. No—for Jesus Christ, in his capacity as redeemer, is perhaps not the master of all people, and so, insofar as it depends on him, he is the redeemer of all.

81. In 1631, the Jesuits had tried to have the Cistercian nuns of the Abbey of Voltigerode (in Lower Saxony) removed in order to have it for their own use as a novitiate.

82. *Jesu, Redemptor omnium.* The beginning of a well-known hymn sung at first vespers of Christmas.

[XXXIII] Miscellany

452

When in a discourse we find words repeated, and, in trying to correct them, we discover that they are so appropriate that we would spoil the discourse, we must leave them as they are, that is the mark of their propriety. And this is where envy plays a major role, as it is blind and does not know that repetition is not a defect in that instance. For there is no general rule.

We desire certainty, we want the pope to be infallible in matters of faith, and grave, learned men to be the same in matters of morality, so that we may be reassured.

If Saint Augustine walked the earth today and had as little authority as his defenders,[1] he would accomplish nothing. God conducts his church wisely by having sent him before and with authority.

Pyrrhonism

Extreme wisdom is accused of folly, just like extreme lack of it. Only the mean[2] is good: it has been established by the plurality, which bites whoever escapes it at either end. I will not insist. I fully consent to be placed there, and refuse to be at the low end, not because it is low but because it is an end, for I would also refuse to be placed at the higher end. To leave the middle is to leave humanity.

The greatness of the human soul consists in knowing how to remain there. Greatness does not lie in leaving the mean, far from it: it is in not moving away from it.[3]

1. The theologians of Port-Royal.
2. The "middle way" constitutes an ideal. Aristotle defines virtue as a just mean between excess and defect (*Nicomachean Ethics*, II, 5, 1, 106 ab). In the seventeenth century the concept would be integrated into the ethical ideal of *honnêteté*.
3. Montaigne, *Essays*, III, 2, 745: "The value of the soul consists not in flying high, but in an orderly pace. Its greatness is exercised not in greatness but in mediocrity." See frs. 453, 560, and 645.

453[4]

(*Nature not . . .*

Nature has placed us so exactly in the middle that if we alter one side of the scale, we also alter the other: I ARE, ZOA TREKEI.[5]

This leads me to believe that there are springs in our heads that are disposed in such a way that whoever triggers one also triggers the opposite.

———

I spent much of my life believing that justice existed, and in that I was not mistaken, for it does exist, insofar as God has been pleased to reveal it to us. But I did not understand it that way, and in this I was mistaken, for I believed that our justice was essentially just and that I had in me the wherewithal to know and to judge it. But I found myself so frequently lacking in good judgment that at last I began to doubt myself, and then others.[6] I have seen changes take place in all countries and all men. And thus, after many changes in judgment concerning true justice, I realized that our nature is but continuous change, and I have not changed since then.[7] And if I did change, I would confirm my opinion. Arcesilaus the Pyrrhonian,[8] who becomes a dogmatist again.

———

It may be that there are true demonstrations, but that is not certain. And so this shows nothing other than that it is not certain that all is uncertain. To the glory of Pyrrhonism.

———

How is it that this man who is so afflicted by the deaths of his wife and of his only son, who has some great feud that torments him, at this very moment is not sad and we see him free of those distressing and disturbing thoughts? We must not be surprised, he has just been served a ball and must return the volley to his opponent, and he is busy getting the ball on the rebound to win the point. How can he possibly think of his own affairs when he has this other affair to handle? Here is a

4. Pascal strikes this entire fragment, written on the reverse side of the sheet on which 452 appears.

5. "The animals 'runs.'" Ancient Greek puts into the singular verbs whose subject is a collective neutral. Transversely, French peasants use the first-person plural verb with the first-person singular pronoun: "JE FAISONS." Hence our approximate translation "I ARE."

6. Montaigne, *Essays*, III, 13, 1001: "He who remembers having been mistaken so many, many times in his own judgments, is he not a fool if he does not distrust it forever after?"

7. Montaigne, *Essays*, I, 26, 141: "So many humors, sects, judgments, opinions, laws and customs teach us to judge sanely of our own, and teach our judgment to recognize its own imperfection and natural weaknesses, which is no small lesson. So many state disturbances and changes of public fortune instruct us on not to make a great miracle of our own."

8. Arcesilaus (316–241 BCE) was the founder of the New Academy, which inflected philosophical doctrines of Platonic origins in the direction of skepticism. See Montaigne, *Essays*, II, 12, 529: "Arcesilaus used to say that to suspend the judgment and keep it upright and inflexible is a good thing, but to consent and incline it is a vice and a bad thing. It is true that by establishing this as a certain axiom, he was departing from Pyrrhonism." Arcesilaus did not profess a dogmatic philosophy, but he dogmatically professed Pyrrhonism.

care worthy of captivating this great soul and of removing every other thought from his mind. This man born to know the universe, to judge all things, to rule a state, here he is occupied and wholly engrossed in the care of catching a hare. And were he not to lower himself to that and chose instead to remain concentrated, he would be even more foolish, because he would wish to raise himself above humanity, and he is but a man, when all is said and done,[9] *that is, he is capable of little and of much, of everything and of nothing. He is neither angel nor beast, but a man.*[10]

One single thought occupies us. We cannot think of two things at once. Which is good for us, according to the world, not according to God.

We must judge soberly divine ordinances,[11] *Father. Saint Paul on the isle of Malta.*[12])

454[13]

Montaigne is wrong. Custom must be followed only because it is custom, and not because it is reasonable or just. But the people follow it for this reason alone, that they think it is just.[14] Otherwise they would not follow it anymore, even though it be custom. For we want to be subjected to reason or justice alone. Otherwise custom would pass for tyranny, but the rule of reason and justice is no more tyrannical than that of delectation. Those are the principles natural to man.

It would be good if we obeyed laws and customs because they are laws, if we knew that none could be introduced that are true or just, that we know nothing about the matter and therefore simply have to follow those that are established. In this way, we would never let go of them. But the common people are unable to grasp this doctrine. And thus, because they believe that truth can be found and that it lies in the laws and customs, they believe them and take their antiquity as proof of their truth (and not simply of their authority

9. Montaigne, *Essays*, II, 12, 457: "'O what a vile and abject thing is man,' he [Seneca] says, 'if he does not raise himself above humanity!' That is a good statement and a useful desire, but equally absurd." And *Essays*, II, 2, 303: "For all his wisdom, the sage is still a man: what is there more vulnerable, more wretched, more null?"

10. See fr. 557.

11. Montaigne, *Essays*, I, 32, bears the title: "We Should Meddle Soberly with Judging Divine Ordinances."

12. Saint Paul was shipwrecked on Malta and bitten by a viper. The inhabitants thought him pursued by divine vengeance. When they saw that he was not harmed, they thought him a god.

13. See fr. 94.

14. Montaigne, *Essays*, III, 13, 1000: "Laws remain in credit not because they are just but because they are laws." "Whoever obeys them because they are just does not obey them for just the reason he should." See fr. 100.

without truth). Thus the people obey them, but they are liable to revolt as soon as they are shown that the laws are worth nothing, which can be shown in all cases by examining them from a certain point of view.

Evil is easy, and its varieties are infinite, the good is almost unique.[15] But a certain kind of evil is just as difficult to find as what is called the good, and often that particular evil is passed off as good on that account. In fact, it takes a certain exceptionally great soul to reach it as much as to reach the good.[16]

The examples that we use to prove other things, if in turn we wanted to prove the examples, we would take the other things as their examples.

For, since we always believe that the difficulty lies in what we want to prove, we find the examples clearer and helpful in that demonstration. Thus, when we want to prove something general, we must give the particular rule of one case. But if we want to prove one particular case, we have to begin with the particular rule.[17] For we always find the thing that we want to prove obscure and that which we use to prove it clear. For when we propose to prove something, we are immediately taken over by the imaginary view that it is therefore obscure, and on the contrary that which we use to prove it is clear, and thus we understand it easily.

I have always been uncomfortable with these civilities: "I have given you much trouble. I am afraid I am bothering you. I fear that this may be too long."—Either we influence or we irritate.

It is so difficult to submit something to someone else's judgment without corrupting that judgment by the manner in which we submit it. If we say: "I find it beautiful, I find it obscure," or some such thing, we carry the imagination toward that judgment or we drive it by irritation in the opposite direction. It is better to say nothing, and then he judges the thing as it is, that is, according to what it is then and according to whatever other circumstances in which we had no part will have added to it. But at least we will have had no part in

15. Montaigne, *Essays*, I, 9, 28: "the Pythagoreans make the good to be certain and finite, evil infinite and uncertain. A thousand paths miss the target, one goes to it."

16. Montaigne, *Essays*, I, 49, 264: "Our powers are no more capable of matching them [the Ancients] in those vicious parts than in the virtuous ones; for both proceed from a vigor of soul which was incomparably greater in them than it is in us; and the weaker soul, the lesser its power to do either very well or very ill." *Essays*, III, 9, 730: "I see not one action, or three, or a hundred, but morals in common and accepted practice so monstrous [...] that I have not the heart to think of them without horror; and I marvel at them almost as much as I detest them. The practice of these arrant villainies bears the mark of vigor and strength of soul as much as of error and disorder." See La Rochefoucauld, *Maximes* [Maxims], no. 185: "Il y a des héros en mal comme en bien" [There are heroes in evil as well as in good] (La Rochefoucauld, *Maximes et réflexions diverses*, ed. Truchet, 61).

17. Pascal must have meant "general" and written "particular" by mistake.

it. Unless this silence also has an effect of its own, according to the turn and interpretation that he will be in the mood to give it, or according to whatever conjectures he may draw from our facial movements and expression, or from our tone of voice, depending on whether or not he is a physiognomist. It is so difficult not to knock a judgment off its natural seat, or rather how rarely is judgement's seat naturally firm and stable!

455

All of our reasoning comes down to giving in to feeling.

But fancy is similar and contrary to feeling, so that we cannot distinguish between those opposites. One says that my feeling is fantasy, the other that his fantasy is feeling. We need a rule. Reason offers itself, but it is pliable in all directions.[18]

And thus there is no rule.

456

Those things that have the most hold on us, such as concealing our lack of wealth, often amount to practically nothing. They are a mere nothing that our imagination expands into a mountain: another turn of the imagination reveals this to us without difficulty.

457

Pyrrhonism

I will write my thoughts here without order, and yet not perhaps in an unplanned confusion. That is the true order, and which will at all times reveal my intent by the disorder itself.

I would confer too much dignity on my subject if I treated it in order, since I wish to show that it is incapable of it.

We imagine Plato and Aristotle only in the full, flowing robes of pedants. They were men of the world like the rest, laughing with their friends. And when they found diversion in writing their *Laws* and *Politics*, they did so as a game.[19] That was the least philosophical and the least serious part of their lives, the most philosophical was to live simply and peacefully. If they wrote about politics, it

---

18. Montaigne, *Essays*, II, 12, 516: reason "is an instrument of lead and of wax, stretchable, pliable, and adaptable to all biases and all measures."

19. Montaigne, *Essays*, II, 12, 457: "Chrysippus said that what Plato and Aristotle had written about logic they had written as a game and for exercise, and could not believe that they had spoken seriously of such an empty matter."

was like putting a madhouse in order. And if they pretended to treat it as an important matter, it is because they knew that the madmen to whom they spoke thought themselves kings and emperors. They entered into their principles so that they might limit their madness to the least pernicious form possible.

Those who judge a work without any rule are, with respect to others, like those who own a watch with respect to those without one. One says: "it has been two hours."—Another says: "it has only been three quarters of an hour."—I look at my watch and say to the first "you are bored," and to the other: "time flies by for you, for it has been an hour and a half."—And I laugh at those who say that time drags on for me and that I judge it according to whim.

They do not know that I judge it by my watch.

There are vices that hold on to us only through others, and which, by removing the trunk, are carried away like branches.

458

God and the apostles, foreseeing that the seeds of pride would give rise to heresies and not wishing to give them the opportunity to emerge from terms themselves, placed in the scriptures and in the prayers of the Church opposing words and seeds that would bear their fruits in due time.

Just as he gives charity in morality, which bears fruit that counters concupiscence.

When wickedness has reason on its side, it becomes proud and displays reason in all of its luster.

When austerity or stern choice has not succeeded in attaining the true good and it is necessary to revert to following nature, it becomes proud by this reversal.

He who knows the will of his master will be beaten with more blows because of the power that he has through knowledge. *He that is just, let him be justified still,*[20] because of the power that he has through justice.

Of him who has received the most will the strictest account be demanded, because of the power that he has through that succor.

There is a universal and essential difference between acts of the will and all others.

---

20. Revelation 22:11: "He that hurteth, let him hurt still: and he that is filthy, let him be filthy still: and *he that is just, let him be justified still:* and he that is holy, let him be sanctified still."

The will is one of the principal organs of belief, not because it creates belief, but because things are true or false according to the side from which we view them. The will that delights in one more than the other will turn the mind away from considering the qualities of the one that it does not wish to see. And thus the mind, marching in step with the will, looks no further than the side that it likes, and thus it judges by what it sees there.

_____

All of the good maxims are abroad in the world: we only fail to apply them.

For example, no one doubts that one must risk one's life to defend the public good, and several actually do, but not for religion.

_____

It is necessary there be inequality among men. That is true, but once this is granted, the door is opened not only to the utmost sovereignty, but also to the utmost tyranny.

It is necessary to relax the mind somewhat, but that opens the door to the greatest excesses.

Let the limits be marked. There are no boundaries for things: laws intend to set them, but the mind cannot tolerate it.[21]

459

(*Nature diversifies and imitates. Artifice imitates and diversifies.*

Chance gives thoughts and chance takes them away: no art for keeping or for acquiring.

_____

Thought that escaped, I wanted to write it down: I write instead that it has escaped me.)

460

All the country of Judea, and all they of Jerusalem, and were baptized.[22] Because of all of the conditions of men who came there.

_____

Stones CAN be children of Abraham.[23]

_____

21. Montaigne, *Essays*, II, 12, 511: "it is not easy to set limits to our mind: it is curious and insatiable, and has no occasion to stop at a thousand paces rather than at fifty."

22. Mark 1:5. "And there went out to him [John the Baptist] *all the country of Judea, and all they of Jerusalem, and were baptized* by him in the river of Jordan, confessing their sins."

23. Mathew 3:9: "And think not to say within yourselves, We have Abraham for our father. For I tell you that God is able of these *stones* to raise up *children* to *Abraham*."

Everything that is in the world is concupiscence of the flesh or concupiscence of the eyes or pride in life.[24] *Desire for sensation, desire for knowledge, desire for domination.* Wretched is the accursed land that those three fiery rivers set ablaze rather than refresh! Happy are they who, being on those rivers, not immersed in them, not swept along by them, but stable and immobile upon those waters, not standing but seated, in a low and secure balance, from which they do not rise before the light, but after having rested there in peace, they extend their hands to him who will raise them to allow them to stand upright and stable at the threshold of holy Jerusalem, where pride will no longer be able to beset them and strike them down. And who nevertheless weep, not to see passing all the perishable things that those torrents sweep away, but in the remembrance of their dear homeland, of celestial Jerusalem, which they remember constantly throughout the length of their exile.[25]

The elect will not know their virtues, and the damned, the magnitude of their crimes: *Lord, when have we seen you hungry, thirsty,*[26] etc.

Jesus Christ wanted no testimony from demons or from those who had no vocation, but from God and John the Baptist.

If we converted, God would heal and pardon us: *Lest they be converted and that I may heal them,* Isaiah.[27] *Their sins should be forgiven them,* Mark 3.[28]
Jesus Christ never condemned without hearing.
To Judas: *Friend, what art thou come to do?*[29] To him who did not have the nuptial robe, the same.[30]

---

24. 1 John 2:16. Quoted in French.

25. Reminiscences of Augustine's commentaries on Psalms 136 and 126. Sellier offers a particularly memorable analysis of the fragment in "By the Waters of Babylon: the Fluidity of the World and the Search for Permanence in the *Pensées*" (translated from the French) in Wetsel, ed., *Meaning, Structure and History in the Pensées of Pascal,* Biblio 17 (Tubingen: Papers on French Seventeenth-Century Literature, 1990), 33–44.

26. Matthew 25:44. Quoted in French.

27. Jesus cites Isaiah 6:10 in Matthew 13:15: "For the heart of this people is grown gross, and with their ears they have been dull of hearing, and their eyes they have shut: lest at any time they should see with their eyes, and hear with their ears, and understand with their heart, and be converted, and I should heal them."

28. In fact, Mark 4:12: "That seeing they may see, and not perceive; and hearing they may hear, and not understand: *lest they be converted, and that I may heal them.*"

29. Matthew 26:50: Jesus to Judas at his arrest: "And Jesus said to him: *Friend, what art thou come to do?* Then they came up, and laid hands on Jesus, and held him."

30. Matthew 22:12: In the parable of the marriage feast, the king asks, "Friend, how camest thou in hither not having a wedding garment?"

461

Pray, lest ye enter into temptation.[31] It is dangerous to be tempted. And those who are, it is because they do not pray.

Being once converted, confirm thy brethren. But before that, *Jesus looked turning on Peter.*[32]

Saint Peter asks permission to strike Malchus, and strikes before hearing the answer. And Jesus Christ answers afterwards.[33]

The word GALILEE that the crowd of Jews pronounced as if by chance when they accused Jesus Christ before Pilate gave Pilate the excuse to send Jesus Christ to Herod.[34] In this way, the mystery that he was to be judged by the Jews and the Gentiles was accomplished. It appeared as though chance had been the cause of the accomplishment of that mystery.

Imagination enlarges small objects to the point of filling our souls through a fantastic evaluation, and through an insolent temerity it reduces great things to its own size, as when speaking of God.

The light he sends down to make earth bright.[35] The weather and my humor have little connection: I have my fogs and my fine weather inside of me.[36] Even good and bad fortune in my affairs has little effect. I sometimes struggle willingly against my fate: the glory of overcoming it allows me to do so gaily, whereas I sometimes act as if I were disgusted in good fortune.

---

31. Luke 22:40: "And when he was come to the place, he said to them: *Pray, lest ye enter into temptation.*"

32. Luke 22:32: Jesus said to Peter: "But I have prayed for thee, that thy faith fail not: and thou, *being once converted, confirm thy brethren.*" And Luke 22:61: "And the Lord *looked turning on Peter.* And Peter remembered the word of the Lord, as he had said: Before the cock crow, thou shalt deny me thrice."

33. Luke 22:49–51: "And they that were about him, seeing what would follow, said to him: Lord, shall we strike with the sword? And one of them struck the servant of the high priest, and cut off his right ear. But Jesus answering, said: Suffer ye thus far. And when he had touched his ear, he healed him."

34. Luke 23:5–8: "But they were more earnest, saying: He stirreth up the people, teaching throughout all Judea, beginning from Galilee to this place. But Pilate hearing Galilee, asked if the man were of *Galilee?* And when he understood that he was of Herod's jurisdiction, he sent him away to Herod, who was also himself at Jerusalem, in those days. And Herod, seeing Jesus, was very glad; for he was desirous of a long time to see him, because he had heard many things of him; and he hoped to see some sign wrought by him."

35. Montaigne, *Essays*, II, 12, 515: "The very air and the serenity of the sky brings us some change, as this Greek verse in Cicero says: 'Such are the minds of men as is the fertile *light* / That Father Jove himself *sends down to make earth bright.*'" These lines are translated from the *Odyssey*, XVIII, 135.

36. Montaigne, *Essays*, II, 1, 291: "Every day a new fancy, and our humors shift with the shifts in the weather."

462

Write against those who investigate too deeply the sciences. Descartes.[37]

463

Power, and not opinion, is the ruler of the world. But opinion is that which makes use of power.

It is power that makes opinion. In our opinion, indolence is beautiful. Why? Because he who wishes to dance upon a rope will be alone.[38] And I will create a stronger cabal of people who will say that that is not beautiful.

464

There are those who speak well but do not write well. It is because the place, the audience excite them and stir in their minds more than they could elicit without that excitement.[39]

465

Languages are ciphers, in which instead of letters being changed into letters, words are changed into words. So that an unknown language becomes decipherable.

———

Diversity is so wide that all tones of voice, all gaits, coughs, nose-blowings, sneezes [are different]. We distinguish among fruits grapes, and among them Muscat grapes, and then those of Condrieux, and then of Desargues,[40] and then a particular vine. Is that all? Has it ever produced two identical bunches? And does one bunch have two grapes that are the same?[41] etc.

I have never judged the same thing in exactly the same way. I cannot judge a work while creating it: I must do as painters do and move back, but not too much. How much then? Guess.

37. See fr. 196.

38. Epictetus, *Discourses*, III, 12: "It is difficult to walk on a taut rope, and not only difficult, but also dangerous. Is that a reason for us to walk on the rope […]? Not at all."

39. Montaigne, *Essays*, I, 10, 31: the soul, for some, needs "to be not shocked; but roused and warmed up by external, present, and accidental stimuli. If it goes along all by itself, it does nothing but drags and languishes. Agitation is its very life and grace. I have little control over myself and my moods. Chance has more power here than I. The occasion, the company, the very sound of my voice, draw more from my mind than I find in it when I sound it and use it myself. Thus its speech is better than its writings, if there can be choice where there is no value."

40. The mathematician, Girard Desargues, a friend of Pascal's, had property at Condrieux, a small town near Lyon, whose wines were renowned.

41. Montaigne, *Essays*, II, 37, 725: "And there were never in the world two opinions alike, any more than two hairs or two grains. Their most universal quality is diversity."

466
Miscellany
Language

Those who produce antitheses by forcing words are like those who add false windows for the sake of symmetry.

Their rule is not to speak appropriately, but to produce appropriate rhetorical figures.

467

The sepulcher of Jesus Christ.

Jesus Christ was dead, but seen, on the cross. He was dead and hidden in the sepulcher.

Jesus Christ was only buried by saints.

Jesus Christ performed no miracle at the sepulcher.

Only saints enter there.

Here does Jesus Christ assume a new life, not on the cross.

This is the last mystery of the Passion and the redemption.

(*Jesus Christ teaches alive, dead, buried, resurrected.*)

Jesus Christ had nowhere to rest on earth save in the sepulcher.

His enemies ceased tormenting him only at the sepulcher.

468

They say that eclipses presage misfortune because misfortunes are ordinary. So that bad things occur so frequently that they forecast frequently, and if instead they claimed that eclipses presaged good fortune they would frequently lie. They anticipate good fortune only in rare celestial events. Thus they rarely fail in their forecasts.

469

There are but two kinds of men: those who are righteous, who believe themselves sinners; and those who are sinners, who believe themselves righteous.

470
Heretics

Ezekiel.[42]

42. Ezekiel 22.

All of the heathen spoke ill of Israel, and the prophet too. And so far were the Israelites from having the right to say to him: "You speak like the heathen," that he derives his greatest force from the fact that the heathen speak like him.

471

The true and unique virtue is to hate oneself, for we merit hate through our concupiscence, and to seek a being truly deserving of love so that we may love him. But since we cannot love that which is outside of us, we must love a being who is in us, and who is not us. And this is true of each and every man. Now only the universal Being is such. The kingdom of God is within us.[43] The universal good is within us, is ourselves and is not us.

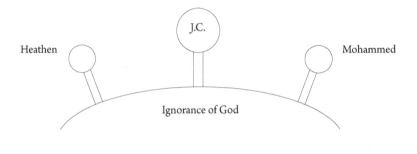

472

Everything turns to good for the elect.[44]

Even the obscurities of scripture, for they honor them because of what is divinely clear. And everything turns out badly for the others, even what is clear; for they blaspheme against them, because of the obscurities they do not understand.

473

One must not judge what the pope is by a few words of the Fathers (as the Greeks said at a Council, *Important Rules*), but by the actions of the Church and of the Fathers and by the canons.

———

43. Luke 17:21: "Neither shall they say: Behold here, or behold there. For lo, *the kingdom of God is within you*."

44. Romans 8:28. Quoted in French.

Unity and the multitude: *Two or three*[45] *into one*.[46] It is an error to exclude one of the two, as the papists do, who exclude the multitude, or the Huguenots, who exclude unity.

———

It is not possible to have a reasonable belief against miracles.

———

The pope is first in rank. Who else is known by all? Who else is recognized by all, having power to insinuate into the whole body because he holds the primary branch, which insinuates itself everywhere.

How easy it was to let this degenerate into tyranny! That is why Jesus Christ set down this precept: *But you shall not be so*.[47]

474

Jesus Christ figured by Joseph.[48]

Beloved of his father, sent by the father to see his brothers, he is innocent, sold by his brothers for twenty farthings, and from there having become their lord, their savior and the savior of strangers and the savior of the world. Which would not have happened without the intent to destroy him, the selling and the reprobation that they undertook.

———

In prison, the innocent Joseph between two criminals; Jesus Christ on the cross between two thieves. He foretold the salvation of one and the death of the other on the same appearances; Jesus Christ saves the elect and damns the reprobate for the same crimes. Joseph only foretells, Jesus fulfills. Joseph asks him who will be saved that he remember him when he comes in his glory; and he whom Jesus Christ saves asks him to remember him when he comes into his kingdom.[49]

———

There is heresy in always interpreting *omnes* as "all," and heresy in not interpreting it sometimes as "all." *Drink ye all of this*[50]: the Huguenots are her-

---

45. Matthew 18:20: "For where *two or three* are gathered in my name, there am I in the midst of them."
46. 1 Corinthians 14:23: "If therefore the whole church come together into one place, and all speak with tongues, and there come in unlearned persons or infidels, will they not say that you are mad?"
47. Luke 22:25–26: "And he said to them: 'The kings of the Gentiles lord it over them; and they that have power over them, are called beneficent. *But you shall not be so*: but he that is the greater among you, let him become as the younger; and he that is the leader, as he that serveth.'"
48. Genesis 37 to 50. Pascal lifts the veil from the story of the patriarch, seeing in it the succession of the Incarnation: from the life of the Trinity and the mission of the Word up to the Passion.
49. The good thief crucified with Jesus. Luke 23:42–43: "And he said to Jesus: Lord, remember me when thou shalt come into thy kingdom. And Jesus said to him: Amen I say to thee, this day thou shalt be with me in paradise."
50. Matthew 26:27–28. At the Last Supper.

etics in interpreting it as "all." *For that all have sinned*[51]: the Huguenots are heretics by excluding the children of the faithful. We must, then, follow the Fathers and tradition in order to know when to do which, since there is heresy to fear on both sides.[52]

475

Miscellany.

Manner of speaking.
I had wanted to devote myself to that.

476

The Synagogue did not perish because it was the figure. But because it was only the figure, it fell into servitude. The figure subsisted until the truth was revealed, so that the Church would always be visible, either in the representation that foretold it or in reality.

477

A miracle, we say, would firm up my belief.[53] We say it when we do not see one. The reasons, which, seen from afar, seem to limit our sight—but once we arrive there, we begin to see even beyond that: nothing stops the volatility of our mind.[54] It is said that there is no rule that does not have an exception, nor any truth so absolute that there is no perspective from which it falls short. It suffices that it not be absolutely universal to give us cause to apply the ex-

---

51. Romans 5:12. "Wherefore as by one man sin entered into this world, and by sin death; and so death passed upon all men, *for that all have sinned*." The Augustinians and Jansenists rigorously interpreted original sin as a kind of hereditary genetic defect that has infected, and will always infect, all human beings who have ever lived, or will ever live.

52. Pascal is underlining the ambiguity of the word "*omnes*" ("all") in the two formulae he cites. "*Bibite ex hoc omnes*": the Huguenots, Pascal argues, are heretical in their insistence on the necessity of communion in two kinds as opposed to the Catholic practice of withholding the cup from the laity. In fact, the Catholic practice is only one of discipline, not of doctrine. With regard to the second citation—"*In quo omnes peccaverunt*"—the Huguenots are heretical in their exemption of the anabaptized children of the faithful from the burden of original sin. In other words, only the Catholic Church, relying upon the Church Fathers and "holy tradition," has the authority to resolve the ambiguity of a word found in scripture. For Pascal, the only authoritative word must be the Latin word *omnes*. The Council of Trent had declared the Latin Vulgate, and not the Greek original, to be the exclusive and definitive version of scripture. Moreover, Pascal assumes that the Calvinists did not know the Fathers and ignores their rigorous teachings on original sin.

53. See fr. 410.

54. Montaigne, *Essays* I, 26, 130: "My conceptions and my judgment move only by groping, staggering, stumbling, and blundering; and when I have gone ahead as far as I can, still I am not at all satisfied: I can still see country beyond." The expression *the volatility of our mind* is found in the *Essays* III, 11, 961.

ception to the current case and say: that is not always true, therefore there are cases where it is not. It only remains to show that this is one of them. And we are indeed awkward or unfortunate if we do not find some angle.

478

Extravagances of the apocalyptics and the pre-Adamites, millenarians,[55] etc.

Whoever wishes to base extravagant opinions upon the scriptures will base them, for example, upon this:

It is said that THIS GENERATION SHALL NOT PASS, TILL ALL THESE THINGS BE DONE.[56] Upon which I will say that after this generation, another generation will come, and so on successively.

In 2 Chronicles[57] Solomon and the king are referred to as if they were two different people. I will say that they were two.

479

The two contrary reasons.[58] It is necessary to begin from there: without that we understand nothing, and everything is heretical.

Similarly, at the end of every truth, it is necessary to add that we remember the opposing truth.

480

If we had to take action only for what is certain, we would have to do nothing for religion, for it is not certain. But how many things do we undertake for what is uncertain: sea voyages, battles! I say then that we should do

---

55. See Wetsel, *Pascal and Disbelief*, 131–76, for an extended discussion of Isaac de La Peyrere and his thesis of the "pre-Adamites." The Apocalyptics, like John of Leyden and those espousing the doctrine of "left-behind" today, prophesized the imminent end of the world and the Second Coming. The Millenarianists, such as the Adventists and the Restorationists today, literally interpreted Revelation 20:3: "And he cast him into the bottomless pit, and shut him up, and set a seal upon him, that he should no more seduce the nations, till the thousand years be finished." They believe that the Messiah will rule for a thousand years on earth with his elect before the Last Judgment. According to modern biblical scholarship, all these sects erroneously take the book of Revelation, a mystical account of Christian martyrdom under the Roman persecutions grounded in its own time, to be a guide to imminent events today.

56. Matthew 24:34.

57. 2 Chronicles 1:13–14: "Then Solomon came from the high place of Gabion to Jerusalem before the tabernacle of the covenant, and reigned over Israel. And he gathered to himself chariots and horsemen, and he had a thousand four hundred chariots, and twelve thousand horsemen: and he placed them in the cities of the chariots, and with the king in Jerusalem."

58. Allusion to Montaigne, *Essays*, II, 15, 563: "There is no reason that does not have its opposite, says the wisest school of philosophy" (i.e., that of the Skeptics).

nothing at all, for nothing is certain, and there is more certainty to religion than that we will live to see tomorrow.

For it is not certain that we will live to see tomorrow, but it is certainly possible that we will not. One cannot say the same for religion. It is not certain that it is, but who will dare say that it is certainly possible that it is not? Now when we work for tomorrow and for the uncertain, we act according to reason.

———

For one must work for the uncertain, by the laws of probability,[59] which are demonstrable.

———

Saint Augustine saw that we labor for the uncertain: at sea, in battle, etc.,[60] but he did not see the laws of probability, which demonstrate that we must do so. Montaigne saw that we are offended by a lame mind and that custom is all powerful,[61] but he did not see the reason for that effect.

All of those people saw the effects, but they did not see the causes.[62] They are to those who have discovered the causes as those who have only eyes are to those who have minds: for the effects can indeed be felt by the senses, whereas the causes are visible only to the mind. And although those particular effects are visible to the mind, this mind is, to the mind that sees causes, as the bodily senses are to the mind itself.

481

Eloquence is a portrait of thought. And thus those who, after having painted, add more, create a picture rather than a portrait.

482

Carriage overturned or turned over, according to the intention.[63]

———

Spill out, or pour out, according to the intention.

———

Defense of M. Le Maître for the Franciscan forced into that order.[64]

———

59. See frs. 186, 187, 680.

60. In *Sermon* 170 Saint Augustine evokes the case of soldiers, who expose themselves to the barbarity of war in the hope of a peaceful and fruitful retirement; then that of ship-owners, who risk everything in storms to acquire riches, which are no more than a gust of wind. Pascal's "etc." refers to other of Augustine's examples: hunters, students . . .

61. Montaigne, *Essays*, I, 23, 100: "there is nothing that custom will not or cannot do, and with reason Pindar calls her, so I have been told, the queen and empress of the world."

62. Pascal's reference is to the philosophers of antiquity (Cicero, Plato), who realized the lamentable state of humanity ("the effects") but remained ignorant of its "causes," i.e., original sin and the Fall.

63. I.e., whether it was intentional or not.

64. Antoine Le Maistre, before retiring to Port-Royal as a solitary, had been a famous lawyer. The

Symmetry,

in what we see at a single glance,

based on the fact that there is no reason to do otherwise.

And based also on the human shape.

And hence we seek symmetry in width only and not in height nor in depth.[65]

483

Scaramouch,[66] who thinks of only one thing.

The *Dottore*[67] who speaks for another quarter of an hour after having said everything. So consumed is he by the desire to speak.

484

Changing the figure, because of our weakness.

485

Guessing/ How much I share in your affliction.[68]
The cardinal did not wish to be second guessed.

————

My mind is filled with anxiety. I am filled with anxiety is more appropriate.

————

Eloquence that persuades gently, and not imperiously, as a tyrant, not as a king.

486

There is a certain model of attractiveness and of beauty that consists of a certain relation between our nature, weak or strong as it may be, and the thing that pleases us.[69]

Everything that is designed according to that model pleases us: be it a

————

reference is to a published version of Le Maistre's summation in defense of a son who had been forced into a religious order. Pascal was said to have mocked his baroque oratory, dating from early in the seventeenth century, in the speech.

65. Saint Augustine, *The True Religion*, 30.

66. Scaramouch was a character of the *Commedia dell'arte*, played on the Paris stage in 1653 by Tiberio Fiorelli, whose performance strongly influenced Molière.

67. The *Dottore* is another character of the *Commedia dell'arte*: that of the pedant Dr. Graziano.

68. The Chevalier de Méré (see introduction, n. 97) mocked the banality of the expression, which may be found in contemporary letters of condolence.

69. See E. Koch, *Pascal and Rhetoric: Figural and Persuasive Language in the Scientific Treatises, the Provinciales, and the Pensées* (Charlottesville: Rockwood Press, 1997), 22–30.

house, song, discourse, verse, prose, woman, birds, rivers, trees, rooms, clothing etc.

———

Everything that is not made according to that model displeases those who have good taste.

———

And, just as there is a precise relation between a song and a house that are made according to that good model, because they resemble that unique model although each in its own way, there is similarly a precise relation among things made according to the bad model. It is not that there is a single bad model, for there are an infinite number of them. But every bad sonnet, for example, on whatever wrong model it is made, resembles precisely a woman dressed according to that model.

———

Nothing makes clearer how much a bad sonnet is ridiculous than to consider both nature and the model, and then to imagine a woman or a house based on that same model.

Poetic Beauty

Just as we say poetic beauty, we should also say geometric beauty or medicinal beauty. But we do not say that, and the reason why is that we know what the object of geometry is and that it consists in proofs, and what the object of medicine is, and that it consists in healing. But we do not know what attractiveness, the object of poetry, consists in. We do not know what constitutes that natural model to be imitated, and for lack of that knowledge, we have invented certain bizarre terms: "golden age," "wonder of our times," "fatal," etc. And we call that jargon poetic beauty.

But whoever imagines a woman on that model, which consists in saying small things with big words, will see a pretty young woman resplendent in mirrors and chains, at whom we will laugh, for we know better what constitutes the attractiveness of a woman than the attractiveness of verse. But those who know no better would admire her in her attire, and there are many villages in which she would be taken for the queen. And that is why we call sonnets written according to that model "village queens."

———

We do not pass in the world for experts on verse if we do not sport the emblem of the poet, of the mathematician, etc. But universal people want no such identifying emblem, and they hardly make any difference between the profession of poet and that of embroiderer.

Universal people are called neither poet nor geometer, etc. But they are all of those things, and judge all of those people. They are difficult to find out. They will speak about the topic under discussion when they arrive. One cannot perceive in them one quality rather than another, beyond the necessity of putting it to use. But then we remember it, for it is equally part of that character that we do not say that they speak well, when language is not the matter at hand, and that we say that they speak well when it is.[70]

It is thus false praise that we confer on a man when we say of him, upon his arrival, that he is very capable in poetry. And it is a bad sign when we do not have recourse to that man when the matter at hand is to judge some verse.

487

Faith is a gift of God. Do not believe that we said that it is a gift of reasoning. The other religions do not say that about their faith. They give only reasoning as the means to achieve it, which nonetheless does not lead to it.

488

The devil troubled the zeal of the Jews before Jesus Christ because he might have done them good, but not afterwards.

The Jewish people, mocked by the Gentiles; the Christian people, persecuted.

489

Adam a figure of him who was to come.[71] The six days to make the one, the six ages to form the other. The six days that Moses portrays for the formation of Adam are only the image of the six ages to form Jesus Christ and the Church. If Adam had not sinned and Jesus Christ had not come, there would have been only one covenant, only one age of man, and Creation would have been portrayed as completed at a single moment.

---

70. This capacity of "universal people" to talk competently, but unobtrusively, of any topic in a conversation is reminiscent of the definition of the *honnête homme* in the seventeenth century. On the terms *honnête homme* and *honnêteté*, see the editor's preface.

71. Romans 5:14: "But death reigned from Adam unto Moses, even over them also who have not sinned after the similitude of the transgression of *Adam*, who is *a figure of him who was to come.*"

490

If they were being led by terror, without guidance. It would seem like wicked domination. Augustine, Letter 48 or 49.[72]

———

Fourth volume: *Against Lying,* to Consentius.[73]

72. Saint Augustine's *Letter to Vincent,* 93. Pascal refers to Augustine's admonition that instruction must accompany that torture which proved a last resort in converting the Donatists. Pascal, who rejects all calls for tyranny in religious matters, probably made this notation in view of developing the same theory of tyranny he outlines in frs. 91–92 and 485. Pascal was the first modern Catholic theologian to reject tyranny as a means to religious conversion.

73. A reference to Saint Augustine's *Against Lying.* The Spanish bishop Consentius had proposed infiltrating the Priscillian heretics with covert Catholics in order to subvert their sect. Augustine rejects such methods of espionage and subterfuge. Truth, writes Augustine, has no need of deceit. Pascal, in setting down this parallel between this text and that of the preceding reference, seeks to set Augustine in contradiction with himself with regard to the use of force in religious conversion. Priscillianism was a heretical doctrine, derived from the Gnostic-Manichaeism, promulgated in Roman Hispania in the fourth century by the ascetic Priscillian. His followers denied the pre-existence of Christ and his real humanity and forbade marriage and procreation. Among their odder practices was that of fasting on Sundays.

[XXXIV Assorted Thoughts 2]

491

General conduct of the world toward the Church.

God wishing to blind and to enlighten.

The outcome having proved the divine origins of the prophecies, the rest of it must be believed. And from there we see the order of the world in this fashion.

———

The miracles of the Creation and the Flood being forgotten, God sent the law and the miracles of Moses. The prophets who prophesy particular things[1]: and to prepare for a lasting miracle he prepares the prophecies and their fulfillment. But the prophecies can be suspect, he wishes to make them non-suspect, etc.[2]

———

If one does not know oneself to be full of pride, ambition, concupiscence, weakness, wretchedness, and injustice, one is truly blind. And if, knowing it, one does not desire to be delivered from them, what can be said of a man ... ?

What can we have if not esteem for a religion that knows so well the faults of man, and desire for the truth of a religion that promises such welcome remedies for them?

492

If the Jews had all been converted by Jesus Christ, we would have only suspect witnesses left. And if they had been exterminated, we would have none at all.

493

The Jews reject him, but not all of them: the saints, and not the carnal, accept him. Far from taking away from his glory, it is the final stroke that brings

———

1. See ch. XXVI, "Particular Figures," and frs. 660 and 719.
2. By the hostile testimony of the Jews.

it to perfection. As the reason that they cite, and the only one to be found in all their writings, in the Talmud and among the rabbis, is that Jesus Christ did not conquer the nations with weapons in hand—*Your sword, O most mighty*[3]—is that all they have to say? Jesus Christ was slain, they say, he succumbed, he did not conquer the heathen by force, he did not give us their spoils, he gives us no riches: is that not all they have to say? That is what makes him lovable to me. I would not want the one whom they picture. It is clear that it was only their vice that kept them from accepting him. And through that rejection they are unimpeachable witnesses, and, what is more, through it they are fulfilling the prophecies.

(*By means of this people not accepting him, the following miracle was brought about:*

The prophecies are the only lasting miracles that can be accomplished, but they are subject to being contradicted.)

————

(*By those who are unhappy to find themselves without faith we see that God does not enlighten them. But for the others, we see that there is a God who blinds them.*)

494

The self is hateful.[4] You, Miton,[5] cover it up, but that does not mean that you remove it: you are, therefore, still hateful.

"Not at all. For in acting, as we do, obligingly to all, there is no cause for hating us any longer."—That is true, if we hated in the self only the displeasure that we derived from it.

But if I hate the self because it is unjust, because it makes itself the center of all things, I will always hate it.

In a word, the self has two qualities: it is unjust in itself, in that it makes itself the center of all things; it is a nuisance to others, in that it wishes to subjugate them, for every self is the enemy and would like to be the tyrant of all others. You remove the nuisance from the self, but not the injustice.

And thus you do not make it lovable to those who hate its injustice. You make it lovable only to the unjust, who no longer find it their enemy. And thus you remain unjust, and can please only the unjust.[6]

3. See fr. 282.

4. For Pascal, the "self," man's very *ego*, is that hereditary residue of original sin, that pathology responsible for the entire flawed human condition, which makes it impossible for man to truly love God.

5. On Miton, see "Religious Challenges to the Modern Reader," in the introduction, especially n. 97. Miton's code of *honnêteté* only bandages over that fatal cancerous lesion, the *ego*, which afflicts man because of original sin. The *ego*, the self, must be surgically extirpated, so to speak, in order to free humanity from the curse of Adam.

6. This is perhaps Pascal's most radical analysis of man in the entire *Pensées*. So radical that the editors

495

What spoils comparisons for us between the state of the Church in former times and its present condition is that we usually regard Saint Athanasius,[7] Saint Theresa, and the others as crowned with glory and [...][8] judged like gods before our time. Now that time has cleared things up, it does so appear. But at the time when he was being persecuted this great saint was only a man called Athanasius and Saint Theresa was considered insane.[9] *Elias was just a man like us,* subject to the same passions as we are, said Saint Peter[10] in order to disabuse Christians of the erroneous idea that makes us reject the example of the saints as bearing no proportion to our state. "They were saints" we say, "and not as we are." What happened then in those times? Saint Athanasius was just a man called Athanasius, accused of a number of crimes, condemned by such and such a council; all the bishops agreed, and ultimately the pope. What were dissenters told? That they were disrupting the peace, creating schism, etc.

Zeal, light. Four kinds of people: zeal without knowledge; knowledge without zeal; neither knowledge nor zeal; both zeal and knowledge.

The first three condemn him,[11] the last acquit him and are excommunicated by the Church and nonetheless save the Church.

496

But is it probable that probability yields assurance?

Difference between tranquility and certainty of conscience. Nothing gives assurance, but truth. Nothing gives tranquility, but the sincere search for the truth.

497

The corruption of reason is revealed by so many different and extravagant *mores.* Truth had to come so that man would no longer live just for himself.

---

of the original *Edition of Port-Royal* inserted the following disclaimer: "The word MOI used by the author in this thought means only 'self-love.'" In the *Logic of Port-Royal* (III, 20), we find the following extraordinary testimony: "The late Monsieur Pascal, who knew more about true rhetoric than anyone has ever known . . . insisted on the principle that an *honnête homme* should avoid referring to himself and even pronouncing the words *I* and *me.* He was accustomed to saying with regard to this subject that Christian piety annihilates the human self and that proper civility hides and suppresses it." Arnauld and Nicole, *Logic,* trans. Baynes, 268. Again, see ch. XVII, fr. 253 and n. 23.

7. See ch. XXXII, n. 15.
8. Undecipherable word.
9. Theresa of Avila (1515–82), *Life Written by Her Own Hand,* ch. 32.
10. In fact, James 5:17.
11. I.e., Athanasius.

498

The casuists submit decisions to corrupt reason and the choice of decisions to corrupt will, so that all that is corrupt in man's nature play a part in his conduct.

499

You[12] want the Church to judge neither the interior because that belongs only to God, nor the exterior, because God considers the interior alone. And thus, taking away from it all choice of men, you keep within the Church the most dissolute people and those who so dishonor it that the Jews' synagogues and the philosophers' sects would have exiled them as unworthy and would have abhorred them as impious.

500

Whoever wishes it is ordained a priest, as under Jeroboam.[13]

It is a horrific thing that the discipline of today's Church is presented as so good, that wanting to change it has been made a crime. In former times it was infallibly good, and we find that it could be changed without sinning. And now, in the state it is in, we are not supposed to want it changed?

It was certainly permitted to change the custom of ordaining priests only with such circumspection that you could hardly find anyone worthy. And it will not be permitted to complain of the custom that allows so many who are unworthy?[14]

———

Abraham took nothing for himself, but only for his servants.[15] Thus the righteous takes nothing for himself from this world or from the world's acclaim, but only for his passions, which he uses as master, saying to one: *Go and Come.*[16] *The lust thereof shall be under thee.*[17] His passions thus overcome are virtues: avarice, jealousy, anger, God too attributes them to himself;[18] and

12. Pascal here addresses the Jesuits.

13. 1 Kings 12:31: To prevent his subjects from making pilgrimages to the Temple in Jerusalem, King Jeroboam "made temples in the high places, and priests of the lowest of the people, who were not of the sons of Levi."

14. Pascal's ideas on the priestly vocation were strongly impregnated by a letter of Saint-Cyran published in 1648.

15. After his victory over the coalition of four kings. Genesis 14:22–24.

16. Luke 7:7–8. The centurion who comes and asks that his servant be healed has faith that Jesus can cure his servant from where he stands: "but say the word, and my servant shall be healed. For I also am a man subject to authority, having under me soldiers: and I say to one, *Go*, and he goeth; *and* to another, *Come*, and he cometh." Pascal quotes these two imperatives in French.

17. Genesis 4:7. God's warning to Cain before he kills Abel.

18. For instance, Exodus 20:5.

they are virtues as much as clemency, pity, constancy, which are also passions. They must be used like slaves, and, leaving them their food, the soul must be prevented from partaking of it. For when the passions are masters, they are vices, and then they give the soul some of their food, and the soul feeds on it and poisons itself.

501
Church, pope
Unity/multitude

In considering the Church as a unity, the pope, who is its head, is like the whole. In considering it as a multitude, the pope is but a part. The Fathers considered it sometimes in the one manner, sometimes in the other, and thus spoke in diverse ways about the pope.

Saint Cyprian, PRIEST OF GOD.[19]

But in establishing one of these truths, they did not exclude the other.

The multitude that is not reducible to unity is confusion. Unity that does not depend on the multitude is tyranny.

There is almost nowhere now except France where it is permissible to say that the council is above the pope.

502

Man is full of needs. He loves only those who can fulfill them all. He is a good mathematician, we might say, but I have no use for mathematics: he would take me for a proposition. He is a good warrior: he would take me for a place under siege. What is needed therefore is an *honnête homme*, who be able to adapt to all my needs in general.

A true friend is such an advantageous thing, even for the highest dignitaries, so that he might speak well of them and support them even in their absence, that they must do everything to gain one. But let them choose wisely! For if they expend their efforts on fools, it will be useless, whatever good they say of them; moreover, they will not speak well of them if they are the weakest party, for they have no authority, and thus they will speak ill of them in order to be part of the majority.

---

19. Saint Cyprian, *Letter* 63: "If Jesus Christ, our Lord and our God, is himself the sovereign *priest of God* the Father, if he first offered himself in sacrifice to the Father and asked that we do the same in memory of him, he plays everywhere the role of Christ, the priest who imitates what Christ did." In *St. Cyprian, Letters 1–81*, trans. Sr. Rose Bernard Donna, Fathers of the Church 51 (Washington, D.C.: The Catholic University of America Press, 1964).

503

(*See the discourses of the Jansenist in the 2nd, 4th, and 5th:*[20] *this is lofty and serious.*)

———

(*I hate equally the buffoon and the overblown person.*) One would not be friends with one or the other.

———

We consult only the ear because we lack heart.

———

The rule is *honnêteté.*[21]

———

Poet, and not an *honnête homme.* [22]

———

Beauties of omission, of judgment.

504

Figures.

Savior, father, sacrificing priest, sacrificial offering, food, king, wise man, lawgiver, oppressed, poor, having to form a people, whom he had to lead and feed, and bring into its own land.

Jesus Christ. Offices.

He alone had to form a great elect people, holy and chosen, lead it, feed it, bring it to a place of rest and holiness, make it holy to God, make it the temple of God, reconcile it to God, save it from the wrath of God, deliver it from the servitude of sin that reigns visibly in man, give laws to this people, inscribe those laws in their hearts, give himself to God for them, sacrifice himself for them, be a spotless offering, and himself the sacrificing priest, having to offer his own body and his blood, and nevertheless offer bread and wine to God.

When he cometh into the world.[23]

Stone upon stone.[24]

———

What preceded, what followed. All of the Jews surviving and wandering.

———

20. I.e., in the second, fourth, and fifth *Provincial Letters.*
21. On this word, see the section "French Words" in the editor's preface.
22. After this line, there is a struck passage not transcribed by C2.
23. Hebrews 10:5–6: "Wherefore *when he cometh into the world,* he saith: Sacrifice and oblation thou wouldest not: but a body thou hast fitted to me. Holocausts for sin did not please thee."
24. Mark 13:2: Jesus, before the Temple of Jerusalem says: "Seest thou all these great buildings? There shall not be left a stone upon a stone that shall not be thrown down."

They pierced: Zechariah 12:10.[25]

Prophecies.

That a Liberator would come who would crush the head of the demon, who would deliver his people from its sins, *from all its iniquities*.[26] That there would be a new Testament that would be eternal, that there would be another priesthood *according to the order of Melchizedek*,[27] that that one would be eternal, that the Christ would be glorious, powerful, strong, and nevertheless so piteous that he would not be recognized,[28] that he would not be taken for what he is, that he would be rejected, that he would be killed, that his people who would have renounced him would no longer be his people, that the idolaters would receive him and would have recourse to him, that he would leave Zion to rule in the midst of idolatry, that nevertheless the Jews would still subsist, that he would be of Judah, and when there would be no more kings.

505

Whether the soul is mortal or immortal must indubitably make all the difference in morality. And nevertheless philosophers have deduced their morality independently of that!

———

They deliberate to pass one hour.

———

Plato, to dispose people towards Christianity.[29]

506

Greatness, wretchedness

As we acquire more wisdom, we discover more greatness and more wretchedness in man.

The common man.

Those who are more elevated.

The philosophers.

They astonish the common man.

Christians. They astonish the philosophers.

25. Prediction of Zechariah cited in John 19:37: "They shall look on him whom *they pierced*." The crucified Jesus is pierced with a lance by a Roman soldier to make sure he is dead. Mary and John see blood and water flow from the wound.

26. Psalm 130:8: "And he shall redeem Israel *from all his iniquities*."

27. Genesis 14:18: Melchisedek's offering of bread and water prefigures the Eucharist.

28. Isaiah 53:3.

29. Following Jansenius and Saint Augustine, Pascal considers Plato the pagan philosopher who came closest to perceiving Christian truth.

Who indeed will be surprised to see that religion only allows us to know more fully that which we recognize as we acquire more wisdom.

507
Figurative

God made use of the Jews' concupiscence to have them serve Jesus Christ (*who brought the cure for concupiscence*).

508
Figurative

Nothing is so similar to charity than cupidity, and nothing so contrary to it. Thus the Jews, puffed up with the possessions that flattered their cupidity, were in conformity with Christians, and most contrary to them. And in this way they had the two qualities that they had to have to be in conformity with the Messiah, in order to figure him, and most contrary to him, in order to be witnesses above suspicion.

509

Concupiscence has become natural to us and has made our second nature. Thus, there are two natures in us: one good, the other evil. Where is God? Where you are not. And *the kingdom of God is in you.*[30] Rabbis.

510

He who does not hate in himself his self-love and that instinct that leads him to make himself God, is truly blinded. Who does not see that nothing is so opposed to justice and truth? For it is false that we deserve that, and it is unjust and impossible to attain it, for all ask for the same thing. It is therefore a manifest injustice in which we are born, from which we cannot separate ourselves and from which we must separate ourselves.

Yet no religion has noted that this was a sin, or that we were born to it, or that we were obliged to resist it, nor has any thought of providing remedies for it.

511

If there is a God, we must love only him and not transient creatures. The reasoning of the impious in *Wisdom* is founded only on the contention that there is no God. "That posited, he says, *let us enjoy the creatures.*"[31]

30. Luke 17:21.
31. Wisdom 2:6: "Come therefore, and *let us enjoy* the good things that are present, and let us speedily use *the creatures* as in youth."

It is only for lack of a better alternative. But if there were a God to love, he would not have concluded that, but quite the contrary. And it is the conclusion of the wise that "there is a God, let us thus not take pleasure in creatures."

———

Thus everything that incites us to become attached to creatures is bad, for that prevents us either from serving God, if we know him, or from searching for him, if we do not know him. Now we are full of concupiscence, thus we are full of evil, thus we should hate ourselves and everything that excites us to any attachment other than to God alone.

512

All of their principles are true, those of Pyrrhonians, Stoics, atheists, etc. But their conclusions are false, because the opposing principles are also true.

513

Man is obviously made to think. That is his whole dignity and his whole merit, and his whole duty is to think properly. Now the order of thought is to begin with oneself and one's creator and one's end.

Now what do people think about? Never about that! But about dancing, playing the lute, singing, writing verse, running at the ring,[32] etc., fighting, making oneself king, without thinking about what it is to be a king, and to be a man.

514

Internal warfare in man between reason and the passions.

If only there was reason without passions.

If only there were passions without reason.

But having one and the other he cannot exist without war, not being able to be at peace with one without being at war with the other.

Thus, he is always divided and contrary to himself.

515

Ennui

Nothing is so unbearable to man than being in complete tranquility, without passions, without concerns, without diversion, without effort. He then feels his nothingness, his abandonment, his insufficiency, his dependence, his

32. Running at the ring: a game in which the knight must capture a ring suspended on a picket with the end of his lance. It was a way for men to prove their worth in the courtship rituals.

powerlessness, his emptiness. Immediately, he will find emerging from the depths of his soul *ennui*, darkness, sadness, sorrow, resentment, and despair.

516

If it is a supernatural blindness to live without searching for what one is, it is a terrible blindness to live badly while believing in God.

517

Prophecies

That Jesus Christ will be on the right while God subjugates his enemies under him.[33]

Therefore he will not subjugate them himself.

518

Injustice

That presumption should be added to wretchedness, this is extreme injustice.

519

Search for the true good

Common man situates true good in fortune and in outward goods, or at least in diversion.

Philosophers have shown the vanity of all that, and placed it where they could.

520

Vanity is so entrenched in man's heart that a soldier, a military valet, a cook, a baggage carrier brags and wishes to have admirers, and philosophers too want them, and those who write against them want the glory of having written well, and those who read them want the glory of having read [them], and I who write this perhaps have that desire, and perhaps those who will read it . . .[34]

---

33. Psalm 110:1–2.

34. Montaigne, *Essays*, 1, 41, 227: "Of all of the illusions in the world, the most universally received is the concern for reputation and glory, which we espouse even to the point of giving up riches, rest, life, and health, which are effectual and substantial goods, to follow this vain phantom and mere sound that has neither body nor substance [. . .]. And of the irrational humors of men, it seems that even the philosophers get rid of this one later and more reluctantly than any other [. . .]. There is hardly any other illusion whose vanity reason condemns so clearly; but it has such live roots in us that I do not know whether anyone yet

521

On the desire to be esteemed by those with whom one finds oneself.

Pride holds us with such a natural possession[35] in the midst of our wretchedness, error, etc., that we even happily lose our lives provided that people talk about it.

Vanity: gaming, hunting, visits, theater, false perpetuity of a name.

522

This duality of man is so visible that there are those who have thought that we had two souls.

A simple subject seems to them incapable of such sudden variations: from boundless presumption to a horrible dejection of the heart.[36]

523

The nature of man is: all nature. *Every beast.*[37]

There is nothing that cannot be made natural. There is nothing natural that cannot be effaced.

524

It is good to be wearied and fatigued by the pointless quest for the true good, in order to extend one's arms to the Redeemer.

525

Man's sensibility to small things and insensibility to great things: the mark of an extraordinary reversal.[38]

---

has ever been able to get clean rid of it [...]. For as Cicero says, even those who combat it still want the books that they write about it to bear their name on the title page, and want to become glorious for having despised glory."

35. See Montaigne, *Essays* III, 1, 726: "Our being is cemented with sickly qualities: ambition, jealousy, envy, vengeance, superstition, despair, dwell in us with a possession so natural that we recognize their image also in the beasts."

36. Montaigne, *Essays*, I, 1, 293: "These supple variations and contradictions that are seen in us have made some imagine that we have two souls, and others that two powers accompany us and drive us, each in its own way, one toward good, the other toward evil; for such sudden diversity cannot well be reconciled with a simple subject." The advocates of the duality of the soul were first and foremost the Manicheans, Augustine's target in the treatise *On the Two Souls*.

37. Ecclesiastics 13:19: "*Every beast* loveth its like: so also every man him that is nearest to himself." Here, as in fr. 545, Pascal's interpretation of the Latin phrase, *omne animal*, seems to differ from its source, as it is a gloss of the phrase "all nature," therefore meaning *wholly a beast*.

38. I.e., the Fall. See fr. 681, par. 19.

526

Despite the sight of all our miseries, which touch us, which hold us by the throat, we have an instinct that we cannot repress [and] that raises us.

527

The most important thing in all of life is the choice of a profession: chance decides it. Custom makes masons, soldiers, roofers. He is an excellent roofer, they say. And in speaking of soldiers: they are quite mad, some say. And others, on the contrary: the only noble venture is war, the rest of men are scoundrels. Constantly hearing some professions praised and others excoriated since childhood, we make our choice. For naturally we love virtue and hate folly. Those words themselves are moving, and we fall short only in their application. So great is the force of custom that, where nature only created men, we create all conditions of man.[39]

For some countries are comprised wholly of masons, others of soldiers, etc. No doubt nature is not so uniform. It is custom then that accomplishes all of that, for it constrains nature. And sometimes nature overpowers it and holds man to his instinct, despite all custom, good or bad.

---

39. Montaigne, *Essays*, III, 13, 1008: "It is for habit to give form to our life, just as it pleases: it is all powerful in that; it is Circe's drink, which varies our nature as it sees fit."

[XXXV Assorted Thoughts 3]

528

We like to see the error, the passion of Cléobuline, because she does not recognize it.[1] She would be displeasing if she were not deceived.

Prince is pleasing to a king because it diminishes his rank.

529

Extinguish the flame of sedition: too florid.

The restlessness of his genius: two daring words too many.

If we are in good health, we can hardly imagine how we would cope if we were ill. When we are ill, we take medicine happily: ill health resolves us to it; we no longer have the passions and desires for diversions and strolls that good health gave us, and which are incompatible with the necessities of ill health. Nature gives us passions and desires that conform to our present state. It is only the fears that we, and not nature, give us that trouble us because they link the state that we are in to the passions of the state in which we are not.[2]

Since nature always renders us unhappy in all states, our desires represent for us a state of happiness, because they link the state that we are in to the pleasures of the state in which we are not. And should we ever attain those pleasures, we would still not be happy, for we would have desires in conformity with that new state.

It is necessary to particularize this general proposition.

1. In *Le Grand Cyrus* (1649–53), a novel by Madeleine de Scudéry, Cléobuline, queen of Corinth, is in love, without realizing it, with one of her subjects. She was thought to be a portrait of Queen Christina of Sweden, to whom Pascal had sent one of his mathematical machines. Pascal himself asserted in the fourteenth *Provincial Letter* that he had never read a single "novel."

2. Montaigne had developed this idea several times: See *Essays* I, 20, II, 37, and particularly II, 6, 325: "Many things seem to us greater in imagination than in reality. I have spent a good part of my life in perfect and entire health: I mean not merely entire, but even blithe and ebullient. This state full of verdure and cheer, made me find the thought of illnesses so horrible that when I came to experience them I found their pains mild and easy compared with my fears."

529b

Those who, in troublesome cases, always keep their hopes up and rejoice when events turn out well, if they are not equally tormented when things turn out badly, may be suspected of being pleased at this outcome; and they are delighted to find those pretexts for optimism to show that they take interest in it, and to conceal with feigned joy their actual joy at seeing that their case is lost.

Our nature consists in movement, complete rest is death.

Miton[3] sees clearly that nature is corrupt and that men are the reverse of what *honnêteté* prescribes. But he does not know why they cannot fly higher.[4]

Hidden noble deeds are the most worthy of esteem. When I see some in history, such as on page 184,[5] they delight me; but then again they were not completely concealed, since they were discovered. And, whatever may have been done to hide them, the little that reveals them spoils everything. For this is the most beautiful—to have wished to conceal them.

Can it be anything but the world's acquiescence that makes you find things probable? Will you have us believe that it could be the truth, and that, were duels not a fad, you would find it probable that men could fight, by considering the thing itself?[6]

530

Justice is what is established. And thus all of our established laws will necessarily be held as just without being examined, because they are established.

---

3. On Miton, see introduction, nn. 97 and 98.

4. Miton agrees that nature is corrupt, but he knows neither how nor why. He does not understand that hereditary original sin has corrupted all humanity and prevents human beings from transcending their uncivilized state—a recurring analysis of the superiority of the Christian religion.

5. A reference to the pagination of the 1652 edition of Montaigne's *Essays*, where Pascal read the following two accounts: "Catullus Luctatius, in the war against the Cimbrians, after making every effort to stop his soldiers from fleeing before the enemy, himself joined the fugitives and played the coward, so that they should seem rather to be following their captain than fleeing from the enemy. That was abandoning his reputation to cover the shame of others. When the Emperor Charles V came into Provence in the year 1537, they say that Antonio de Leyva, seeing his master resolved on this expedition and believing that it would add wonderfully to his glory, nevertheless expressed a contrary opinion and advised him against it; to this end, that all the glory and honor of this plan should be attributed to his master, and that it might be said that his good judgment and foresight had been such that, against the opinion of everyone, he had carried out such a splendid enterprise: which for de Leyva was to honor his master at his own expense." Montaigne, *Essays*, I, 41, 227–28.

6. The maxims of the casuists on duels are reported in the seventh *Provincial Letter*.

531
Feeling

Memory, joy are feelings. And even geometric propositions become feelings, for reason makes feelings natural and natural feelings are effaced by reason.

532
Honnête homme

We should be able to say of him not that he is a mathematician, or a preacher, or eloquent; but that he is an *honnête homme*.[7] This universal quality alone pleases me. When on seeing a man we remember his book, it is a bad sign. I would like a quality to be apparent only when the occasion arises to use it, NOTHING IN EXCESS for fear that one quality prevail and become an identifying trait. Let us not be made aware that he speaks well, unless speaking well is called for. But then let us be made aware of it.

533
Miracles

The people conclude this for themselves, but if it is necessary to give you a reason . . .

———

It is unfortunate to be the exception to the rule. It is even necessary to be severe and opposed to the exception. But nevertheless, as it is certain that there are exceptions to the rule, we must judge severely, but justly.[8]

534
Montaigne

What good there is in Montaigne can only be acquired with difficulty. What is bad in him, I mean apart from morals, could have been corrected in a moment, had he been alerted to the fact that he told too many tales and spoke too much about himself.[9]

---

7. See La Rochefoucauld, *Maximes* [Maximes], no. 203: "Le vrai honnête homme est celui qui ne se pique de rien [The true *honnête homme* is one who does not pride himself upon anything.]" La Rochefoucauld, *Maximes*, no. 203, trans. J. Farrell, in *Paranoia and Modernity: Cervantes to Rousseau* (Ithaca, Cornell University Press, 2006), 170.

8. As opposed to the laxity of the casuists, who go as far as to authorize homicide.

9. Montaigne, *Essays*, III, 8, 875: "I dare not only to speak of myself, but to speak only of myself: I go astray when I write of anything else and get away from my subject."

535

Have you never seen people who, to complain of how little you think of them, liberally boast to you of people of rank who hold them in esteem? I would respond to that: "Show me the merit by which you charmed those people, and I too will hold you in esteem."

536

Memory is necessary for all of the operations of reason.

When a natural discourse paints a passion or an effect, we find in ourselves the truth of what we hear, a truth that we did not know was there, such that we are led to love the person who made us perceive it, for he has not shown us his riches, but our own. And thus that good deed makes him agreeable to us, beyond the fact that the community of understanding that we share with him necessarily inclines our heart to love him.

537

Probability

All can contribute, none can remove.[10]

538

You never accuse me of falsehood about Escobar,[11] because he is commonly known.[12]

539

Discourses about humility are a matter of pride for the prideful and of humility for the humble. Thus those about Pyrrhonism are a matter of assertion for the assertive. Few speak of humility humbly, few of chastity chastely, few of Pyrrhonism with doubt.[13] We are but deceit, duplicity, contrariety, and we hide and disguise ourselves from ourselves.

---

10. See the thirteenth *Provincial Letter*. The casuists contradict one another. Any recognized theologian may assert his opinions as "probable." The Jesuits teach, or so Pascal claims, that confessors are thus compelled to absolve penitents even of sins that most other theologians condemn.

11. On Escobar, see ch. XXXII, "Miracles [3]," n. 16.

12. Escobar had published forty-one works, among them his 1644 *Liber theologiæ moralis* [Moral theology]. Anyone, Pascal asserts, can verify the accuracy of his own citations from Escobar's works in his *Provincial Letters*.

13. Montaigne, *Essays*, II, 12, 477: "I can see why the Pyrrhonian philosophers cannot express their general conception in any manner of speaking; for they would need a new language. Ours is wholly formed of affirmative propositions, which to them are utterly repugnant; so that when they say 'I doubt,' immediately you have them by the throat to make them admit that at least they know and are sure of this fact that they doubt."

540

In writing down my thought, it slips away sometimes, but that reminds me of my weakness, which I forget constantly. That teaches me as much as the forgotten thought, for I am interested only in knowing my nothingness.[14]

541

Pitying the unfortunate is not opposed to concupiscence. On the contrary, we are quite pleased to have to give this token of friendship and to earn a reputation for kindness without giving anything.

542

Conversation

Great words for religion: "I deny it."

Conversation

Pyrrhonism serves religion.[15]

543

Is it right to kill in order to prevent there being evil people?

It is to create two in the place of one. OVERCOME EVIL BY THE GOOD, Saint Augustine.[16]

14. See Montaigne, *Essays*, III, 13, 1001–1002: "When I find myself convicted of a false opinion by another man's reasoning, I do not so much learn what new thing he has told me and this particular bit of ignorance—that would be small gain—as I learn about my weakness in general and the treachery of my understanding; whence I derive the reformation of the whole mass. [...] To learn that we have said and done a foolish thing, that is nothing; we must learn that we are nothing but fools, a far broader and more important lesson."

15. In the Apology, skepticism will serve to neutralize anti-religious bias, making way for Pascal's exposition of Christian revelation. In the *Exchange with M. de Sacy*, Sacy compares Pascal to a skilled physician who knows how to extract powerful medicines from the most virulent poisons, i.e., "skepticism."

16. Saint Augustine, *Sermon* 302: "Why do you unleash yourself against evil doers? [...] You make yourself one of them in unleashing yourself against them. [...] *There will then be two evils, both to be overcome.* Do you not hear the counsel of your Lord, through the voice of the Apostle: 'Do not let yourself be overcome by evil, but *overcome evil by the good*.'" See Romans 12:21.

544

Spongia solis[17]

When we see an effect always occur in the same way, we conclude that it is a natural necessity, such as that tomorrow the sun will rise, etc. But frequently nature proves us wrong and does not obey its own rules.

The mind naturally believes, and the will naturally loves. So that lacking any true objects, they must attach themselves to false ones.[18]

Grace will always exist in the world, and also nature, so that grace is in some way natural. And thus there will always be Pelagians,[19] and always Catholics, and always conflict.

Because the first birth makes the former, and the grace of the second birth makes the latter.

Nature always renews the same things: years, days, hours; and so it goes with spaces; numbers are continuous and follow one another in sequence. Thus is produced a kind of infinity and eternity. Not that there is anything in all this that is infinite and eternal but those finite entities multiply themselves infinitely. Thus, it seems to me, only number, that multiplies them, is infinite.

545

Man is properly speaking *every beast*.[20]

546

Dominion founded on opinion and imagination rules for a time, and that dominion is gentle and voluntary. That of force rules forever. Thus opinion is like the queen of the world,[21] but force is its tyrant.

547

He will be well condemned who is condemned by Escobar!

---

17. "Sponge of the sun." A phosphorous rock discovered in 1604, which becomes luminous when exposed to light and even more so when exposed to the rays of the sun. This phenomenon contradicted the scientific consensus that light was always accompanied by heat and therefore could never go through opaque surfaces.

18. Perhaps a reference to the title of an essay of Montaigne: "How the Soul Discharges Its Passions on False Objects, When the True Are Wanting."

19. See the introduction, nn. 29 and 30. For Pascal, the Jesuits are neo-Pelagians.

20. On this phrase, and Pascal's interpretation, see ch. XXXIV, n. 37.

21. See ch. III, n. 30.

Eloquence

The pleasant and the real are both necessary, but the pleasant itself must be derived from the true.[22]

Everyone is everything to himself, for, once dead, everything is dead for oneself.[23] And for this reason everyone believes that he is everything to all people. We must not judge nature according to ourselves but according to it.

548

In all dialogues and discourses we must be able to say to those who take offense: "What are you complaining about?"

549

Great wit, bad character.

550

Do you wish others to think well of you? Do not speak well of yourself.

551

Not only do we look at things from other sides, but with other eyes. We are far from finding them the same.[24]

552

He no longer loves that person whom he loved ten years ago. I can well believe it: she is not the same, nor is he. He was young and so was she: she is completely different. He would perhaps still love her as she was then.

553

We do not keep to virtue by our own strength, but by the counterweight of two opposing vices, just as we stand upright in two opposing winds. Remove one of those vices, and we fall into the other.

---

22. Saint Augustine, *On Christian Doctrine*, IV, 28: "The man who does not strive about words, whether he speak quietly, temperately, or vehemently, uses words with no other purpose than to make the truth plain, pleasing, and effective [...]. But the man who cannot speak both eloquently and wisely should speak wisely without eloquence, rather than eloquently without wisdom." Translated by James Shaw, from Nicene and Post-Nicene Fathers, 1st. ser., vol. 2, ed. Philip Schaff (Buffalo, N.Y.: Christian Literature Publishing Co., 1887); rev. and ed. for *New Advent* by Kevin Knight, http://www.newadvent.org/fathers/12024.htm.

23. Montaigne, *Essays*, I, 20, 77: "As our birth brought us the birth of all things, so will our death bring us the death of all things."

24. Montaigne, *Essays*, I, 38, 210–11: "There is nothing changed, but our soul looks on the thing with a different eye, and represents it to itself in another aspect, for each thing has many angles and many lights."

554
Style

When we see a natural style, we are astonished and delighted, for we expected to see an author and instead we find a man. Whereas those who have good taste and who, when they see a book, expect to find a man, are quite surprised to find an author: YOU SPOKE MORE AS A POET THAN AS A MAN.[25] They truly honor nature, they who show it that it can speak about all things, and even about theology.

555

The world must indeed be blind, if it believes you.

556

The pope hates and fears learned men who have not sworn obedience to him.

557

Man is neither angel nor beast, and unfortunately whoever tries to play the angel plays the beast.[26]

558
Prov.[27]

Those who love the Church complain of seeing morals corrupted: but at least the laws remain. But these people corrupt the laws. The model is spoiled.

559
Montaigne

Montaigne's faults are considerable. Lascivious words: that is worthless, despite Mademoiselle de Gournay.[28]

---

25. "You've talked more often like a poet than you have like a human being!" Petronius, *Satyricon*, 90; *The Satyricon of Petronius Arbiter*, trans. W. C. Firebaugh, available online through Project Gutenberg, https://www.gutenberg.org/files/5225/5225-h/5225-h.htm#linkVOLUME_III.

26. Montaigne, *Essays*, III, 13, 1044: "They want to get out of themselves and escape from the man. That is madness: instead of changing into angels, they change into beasts; instead of raising themselves, they lower themselves." See frs. 153–54.

27. Prov.: *Provincial Letters*. In C2, the word is completed by an unknown hand.

28. Marie Le Jars de Gournay (1566–1645), Montaigne's "covenant daughter" (see *Essays* II, 17, 610), presided over the *Essays*' posthumous fate. In the preface that she prepared for the 1635 edition, she justifies Montaigne's use of what Pascal calls "lascivious words": "One proscribes afterwards not only as

Credulous: PEOPLE WITHOUT EYES.[29] Ignorant: SQUARING THE
CIRCLE, A GREATER WORLD.[30] His opinions on voluntary homicide, on
death. He inspires a carelessness about salvation, WITHOUT FEAR AND
WITHOUT REPENTANCE. [31] Since his book was not written to lead to piety, he was not obliged to do so; but one is always obliged not to turn others
away from it. We may excuse his somewhat free and voluptuous views in some
of life's circumstances—730, 331[32]—but we cannot excuse his wholly pagan
views on death. For we must renounce all piety if we do not at least want to
die as a Christian should. And he envisions only dying in a cowardly and weak
way throughout his book.

560

I do not at all admire the excess of a virtue, such as valor, if I do not at the
same time see the excess of the opposite virtue, as in Epaminondas,[33] who had
extreme valor and extreme kindness. For otherwise it is not rising but falling.
We do not show our greatness by being at one extreme, but by touching the
two at the same time and filling the space in between.

But perhaps it is only a sudden movement of the soul from one extreme
to the other, and it never resides anywhere but in one point, like a spark of fire.
So be it, but at least that marks the agility of the soul, if it does not mark its
breadth.

561

Infinite movement

Infinite movement, the point that fills all, movement in rest, the infinite
without quantity, the indivisible and infinite.

---

unrestrained and dangerous, but also for its nefarious *je-ne-sais-quoi*, if we may use the term, his liberty of
anatomizing love. [...] It is not the frank and speculative discourses on love that are dangerous, it is the soft
and delicate, the artistic and tickling narratives of passions of love, which are found in novelists, in poets and
such types of writers." See *Les Essais de Michel, Seigneur de Montaigne, édition nouvelle* (Paris:Pierre Rocolet,
1635); translation by Pierre Zoberman

    29. Montaigne, *Essays*, II, 12, 475: "If we want to believe Pliny and Herodotus, '[...] there are countries
where the men are born without heads, wearing their eyes and mouth in their chest [...]; where they have
only one eye in their forehead.'"

    30. Montaigne, *Essays*, II, 14, 563. The source of "a greater world" has yet to be identified.

    31. See Montaigne, *Essays*, III, 2, 752: "I rarely repent" (p. 742). "I have neither tears for the past nor
fears for the future."

    32. These references to the page numbers of the 1652 edition of Montaigne's *Essays* would serve to
illustrate what for Pascal is Montaigne's essentially "pagan" attitude toward death (Montaigne, *Essays*, III,
9, 911–15, and II, 12, 410).

    33. Epaminondas was a general and statesman (fifth to fourth century BCE) who defeated the Spartans
and gave Thebes hegemony over Greece. Pascal read his eulogy in Montaigne, *Essays*, III, 1, 738.

562
Order

Why should I undertake to divide my moral doctrine into four parts rather than six? Why should I establish virtue in four rather than in two or in one? Why in BEAR AND FORBEAR[34] rather than FOLLOW NATURE[35] or CARRY OUT YOUR PRIVATE AFFAIRS WITHOUT INJUSTICE, like Plato,[36] or something other?

But there, you will say, is the whole matter captured in a word. Yes, but it is useless if it is not explained. And when we come to explain it, as soon as we open that precept that contains all the others, they emerge in the original confusion that you wanted to avoid. Thus, when they are enclosed in one, they are hidden and useless, as if they were in a chest, and never appear but in their natural confusion. Nature established them all, without enclosing one in another.

563
Order

Nature placed all of its truths each in itself. Our art encloses them in one another, but this is not natural. Each holds its own place.

564
Glory

Animals do not admire one another. A horse does not admire its companion. Not that they will not vie to outrace one another, but it is without consequence, for back in the stable the heavier and the less powerfully built does not give up its oats to the other, as men consider it their due. Their virtue is self-sufficient.

34. Stoic maxim. See Charron, *De la sagesse*, II, 7: "What the great philosopher Epictetus meant, encompassing all of moral philosophy in two words, *sustine et abstine*: *endure* all evils, that is, adversity; *abstain* from material goods, that is, from voluptuous pleasures."

35. Precept shared by the Epicureans and Stoics of antiquity, who nevertheless disagreed on what "nature" means. See Montaigne, *Essays*, III, 12, 988: "As I have said elsewhere, I have very simply and crudely adopted for my own sake this ancient proverb: that we cannot go wrong by following nature, that the sovereign precept is to conform to her."

36. Montaigne, *Essays*, III, 9, 885: Plato "thinks the happiest occupation for each man is to carry on his own affairs without injustice."

565

When it is said that heat is merely the movement of certain globules[37] and light the EFFORT TO MOVE AWAY[38] that we feel, those observations astonish us. What! that pleasure is nothing more than the dance of the spirits?[39] We had conceived such a different idea of it! And those sensations seem so distant from the others that we say are the same as those with which we compare them! The sensation of fire, that heat that affects us in a way entirely other than touch, the reception of sound and of light, all of that seems mysterious, and nevertheless it is as crude as being hit by a stone. It is true that, in their smallness, the spirits that enter pores touch other nerves, but it is still nerves that are touched.

566

I had spent a long time in the study of abstract sciences, and had been put off by how little communication one can have about them. When I began the study of man, I saw that the abstract sciences are not appropriate for man, and that by delving into them deeply I was straying farther from my condition than other people were by their ignorance of them. I forgave other people for knowing so little about them. But I thought that I would at least find many companions in the study of man, and that this is the true study that is appropriate for him. I was wrong: there are even fewer who study man than geometry. It is only for the lack of knowing how to study that subject that we pursue the rest. But does it not mean that this is still not the knowledge that man should have, and that it is better for him to be ignorant of himself in order to be happy?

37. Descartes, in his *Principles of Philosophy* (IV, 29), proposed a purely mechanist explanation of sensation. For instance, heat is an "agitation of particles of terrestrial bodies . . . [that] stimulates our senses; for the term *heat* particularly concerns the sense of touch." *Principia philosopiæ*, vol. 8 of *Œuvres completes de Descartes*, ed. Ch. Adam and P. Tannery (Paris: Léopold Cerf, 1905), 108 (translation courtesy of P. Zoberman).

38. According to Descartes, the *conatus recedendi* [effort to move away] is the effort of bodies moving in a circle to recede from their centers of motion, and light is the result of that effort. See Descartes, *Principles of Philosophy*, III, 54–55: "it is in that effort alone that the nature of light consists." In *Œuvres completes*, ed. Adam and Tannery, 8:218 (translation by Pierre Zoberman).

39. On those "animal spirits," which were thought to be minuscule bodies that pass from the blood to the brain and from the brain to the muscle through the nerves, see Descartes's treatise, *Passions of the Soul*, I, 10–13.

567

What is the self?

A man who goes to the window to see the passersby, if I walk by, can I say that he went there to see me? No, for he is not thinking of me in particular. But someone who loves another because of that person's beauty, do they love that person? No, for smallpox, which will kill beauty without killing the person, will result in them not loving that person anymore.

And if I am loved for my judgment, for my memory, am I truly loved? No, for I can lose those qualities without losing myself. Where then is this self if it is neither in the body nor in the soul? And how is it possible to love the body or the soul if not for those qualities, which do not make the self, since they are perishable? For would we love the substance of a person's soul abstractly, and whatever qualities were there? That cannot be and would be wrong. Then we never love a person but only some qualities.

Let us no longer mock, then, those who make themselves honored for their appointments and their offices! For we love no one save for their borrowed qualities.

568

It is not in Montaigne but in myself that I find all that I see in him.[40]

569

May God not impute our sins to us:[41] that is, all of the consequences and results of our sins, which are horrifying in the smallest faults, if we make a ruthless effort to track them down.

570

Pyrrhonism

Pyrrhonism is the truth. For, after all, men, before Jesus Christ, did not know where they stood, nor whether they were great or small. And those who said one or the other knew nothing about it and guessed without reason and by chance and indeed always erred by excluding one or the other.

What therefore, you seek without knowing it, this religion proclaims to you.[42]

---

40. Montaigne, *Essays*, I, 26, 135: "Truth and reason are common to everyone, and no more belong to the man who first spoke them than to the man who says them later. It is no more according to Plato than according to me, since he and I understand it and see it in the same way."

41. Psalm 32:2: "Blessed is the man to whom *the Lord hath not imputed sin,* and in whose spirit there is no guile."

42. Free translation of Paul's discourse at the Aeropagus in Acts 17:23: "For passing by, and seeing your

571

Montalte[43]

Lax opinions are so pleasing to men that it is strange that theirs[44] should displease. It is because they have exceeded all limits. And moreover there are many people who see the truth and who cannot attain it, but there are few who do not know that the purity of religion is contrary to our corruption. Ridiculous to say that an eternal reward is offered for Escobar's morals.

572

The easiest walks of life to live in, according to the world, are the most difficult to live in according to God. And, on the contrary, nothing is so difficult, according to the world, than religious life, and nothing is easier than to pursue it according to God. Nothing is easier than holding a high office and great wealth, according to the world. Nothing is harder than to live such a life according to God and without taking any interest in or taste for it.

573

Order

I would have gladly written this discourse in the following order, to show the futility of all walks of life: showing the vanity of common lives, and then the vanity of philosophical lives, Pyrrhonian and Stoic. But the order would not have been kept. I know a bit about it, and how few people understand it. No human science can keep it. Saint Thomas did not keep it. Mathematics keeps it, but it is useless in its depth.

574

Original sin is folly before men, but it is presented as such. You should not reproach me, then, for the lack of reason in that doctrine, for I present it as without reason. But that folly is wiser than all of the wisdom of men, *wiser than men*.[45] For without that what would we say man is? All of his condition depends on that imperceptible point. And how would he have seen it by reason, for it is something contrary to his reason and his reason, far from discovering it by its own means, turns away from it when it is presented with it.

---

idols, I found an altar also, on which was written: To the unknown God. *What therefore you* worship, *without knowing it*, that I preach to you."

43. "Louis de Montalte" was the pseudonym used by Pascal in publishing *The Provincial Letters*. See also ch. XXXVI, fr. 618, n. 20.

44. *Theirs*: those of the Jesuits.

45. 1 Corinthians 1:25.

575

Let it not be said that I have said nothing new: the disposition of the material is new. When they play ball, it is with the same ball that both players play, but one places it better.

I would just as soon have someone say that I have used old words. As if the same thoughts did not constitute another body of discourse when ordered differently, just as the same words form other thoughts when ordered differently.

576

Those who lead disorderly lives say to those who lead orderly ones that they are the ones who are turning away from nature, and they believe that they themselves are following it: just as people on a boat believe that those who are on the shore are moving away. The language is the same on all sides. We need a fixed point to settle the matter. The port settles things for those who are on a ship. But where will we find a port in morals?

577

Nature imitates itself

Nature imitates itself: a seed, cast into good earth, will bear fruit; a principle, cast into a good mind, will bear fruit.

Numbers imitate space, even though the two are of such a different nature.

All is made and directed by the same master: the root, the branches, the fruits, the principles, the consequences.

When everything moves equally, nothing appears to move, like on a ship.[46] When all move towards debauchery, none seems to go there: he who stops draws attention to the frenzy of the others, like a fixed point.

578

Generals[47]

It is not enough for them to introduce such conduct into our temples, INTRODUCE THEIR WAYS INTO THE TEMPLES. Not only do they want to

---

46. See Descartes, *Principles of Philosophy*, II, 13: "In the same way as, if you sit at the stern when a ship is carried out to sea, you always remain in one place if one considers the parts of the ship where you remain seated, yet you constantly change position if one considers the shores, since you are constantly getting further away from one and closer to the other." In *Œuvres completes*, ed. Adam and Tannery, 8:47 (translation by Pierre Zoberman).

47. Generals: the superiors of religious orders.

be tolerated in the Church, but, as they become the stronger party, they wish to drive out those [customs] that are not theirs. . . .[48]

MOHATRA,[49] ONE IS NOT A THEOLOGIAN IF ONE IS ASTONISHED BY IT.

Who would have said to your generals[50] that a time was so near when they would offer such customs to the universal Church, and call the rejection of those disorders an act of war? SO MANY AND SO GREAT EVILS, PEACE.[51]

579

When we want to correct another usefully and show that he is mistaken, we must observe from what perspective he envisions the matter, for ordinarily it is true from that perspective, and acknowledge that truth, but show him the perspective from which it is false. He is satisfied with that, for he sees that he was not mistaken but only failed to see all of the perspectives. Now we do not get angry about not seeing everything, but we do not like to be mistaken. And perhaps that derives from the fact that naturally man cannot see all, and that naturally he cannot be mistaken from the perspective he envisions, since the perceptions of the senses are always true.

580

Movements of grace, hardness of the heart, external circumstances.

581

Grace

Romans 3:27: vainglory dismissed. *By what law? Of works? No, but by faith.* Thus faith is not in our power like the works of the law, and it is given to us in another manner.

---

48. Pascal speaks in the name of a group of priests. See *Factum pour les curés de Paris* [Brief for the Parisian clergy], 1658. "This is the summit of insolence, the degree to which the Jesuits have raised the casuists. After having abused the moderation of ministers of the Church to introduce their impious opinions"—echoed by the Latin phrase, "*templis inducere moris*," translated by "to introduce their ways into the temples"—"they have now sought to chase from the ministry of the Church those who refuse to consent to them." In Pascal, *Œuvres completes*, ed. Lafuma, 475 (translation by David Wetsel).

49. According to Pascal's eighth *Provincial Letter*, "*Mohatra* is the name of a contract by which someone purchases fabric at a high price on credit in order to resell it at once to the same person for cash at a lower price." See Pascal, *The Provincial Letters*, transl. A. J. Krailsheimer, (London: Penguin, 1967), 121. Pascal condemns such contracts, permitted by Escobar, as an indirect means of practicing usury, forbidden by the Church.

50. Here, Pascal refers to the early superiors of the Jesuits. He contrasts the evangelization undertaken by the first Jesuit superiors with the indolence of those of his time.

51. Wisdom 14:22: "And it was not enough for them to err about the knowledge of God, but whereas they lived in a great war of ignorance, they call *so many and so great evils peace*." A vestige of Pascal's preparation of the *Second Brief for the Parisian Clergy*.

582

Venice[52]

What advantage will you gain from it, if from the need that princes have of it and the horror of the people for it … ? If they had asked you, and if to obtain it they had implored the assistance of the Christian princes, you might have validated this request. But that for fifty years all of the princes had worked for it to no avail and there had to be such a pressing need to obtain it … !

583

People of high and low rank have the same setbacks, the same vexations, the same passions. But one is at the top of the wheel, and the other close to the center, and thus less agitated by the same movements.[53]

584

Binding and loosening[54]

God did not wish to absolve without the Church: as it partakes of the offence, so does he wish that it partake in the forgiveness. He associates it with that power as kings do with parliaments. But if it absolves or binds without God, it is no longer the Church. The same in parliament: for although the king may have granted a man the royal pardon, still it must be ratified; but if the parliament ratifies without the king or if it refuses to ratify the king's order, it is no longer the king's parliament but a rebellious body.[55]

52. Venice, which had banished the Jesuits from its territory in 1606, consented, on the insistence of the pope and the King of France, to their return during the Republic's war against the Turks. Pascal learned this from an article in the *Gazette* of February 17, 1657.

53. Montaigne, *Essays*, II, 12, 424–25: "The souls of emperors and cobblers are cast in the same mold. Considering the importance of the actions of princes and their weightiness, we persuade ourselves that they are produced by some causes equally weighty and important. We are wrong: they are led to and fro in their movements by the same springs as we are in ours. The same reason that makes us bicker with a neighbor creates a war between princes; the same reason that makes us whip a lackey, when it happens in a king makes him ruin a province. Their will is as frivolous as ours, but their power is greater. Like appetites move a mite and an elephant."

54. Matthew 16:19: Jesus tells Peter: "And I will give to thee the keys of the kingdom of heaven. And whatsoever thou shalt bind [condemn] upon earth, it shall be bound also in heaven; and whatsoever thou shalt loose [from sin] upon earth, it shall be loosed also in heaven."

55. The *parliament* in its French sense before the Revolution had little or no link to the way that *parliament* is used in modern times: the French parliaments were courts of appeal in the French judicial system. At the top of the hierarchy, the parliament of Paris, which was both the highest court and the final court of appeal. Pascal refers here to the other function of parliaments at the time: they had to *register* official acts, after verifying the phrasing (hence recurring conflicts with the kings when parliaments presented themselves as guarantors, not only of the language of the law, but more generally of the law itself. On the most recent conflict on a large scale, the *Fronde*, and Louis XIV's long term resentment, see *The Life of Monsieur Pascal*, n. 18, and ch. VI, fr. 119 and n. 9.

585

They cannot have perpetuity and they seek universality. And to that end they make all the Church corrupt so that they may be saints.

586

Popes

Kings dispose of their authority, but popes cannot dispose of theirs.

587

We know ourselves so poorly that many believe they are about to die when they are in good health, and several believe they are in good health when they are near dying, not feeling the impending fever or the abscess that is about to form.

588

Language

We must not divert the mind elsewhere, except for relaxation, but only when it is in a timely fashion: relaxation when necessary and not otherwise. For he who relaxes in an untimely fashion, wearies; and he who wearies in an untimely fashion relaxes, for one lets go of everything in such cases. So much does the maliciousness of concupiscence delight in doing the opposite of what is wanted from us without giving us pleasure, which is the currency for which we give everything wanted of us.

589

Force

Why do we follow the majority? Is it because they have more reason? No, but more force.

Why do we follow ancient laws and ancient opinions? Are they the soundest? No, but they are unique and remove from us the basis for disagreement.

590

A person said to me one day that he felt great joy and confidence when coming out of confession. Another said to me that he remained in fear. Upon this, I reflected that from those two one good person might be formed, and that each was lacking in not having the feeling of the other. This often happens in other matters as well.

591

It is not absolution alone that remits sins, in the sacrament of penance, but also contrition, which is not authentic unless it seeks the sacrament.

Similarly, it is not the nuptial blessing that prevents sin in procreation, but the desire to engender God's children, which is genuine only in marriage.

And as a contrite person without the sacrament is more disposed to absolution than an impenitent with the sacrament, thus the daughters of Lot, for example, who only had the desire for children, were more pure without marriage than married people without the desire for children.[56]

592

P.P.[57] pope

There is a contradiction, for on the one hand, they[58] say that it is necessary to follow tradition and would not dare deny that, and, on the other, they will say what they please. We will always believe the former, since it would go against them not to believe it anyway.

593

Principal talent that determines all of the others.

594

Fear death when out of peril, and not when in peril, for one must be a man.

595

Rivers are paths that walk, and that carry one where one wants to go.

596

The five propositions were equivocal, and they no longer are.[59]

---

56. Summary of Augustine's commentary on Genesis 19:30–38 in his *Against Faustus* 22, 43.

57. Meaning unclear.

58. The Jesuits.

59. It was possible for the five propositions attributed to Jansenius (which the pope had erroneously declared were actually to be found in the *Augustinus*) to be interpreted in either an orthodox or in a heretical sense. However, the miracle of the holy thorn at Port-Royal henceforth showed them to be orthodox. See ch. XXXII, fr. 443.

597

I have left me seven thousand.[60] I love those worshippers unknown to the world and even to the prophets.

598

Universal

Morality/ and language/ are particular sciences, but universal.

Probability

The ardor of the saints to seek the truth was useless, if the probable is certain.

The fear of the saints who had always followed the most certain.

Saint Theresa having always followed her confessor.

599[61]

It is in vain that the Church established these words, anathema, heresies, etc.: they are being used against it.

600

Probable

See whether you sincerely seek God by the comparison of the things you care for!

It is probable that this food will not poison me.

It is probable that I will not lose my legal case by not making pressing entreaties.

601

Two infinites. Middle.

When we read too quickly or too slowly, we understand nothing.

602

Will you really dare thus to make light of the king's edicts? As when you say that to go to a field and wait for a man is not fighting a duel.[62]

---

60. 1 Kings 19:18. Elijah believed that all of Israel had forsaken the covenant with God. However, he received a revelation that God would reserve unto himself those "seven thousand men in Israel, whose knees have not been bowed before Baal."

61. The Copies show that frs. 598 and 599 were a single fragment. They were separated only in 1711 when pasted into the Original Collection. See the introduction, "A Brief History of Pascal's Text."

62. A subterfuge imagined by the casuist Hurtado de Mendoza: "What harm is there in going to a

603
Probable

Even if it were true that solemn authors and reasons were sufficient, I say that they are neither solemn nor reasonable. What! A husband may profit from his wife according to Molina! Is the reason that he gives reasonable? And is Lessius's opposite reason any more so?[63]

604[64]

That the Church has indeed prohibited dueling, but not taking a walk.[65]
And also usury, but not...[66]
And simony, but not...[67]
And vengeance, but not...[68]
And sodomites, but not...[69]
And the *as soon as possible*, but not...[70]

---

field, to wander there while waiting for a man and defending oneself if attacked?" See the seventh *Provincial Letter*.

63. Escobar presents the following case of conscience in his *Liber theologiæ moralis* [Moral theology] (Brussels: Franciscus Vivienus, 1651), 147: "Is a wife who receives profit from adultery required to give it to her husband?" Molina affirms this by virtue of the right of the husband to be the master of the conjugal acts of the wife. But Lessius is of the opposite opinion, because the offense of adultery cannot be compensated by money.

64. Casuistries Pascal attributes to the Jesuits.

65. See above, fr. 602, n. 62.

66. Escobar, cited in the eighth *Provincial Letter*, had written: "It would be usury to make a profit from those to whom one lends if one demanded it as legally due; but if one demands it as due out of gratitude. it is not usury." See Pascal, *The Provincial Letters*, trans. A. J. Krailsheimer, 121.

67. Valencia, cited in the sixth *Provincial Letter*: "If anyone gives a temporal good for a spiritual good (that is, money for a benefice) and gives money as the price for a benefice, this is obviously simony. But if the money is given as a motive inducing the incumbent to resign the benefice... it is not simony, even if the person resigning considers and expects the money as his main object." Pascal, *The Provincial Letters*, trans. A. J. Krailsheimer, 94.

68. Lessius, cited in the seventh *Provincial Letter*: "Someone who has been slapped may not have the intention of avenging himself; but he may very well have that of avoiding infamy, and to that end repel such an insult at once, even at the point of the sword." Pascal, *The Provincial Letters*, trans. A. J. Krailsheimer, 105.

69. Pascal makes a scandalized reference to the subject in the sixth *Provincial Letter*. No casuist appears to have ever justified sodomy. But the mere mention of the sin reveals how far a horrified Pascal imagines the Jesuits to have fallen into heresy—and it reveals the rhetorical strategy of hyperbole he chose to oppose their theology (given his rhetorical skills and awareness, singularly emphasized by Arnauld and Nicole in the *Port-Royal Logic*; see the Introduction to the present translation, n. 95). For indications of Pascal's awareness of his writing skills, see, above, fr. 575, and, below, fr. 618, and n. 20.

70. Mascaren, an obscure casuist, whose name is cited at the end of fragment 801, had attempted to circumvent the rule promulgated by the Council of Trent that a priest, even though in a state of sin, is obligated to celebrate Mass. But he is constrained to go to confession *as soon as possible* (*quam primum*). Masaren argues that the rule applies only to priests who have omitted confession out of malice, but not to those who have done so out of necessity.

605

What a man's virtue can accomplish should not be measured by his efforts but by his ordinary behavior.[71]

606

Sinners without penitence.

Righteous people without charity.

A God without power over the wills of men. Predestination without mystery.

607

P.P.[72] pope

God does not perform miracles in the ordinary guidance of his Church. It would be an extraordinary miracle if infallibility were in one single man. But for it to reside in the multitude, that seems so natural, that God's guiding hand is hidden under nature, as it is in all of his other works.

608

They make the rule out of the exception. The ancients gave absolution before penance? Do so in the spirit of the exception. But of the exception you make a rule without exceptions, so that you no longer even want the rule to be an exception.

609

Miracles

Saint Thomas, vol. 3, 1, 8, c. 20.[73]

---

71. An idea dear to Montaigne. See *Essays*, II, 1, 294: "Therefore one courageous deed must not be taken to prove a man valiant; a man who was really valiant would be so always and on all occasions. If valor was a habit of virtue, and not a sally, it would make a man equally resolute in any contingency, the same alone as in a company, the same in single combat as in battle." And *Essays*, II, 29, 647: "It happens even to us, who are but abortions of men, to launch our soul, aroused by the ideas or examples of others, very far beyond her ordinary range; but it is a kind of passion that impels and drives her, and which to some extent tears her out of herself [...]. For this reason, say the sages, to judge a man truly properly, we must chiefly examine his ordinary actions and surprise him in his everyday habit."

72. Again, the meaning of these letters is unclear.

73. This is a reference to a chapter examining Aquinas's theology in Jansenius's *Augustinus*, which is cited in the eighteenth *Provincial Letter*: "one always has the power to resist grace." Pascal, *The Provincial Letters*, trans. A. J. Krailsheimer, 286.

610

All of the false beauties that we condemn in Cicero have admirers, and in great numbers.

611

Casuists

Considerable alms, a reasonable penance: even though we cannot determine what is just, we can certainly see what is not. The casuists are ridiculous to think that they can interpret it as they do.

———

People who get accustomed to speaking and thinking badly.

———

Their great numbers, far from marking their perfection, mark the opposite.

———

The humility of a single one reveals the pride of the many.

The Last Folders
of "Assorted Thoughts,"
July 1658 to
June 1662

[XXXVI Assorted Thoughts 4]

612

CC. *thou, being a man, maketh thyself God.*

—————

CC. *It is written: you are gods ... and the scripture cannot be broken.*[1]

—————

CC. *This sickness is not unto death.*[2]
And yet this sickness is unto death.

—————

Lazarus our friend sleepeth. And then Jesus said to them plainly: Lazarus is dead.[3]

613[4]

These people lack heart.

—————

—————

One would not make them one's friends.

—————

A poet and not an *honnête homme.*

614

The Church has always been assailed by opposing errors. But perhaps never at the same time as is the case now. And if, as a result, the Church suffers more because of the multiplicity of errors, it derives this advantage from it, that they destroy each other.

—————

1. John 10:33–5. The Jews took up stones to stone him for blasphemy: "For a good work we stone thee not, but for blasphemy; and because that *thou, being a man, maketh thyself God.* Jesus answered them: 'Is it *not written* in your law: I said *you are gods?* If he called them gods, to whom the word of God was spoken, *and the scripture cannot be broken.'"*

2. John 11:4. Jesus says to the sisters of Lazarus, who is ill: *"This sickness is not unto death."* Pascal adds: "and yet it is unto death."

3. John 11:11 and 14. Jesus "said to them: *Lazarus our friend sleepeth* [...] *Then* therefore Jesus *said to them plainly: Lazarus is dead."*

4. See fr. 503.

It complains of the two, but much more about the Calvinists, because of the schism.[5]

_____

It is certain that many on the two opposing sides are misled. They must be disabused.

_____

Faith embraces many truths that seem to contradict each other: *Time to laugh, to weep,*[6] etc., *answer, do not answer,*[7] etc.
The source of these is the union of the two natures in Jesus Christ.

_____

And also the two worlds, the creation of a new heaven and new earth,[8] new life, new death. All things doubled, and the same names remaining.

_____

And finally the two men who are among the just, for they are the two worlds and a member and image of Jesus Christ. And there for them all names are suitable: just sinners, living dead, dead living, condemned elect, etc.

_____

There are therefore a great number of truths in matters of both faith and morals that are in conflict, and that all endure nonetheless in an admirable order.

_____

The source of all heresies is the exclusion of some of these truths.

_____

And the source of all the objections that the heretics raise against us is the heretics' ignorance of some of our truths.

_____

And it ordinarily comes about that, unable to understand the relationship between two opposing truths and believing that to admit the one means to exclude the other, they cling to one and exclude the other, assuming that we do the opposite. But the exclusion they make is the cause of their heresy; and their ignorance that we hold the other truth causes their objections.

_____

First example: Jesus Christ is God and man. The Arians,[9] unable to reconcile these things, which they believe incompatible, say that he is man: in

_____

5. The two: the Molinists (Jesuits) and the Calvinists. The Jesuits at least nominally remain within the Church.

6. Ecclesiastes 3:4.

7. Proverbs 26:4–5. "*Answer not* a fool according to his folly, lest thou be made like him. *Answer* a fool according to his folly, lest he imagine himself to be wise."

8. In Isaiah 65:17 God promises: "For behold I create *new heavens, and* a *new earth*: and the former things shall not be in remembrance, and they shall not come upon the heart." Revelation 21:1: "And I saw *a new heaven and a new earth* for the first heaven and the first earth was gone [...]."

9. See fr. 317, n. 12. The Arians believed the Son to be inferior to the Father.

that they are Catholic. But they deny that he is God: in that they are heretical. They claim that we deny his humanity: in that they are ignorant.

———

Second example: concerning the Blessed Sacrament. We believe that Jesus Christ is really present therein, the bread's substance being changed and transubstantiated into that of the body of Our Lord: this is one of our truths. Another is that this sacrament is also a figure of the truth of the cross and of glory, and a commemoration of the two. This is the Catholic faith, which includes these two truths that appear to oppose each other.[10]

Today's heresy, not conceiving that this sacrament contains both the presence of Jesus Christ and his figure; and that it is a sacrifice and a commemoration of sacrifice, believes that one of these truths cannot be admitted without excluding the other for the same reason.

They cling to this sole point, that this sacrament is figurative: and in that they are not heretical. They think that we exclude this truth: and this is the reason why they raise so many objections against us concerning the passages in the Fathers who do say it. Finally, they deny the presence: and in that, they are heretical.[11]

———

Third example: indulgences.

———

That is why the shortest way to forestall heresies is to teach all our truths. And the surest way to refute them is to declare them all.

For what will the heretics say?

In order to know whether an opinion is that of a Father . . .

615

Why it is that people believe so many
liars who say that they have
seen miracles and that they do not
believe any one of those who say

10. Catholic orthodoxy maintains that the consecrated elements are literally the true Body and true Blood of Jesus Christ (the real presence). The consecration of the Mass is a true and real repetition of Christ's sacrifice on the cross. Pascal adds that the sacrament itself is a *figure* of both Christ's sacrifice and the beatitude to which it leads.

11. For Pascal, as for Catholics today, nothing can be more heretical than denying the real presence of Christ in the Blessed Sacrament and in the sacrifice of the Mass. Pascal grants that the Protestants, while committing heresy by denying the real presence, are not in fact heretics in their understanding that their Lord's Supper is a "figure" of the beatitude it portends. For Pascal, heresy results from understanding only one side of the equation. The Arians could not accept Christ as "True Man" and "True God." The Protestants fail to understand that the sacrament is both real and figurative.

that they have secrets for
making man immortal or
restoring youth.

Having considered why people put so much faith in so many impostors who say that they possess remedies, often to the point of putting their own lives in their hands, it seems to me that the true cause is that there are some remedies that are true. For it would not be possible that there be so many false ones and that people put so much faith in them if none were true. Had there never been any remedy for any ill and had all ills been incurable, it is impossible that people would have imagined that they could provide any; and what is more, that so many other people would have given credence to those who might have boasted of having any. Likewise, if a man boasted of preventing death, no one would believe him, because there is no example of it. But as there have been numerous remedies that were in fact found to be real, to the very knowledge of the greatest men, men's credence has inclined toward this. And since it was known to be possible, they have concluded from this that it was. For ordinarily the common people reason in the following way: a thing is possible, therefore it is. Because the thing cannot be denied in general, since there are particular effects that are real, the common people, who cannot distinguish which among these particular effects are the real ones, believe them all. Likewise, what makes people believe so many of the moon's false effects, is that there are some that are true, like the ocean's tides.

It is the same with prophecies, miracles, divinations by dreams, spells, etc. For, if nothing in these had ever been real, none of it would have been believed. And so, instead of drawing the conclusion that there are no true miracles because there are so many false ones, one must on the contrary say that there certainly are true miracles since there are so many false ones, and that there are false ones for this very reason, that there are true ones. One must reason in the same way for religion, for if there were not a true one, it would not be possible for men to have imagined so many false religions. The objection to this is that savages have a religion. But we answer to this that it is because they have heard of it, as it appears from the flood, circumcision, Saint Andrew's cross, etc.[12]

---

12. Pascal alludes to Montaigne's *Essays*, II, 12, in which Montaigne is fascinated by the fact that a cross was found among the Indians of Peru and that they had their own myth of the flood. Whereas Montaigne sees these phenomena among the heathen as resulting from superstitious parallels in the human imagination, Pascal insists that men would not be capable of inventing such false religions if a true one did not exist. Pascal, like his mentor Le Maistre de Sacy, will come to believe that these phenomena are but Satan's mockery of Christian truth. See Wetsel, *L'Écriture et le Reste: The Pensées of Pascal in the Exegetical Tradition of Port-Royal* (Columbus: Ohio State University Press, 1981), 59 and 64–65. See also ibid. for various aspects of Pascal's discussion, such as the role and place of reason (see also above, ch. XIV), etc.

616[13]

Having considered why it is that there are so many false miracles, false revelations, spells, etc., it seemed to me that the real cause is that there are true ones. For it would not be possible that there be so many false miracles if there were no true ones, nor so many false revelations if there were no true ones, nor so many false religions if there were not a true one. For if none of this had ever been, it is practically impossible that men would have imagined it, and even more impossible that so many others would have believed it. But because there have been very great things that were true and they have therefore been believed by great men, this impression has caused almost everyone to become susceptible of believing the false ones too. And so, instead of drawing the conclusion that there are no true miracles since there are so many false ones, we must on the contrary say that there are true ones since there are so many false ones; and that there are false ones for this reason only; and that, likewise, there are false religions but only because there is a true one.

The objection to this: savages have a religion. But that is because they have heard of the true one, as it appears from Saint Andrew's cross, the flood, circumcision, etc.[14]

This arises from the fact that the mind of man, finding itself inclined in that direction by the truth, therefore becomes susceptible to all the falsehoods of this ...

617

When one is accustomed to using wrong reasons to prove nature's effects, one is no longer willing to accept valid ones when they are discovered. The example given for this was about the circulation of the blood, to explain why a vein swells below a ligature.[15]

———

Ordinarily, one is better persuaded by reasons that one has discovered oneself than by those that occurred to others.

———

Liancourt's story of the pike and the frog—they always act like this, and never otherwise, nor display any other sign of intelligence.[16]

———

13. This fragment is written on the back of a letter written to Pascal dated February 19, 1660. It constitutes one of the few of the *Pensées* that can be dated with relative certainty.

14. See above, n. 12.

15. Harvey had discovered the circulation of the blood in the 1620s. Those who tried to contradict his theory explained the swelling of the vein as due to pain, heat, and nature's alleged abhorrence of a vacuum.

16. Pascal and Arnauld, following Descartes, thought that animals were purely machines, like watches. The Duke of Liancourt was of the reverse opinion, citing an anecdote from Isaac Walton's *The Compleat*

Truth is so dimmed and falsehood so well established in these times, that unless one loved the truth, one would not be able to recognize it.[17]

———

Weaklings are people who know the truth, but who maintain it only insofar as their own interest is concerned. Beyond that, they abandon it.

———

The arithmetic machine[18] produces results that come closer to thought than anything that animals do. But it accomplishes nothing that can make one say that it has will like animals.

Although people may have nothing at stake in what they say, one must not thereby absolutely conclude that they are not lying. For there are people who lie merely for the sake of lying.

———

There is pleasure in being in a vessel tossed by the storm, when one is assured of not perishing. The persecutions that assail the Church are of this nature.

618

Whenever one does not know the truth of a thing, it is good that there be a common error to settle men's minds, as, for example, the moon, to which one attributes the change of seasons, course of sickness, etc. For man's main sickness is his restless curiosity over things that he cannot know.[19] And it is not so bad for him to be in error as to be in this pointless curiosity.

———

Epictetus, Montaigne, and Salomon de Tultie[20] all have a manner of writing that is the most common, which best insinuates itself, which remains most in one's memory and is the most quoted, because it is composed entirely of thoughts derived from the conversations of daily life. For example, when someone discusses the common error that prevails in the world that the moon is the cause of everything, unfailingly, someone will say that Salomon de Tultie says that, when one does not know the truth of a thing. It is good that there be a common error, etc., which is the thought on the other side.

———

Angler (1655). Walton recounted that in a combat between frogs and pikes, the frogs customarily put out the eyes of their adversaries. See Antony McKenna, "L'histoire du brochet et de la grenouille: Pascal et Isaac Walton" [The story of the pike and the frog: Pascal and Isaac Walton], *Courrier du Centre International Blaise Pascal,* December 1990, 18–19, http:// journals.openedition.org/ccibp/637 ; doi: 10.4000/ccibp.637.

17. See Saint Augustine, *Against Faustus,* 32, 18: "One enters into truth only by way of love."

18. A kind of calculator invented by Pascal in 1642–43.

19. On Montaigne's opposition to "restless curiosity," see *Essays,* II, 12, 460, where he examines "the vain picture of this morbid curiosity"—"this passion for study, which keeps us amused in pursuit of things of whose gain we have no hope."

20. An anagram of "Louis de Montalte," the pseudonym used by Pascal in publishing *The Provincial Letters.*

619

On the fact that neither Josephus[21]
nor Tacitus[22] nor
the other historians
spoke of Jesus Christ.

Far from being an argument against him, on the contrary it is an argument for him. Because it is certain that Jesus Christ existed, and that his religion made a great stir, and that those people were not ignorant of this, and therefore it is clear that they either concealed it on purpose or did speak of it, but it was censored or changed.

620

On the Christian religion not being unique

Far from that being a reason to make one believe that it is not the true one, it is, on the contrary, what makes one see that it is.

621

Objection: those who hope for their salvation are happy in that, but they have the fear of hell as counterweight.—Response: Who has more reason to fear hell, one who ignores whether there is a hell and is in the certainty of damnation if there is? or one who is fully convinced that there is a hell, and hopes that he will be saved, if there is?[23]

622

How wayward is the judgment that there is no one who fails to put himself above the rest of the world, to prefer his own good and the continuing duration of his happiness and of his life over that of the rest of the world!

———

Cromwell was ready to lay waste to all Christendom, the royal family was lost, and his own family forever powerful—but for a small grain of sand entering his ureter. Rome itself was about to tremble under him. But this small bit

---

21. See ch. XXIII, n. 7.

22. See ch. XXV, n. 31. For Pascal, the fact that secular sources hardly mention Christ at all is a function of the great truth of the *Deus absconditus*.

23. The objection is that of Pascal's adversary; the response that of the apologist.

of gravel having got itself lodged in him, he died, his family humbled, everything in peace, and the king restored.[24]

Those who are accustomed to judging by feeling understand nothing in matters of reasoning. For they want to get to the heart of the matter immediately at a glance and are not accustomed to searching for principles. And the others, on the contrary, who are accustomed to reasoning by principle, understand nothing in matters of feeling, searching for principles and unable to comprehend things at a glance.[25]

Two kinds of people make all things equal, like feast days and work days, Christians and priests, all sins among themselves, etc. And hence some people conclude that what is bad for priests is also bad for Christians, while others conclude that what is not bad for Christians is permissible for priests.

623

When Augustus learned that among the children whom Herod had had put to death below the age of two years there was Herod's own son, he said that it was better to be Herod's pig than his son. Macrobius,[26] book II, *Saturnalia*, c. 4.

624

First degree: to be blamed for doing evil and praised for doing good.
Second degree: to be neither blamed nor praised.

625

Each forges his own God.[27]
Disgust.

---

24. The writing of this fragment, along with that of fr. 616, must date from after the time Charles II ascended the throne of England on May 25, 1660.

25. See fr. 670.

26. Macrobius was a Roman grammarian and neo-Platonist philosopher who flourished during the reigns of Honorius and Arcadias (395–423 CE).

27. See Wisdom 15:8: "And of the same clay by a vain labor he maketh a god," and Wisdom 16: "For man made them: and he that borroweth his own breath fashioned them. For no man can make a god like to himself."

626
Thought

All of man's dignity is in thought. But what is this thought? That it is silly?

Thought is therefore an admirable thing and incomparable by its nature. It must have possessed extraordinary defects to be contemptible. But it has some that are such that nothing is more ridiculous. How great it is by its nature, how base it is by its defects.

Flowing away.

It is a horrible thing to feel that all that we possess is flowing away.

627
Light, darkness

If truth had no visible sign, there would be too much darkness. But it is a wonderful sign always to be in a visible Church and assembly. There would be too much light if in this Church there were only one opinion. The true opinion is the one that has always been there. For the true opinion has always been there and no false one has always been there.

628

Thought makes man's greatness.

629

Objection[28]: Scripture visibly full of things not dictated by the Holy Spirit. Response: They therefore do not harm faith.

Objection: But the Church has decided that everything is of the Holy Spirit.

Response: I answer two things, that the Church has never decided that; the other, that even had it decided that, it could be maintained.

———

There are many false minds.

———

Denys[29] has charity. He was in place.

———

28. Again, the objection is that of the unbeliever.

29. Denys was a Christian philosopher of the late fifth and early sixth centuries, thought later to be Dionysius the Areopagite, the Athenian convert of Saint Paul mentioned in Acts 17:34. He had been tradi-

The prophecies quoted in the Gospel: do you believe that they are cited to make you believe? No, it is to make you less likely to believe.

630[30]

All great diversions are dangerous obstacles for leading a Christian life. But among all those invented by the world, there is none more to be feared than the theater. It is so natural and so delicate a *representation* of the passions that this representation *stirs* them and generates them in our heart; especially that of love, primarily when one *represents it* as *very* chaste and very proper, for the more it appears innocent to innocent souls, *the more* they are liable to be moved by it. *Its violence pleases our self-love, which immediately forms a desire of causing the same effects that one sees represented so well. And at* the same time, one derives a perfectly clear conscience from the propriety[31] *of the feelings that one sees, which remove any fear from pure souls, who imagine* that it is not offending their purity to love with a love that *seems to them* so prudent.

Thus, one *leaves* the theater with one's heart so full of all the beauties and all the blandishments of love, and *one's soul* and mind so persuaded of its innocence, that one is quite prepared to receive its first impressions, or rather, to seek the opportunity to produce them in the heart of someone else, in order to receive the same pleasure and the same sacrifices that one has seen so well *depicted in the theater.*

631

If lightning fell on low places, etc.

Poets[32] and those who can reason only from the things of this nature would lack proofs.

There are many people who listen to a sermon in the same way that they listen to vespers.

632

Since duchies and kingdoms and offices are real and necessary (because everything is ruled by might), they exist always and everywhere. But because

---

tionally considered as the first bishop of Paris and the author of influential mystical works, which were in fact composed, most likely, by an anonymous Greek author of the fifth or sixth century.

30. A text by Mme de Sablé, who had sent it to Pascal for his opinion and corrections. The words added by Pascal are in italics. The autograph has been lost, but it appears in the Second Copy. A rigorous polemic against the theatre, it was published among her *Maximes* in 1678.

31. The French reads "*honnêteté,*" closer here to the moral usage of the term. On the word *honnêteté,* see the section "French Words" in the preface of this edition.

32. For instance, in Lucretius's *De rerum natura,* V, 1120–28.

only fancy decides that this or that person will be such, this is not uniform; this is subject to variation, etc.

633

Reason commands us much more imperiously than a master, for if you disobey the latter, you are unhappy, and if you disobey the former, you are a fool.

634

(*Stand ye on the ways and ask for the old paths and walk ye in them. And they said: we will not walk,*[33] *but we will follow our own minds. They*[34] *have said to the nations: Come with us. Follow the opinions of the new authors. Natural reason will be our guide. We shall be like the other nations, who each follow their natural light. The philosophers have . . .*)

All the world's religions and sects have had natural reason as their guide. Only Christians have been constrained to take their rules from outside of themselves and to acquaint themselves with the ones that Jesus Christ left to the first Christians so that they be transmitted to the faithful. This constraint fatigues these good Fathers; they want to have, like other nations, the freedom to follow their imaginations. It is in vain that we cry out to them, as the prophets of old told the Jews: *Go into the middle of the Church. Ask ye of the ways which the ancients have left to it and walk ye in those paths. They have answered like the Jews: We will not walk in them, but we will follow the thoughts of our own hearts. And they have said: We will be like the other nations.*[35]

---

33. An abridged Latin [in Pascal's text] citation from Jeremiah 6:16: "Thus saith the Lord: *Stand ye on the ways, and* see and *ask for the old path which is* the good way, *and walk ye in* it: and you shall find refreshment for your souls. *And they said: we will not walk.*" Pascal gives the translation at the end of the fragment, replacing "*Stand ye on the ways*" (*state per vias*) by "Go into the middle of the Church."

34. *They*: the Jesuits.

35. 1 Kings 8:20: "And *we* also *will be like* all *nations.*"

[XXXVII Assorted Thoughts 5]

635

The example of Alexander's chastity has not made as many people continent as the example of his drunkenness has made people intemperate. No one need be ashamed at not being as virtuous as he, and it seems excusable to be no more vicious than he. We do not think ourselves entirely given over to the vices of the common people, when we see ourselves sharing those of great men. And yet we fail to realize that in that respect they are no different from the common man. We cling to that side of them by which they themselves stoop to the tastes of the common people; for exalted as their position may be, they are still somehow tied to the lowliest mortal.[1] They are not suspended in mid-air without any contact with our society. Far from it. If they are greater than we, it is because they carry their heads higher, but their feet are planted on the ground like our own. They are all on the same level and supported by the same earth. And at this extremity they are as low as we are, as the most insignificant of people, as children, as beasts.

636

Continual eloquence bores.

———

Princes and kings sometimes play. They are not always on their thrones, as they would become bored. Greatness must be put aside in order to be appreciated. Continuity in all things brings surfeit. The cold is agreeable so that we may get warm.

———

Nature acts by progress, *back and forth*. It moves forward and backward, then goes farther, then regresses twice as much. Then moves forward more than ever, etc.

$$\lessgtr$$

———

1. Montaigne, *Essays*, III, 13, 1044: "Yet there is no use our mounting on stilts, for on stilts we must still walk on our own legs. And on the loftiest throne in the world, we are still only sitting on our rump."

Ocean tides flow like this, and this is the way the sun seems to go.

You are ungracious: "Please excuse me." Without that apology I would not have noticed that there was any offense.

"No offence": there is nothing wrong but their apology.

637

The contest, not the victory, pleases us.

We like to see animals fight, not the victor relentlessly ripping into the loser. What did we want to see, if not the final victory? And, as soon as it comes, we have had enough. The same goes for gambling, the same with the pursuit of truth: in disputes, we like to see the clash of opinions, but not at all to contemplate the truth once it has been found. To point it out with pleasure, it must be seen to emerge from the dispute. Similarly with passions: there is pleasure in seeing the collision of two opposites, but when one of them gains mastery over the other, it becomes nothing but sheer brutality. We never pursue things themselves, only the pursuit of things.[2] Likewise in the theater. Happy scenes without fear are worthless, as are those of extreme hopeless misery, brutal love affairs, or bitter cruelty.

638

**Against those who, trusting in
God's mercy, remain
in a state of apathy without
undertaking good works.**

Since the twin sources of our sins are pride and sloth, God has revealed to us two of his qualities to cure them: his mercy and his justice. The essence of justice is to strike down pride, however holy the works may be. AND ENTER NOT INTO JUDGMENT,[3] etc.; and the characteristic of mercy is to counter sloth by inviting us to perform good works, in accordance with the passage: GOD'S MERCY INVITES REPENTANCE,[4] and the other one of the

---

2. See fr. 168: "We prefer the hunt to the catch."

3. Psalm 142:2: "*And enter not into judgment* with thy servant; for in thy sight no man living shall be justified."

4. Romans 2:4: "Or despisest thou the riches of his goodness, and patience, and longsuffering? Knowest thou not, that *the benignity of God* leadeth thee *to penance?*"

Ninevites:[5] LET US DO PENANCE TO SEE IF PERCHANCE HE WILL HAVE PITY UPON US.[6] Far from authorizing moral laxity, mercy, on the contrary, is the quality that formally combats it. So, instead of saying: if there were no mercy in God, we should have to make every kind of effort toward virtue; we must say on the contrary that it is because there is mercy in God that we must make all kinds of efforts.

639

**Against those who abuse the passages of
the scriptures and who take advantage of any they might find
to countenance their errors.**

The chapter for vespers, Passion Sunday, the *Prayer for the King*.[7]

640

**Explanation of these words: *He who is not with me, is against me*. And of these others:
He that is not against you, is for you.**[8]

A person who says: "I am neither for nor against." We must reply . . .

641

The history of the Church should properly be called the history of truth.

642

One of the antiphons of Christmas vespers: *To the righteous a light is risen up in darkness*.[9]

643

Men are not taught to be *honnêtes hommes*, and they are taught all the rest. And they never pride themselves so much on anything but being *honnêtes hommes*. They only pride themselves on knowing the one thing that they never learn.

---

5. The book of Jonah depicts Nineveh as a wicked city worthy of destruction. God sent Jonah to preach, and the Ninevites fasted and repented. As a result, God spared the city.

6. Jonah 3:9: "Who can tell if God will turn, and forgive: and will turn away from his fierce anger, and we shall not perish."

7. Several liturgical texts from the now suppressed "Sunday of the Passion" [the Sunday before Palm Sunday in the Tridentine Rite] emphasize that it is only from within the Church that one hears the true word of God. The *Oratio ad regem* . . . was a pamphlet written in 1603 by Antoine Arnauld, father of *le grand Arnauld*, in which he argued that the Jesuits had deformed the relevant scriptural texts in order to minimize the authority of kings.

8. Matthew 12:30 and Mark 9:39.

9. Psalm 112:4.

Children who are frightened by the face that they daubed are only children.[10] But how will someone so weak in childhood become really strong at a greater age? Only the fancies have changed. Anything that is perfected by progress also perishes by progress. Anything that has once been weak can never become absolutely strong. We may well say: he has grown, he has changed. He is also the same.

644[11]
Preface to the first part

Discuss those who have addressed self-knowledge: Charron's divisions,[12] which are depressing and tedious; the confusion of Montaigne: that he truly felt the lack of proper method, that he avoided it by jumping from subject to subject, that he sought to look good.

What a foolish project in painting himself! And this is not in passing and against his own maxims, just as anyone may make mistakes, but by his own maxims, by a prime and principal design. For to say foolish things by chance or out of weakness, that is an ordinary failing. But to say them by design, that is not tolerable.[13] And to say such as these. . .

Preface to the Second Part

Speak of those who have addressed this matter.

I wonder at the boldness with which these people undertake to speak of God. In addressing their discourses to the impious, their first chapter aims at proving divinity through the works of nature. I should not be surprised by this undertaking if they addressed their discourses to the faithful, for it is certain that those who possess living faith in their hearts see immediately that all existence is nothing other than the work of the God they adore. But for those in whom that light is extinguished and in whom we are trying to rekindle it,

---

10. See fr. 168.

11. These two "Prefaces" should not be confused with the quite finished "Overture" to the entire Apology constituted by fragment 681. This "Overture," which takes the form of a Classical Greek protreptic (or exhortation), prompts the unbeliever to at least "seek" the truth. Fragment 644 is completely different. The "Preface to the First Part," principally a critique of Montaigne, contains little that would allow us to speculate where it was to have been set or what it would have contained. The "Preface to the Second Part" introduces the only possible way to "prove" God, a hidden God accessible only through Jesus Christ. Echoing fragment 690, it represents Pascal's outline of an essential theme of the Apology: Christ as the unique Mediator between man and God.

12. In his treatise *De la sagesse* [On wisdom].

13. Montaigne, *Essays*, II, 17, 602: "I am not obliged not to say stupid things, provided I do not fool myself and that I recognize them as such. And to slip up knowingly is so common for me that I scarcely ever slip up in any other way; I never slip up accidentally."

those people destitute of faith and of grace, who, seeking with all of their light everything they perceive in nature that might lead them to this knowledge, find only obscurity and darkness. To tell them that they need only look at the smallest things surrounding them and that they will see God there in plain sight, to give them as the only proof of this great and important matter the course of the moon and the planets, and claim to have achieved that proof with such an argument, is to give them grounds for believing that the proofs of our religion are very weak indeed. Reason and experience inform me that nothing is more likely to make them despise it. This is not the way that scripture, which has a better knowledge of the things that are of God, speaks of this. It says, on the contrary, that God is a hidden God, and that, since the corruption of nature, he has left us in a state of blindness out of which they can emerge only through Jesus Christ, without whom all communication with God is cut off: *No one knoweth the Son, but the Father: neither doth any one know the Father, but the Son, and he to whom it shall please the Son to reveal him.*[14]

This is what scripture indicates to us, when it says in so many places that those who seek God find him. We do not speak of that light as if it were daylight at high noon. We do not say that those who seek daylight at high noon or water in the sea will find it. And thus it must necessarily follow that the evidence of God must not be of this kind in nature. Also it tells us elsewhere: *Verily thou art a hidden God.*[15]

645

How many beings has the telescope revealed to us that did not exist for the philosophers who preceded it. Holy scripture was squarely attacked on the great number of stars. It was said: "There are only 1022[16] of them, we know that."

———

"There are grasses on the earth, we see them. From the moon, they could not be seen. And on those grasses there are cilia, and on those cilia, tiny creatures; but beyond that, nothing." Oh, presumptuous man!

"Mixed substances are made up of elements; but not the elements." Oh, presumptuous man! Here is a subtle point. We must not say that there is something that we do not see. We must then talk like others, but not think like them.

———

When we wish to pursue virtues all the way to their extreme, on both sides we are faced with vices that insinuate themselves imperceptibly,[17] in their

14. Matthew 11:27. This argument appears to anticipate the opening of the "Overture" (fr. 681, par. 1).

15. Isaiah 45:15. The overarching theology of the Apology.

16. The number given by Ptolemy in his *Almagest*. See *Ptolemy's Almagest*, trans. G. J. Toomer (London, Duckworth, 1984), 399.

17. See Montaigne, *Essays*, I, 15, 56: "Valor has its limits like the other virtues, and these limits once

imperceptible paths on the side of the infinitely small. And we are faced with vices in a multitude on the side of the infinitely great. So that we become lost in the vices and no longer see the virtues.

We get entangled in perfection itself.[18]

———

Words differently arranged produce a different meaning. And meanings arranged differently produce different effects.

———

Fear not little flock.[19] *With fear and trembling.*[20]
Quid ergo, ne timeas, modo timeas.
Do not fear, provided you fear.[21] But if you do not fear, fear.

———

Whosoever shall receive me, receiveth not me, but the one who sent me.[22]

———

No man knoweth, [...] *not the Son.*[23]

———

If there is ever a time when we must profess two contrary truths, it is when we are accused of omitting one. Thus the Jesuits and the Jansenists are wrong to conceal them, but the Jansenists more so, for the Jesuits have been better at professing both.[24]

———

M. de Condren:[25] There is no comparison, he says, between the union of saints and that of the Holy Trinity.

Jesus Christ says the contrary.[26]

———

transgressed we find ourselves on the path of vices, so that we may pass through valor to temerity, obstinacy, and madness, unless we know the limits well."

18. See Montaigne, *Essays* I, 30, 177: "We can grasp virtue in such a way that it will become vicious if we embrace it with too sharp and violent a desire. [...] A man can love virtue too much, and perform excessively in a just action. The Holy Writ fits this bias: 'Be not wiser than you should, but be soberly wise.' [Rom 23:31] [...] Immoderation, even in the direction of the good, if it does not offend me, astonishes me, and gives me trouble to name it."

19. Luke 12:32.

20. Philippians 2:12. "*With fear and trembling* work out your salvation."

21. Translation of the preceding line, except for *quid ergo* ("what then?").

22. Mark 9:36.

23. Mark 13:32: "But of that day or hour [of the Last Judgment], *no man knoweth*, neither the angels in heaven, *nor the Son*, but the Father."

24. Any truly Catholic theology of grace must simultaneously affirm both man's freedom and divine omnipotence. Pascal thinks that the Molinist expositions of this doctrine have been better written than those of the Jansenists. In order to reverse this rhetorical inferiority, Pascal undertakes his *Écrits sur la grâce* [*Writings on Grace*].

25. Charles de Condren (1588–1641) was a mystical writer and successor of Bérulle as the head of the Oratory. The passage to which Pascal refers can be found in his *Lettres et discours* [Letters and discourses] (1642), letter 17.

26. In John 17:21–23, Jesus prays "That they all may be one, as thou, Father, in me, and I in thee; that they may be also one in us; that the world may believe that thou hast sent me. And the glory that thou hast given me, I have given to them; that they may be one, as we also are one."

The dignity of man consisted, in his innocence, in using and exerting his domination over creatures, but today in separating himself from them and submitting to them.

———

Meanings.

The same meaning changes according to the words expressing it.

Meanings receive their dignity from words instead of giving it to them. We must search for examples.

———

I believe that Joshua is the first among the people of God to bear that name, as Jesus Christ is the last among the people of God.[27]

———

A bright cloud OVERSHADOWED.[28]

———

Saint John [the Baptist] was to turn the hearts of the fathers to the children,[29] and Jesus Christ to plant division.[30]

Without contradiction.

———

The effects *in general* and *in particular*. The semi-Pelagians err in saying about things *in general* what is true only *in particular*, and the Calvinists in saying *in particular* what is true *in general* (it seems to me).[31]

27. Joshua, a variant of the name Jesus. Both signify "Savior." In the Old Testament, Joshua succeeds Moses and leads the chosen people into the Promised Land, prefiguring Christ's leading men to salvation.

28. Matthew 17:5. The Transfiguration: "And as he was yet speaking, behold a bright cloud *overshadowed* them. And lo, a voice of the cloud saying: This is my beloved Son, in whom I am well pleased: hear ye him."

29. Luke 1:17: "And he [John the Baptist] shall go before him in the spirit and power of Elias; that he may turn *the hearts of the fathers unto the children,* and the incredulous to the wisdom of the just, to prepare unto the Lord a perfect people."

30. Matthew 10:35: "For I came to set a man at variance against his father, and the daughter against her mother, and the daughter in law against her mother in law."

31. Pascal takes up the age-old controversy in which Saint Augustine and Pelagius were embroiled. (See the introduction, n. 29.) Is that justification leading to salvation attained by grace or by works? According to Saint Thomas Aquinas, one may take into consideration either the whole of justification (*in communi*) or the different stages of justification (*in particulari*). In the first instance, the justification of the elect is the work of God alone. In the second, there is room for works. The semi-Pelagians err by giving the initiative to man for the whole of justification and by excluding the mysterious work of grace. The Calvinist doctrine of "justification by faith (grace) alone" is heretical because it reserves for God alone every step in the unfolding of justification. Good works count for nothing. The Jansenists (and particularly Jansenius) were often accused of embracing this Calvinist doctrine of justification by Grace alone. In effect, the strict doctrine of predestination, inherited from Saint Augustine and Jansenius and so prominent in Pascal's theology, might be taken to imply the Protestant doctrine of *sola fides*. The orthodox Catholic understanding of justification had always made room for works as well as grace. It is not surprising that the Jesuits sought (to the horror of Pascal) to moderate and even marginalize the doctrine of predestination and particularly the dogma of the small number of the elect. In their worldwide missionary efforts they could hardly preach that works were fruitless and that, as Pascal holds, only a few elect would be saved. In his landmark study, *God Owes Us Nothing*, L. Kolakowski argues that the Jansenists lost the entire battle and that in the succeeding centuries the Catholic Church gradually moved toward semi-Pelagianism.

[XXXVIII Assorted Thoughts 6]

646

I submit as a fact that, if all men knew what they say of one another, there would not be four friends in the entire world. This can be seen from the quarrels caused by indiscreet disclosures that are sometimes made.

———

Hence, I refuse all other religions.[1]

———

In this way, I find an answer to all objections.

———

It is right that a God so pure should reveal himself only to those whose hearts are purified.[2]

———

Hence this religion is attractive to me, and I find it is already sufficiently authorized by the divine nature of its morality. But I find more to it than that: I find the decisive fact that as far back as man can remember, a people more ancient than any other people has existed. It has been constantly declared to mankind that they are universally corrupt, but that a redeemer will come. It is not just one man saying this, but innumerable men, and a whole people, expressly prophesying this for four thousand years. And an entire people, prophesying and created for that purpose. Their books are scattered for four hundred years. Finally, this people without idols or king.

An entire people foretell him before his coming. After his coming, an entire people worship him.

The more I examine this, the more I find truths in it: both what has preceded and what has followed; both this synagogue that preceded him, and this wretched synagogue (*this number of Jews*) without prophets who came after him and who, being enemies, are wonderful witnesses of the truth of these prophecies, in which their wretchedness and blindness are foretold.[3]

———

1. See ch. XVII, "Falsity of Other Religions."

2. Echo of the sixth beatitude: "Blessed are the clean of heart [RSV: pure in heart]: for they shall see God." Matthew 5:8.

3. As seen earlier (for instance, ch. XX, fr. 293, n. 26), Pascal believes, following the apologetics of the

The frightful darkness of the Jews foretold: *And you shall always grope at midday.*[4] *A book men delivered to one that is learned, and he said: I cannot read.*[5]

———

The scepter still in the hands of the first foreign usurper.[6]

———

The rumor over the coming of Jesus Christ.

I find this continuity, this religion wholly divine in its authority, in its duration, in its perpetuity, in its morality, in its conduct, in its doctrine, in its effects. So I stretch out my arms to my Savior, who, having been foretold for four thousand years, came to suffer and to die for me on earth, in the time and all the circumstances foretold. And through his grace, I await death in peace, in the hope of being united to him eternally, and yet I live with joy, whether in the blessing he chooses to bestow upon me, or in the afflictions he sends me for my own good and which he has taught me by his example to endure.

647

It is amusing to consider that there are people in the world who, having renounced all the laws of God and nature, have made laws for themselves that they obey scrupulously, as, for example, Mohammed's soldiers, thieves, heretics, etc. And likewise logicians.

It seems that their license must be without bounds or barriers, since they have broken through so many that were so just and holy.

648

Sneezing absorbs all the soul's functions, as does the sexual act.[7] But we do not derive from it the same arguments to refute man's greatness, because it occurs against his will. And although we bring it about, it is nevertheless done against our will: not for the sake of the act itself, but for another end. And therefore it is not a sign of man's weakness and his subjection to that act.

———

Church Fathers, that the testimony of the Jews as to the authenticity and historicity of the Old Testament can be considered trustworthy because the Jews are hostile witnesses who could not have possibly participated with the first Christians in the fabrication of a fraudulent text.

4. Deuteronomy 28:29.

5. Isaiah 29:11.

6. Herod the Great.

7. Montaigne, *Essays*, III, 5, 812: "Sleep suffocates and suppresses the faculties of our mind; the sexual act likewise absorbs and dissipates them. Truly it is a mark not only of our original corruption; but also of our inanity and deformity."

It is not shameful for man to yield to pain, but it is shameful for him to yield to pleasure. This is not because pain comes to us from outside and we ourselves seek pleasure; for one can look for pain and yield to it on purpose without such baseness. Why then does reason find glory in succumbing to the workings of pain and shame in yielding to the workings of pleasure? It is because it is not pain itself that tempts and attracts us. It is we ourselves who choose it willingly and want to have it prevail over us, so that we remain the masters of the situation. Man is thus yielding to himself. But in the case of pleasure, man is yielding to pleasure. And only mastery and control bring glory, only servitude brings shame.

<h2 style="text-align:center">649[8]</h2>

God
created everything for himself,
provided the power of pain and blessing for himself.

———

You can apply this to God or to yourself.

———

If to God, the Gospel is the rule.

———

If to yourself, you would be taking the place of God.

———

As God is surrounded by people full of charity, who ask him for the blessings of charity that are in his power, so . . .

———

Know yourself therefore, and know that you are only a king of concupiscence and follow the ways of concupiscence.

<h2 style="text-align:center">650</h2>

King and tyrant.

———

I too will have my thoughts in the back of my mind.

———

On each journey, I will watch out.

———

8. Frs. 649–59 are notes composed for the education of the young Duc de Chevreuse, the son of the Duc de Luynes. Nicole tried to reconstitute Pascal's ideas in the *Discours de la condition des grands* [Discourses on the condition of the great], attributed to Pascal, and published in 1670 as the *Traite de l'education d'un prince* [Treatise on the education of a prince]. Lafuma dates these notes from 1660. The *Epigrammatum delectus* [Excerpted epigrams], in which Pascal presumably read Martial was published only in August of 1659. The watermark on the sheet on which fr. 650 is written is that of "Auvergne," where Pascal spent the summer of 1660.

Greatness by convention, respect by convention.

The pleasure of the great is the ability to make people happy.

The specific function of riches is to be given away liberally.

The specific function of everything must be sought. The specific function of power is to protect.

When force attacks dissimulation, when a mere soldier snatches the square cap of a presiding judge and sends it flying through the window.

Epigrams of Martial[9]

Man loves malevolence, but it is not against the half-blind or the unfortunate, but against the fortunate and arrogant. Otherwise, we go wrong. For concupiscence is the source of all our movements, and humanity ...

We must please those who have humane and tender feelings.

The epigram about the two half-blind people is worthless, for it does not console them and only serves to produce a witticism, for the reputation of the author.[10]

What is only for the sake of the author is worthless.

Ambitious ornaments he'll lop away.[11]

---

9. The following notes are Pascal's reflections on the *Epigrammatum delectus* [Excerpted epigrams], an anthology of Latin verse published for the Petites Écoles [Little schools] in 1659. Pierre Nicole wrote a preface, entitled *De vera pulchritudine et adumbrate* [On true and represented (i.e., as in a drawing) beauty], in which he criticizes the malevolent character of the epigrams of Martial. Pierre Nicole, *La vraie beauté et son fantôme* [*Dissertatio de vera pulchritudine et adumbrata*], ed. and trans. B. Guion (Paris: Champion, 1996).

10. This Latin epigram (VI, 30) of Geronimo Amaltei had been adapted by Joachim du Bellay.

11. Horace, *Epistle to the Pisons*, v. 447–48. See Horace, *The Art of Poetry: An Epistle to the Pisons*, trans. George Colman (London: T. Cadell, 1783), 78. Cited in the *Epigrammatum delectus*, no. 110.

[XXXIX Assorted Thoughts 7]

651

Genesis 17: *And I will establish my covenant between me and thee by a perpetual covenant: to be a God to thee. And thou shalt keep my covenant.*[1]

652

Scripture has provided passages to console every condition, and to inspire fear in every condition.

Nature seems to have done the same by the two infinites, natural and moral; for we will always have the higher and lower, the more able and the less able, the more exalted and the more wretched, in order to humble our pride and exalt our abjection.

653

Bewitching.[2]
Their sleep.[3]
The fashion of this world.[4]

—————

The Eucharist.

Thou mayest eat THY *bread /* OUR *bread.*[5]

—————

The enemies of the Lord shall lick the dust.[6] Sinners lick the dust, that is to say, love earthly pleasures.

—————

1. Genesis 17:7 and 9. God's pact with Abraham.
2. Wisdom 4:12. "For the *bewitching* of vanity obscureth good things." A verse often cited at Port-Royal.
3. Psalm 75:6. "All the foolish of heart were troubled. They have slept *their sleep*; and all the men of riches found nothing in their hands."
4. 1 Corinthians 7:31. "The *fashion of this world* passeth away."
5. Deuteronomy 8:9: "Here *thou mayest eat thy bread.*" Moses, prophesying the Promised Land. Luke 11:3: "Give us this day *our* daily *bread*" (Lord's Prayer).
6. Psalm 72:9: "Before him the Ethiopians shall fall down: and *his enemies shall lick the ground.*"

The Old Testament contained the figures of the joy to come, and the New contains the means of attaining it.

The figures were of joy, the means of penitence; and yet the paschal lamb was eaten *with bitter things, cum amaritudinibus.*[7]

_____

I am alone until I pass.[8] Jesus Christ before his death was almost the sole martyr.

_____

Time heals grief and quarrels, because we change. We are no longer the same person. Neither the offender nor the offended are themselves anymore. It is like a people we have angered but meet again after two generations; they are still French, but not the same ones.

_____

If we had the same dream every night, it would affect us as much as the objects we see every day. And if a craftsman were to dream every night for twelve hours that he was a king, I believe he would be nearly as happy as a king dreaming every night for twelve hours that he was a craftsman.

If we dreamed every night that we were being pursued by enemies and harassed by these painful phantoms, or that we spent every day in different occupations, as when travelling, we would suffer almost as much as if it were real, and we would dread going to sleep as we dread waking up when we are afraid to encounter such mishaps in reality. And, indeed, this would produce just about the same woes as reality.

But because dreams are all different, and there is change even within a single dream, what we see in them affects us much less than what we see when we are awake, on account of continuity, which is not, however, so continuous as not to change too, though less abruptly, except on rare occasions, as when we are travelling; and then we say: I feel as if I were dreaming. For life is a dream, a little less unstable.[9]

_____

Shall we say that, because they have said that justice has fled the earth, men knew of original sin? *No man happy till his death:*[10] is this to say that they realized that eternal and essential happiness begins at death?

_____

7. Pascal adds the Latin to his translation. Exodus 12:8: "And they shall eat the flesh that night [of Passover] roasted at the fire, and unleavened bread with bitter herbs." Pascal follows the Latin (*amaritudinibus*) of the Vatable Bible. (On the Vatable Bible, see ch. XXXI, n. 76).

8. Psalm 141:10, traditionally considered a prophecy of Christ's agony in the garden. This is a note taken from Augustine's *On Psalm 141*, nos. 25–26.

9. The passage recalls Calderon's religious play *Life Is a Dream* (1633).

10. Ovid, *Metamorphoses*, III, 135. Cited in Montaigne, *Essays*, I, 19: "No man should be called happy till his death." The warning had been given by Solon to Croesus, who was eventually defeated by Cyrus, and who, about to be executed, was in a position to verify the wisdom of Solon's words.

By knowing each person's dominant passion, we can be sure of pleasing them. And yet everyone has fancies contrary to their own good, according to their very idea of good. This is a bizarre disposition that puts us off the scale.[11]

———

We are never satisfied with the reality of our life and our own being. We want to live an imaginary life in the minds of others, and for this purpose we struggle to make an impression. We strive incessantly to embellish and preserve our imaginary being, and we neglect our true one.[12] And if we possess equanimity, or magnanimity, or fidelity, we are eager to make it known, so as to attach these virtues to our other being, and would rather separate them from ourselves to unite them with the other. We would gladly be cowards if it earned us the reputation of being brave.[13] This is a great sign of the nothingness of our own being, that we are not satisfied with the one unless we have the other, and often exchange the one for the other! For whoever would not die in order to save his honor would be infamous.

654

John 8

MANY BELIEVED IN HIM—*Jesus said to them: If you continue ... You shall be my disciples* INDEED ... AND THE TRUTH SHALL MAKE YOU FREE ...

They answered him: We are the seed of Abraham, and we have never been slaves to any man.[14]

There is a great difference between disciples and TRUE disciples. You can recognize them by telling them that the truth will set them free. For if they answer that they are free, and that it is within their own power to escape enslavement to the devil they are indeed still disciples, but not true disciples.

11. See fr. 88.

12. See Montaigne, *Essays* II, 16, 579: "Even of those whom we see doing bravely, three months or three years after they have been left on the field, you hear no more talk than if they had never been. [...] And for three years of this fanciful and imaginary life shall we go and lose our real and essential life and engage ourselves in a perpetual death?"

13. Montaigne, *Essays*, III, 9, 886: "Whatever it is, whether art or nature, that imprints in us this disposition to live with reference to others, it does us much more harm than good. We defraud ourselves of our own advantages to make appearances conform to public opinion. We do not care so much what we are in ourselves and in reality as what we are in the public mind." Also, *Essays*, III, 5, 780: "A man who does everything for honor and glory, what does he think to gain by presenting himself to the world in a mask, concealing his true being from public knowledge? Praise a hunchback for his handsome figure, and he is bound to take it as an insult. If you are a coward and people honor you as a valiant man, is it you they are talking about?"

14. John 8:30–33: "When he spoke these things, *many believed in him. Then Jesus said* to those Jews, who believed him: *If you continue in my word, you shall be my disciples indeed. And you shall know the truth, and the truth shall make you free ... They answered him, we are the seed of Abraham and we have never been slaves to any man;* how sayest thou: you shall be free?"

655

There are three ways to believe: reason, custom, inspiration. The Christian religion, which alone has reason on its side, does not admit as its true children those who believe without inspiration. Not that it excludes reason or custom. On the contrary. But we must open our minds to the proofs, confirm them through custom, and offer ourselves in humility to inspirations, which alone can bring about a true and salutary effect. *Lest the cross of Christ should be made of no effect.*[15]

656

It is incomprehensible that God should exist and incomprehensible that he should not; that the soul should be joined to the body, that we should have no soul; that the world should have been created, that it should not, etc.; that original sin should be a fact, that it should not.

657

What will become of men who despise small things and do not believe in the greater?[16]

658

The two oldest books in the world are Moses and Job, one Jewish, the other heathen, which both consider Jesus Christ as their common center and object:[17] Moses by relating God's promises to Abraham, Jacob, etc., and his prophecies; and Job: *Who will grant me, etc.—I know that my Redeemer liveth, etc.* . . .[18]

———

The style of the Gospel is admirable in so many ways, among others in that it never resorts to invective against the killers and enemies of Jesus Christ. For the [Gospel] historians include none against Judas, or Pilate, or any of the Jews.

———

15. 1 Corinthians 1:17. A Pauline doctrine of primary importance in shaping the early Church. Without Christ's saving work on the cross, there can be no salvation or reason for preaching the Gospel.

16. Saint Augustine, Letter 137, 4, no. 14. Sellier notes, "The greater works are the Resurrection and the Ascension of Christ" (Pascal, *Pensées*, ed. Sellier, 2010, 483n2).

17. I.e., the Pentateuch, of which Moses was still universally taken to be the author. Job is called a heathen book presumably because Job himself is not a Jew: he comes from the land of Uz, probably in the south of Edom.

18. Job 19:23–25: "*Who will grant me* that my words may be written? Who will grant me that they may be marked down in a book? With an iron pen and in a plate of lead, or else be graven with an instrument in flint stone. For *I know that my Redeemer liveth*, and in the last day I shall rise out of the earth."

If this moderation on the part of the writers of the Gospel had been assumed, along with all the other distinguishing marks of so noble a character, and they had only assumed it to attract notice, even if they had not dared to draw attention to it themselves, they would not have failed to enlist friends to make such remarks for their benefit. But as they acted in this way without pretense, and from purely disinterested motives, they did not point it out to anyone. I believe that several of these things have never been noticed until now. This is a testimony to the dispassionate spirit with which it was done.

———

We never do evil so wholeheartedly and as cheerfully as when we do it out of conscience.

———

Just as we corrupt our minds, we also corrupt our feelings.

———

Our minds and feelings are improved through the company we keep; our minds and feelings are corrupted through the company we keep. Thus good and bad society improves or corrupts them.[19] So it is therefore of the utmost importance to know how to choose well, so as to improve and not to corrupt them. And we cannot make the right choice unless we have already improved and not corrupted them. So we find ourselves in a vicious circle, and those who escape it are really fortunate.

659

Ordinary people have the power not to think about what they do not want to think about. "Do not think about the passages concerning the Messiah," said the Jew to his son. Our own people often do the same. This is how false religions are preserved, and the true one as well, with respect to many people.

But there are some who do not have the power to prevent themselves from thinking, and who think all the more because it is forbidden to do so. They shake off the false religions, and even the true one, if they do not find solid arguments.

———

I would soon have given up my pleasures, they[20] say, if I had faith. And what I say to you is this: you would soon have faith, if you had given up your pleasures. Now, you have to go first. If I could, I would give you faith. I cannot

———

19. Montaigne, *Essays*, III, 8, 855: "As our mind is strengthened by communication with vigorous and orderly minds, so it is impossible to say how much it loses and degenerates by our continual association and frequentation with mean and sickly minds. There is no contagion that spreads like that one."

20. The unbelievers. See "The Wager" (fr. 680), par. 9.

do so, nor can I test the truth of what you say. But you can indeed renounce pleasures, and test whether what I say is true.

You may well say: we must admit that there is something extraordinary about the Christian religion. "You say that because you were born into it," they will say. Far from it: I make myself resist it for this very reason, for fear this prejudice may lead me astray. But, although I was born into it, I still find something extraordinary about it.

660

Victory over death.[21]
For what shall it profit a man if he gains the whole world and loses his soul?
Whosoever will save his soul shall lose it.[22]
I have come not to destroy the law but to fulfill it.[23]
Lambs did not take away the sins of the world, but I *am the Lamb who taketh away the sins.*[24]
Moses gave you not bread from heaven.[25]
Moses did not deliver you from captivity and did not make you *truly free.*[26]

The prophecies of particular things are mingled with those concerning the Messiah, so that the prophecies of the Messiah should not be without proof and the particular prophecies should not be without fruit.

There are two ways of persuading people of the truths of our religion: one, by the power of reason, the other, by the authority of the speaker.

We do not use the latter, but the former. We do not say, this must be believed, because scripture, which says it, is divine. We say that it must be believed for such and such a reason, which are feeble arguments, because reason is completely malleable.[27]

21. 1 Corinthians 15:54: "Death is swallowed up in victory."
22. Luke 9:24–25.
23. Matthew 5:17: "Do not think that I am come to destroy *the law,* or the prophets. *I am not come to destroy, but to fulfill.*"
24. Paraphrase of John 1:29. At the elevation in the Mass, the priest recites: "Behold the Lamb of God, behold *him who taketh away the sin* of the world."
25. John 6:32. The verse continues: "but my Father *giveth* you the true bread from heaven." The manna that fell from heaven to feed the starving Hebrews during their forty years in the desert (Exodus 16:4) was but a *figure* of the Body of Christ consumed in the Eucharist.
26. John 8:36: "If therefore the son shall make you free, you shall be *free indeed.*" Moses's deliverance of the Hebrews from Egypt was only a figure of the redemption wrought by Jesus' salvific work on the cross, which rendered men "free indeed."
27. Montaigne, *Essays,* II, 12, 652: "How pliable our reason is to all sorts of ideas."

[XL Assorted Thoughts 8]

661

For we must make no mistake about ourselves: we are as much automata[1] as minds. And this is why demonstration is not the only instrument of persuasion. How few things are demonstrable! Proofs convince only the mind. Custom is the source of our strongest and most firmly believed proofs. It inclines the automaton, which drags the unwitting mind with it. Who has ever demonstrated that tomorrow will dawn and that we shall die? And is there anything more widely believed? It is custom, then, that so persuades us and makes so many Christians. It is custom that makes Turks, heathen, trades, soldiers, etc. (What Christians have, over and above what heathen have, is the faith they receive in baptism.) In the end, we have to turn to custom once the mind has seen where the truth lies, in order to quench our thirst and steep ourselves in this belief, which slips away from us at every turn. For always to have the proofs before us is too much trouble. We have to acquire an easier belief, which is that of habit, which, without violence, art, or argument, makes us believe things and inclines all our faculties to this belief, so that our soul settles into it naturally. When we believe only through the strength of conviction, and the automaton is inclined to believe the opposite, it is not enough. So we have to get the two parts of ourselves to believe: the mind, by reasons, which it is enough to have grasped once in one's lifetime, and the automaton, through custom, and by not allowing it any inclination to the contrary.

O Lord, incline my heart . . .[2]

Reason acts slowly, and with so many perspectives, on so many principles, which have to be in sight all the time, that it is constantly dozing off and losing its way, because of its inability to keep all its principles in sight. This is not how feeling acts: it acts in a moment, and is always ready to act. Thus we must place our faith in feeling; otherwise it will always be vacillating.

------

1. The "machine." See frs. 39, 41, 45, 59, 118, 617, and 680 ("Discourse on the Machine).

2. Liturgical response based on Psalm 119:36: "*Incline my heart* into thy testimonies and not to covetousness."

329

662[3]

(*We should feel pity for both these kinds of people. But for the first kind we should feel a pity derived from affection, for the second kind a pity derived from scorn.*[4]

———

One has to be wholly filled with the religion they despise in order not to despise them.[5]

———

These are not the manners of the world.

———

That shows that there is nothing to be said to them; not out of scorn, but because they lack common sense. They will have to be touched by God.

———

This kind of people are academics, scholars, the most worthless category of people I know.

———

You will convert me.[6]

———

I do not accept this out of superstition, but out of the makeup of the human heart; not out of zeal for piety or detachment from the world, but out of a purely human motive and motives of self-interest and self-love.[7]

———

It is beyond doubt that there is no real happiness without the knowledge of God, that as one gets closer to him, one is happy, and that the supreme happiness is to know him with certainty, that as one gets further away from him one is unhappy, and that the ultimate unhappiness would be the certainty of the contrary.[8]

———

3. This entire fragment is constituted by preparatory notes for fr. 681, the preface to the entire Apology. To borrow Sellier's phrase, Pascal uses them to "orchestrate" the "Letter Urging the Search for God." How these fragments came to be inserted in this chapter remains a mystery.

4. Fr. 681, par. 5–7: "I can feel only compassion for those who sincerely bemoan their doubt [...]. But as for those who drift through life without a thought for the final end of life, [....] [their] negligence [...] arouses my indignation more than my sympathy."

5. Fr. 681, par. 24: "One needs all the charity of the religion they despise not to despise them even to the point of abandoning them to their folly...."

6. Fr. 681, par. 22: "'If you carry on holding forth like this,' he remarked, '*you will end up by converting me.*'" Satire on the part of the hardened disbeliever, reacting to the inept arguments of those "*pseudo-libertins*" professing disbelief in order to appear witty. A *bon mot* either overheard by, or recounted to, Pascal.

7. Fr. 681, par. 7: "I do not say this prompted by *the pious zeal of a devout spirituality*. I mean, on the contrary, that we ought to have this feeling *out of sheer human self-interest and self-love.*"

8. Fr. 681, par. 9: "then say whether it is not beyond doubt that *the only true good in this life is the hope of a life to come; that we become happy only insofar as we draw nearer to it*, and that, just as no more unhappiness awaits those who had a firm belief in eternity, so there is no happiness for those who are altogether in the dark about it."

So doubt is an unhappy state, but it is an indispensable duty to seek when one doubts. So someone who doubts and does not seek is unhappy and unjust at the same time. But if, along with that, he is cheerful and arrogant, then I cannot find words to describe so absurd a creature.)[9]

Yet, it is certain that man is so divided from his nature that there is a seed of joy in his heart.

(Is it a thing to be said joyfully? No: so it is a thing to be said sadly.[10]

What a reason to rejoice, to boast, with one's head held high and say: "So let us make merry, let us live without fear and without anxiety, and let us just wait for death, because it is all uncertain, and that will be time enough to find out what is going to happen to us." I cannot see the logic in that.)

Is it not enough that miracles occur in one place and that Providence appears in one people?

Good manners promote a lack of forbearance for others; good piety promotes forbearance for others.

(Is it courage for a dying man, weak and in his death throes, to confront an all-powerful and eternal God?)[11]

How happy I would be, if I were in that state, and someone took pity on my foolishness and had the goodness to drag me out of it whether I wanted or not![12]

(Not to be distressed by it, not to love, is a proof of such weakness of mind and such evil in the will.)

What kind of reason for joy is there when all you can expect is irremediable wretchedness? What consolation is there, when you despair of there being anyone to bring consolation?

9. Fr. 681, par. 10: "But if, in addition, he is calm and satisfied, if he professes to be so, and if he regards such a state as something to boast about; if this very state is in fact the cause of his joy and his vanity, *I lack the words to describe so extravagant a creature.*"

10. Fr. 681, par. 21: "*Is this a thing to be said cheerfully?* Is it not rather something *to be said sadly,* as the saddest thing in the world?"

11. Fr. 681, par. 23: "There is nothing more cowardly than to want to brazen it out with God."

12. Fr. 681, par. 24: "we must do unto them what we would wish to be done unto us were we in their place" (The Golden Rule).

But these very people who seem most opposed to the glory of religion will constitute our first argument to prove that there is something supernatural about all this. Their example will not be without value for others.[13] For blindness of this kind is not a natural thing. And if their folly drives them to act so rashly against their own good, it will be a salutary deterrent for other people, horrified by such a deplorable example and by a folly so deserving of compassion. Are they so strong-minded as to be unaffected by anything that concerns them? Test them: how would they behave if they lost their property or their honor? You see! It's a spell . . .[14]

663

History of China[15]

The only histories I believe are those whose witnesses would have their throats cut.[16]

(*Which is the more credible of the two: Moses or China?*)[17]

I am not talking of some general overview here: I tell you that there is enough to blind, and enough to enlighten.

These words alone are enough for me to wreck all your arguments.—"But," you say, "China obscures the issue." And I answer: "China obscures the issue, but there is light to be found. Look for it.

In this way, everything you mention contributes to one of the purposes, and does not go against the other. In this way, it helps, and does no harm.

Therefore we have to look at the matter in detail, we have to lay our documents on the table."[18]

---

13. Fr. 681, par. 18: "In truth, it is glorious for our religion to have as enemies men so unreasonable."

14. Fr. 681, par. 20: "It is an incomprehensible *spell*, a supernatural torpor that points to an all-powerful force as its cause."

15. This brief exchange between Pascal and an imaginary interlocutor has no discernible context in the chapter in which it is filed. According to documents discovered by the Jesuits during their first mission to China, the world was far older than 4404 BCE, the date established by the Christian chronologists of Pascal's day. Unlike the Jesuits, Pascal refuses any attempt to reconcile "pagan" and Christian history. Like those of the Greeks and Egyptians (fr. 688), the "histories" of the Chinese are but "fables" since they are not founded upon the testimonies of contemporary witnesses (fr. 327). Pascal's source is usually thought to be the Jesuit M. Martini's *Sinicæ historiæ* (1658). However, in Rouen in 1647, the young Pascal had already denounced as heretical a certain Pere Forton, who had argued, among other things, that the Chinese had written records dating back 36,000 years and that Biblical chronologies were metaphors. See Wetsel, "Histoire de la Chine: Pascal and the Challenge to Biblical Time," in *The Journal of Religion* 69, no. 2 (1985), 199–219.

16. The martyrdom of the apostles, witnesses of Christ's life and Resurrection, is likewise a testimony to their belief in the veracity of the Old Testament, including its chronologies.

17. In chapter XXIII, "Proofs of Moses," and particularly in fr. 327, Pascal takes great pains to establish the veracity and historicity of the Pentateuch and its chronologies. Until the advent of modern criticism, Moses was always accepted as the unique author of the Pentateuch. In chapters XLVIII–LII Pascal repeatedly argues that the Jews were the oldest people to appear on earth.

18. Pascal's admonitions about "blinding" and "enlightening" refer, of course, to the apologetic theme

664

An heir finds the title-deeds to his house. Is he going to say: "They may not be authentic," and not bother to verify them?

665

The law required what it did not give us; grace gives us what it requires of us.

666

Seems to refute.

To the humble giveth grace.[19] But did he not give them humility?[20] *His own received him not.*[21] However many did not receive him. Were they not his own?[22]

---

of the *Deus absconditus*. God hides the clues to revelation so that only those who "seek" will find them. "Lay out our documents on the table" has the sense of "discerning more closely." Here, "China obscures the issue." Only those seeking the truth will discern that the Chinese chronologies are but a fictitious obstacle to truth conjured up by Satan. See fr. 615 and n. 12.

19. 1 Peter 5:5: "For God resisteth the proud, but *to the humble giveth grace.*"

20. "But did he not give them humility?" is Pascal's addition in Latin.

21. John 1:11: "He came unto his own, and *his own received him not.*"

22. "However many did not receive him. Were they not his own?" is, again, Pascal's addition, in Latin.

[XLI Assorted Thoughts 9]

667

Make all things according to the pattern which was shewn thee on the mount.[1]

The religion of the Jews was thus formed on the pattern of the truth of the Messiah. And the truth of the Messiah was recognized from the religion of the Jews, of which it was the figure.

Among the Jews the truth was only figurative. In heaven it is revealed.

In the Church it is covered, and recognized by its relation to the figure.[2]

———

The figure was fashioned from the truth, and the truth was recognized from the figure.

———

Saint Paul himself says that people will forbid marriage, and he himself speaks of it to the Corinthians[3] in a manner that is a trap. For if a prophet had said one thing and Saint Paul had then said another, he would have been accused.

668

The bonds that bind the respect of men to one another are, generally speaking, bonds of necessity. For there must be different ranks, all men wishing to dominate, and not all, but some, being able to.

Let us then imagine that we can see them beginning to take shape. There is no doubt that they will fight until the stronger party subjugates the weaker, and a dominant party is finally established. But when this has been settled once and for all, the masters, who do not want the strife to continue, then

---

1. Exodus 25:40. Pascal cites from Hebrews 8:5. See fr. 279.

2. See the sixteenth *Provincial Letter*. "God made himself three tabernacles: the synagogue, in which there are only figures but not truth; the Church, which has both truth and figures; and heaven, where there is truth alone."

3. 1 Timothy 4:1–3 and 2 Corinthians 7:29–35. In the first text, a sect hostile to marriage is denounced as heretical. In the second, Paul exhorts avoiding marriage.

decree that the power on their hands shall pass down as it pleases them: some opt for election by the people, others for hereditary succession, and so on.

And this is where imagination enters the scene. Until now, pure power did it. But now, power is sustained by the imagination in the hands of a certain party: in France the nobility, in Switzerland the commoners,[4] and so forth.

These bonds that bind the respect of men to this or that particular person are therefore bonds of imagination.

———

These great mental efforts on which the soul sometimes alights are things on which it does not take hold. It can only leap up to them, not like one ascending a throne forever, but only for a moment.

4. See fr. 83. In certain cantons (Basel, Zürich) the nobility were in the minority.

[XLII] Geometry/Intuition [1][1]

669

To mask and disguise nature: no more king, pope, bishop, but "august monarch," etc. No more Paris, but "capital of the realm."

There are places where we should call Paris, Paris, and others where we must call it the capital of the realm.

———

The greater one's mind, the more variety one finds among men. The common people discern no difference among men.

———

Different kinds of right thinking: some in a certain order of things, and not in others, where they spout nonsense.

———

Some are good at drawing consequences from few principles, and this is a capacity to think logically.

Others are good at drawing consequences properly from things involving many principles.

For example, the former understand properly the effects of water,[2] which involve few principles; but the consequences there are so subtle that only a very logical mind can reach them. And, in spite of that, these people might not be great geometers, because geometry comprises a great number of principles, and a mind may be of such a nature that it could get all the way to the bottom of a few principles without in the least being able to get anywhere in matters involving many principles.

There are therefore two types of minds: the one, penetrating swiftly and profoundly the consequences of principles, is the logical mind; the other, grasping a great number of principles without confusing them, is the geometric mind. The first is characterized by strength and the capacity to think straight, the second by breadth of mind. Now, one can exist without the other; the mind can be strong and narrow, and also broad and weak.

---

1. Sellier advances the hypothesis that the following two chapters are linked to *liasse* "[XIV] Submission and Use of Reason." There as well Pascal attacks the so-called proof by general consent.

2. As does Pascal himself, in his *Traité de l'équilibre des liquides* [On the equilibrium of liquids].

[XLIII] Geometry/Intuition [2]

670

Difference
between the geometric
and the intuitive mind[1]

In the former, the principles are palpable, but remote from common usage, so that it is difficult to turn our head in that direction, for lack of habit. But only turn it that way, and you see the principles in full. And one would need to have a completely defective mind to reason wrongly from principles so evident that it is almost impossible to miss them.

But for the intuitive mind, the principles are in common usage and in plain sight for everybody. There is no need to turn one's head, or constrain oneself. It is only a question of having good sight. But it must be good, for the principles are so subtle and so numerous that it is almost impossible not to miss some. Now, skipping one principle leads to error. Thus we must have clear vision to see all of the principles, and then an accurate mind in order not to reason falsely from those known principles.

All geometric minds would thus be intuitive, if they had clear vision, for they do not reason falsely from principles that they know. And the intuitive minds would be geometers, if they could bend their sight to the unfamiliar principles of geometry.

The reason why some intuitive minds are not geometers is that they cannot at all apply themselves to the principles of geometry. But the reason why geometers are not intuitive is that they do not see what is in front of them and, being accustomed to the clear and unsubtle principles of geometry, and to reasoning only after having seen clearly and having handled their principles,

---

1. *Intuition/intuitive* are only an approximation, meant to refer to a non-mathematical subtlety. It might be argued that the French word *finesse* and its adjectival cognate *fin* refer to qualities usually prized in polite society, which cannot fully be accounted for. They are linked with *honnêteté* and the *je ne sais quoi* often mentioned in the literature of the second half of the century. On *honnêteté*, see "French Words" in the preface. On the *je ne sais quoi*, see ch. I (the "Table-*liasse*"), fr. 32, n. 17.

they get lost in matters of intuition, where principles cannot be handled thus. They are barely seen, or rather they are felt rather than seen. It is infinitely difficult to make them felt by those who do not feel them themselves. These matters are so delicate, and so numerous, that one must have a very clear and delicate sense to feel them, and to judge rightly and correctly according to that feeling, most often without being able to set out proofs in an orderly fashion, as in geometry, because we do not have a grasp on their principles in the same way, and because it would be a never-ending undertaking. The matter must be seen all at once, at a single glance, and not by gradual reasoning, at least to a certain degree. And thus it is rare for people with a geometric mind to be intuitive, and rare for those with an intuitive mind to be geometers, because geometers want to treat matters of intuition in geometrical fashion, and they make themselves ridiculous, wanting to begin from definitions, and then by principles.[2] This is not the way to go about that sort of reasoning. It is not that the mind does not do this, but it does it tacitly, naturally, and without art, for its expression is beyond the capacity of all men, and the perception of it belongs only to a few.

Intuitive minds, on the contrary, being thus accustomed to judge at a single glance, are so baffled, when they are presented with propositions in which they understand nothing, and to gain access to which, they must go through definitions and principles so sterile, which they are not accustomed to seeing in such detail, that they are discouraged and put off by them.

But unsound minds are never either geometric or intuitive.

Geometers who are only geometers thus reason correctly, provided that all matters are explained to them by definitions and principles. Otherwise they are wrong and insufferable, for they are right only when reasoning from well clarified principles.

And the intuitive minds who are only intuitive cannot have the patience to push all the way to the first principles in matters of speculation and imagination, which they have never seen in the world, and which are completely outside common experience.

---

2. The method presented in *De l'esprit géométrique* [On the geometrical mind], which concludes in a third moment on "demonstrations." English translation: *The Provincial Letters, Pensées, Scientific Treatises by Blaise Pascal*, in Great Books of the Western World 33, Pascal (New York: Encyclopedia Britannica, 1952), 430–46.

671

Geometry/intuition

True eloquence cares nothing for eloquence. True morality cares nothing for morality, that is, the morality of judgment cares nothing for the morality of the mind, which has no rules.[3]

For sentiment belongs to judgment, just as the sciences belong to the mind. Intuition is the province of judgment, and geometry is that of the mind.

To care nothing for philosophy is to be a true philosopher.[4]

———

Nourishment of the body is incremental.

Plenty of nourishment, and little substance.

3. The context invites us to make the antecedent of "which has no rules" the "morality of judgment," not "the morality of the mind." The references that follow—to the sciences, to geometry—show that the products of the mind are eminently characterized by a rule-based functioning.

4. Montaigne, *Essays*, II, 12, 461: "An ancient who was reproached for professing philosophy, of which nevertheless in his own mind he took no great account, replied that "this was being a true philosopher.""

[XLIV] Authority

672

Authority

They hide in the crowd and call on the multitude to help them.[1]

Uproar.

Far from making it a rule to believe something because you have heard it, you ought to believe nothing without putting yourself into the position you would have been if you had never heard it.

It is your own assent to yourself and the steadfast voice of your own reason, and not that of others, which should make you believe.

Belief is so important.

A hundred contradictions might be true.

If the rule was that you can only believe what is old, then the ancients had no rule for their beliefs.

If universal consent, if men had perished?

False humanity, pride.

Punishment of those who sin: error.

Lift the curtain.

It is no use trying: you still must believe, or deny, or doubt.

Shall we then have no rule?

We are able to judge whether an animal's action is performed well. Will there be no rule for judging men?

To deny, to believe, and to doubt well are to a man what running is to a horse.

673

What he sees often, does not astonish him, even if he does not know why it is. If something happens that he has not seen before, he thinks it is a prodigy (Cicero).[2]

---

1. Montaigne, *Essays*, III, 11, 957: "It is unfortunate to be in such a pass that the best touchstone of truth is the multitude of believers, in a crowd in which the fools so far surpass the wise in numbers."
2. Cicero, *On Divination*, II, 22. All these citations in italics are in Latin in Pascal's text and are taken from the 1652 edition of Montaigne's *Essays*. Here, II, 30, 654.

674

583.—*Indeed this man will take great pains to speak great foolishness* (Terence).³

*As if anything was more unhappy than a man dominated by the figments of his imagination*⁴ (Pliny).⁵

675

588.—*It is by virtue of decrees of the Senate and of plebiscites that crimes are committed* (Seneca).⁶

Nothing so absurd can be said that it has not been said by some philosopher (*On Divination*).⁷

Devoted to certain set and fixed opinions, so that they are reduced to defending even those things of which they do not approve (Cicero).⁸

We suffer from an excess of literature as from an excess of anything (Seneca).⁹

588.—"*What most becomes a man is what is most natural to him.*¹⁰

These manners nature first ordained (*The Georgics*).¹¹

*Wisdom does not demand much teaching.*¹²

*If a thing is not shameful in itself, still it is not free from shame when it is praised by the multitude.*¹³

That is my practice: do as you see fit (Terence).¹⁴

676

*For it is rare for anyone to respect himself enough.*¹⁵

---

3. The page numbers ("583," etc.) refer to the 1652 edition of the *Essays*. Here, III, 1, 726. Montaigne's source is Terence's *Heauton Timoroumenos* [The self-tormentor], III, v. 8.

4. Cited by Montaigne, *Essays*, II, 12, 479.

5. Pascal attributes the maxim to Pliny the Elder (the author of the *Natural History*, who died in the 79 CE eruption of Vesuvius), but the actual reference is to Augustine, *The City of God*, VIII, 22; see Augustine, *The City of God*, vol. 3, *Books 8-11*, trans. David S. Wiesen, Loeb Classical Library 413 (Cambridge, Mass.: Harvard University Press, 1968), 110.

6. Seneca, Letter 106, cited by Montaigne in *Essays*, III, 12, 732. See frs. 94 and 796.

7. *On Divination*, II, 58, cited by Montaigne in *Essays*, II, 12, 496.

8. Pascal shortens the citation. Cicero, *Tusculan*, II, 2, cited by Montaigne in *Essays*, II, 12, 510.

9. Seneca, Letter 106, cited by Montaigne in *Essays*, III, 12, 966.

10. Cicero, *On Duties*, I, 31, cited by Montaigne in *Essays*, III, 1, 732.

11. Virgil, *Georgics*, II, 20, cited by Montaigne in *Essays*, I, 31, 186.

12. Seneca, Letter 106, cited by Montaigne in *Essays*, III, 12, 967.

13. Cicero, *On the ends* [*of good and evil*], II, 15, cited by Montaigne in *Essays*, II, 16, 574.

14. *Heauton Timoroumenos*, I, 1, 80, cited by Montaigne in *Essays*, I, p. 173.

15. Quintilian, *Institutes of oratory*, X, 7, cited by Montaigne in *Essays*, I, 39, 216.

677

So many gods in an uproar about a single head.[16]

678

Nothing is more shameful than to affirm before knowing (Cicero).[17]

679

Nor am I ashamed, as are these men, to admit that I do not know what I do not know.[18]

It is better not to begin.[19]

16. Seneca The Elder, *Suasoriæ,* 4, cited by Montaigne in *Essays,* II, 13, 557.

17. *Academics,* I, 12, cited by Montaigne in *Essays,* III, 13, 2003. Pascal omits the words *"assertion and proof precede knowledge and perception."*

18. Cicero, *Tusculan Disputations,* I, 25, cited by Montaigne in *Essays,* III, 11, 962.

19. Seneca, Letter 72, cited by Montaigne in *Essays,* III, 10, 945.

Developments

from July 1658

to July 1662

[Proofs of religion
from the Jewish people, prophecies,
and some discourses][1]

---

1. This title, missing from C1, is most likely not Pascal's. It covers *developments* later than the June 1658 sketch: two important groups, "The State of the Jews" and "Prophecies," to which ch. LXI, "The Law Was Figurative," as well as three discourses, "Discourse on the Machine" (XLV), the "Letter Urging the Search for God" (XLVI), and the "Preface to the Second Part" (XLVII) are linked. Various notes pertaining to these five groups either accompany the discourses or form separate units (LIII and LX).

[XLV] Discourse on the Machine[1]

680[2]

Infinity, nothingness.[3]

1. This is the "Letter about removing obstacles, which is the discourse on the machine," anticipated in fr. 45 and commonly known as the "Wager." Pascal seeks to reveal to the unbeliever an entire dimension of his being of which he is unaware: "the machine," i.e., the routine of self-destructive habits in the form of the passions, which prevent belief and Christian charity from taking root. Once disabused of the naive rationalism of believing himself capable of free will, the unbeliever is made capable of at least *wishing* Christianity were true. No fragment in the entire *Pensées* has been more often read, taught, excerpted, and anthologized, yet misunderstood and abused. It has become almost a commonplace among readers that the "Wager" was to have been Pascal's ultimate proof of the existence of God and is the centerpiece of the *Pensées*. In fact, according to Pascal's own schema in fr. 45, this "Discourse on the machine" would have constituted the second chapter of the Apology, immediately following the preface adumbrated in fr. 681. Philippe Sellier constantly reminds us that this discourse is in no sense a proof of the existence of a Christian God. It is nothing more than a proof (like Descartes's) of the God of deism—and Christianity "abhors almost equally" deism and atheism (see fr. 690). Rather, as Laurent Thirouin demonstrates in his authoritative *Le Hasard et les Règles: Le modèle du jeu dans la pensée de Pascal* [Chance and rules: The model of game theory in the thought of Pascal] (Paris: Vrin, 1991), the "wager" is a kind of "lure." Its function is to have the Apology be read by those who could never otherwise be convinced to take up any other kind of defense of Christianity but who, like Méré and Miton (see, in the introduction, "Religious Challenges to the Modern Reader," esp. n. 97), are fascinated with Pascal's theory of probability. Whereas the great majority of readers, who have never seen the discourse as it appears on the sheets found in the Original Collection, suppose the text definitive, the reverse is the case. In the autograph, the text of the "Wager" appears as an unreadable and total scramble of almost undecipherable and tentative notes, written in every direction on the page. Jean Mesnard reminds us: "The text is little more than a rough draft, so far from completion that it would most certainly have undergone significant rewriting." Jean Mesnard, *Les Pensées de Pascal* (Paris: S.E.D.E.S, 1976), 316. (See plate 1.)

2. No study comparable to that of Laurent Thirouin exists in English. The following, though sometimes flawed, may be of help to the reader: Jeff Jordan, *Pascal's Wager: Pragmatic Arguments and Belief in God* (Oxford: Oxford University Press, 2006); Jon Elster, "Pascal and Decision theory," in *The Cambridge Companion to Pascal*, ed. Nicholas Hammond, 53–74 (Cambridge: Cambridge University Press, 2003); Leslie Armour, *"Infini Rien": Pascal's Wager and the Human Paradox* (Carbondale: Southern Illinois Press, 1993); Bernard Howells, "The Interpretation of Pascal's '*Pari*,'" *The Modern Language Review*, 79 (1984), 35–63. Sara Melzer offers an unorthodox but highly challenging modernist interpretation of the discourse in her *Discourses of the Fall: A Study of Pascal's Pensées* (Berkeley, University of California Press, 1986), 58–64.

3. In his contribution to *Blaise Pascal: L'Homme et l'œuvre*, Jean Orcibal has demonstrated that everything from this point until the first intervention of Pascal's interlocutor in par. 15 was inspired by Pierre Charron's *Les Trois Vérités* [Three truths]. See *Blaise Pascal: L'Homme et l'œuvre* [The man and his works], Cahiers de Royaumont, Philosophie 1 (Paris: Editions de Minuit, 1956), 159–86. In the same volume, we find three eminent Pascal scholars disagreeing over the identity of Pascal's interlocutor. Lucien Goldman insists that the "wager" cannot possibly have been written for the *libertin*. Henri Gouhier, pointing to fr. 681, argues that Pascal's interlocutor must be "one who has started to seek God or who at least is unhappy." Paul Benichou sees a "pure and simple skeptic." Gouhier's conclusion is that animating the Sellier edition.

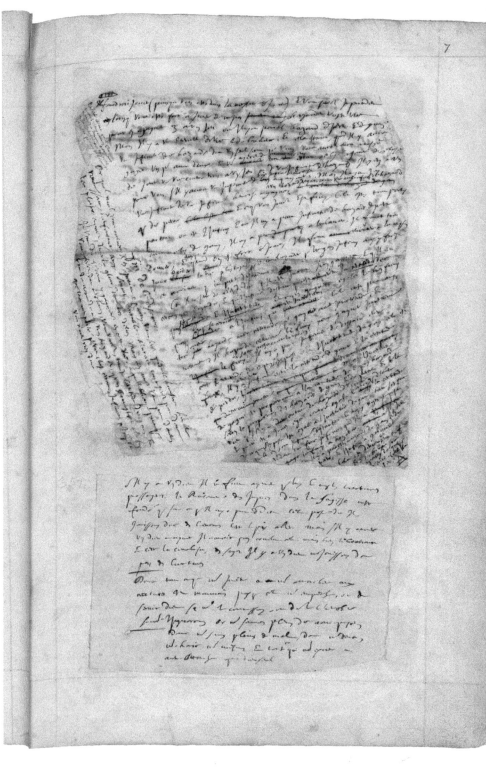

Plate 1. Autograph manuscript for fr. 680. Bibliothèque nationale de France.

Our soul is cast into the body, where it finds number, time, and dimensions. It reasons about these things and calls them nature, necessity, and can believe nothing else.

———

Adding one to infinity does not increase it at all, no more than adding a foot to an infinite distance does. What is finite is obliterated in the face of infinity and becomes pure nothingness. So it is with our mind before God and with our justice before divine justice. The disproportion between our justice and God's justice is not as great as the disproportion between one and infinity.

———

God's justice must be immense, like his mercy. Yet, his justice towards the reprobate is less immense and ought to shock less than his mercy towards the elect.

———

We know that there is an infinite, and yet we do not know its nature; just as we know that it is not true that numbers are finite, and therefore it is true that numerical infinity exists, and yet we do not know what it is. It would be false to say either that it is an even number or that it is an odd number, since adding one to it does not change its nature; and yet it is a number, and each and every number is either even or odd (this refers, it is true, to any finite number).

In the same way one may well recognize that there is a God without knowing what he is.

Is there no substantial truth, seeing that so many things are true that are not truth itself?

———

We know the existence and nature of the finite, because we are finite and have extension, as it does.

We know the existence of the infinite and do not know its nature, because like us, it has extension, but unlike us, it has no limits.

But we know neither the existence nor the nature of God, because he has neither extension nor limits.

———

But through faith we know his existence. And through heavenly glory we will know his nature.

Now, I have already shown that one may well know the existence of a thing without knowing its nature.

Let us now speak according to the natural light.

If there is a God, he is infinitely incomprehensible, since, having neither parts nor limits, he bears no relation to us. We are therefore incapable of knowing either what he is or whether he is. This being the case, who would dare to try and resolve the question? Not we, who bear no relation to him.

Who, then, will blame Christians for being unable to account for their belief, they who profess a religion for which they cannot account? They declare, when presenting it to the world, that it is foolishness, *stultitiam*;[4] and then you complain that they cannot prove it! If they were to prove it, they would not be keeping their word. It is in lacking proofs that they prove they do not lack sense—"Yes, but even if this excuses those who offer it in this way and takes away the blame for bringing it forth without reasons, it hardly excuses those who accept it."

Let us examine this point, and say: either God does or does not exist. Which way should we lean? Reason can settle nothing here. An infinite chaos separates us. A game is being played, right at the other end of that infinite distance, which will come down either heads or tails: which way will you wager? Reason does not allow you to do the one or the other; reason justifies neither of the two.

Do not, then, accuse those who have made a choice of being wrong, since you know nothing whatsoever about it!—"No, but I will blame them for having made, not this or that choice, but any choice at all. For even if the person making one choice and the person making the other are equally mistaken, they are both mistaken. The right course is not to wager."

Yes, but you must wager. *That* is not your decision, you are already embarked. What, then, are you going to call? Let us see. Since a choice has to be made, let us see on which side you have less to lose. You have two things to lose: the true and the good; two things to stake: your reason and your will, your knowledge and your happiness; while there are two things that your nature prompts you to shun: error and wretchedness. Since it is absolutely necessary to choose, your reason is no more injured by one choice than by the other. That point is settled. But what about your happiness? Let us weigh up what you stand to win and lose if you bet on heads that God exists. Let us consider the following two situations: if you win, you win everything; and if you lose, you lose nothing. So go ahead and gamble on God existing![5]—This

---

4. 1 Corinthians 1:18: "For the word of the cross, to them indeed that perish, *is foolishness*; but to them that are saved, that is, to us, it is the power of God." Pascal uses both the Latin word, *stultitiam*, and its French equivalent, "*sottise*."

5. Jean Mesnard qualifies Pascal's response as particularly adapted to the mentality of such *honnêtes gens* as Miton and Méré (see "Religious Challenges to the Modern Reader," in the introduction). Built into the argument that follows is a proposition that the *honnête homme*, whose rule is to seek the greatest possible happiness and avoid the greatest possible pain, cannot resist. Jean Mesnard, *Les Pensées de Pascal*, 126.

is astounding! Yes, I must wager.[6] But I may be staking too much."[7]—Well, let us see. Since the chances of winning and losing are equal, even if you stood to win only two lives for one, you could still wager. But if there were three lives to be won, you would have to play (being of necessity obliged to play), and you would be foolish, when forced to play, not to put your life at stake in order to win three in a game where the chances of winning and losing are equal. But there is an eternity of life and of happiness to be won. This being so, even if there were an infinite number of chances and just one in your favor, you would still be right to stake one in order to win two, and you would be quite misguided, being obliged to play, if you refused to stake one life on three in a game in which, among the infinite number of chances, there is one for you, if there were an infinity of infinitely happy life to win. But, in this case, there is an infinity of infinitely happy life to win, one chance of winning against a finite number of chances of losing, and what you are staking is finite. This removes any consideration of odds; for, wherever there is infinity to be won and the chances of losing (compared to that of winning) are not infinite in number, there is no hesitating. One should stake everything one has. And so, being forced to play, one would have to be mad to cling to life rather than risk it for an infinite gain that is just as likely to result as the loss of nothingness.

For it is no use saying that it is uncertain that you will win, while it is certain that you are taking a chance, and that the infinite distance between the CERTAINTY that you are playing and the UNCERTAINTY that you will win is equal to the finite good that it is certain you are staking on an infinity that is uncertain. Such is not the case. Every gambler takes a chance with certainty so as to win with uncertainty; and yet, in certainly chancing something finite so as uncertainly to win something finite, he in no way errs against reason. There is not an infinite distance between the certainty that you are taking a chance and the uncertainty that you will win. It is not so. There is, it is true, an infinite distance between the certainty that you will win and the certainty that you

6. The unbeliever's third response is problematic. What does he mean by "this is astounding"? Can he mean that he suddenly understands Pascal's diagnosis of his dilemma? He appears oblivious to the theological implications of the proposition he is being asked to accept. He agrees only to abide by the rules of the game, without explaining why he has suddenly abandoned his detachment and instinct that wagering is unreasonable.

7. The unbeliever hesitates because he obviously fears giving up his earthly and "carnal" pleasures. He is very much in character with the victim of "diversion" portrayed in ch. IX. At this point, Pascal embarks on a far more difficult argument (the second version of the wager) designed to strengthen his case. He restates the wager in mathematical terms that recall his formulation of the rules for calculating probability in his letters to Fermat in 1654. Whereas the first version of the wager can be analyzed from a psychological perspective, the second version that follows can be explained only by a mathematical exegesis that deliberately leaves aside all psychological aspects.

will lose. But the uncertainty that you will win is in proportion to the certainty that you are taking a chance, in accordance with the proportion of chances of winning and losing. It follows, if there are as many chances on one side as on the other, that the game is equally balanced. Thus, the certainty that you are taking a chance is in fact equal to the uncertainty that you will win: thus it is far from being infinitely distant. And thus our position is one of infinite force, since what is staked is finite, in a game where the chances of winning and losing are equal and where there is infinity to be won.[8]

This is conclusive, and if humans are capable of any truth, this is it.[9]

"I confess, I admit it, but all the same ... Is there no way to take a peek at the cards that have been dealt?"—"Yes, the scriptures and the rest, etc."—"Yes, but my hands are tied and my tongue is mute. I am being forced to wager, and yet I do not have a free hand; I am being offered no respite. And I was made in such a way that I cannot believe. So what would you have me do?"—"All this is true. But you might at least learn that your inability to believe—since reason prompts you and yet you cannot do so—comes from your passions. Work, therefore, at persuading yourself not by accumulating proofs of the existence of God but by diminishing your passions. So you want to find faith but do not know the way? You want to be cured of your lack of faith and you are asking for the remedy? Learn from those who once were shackled like you and who now wager all they have. These are people who know the path you would like to follow and are cured of the ill of which you wish to be cured. Do as they did when they started: which was to act in all respects as if they already believed, by taking holy water, having masses said, and so on. Naturally and of itself, this will make you believe, and will tame you."[10]—"But that is precisely what I'm afraid of."—"Why so? What have you got to lose? But, so as to show you that it leads you there, this is because it diminishes your passions, which are your greatest stumbling-blocks, etc."—"Oh how these words transport me, delight me, etc."—"If these words please you and strike you as powerful, know that they were composed by a man who went down on his knees, beforehand and afterwards, to beseech the infinite and indivisible Being, to whom he submits

---

8. In this long paragraph, Pascal seems to broaden his perspective in order to adapt his wager demonstration for a larger audience.

9. At this point, Pascal draws a practical conclusion on behalf of his silent interlocutor. Rational behavior demands wagering in favor of God's existence. Deciding not to wager one's life rather than wagering it would amount to renouncing the use of reason itself.

10. Literally "will make you into an animal," i.e., will bring the unbeliever into a state akin to that of trained animals, in which the "machine" (fr. 41) of the body predominates and which, through sheer force of habit, inclines the "automaton" (fr. 661) to believe. The taming of his intellectual powers is precisely, as his reply shows, what the unbeliever fears. *Abêtir*, the French verb translated here by *tame*, is far stronger. See Melzer, *Discourses of the Fall*, 63–64; and Howells, "The Interpretation of Pascal's 'Pari,'" 58–59.

all that he has, to take to himself also all that you have, for your good and his glory, and that in this way strength accord with lowliness."

End of this Discourse[11]

What harm will you come to through taking this course of action? You will be loyal, virtuous, humble, grateful, kind, a friend sincere and true. It is true that you will not be surrounded by tainted pleasures, glory, and worldly delights. But will you not have others?[12]

I tell you that you will gain from this even in this life, and that at each step of the way you will discover that the gain is so certain and the risk so meaningless that you will eventually understand that you have wagered on something certain and infinite for which you have given up nothing.

We are truly obliged to those who point out our faults, for they mortify us. They teach us that we have been despised, but they do not prevent us from being so again in the future, since we have many further faults for that. They prepare us for the exercise of correction and for the removal of a fault.

Habit is our nature. Whoever makes a habit of faith comes to believe it, can no longer avoid fearing hell, and can believe nothing else. Whoever makes a habit of believing that the king is terrifying, etc. Who therefore can doubt that our soul, being in the habit of seeing number, space, and movement, believes these, and only these, things?

Do you believe that it is impossible for God to be infinite and indivisible?—"Yes." I am going to show you then (*an image of God in all his immensity*) an infinite and indivisible thing. It is a point moving everywhere at infinite speed.

11. Only the first two paragraphs, which follow (down to the line) and which conclude Pascal's counsel to the unbeliever, belong to the "wager" discourse as sketched in fr. 680. Those fragments that follow are notes destined for some future version. Henri Gouhier warns us that "trying to incorporate them into Pascal's initial version of the "wager" will interrupt its continuity and render it unintelligible." Henri Gouhier, *Biaise Pascal: Commentaires* Bibliothèque d'Histoire de la Philosophie (Paris: J. Vrin, 1966), 274. These originally eight fragments are written on the last two sheets of the discourse in the autograph. The editors of C1 and C2, attempting to ascertain where they should be transcribed, order them in different ways. In the present text, Sellier incorporates them into the end of the discourse. Lafuma, following C1, assigns them new fragment numbers: 419–26. This is the numbering found in the Krailshimer Penguin translation and in all other English translations based upon the Lafuma edition. See the bibliography.

12. Here we see Pascal's relative esteem of *honnêteté* as a means to a Christian way of life (in fact, the term *virtuous* in the list translates the French *honnête*). Sellier cites a line from Méré's *De la vraie Honnêteté* [Concerning true *Honnêteté*] (1668): "*Honnêteté* is not entirely without its uses in the matter of salvation." See Méré, "Discours II. Suite de la vraie honnesteté," in *Œuvres posthumes de M. le Chevalier de Méré* (Paris: Jean and Michel Guignard, 1700), 92. An external behavior as close as possible to that produced by true "charity" serves to drive the "machine" towards Christianity.

For he is one and the same in all places and entire in each.[13]

Let this effect of nature, which seemed impossible to you before, teach you that there may be others that you do not yet know. Do not conclude from what you have already learned that there is nothing left for you to know, but that there is infinitely more for you to know. '

It is not true that we are worthy of the love of others. It is unjust of us to want it. If we were born reasonable, dispassionate, and truly knowing ourselves and others, we would not incline our wills in this direction. But we are born that way. We are therefore born unjust. For everything tends towards itself and this goes against any kind of order. One should tend towards the general, whereas the inclination towards oneself is the beginning of all disorder: in war, in society, at home, in the individual human body.

The will is thus depraved. If the members of natural and civil corporations tend towards the good of the whole body, the corporations themselves should tend towards a still more general body of which they are members. One should therefore tend towards the general. We are therefore born unjust and depraved.[14]

No religion but ours has taught that man is born in sin. No philosophical sect has said it. None, therefore, has told the truth.

No sect or religion has always been on earth, except for the Christian religion.[15]

The Christian religion alone makes man at once LOVABLE and HAPPY. In the polite commerce of the world, one cannot be at once lovable and happy.[16]

It is the heart that perceives God, and not reason: that is what faith is. God perceptible to the heart, not to reason.

The heart has its reasons, which reason cannot know. We see this in a thousand things.[17]

I say that the heart loves the universal Being naturally, and itself naturally, according to which of the two it embraces. And it hardens itself against the

13. Clearly, these two sentences do not belong here. They may be destined for some future mathematical introduction to the wager.

14. This paragraph and everything that follows do not belong to the wager text and represent Pascal's extemporaneous notation of ideas meant to figure elsewhere. This particular paragraph might be destined for the chapters "Ennui" or "Corruption."

15. Again, the foregoing two sentences have nothing to do with the "wager." Rather, they may be destined for any number of fragments and chapters that define the uniqueness of Christianity or the unity of the two Testaments.

16. The first of these two sentences anticipates ch. XVIII, "Make Religion Lovable." The second is obviously a critique of honnêteté (which is here translated so as to heighten the opposition between "religion" and "the world"—hence "the polite commerce of the world").

17. One of Pascal's most celebrated pensées and certainly one known to many readers, this fragment has inevitably been associated with the "Wager." But it would have figured elsewhere.

one or the other by choice. You have rejected one and preserved the other: is it rational for you to love yourself?[18]

The only kind of knowledge that goes against common sense and human nature is the only one that has always existed among humans.

18. These three sentences clearly anticipate and might have figured in such fragments as 391, 484, 502, 510, and 548–50.

[XLVI] Letter Urging the Search for God[1]

681

... Let them[2] at least find out what the religion they mean to attack is about before they start attacking it. If this religion boasted that it possessed a clear vision of God, and possessed it in an obvious and transparent form, then this religion could indeed be challenged by arguing that we see nothing in the world that shows it with such clarity. But, since on the contrary this religion proclaims that men live in darkness far removed from God, that God has hidden himself from them, that this is the very name he gives himself in scripture, A HIDDEN GOD;[3] in short if this religion strives equally to establish these two things: that God has left perceptible signs in the Church so that he can be recognized by those who sincerely seek him; and that he has nevertheless veiled these signs in such a way that he will be perceived only by those who seek him with all their hearts, what advantage can they claim to obtain, when, in their professed indifference to the search for truth, they proclaim that nothing reveals it, because the darkness in which they find themselves and which they use as an objection against the Church only proves one of the two things this religion affirms while leaving the other intact, and, far from proving her doctrine false, confirm it?[4]

In order to attack it, they would have to protest that they have made every effort to seek it everywhere, even in what the Church offers by way of instruction, but without any satisfaction. If they spoke in this way, they would

---

1. Jean Mesnard has called this discourse the most finished and beautiful of all the *Pensées*. Sellier's conclusion that this "letter" was to have served as the "overture" to the entire Apology has now gained widespread acceptance. In fr. 45, Pascal clearly states that this "preface" will precede the so-called "wager" (fr. 680). Significantly, the editors of the *Edition de Port-Royal* of the *Pensées* set this discourse at the very beginning of their edition. In fr. 662, a notation of key words and phrases appears to anticipate this discourse: "You will convert me," "zeal of devotion," "one must pity," etc.

2. The aggressive atheists.

3. *Deus absconditus*, a fundamental (and recurring) reference in Pascal: Isaiah 45:15. See ch. VIII, n. 17.

4. Pascal intends to render the hardened unbelievers speechless in the first five sentences of the Apology. The atheists make the traditional argument that we never see God intervening in the world. Therefore he does not exist. Pascal rejoins that their conclusion squares exactly with Christian doctrine. According to scripture, God has indeed hidden himself from men because of Adam's sin.

indeed be attacking one of the Church's claims. But I hope to show here that no reasonable person could speak in such a way. And I even venture to say that no one has ever done so. We know perfectly well how people who adopt this attitude behave. They think they have made an extraordinary effort to inform themselves, when they have spent a few hours reading some book of scripture, and questioned some priest about the truths of faith. That done, they brag that they have sought in vain in books and from the mouths of men. But in fact I would tell them what I have often said: that such negligence is intolerable. We are not talking here about something that slightly affects some people who are nothing to us. This is about us, and about our whole being.

The immortality of the soul is something of such consequence to us, something that touches us so profoundly, that only someone who has lost all sense could be indifferent to finding out whether it is true or not. All our actions and thoughts must take such different paths according to whether there is hope for eternal blessing or not, that the only possible way of acting with common sense and judgment is to decide our course in light of this mystery, which ought to be our ultimate objective.

So nothing is more urgent, from the point of view of both self-interest and duty, than to enlighten ourselves on this point, on which the whole of our conduct depends. And this is why, with respect to those who are not convinced, I draw a stark distinction between those who strive with all their might to inform themselves and those who live without worrying or thinking about it.[5]

I can feel only compassion for those who sincerely bemoan[6] their doubt, who regard it as the worst of misfortunes, who spare no effort to escape it, and who seek to make this search their principal and most serious endeavor.

But as for those who drift through life without a thought for the final end of life, and who, solely for the reason that they fail to find within themselves[7] the light of conviction, neglect to look elsewhere,[8] and to examine thoroughly whether this opinion is one of those that the common people accept out of credulous simplicity or one of those that, although obscure in themselves, are nonetheless built upon a very solid and unshakeable foundation, I consider them in a very different light.

---

5. See Montaigne, *Essays,* I, 20, 69–71.

6. On the use of the verb *gémir* here, see the introduction, n. 57. Men are oppressed by their doubt, just as their passions are their real enemies (a statement that recurs in the *Pensées*). See, among other fragments, 291, 300.

7. See chapter X, "Philosophers." The ancient sages were completely wrong. Introspection, Pascal is certain, can never serve to arrive at the truth. The Fall corrupted both the human mind and soul. The proofs of Christianity lie *outside* the human psyche.

8. I.e., in scripture and holy tradition.

This negligence in a matter in which they themselves, their eternity, their all, are at stake, arouses my indignation more than my sympathy. It astonishes and appalls me. To me it is monstrous. I do not say this prompted by the pious zeal of a devout spirituality. I mean, on the contrary, that we ought to have this feeling out of sheer human self-interest and self-love. For that we only need to see what even the least enlightened people see.[9]

You do not need to possess a very lofty soul to realize that this life is the source of no true or lasting satisfaction, that all our pleasures are but vanity, that our sufferings are infinite, and that finally death, which threatens us at every moment, will in but a few years infallibly present us with the horrible necessity of being forever either annihilated or unhappy.

There is nothing more real than this, nothing more terrible. We can be as heroic as we like; that is the end that awaits the most noble life in the world. Let us reflect upon these things and then say whether it is not beyond doubt that the only true good in this life is the hope of a life to come; that we become happy only insofar as we draw nearer to it, and that, just as no more unhappiness awaits those who had a firm belief in eternity, so there is no happiness for those who are altogether in the dark about it.

It is assuredly a great misfortune to be in such a state of doubt. But it is at least an indispensable duty to seek when we are in this doubt. And thus someone who doubts and does not seek is altogether completely unhappy and completely wrong. But if, in addition, he is calm and satisfied, if he professes to be so, and if he regards such a state as something to boast about, if this very state is in fact the cause of his joy and his vanity, I lack the words to describe so extravagant a creature.[10]

Where could such feelings come from? What reason for joy in anticipating nothing but irremediable misery? Why brag about being plunged into impenetrable darkness? How might a reasonable man subscribe to such an argument as this?[11]

---

9. To the free-thinker's scorn for the ignorant and credulous populace (alluded to in the previous paragraph) Pascal replies by invoking the basic common sense of the "poor in spirit." See frs. 117, 128, 129, and 134.

10. See Montaigne, *Essays*, II, 12, 394–95: "Atheism being a proposition as it were unnatural and monstrous, difficult too and not easy to establish in the human, however insolent and unruly it may be, plenty of men have been seen, out of vanity and pride in conceiving opinions that are not common and that reform the world, to affect to profess it outwardly, who, if they are mad enough, are not strong enough nevertheless to have implanted it in their conscience."

11. The quotation marks that follow are not in the autograph. Sellier furnishes them to clarify that the speaker in this tableau is not Pascal himself but an indolent skeptic. A Romantic tradition, which regarded the *Pensées* as Pascal's intimate spiritual journal, attributed this profession to Pascal himself and has misled generations of readers. In the course of fr. 681, destined to become the preface to the entire Apology, Pascal produces several tableaux in which the unbelievers are permitted to testify, primarily this skeptic.

"I do not know who put me into the world, nor what the world is, nor what I am myself. I am greatly ignorant about everything. I do not know what my body is, nor my senses, nor my soul, nor even that very part of me that thinks what I am saying, that reflects on everything and on itself and does not know itself any better than it knows anything else. I see those terrifying spaces of the universe that hem me in, and I find myself planted in a tiny corner of this vast expanse, without knowing why I have been put in this place rather than in another, or why the brief span of life that is mine has been allocated to me at this point rather than another in all the eternity of time that will come after me.

"I see nothing but infinity on every side, surrounding me like an atom and like a shadow that lasts but an instant and returns no more.

"All I know is that I must soon die, but what I know least is this very death from which there is no escape.

"Just as I do not know whence I came, so I do not know whither I go, and I know only that upon leaving this world I shall fall forever either into nothingness or into the hands of an angry God, without knowing which of these two conditions will be my lot for all eternity. Such is my state, full of weakness and uncertainty. And the only conclusion I draw from all this is that I shall spend the whole of my life without trying to find out what is to become of me. Perhaps I could find some illumination in my doubt, but I do not want to be bothered or take a step to seek it. And afterwards, contemptuous of those who are striving toward this end, I want to go without foresight and without fear to confront so great an event, and let myself be led unresisting off to death, uncertain as to the eternity of my future condition."[12]

Who would wish to have a man who talks in this way as a friend? Who would choose him over others to tell him of his affairs? Who would have recourse to him in adversity?

And indeed, what use could he possibly be to anyone in life?

In truth, it is glorious for our religion to have as enemies men so unreasonable. And their opposition to it is so little dangerous (whatever certainty they possess, it is a reason for despair rather than vanity), that it serves, on the contrary, to establish its truths. For the Christian faith serves almost wholly to establish these two things: the corruption of nature and the redemption wrought by Jesus Christ. Now, I contend that if these men do not demonstrate the truth of the redemption by the sanctity of their behavior, they at least admirably serve to demonstrate the corruption of nature by sentiments so unnatural.

12. The skeptic's testimony ends here, followed by the apologist's devastating critique of his discourse.

Nothing is of more importance to man than his state; nothing so terrifying to him than eternity. And thus the fact that there exist men indifferent to the loss of their very being and to the peril of everlasting suffering is not natural. They behave quite differently with regard to everything else. They are afraid of the most insignificant things, foresee them, feel them. And this same man who spends so many days and nights in rage and despair at the loss of some office, or because of some imaginary insult to his honor, is the very one who knows, without anxiety and without emotion that he will lose everything by death. It is a monstrous thing to see one and the same heart at once so sensitive to minor things and so strangely insensitive to the greatest.

It is an incomprehensible spell, a supernatural torpor that points to an all-powerful force as its cause.

There must have been a strange upheaval[13] in the nature of man for him to boast of being in that state in which it seems inconceivable that anyone could exist. However, experience has shown me so great a number of such men that it would be surprising, if we did not know that the majority of them in fact feign their feelings and are really not what they seem.[14] These are people who have heard that the worldly manners of polite society require them to display such extravagance. They call it "throwing off the yoke"[15] and this is what they try to imitate. It would not be difficult to show them how mistaken they are to court esteem in this way. This is not the way to acquire it, especially I would say, among men of the world who judge things sensibly and who know that the only way to succeed in society is to appear honorable, loyal, judicious, and capable of helping one's friends, because by nature men love only what may be of use to them. Now, what advantage do we derive from hearing someone say that he has now "thrown off the yoke," that he does not believe there is a God watching over our actions,[16] that he considers himself the sole master of his actions, and that he thinks he is accountable only to himself? Does he think that he has persuaded us in this way to have complete confidence in him from now on, and to look to him for consolation, advice, and assistance in life's difficult moments? Do they think that that they have cheered us up, by telling us that they hold our soul to be no more than wind or smoke,[17] and

13. I.e., the Fall.

14. At this point Pascal turns away from the hardened atheists to those whom Wetsel calls the "pseudo-*libertins*." They adopt skepticism about religion because they think it will make them stand out in high society. They are not yet atheists. Pascal will call them to the vocation of seeking.

15. Here the speaker uses ironic and irreligious citation, mocking Matthew 11:30, in which Jesus consoles his disciples, "For my *yoke* is sweet and my burden light."

16. The pseudo-*libertin* might be invoking deism, in which God cares about nothing of what happens in the world, but he probably envisages pure atheism.

17. Wisdom 2:1–6.

moreover by saying it in a haughty and self-satisfied tone? Is this a thing to be said cheerfully? Is it not rather something to be said sadly, as the saddest thing in the world?

If they thought about it seriously, they would see that it creates the worst possible impression, that it is so contrary to common sense, so opposed to true *honnêteté* and so remote in every way from the fine impression they are seeking, that they would be more likely to reform rather than corrupt those who might have any inclination to follow them. Make them account for their feelings and their reasons for doubting religion. They will come out with things that are so feeble and pathetic arguments that they would persuade you that the opposite is true.[18] That was what someone said very aptly to them one day. "If you carry on holding forth like this," he remarked, "you will end up by converting me."[19] And he was quite right. For who would not be horrified to find oneself in the company of such despicable people![20]

Thus those who are only feigning these sentiments would indeed be extremely miserable if they had to constrain their natural instincts and thus make themselves the most foolish of men. If they are troubled in the depth of their heart not to have more light, let them not disguise it. There would be no shame in admitting it. There is no shame except in having none.[21] There is no more sure a sign of extreme weakness of mind than the failure to recognize the unhappy state of a man without God. There is no more sure a sign of an evil heart than the failure to desire the truth of the eternal promises.[22] There is nothing more cowardly than to want to brazen it out with God.[23] So let them

18. This sentence refers to those pseudo-*libertins* who attempt to impress *le beau monde* by affecting free-thinking and a facade of *libertinage* and fare poorly at it. They do not understand those traditional religious arguments formulated by classical atheism and its contemporary erudition. They attempt to disguise their ignorance by uttering embarrassingly "low" blasphemies and sacrileges.

19. This sarcastic comment on the part of a hardened atheist was probably either heard by Pascal himself or recounted to him. In fr. 662, par. 6, he noted: "You will convert me," to use it later.

20. Pascal is a merciless satirist, going so far as to pretend to take the side of the hardened atheist, embarrassed by the garbled and silly arguments of his would-be imitators.

21. Here Pascal issues a kind of invitation to the first step toward conversion. Those pseudo-*libertins* who have genuine scruples or doubts about Christianity are invited to make a clean confession of their spiritual state. In fact, being disturbed by having so little inner light is a positive sign. One's natural instincts prompting the search for a lost God are still operative. Feeling no shame at all would be a very bad sign indeed.

22. Even "wishing" that Christianity might be true is a powerful marker of the "seeker." The reprobates cannot even be led to *wish* for an afterlife of blessings. In fr. 46, Pascal sums up his entire apologetic scheme. "Men despise religion; they detest it and are afraid that it might be true. [...] Start by showing that religion is not at all contrary to reason. [...] Next make it worthy of love, make good people *wish* that it were true, and then show that it is true" (fr. 46, emphasis added).

23. Montaigne, *Essays*, II, 18, 614: "what can you imagine uglier than being a coward toward men and bold toward God?"

leave these impieties to those so ill-born[24] as to be truly capable of them. Let them at least be *honnêtes gens* if they cannot be Christians.[25] And lastly, let them acknowledge that there are only two kinds of people whom we can call rational: those who serve God with all their heart because they know him, and those who search for him with all their heart because they do not know him.

As for those who go through life without either knowing or seeking him,[26] they judge themselves so little worthy of their own care that they are not worthy of the care of others. One needs all the charity of the religion they despise not to despise them even to the point of abandoning them to their folly. But as this religion obliges us to consider them, as long as they are in this life, as capable of receiving that grace which might enlighten them, and to believe that they may in an instant be more filled with faith than we are, while we on the other hand, may be stricken by the same blindness that is now theirs, we must do unto them what we would wish to be done unto us were we in their place.[27] We must appeal to them to take pity on themselves and to take at least a few tentative steps in quest of enlightenment. Let them spend on reading what follows a few of the hours they fritter away so pointlessly on other things. However reluctantly they approach the task, perhaps they will hit upon something. At least they will not be losing much. But as for those who approach that which follows in perfect sincerity and with a genuine desire to find the truth, I hope that they will be satisfied and convinced by the proofs of so divine a religion, which I have collected here, and in which I have followed more or less this order . . .[28]

24. Is Pascal merely using social disapprobation as a wedge between the true and pseudo libertins? Or does *mal nés* ("ill-born") echo Augustinian theology? Some men, of course, are born in the world only to be damned.

25. On *honnêtes gens* and *honnêteté*, see the section "French Words" in the preface. Pascal will later convert the *honnête homme* into a seeker by showing him the defects inherent in *honnêteté*. See fr. 494.

26. Not the hardened professional skeptics. According to Sellier's mentor René Pintard, those whom Pascal sought to convert were those "brilliant and impertinent intellects endowed with lusts, joys, disappointments, and weaknesses, who fall into [Pascal's] grasp because of these very qualities." *Le Libertinage érudit dans la première moitie du XVIIe siècle* [Scholarly disbelief in the first half of the seventeenth century], 81.

27. Pascal invokes not only the Golden Rule but the fact that God owes us nothing. God *necessarily* damns whomever he wishes. He must, to preserve his absolute freedom. See the introduction, "Predestination." Those who have led exemplary and even charitable lives may have grace withdrawn from them during their last gasp for breath, whereas repentant murders may receive God's inscrutable grace at the same moment.

28. Anthony Pugh suggests that this preface to the Apology might have been completed by the lists of proofs found in fragments 402 and 484. See Pugh, *Composition of Pascal's Apologia* (Toronto: University of Toronto Press, 1984), 155–58.

682[29]

Before I embark on the proofs of the Christian religion, I feel impelled to point out how wrong those people are who live their lives with no interest in seeking the truth of a matter that is so important to them and touches them so closely.

Of all their aberrations, this doubtless is the one that most convicts them of madness and blindness, and in which it is easiest to confound them with the most basic promptings of common sense and natural feelings. For it is beyond doubt that this life lasts no more than an instant, that the state of death is eternal, whatever form it may take, and that therefore all our actions and thoughts should take such different directions, depending on the state of this eternity, that it is impossible to pursue a single course of action with good sense and good judgment, without keeping in view that point, which should be our ultimate objective.

Nothing can be more obvious than this, from which it follows, according to the principles of reason, that the conduct of men is utterly irrational if they follow any other course of action. From this perspective, let us judge those who, paying no attention to this ultimate goal of life, submitting themselves to their inclinations and their pleasures, without thought or anxiety, act as if they could annihilate eternity simply by turning their minds away from it, only thinking of how to be happy in the present moment.

And yet this eternity exists, and death, which must open it up before them and which threatens them at every moment, will inevitably and before very long confront them with the horrible inevitability of being eternally either annihilated or wretched, without their knowing which of these two eternities has been prepared for them since the beginning.

Here we have a doubt of terrible import. They are in danger of an eternity of wretchedness, and yet their reaction to this, as if the thing were not worth the trouble, is to neglect to examine whether this is one of those opinions accepted by the people in their credulous simplicity, or one of those, that, though mysterious in themselves, have none the less a very solid foundation, albeit one that is hidden. Thus they do not know whether the thing is true or false, or whether the proofs of it are strong or weak. They have these proofs before their eyes. They refuse to look at them, and in this ignorance they take the decision to do everything it takes to fall into this misfortune, supposing it exists, to wait until the moment of death to put the matter to the test, and

---

29. Sellier views this discourse, though remarkably similar to fr. 681, not as a draft of that preface, but as another letter.

meanwhile to be perfectly comfortable in this state, to proclaim they are in it, and indeed to pride themselves on it. Can one seriously think about how important this issue is without being horrified by such insane behavior?

This blissful ignorance is a monstrous thing, the inanity and stupidity of which we have to get across to those people who spend their lives in this state, by bringing it clearly before their eyes, so as to confound them by the recognition of their folly. For this is how human beings reason when they choose to live their lives in ignorance of what they are, without seeking for enlightenment: "I do not know ..." they say.

"This is what I see and this is what troubles me. I look in all directions, and all I see is darkness. Nature offers me nothing that is not an object for doubt and anxiety. If I could see no traces of a divinity in it, I would decide in the negative. If everywhere I could see traces of a Creator, I would rest in peace in faith. But, seeing as I do too much to be able to deny, and too little to be able to be certain, I am in a pitiable state, in which I have wished a thousand times that if there is a God who keeps nature in being, it would reveal him beyond doubt; and that, if the signs of him it gives are deceptive, that nature should eliminate them altogether; that it would say everything or nothing, so that I could see on which to wager. Whereas in the state in which I am, not knowing what I am and what I ought to do, I know neither my condition nor my duty. My whole heart aspires to know where the true good resides, so that it can pursue it. There is no price I would not pay for the sake of eternity.

"I envy those I see who have faith and who take it so much for granted, making such bad use of a gift of which it seems to me I would make far better use."[30]

683

No one else has acknowledged that man is the most excellent of creatures. Some, who have fully acknowledged the reality of his excellence, have seen people's naturally low estimate of themselves as a sign of weakness and ingratitude.[31] Others, who have fully acknowledged the truth in this low estimate, have treated the sense of greatness, which is equally natural to man, as a sign of ridiculous arrogance.[32]

"Raise your eyes to God," say the former. "Behold him whom you resemble and who made you to worship him. You can make yourselves like him.

---

30. In the last two paragraphs of fr. 682, the spoken discourse cited by Pascal is pronounced by a seeker of truth, not by the indifferent against whom Pascal has just inveighed.

31. The Stoics.

32. The Epicureans. See fr. 240.

Wisdom will make you equal to him, if you are willing to follow him."—"Lift up your heads, free men," says Epictetus.[33] And the latter say to him "Cast your eyes down to the ground, wretched earthworm that you are, and gaze at the beasts whose fellow you are." So what will become of man? Will he be equal to God, or to the beasts? What an appalling distance there is between them! So what are we to be? Who cannot see in all of this that man has lost his way, that he has fallen from his true place, that he is searching anxiously for it, that he cannot find it again? And who is there that can direct him to it? The greatest of men have been unable to do so.

We can comprehend neither the glorious state of Adam nor the nature of his sin, or how it has been transmitted to us. These are things that took place in the sphere of a nature completely different from ours and are beyond our present capacity to grasp.

Knowing all this would make no difference as to our chances of getting out of this state. And all that matters for to us to know is that we are wretched, corrupt, cut off from God, but redeemed by Jesus Christ. And of this we have admirable proofs on this earth.

Thus the two proofs we have of the corruption of human nature and the redemption are derived from unbelievers, who live in a state of indifference to religion, and from the Jews, who are its irreconcilable enemies.

684[34]

(*Self-love, and because it is a thing that concerns us closely enough to arouse our emotions, to be certain that after all the sufferings of life an inevitable death, which threatens us at every moment, must necessarily in a few years ... in the horrible inevitability ...*)

The three conditions.[35]

We should not say that this is a proof of rationality.

That is all a man could do if he were certain this revelation were false. Even so he should not be joyful about it, but struck down by it.

Nothing else is important, and nothing else is treated as unimportant.

Our imagination so magnifies the present moment, because we are constantly thinking about it, and so minimizes eternity, because we never think about it, that we regard eternity as a nothing, and what is nothing as an eterni-

---

33. Epictetus was a Stoic philosopher of the first century CE. See the introduction to Fontaine's *Exchange with M. de Sacy* at the end of this edition.

34. C2 properly places frs. 684–87 in chapter XLVI, as the copyist notes in the margin. These notes were obviously set down in preparation for the writing of the letter constituted by fr. 662.

35. See fr. 192 and "The Three Orders" in the introduction of this edition.

ty. And the roots of this are so deeply in us that the whole of our reason cannot defend us against it and that . . .

I would ask them if it is not true that they themselves bear witness to the fundamental truth of the faith they are challenging, namely that the nature of man is in a state of corruption.[36]

685

Then Jesus Christ comes to tell men that they have no other enemies beside themselves, that it is their passions that cut them off from God, that he has come to destroy these passions and to give them his grace, so as to transform all of them into a holy Church.

That he has come to bring the heathen and the Jews into this Church, that he has come to destroy the idols of the former and the superstition of the latter. But all men oppose this, not only on account of concupiscence, which is naturally opposed to it, but above all the kings of this earth join together to wipe out this religion at its birth, as had been foretold. (Prophecy: *Why have the Gentiles raged . . . the kings of the earth . . . against his Christ.*)[37]

All that is great on this earth joins together: scholars, wise men, kings. Some write, others condemn, others kill. And yet in spite of all this opposition, these simple and powerless people resist all these powers, and win over even those kings, scholars, wise men, and sweep the whole earth clean of idolatry. And all this comes to pass through the very power that foretold it.

686

Imagine a number of men in chains, all condemned to death, some of whom are slaughtered every day, in full view of the others. Those who are left perceive their own condition in that of their fellows, and gazing at one another in grief and without hope, they wait their turn!

687

Since the Creation and the Flood were past, and God no longer supposed to destroy the world again, nor create it afresh, nor give such great signs of himself, he began to establish a people on the earth, a people formed for this purpose, which was to last until the Messiah formed a people by his Spirit.

---

36. In fr. 529b, Pascal's friend, the *honnête homme* Damien Miton, is willing to admit that nature is corrupt, but he cannot understand why man cannot transcend his condition. On Miton, see the introduction, nn. 97 and 98.

37. Psalm 2:1–2.

[XLVII] Discourse on Corruption[1]

688
The antiquity of the Jews

What a difference there is between one book and another! It does not surprise me that the Greeks produced the *Iliad* or the Egyptians and the Chinese their histories.

You only have to see how the whole thing came about. Their fabled historians were not contemporary with the events they describe. Homer composed a story, which he presented as such. It is received as such, because no one ever considered that Troy and Agamemnon existed, any more than the golden apple.[2] He never thought of writing history, merely entertainment. He is the only writer of his age; the beauty of the work has made it immortal; everyone learns it and talks about it. We have to know it, and indeed everyone knows it by heart. Four hundred years later, the people who witnessed the events are no longer alive. No one can tell from first-hand knowledge whether it is fact or fiction. It has simply been handed down from generation to generation and might easily pass for fact.

All history that is not contemporary is suspect. Thus, the books of the Sibyls,[3] Trismegistus,[4] and many others that have enjoyed a great reputation

---

1. This dossier is missing from the Original Collection. Like the autograph of the "Overture" (fr. 681)—an incalculable loss to scholars—it may well have been kept by his sister Gilberte or by another of his intimates as a kind of relic. Fr. 688 on the Jews was misfiled into this dossier. Fr. 690 might well have been destined for the chapter in the table-*liasse* entitled "Nature is corrupt." The copyist of C2 found no dossier in the *liasses* arranged in 1658 corresponding to this title and signaled his perplexity with an asterisk. In most editions, this title is merged with the title "The falsity of other religions" as the title of chapter XVII. Fr. 690 might well have constituted that separate chapter, which is listed in the table-*liasse* but not found by the copyist in the dossiers that had been organized. Evidently the copyist never thought to look for it in the untitled dossiers since all the other titles corresponded to the titled dossiers arranged in 1658.

2. The golden apple: found in the garden of the Hesperides, Hera's orchard.

3. A collection of oracles from different periods attributed to various sibyls, the *Sibylline Oracles* became a part of apocalyptic literature in both the Jewish and Christian traditions.

4. *Trismegistus*: The "thrice-great" Hermes, a legendary figure long thought in the West to be the author of a body of literature known as the *Corpus Hermeticum* and to be a pagan prophet contemporary with Moses.

for veracity, are false and seen to be false with the passing of time. The position of contemporary writers is not the same.

There is a considerable difference between a book that an individual creates and then casts among the people, and a book that itself creates a people.[5] There can be no doubt that the second kind of book is as old as the people.

689

Without sensations, we are not wretched. A house in ruins is not wretched. Only man is wretched. *I am the man that see* [my own wretchedness].[6]

690[7]

Now if God's mercy is so great that he offers us salutary instruction even when he is hiding, what illumination can we not expect from him when he reveals himself?

Recognize, then, the truth of the Christian religion in its very obscurity, the scant illumination we have of it, and the indifference we show towards understanding it.

The eternal Being exists forever, if he ever once existed.

All the objections of this or that side only go against themselves, and most certainly not against religion. Everything the unbelievers say.

Thus the entire universe teaches man either that he is corrupt or that he is redeemed. Everything leads him to understand his greatness or his wretchedness. God's abandonment can be seen in the heathen, God's protection in the Jews.

All of them err the more dangerously in that they each follow one truth. Their mistake lies not in following a falsehood, but in not following another truth.

It is true, then, that everything instructs man as to his condition, but this instruction must be properly understood; for it is not true that everything reveals God, nor is it true that everything hides God. However, it is simultaneously true that he hides from those who tempt him and reveals himself

---

5. The Old Testament. See fr. 716.

6. Lamentations 3:1.

7. In this Christocentric discourse, which could very well have served as a preface to the second part of the Apology, Pascal recapitulates the great leitmotiv of the "overture" to the Apology (fr. 681) in more theological terms. He rejects traditional apologetics and focuses intensely on the God of scripture and on the absolute necessity of proving his Incarnation in Jesus Christ, without whom any apologetic enterprise is but folly.

to those who seek him,[8] because men are at once unworthy and capable of God: unworthy on account of their corruption and capable on account of their first nature.[9]

What should we conclude from the obscurities that surround us, if not our own unworthiness?

If there were no obscurity, man would not feel his corruption. If there were no light, man would not hope for a remedy. Thus, it is not only right but also useful for us that God should be partly hidden and partly revealed, since it is equally dangerous for man to know God without knowing his own wretched state and to know his own wretched state without knowing God.[10]

The conversion of the heathen was solely reserved for the grace of the Messiah. The Jews to no avail contended with them for so long! Everything Solomon and the prophets said about it was useless. Philosophers, such as Plato and Socrates, were unable to persuade them.[11]

If nothing had ever appeared of God, this perpetual privation would have been ambiguous, since it could be explained equally well by the absence of any deity or by the unworthiness of man to know him. But the fact that God appears from time to time, but not always, removes the ambiguity. If he appears once, he exists forever. And thus we can only conclude that there is a God and that men are unworthy of him.

They blaspheme against something that they do not know.[12] The Christian religion consists of two principles.[13] It is equally important for men to know them both; not knowing them is equally dangerous.

And it is equally merciful of God to have given indications of both.

Yet they take it upon themselves to conclude that one of those principles is not true from the fact that ought to make them accept the other.

The philosophers who said that there is only one God were persecuted, the Jews were hated, and the Christians even more so.

They saw by the natural light that, if there is a true religion on earth, all things ought to tend towards it as their center.

(The object of the entire course of things should be the establishment and the greatness of religion. Men's feelings should conform to the teachings of religion. In short, it ought to be so much the object and center towards which

---

8. Pascal again recapitulates the great leitmotiv of "seeking," which animates the "Overture" constituted by fr. 681.

9. *Their first nature*: that which existed before the Fall.

10. See fr. 225.

11. On Plato, see fr. 370.

12. See fr. 681, par. 1.

13. See below fr. 690, par. 20: (1) "there is a God of whom men are capable" and (2) "there is a corruption in their nature that renders them unworthy of him."

all things gravitate, that whoever knows the principles will be able to provide an explanation of both the whole nature of man in particular, and the whole direction of the world in general.)[14]

And starting from this assumption, they take it upon themselves to blaspheme against the Christian religion because they do not possess a proper knowledge of it. They imagine it consists simply in worshipping a God considered to be great and powerful and eternal. But this is essentially deism,[15] which is almost as far removed from the Christian religion as atheism, the exact opposite of it. From this they go on to conclude that the Christian religion is not true, because they fail to perceive that all things help to establish this fact: that God does not reveal himself to men as clearly as he could.[16]

But let them conclude what they will against deism. They will conclude nothing against the Christian religion, the essence of which lies in the mystery of a Redeemer who, by uniting within himself two natures, one human and one divine, has saved man from the corruption of sin in order to reconcile them with God in his divine person.

It therefore teaches men these two truths at the same time: that there is a God of whom men are capable and that there is a corruption in their nature that renders them unworthy of him.[17] It is equally important for man to grasp both these points, and it is equally dangerous for man to know God without being aware of his own wretchedness, and to be aware of his own wretchedness without knowing the Redeemer who can cure him of it. Knowing just one of these principles gives rise either to the pride of the philosophers,[18] who knew God but not their own wretchedness, or to the despair of the atheists, who know their own wretchedness but not the Redeemer.

And just as it is equally necessary for mankind to be aware of both these things, it is equally a sign of God's mercy to have taught men both these things. This is what the Christian religion does. That is its essence.

Let us examine the order of the world to see whether all things do not tend to establish the two main tenets of our religion![19]

(Jesus Christ is the purpose of everything and the center towards which all things gravitate. He who knows him knows the reason for all things.)[20]

---

14. The passage in parentheses is a marginal addition. *The course of the world*: the final argument in the "proofs" of the Christian religion listed in fr. 717.

15. See Wetsel, *Pascal and Disbelief*, 90–110.

16. See again, fr. 681, par. 1.

17. This central theme of corruption is linked to that of the *clair / obscur* [plain to see / obscured]. God is hidden, but because of his inscrutable mercy he reveals himself to the elect.

18. See frs. 221–22.

19. *Heads*: the "two truths" set down above in par. 20.

20. See T. S. Eliot's beautiful, though not literal, rendition: "He is the stillpoint of the turning world"

Those who go astray do so only because they fail to see one of these two things. We can therefore easily know God without our wretchedness and our wretchedness without God. But we cannot know Jesus Christ without knowing both God and our wretchedness.

And this is why I will not undertake to prove by reasons drawn from nature either the existence of God, or the Trinity, or the immortality of the soul, or anything of that sort.[21] This is not only because I would not feel sufficiently well-equipped to discover anything in nature that will convince hardened atheists, but also because without Jesus Christ such knowledge is useless and vain.[22] Even if a man were convinced that numerical proportions were immaterial and eternal truths dependent on a first truth in which they subsist and which we call God, I should not consider that he had made much progress towards salvation.

The God of the Christians is not a God who is merely the author of geometrical truths and the order of the elements: that is the lot of the heathen and the Epicureans. Nor is he merely a God whose providence watches over the lives and fortunes of men, bestowing a happy span of years upon those who worship him: that is the lot of the Jews. But the God of Abraham, the God of Isaac, the God of Jacob,[23] the God of Christians is a God of love and consolation. He is a God who fills the heart and soul of those he possesses. He is a God who makes them inwardly aware of their wretchedness and of his infinite mercy; who unites himself with them in the depths of their soul; who fills it with humility, with joy, with trust, with love; who renders them incapable of any other end but him.

All who seek God outside Jesus Christ, and who go no further than nature, either find no enlightenment to satisfy them or come to fashion for themselves a means of knowing God and serving him without a mediator.[24] In this way, they fall into either atheism or deism, two things that the Christian religion abhors almost equally.

Without Jesus Christ, the world would not continue to exist. It would either be destroyed or be like a living hell.[25]

("Burnt Norton," in *The Four Quartets*). The parenthetical phrases are placed inside a block in the two Copies and in the margin in the Original Collection. They do not figure in the unfolding of this text and stand apart from its argument. Yet they sum up the entire argument of this remarkable discourse.

21. As in most traditional post-Patristic Christian apologetics. However, in the preface to the Apology constituted by fr. 681, Pascal argues that finding out whether the soul is immortal or mortal is the most important question the seeker must resolve. See fr. 681, pars. 3–4.

22. Cf. fr. 445: "Descartes—useless. . ." Descartes's proofs of God's existence never lead to Jesus Christ and demonstrate only the existence of the God of the deists.

23. See Pascal's own revelation in his *Memorial* (fr. 742): "*God of Abraham, God of Isaac, God of Jacob,* / not of philosophers and scholars."

24. The approach attacked in ch. XV, "Excellence of this manner of proving God."

25. See fr. 35.

If the world existed in order to instruct men in the knowledge of God, his divinity would shine everywhere in an undeniable manner. But since it only continues to exist through and for Jesus Christ, and to bring men knowledge both of their corruption and of their redemption, everything in it is bursting with the proofs of those two truths.

What can be seen is not a sign either of a total absence, or of the manifest presence of the divinity, but of the presence of a God who hides himself. Everything bears this character.

Will the only one who knows nature know it only to be wretched?

Will the only one who knows it be the only one to be unhappy?

He must not see nothing at all. He must also not see so much that he believes that he possesses God, but he must see enough to know that he has lost him.[26] For to know of loss, one must see and not see and that is precisely the current state of nature.

Whatever side he takes, I shall not leave him in peace there.[27]

The true religion must teach greatness and wretchedness, lead to self-esteem and self-contempt, to love and to hate.[28]

---

26. There remains in human consciousness only an "empty mark and trace" of our happiness before the Fall (fr. 181). Man's endless and fruitless search for happiness testifies to his innate feeling of some great void in his being.

27. See fr. 163. Throughout the Apology Pascal carries out the strategy outlined in the great preface to the Apology (fr. 681). His interlocutor is over and over again forced to awaken from his lethargy and prompted to "seek." In the course of the titled *liasses* he is methodically transformed into what Wetsel calls the *chercheur* (seeker). The hardened atheists are left behind to await their condemnation. See Wetsel, *Pascal and Disbelief*, 327–35.

28. See fr. 248 and fr. 494: "The self is hateful." See also ch. XXXIV, n. 6.

[XLVIII] The State of the Jews [1]

691
Advantages of the Jewish people

In this search, the Jewish people immediately attract my attention by a number of wonderful and singular qualities apparent in them.

First of all, I see that they are a people consisting wholly of brothers. And, whereas all other peoples are composed of an infinite number of families, the Jewish people, though strikingly fertile, are all descended from a single man,[1] and since they are all of one flesh and are members of one another, they form a powerful state built out of a single family. That is unique.

This people is the most ancient known to mankind. I consider that this calls for special veneration, above all in the enquiry in which we are engaged, since, if God has revealed himself to men throughout time, it is this people whom we must consult in order to learn about tradition.

This people is not only remarkable by virtue of its antiquity; it is also singular owing to the manner in which it has survived and has continued unbroken from its origins down to the present day. For unlike the peoples of Greece and Italy, of Sparta, Athens, Rome and the others who came much later and disappeared long ago, the Jews survive to this day. And, despite the assaults of so many powerful monarchs who have tried, on countless occasions, to bring about their ruin, as their historians record, and as it is easy to judge from the natural order of things during such a long stretch of time, they have nonetheless always been preserved (and this preservation was foretold). And, extending from the earliest times to the most recent, their history contains in its duration all our histories.

The law that governs this people is at once the most ancient law in the world, the most perfect, and the only one that has always been observed without any interruption in any state. That is what Josephus[2] demonstrates

---

1. Abraham. In this *liasse* and the four that follow, Pascal brings to fruition the project of fragment 42, to which fragment 688 also belongs.
2. See ch. XXIII, n. 7.

admirably against Apion,[3] as does Philo Judæus,[4] in the various places where they show that it is so ancient that the very name of law was not known to the most ancient of the other peoples until more than a thousand years later; so that Homer, who wrote the history of so many nations, never used it. And it is easy to gauge its perfection by simply reading it, which shows that every contingency has been provided for with such wisdom, such equity, such judgment, that the earliest of the Greek and Roman legislators, when they gained some knowledge of it, borrowed their principal laws from it. This is apparent from what they call the Twelve Tables, and the other proofs given by Josephus.[5]

In so far as it deals with the practice of religion, their law is the strictest and most rigid of all laws. In order to keep them on the path of duty, it compels them to submit, on pain of death, to a thousand special and onerous observances. It is therefore astonishing that it should have always been preserved unchanged through so many centuries by such a rebellious and impatient people as the Jews, while all the other states have changed their laws from time to time, though their laws were altogether more lenient.

The book that contains this law, the first of all laws, is itself the oldest book in the world because those of Homer, Hesiod, and others only came six or seven hundred years later.

3. *Against Apion*, 11, 15, and 31. Apion (30 BCE–45 CE) was a Hellenized Egyptian commentator on Homer whose criticisms of Jewish culture and history were refuted by Josephus in this work.

4. See ch. XXV, n. 40. Philo Judæus, *Life of Moses*, 11, 12–15.

5. In book 2 of *Against Apion*. The idea is taken up, among others, by Grotius: "the most ancient Attic laws, from whence the Roman were afterwards taken, owe their original to the law of Moses." Grotius, *The Truth of the Christian Religion*, I, 15, 26.

[XLIX] The State of the Jews [2]

692
Sincerity of the Jews

They have preserved with loving care the book in which Moses declares that they have been ungrateful to God all their lives; that he knows that they will be still more ungrateful after his death; but that he calls upon heaven and earth to bear witness against them,[1] that he has impressed it on them sufficiently.

Finally, he declares that God will grow angry with them, will scatter them among all the peoples of the earth; that, since they have angered him by worshipping gods that were not their God, so he will provoke them by calling a people who are not his people;[2] and wishes all his words to be preserved eternally, and his book to be placed in the ark of the covenant so that it will serve for all time as a witness against them.[3]

Isaiah: Isaiah says the same thing, 30:8.

1. Deuteronomy 31:27–28.
2. Deuteronomy 32:21.
3. Deuteronomy 31:26.

374

[L] The State of the Jews [3]¹

693
To show that true Jews
and true Christians have but
one and the same religion²

The religion of the Jews appeared to consist essentially in the fatherhood of Abraham, in circumcision, in sacrifices, in ceremonies, in the ark, in the temple, in Jerusalem; in short, in the law and the covenant of Moses.

I say that it did not consist in any of those things, but only in the love of God, and that God rejected all other things.

That God did not make any exception for the posterity of Abraham.

That the Jews will be punished by God in the same way as strangers, if they have offended him.

Deuteronomy 9:19[20]³: *But if thou forget the Lord thy God, and follow strange gods I foretell thee that thou shalt perish as the nations, which the Lord destroyed before you.*

That strangers will be welcomed by God in the same way as the Jews, if they love him.

Isaiah 56:3[–7]: *Let not the stranger say: "The Lord will not welcome me." Strangers who turn to God will not fail to love and serve him. I will lead them to my holy mountain and will receive sacrifices from them. For my house is a house of prayer.*

That true Jews could only consider their merit as coming from God, not from Abraham.

Isaiah 63:16: *For thou art truly our father, and Abraham hath not known us, and Israel hath been ignorant of us: but thou art our Father and our Redeemer.*

---

1. In this *liasse*, Pascal assembles a list of Old Testament prophecies, which he interprets as predicting the reprobation of the Jews and the abrogation of the Old Covenant.

2. A theme to which Pascal returns again and again. The "spiritual" Jews, such as the Patriarchs and Prophets, are, as Le Maistre de Sacy often repeated, "Christians by an anticipation of grace."

3. In fact, this is Deuteronomy 8:19[20].

Even Moses told them that God would not regard persons.

Deuteronomy 10:17: *God said: "I regard neither persons nor sacrifices."*

The Sabbath was only a sign, Exodus 31:13; and in memory of the exodus from Egypt, Deuteronomy 5:15. So it is no longer necessary, since we must forget Egypt.

Circumcision was only a sign, Genesis 17:11.

And hence it follows that, when they were in the desert they were not circumcised,[4] because they could not be confused with other peoples; and that, since the coming of Jesus Christ, circumcision is no longer necessary.

That circumcision of the heart is ordained.[5]

Deuteronomy 10:17: Jeremiah 4:[4]: *You must be circumcised in your hearts. Excise what is superfluous from your hearts and do not let yourselves become hardened. For your God is a great God, strong and terrible, who does not regard persons.*

That God said that he would do it one day.

Deuteronomy 30:6: *God will circumcise your hearts, and those of your children, so that you love him with all your heart.*

That the uncircumcised in heart will be judged.

Jeremiah 9:26: For God will judge the uncircumcised peoples and the whole people of Israel, *because their hearts are uncircumcised.*

That the external is worth nothing without the internal.

Joel 2:13: *Rend your hearts*, etc.,[6] Isaiah 58:3–4, etc.

The love of God is enjoined throughout Deuteronomy.

Deuteronomy 30:19[–20]: *I call heaven and earth to witness, that I have set before you life and death, so that you choose life and that you may live and that you may love the Lord your God, and obey him. For God is your life.*

That the Jews, for lack of that love, would be rejected for their offenses and the heathen chosen in their place:

Hosea 1:10 [9].

Deuteronomy 32:20: *I will hide myself from them in the light of their latest crimes. For this is a wicked and unfaithful nation. They have provoked me to anger by things that are not gods, and I will provoke them to jealousy by a people that is not my people, and by a nation without knowledge or intelligence.*

Isaiah 65.[7]

---

4. Joshua 5:5–6.

5. Romans 2:25–31.

6. "*Rend your hearts*, and not your garments." A text omnipresent in the Lenten liturgies.

7. Pascal quotes Isaiah 65 at length in fr. 735, in a section entitled "Rejection of the Jews and conversion of the Gentiles."

That temporal goods are false, and that the true good is to be united with God:

Psalm 144:15.

That their feasts are displeasing to God:

Amos 5:21.

That the sacrifices of the Jews are displeasing to God:

Isaiah 66.[8]

1:11.[9]

Jeremiah 6:20.

David, *Have mercy on me.*[10]

Looking for.[11]

Even among good men:

Psalms 50, 8, 9, 10, 11, 12, 13, and 14.

That he only established them on account of their obstinacy:

Micah admirably, 6.

1 Kings 15:22.[12]

Hosea 6:6.

That the sacrifices of the heathen will be received by God, and that God will withdraw his favor from the sacrifices of the Jews:

Malachi 1:11.

That God will make a new covenant through the Messiah, and that the old one will be rejected:

Jeremiah 31:31.

———

Statutes that were not good. Ezekiel.[13]

———

That the former things will be forgotten:

Isaiah 43:18–19.

65:17–18.

That the Ark will no longer be remembered:

Jeremiah 3:15–16.

That the temple will be rejected:

Jeremiah 7:12, 13, 14.

8. Isaiah 66:3.

9. Isaiah 1:11.

10. Psalm 51, designated here by its first word, contains a rejection of ritual sacrifices in verses 17–18.

11. Psalm 40:9–10.

12. This is the First Book of Kings in the Vulgate, i.e., the First Book of Samuel.

13. In Ezekiel 20:25: "Therefore I also gave them *statutes that were not good*, and judgments, in which they shall not live."

That the sacrifices would be rejected, and other pure sacrifices established:

Malachi 1:11.

That the priesthood of Aaron will be reproved, and that of Melchizedek introduced by the Messiah: *The Lord said.*[14]

That this priesthood would be eternal:

Ibid.

That Jerusalem will be reproved and Rome admitted:

The Lord said.[15]

That the name of the Jews will be cast out and a new name given:

Isaiah 65:15.

That this last name will be better than that of the Jews, and everlasting:

Isaiah 56:5.

That the Jews were to be without prophets:

Amos.[16]

Without king, prince, sacrifice, or idol.[17]

That the Jews will nevertheless always remain as a people:

Jeremiah 31:36.

---

14. Aaron, the brother of Moses, the first high priest of the Hebrews. Psalm 110, designated here by its first words (*"The Lord said* to my Lord"), announces in its fourth verse the supreme priesthood of the Messiah: "The Lord hath sworn, and he will not repent: Thou art a priest for ever according to the order of Melchisedech." Melchizedek, king of Salem and priest of the Most High God, offers bread and wine in Genesis 14:18, traditionally interpreted as a prefiguring the Eucharist. See fr. 504. See also the [Roman] Canon of the Mass: "Deign to look upon these offerings . . . as you did those offered you by your high-priest Melchizedek."

15. A liturgical designation of Psalm 110:2: "The Lord will send forth the scepter of thy power [that of the Messiah] out of Sion: rule thou in the midst of thy enemies."

16. See fr. 718.

17. See fr. 294.

[LI] The State of the Jews [4]

694

I see the Christian religion, founded on a previous religion, and this is what I find as fact.[1]

I am not speaking here about the miracles[2] of Moses, of Jesus Christ, and the apostles, because they do not at first appear convincing. Here I only want to put into evidence all the foundations of this Christian religion that are indubitable, and that cannot be called into doubt by anyone whosoever.

It is certain that in several parts of the world, we see a peculiar people, separate from all the other peoples of the world, called the Jewish people.

I therefore see makers of religions in several parts of the world, and in every age. But they have neither a morality that can please me nor proofs that can convince me. And therefore I would equally have rejected the religion of Mohammad,[3] and that of China,[4] and of the ancient Romans,[5] and of the Egyptians,[6] for the sole reason that since none of them bears greater marks of truth than the others, nor anything that would determine me irresistibly, reason cannot incline towards one rather than towards the other.

But when reflecting upon this changeable and strange variety of customs and beliefs at different times, I find in one corner of the world a peculiar people, separated from all the other peoples of the earth, who are the most ancient of all and whose histories precede by several centuries the most ancient histories we have.[7]

1. This claim on Pascal's part is of course rhetorical and designed to appear to the reader as if he had just discovered what follows.

2. Pascal had long already decided that an Apology based upon miracles, his first inclination (reflected in frs. 419–51), would not have been convincing when presented to the unbeliever. See ch. XXX, n. 1.

3. Pascal repudiates Islam in ch. XVII.

4. See fr. 663 and notes.

5. See fr. 688.

6. See frs. 278, 300.

7. Pascal never fails to insist that the Jews are the oldest people in the world, that the Pentateuch is the oldest book in history, and that the biblical chronologies are the only authentic ones. No one before or in Pascal's time ever suspected that the world was over sixty-five hundred years old. Hence Pascal's need

I find then this great and numerous people, descended from a single man,[8] who worship one God, and who live by a law, which they say was received by them from his hand. They maintain that they are the only people in the world to whom God has revealed his mysteries, that all men are corrupt and in disgrace in the sight of God, that they have given themselves over to sensual pleasures and their own wayward spirit, instead of remaining steadfast in their conduct, which produces strange errors and continual changes in both religion and custom; but that God will not always leave the other peoples in their state of darkness, that a Liberator will come for all men, and that the Jews are in the world to proclaim his coming to men, that they were created precisely in order to be the forerunners and heralds of this great advent, and to call all peoples to unite with them in their expectation of the Savior.

The encounter with this people astounds me and seems worthy of my attention.

I examine the law, which they boast they have received from God, and find it admirable. It is the first of all laws, and of such a kind that the Jews had received it and observed it nearly a thousand years before the word "law" was used by the Greeks. So I find it strange that the first law in the world should also turn out to be the most perfect, so that the greatest legislators borrowed their own laws from it, as we can see from the law of the Twelve Tables of Athens, which was later taken up by the Romans, as could easily be shown if Josephus and others had not adequately dealt with this subject.[9]

695

(Prophecies

Oath that David will always have successors. Jeremiah.[10])

---

to argue that the recently discovered chronologies of the Chinese, Chaldeans, Greeks, and Egyptians are fictional.

8. I.e., Abraham.

9. On Josephus, see ch. XXIII, n. 7. See fr. 691.

10. Jeremiah 33:20–23.

[LII] The State of the Jews [5]

696

This is plain fact:

While all the philosophers are divided into different sects, we find in one corner of the world a people who are the oldest people in the world declaring that the whole world is in error, that God had revealed the truth to them, and that it will always exist on earth. Indeed, although all other sects have come to an end, this one still endures. And for four thousand years they declare that they hold from their ancestors that man has fallen from communication with God into a state of complete estrangement from him, but that God has promised to redeem him, that this doctrine would always exist on earth, that their law has a double meaning.[1]

That for sixteen hundred years they had men whom they believed to be prophets, who have foretold the time and the manner.[2]

That four hundred years later they were scattered over the face of the world; because Jesus Christ had to be announced everywhere.[3]

That Jesus Christ came in the manner and at the time foretold.[4]

That, ever since, the Jews have been scattered abroad under a curse and nevertheless subsisting.[5]

Hypothesis that the apostles were impostors.[6]

1. See ch. XX in the titled *liasses*, "That the Law Was Figurative." On the specific nature of liasses, see the section "A Brief History of Pascal's Text" in the introduction, and more particularly note 111.

2. Of the coming of the Messiah. Pascal calculates that the time from Adam to the last of the prophets amounted to only sixteen hundred years.

3. Prior to the coming of Christ, the Jewish people were scattered into all nations after the destruction of the Temple by the Babylonians in the fifth century BCE. In this Diaspora they prepared the way for the Messiah by serving as living, and later hostile, witnesses that their scriptures were authentically historical. Hence, the prophecies of the coming of Christ could not have been forged and invented after the fact by the early Christians.

4. See ch. XXV, n. 34.

5. For Pascal, the survival of the Jewish people is a living miracle ordained by God. This is a constant theme of "The State of the Jews" [1]–[4], chs. XLVIII–LI.

6. See fr. 341. The apostles could not have forged the prophecies of the Messiah after the fact, since the Jews had long before spread them abroad. After Jesus' death, the disheartened apostles could not possibly have invented the story of his Resurrection had they not seen him with their own eyes. Nor would they

The time clearly, the manner obscurely.[7]

___

Five proofs of the figurative[8] [meanings of scripture].

___

$$2000 \begin{cases} 1600\text{—prophets.} \\ 400\text{—scattered.}^9 \end{cases}$$

___

have endured torture and death without recanting had they not seen the accomplishment of the messianic prophecies.

7. See ch. XXV, "Prophecies." While appearing in the very year foretold by the prophets, Christ came, not as a great king, but as a lowly and obscure figure whose very existence was hardly noticed by the great historians of the time.

8. See fr. 305. These particular proofs would be greatly revised by Pascal in the course of writing the Apology. Only foreordained "seekers" would come to pierce the veil and discern the "figurative" meanings embedded in the literal text of the Old Testament.

9. See above, n. 2. The chronologists of Pascal's time generally agreed that Christ came in the Year of the World "2000." The Diaspora of the Jews during four hundred years after the cessation of the prophecies was an indispensable preparation for his coming.

[LIII Around Corruption]

697[1]

Contradictions
Infinite wisdom and folly of religion.

Zephaniah[2] 3:9: *I shall offer my words to the Gentiles, so that all may serve me with one shoulder.*

Ezekiel 37:25: *My servant David shall be forever king over them.*

Exodus 4:22: *Israel is my first-born son.*

Jeremiah 7:4: *Trust not in the lying words of those who say to you: "The temple of the Lord, the temple of the Lord, they are the temple of the Lord."*[3]

698[4]

These are the effects of the sins of the peoples and the Jesuits. The powerful have wished to be flattered; the Jesuits wanted to be loved by the powerful.

They deserved to be abandoned to the spirit of lies, the ones to deceive, the others to be deceived. They have been greedy, ambitious, and lustful. *They will heap to themselves teachers.*[5]

Worthy disciples of such teachers. *They are worthy.*[6]

They have sought flatterers and have found them.

1. The autograph is missing from the Original Collection. The two Copies give the two titles, then the quotations (translated into French by Pascal) separated by blank spaces.

2. Zephaniah is the ninth of the twelve minor prophets in the canon of the Old Testament. Zephaniah preached and wrote in the second half of the seventh century BCE and was a contemporary and supporter of Jeremiah.

3. The Vulgate gives the singular "*is.*" The Jews congratulate themselves by repeating this acclamation three times from the sanctuary of Jerusalem: "This *is* the temple of the Lord." Pascal takes the third-person plural "are" from the Bible of Vatable, whose translator considers the triple mention of the temple as referring to the three different parts of the building.

4. This anti-Jesuit fragment, of which the original is lost, is found only in C2 and not in the Original Collection. It does not belong to the Apology at all, but was an independent paper. Sometime after 1731, Guerrier transcribed it on the blank reverse side of a paper, which precedes the beginning of this dossier, but lost the original autograph. Louis Périer already had it copied in C2 sometime between 1680 and 1711.

5. 2 Timothy 4:3: "For there shall be a time, when they will not endure sound doctrine; but, according to their own desires, *they will heap to themselves teachers*, having itching ears."

6. Romans 1:32: "Being filled with all iniquity, malice, fornication, avarice, wickedness, full of envy,

699

The Christian God is a God who makes the soul feel that he is its unique good, that all its rest is in him, that it will find joy only in loving him; and who at the same time makes it abhor the obstacles that are holding it back and preventing it from loving God with all its might. Self-love and concupiscence, which hinder it, are unbearable to it. This God makes the soul feel that it has this underlying self-love that is destroying it, and that he alone can cure.

700

The world exists for the exercise of mercy and judgment, not as if the men in it came from the hands of God, but as if they were the enemies of God, to whom he grants by grace enough light to return, if they choose to seek and follow him; but also for punishing them if they refuse to seek or follow him.[7]

701

The prophets foretold and were not foretold. Then the saints were foretold, but did not foretell. Jesus Christ: foretold and foretelling.

702

It is a remarkable thing that no canonical author has ever made use of nature to prove God.[8] All of them aim to produce belief in him: David, Solomon, and the others never said: "There is no vacuum, therefore there is a God."[9] They must have been shrewder than the shrewdest people to come after them, all of whom have made use of this argument.[10]

This is truly noteworthy.

---

murder, contention, deceit, malignity, whisperers [...].Who, having known the justice of God, did not understand that they who do such things, *are worthy* of death; and not only they that do them, but they also that consent to them that do them."

7. A favorite liturgical text at Port-Royal was a line from the *Exultet,* sung at the beginning of the Easter Vigil: "O happy fault which merited so great a Redeemer." God created the world only to work out his drama of salvation. From that perspective, even the Fall was "happy." The world *continues to exist* only so that God may exercise mercy and judgment. The leitmotiv of "seeking" animates the entire Apology.

8. "Canonical": biblical. Pascal is contrasting canonical authors to most other apologists, even Aquinas, who employ ontological and cosmological proofs of the existence of God. See fr. 690, par. 25: "The God of the Christians is not a God who is merely the author of mathematical truths and the order of the elements: that is the portion of the heathen and the Epicureans."

9. A reminiscence of Pascal's quarrel with Father Noël, who rejected the results of Pascal's experiments on the vacuum, arguing that since God fills all things, no vacuum is possible in nature.

10. I.e., Father Noël's argument concerning the vacuum. By reversing Fr. Noël's thesis, Pascal ridicules those who use it. In fr. 38, the unbeliever asks Pascal if he had not said that he was going to use "the argument by design." Pascal replies with a firm "No."

703

I will not suffer him to rest in either one or the other, so that being without a resting place and without rest . . .[11]

———

These children, astonished, see their classmates respected . . .[12]

———

If it is a sign of weakness to prove God by nature, do not scorn scripture for it. If it is a sign of strength to have known these contrarieties, respect scripture for it.

704
Order

After corruption,[13] say: it is right that all those who are in this state should know what it is, both those who are content and those who are not content with it. But it is not right that they all should see redemption.[14]

705

There is nothing on earth that does not reveal either the wretchedness of man or the mercy of God, man's weakness without God or man's power with God.

706

God has used the blindness of this people for the benefit of the elect.

707

Man is at his most base in his quest for glory. But this is also the greatest mark of his excellence; for, whatever possessions he may have on earth, whatever health or material ease, he is not satisfied if he does not also enjoy men's esteem. So highly does he esteem human reason that, whatever other advantages he may possess on earth, he is not content if he does not also enjoy an advantageous place in human reason. This is the finest position in the world.

11. This echoes a key line from Augustine's *Confessions*: "You shall not rest until you rest in me." The line not only resonates with the penultimate sentence of fr. 690 ("Whatever side he takes, I shall not leave him in peace there") but it anticipates the entire strategy of the Apology.
12. See fr. 136.
13. An echo of ch. XVII. It is just that both those satisfied with man's state of corruption and those unhappy with it should be in this same state since all men are damned by original sin.
14. See fr. 264: "One understands nothing of the works of God unless one takes as a principle that his intention was to blind some and enlighten others."

Nothing can deflect him from that desire, and this is the most indelible quality of the human heart.

Even those who most despise men, and rank them with the beasts, still want to be admired and believed by them. They contradict themselves by their own feelings; for their nature, which is stronger than anything, convinces them more strongly of the greatness of man than reason can convince them of their baseness.[15]

708

As for me, I confess that as soon as the Christian religion reveals the principle that human nature is corrupt and fallen from God, it opens one's eyes to see the mark of this truth everywhere: for nature is such that it bears the traces of a lost God everywhere, both within and outside man.[16]

And a corrupt nature.

709

Greatness

Religion is such a great thing that it is only right that those who would not take the trouble to seek it, if it is obscure, should be deprived of it. What then is there to complain about, if it is the kind of thing that can be found by seeking?

710

Comprehension of the words good and evil.[17]

711

Since the creation of the world was beginning to be distant, God provided for a single contemporary historian,[18] and entrusted an entire people with safeguarding this book, so that this history would be the most authentic in the

15. See Montaigne, *Essays*, I, 41, 227: "Of all the illusions in this world, the most universally received is the concern for reputation and glory, which we espouse even to the point of giving up riches, rest, life, and health [...]. And of the irrational humors of men, it seems that even the philosophers get rid of this one later and more reluctantly than any other. It is the most contrary and stubborn of all [...]. For, as Cicero says, even those who combat it still want the books they write about it to bear their name on the title page and want to become glorious for despising glory."

16. See fr. 181. There remains in the human unconscious only an "empty mark and trace" of his happy pre-lapsarian state.

17. Genesis 3:5. The serpent says to Eve that as soon as she and Adam eat of the forbidden fruit they will be "like gods, knowing good and evil."

18. Moses, the presumed author of the Pentateuch. See ch. XXIII, n. 1.

world and all men might learn from it something so necessary to know and that could not be known in any other way.

The veil drawn over these books for the Jews is there also for bad Christians and for all those who do not hate themselves.[19]

But how well disposed are we to understand them and to know Jesus Christ, when we truly hate ourselves.[20]

I am not saying that the *mem* is mysterious.[21]

712

Pride counterbalances and banishes all wretchedness. Here indeed is a strange monster,[22] and a glaring error! No sooner has it fallen from its place than it looks anxiously for it again. That is what all men do. Let us see who will find it.

713

Without examining each particular occupation in turn, it is enough to include them all under the heading of diversion.

714

For the philosophers, two hundred and eighty kinds of sovereign good.[23]

715

As regards religions, it is important to be sincere: true heathen, true Jews, and true Christians.[24]

19. Two essential leitmotifs of the Apology. The "spiritual" Jews (the patriarchs and prophets) and the "spiritual" Christians share the same religion. When it comes to understanding the "spiritual" meanings embedded in the Old Testament, the eyes of the "carnal Christians" are just as veiled as were those of the masses of the Jews. The same is true of those unwilling to immolate their egos in order to behold the Beatific Vision.

20. On Pascal's radical admonition of self-hatred, see ch. XXXIV, nn. 4 and 6.

21. Fr. 711 consists of three unrelated notes: Moses's writing of the Pentateuch; "carnal" vs. spiritual Jews and Christians (and the corollary of self-hatred); and a completely unrelated note summing up frs. 287 and 303. On the complexities of the Hebrew *mem*, see ch. XX, nn. 17 and 59.

22. See P. Charron, *Of Wisdom*, I, ch. 35: "These Two Qualities, I confess, seem utterly inconsistent, and destructive of each other. For what in appearance more distant, what more contradictious than Emptiness and Presumption, than Misery and Pride? So strange, so monstrous a Composition is *Man*, in which these wide Extremes are Ingredients." P. Charron, *Of Wisdom*, trans. George Stanhope, 3rd ed. (London, 1729), 323.

23. See fr. 27, n. 14.

24. See fr. 318. Pascal's notation is enigmatic, see also fr. 693: "True Jews and true Christians have but one and the same religion." But what of the "true heathen"? Port-Royal, and particularly Arnauld in *On the Necessity of Faith in Jesus Christ*, conducted a fierce campaign against La Mothe le Vayer's *De la vertu des*

716

Against the history of China.[25]

Histories of Mexico, and of the five suns, the last of which was only eight hundred years ago.[26]

Difference between a book that is accepted by a people and a book that forms a people.[27]

717

Proofs.

1. The Christian religion, by its establishment: by establishing itself so strongly, so gently, being so contrary to nature.

2. The holiness, loftiness, and humility of a Christian soul.

3. The wonders of holy scripture.

4. Jesus Christ in particular.

5. The apostles in particular.

6. Moses and the prophets in particular.

7. The Jewish people.

8. The prophecies.

9. Perpetuity. No other religion has perpetuity.

10. Doctrine, which explains everything.[28]

11. The sanctity of this law.

12. Through the conduct of the world.[29]

---

payens [On the virtue of the pagans] (1642). Le Vayer had argued that the virtuous lives of Plato, Aristotle, Confucius, and the other pre-Christian sages constituted an implicit faith that saved them from damnation. Dante had reserved a not unpleasant corner of hell for them, but the Augustinian tradition, renewed by Jansenius, staunchly maintained that only those who have an *explicit* faith in Christ might be numbered among the elect. In fragment 796, Pascal's position is exactly that of Arnauld: "The pagan sages erected a building equally beautiful on the outside, but upon an unsound foundation. And the devil deceives men by this apparent resemblance."

25. See fr. 663 and n. 15.

26. See Montaigne, *Essays*, III, 6, 847–48: "The peoples of the Kingdom of Mexico [...] believed that the existence of the world was divided into five ages and into the life of five successive suns, of which four had already run their time, and that the one which gave them light was the fifth." The beginning of the fifth period "coincides with that great conjunction of stars which produced, some eight hundred years ago, according to the reckoning of our astrologers, many great alterations and innovations in the world." In fragment 663, Pascal rejects the pretentions of the Chinese chronologies to pre-biblical antiquity. Here, he seems to entertain the notion that the chronologies of the Aztecs might confirm those of the Bible. Both refer to a universal flood at the end of the first age, both speak of this age as the last in the history of the world (see fr. 315), and both see it as having started relatively recently.

27. This note clearly resonates with fr. 688: "There is a great difference between a book composed by an individual and given to a people and a book that itself creates a people."

28. The doctrine of the Fall, especially, explains humanity's tragic situation and constitutes what, for Pascal, is the true Christian theodicy.

29. Pascal will not in fact develop all of these proofs at length, much less as chapters or in the order of

Without a doubt, after considering what life is and what this religion is, we must not reject the inclination to follow the latter, if it comes into our heart. And there are certainly no grounds for mocking those who follow it.

---

the "titled" *liasses*. Number 10 will hardly be developed and numbers 2 (though a key theme) and 5 appear only in scattered fragments. Number 12, "the conduct of the world," may be seen in one sense as anticipating the entire analysis of human behavior in the anthropological chapters, III–XVI, though the phrase also refers to the course of the world, according to God's conduct of it (see fr. 738).

[LIV] Prophecies [1]

718[1]

215. In Egypt.

———

Talmud (Pugio, 659[2]):

It is a tradition among us that, when the Messiah will come, the house of God destined for the dispensation of his word will be filled with filth and impurity, and that the wisdom of the scribes will be corrupt and putrid. Those afraid to sin will be rejected by the people and treated as madmen and fools.

Isaiah, 49:[3]

Give ear, ye islands, and hearken, ye people from afar. The Lord hath called me by my name from the womb, from the bowels of my mother. In the shadow of his hand he hath protected me, he hath made my mouth like a sharp sword; and he said to me: "Thou art my servant, for in thee will I glory." And I said: "Lord, have I labored in vain? Have I spent my strength uselessly? Therefore my judgment is with the Lord, and my work with my God."—And now saith the Lord, that formed me from the womb to be his servant, that I may bring back Jacob and Israel unto him: "Thou shalt be glorified in the eyes of the Lord, and thy God is made thy strength. It is a small thing that thou shouldst convert the tribes of Jacob. Behold, I have raised thee to be the light of the Gentiles, that thou mayst be my salvation even to the farthest part of the earth."—Thus saith the Lord to the soul that has humbled itself, that is despised, to the nation that is abhorred by the Gentiles, to the servant of rulers: Kings and princes shall adore thee because the Lord, who hath chosen thee, is faithful."

Thus saith the Lord: "In the day of salvation and mercy I have heard thee, and I have given thee to be a covenant of the people, that thou mightest possess the

---

1. This collection of prophetic texts comes from the Talmud. See ch. XXI, n. 9.

2. Pascal translates this commentary from the Latin edition of the *Pugio fidei* published by J. de Voisin in 1651. Pascal considerably modifies the biblical text. Here, and throughout the "Prophecies" chapters, this translation seeks to reflect what Pascal wrote (in French, except for ch. LVII). On the *Pugio fidei*, see ch. XXI, fr. 308, and n. 2.

3. A passage traditionally interpreted as a prophecy of Christ's bringing the Gentiles to salvation.

nations most abandoned; that thou mightest say to them that are bound: 'Come out and be free': and to them that are in darkness: 'Come forth into the light and you shall feed in the ways, and your pastures shall be in every plain.'" They shall not hunger, nor thirst, neither shall the heat nor the sun strike them: for he that is merciful to them shall be their shepherd, and at the fountains of waters he shall give them drink and he shall make all his mountains a way. Behold these shall come from afar, and behold these from the east and from the west, these from the north and from the south country. Give praise, O ye heavens, and rejoice, O earth, give praise with jubilation: because the Lord hath comforted his people, and will have mercy on his poor ones, who placed their hope in him!

Yet, Zion dared to say: "The Lord hath forsaken me, and the Lord hath forgotten me."—Can a mother forget her infant, so as not to have pity on the son of her womb? and if she should forget, yet will not I forget thee. Behold, I have graven thee in my hands: thy walls are always before my eyes. Thy builders are come: they that destroy thee and make thee waste shall go out of thee. Lift up thy eyes round about, and see all these are gathered together, they are come to thee: I swear, thou shalt be clothed with all these forever as with an ornament. For thy deserts, and thy desolate places, and the land of thy destruction shall now be too narrow by reason of the inhabitants, and the children of thy barrenness shall still say in thy ears: "The place is too strait for me, make me room to dwell in."—And thou shalt say in thy heart: "Who hath begotten these? I was barren and brought not forth, led away, and captive: and who hath brought up these? I was destitute and alone: and these, where were they?" And the Lord God shall say: "Behold I have lifted up my hand to the Gentiles, and have set up my standard to the people. And they shall bring thee children in their arms and on their breasts. And kings shall be thy nursing fathers, and queens thy nurses: they shall worship thee with their face toward the earth, and they shall lick up the dust of thy feet. And thou shalt know that I am the Lord, for they shall not be confounded that wait for him. Shall the prey be taken from the strong and mighty? Yet, that which was taken by the strong and mighty, shall be delivered, and thy children I will save and thy enemies I will destroy. And all flesh shall know, that I am the Lord that save thee, and thy Redeemer the Mighty One of Jacob."

Isaiah, 50:[4]

Thus saith the Lord: "What is this bill of divorce, with which I have repudiated the synagogue? or why have I given her into the hands of thy enemies? Is it not for her iniquities, and for her wicked deeds have I put your mother away? Because I came, and there was not a man: I called, and there was none that would hear. Is my hand shortened and become little, that I cannot save?

---

4. The synagogue shall be divorced for her iniquities. Christ will endure ignominious afflictions for her sake.

"Behold at my rebuke I will clothe the heavens with darkness, and will make sackcloth their covering."

The Lord hath given me a learned tongue, that I should know how to uphold by word him that is weary: He wakeneth my ear, that I may hear him as a master.

The Lord God hath opened my ear, and I do not resist.

I have given my body to the strikers, and my cheeks to them that plucked them: I have not turned away my face from them that rebuked me, and spit upon me. The Lord God is my helper, therefore am I not confounded: therefore have I set my face as a most hard rock, and I know that I shall not be confounded.

He is near that justifieth me, who is he that shall condemn me? Behold the Lord God is my helper.

Lo, all men shall pass and be consumed by time. Who is there among you that feareth the Lord, that heareth the voice of his servant, that hath walked in darkness, and hath no light? Let him hope in the name of the Lord, and lean upon his God. Behold all you that kindle God's wrath, encompassed with flames, walk in the light of your fire, and in the flames which you have kindled: this is done to you by my hand, you shall die in your sorrows.

[Isaiah 51][5]

Give ear to me, you that follow that which is just, and you that seek the Lord: look unto the rock whence you are hewn, and to the hole of the pit from which you are dug out. Look unto Abraham your father, and to Sara that bore you. Behold, he was alone and childless when I called him, and blessed him, and multiplied him. See how I comforted Zion, and how many blessings and graces I have bestowed upon her.

Consider all these things, O my people, and give ear to me, for a law shall go forth from me, and my judgment shall rest to be a light of the nations.

Amos, 8[6]

The prophet, having enumerated the sins of Israel, says that God has sworn to take vengeance on them.

He says this:

And it shall come to pass in that day, saith the Lord God, that the sun shall go down at midday, and I will make the earth dark in the day of light. And I will turn your feasts into mourning, and all your songs into lamentation.

---

5. Interpreted by Christian scholars as an exhortation to trust in Christ, who will protect the children of his Church.

6. The approaching desolation of Israel is predicted because of its avarice and injustice.

Ye shall all be in sadness and in sorrows, and I will make it as the mourning of an only son, and the latter end thereof as a bitter day. Behold the days come, saith the Lord, and I will send forth a famine into the land: not a famine of bread, nor a thirst of water, but of hearing the word of the Lord. And they shall go wandering from sea to sea, and from the north to the east: they shall go about seeking the word of the Lord, and shall not find it.

In that day the fair virgins, and the young men shall faint for thirst. They that swear by the sin of Samaria, and say: Thy God, O Dan, liveth: and the way of Bersabee liveth: and they shall fall, and shall rise no more.

Amos 3:3[2]

You only have I known of all the nations of the earth.

Daniel 12:7

Having described the entire extent of the Messiah's reign, Daniel says:

And when the scattering of the band of the holy people shall be accomplished, all these things shall be finished.

Haggai 2:4[7]

Who is left among you, that saw this house in its first glory? and how do you see it now? is it not in comparison to that as nothing in your eyes? Yet now take courage, O Zorobabel, saith the Lord, and take courage, O Jesus the high priest, and take courage, all ye people of the land, saith the Lord of hosts: and perform. The word that I covenanted with you when you came out of the land of Egypt: and my spirit shall be in the midst of you: fear not. Do not lose hope, for thus saith the Lord of hosts: Yet one little while, and I will move the heaven and the earth, and the sea, and the dry land (a figure of speech to mark a significant and extraordinary change);[8] *and I will move all nations. And the desired of all nations shall come: and I will fill this house with glory, saith the Lord of hosts.*

The silver is mine, and the gold is mine, saith the Lord of hosts (this means that it is not in this way that I want to be honored; and as it is written elsewhere:[9] *For all the beasts of the fields are mine, what advantage is it to me that*

---

7. Haggai was one of those who returned from the Babylonian captivity. He was sent by the Lord to exhort Zorobabel the prince of Judah, and Jesus the high priest, to the rebuilding of the temple. They had begun, but left off because of the opposition of the Samaritans. In consequence of the exhortation they took up the work again and finished the temple. The prophet was commissioned by the Lord to assure them that this second temple should be more glorious than the former, because the Messiah should honor it with his presence.

8. Pascal's commentary.

9. Pascal's commentary.

they are offered to me in sacrifice?[10]); *great shall be the glory of this new temple more than of the first, saith the Lord of hosts: and in this place I will establish my house, saith the Lord."*[11]

[Deuteronomy 18:16]

In Horeb, when the assembly was gathered together, and saidst: Let me not hear any more the voice of the Lord my God, neither let me see any more this exceeding great fire, lest I die. And the Lord said to me: They have spoken all things well. I will raise them up a prophet out of the midst of their brethren like to thee: and I will put my words in his mouth, and he shall speak to them all that I shall command him. And he that will not hear his words, which he shall speak in my name, I will be the revenger.

Genesis 49[12] [8, 10]

Juda, thee shall thy brethren praise: thy hands shall be on the necks of thy enemies: the sons of thy father shall bow down to thee. Juda is a lion's whelp: to the prey, my son, thou art gone up: resting thou hast couched as a lion, and as a lioness, that shall awaken.

The scepter shall not be taken away from Juda, nor a ruler from his thigh, till Shilo come, and the nations shall gather to obey him.

---

10. Psalm 49:10.
11. See above, n. 7.
12. Jacob's prophetical blessings of his twelve sons.

[LV] Prophecies [2]

719

Prediction of Specific Things[1]

They were foreigners in Egypt, without any possessions of their own either in that country or elsewhere (*there was not the least sign of kingship, which came so long afterwards, nor of that supreme council of seventy judges called the* SANHEDRIN *which being instituted by Moses, lasted until the time of Christ. All these things were as far removed from their current state as they could have been*), when Jacob, dying and blessing his twelve children, told them they would enjoy possession of a great land, and in particular foretold to the family of Judah that the kings who should one day govern them would be descended from him, and that all of his brothers would be subject to him (*and that even the Messiah who would be expected by the nations would be born of him, and that the scepter would not be taken from Judah, nor the governor and lawgiver from his descendants, until this expected Messiah had appeared into his family*).

This same Jacob, dividing up this future land as if he were already its master, gave a greater lot to Joseph than to the others: "I BEQUEATH THEE ONE PORTION TO WHICH THY BRETHREN SHALL HAVE NO CLAIM." And blessing his two children, Ephraim and Manasseh, whom Joseph had presented to him, with the eldest, Manasseh, at this right, and the youngest, Ephraim, at his left, he crossed his arms, and, placing his right hand on Ephraim's head and his left on that of Manasseh, he blessed them in [this] way. When Joseph pointed out to him that he was giving preference to the younger, he answered with an admirable resolve: "I know it, my son," said he, "I know it very well, but Ephraim will increase much more than Manasseh." So true did this turn out to be that, since Ephraim alone was almost as fruitful as two families composing a whole kingdom, they were usually called simply Ephraim.[2]

---

1. See ch. XXVI, "Particular Figures" (frs. 381–82). Pascal cites Genesis 48–50; Deuteronomy 28–32; and Numbers 34:17 and 35:6. In this chapter, as opposed to the preceding one, the lines in italics represent lines struck out by Pascal. The scriptural citations are marked by quotation marks. Pascal's interpolations are in regular print.

2. Ephraim became the largest and the predominant people of the northern kingdom, which is often called by his name.

This same Joseph, when he was dying, charged his children to carry his bones with them when they left for this land where they only arrived two hundred years later.

Moses, who wrote all of these things so long a time before they came to pass, himself assigned to each family portions of that land before they entered it, as if he had been its ruler, (*and he predicted exactly to them all that was to happen to them in the land they were to enter after his death: the victories that God would give them, their ingratitude towards God, the punishments they would receive for it, and the rest of their adventures*).

He gave them judges to oversee the partitioning. He prescribed the entire form of political government that they were to observe, the cities of refuge they were to build, etc.

[LVI] Prophecies [3]¹

720
Daniel 2²

The secret that the king desireth to know, none of the wise men, or the philosophers, or the diviners, or the soothsayers can declare to the king. (He must really have taken this dream to heart.) ³

But there is a God in heaven that can, who hath shewn to thee, what is to come to pass in the latter times. To me this secret is revealed, not by any wisdom that I have more than all men alive: but by the same God, that the interpretation might be made manifest in your presence.

Thy dream, therefore, was of this kind: Thou sawest, and behold there was a great statue: this statue, which was great and high, tall of stature, stood before thee, and the look thereof was terrible. The head of this statue was of fine gold, but the breast and the arms of silver, and the belly and the thighs of brass: And the legs of iron, the feet part of iron and part of earth (clay). Thus thou sawest, till a stone hewn out without hands: and it struck the statue upon the feet thereof that were of iron and of clay, and broke them in pieces.

Then was the iron, the clay, the brass, the silver, and the gold broken to pieces together, and they vanished into the air: but the stone that struck the statue, became a great mountain, and filled the whole earth. This is the dream: we will also tell the interpretation thereof before thee.

Thou who art a king of kings and to whom the God of heaven hath given strength, and power such that all the nations are in awe of thee, thou art figured by the head of gold on the statue that thou sawest.

---

1. The numerology in the chapter, accepted as proving the time of the coming of Christ as predicted in the Old Testament, remains completely enigmatic to all but those Old Testament scholars familiar with pre-modern biblical exegesis. While recognizing that this numerology has nothing to do with a prediction of the advent of Christ, they attempt to integrate it into its Old Testament context. See ch. XXV, n. 34, for Le Maistre de Sacy's far more comprehensible explanation of the prediction as traditionally accepted.

2. Daniel 2:27–46.

3. The phrases in Roman type and sometimes in parentheses are Pascal's own interpolations. They are written in the margins of the Original Collection. The text in italics is that of the scriptural citation, sometimes cited by Pascal from memory.

But after thee shall rise up another kingdom,[4] inferior to thee. And then another third kingdom[5] of brass, which shall rule over all the world.

But the fourth kingdom[6] shall be strong as iron; and, just as iron breaketh into pieces, and pierceth all things, so shall that break and destroy all these.

And whereas thou sawest the feet, part of potter's clay, and part of iron: it is a sign that this kingdom shall be divided, and shall be partly strong, like iron, and partly breakable, like earth.

But whereas iron cannot be mixed solidly with earth, so those who figured by the iron and by the earth shall not establish a lasting alliance, even though they shall be mingled indeed together by marriages.

But in the days of those kingdoms the God of heaven will set up a kingdom that shall never be destroyed, and his kingdom shall not be delivered up to another people. It shall break in pieces, and shall consume and bring to their end all these kingdoms, and itself shall stand for ever, according to what hath been revealed to thee concerning the stone, which was cut out of the mountain without hands, and broke in pieces, the iron, the clay, and the brass, and the silver, and the gold.

This is what, the great God hath shewn thee about what shall come to pass hereafter. This dream is true, and the interpretation thereof is faithful.

Then king Nabuchodonosor fell on his face, etc.

Daniel 8[7]

When Daniel had seen the combat between the ram[8] and the he-goat,[9] which conquered the ram and ruled over the land, and when its chief horn[10] had fallen, four others[11] had emerged pointing towards the four winds of heaven, from one of which a "little horn"[12] emerged, which grew bigger towards the south, towards the east and towards the land of Israel, and rose up against the army of heaven, and threw down the stars and crushed them under its feet, and finally felled the prince,[13] and brought the perpetual sacrifice to an end, and reduced the sanctuary to desolation.

4. "The Chaldeans," the astrologers, that pretended to divine by stars.

5. "Third kingdom," that of Alexander the Great.

6. Some understand this as the successors of Alexander, the kings of Syria and Egypt, others of the Roman empire, and its civil wars.

7. Pascal summarizes verses 3–17 and translates verses 20–25.

8. "A ram" refers to the empire of the Medes and Persians.

9. "A he goat" refers to the empire of the Greeks, or Macedonians.

10. "Chief horn": Alexander the Great.

11. "Four others": Seleucus, Antigonus, Philip, and Ptolemeus, the successors of Alexander, who divided his empire among them.

12. "A little horn": Antiochus Epiphanes, a descendant of Seleucus. He grew against the south, and the east, by his victories over the kings of Egypt and Armenia.

13. "The prince": the angel guardian of Persia, who according to his office, in seeking the spiritual good of the Persians was desirous that many of the Jews should remain among them.

This is what Daniel saw. He sought for an explanation, *and he heard a crying thus: "Gabriel, make this man to understand the vision that he had."—And Gabriel said to him:*

"The ram, which thou sawest, is the king of the Medes and Persians, and the he goat, is the king of the Greeks, and the great horn that was between his eyes, the same is the first king of that kingdom. And whereas when that was broken, there arose up four for it: four kings shall rise up of his nation, but not with his strength.

But, after their reign declined, when iniquities shall be grown up, there shall arise a king of a shameless face, and a strong power, but not strengthened by his own force: and he shall prosper in all things according to his will. And he shall destroy the people of the saints, lay all things waste, and shall be successful in his enterprises with craft and deceit, and he shall kill many: and he shall rise up against the prince of princes. But he shall be broken miserably, yet without a violent hand."

Daniel 9:20

Now while I was praying to God with all my heart, and laying prostrate before my God, confessing my sins, and the sins of my people of Israel, behold Gabriel, whom I had seen in the vision at the beginning, came to me and touched me at the time of the evening sacrifice. And he instructed me, and spoke to me, and said: "O Daniel, I am now come forth to teach thee, and that thou mightest understand. From the beginning of thy prayers, I am come to shew to thee what thou desirest, because thou art a man of desires:[14] *therefore do thou mark the word, and understand the vision. Seventy weeks*[15] *are ordained and determined upon thy people, and upon thy holy city, that transgression may be finished, and sin may have an end, and iniquity may be abolished; and everlasting justice may be brought; and vision and prophecy may be fulfilled; and the saint of saints may be anointed."*

(After which, this people will no longer be your people, nor this city the holy city.

The time of anger will have passed, and the years of grace will come forever.)

Know thou therefore, and understand, that from the going forth of the word,[16] *to build up Jerusalem again, unto Christ the prince, there shall be seven weeks, and sixty-two weeks:* (the Hebrews followed the practice of dividing numbers, and of putting the smaller one first. So these 7 and 62 make up 69 out of the 70. So

---

14. "Man of desires": that is, ardently praying for the Jews then in captivity.

15. "Seventy weeks": Weeks of years, seventy times seven, that is, 490 years. See ch. XXV, "Prophecies," n. 34.

16. "From the going forth of the word": That is, from the twentieth year of king Artaxerxes, when by his commandment Nehemiah rebuilt the walls of Jerusalem, 2 Esdras 2. From which time, according to the best chronology, there were just sixty-nine weeks of years, that is, 483 years to the baptism of Christ (traditional interpretation).

that leaves the seventieth, in other words the seven last years of which he will go on to speak.) *After the square and the walls have been built, in a time of trouble and affliction, and after these 62 weeks* (that will have followed the first 7), *the Christ will be killed* (so the Christ will be killed after 69 weeks, that is to say in the last week),[17] *and a people come,*[18] *shall destroy the city and the sanctuary and shall submerge everything: and the end of the war shall bring the appointed desolation.*

Thus in one week (which is the seventh, which remains) *an alliance with many shall be established* and *even in the half of the week*[19] (that's to say the last three and a half years) *the victim and the sacrifice*[20] *shall fall: and there shall be in the temple an abomination of astonishing magnitude*[21] that will spread and endure over those same people who will be astonished and the desolation shall continue *even to the consummation, and to the end.*

Daniel 11[22]

The angel said to Daniel:

Behold there shall (after Cyrus, under whom this is written) *stand yet three kings in Persia* (Cambyses, Smerdis, Darius). And *the fourth* (Xerxes) *that shall come after them shall be enriched and strengthened exceedingly above them all, and he shall stir up all against the Greeks.*

But there shall rise up a strong king (Alexander) *and shall rule with great power: and he shall succeed in all his enterprises and shall do what he pleaseth. And when he shall come to his height, his kingdom shall be broken, and it shall be divided towards the four winds of the heaven* (as he had said previously: 7:6; 8:8), *but not to his posterity. And his successors shall not be as powerful, for even his kingdom shall be rent in pieces, even for strangers, beside these* (the four principal successors).

And the king of the south (Egypt: Ptolemy, son of Lagus) *shall be strengthened, but another* (Seleucus, king of Syria) *shall prevail over him.* (Appian[23] says that he is the most powerful of Alexander's successors).

And after the end of years they shall be in league together: and the daughter of the king of the south (Berenice, the daughter of Ptolemy Philadelphus, the son

---

17. Again, see ch. XXV, n. 34.

18. Titus and the Romans.

19. "In the half of the week": In the middle of the week, etc. Christ preached three years and a half: and then by his sacrifice upon the cross abolished all the sacrifices of the law (traditional interpretation).

20. The sacrifices of the Temple.

21. The bringing of the pagan Romans' ensigns and standard into the Temple.

22. Verses 2–24.

23. Appian the Greek historian (1st–2nd cent. CE) was the author of a *Roman History,* in which he relates the wars between Rome and the states that became provinces of the empire.

of the other Ptolemy) *shall come to the king of the north* (Antiochus Deus, king of Syria and Asia, the nephew of Seleucus Lagidas) *to make friendship between these princes.*

But neither she nor her seed shall be strengthened for long; for she shall be given up unto death, and her young men that brought her. (Berenice and her son were killed by Seleucus Callinicus). *And a plant*[24] *of the bud of her roots, shall stand up: and he shall come with an army, and shall enter into the province of the king of the north: and he shall prevail. And he shall also carry away captive into Egypt their gods, and their princes, and their gold and silver, and all their most precious spoils; and for several years the king of the north*[25] *shall have no power against him* (if he had not been called back to Egypt for domestic reasons, he would have stripped Seleucus of all his possessions, according to Justin[26]).

And thus he shall return to his own land. But the sons of the other (Seleucus Ceraunius, Antiochus the Great[27]) *shall be provoked, and they shall assemble a multitude of great forces.*

And their army shall come and bring destruction on everything. And the king of the south (Ptolemy Philopator) *being provoked shall prepare an exceeding great multitude, and shall fight against him* (Antiochus the Great) *and shall defeat him* (at Rapham). *And his forces shall become arrogant and his heart shall be lifted up* (the same Ptolemy desecrated the Temple: Josephus), *and he shall cast down many thousands: but he shall not prevail for long.*

For the king of the north (Antiochus the Great) *shall return and shall prepare a multitude much greater than before, and in those times many shall rise up against the king of the south* (the young Ptolemy Epiphanes being on the throne), *and even some apostates* (those who abandoned their religion in order to please Evergetes when he sent his forces to Scopas), *violent men, of thy people shall lift up themselves to fulfill the visions, and they shall fall* (for Antiochus shall take Scopas back and shall defeat them).

And the king of the north shall come, and shall bring down the walls and the best fenced cities: and the arms of the south shall not withstand.

And all shall yield to his will. He shall stand in the land of Israel, and it shall yield to him.

And he shall set his face to come to possess all the empire of Egypt (despising the youth of Epiphanes, according to Justin).

And for this he shall enter into an alliance with him and shall give him his

---

24. "A plant" refers to Ptolemy Evergetes, the son of Philadelphus.
25. Seleucus Callinicus.
26. Justin was a Roman historian of the second century who wrote a *Universal History*.
27. The sons of Callinicus.

daughter (Cleopatra, so that she should betray her husband. On which subject Appian says that, uncertain of being able to gain mastery of Egypt by force because of Roman protection, he wanted to take it by cunning). *He shall want to corrupt her, but she shall not follow his designs. Therefore he shall throw himself into other projects and he shall turn his face to the islands* (that is to say, places on the seaboard), *and he shall take several of them* (as Appian says).

But a great chief shall oppose his conquests, and shall put an end to the shame that he would incur from it (Scipio the African, who will halt the progress of Antiochus the Great because he was offending the Romans in the person of their allies). *Therefore he shall return to his kingdom and shall perish there and shall be no longer* (he was killed by his own people).

And there shall stand up in his place one most vile, and unworthy of kingly honor, who shall make his way in by cunning and blandishments.

All the armies shall fold before him, he shall defeat them, and even the prince with whom he had made *an alliance. For, having renewed the alliance with him, he will deal deceitfully with him and, arriving with few troops in his peaceful provinces, he shall take the best places and shall do more than his forefathers had ever done. And, bringing devastation everywhere, he shall turn his face to great projects during his time.*

25.[28]

28. Having just translated Daniel 11, verses 2–24, Pascal notes the verse at which he intends to resume his translation.

[LVII] Prophecies [4]¹

721

Isaiah 1:21: Change from good to evil, and God's vengeance.

––––––

Isaiah 10:1: *Woe to them that make wicked laws.*

––––––

Isaiah 26:20: Go, my people, enter into thy chambers, shut thy doors upon thee, hide thyself a little for a moment, until the indignation pass away.

––––––

Isaiah 28:1: *Woe to the crown of pride.*

––––––

Miracles. *The land hath mourned, and languished: Libanus is confounded and become foul, etc.*: Isaiah [33:]9.

*Now will I rise up, saith the Lord: now will I be exalted, now will I lift up myself.*²

––––––

All as if they had no being at all: Isaiah 40:17.³

722

Who hath declared from the beginning, that we may know: and from time of old, that we may say: "Thou art just"? Isaiah 41:26.⁴

––––––

I will work, and who shall turn it away? Isaiah 43:13.

1. The prophecies anticipating the reprobation of the Jewish people tie together this chapter. Why, with exception of a few explanatory phrases, the verses of the entire chapter are all copied out in Latin is not evident.

2. In fact, Isaiah 33:9–10: "Libanus is confounded and become foul, and Saron is become as a desert [...]. *Now will I rise up, saith the Lord: now will I be exalted, now will I lift up myself.*"

3. The actual text reads: "*All nations* are before him *as if they had no being at all.*"

4. Pascal provides his own translation of this verse in fr. 735.

723

Thou shalt not prophesy in the name of the Lord, and thou shalt not *die in our hands.*

Therefore thus saith the Lord: Jeremiah 11:21.[5]

And if they shall say unto thee: "*Whither shall we go forth? thou shalt say to them: Thus saith the Lord: Such as are for death, to death: and such as are for the sword, to the sword: and such as are for famine, to famine: and such as are for captivity, to captivity.*" Jeremiah 15:2.

The heart is perverse above all things, and unsearchable, who can know it? (that is to say: who will know the extent of the wrongdoing? For it is already known that he is wicked.)

I am the Lord who search the heart and prove the reins.—Jeremiah 17:9.[6]

And they said: "*Come, and let us invent devices against Jeremias: for the law shall not perish from the priest, nor counsel from the wise, nor the word from the prophet.*"[7]

Be not thou a terror unto me, thou art my hope in the day of affliction: Jeremiah 17:17.

724

Assurance in external sacraments.—Jeremiah 7:14.

I will do to this house, in which my name is called upon, and in which you trust, and to the places which I have given you and your fathers, as I did to Silo.

Therefore, do not thou pray for this people.[8]

725

External sacrifice is not the essential thing.—Jeremiah 7:22.

For I spoke not to your fathers, and I commanded them not, in the day that I brought them out of the land of Egypt, concerning the matter of burnt offerings and sacrifices.

But this thing I commanded them, saying: Hearken to my voice, and I will be

---

5. Actually, the last fragment is the beginning of verse 22. Verse 21 ends with the preceding quotation.
6. Jeremiah 17:9–10.
7. Jeremiah 18:18.
8. Jeremiah 7:16. Translated by Pascal in fr. 735.

your God, and you shall be my people: and walk ye in all the way that I have com-
manded you, that it may be well with you. But they hearkened not.[9]

A multitude of doctrines.   Jeremiah 11:13.

For according to the number of thy cities were thy gods, O Juda: and according
to the number of the streets of Jerusalem thou hast set up altars of confusion.

Therefore, do not thou pray for this people.[10]

726

And he will not say: "Perhaps there is a lie in my right hand." Isaiah 44:20.

Remember these things, O Jacob, and Israel, for thou art my servant. I have
formed thee, thou art my servant, O Israel, forget me not.

I have blotted out thy iniquities as a cloud, and thy sins as a mist: return to me,
for I have redeemed thee.—44:21, etc.

Give praise, O ye heavens, for the Lord hath shewn mercy: shout with joy, ye
ends of the earth: ye mountains, resound with praise, thou, O forest, and every tree
therein: for the Lord hath redeemed Jacob, and Israel shall be glorified. Thus saith
the Lord thy Redeemer, and thy maker, from the womb: "I am the Lord, that make
all things, that alone stretch out the heavens, that establish the earth, and there is
none with me."—44:23–24.

727

In a moment of indignation have I hid my face a little while from thee, but with
everlasting kindness have I had mercy on thee, said the Lord thy Redeemer.—Isaiah
54:8.

728

He that brought out Moses by the right hand, by the arm of his majesty: that
divided the waters before them, to make himself an everlasting name.—Isaiah
63:12.

So didst thou lead thy people to make thyself a glorious name. 14.

For thou art our father, and Abraham hath not known us, and Israel hath been
ignorant of us.—Isaiah 63:16.[11]

---

9. Jeremiah 7, verses 22 and 23, is translated freely in fr. 735. Pascal adds the beginning of verse 24 here: "And did they listen? *Hearing they gave me none . . . ."*

10. Jeremiah 11, verses 13 (the final words "altars to offer sacrifice to Balaam," are omitted) and 14.

11. Translated in fr. 693.

Why hast thou hardened our heart, that we should not fear thee?—Isaiah 63:17.

————

"They that were sanctified, and thought themselves clean . . . they shall be consumed together," saith the Lord.—Isaiah 66:17.

————

And thou hast said: "I am without sin and am innocent: and therefore let thy anger be turned away from me."

Behold, I will contend with thee in judgement, because thou hast said: I have not sinned."—Jeremiah 2:35.

————

They are wise to do evil, but to do good they have no knowledge.—Jeremiah 4:22.

729

I beheld the earth, and lo it was void, and nothing: and the heavens, and there was no light in them.

I looked upon the mountains, and behold they trembled: and all the hills were troubled. I beheld, and lo there was no man: and all the birds of the air were gone. I looked, and behold Carmel was a wilderness: and all its cities were destroyed at the presence of the Lord, and at the presence of the wrath of his indignation.—Jeremiah 4:23, etc.[12]

730

For thus saith the Lord: "All the land shall be desolate, but yet I will not utterly destroy."[13]

Jeremiah 5:4: *But I said: "Perhaps these are poor and foolish, that know not the way of the Lord, the judgement of their God."*

I will go therefore to the great men, and I will speak to them: for they known the way of the Lord.

And behold these have together broken the yoke more, and have burst the bonds.

Wherefore a lion out of the wood hath slain them, hath spoiled them, a leopard watcheth for their cities."[14]

12. Jeremiah 4:23–26.
13. Jeremiah 4:27.
14. Pascal drops a few words from the text he is citing: ". . . slain them, a wolf in the evening, a leopard."

730

Shall I not visit for these things, saith the Lord? or shall not my soul take revenge on such a nation?—Jeremiah 5:29.

Astonishing and wonderful things have been done in the land.

The prophets prophesied falsehood, and the priests clapped their hands: and my people loved such things: what then shall be done in the end thereof?—Jeremiah 5:30.[15]

Thus saith the Lord: "*Stand ye on the ways, and see and ask for the old paths which is the good way, and walk ye in it: and you shall find refreshment for your souls. And they said: we will not walk.*

"*And I appointed watchmen over you, saying: Hearken ye to the sound of the trumpet. And they said: We will not hearken.*

"*Therefore hear, ye nations, and know, O congregation, what great things I will do to them,*" etc.—Jeremiah 6:16.[16]

733

From the prophets of Jerusalem corruption has gone forth into all the land.—Jeremiah 23:15.[17]

They say to them that blaspheme me: The Lord hath said: "*You shall have peace*": *and to every one that walketh in the perverseness of his own heart, they have said:* "*No evil shall come upon you.*"—Jeremiah 23:17.

---

15. Actually, Jeremiah 5:30–31.

16. Jeremiah 6:16–19. Verse 16 is freely translated in fr. 634.

17. Corruption has spread from the heart of Jerusalem to the face of the entire world.

[LVIII] Prophecies [5]¹

734
During the lifetime of
the Messiah

Put forth a riddle: Ezekiel 17.[2]

His precursor: Malachi 2.

He will be born as a child: Isaiah 9.

He will be born in the town of Bethlehem: Micah 5.[3] He will appear mainly in Jerusalem, and will be born of the family of Judah and David.

He will blind wise and learned men: Isaiah 6; Isaiah 8; Isaiah 29,[4] and announce the Gospel to the poor and meek, opening the eyes of the blind: Isaiah 29; Isaiah 61,[5] heal the sick and lead those who languish in darkness into the light: Isaiah 61.[6]

He is to teach the way of perfection and be the teacher of the Gentiles: Isaiah 55; 42:1–7.

The prophecies are to be incomprehensible to the ungodly: Daniel 12;[7] but comprehensible to the learned: Hosea, last, 10.

The prophecies that depict him as poor, depict him as ruler of the nations: Isaiah 52:[13], etc.; 53; Zechariah 9:9.

The prophecies that foretell the time only foretell him as master of the Gentiles and suffering, and not as in the clouds, nor as a judge. And those that depict him thus as a judge and in glory do not indicate the time.

That he is to be a victim for the sins of the world: Psalm [40]; Isaiah 53, etc.

---

1. Pascal continues to translate passages he will need as proof of the accomplishment of the Old Testament prophecies in the New Testament. Many of these passages are in fact already cited by the authors of the Gospels themselves to the same end.

2. Ezekiel 17:2: "Son of man, *put forth a riddle*, and speak a parable to the house of Israel."

3. For the three references, Micah 5:1, 5:6, and 5:2.

4. Isaiah 6:10; Isaiah 8:14–15; Isaiah 29:10.

5. Isaiah 29:18–19 and Isaiah 61:1.

6. Isaiah 61:3.

7. Daniel 12:10. Cited in fr. 735.

He is to be the precious cornerstone: Isaiah 28:16.

He is to be the stone of stumbling, the rock of offence: Isaiah 8.[8]

Jerusalem is to dash itself against this stone.

The builders are to reject this stone: Psalm [118]:22.

God is to make this stone the chief cornerstone.

And this stone is to grow into an immense mountain and must fill all the earth: Daniel 2.[9]

That he is thus to be rejected, not recognized, betrayed: [Psalm] [109]:8; sold, Zechariah 11:12; spat upon, struck, mocked, afflicted in countless ways; given gall to drink: Psalm [69]:22; Zechariah 12:10; his hands and feet pierced, slain, and lots cast for his raiment: Psalm [22].[10]

That he would rise again: Psalm [16];[11] the third day: Hosea 6:3.

That he would ascend into heaven to sit at the right hand: Psalm [110].[12]

That kings would take up arms against him: Psalm [2].

That, being seated at the right hand of the Father, he would be victorious over his enemies.

That the kings of the earth and all the peoples would worship him: Isaiah 60.[13]

That the Jews will continue as a nation: Jeremiah.[14]

That they will wander, without kings, etc.: Hosea 3.[15]

Without prophets: Amos.[16]

Waiting for salvation and not finding it: Isaiah.[17]

By slaying him and by continuing to deny him, the Jews have given him the final proof of being the Messiah.

And, by continuing not to recognize him, they have made themselves unimpeachable witnesses.

And, by killing him and continuing to deny him, they have fulfilled the prophecies.

8. Isaiah 8:14.

9. Daniel 2:35.

10. Psalm 22:10 and 17 for the two references.

11. Psalm 16:10.

12. Psalm 110:1.

13. Isaiah 60:14.

14. Jeremiah 31:36.

15. Hosea 3:4.

16. Amos 9:9.

17. Isaiah 69:9.

The calling of the Gentiles by Jesus Christ: Isaiah 52:15; Isaiah 55;[18] Isaiah 60.[19]

Psalm [72].[20]

Hosea 1:9: *You will be no longer my people, I will no longer be thy God, when you are multiplied after the dispersion. In the places where it was said "Not my people," I will call them my people.*

18. Isaiah 55:5.
19. Isaiah 60:4.
20. Psalm 72:11–18.

[LIX] Prophecies [6]

735
Captivity of the Jews without return

Jeremiah 11:11: *I will visit upon Juda evils from which they shall not be able to escape.*

Figures

The Lord had a vineyard and was waiting for its grapes, it produced nothing but sour grapes. "Thus I will disperse and destroy it. The earth will only give thorns, and I will prevent the heavens from [raining down]."[1]

Isaiah 5:7: For the vineyard of the Lord of hosts is the house of Israel: and the men of Juda, its delectable seed. And I looked that they should do acts of justice, and behold they yield only iniquity.

Isaiah 8:[2]

Sanctify the Lord with fear and trembling. Fear him alone and you will be sanctified. He will be a stone of scandal and a stone of stumbling unto the two houses of Israel. He will be for a snare and a ruin to the inhabitants of Jerusalem. And many of them will stumble upon it, fall upon it, be broken in pieces upon it, and shall be snared and shall perish.

Veil my words and seal my law for my disciples.

I will wait in patience for the Lord, who veils himself and hides from the house of Jacob.

Isaiah 29:[3] *Be bewildered and astonished, nation of Israel, and wander, waver, and stagger: be drunk, and not with wine: stagger, and not with drunkenness. For the Lord hath mingled for you the spirit of a deep sleep, he will shut up your eyes, he will cover your prophets and princes, that see visions.*

---

1. Synopsis of Isaiah 5, verses 1 to 6.
2. Isaiah 8:13–17. Pascal cites only in part.
3. Isaiah 29:9–14, broken by two marginal additions: Daniel 12:10 and Hosea 14:10.

—Daniel 12: *none of the wicked shall understand, but the learned shall understand.*

———

—Hosea, last chapter, last verse, after many temporal blessings says: *Where is the wise man, and he shall understand these things?* etc.

And the visions of all the prophets shall be unto you as the words of a book that is sealed, which when they shall deliver to one that is learned and that could read it: he shall answer: "I cannot read it, for it is sealed." And when the book shall be given to those that know no letters, they shall answer: "I know no letters."

And the Lord said to me: "Forasmuch as this people honor me with their mouth, and with their lips glorify me, but their heart is far from me, and they have served me with doctrines of men: (and thus the reason and the cause of it; had they but worshipped God with their hearts, they would have understood the prophecies).

Therefore behold I will proceed to cause an admiration in this people, by a great and wonderful miracle: for wisdom shall perish from their wise men, and their understanding shall be hid.

Prophecies proving the divinity

Isaiah 41:[4]

If ye are gods, come, and tell us the things that are to come, and we will set our heart upon your words. Tell us the things that were at the beginning, and tell us the things that are to come.

Thus we shall know that ye are gods. Do ye also good or evil, if you can: and let us see, and reason together.

Behold, you are of nothing, you are nothing but an abomination, etc. Who among you teaches (through contemporary authors) *us the things that were from the beginning and from time of old, that we may say: "Thou art just."*[5]

———

Isaiah 42:[6] *I who am the Lord will not give my glory to another. I had the things that are come foretold: and new things do I declare: before they spring forth. Sing ye to the Lord a new song throughout the earth.*

———

Isaiah 43:[7] *Bring forth the people that are blind, and have eyes: that are deaf, and have ears. Let all the nations be assembled together: who among them and their gods can make us hear the former things and the things that are to come?*

4. Isaiah 41:21–26.
5. Pascal cites loosely from Isaiah 41, verses 21–24 and 26.
6. Isaiah 42:8–10.
7. Free translation of Isaiah 43, verses 8 to 27.

let them bring forth their witnesses, let them be justified! Or let them hear, and say: It is truth.

You are my witnesses, saith the Lord, and my servant whom I have chosen: that you may know, and believe me, and understand that I myself am.

I have foretold, I have saved. I have by my own power produced all these wonders in your sight. You are my witnesses, saith the Lord, and I am God.

For your sake I brought down all the Babylonians' forces. I sanctified you and I created you.

I made a way and a path for you in the middle of the sea and the mighty waters and I brought down forever the powerful enemies that resisted you.

But remember not former things, and look not on things of old.

Behold I do new things, and now they shall spring forth, verily you shall know them: I will make deserts places to live and places of delights.

This people have I formed for myself, I have established them that they shew forth my praise.

But I am he that blot out thy iniquities for my own sake, and I will not remember thy sins. As for thyself, put thyself in remembrance of all thy ingratitude, and see whether thou hast any thing to justify thyself.

Thy first father sinned, and thy teachers have transgressed against me.

Isaiah 44:[8] "I am the First, and I am the Last. Who is like to me? let him set before me the order of things since I appointed the ancient people: and let them shew unto them the things to come. Fear ye not. have I not made thee to understand all these things? You are my witnesses."

Cyrus's prediction

For the sake of Jacob, my elect, I have even called thee by thy name.[9]

Isaiah 45:21: Come, and let us consult together: who hath declared this from the beginning? Who hath foretold this from that time? Have not I, who am the Lord?

Isaiah 46:[10] Remember the former age, and know that there is nothing that is like to me, who shew from the beginning the things that shall be at last, and from the origin of the world. My counsel shall stand, and all my will shall be done.

8. Isaiah 44:6–8.
9. Isaiah 45:4.
10. Isaiah 46:9–10.

Isaiah 42:9: *The things that were first, behold they are come in the manner they had been foretold: and new things do I foretell, and I declare them before they spring forth.*

Isaiah 48:3:[11] *The former things I have made to be foretold and then I did them, and then they came to pass in the manner I had declared, for I knew that thou art stubborn, and thy spirit rebellious, and thy forehead shameless. Therefore, I foretold thee of old, before they came to pass, lest thou shouldst say that these things were the work of thy gods and the effect of their order.*

You see now all the things which were foretold come to pass: will you not declare them? Now I declare new things which are kept in my power and which thou knowest not: they are created only now, and not of old. I kept them hidden from thee, lest thou shouldst boast of having foretold them by thy own power.

Thou hast neither heard, nor known, neither was thy ear opened of old. For I know thou art full of transgressions, and I have called thee a transgressor from the first moments of thy birth.

Rejection of the Jews and conversion of the Gentiles

Isaiah 65:[12]

They have sought me that before asked not for me, they have found me that sought me not. I said: Behold me, behold me, to a nation that did not call upon my name.

I have spread forth my hands all the day to an unbelieving people, who walk in a way that is not good after their own thoughts. A people that continually provoke me to anger by the evil they did before my face, who betook themselves to sacrifice to idols, etc.

Those will be dissipated in smoke on the day of my wrath, etc.

I will gather your iniquities, and the iniquities of your fathers together, and I will give back to you according to your works.

Thus saith the Lord: "For the sake of my servants I will not destroy the whole of Israel, but I will set aside a few, as one sets aside a grain found in a cluster, of which it is said: 'Destroy it not, because it is a blessing.'

And I will bring forth a seed out of Jacob, and out of Judah a possessor of my mountains that my elect and my servants shall inherit it, as they shall my fertile and incredibly plentiful lands.

---

11. Isaiah 48:3–18.
12. Isaiah 65:1–19 and 24–25.

But I shall slay all the others, because I called and you did not answer: I spoke, and you did not hear, and you have chosen the things I had forbidden.

Therefore thus saith the Lord God: Behold my servants shall eat, and you shall be hungry. Behold my servants shall rejoice, and you shall be confounded: behold my servants shall praise for joyfulness of heart, and you shall cry for sorrow of heart, and shall howl for grief of spirit.

And you shall leave your name for an execration to my elect: and the Lord God shall slay thee, and call his servants by another name, in which he that is blessed upon the earth, shall be blessed in God, etc.

Because the former distresses are forgotten.

For behold I create new heavens, and a new earth: and the former things shall not be in remembrance, and they shall not come upon the heart.

But you shall be glad and rejoice forever in these things, which I create: for behold I create Jerusalem a rejoicing, and the people thereof joy. And I will rejoice in Jerusalem, and in my people, and the voice of weeping shall no more be heard in her, nor the voice of crying.

And it shall come to pass, that before he calls, I will grant his prayer; as they are only beginning to speak, I will hear. The wolf and the lamb shall feed together; the lion and the ox shall eat the same straw; and dust shall be the serpent's food: they shall not hurt nor kill in all my holy mountain."

Isaiah 56:[13]

(Thus saith the Lord: "Keep ye judgment, and do justice: for my salvation is near to come, and my justice to be revealed.

Blessed is the man that doth this, and the son of man that shall lay hold on this: that keepeth the Sabbath from profaning it and keepeth his hands from doing any evil.)

And let not the son of the stranger that adhereth to the Lord speak, saying: "The Lord will divide and separate me from his people."

For thus saith the Lord to the eunuchs, "They that shall keep my Sabbaths, and shall choose the things that please me, and shall hold fast my covenant: I will give to them in my house, a place, and a name better than the name I gave my children: I will give them an everlasting name which shall never perish."

[Isaiah 59:9–11]

Because of our crimes is justice gone away from us. We looked for light, and behold darkness: brightness and we have walked in the dark.

We have groped for the wall, and like the blind we have groped as if we had no

13. Isaiah 56:1–5.

eyes: we have stumbled at noonday as in darkness; we are in dark places as dead men.

We shall roar all of us like bears, and shall lament as mournful doves. We have looked for judgment, and there is none: for salvation, and it is far from us.

Isaiah 66:18:

But I know their works, and their thoughts, when I come that I may gather them together with all nations and tongues. And they shall see my glory.

And I will set a sign among them, and I will send of them that shall be saved, to the nations: into Africa, into Lydia, into Italy, into Greece, and to them that have not heard of me, and have not seen my glory. And they shall declare my glory to the Gentiles: And they shall bring all your brethren.

Jeremiah 7:[14] Reprobation of the Temple.

Go ye to my place in Silo, where my name dwelt from the beginning: and see what I did to it for the wickedness of my people (for I have rejected them and made a temple elsewhere).

And now, saith the Lord because you have done the same evil works, I will do to this temple, in which my name is called upon, and in which you trust, and to the places that I myself have given your fathers, as I did to Silo.

And I will cast you away from before my face, as I have cast away all your brethren, the whole seed of Ephraim (rejected definitively).

Therefore, do not thou pray for this people.

———

Jeremiah 7:22: *For what use is it to you to make sacrifice upon sacrifice? For I spoke not to your fathers, and I commanded them not, in the day that I brought them out of the land of Egypt, concerning the matter of burnt offerings and sacrifices. But this thing I commanded them, saying: Hearken obediently and faithfully to my commandment, and I will be your God, and you shall be my people* (it was only after they had sacrificed to the golden calf that I ordained sacrifices to me, in order to sanctify a bad tradition).

———

Jeremiah 7:[15] *Trust not in the lying words of those who say to you: The temple of the Lord, the temple of the Lord, they are the temple of the Lord.*

14. Jeremiah 7:12–16.
15. Jeremiah 7:4. See fr. 697.

[LX] Prophecies, Jews, Corruption[1]

736

Corrupt nature

Man does not act with his reason, the thing that defines his being.

We have no other king save Caesar.[2]

Jews as God's witnesses: Isaiah 43:9, 44:8.

It is obviously a people created specifically to act as witnesses to the Messiah: Isaiah 43:9, 44:8. They possess the books, and love them yet do not understand them.

And all of this is foretold: that God's judgments are entrusted to them, but as a sealed book.[3]

Harden their hearts.[4] And how? By flattering their concupiscence and making them hope to satisfy it.

The sincerity of the Jews

Since the time that they have no more prophets: Maccabees.

Since Jesus Christ, Masoretes.[5]

This book shall be in the latter days for a testimony.[6]

The defective and final letters.[7]

---

1. In this short chapter, Pascal gathers the texts and ideas he will use as one of cornerstones of the Apology. The Jews, dispersed throughout the world, prepare the advent of the Gospels by carrying a "sealed book" (the Old Testament) whose prophetic meaning they fail to understand. Had the Jews been saved and not scattered as hostile witnesses, Christianity might not have survived the arguments of its detractors. Ironically, the Jews had to reject Christ. Their fate had been a part of God's plan to save his elect since the beginning of time. The hardening of their hearts was an inevitable consequence.

2. John 19:15. See fr. 372.

3. Isaiah 29:11. A fundamental theme developed fully in ch. XX, "That the Law Was Figurative."

4. Isaiah 6:10 and John 12:40.

5. Masoretes. See ch. I, n. 4.

6. Isaiah 30:8.

7. On the defective letters, see ch. XX, fr. 303, n. 59.

Sincere against their honor, and dying for this, is without any precedent in the world and is not rooted in nature.[8]

Prophecy

And you shall leave your name for an execration to my elect and I will call them by another name.[9]

Fulfilled prophecies

3 Kings 13:2.
4 Kings 23:16.

Joshua 6:26.
3 Kings 16:34.

Deuteronomy 33.

Malachi 1:11: The sacrifice of the Jews rejected,[10] and the sacrifice of the heathen (even outside of Jerusalem), and everywhere.

Moses foretells the calling of the Gentiles before dying: 32:21, and the rejection of the Jews.[11]

Moses foretells what will happen to each tribe.

Prophecy

Amos and Zechariah:[12] They have sold the righteous one, and for that they will never be called again.

Jesus Christ betrayed.

There will be no more memory of Egypt: see Isaiah 43:16–17–18–19; Jeremiah 23:6–7.

---

8. See fr. 692, "Sincerity of the Jews." The Jews stubbornly defend and even die for the very Old Testament texts that condemn them. For Pascal, this unprecedented phenomenon, contrary to human nature, has been ordained by God as a powerful clue to the truth of the Christian revelation. The Jews serve as hostile witnesses to the historicity and authenticity of the Old Testament against those who would argue that the Old Testament prophecies had been confected by the Christians. Even the unbelievers are obliged to acknowledge that they cannot explain the singularity of this contradictory "sincerity."

9. Isaiah 65:16, already cited at length in fr. 735.

10. Christ's sacrifice on the cross abrogates the sacrifices of the Temple, doomed to destruction in 70 CE, void. See Hebrews 9.

11. At the end of Deuteronomy.

12. Zechariah 11:12.

Prophecy

The Jews will be dispersed everywhere: Isaiah 27.

New law: Jeremiah 32:32.

The second glorious temple, Jesus Christ will go to it: Haggai 2:7–8–9–10; Malachi—Grotius.[13]

Vocation of the Gentiles: Joel 2:28; Hosea 2:24; Deuteronomy 32:21; Malachi 1:11.

What man was ever shown with more splendor?

The entire Jewish people foretell him before his coming.

The Gentiles adore him after his coming.

These two peoples, Gentile and Jew, consider him as their center.

And yet, which man ever enjoyed less such splendor?

He lived for thirty of his thirty-three years without showing who he was. During those three years, he is treated as an impostor, the priests and leaders reject him, his friends and those closest to him despise him, and finally he dies betrayed by one of his own, denied by another, and abandoned by everyone.

What part therefore does he have in this splendor? Never has a man had so much splendor; never has a man suffered so much ignominy. All of this splendor was only for us, to make him recognizable to us, and not for his own sake.[14]

---

13. Malachi 3:1–5, cited by Grotius, *The Truth of the Christian Religion* (1627), V, 14, interpreting the prophecy of *Haggai*.

14. See the theme of the Three Orders, fr. 339. From the perspective of the first order, Christ's hidden life for thirty-three years reflects the doctrine of the *Deus absconditus*. Only the elect were able to penetrate this veil to see him in the "splendor" of the third order, holiness.

[LXI] Law Was Figurative[1]

737

Figures

In order to show that the Old Testament is—is only—figurative and that the prophets meant other goods when they said temporal goods, to wit: (1) it would be unworthy of God; (2) their discourses promise temporal goods very clearly and yet they say that their discourses are obscure and their meaning will not be understood. Thus it is clear that the secret meaning is not what they were saying overtly and therefore they meant other sacrifices, another Liberator, etc. They say that it will be understood only at the end of time: Jeremiah [30], final verse.[2]

The second[3] proof is that their discourses are in opposition to each other and obliterate each other. Thus if you assume that when they said law and sacrifice they only meant those of Moses, the contradiction is clear and plain. Therefore they meant something else, since they sometimes contradicted themselves even in the same chapter.

Now in order to understand the meaning of an author[4]...

Beautiful to see, with the eyes of faith, the story of Herod, of Caesar.[5]

738

Reasons for the figures

R. (*they had to address a carnal people and make them the depositary of the spiritual testament.*)

1. See ch. XX, "That the Law Was Figurative." In spite of its many affiliations with that titled chapter, it is difficult to say whether the chapter is a redraft of ch. XX, its preliminary draft, or a completely independent document.
2. In fact, the last verse of chapter 30.
3. Initially the second. The present first was added in the margin.
4. Echo of fr. 289: "...one must reconcile all the contrary passages."
5. Augustus, under whom Christ was born. See fr. 348: "How beautiful it is to see with the eyes of faith, Darius and Cyrus. Alexander, the Romans, Pompey and Herod act without knowing it to the glory of the Gospel." The great of the world are but pawns in the divine plan of salvation. According to the prophecies, four great empires had to succeed one another before the Messiah could arrive. See ch. XXIV, n. 34 ("four monarchies").

In order to inspire faith in the Messiah, it was necessary that there should be prophecies beforehand, conveyed by people who were not suspect and also were diligent, faithful, and fervent in a way that was extraordinary and known throughout the earth.

In order to bring this about, God chose this carnal people, and he entrusted them with the prophecies that foretell the Messiah as liberator and giver of the carnal goods that this people loved.

Thus they were extraordinarily enthusiastic about their own prophets and they brought the books that foretold their Messiah to the attention of the entire world. They assured all the nations that he was to come, and in the way foretold in the books they displayed openly for everybody. Thus this people, disappointed as they were by the humble and poor advent of the Messiah, became his bitterest enemies. So much so that they are the people in the whole world who are the least suspect of having a bias in our favor, and also the most rigorous and fervent imaginable regarding his law and his prophets, which they carry unaltered.

So that those who rejected and crucified Christ because he was a scandal to them are those who carry the books that testify about him and say that he will be rejected and a scandal. So that they showed it was him by refusing him, and he was proven both by the righteous Jews who accepted him and the unjust ones who rejected him, both cases having been predicted.

Thus the prophecies have a hidden meaning, the spiritual one, to which this people was hostile, under the carnal, which they welcomed. Had the spiritual meaning been in the open, they would have been unable to love it; thus, being unable to bear it, they would have had no zeal for the preservation of their books and ceremonies. On the other hand, had they loved the spiritual promises and kept them unaltered until the Messiah, their testimony would carry no strength, because it would come from a friendly source.

For that reason, it was good that the spiritual meaning should be veiled. On the other hand, if the meaning had been so hidden as to disappear entirely, it could not have proved the Messiah. What was done then? It was veiled under the temporal meaning in the vast majority of passages, and it was revealed very clearly in some, in addition to the fact that the time and the state of the world were foretold in a way that is clearer than daylight. The spiritual meaning is so clearly stated in some places that in order not to see it, one had to have the sort of blindness that comes to the spirit when it is ruled by the flesh.

This is how God proceeded: the meaning is veiled by another meaning in countless places, and revealed rarely in some, but in such a way that the places where it is hidden are equivocal and can be read both ways, while the places where it is revealed are unambiguous and can be read only spiritually.

Therefore there was no occasion to be mistaken and only a people as carnal as they were could misunderstand.

When goods are promised in abundance, what prevented them from understanding the true nature of these goods, other than their cupidity, which interpreted the promise as referring to earthly goods?

But those who saw their only good in God referred them to God alone.

For the human will is comprised of two principles: cupidity and charity. I do not mean that cupidity cannot be associated with faith in God, and that charity cannot be associated with earthly goods. But cupidity uses God and enjoys the world, while charity does the reverse.[6]

Now the ultimate end is what gives things their names.

All that stands in the way of its accomplishment is called an enemy.

Thus creatures, albeit good, are enemies of the righteous when they distract them from God. And God himself is the enemy of those whose greed he disrupts.

Thus, depending on the ultimate end, the righteous understood the word *enemy* as referring to their passions, and the carnal ones referred it to the Babylonians. Thus those terms were obscure only for the unjust. That is what Isaiah says: seal the law among my disciples.[7] Also that Jesus Christ will be a *stumbling block* but *Blessed is he that shall not be scandalized*[8] by him.

Hosea, last verse,[9] says it perfectly: *"Who is wise? and he shall understand these things. The just shall understand them, for the ways of the Lord are right: but the transgressors shall fall in them."*

At the same time, this testament made to blind the ones and enlighten the others revealed in the very people that were being blinded the truth that was to be known to others. Since the visible goods they received from God were so great and divine, it was apparent that it was in his power to give the invisible goods and a Messiah.

Because nature is an image of grace, and visible miracles are images of invisible ones: *But that you may know, I say to thee: "Arise."*[10]

Isaiah 51 says that redemption will be like the crossing of the Red Sea.[11]

Thus, God has shown, in the escape from Egypt, and from the sea, in the

---

6. The opposition between *uti* (to use) and *frui* (to enjoy) runs through Augustine's works. "To enjoy a reality means to be attached to it lovingly and for its own sake. To use it means to refer what one uses to what one loves and craves" (*On Christian Doctrine,* I, 4, n. 4).

7. Isaiah 8:16.

8. Matthew 11:6.

9. Hosea 14:10: *"Who is wise, and he shall understand these things?* prudent, *and he shall know these things? for the ways of the Lord are right, and the just shall walk in them: but the transgressors shall fall in them."*

10. Mark 2:10–11. See fr. 306.

11. See fr. 306.

defeat of the kings, in the manna and all the genealogy of Abraham, that he was able to save, to rain down the bread from heaven, etc., in such a way that this hostile people is the figure and representation of the very Messiah they fail to recognize.

He taught us at last that all those things were but figures, and the true meaning of *Truly free, True Israelite, True circumcision, True bread from heaven,*[12] etc.

In those promises, each finds what he has in the bottom of his heart: temporal goods or spiritual goods, God or creatures. The difference is that those who look for creatures find them, but with several contradictions, such as the prohibition to love them, and the command to worship only God and to love only him—which are one and the same—and finally that no Messiah has come for them. On the other hand, those who look for God in the prophecies find him, without any contradiction, with the command to love only him and that a Messiah came at the time foretold to give them the goods they were asking for.

Thus the Jews had miracles, and prophecies they saw being accomplished. And the doctrine of their law was to worship and love God alone; it was also perpetual. Thus it had all the signs of the true religion: and it was true indeed. But we must distinguish between the doctrine of the Jews and the doctrine of the law of the Jews.[13] The doctrine of the Jews was not true, even though it had miracles, prophecies, and perpetuity, because it lacked this other point, which is to worship and love God only.

Kirkerus[14]—Usserius.[15]

12. See frs. 285 and 299.
13. See fr. 276: "The Jewish religion must be viewed differently in the tradition of their saints and in the tradition of the people."
14. Konrad Kircher, German pastor and philologist, author of the *Greco-Hebraic Concordances of the Old Testament* (1607).
15. James Usher was the Anglican archbishop of Armagh and author of *The Annals of the World* (1650) and a *Sacred Chronology* (1660). Both chronologists counted backwards through the generations of scripture and arrived at the conclusion that the world was created just over six thousand years before their time. French chronologists known at Port-Royal had reached more or less the same conclusion. No notion of deep time would begin to enter human consciousness until the end of the nineteenth century.

Fragments Not Recorded in the Second Copy

1. Edition of 1678[1]

739

Men often mistake their imagination for their hearts: and they believe they have been converted as soon as they start thinking about conversion.

740

The last thing you discover when you write a book is knowing what you should put first.

---

1. The date of the second edition of the *Pensées*, based closely on the *Edition of Port-Royal* (1670).

2. Autograph Fragment Attached
to the First Copy

741[1]

For, although about two thousand years had elapsed since they had occurred, the small number of generations that had intervened meant that they were as fresh to the men who lived in those times as those which took place about three hundred years ago are currently to us. This is a result of the longevity of the first men. So that Sem, who saw Lamech, and so on.

This proof is enough to convince reasonable people of the truth of the Flood and the Creation. And that in turn shows the providence of God, who, seeing that the Creation was beginning to fade into the distance, supplied a historian who may be described as contemporary, and committed an entire nation to safeguarding his book.

And what is also remarkable is that this book has been unanimously adopted without any argument, not only by the whole Jewish people, but also by all the kings and peoples of the earth, who have accorded it a quite special respect and veneration.

1. This fragment, hastily set down on a page torn out of a book and written in Pascal's own hand, was inserted into the First Copy as a kind of ornament, perhaps after the 1678 edition. The pages between which it was inserted corresponded to the *liasse* titled, "Proofs of Moses." The unfinished sentence "... Sem, qui a vu Lamech ..." refers back to fr. 327 and the argument that the longevity of the patriarchs made them quasi contemporaries of the Creation and Fall and unimpeachable in their historical testimony.

3. The Périer Manuscript

742

[THE MEMORIAL][1]

The year of grace 1654

Monday November 23, Feast of Saint Clement, pope and martyr, and others of the martyrology.[2]

Eve of Saint Chrysogonus, martyr, and others.

From about half-past ten in the evening to half-past midnight.

Fire

God of Abraham, God of Isaac, God of Jacob,[3]

not of philosophers and scholars.

Certainty, certainty, sensation, joy, peace.[4]

God of Jesus Christ.

Deum meum et Deum vestrum.[5]

Thy God will be my God.[6]

---

1. Upon Pascal's death, a small folded piece of parchment, containing another sheet of paper was found sewn into the lining of his coat—over his heart, according to tradition. On each of these two papers there figured more or less the same text, autographs containing traces of an intense religious experience. Gilberte Périer, Pascal's sister, treated what she called the "Memorial" almost as a true relic. For the last eight years of his life, Pascal had taken meticulous care to un-sew and sew in again the papers every time he changed clothes. The autograph on the parchment has been lost, but around 1692 Louis Périer made a copy of it, which preserves the disposition of the text upon the parchment, and inserted it into the beginning of the Original Collection. This document is referred to hereafter by the initial "P." There has been endless speculation about the nature of the *tremendum* that Pascal experienced (what made him tremble). The authoritative analysis forms an entire long chapter in Henri Gouhier's *Commentaires*.

2. Pascal's reference is to the *Martyrologium Romanum*, a universal martyrology drawn up by Cardinal Baronius under Pope Gregory XIII in the 1580s and published in constant reeditions throughout the seventeenth century. Pascal opens and closes the "P." variant with a cross surrounded by rays.

3. Exodus 3:6. In the theophany of the burning bush, God reveals himself to Moses: ". . . I am the God of Abraham, the God of Isaac, and the God of Jacob." See fr. 690, par. 26.

4. P.: "Certainty, joy, certainty, sensation, sight, joy."

5. John 20:17 (the reference is given in P.). After his resurrection, Jesus appears to Mary Magdalene: ". . . go to my brethren, and say to them: I ascend to my Father and to your Father, to *my God and your God*" (Quoted in Latin by Pascal).

6. Ruth 1:16 (reference partially given in P.): Ruth, the foreigner, turns away from her people's idols and adheres to the God of Israel, the God of her mother-in-law Noemi.

Oblivion of the world and of everything, except God.
He can only be found in the ways taught by the Gospel.

Greatness of the human soul.
Just Father, the world hath not known Thee; but I have known Thee.[7]
Joy, joy, joy, tears of joy.[8]
I have separated myself from him. _____
Derelinquerunt me fontem aquae vivae.[9]
My God, will you forsake me? _____
May I not be eternally separated from him.

_____

This is eternal life, that they know you as the only true God and him you have sent, Jesus Christ.[10]

Jesus Christ _____

Jesus Christ
I separated myself from him, fled, renounced, crucified Him. _____
May I never be separated from him![11]
He can only be kept by the ways taught in the Gospel.
Total, effortless renunciation.
etc.[12]

743

It is in the nature of self-love and of this human ego to love only itself and to care only for itself. But how is it to proceed? It cannot help the fact that the very same object that it loves is full of failings and inadequacies; it wants to be great, but sees that it is small; it wants to be happy, but sees that it is wretched; it wants to be perfect, but sees that it is full of imperfection; it wants to be the object of the love and respect of men, but sees that its failings only warrant

7. John 17:25 (reference partially given in the parchment). The "priestly" prayer of Jesus to the Father, after the Last Supper.

8. P. ". . . joy and tears of joy."

9. Jeremiah 2:13. God complains of the children of Israel: "*They have forsaken me, the fountain of living water.*" P. Omits "living water."

10. John 17:3. Omitted by P.

11. The last words of Pascal, according to the *Life of M. Pascal* written by his sister Gilberte Périer: "May God never abandon me!" See Psalm 26:15, 27–29, and Matthew 27:46.

12. In place of "etc." there appeared three lines on the parchment (P): "Total submission to Jesus Christ and to my director [M. Singlin]. Eternally in joy for one day of exertion on earth. *Non obliviscar sermones tuos* ("May your words always be kept in mind")."

their aversion and their scorn. This dilemma in which it finds itself gives rise to the most unjust and criminal of passions that it is possible to imagine; for it conceives a mortal hatred for the very truth that censures it, and that accuses it of its failings. It would like to annihilate the truth, but, not being able to destroy it in its essence, it destroys it, as far as it can, in the knowledge that it has of itself and that others have of it; in other words, it puts all its efforts into concealing its failings from itself and from others, and cannot bear to have them noticed or pointed out.

It is no doubt a bad thing to be full of failings; but it is a worse thing still to be full of failings and yet not be prepared to acknowledge them, since it adds a supplementary failing in the form of a self-induced illusion. We do not want others to deceive us; and we do not think it fair that they should be accorded more respect by us than they deserve. It is therefore equally unjust if we deceive them and if we wish them to respect us more than we deserve.

So when they find in us only those imperfections and vices that are indeed our own, it is evident that they do us no wrong, since *they* are not the cause of them; rather they are doing us a good deed, since they help us rid ourselves of an ill, in the form of our own ignorance of these imperfections. We must not be angry if they recognize them and despise us for them, since it is right both that they know us for what we are, and that they despise us, if we are despicable.

Such are the feelings that would arise in a heart that was filled with equity and justice. But what can we say of our own hearts, seeing that their disposition is quite the opposite? For is it not true that we hate both the truth and those who speak it to us, that we love them to be mistaken if it is to our advantage, and that we want to be considered by them as being different from what we are in reality?

Here is a proof of it that fills me with horror. The Catholic religion does not require anyone to reveal his sins to one and all with no distinction. It allows people to remain hidden from all other men; but it makes one sole exception, to whom it demands that the depths of one's heart be revealed, so as to be seen as one really is. There is just this single man in the whole world whom it asks us to undeceive, and it commits him to an inviolable secrecy, so that this knowledge is kept within him as if it were not there. Could anything more charitable or more accommodating be imagined? And yet the corruption of man is such that he still sees hardship in this law; and that is one of the principal reasons that has driven a substantial part of Europe into revolt against the Church.[13]

13. The reformed churches' refusal to recognize the sacrament of penance is alleged to have contributed substantially to the success of Protestantism in Europe. Luther, however, continued to recognize penance

How unjust and unreasonable the heart of man is, to resent being asked to do for one man what it would be just, in some respects, to expect it to do for all men! For is it right for us to deceive them?

There are different degrees of this aversion to the truth; but it can be said that it is present in all of us to some degree, because it is inseparable from self-love. It is this false delicacy that drives those who are required to censure others to opt for so many roundabout approaches and accommodations to avoid offending them. They have to make light of our failings, to seem to excuse them, to temper them with praise and with signs of affection and esteem. Even then, this medicine is still a bitter one for self-love to swallow. It takes as little of it as it can, always with distaste, and often indeed with a secret resentment of those who administer it.

It follows from this that, if someone has a vested interest in being liked by us, that person turns away from doing us a service they know we will find unpleasant. People treat us as we want to be treated: we hate the truth, and so it is hidden from us; we wish to be flattered and so we are flattered; we like to be deceived and so we are deceived.

That is why each and every step that makes us rise in the world takes us further away from the truth, because one is more wary of offending those whose affection is more useful and whose aversion is more dangerous. A ruler might be the talk of all Europe, and yet will be the only one unaware of it. It does not surprise me: speaking the truth is useful for him to whom it is spoken, but disadvantageous to those who speak it, because they bring hatred upon themselves. Now, those who live with sovereigns prefer their own interests to those of the sovereign whom they serve; and therefore they take care not to do them a favor so detrimental to themselves.

This misfortune is no doubt greater and more widespread in those in the most exalted positions; but those less exalted positions are not exempt, because there is always something to be gained by making oneself liked by men. So human life is but a perpetual illusion; we just spend our time deceiving and flattering each other. Nobody speaks about us in our presence as he does in our absence. The union that exists between men is based on this mutual deception; and few friendships would survive if everyone knew what his friend said of him when he was not there, even though he spoke on such occasions sincerely and dispassionately.

Man is then nothing but dissimulation, lying, and hypocrisy, with respect both to himself and to others. He therefore does not want to be told the truth.

---

as a sacrament and the practice has persisted in one form or another until the present day in many Lutheran churches.

He avoids telling other people the truth. And all these tendencies, as far removed as they are from justice and reason, are rooted naturally in his heart.

744[14]

Every time the Jesuits deceive the pope, the whole of Christendom will be guilty of perjury.

The pope is easily deceived because of his many concerns and because of the belief he has in the Jesuits. And the Jesuits are very capable of deceiving people because of their calumny.

745

On the strength of the rumor about the Feuillants,[15] I went to see him, my old friend said.[16] He thought that, when speaking of devotion, I had some feeling for it, and that I might well be a Feuillant.

And that I might fruitfully write, particularly at the present time, against innovators.

We moved a little while ago against our chapter general, which decreed that we should sign the bull.[17]

That he wished that God would inspire me.

Father, should I sign?

746

3.

If they[18] do not give up probability, their good axioms are as unholy as their bad ones, since they are founded on human authority. And therefore, if these axioms are more just, they will be more reasonable, but not more holy: they take after the wild stem onto which they are grafted.

If what I say does not serve to enlighten you,[19] it will be of use to the public.

---

14. Here begins a group of unpublished *pensées* constituted under the direction of Louis Périer. Each fragment was assigned a number: 1A, 2B . . . 24Aa, ending with 27 Dd. The number "3" at the top of fr. 746 is a vestige of this numbering.

15. An order of reformed Cistercians.

16. "Old friend": a fictional and anonymous character in the second *Provincial Letter.*

17. The papal bull of May 31, 1653 which condemned the five propositions presented as extracts from Jansenius's *Augustinus.*

18. The Jesuits.

19. Here again, the Jesuits.

If they remain silent, the stones will speak.[20]

Silence is the greatest of persecutions. The saints were never silent. It is true that you need a vocation, but it is not from the decrees of the council that you must learn whether you are called, but rather from the need to speak. Now since Rome has spoken, and people think that it has condemned the truth and that they have written it, and since those books that said the opposite have been censured, we must shout all the louder that we are censured all the more unjustly, and that they are trying to stifle speech all the more violently, until a pope arrives who listens to the two sides and who consults antiquity in order to administer justice.

Thus, the good popes will find that the Church is still in an uproar.

The hope that Christians have of possessing an infinite good is mingled with actual enjoyment as it is with fear. For it is not like those who might hope for a kingdom in which they would possess nothing, because they are subjects; rather they hope for holiness, freedom from injustice; and they have some part of these things.

The Inquisition[21] and the Society: twin scourges of the truth.

Why do you not accuse them of Arianism?[22] For if they have said that Jesus Christ is God, perhaps they do not understand it as meaning by his nature, but as it is said: *You are gods.*[23]

If my *Letters* are condemned in Rome,[24] what I condemn in them is condemned in heaven.

Lord Jesus I appeal to thy tribunal.[25]

You are yourselves corruptible.

------

20. Luke 19:40. Jesus replies to the Pharisees' demand that he silence his disciples: "I say to you, that if these shall hold their peace, *the stones will cry out.*"

21. An attack on the Inquisition developed in a text of June 1, 1657, on which Pascal collaborated: *Lettre d'un avocat au Parlement touchant l'inquisistion qu'on veut établir en France à l'occasion de la nouvelle bulle du pape Alexandre VII* [Letter from a Solicitor at the Parliament to one of his friends, concerning the Inquisition that some want to establish in France on the occasion of the new bull of Pope Alexander VII].

22. See ch. XXII, n. 12.

23. Psalm 82:6: "I have said: You are gods and all of you the sons of the Most High."

24. The *Provincial Letters* were placed on the index on September 6, 1657.

25. Saint Bernard in a letter to his cousin Robert.

I was afraid that I might have written badly, since I was condemned, but the example of so many pious books leads me to believe the opposite. It is no longer permitted to write well.

Such is the corruption or ignorance of the Inquisition.

We ought to obey God, rather than men.[26]

I fear nothing, I expect nothing.[27] It is not so for the bishops. Port-Royal is afraid, but it is bad policy to isolate them, since they will no longer be afraid but will make themselves more feared.

I do not even fear your censures, which are just straw if they are not founded on tradition.

Do you censure everything? What! Even my respect? No. So, say what you censure, or you will achieve nothing, if you do not identify the wrong-doing, and say why it is wrong. And that is what they will have a good deal of difficulty doing.

Probability

They have given a fine explanation of certainty, indeed. For having established that all their ways are certain, they did not call *certain* what leads to heaven, with no risk of not arriving there by following it, but rather what leads there without any danger of straying from their way.

747[28]

Reverend Father[29]

If I have given you some displeasure in my other *Letters* by demonstrating the innocence of those whom you were anxious to besmirch, I will give you cause for rejoicing in this one, by disclosing the pain with which you have filled them. Take comfort, Father, those whom you hate are afflicted. And if our lord bishops act in their dioceses upon the advice that you give them to compel people to swear and to sign to the effect that they believe something

---

26. Acts 5:29.

27. Theme anticipated in the seventeenth *Provincial Letter*.

28. The Périer manuscript reproduces only the marginal notes related to the beginning of the nineteenth *Provincial Letter* (from the end of May 1657). The beginning of the letter was bound among other documents after the Second Copy. It would not make sense not to include the text along with the notes, which start with: "If the Jesuits . . ."

29. The Jesuit Fr. Annat, confessor to Louis XIV.

to be factually true[30] that they do not honestly believe and that they are not obliged to believe, you will reduce your adversaries to the very depths of despair on seeing the Church in such a state. I have seen them, Father, and I confess that I derived the greatest satisfaction from doing so. I did not find them in that state of philosophical nobility of spirit or of stubborn disrespect that makes people follow imperiously what they perceive to be their duty; nor indeed of limp and fearful cowardice that prevents them either from seeing the truth or from following it; but in a state of quiet, robust piety, full of self-questioning, of respect for the Church authorities, of the love of peace, of tenderness and of commitment to the truth, of the desire to know it and defend it, of fear on account of their own infirmity, of regret at having been put to the test in this way, and of hope nonetheless that God will deign to sustain them during it by his light and by his strength, and that the grace of Jesus Christ, that they uphold and on account of which they suffer, will itself be their light and their strength. And I saw in them finally the character of Christian piety, which brings out a strength . . .

I found them surrounded by people known to them, who had also come on this account to persuade them to act for what they believed to be the best in the current state of affairs. I heard the advice they were given. I noted the way in which it was received and the replies that were made. In truth, Father, if you had been present, I think that you would yourself admit that there is nothing in all their actions that is not infinitely far removed from any semblance of revolt and heresy, as everyone will be able to see from the accommodations that they have introduced, and that you will see in evidence here, in order to keep intact those two things that are infinitely dear to them, peace and truth.

For after they were told in general terms about the woes that they will draw upon themselves by their refusal, if they are confronted with this new Constitution to sign, and the scandal to which this will give rise in the Church, they drew attention to. . .

If the Jesuits were corrupt and if it was true that we were alone, that would be all the more reason for us to stay.

The day of judgment.

May that which war has endorsed not be taken away by a false peace.[31]

He is neither moved with blessing nor cursing like an angel of God.[32]

The greatest of Christian virtues, which is the love of truth, is under attack.

---

30. The actual presence of the five propositions in Jansenius's *Augustinus*.

31. Saint Jerome, *Dialogus adversus Pelagianos* [Dialogue against the Pelagians], in J.-P. Migne, ed., Patrologiæ Cursus Completus: Series Latina [henceforth, PL], vol. 23, col. 498.

32. 2 *Kings* 14:17: "For even as *an angel of God*, so is my lord the king, that *he is neither moved with blessing nor cursing.*"

If signing signifies that, let us be allowed to explain it, so that there is no ambiguity: for it has to be acknowledged that many people believe that signing betokens consent.

So that, Father, is what you call the sense of Jansenius![33] So that is what you would have the pope and the bishops believe!

If the reporter did not sign, the ruling would be invalid. If the bull was not signed, it would be valid. So it is not that . . .

You cannot be guilty of not believing something,[34] but you would be guilty of swearing without believing something . . .

Good questions. There . . .

"But perhaps you were wrong?" I swear that I believe that I could have been wrong. But I do not swear that I believe that I was wrong.

I am sorry to say all this to you; I am only telling you what happened.

That, along with Escobar, puts them in the place of honor. But they do not understand it thus, and betray displeasure at seeing themselves between God and the pope . . .

748[35]

The rivers of Babylon flow, and fall, and sweep all away.

O Holy Zion, where all is constant, and where nothing falls!

We must be seated on these rivers, not beneath them or within them, but above them, and not standing, but seated, in order to be humble because we are seated, and in safety because we are above them. But we shall be standing in the hallways of Jerusalem.

See whether this pleasure is constant or fleeting! If it passes, it is a river of Babylon.

---

33. The "sense of Jansenius" is one of several ambiguities. To sign the formulary condemning the five propositions is, for the adversaries of Port-Royal, to condemn Calvin; for Pascal, it is to condemn Saint Augustine. See the eighteenth *Provincial Letter*: "Was this all you meant, then, father? Was it only the error of Calvin that you were so anxious to get condemned, under the name of 'the sense of Jansenius?' Why did you not tell us this sooner? You might have saved yourself a world of trouble; for we were all ready, without the aid of bulls or briefs, to join with you in condemning that error."

34. Something that the pope declares on a point *of fact* (for example, on the presence of the propositions in a book or on the sense its author gave them) cannot be considered infallible. See the seventeenth *Provincial Letter*.

35. Free translation of Saint Augustine's *Commentary* on Psalm 136. See Sellier's enlightening essay (translated into English) on this fragment in *Meaning, Structure and History in the "Pensées" of Pascal*, ed. David Wetsel, Biblio 17 (Tübingen: *Papers on French Seventeenth-Century Literature*, 1990), 33–44.

749
The Mystery of Jesus[36]

In his Passion, Jesus suffers the torments that men inflict on him. But in his agony he suffers the torments that he inflicts on himself. *And troubled himself.*[37] He is not tortured by a human, but by an omnipotent hand. And you have to be omnipotent to endure it.

———

Jesus seeks some consolation, at least from his three dearest friends, and yet they are asleep. He asks them to bear with him a little, and yet they leave him in utter neglect, having so little compassion that it could not even prevent them from sleeping for a moment. And so Jesus was left alone to face the wrath of God.

———

Jesus is alone on earth not only in feeling and in sharing his suffering, but in being aware of it. He shares this knowledge with heaven alone.

———

Jesus is in a garden, not of delights, like the first Adam, where he damned himself and the whole human race, but in a garden of torments, where he saved himself and the whole human race.[38]

———

He endures this suffering and this abandonment in the dread of night.

———

I believe that Jesus only ever complained on this one occasion. But then he complained as if he could no longer contain his excessive suffering: *My soul is sorrowful even unto death.*[39]

———

Jesus looks for company and relief from other men. That is the only time in the whole of his life, it seems to me. But he does not receive either, for his disciples are asleep.

———

Jesus will be in agony until the end of the world. No one should sleep until then.

———

36. The title is not in Pascal's handwriting. At Port-Royal, it was a custom to circulate proposals for meditations on events in the life of Christ. The word "Mystery" points to an event in the life of Jesus, which, over and beyond its concrete realization in history, carries a hidden ("mysterious") significance.

37. John 11:33.

38. The place of agony is the garden of Gethsemane, on the Mount of Olives, contrasted here with the Garden of Eden, that garden of delights ("paradise of pleasure," Genesis 2:15) in which man was placed at the Creation. Jesus Christ is the new Adam, who redeems the fault committed by the first man. See Romans 5:1–21.

39. Matthew 26:38; Mark 14:34.

Jesus, in the midst of this universal abandonment and among the friends he has chosen to stay awake with him, grows angry when he finds them asleep, because of the danger to which they expose not him but themselves, and warns them about their own safety and their own salvation with a heartfelt tenderness for them in spite of their ingratitude, and warns them that *the spirit is willing but the flesh weak.*[40]

Jesus, finding them asleep again, since neither concern for him nor for themselves had held them back from it, has the goodness not to awaken them, and so leaves them to their slumber.

Jesus prays with uncertainty as to the will of the Father, and in fear of death. But once he knows the former, he goes ahead to offer himself up to the latter: *Let us go.*[41] *He went forth.* (John).[42]

Jesus prayed to men and was not heard.

Jesus, while his disciples were sleeping, brought about their salvation.

He did so for all just men while they were asleep and in the nothingness that preceded their birth, and in their sins since they have been born.

He prays only that the chalice might pass away, and then with submission, and twice that it should come if it must.[43]

Jesus in torment.

Jesus, seeing all his friends asleep, and all his enemies vigilant, gives himself over entirely to his Father.

Jesus does not see enmity in Judas, but the order of God, which he loves, and sees so little of his enmity that he calls him his friend.[44]

Jesus tears himself away from his disciples to embark on his agony. We must tear ourselves away from those who are closest and most dear to us, in order to imitate him.

---

40. Matthew 26:41; Mark 14:38.
41. Matthew 26:46; Mark 14:42.
42. John 18:4.
43. Pascal here follows Matthew 26:39–44.
44. These two verses refer to Matthew 26:42 and 50.

Since Jesus is in agony and in the greatest suffering, let us spend longer in prayer. [45]

750

We[46] have not ourselves been able to have general maxims. If you look at our *Constitutions*[47] you will hardly recognize us: they make us out to be beggars, excluded from courts, and yet, etc. But this is not a violation of them, since the glory of God is everywhere.[48]

There are different ways to attain it. Saint Ignatius took some of them, and now we take others. It was better at the outset to propose poverty and retreat from the world. It has been better since to take the remainder. For it would have frightened people to start at the top. That is against human nature.

It is not that the general rule exempts you from keeping to the *Institutions*, otherwise there would be abuses of them. You would find few people like us who can raise ourselves up without vanity.

One and holy.[49]

The Jansenists will suffer for it.

Father Saint-Jure.—Escobar.[50]

Such an important man.[51]

Aquaviva, December 14, 1621. Tanner. q. 2, dub. 5, n. 86.[52]

Clement and Paul V. God is visibly protecting us.[53]

---

45. The "Mystery of Jesus" ends here. Luke 22:44. "Let us": Pascal himself or those who will use the meditation as a devotion.

46. Pascal places these words in the mouth of a fictitious Jesuit.

47. *Constitutions* is the second most important work by Saint Ignatius Loyola, founder of the Jesuits.

48. Allusion to the Jesuit motto: *Ad majorem Dei gloriam* ("For the greater glory of God").

49. The bull *Unam sanctam* (1302) of Boniface VIII declared that the pope is master of temporal as well as spiritual power. This text, which disconcerted the Gallican party (who sought greater national autonomy from the Holy See), is mentioned critically in the *Letter of an advocate* by Le Maistre de Sacy and Pascal (June 1, 1657).

50. Pascal contrasts two types of Jesuits: Escobar (see ch. XXXII, fr. 440, n. 16), the laxest casuist principally attacked in the *Provincial Letters*, and Father Jean-Baptiste Saint-Jure (1588–1657), an eminent spiritual figure, and author de *De la Connoissance et de l'amour du fils de Dieu, Nostre Seigneur Jésus-Christ* [Of the knowledge and love of the Son of God, Our Lord Jesus Christ] (1634).

51. In the *Sixième écrit des Curés de Paris* [Sixth Brief of the Parisian clergy], Pascal records the "dreadful" case of conscience invented by the Jesuit Lamy (Amico): "To know whether a religious who, yielding to weakness, abuses a woman of low condition, who in turn, considering it an honor to have let herself be prostituted by such an important man (*tanto viro*), makes public what has occurred and thus dishonors him. If this religious can kill her in order to avoid that shame?" (July 24, 1658) (Pascal, *Œuvres complètes*, ed. Lafuma, 489).

52. The Jesuit A. Tanner (1578–1632), author of the *Universa Theologia* (1626), is cited in the twelfth *Provincial Letter*. In 1613, Aquaviva, General of the Jesuits, had issued a letter *against* the doctrine of probable opinions.

53. The Jesuits felt themselves protected by Providence, since both Popes Clement VIII and Paul V

Against rash judgments and scruples.

Saint Teresa 474.

Romance, Rose.

False crimes.[54]

Subtlety needed for survival.

All truth on one side. We extend it to both sides.

Two obstacles: the Gospel; the laws of the state. *From the greater to the lesser. Most recent.*[55]

In order to speak of personal vices.

Fine letter of Aquaviva, June 18, 1611, against probable opinions.

Saint Augustine 282.

And for Saint Thomas in the places where he explicitly dealt with these matters.

Clemens Placentinus,[56] 277.

And innovations.

And it is not an excuse for the superiors to say that they did not know about it, because they should have known about it: 194, 197, 279.

For morality: 283, 288.

The Society matters to the Church: 236; for good and for ill: 156.

Aquaviva: how to hear women's confessions: 360.[57]

751

We implore the mercy of God, not so that he leave us to enjoy our vices in peace, but so that he release us from them.

If God gave us masters from his own hand, we should of course have to obey them joyfully. Necessity and the course of events are infallibly such masters.

(see the second *Provincial Letter*) were unable, at the beginning of the seventeenth century, to pronounce the condemnation that they wished to enact against Molina.

54. The fifteenth *Provincial Letter* stigmatizes a thesis defended by the Jesuits at Louvain University in 1645: "It is not a venial sin to calumniate and to impute false crimes (*falso crimine elidere*) in order to destroy the reputation of those who speak ill of you."

55. See fr. 801.

56. Clemens Placentinus is the pseudonym under which Giulio Scotti, a former Jesuit, had written a diatribe against the Society, which became an arsenal of anti-Jesuit propaganda: *De potestate pontificia in Societatem Jesu* [The pontifical power in the Society of Jesus] (Paris: Barthélemy Macé, 1646). The figures refer to the page numbers of this work.

57. Scotti (see above), on page 360 of the book cited above, quotes a stricture of Aquaviva: "Let no one be allowed to hear women's confessions if he has not satisfactorily fulfilled certain offices in the Society."

Console yourself, you would not be seeking me, if you had not already found me.[58]

———

I thought of you in my agony, I shed these drops of blood for you.

———

It is tempting me rather than testing yourself to wonder whether you might do right in some hypothetical circumstance. I will do it within you if it occurs.

———

Let yourself be guided by my rules. Look how well I guided the Blessed Virgin and the saints, who let me act through them.

———

The Father loves all that I do.

———

Do you want it always to cost me the blood of my humanity without you ever shedding any tears?

———

Your conversion is my affair. Do not be afraid, and pray with confidence as if for me.

———

I am present with you in my word through the scriptures, in my spirit through the Church and through inspiration, in my power through the priesthood, and in my prayer through the faithful.

———

Doctors will not heal you, for you will die in the end, but I will heal you and make your body immortal.

———

Endure your chains and bodily servitude, I can only free you from spiritual servitude at present.

———

I am a better friend to you than so and so, for I have done more for you than they have, and they would not suffer what I have suffered at your hands and would not die for you when you were being unfaithful and cruel, as I did and as I am prepared to do and as I do in my chosen ones and in the Blessed Sacrament.

———

58. See Saint Bernard: "He alone can seek you who has already found you." *On the love of God*, in PL 182, col. 887. Pascal himself affirms, in *Sur la conversion du pécheur* [On the conversion of the sinner]: "[God] can only be taken away from those who reject him, because to desire to possess him is to possess him, and to renounce him is to lose him." Pascal, *Œuvres completes* (Paris: Hachette, 1871), vol. 2, p. 39 [the passage does not figure in Sellier's 2010 edition; translation by the editors]. Obviously, the fragment is an assurance to those who seek God but fear they are not included among the elect. But those who seek God must have somehow been touched by grace. Pascal perhaps directs this assurance to the "seeker" in the Apology. But does he direct it to himself? We must be careful not to stumble into the tradition of attributing the seeker's doubts to Pascal himself. But we remember his last words before his death: "May God never abandon me." *The Life of M. Pascal*, par. 88 of this edition.

If you knew your sins, you would lose heart.—I will lose heart then, Lord, for I believe their malice on your assurance.—No, for I, through whom you learn of it, can cure you of it, and that I speak to you about it is itself a sign that I want to cure you of it. As you atone for your sins, so you will become aware of them and you will be told: "Look: here are your sins that are remitted."

Do penance therefore for your hidden sins[59] and for the malice concealed within those of which you are aware.

———

Lord, I give you everything.

———

I love you more fiercely than you loved your filth. *Like those unclean for the clay.*[60]

———

May mine be the glory, not yours, worm and clay.

———

Testify to your director[61] that my own words are for you the cause of evil and of vanity or curiosity.

———

I see in myself an abyss of pride, of curiosity, of concupiscence. There is no link between me and God or between me and Jesus Christ the Righteous. But he has been made sin for me:[62] all your scourges fell upon him.[63] He is more wretched than I am. And yet far from loathing me, he considers himself honored that I go to help him. But he has healed himself and will heal me all the more surely.

I must add my wounds to his and ally myself to him, and he will save me by saving himself.

But I must not add any more in the future.

———

59. See Psalm 19:13: "Who can understand *sins? from my secret ones cleanse me,* O Lord."

60. Isaiah 64:6–8: "And we are all become *as one unclean,* and all our justices as the rag of a menstruous woman: and we have all fallen as a leaf, and our iniquities, like the wind, have taken us away. There is none that calleth upon thy name: that riseth up, and taketh hold of thee: thou hast hid thy face from us, and hast crushed us in the hand of our iniquity. And now, O Lord, thou art our father, and *we are clay*: and thou art our maker, and we all are the works of thy hands."

61. Confessor and spiritual guide.

62. 2 Corinthians 5:21: "*Him, who knew no sin,* he hath *made sin for us,* that we might be made the justice of God in him."

63. See Isaiah 53:3–5: "Despised, and the most abject of men, a man of sorrows, and acquainted with infirmity: and his look was as it were hidden and despised, whereupon we esteemed him not. Surely he hath borne our infirmities and carried our sorrows: and we have thought him as it were a leper, and as one struck by God and afflicted. But he was wounded for our iniquities, he was bruised for our sins: the chastisement of our peace was upon him, and by his bruises we are healed."

You shall be as gods, knowing good and evil.[64] Everybody acts as a god by judging: "this is good or evil," and by being overly distraught or overly joyful on account of the way things turn out.

―――――

Do small things as if they were great ones because of the majesty of Jesus Christ who does them within us and who lives our lives; and do great things as if they were small, easy ones because of his omnipotence.

The false justice of Pilate only serves to make Jesus Christ suffer, because he has him whipped on account of his false justice, and then kills him. It would be better to have killed him first. So it is for the falsely righteous. They do good works and evil ones, so as to please the world and show that they are not entirely given over to Jesus Christ, for they are ashamed of him; and in the end, in their major temptations and occasions of sin, they kill him.

You only understand prophecies when you see things that have happened. So the justification for the value of retreats and direction of conscience, of silence and so on, only becomes apparent to those who have experienced them and who believe in them.

―――――

Saint Joseph so turned inward in an entirely external law.

―――――

External penances dispose you to internal ones, just as humiliations dispose you to humility. So the . . .

752

Every condition, even that of martyrs, should be fearful: according to scripture.

The greatest suffering in purgatory is the uncertainty of judgement.

―――――

Hidden God.[65]

753

It is true that there are some hardships in embarking on a pious life. But these hardships do not arise from the piety that begins to exist within us, but from the impiety that remains. If our senses were not opposed to penance, and our corruption were not opposed to the purity of God, there would be nothing difficult about it. We only suffer in proportion to the degree to which vice, which is natural to us, resists supernatural grace: our hearts feel torn apart by

―――――

64. Genesis 3:5. The serpent's promise to Eve.

65. Isaiah 45:15: "Verily thou art *a hidden God.*" The central doctrine not only of Jansenism, but of the Apology itself. See above, ch. XIX, nn. 4 and 30.

these opposing forces. But it would be unjust to impute this violence to God, who is drawing us towards him, rather than attributing it to the world, which is holding on to us. It is like a child whose mother snatches it from the arms of thieves: [it] must love, in the suffering it endures, the loving and legitimate violence of her who procures its freedom, and hate only the imperious and tyrannical violence of those who hold on to it unjustly. The most cruel war that God can wage against men in this life is to spare them that same war that he came to bring. *I have come to bring war*, he says; and in order to tell us about that war: *I have come to bring a sword and fire.*[66] Before him the world lived in just such a false peace.

On the miracle

Since God has made no family happier, let him now find no family more thankful.[67]

_____

On confession and absolution without signs of regret.

God only considers the internal, the Church only judges by the external. God absolves as soon as he sees penitence in the heart, the Church when it sees it in works. God will make a Church that is pure within, which confounds by its internal and fully spiritual holiness the internal impiety of the arrogant sages and Pharisees. And the Church will make an assembly of men whose external conduct is so pure that it confounds the conduct of pagans. If there are some hypocrites among them, but so well disguised that the Church does not recognize their venom, it will tolerate them. For, even though they are not accepted by God, whom they cannot deceive, they are accepted by men, whom they can. And so the Church is not dishonored by their conduct, which appears to be holy . . .[68]

754

The law has not destroyed nature, but has ordered it. Grace has not destroyed the law, but puts it into practice.

_____

The faith received in baptism is at the origin of all Christian life, and of that of converts.

66. Matthew 10:34 ("I *came* not to *send* peace, but the *sword*"), and Luke 12:49 ("I am come to cast *fire* on the earth; and what will I, but that it be kindled?").

67. Pascal refers to his own extended family, following the miracle of the holy thorn.

68. The Périer manuscript notes that the page is torn here. Completed by the copyist in fr. 499.

755

People make an idol out of truth itself, for truth without charity is not God but is his image and an idol that you must neither love nor worship. And even less should you love or worship its opposite, which is untruth.

———

I might well like total darkness; but if God draws me into a state of semi-darkness, the small amount of darkness that remains displeases me, and since I do not infer from it the merits of total darkness, it does not please me. It is a failing, and a sign that I have made an idol for myself out of darkness, separate from God's order. So any worship must only occur within that order.

756

What use would that be to me?
Abominable.
Singlin.[69]
What use would it be for me to remember that, if it can equally well work for me or against me, and since everything depends on the blessing of God, and since he only grants it to those things that are done for him, according to his rules and following his paths, and since the way we do the deed is thus as important as the deed itself, and perhaps even more so, since God can draw good from evil, and since without God evil can be drawn from good?

———

Do not compare yourself to other people, but to me. If you do not find me in those to whom you compare yourself, you compare yourself to an abominable creature.

If you find me there, compare yourself to what you find.

But what will be your point of comparison? Will it be yourself or myself in you? If it is you, it is an abominable creature. If it is me, you compare me to myself.

For I am God in everything.

———

I often speak to you and advise you, because your director cannot speak to you. And because I do not want you to lack a director.

———

And perhaps I do it at his behest, so that he is guiding you without your seeing it.

———

69. Antoine Singlin (1607–64) was one of the spiritual directors of Pascal and of many of the solitaires.

You would not be looking for me, if you did not already possess me.[70] So do not be anxious.

———

Everything can be fatal to us, even those things made for our benefit, just as in the natural world walls can kill us, and steps can kill us, if we do not look where we are going.

———

The slightest movement affects the whole of nature: the whole ocean changes on account of a pebble. It is the same in matters of grace, where the slightest action has implications for everything, so that everything is important.

———

In every action, we have to consider, along with the action, our past, present, and future state, and that of other people, what is its significance, and see how all this is linked together. And only then shall we be kept properly in check.

External works

Nothing is as dangerous as what pleases God and men, since those states that please both God and men contain one thing that pleases God and another that pleases men, such as the greatness of Saint Teresa. What pleases God is her deep humility during her revelations. What pleases men is her enlightenment. So people go to untold lengths to imitate her utterances, thinking that they imitate her state by so doing, and that they thereby love what God loves, and put themselves in the state that God loves.

———

It is better not to fast, and be humble, than to fast and be self-satisfied. Pharisee. Publican.[71]

757

Why did God institute prayer?

1. To communicate the dignity of causality to his creatures.[72] But to retain his pre-eminence, he gives prayer to those to whom it pleases him.[73]

2. To teach us from whom we derive virtue.

3. To make us merit other virtues by our own efforts.

———

70. See fr. 751, n. 58, above for this key element in the Apology. The seeker is reassured that he would not be seeking had not God already touched his heart.

71. Luke 18:9–14. Notes on the parable of the Pharisee and the publican.

72. Textual citation from Saint Thomas (*Summa theologiæ* I, q. 22, a. 3, and q. 23, a. 8, ad. 2).

73. In the "Lettre sur la possibilité d'accomplir les commandements de dieu" [Letter on the possibility to obey God's commands], 5, Pascal posits that "God never refuses what he is worthily asked for in prayer, and God does not always accord perseverance in prayer: which is in no respect contradictory." See Pascal, *Œuvres complètes* (Paris: Hachette, 1913), vol. 2, 57–81. See also fr. 803.

Objection: but people will believe that prayer comes from within themselves.

That is absurd. For, since even with faith they would not have any virtues, how could they have faith? Is there not a greater distance between faithlessness and faith than between faith and virtue?

―――――

MERITED: this word is ambiguous.

―――――

Merited a Redeemer.[74]

―――――

Merited to touch such holy limbs.[75]

―――――

Worthy to touch such holy limbs.[76]

―――――

I am not worthy.[77] *Who eateth unworthily.*[78]

―――――

Worthy to receive.[79]

―――――

Judge me worthy.[80]

―――――

God only gives according to his promises.
He has promised to grant righteousness in answer to prayers.
He has only promised prayers to the children of the promise.[81]

―――――

74. "O happy fault, which *merited* so great *a Redeemer*." The *Exultet*, from which this verse is taken, is sung at the arrival of the illuminated Easter candle at the altar during the rite of the Easter Vigil. The candle, representing the Light of Christ, is censed while the deacon chants this hymn of praise. The verse itself was much beloved, particularly by M. de Sacy, and was often cited at Port-Royal in sermons. Its implications are nothing less than cosmic. The entire and sole reason God created the entire universe was so that Christ might perform his saving work upon the cross.

75. "Chosen tree that was judged worthy *to touch such holy limbs*." Office for Good Friday. See the anthem, *Vexilla Regis* sung in the Good Friday liturgy, which celebrates the cross, whose "wood was worthy to touch such holy limbs."

76. Office for Good Friday.

77. The exclamation (said three times in the Tridentine Rite known to Pascal) at the elevation of the Host before communion: "Lord, *I am not worthy* that thou shouldst come under my roof" (Luke 7:6) [DR: "Lord, trouble not thyself; for *I am not worthy* that thou shouldest enter under my roof"]. Altered during the revisions of Vatican II, the original verse was restored in the English translation of the Mass by Benedict XVI.

78. Saint Paul wrote, in 1 Corinthians 11:29, concerning the reception of the Eucharist: "For he that *eateth* and drinketh *unworthily* [the Body and Blood], eateth and drinketh judgment to himself, not discerning the body of the Lord."

79. Revelation 5:12: "Saying with a loud voice: The Lamb that was slain is worthy *to receive* power, and divinity, and wisdom, and strength, and honor, and glory, and benediction."

80. Office of the Blessed Virgin: "*Judge me worthy* to praise you, O Blessed Virgin."

81. To the elect.

Saint Augustine said unambiguously that the means will be denied the righteous man.[82]

But it is by chance that he said it. Because the opportunity to say it might not have arisen. But his principles make it clear, since the opportunity did arise, that it was impossible that he did not say it, or at least that he did not say anything to the contrary. So it is more a matter of being forced to say it, since the opportunity arose. The option being between necessity and chance. But both of them are all that can be asked.

758

And that man will make fun of the other man?

Who should be making fun of whom? And yet this man does not make fun of the other man, but has pity on him.

759

I love poverty, because he loved it. I love wealth, because it gives me the means to help the destitute. I keep faith with everybody. I do not return ill to those who do ill to me, but I wish them a condition similar to mine, in which you receive neither good nor ill from the hands of men. I try to be fair, true, sincere, and loyal to all men. And I have a heartfelt affection for those to whom God has united me more closely. And whether I am alone, or in the sight of men, I keep God in view in all my actions, since it is he who will judge them and since I have consecrated them all to him.

These are my feelings.

And I bless my Redeemer every day of my life, since it was he who placed them in me and he who, out of a man full of weakness, wretchedness, concupiscence, pride, and ambition, has made a man free from all these ills by the power of his grace, to which all glory is due, since I find in myself only wretchedness and error.

760

They say that the Church says what she does not say, and that she does not say what she does say.

---

82. "God, to show that without grace nothing can be achieved, left Saint Peter without grace." Saint Augustine, *Sermon* 79, par. 1, PL 39, col. 1899.

761 [83]

Concupiscence of the flesh, concupiscence of the eyes, pride,[84] etc.
There are three orders of things:[85] the flesh, the mind, the will.
The carnal are rich men, kings: their object is the body.
Enquiring and learned men: their object is the mind.
Wise men: their object is justice.
God must reign over all and all must relate back to him.
In matters of the flesh concupiscence reigns fittingly.
In those of the mind, curiosity fittingly.
In wisdom, pride fittingly.

It is not that you cannot glory in wealth and knowledge, but that is not the place for pride. For by granting to a man that he is learned, you may nonetheless not fail to convince him that he is wrong to be arrogant.

The rightful place for pride is wisdom. For you cannot grant to a man that he has become wise and that he is wrong to glory in it. For that is simply his right.

So God alone gives wisdom. *He that glorieth, let him glory in the Lord.*[86]

762

Nature has perfections, to show that it is the image of God, and defects, to show that it is no more than his image.

———

Since men have not been accustomed to create merit, but simply to reward it where they find it, they judge God by their own standards.

763

20 V. The images in the Gospel for the state of the sick soul are sick bodies. But since one body cannot be sufficiently sick to express it properly, there had to be several. So there is the deaf man, the dumb man, the blind man, the paralytic man, the dead Lazarus, the man possessed [by demons]: and all of that put together is present in the sick soul.

83. This entire fragment is closely related to fragment 339 ("The Three Orders"). It seems to sketch only the beginning of that remarkable piece, dealing only with the first order relative to concupiscence. See, in the introduction, the section titled "The Three Orders."

84. See fr. 460.

85. See again fr. 339, "The Three Orders." Each concupiscence corresponds to a different order—concupiscence of the flesh, that of the eyes (curiosity), and that of pride. Wisdom is an order higher than concupiscence but it is still subject to pride. Absent here is the order of holiness, that of Christ, which is central to fr. 339. And, again, see "The Three Orders," in the introduction.

86. Beginning of the Epistle read in the Mass for the Common of Virgins. 2 Corinthians 10:17.

When our passions drive us to do something, we forget our duty: just as if you are enjoying a book, you read it, whereas you should be doing something else. But in order to remember your duty, you have to plan to do something you hate doing, and then you excuse yourself from doing it on the grounds that you have something else to do, and you remember your duty in this way.

764

The servant knoweth not what his master doth,[87] since the master only tells him of the action, and not of the purpose. And that is why the servant submits to it unthinkingly and often sins against the purpose. But Jesus Christ told us the purpose.

And you are destroying that purpose.

765

Jesus Christ did not want to be killed without the due form of justice, since it is far more ignominious to die as a result of justice than by an unjust rebellion.

766

You do not get bored with eating and sleeping every day, because hunger recurs as does weariness. If that were not the case you would get bored.

Similarly, without the hunger for spiritual things, you get bored with them: *hunger after justice.*[88] (Eighth Beatitude)

End.

Are we safe? Is that principle certain? Let us look.

Our own witness worthless. Saint Thomas.

767

It seems to me that Jesus Christ let only his wounds be touched after his resurrection.

Do not touch me.[89]

We should only be united with his suffering.

---

87. John 15:15. Jesus says to his disciples: "I will not now call you servants: for *the servant knoweth not what his lord doth*. But I have called you friends: because all things whatsoever I have heard of my Father, I have made known to you."

88. Matthew 5:6. "Blessed are they that *hunger* and thirst *after justice*: for they shall have their fill."

89. John 20:17. The risen Jesus says to Mary Magdalene "*Do not touch me*, for I am not yet ascended to my Father."

He gave himself in communion as a mortal being at the Last Supper, as a risen man to the disciples at Emmaus, and as ascended into heaven to the whole Church.

———

The external has to be joined to the internal to find favor with God, in other words you have to get down on your knees, pray with your lips, etc., so that the proud man who did not want to submit to God must now submit to the creature. To expect help from this external dimension is to be superstitious. Not to wish to add it to the internal one is to be arrogant.[90]

———

Penitence, alone among all the mysteries, was clearly declared to the Jews, and by Saint John the precursor;[91] and then the other mysteries, to signal that it is in each man and in the whole world that this order has to be observed.

768

25 Bb.[92]—2. To consider Jesus Christ in all people, and in ourselves: Jesus Christ as father in his father, Jesus Christ as brother in his brothers, Jesus Christ as a poor man in the poor, Jesus Christ as a rich man in the rich, Jesus Christ as doctor and priest in priests, Jesus Christ as sovereign in princes, etc. For he is everything that is great on account of his glory, being God, and he is everything that is feeble and abject on account of his mortal life. That is why he took on this wretched condition, to be in all people, and to be the model for all conditions of men.

The just man acts by faith[93] in the least things: when he upbraids his servants, he wishes for their correction by God's spirit and prays to God to correct them, and expects as much from God as from his own reprimands, and prays to God to bless his corrections. And so forth for other actions.

769

You fall away only when you fall away from charity.

———

Our prayers and our virtues are abominable before God, if they are not

90. See "The Machine" (fr. 680). This fragment completes the thirteenth paragraph of the so-called "Wager" (fr. 680), in which Pascal envisages preparing the body to receive grace by admonishing the "seeker" to cross himself with holy water and have masses said for the dead. The admonitions of this fragment (praying with the lips, kneeling) complete those in fr. 680 and explain how these external acts are joined to the "internal." Thinking that the external acts can attract grace is but "superstition." But not *wanting* to submit to God by fervently praying on one's knees that external acts may be joined to their internal significance is "arrogant" and betokens not being numbered among the elect. See frs. 39 and 45.

91. Matthew 3:1–2; Mark 1:2–5; Mark 1:4.

92. A vestige of Périer's numbering of the fragments in this collection. See fr. 744, n. 14, above.

93. Romans 1:17: "*The just man* liveth *by faith*."

the prayers and virtues of Jesus Christ. And our sins will never be the object of God's mercy, but of his justice, if they are not the sins of Jesus Christ.

———

He took on our sins and [welcomed us into his] alliance. For virtues are true to his nature, and sins foreign to it. And virtues are foreign to our nature, and sins true to it.[94]

———

Let us change the rule that we have adopted until now to judge what is good. We used to take our own wills as a rule for it, but let us now take the will of God. All that he wants is good and just. All that he does not want, bad and unjust.

Everything that God does not want is forbidden. Sins are forbidden by the general declaration made against them by God. The other things that remained without a general prohibition and that are known for this reason as permitted, are nonetheless not always permitted since, when God takes one of them away from us and, through the occurrence, which manifests the will of God, it appears that he does not wish us to have something, this thing is thereafter forbidden in the same way as sin, since the will of God no more wishes us to have it than sin. There is just one difference between these two things: it is certain that God will never want sin, whereas it is not certain that he will never want the other thing. But while God does not want it, we must consider it to be a sin, since the absence of the will of God, which is alone all goodness and all justice, renders it unjust and bad.

770

What would the Jesuits be without probability, and what would probability be without the Jesuits?

Take away probability, and you cannot please the world. Introduce probability, and you can no longer displease it. Formerly, it was difficult to avoid sins, and difficult to atone for them. Now, it is easy to avoid them by a whole range of devices, and easy to atone for them.[95]

We have made uniformity from diversity, for we are all uniform, to the extent that we have all become uniform.[96]

94. These three paragraphs develop a fundamental affirmation of Augustinianism, founded on Saint Paul. "For all that is not of faith is sin." (Romans 14:23).

95. Tenth *Provincial Letter*. The fictional Jesuit is speaking: "Having shown you, in our previous conversations, how we have relieved the scruples that troubled people's consciences, by showing how what was believed to be evil is not in fact so, it remains to show you in this one the way to atone easily for what is truly sinful, by making confession as easy now as it was difficult before."

96. The Jesuits are presented as diverse, because the probable opinions that they profess are inconsistent to the point of contradiction, but also as uniform, in that each Jesuit is obliged to accept the probable opinions of all the others. See the thirteenth *Provincial Letter*.

4. Piece Bound Together with the Second Copy

771

Just as peace within states has as its only objective to safeguard their peoples' possessions, so peace within the Church has as its only objective to safeguard the truth that is its possession, and the treasure where its heart lies. And just as it would go against the aims of peace to allow foreigners into a state to pillage it, without opposition, in order not to cause a stir (because, since peace is only just and useful for the security of possessions, it becomes unjust and pernicious when it allows them to be lost, and the war that can serve to defend them becomes both just and necessary), so, in the Church, when truth is offended by the enemies of the faith, and when it risks being torn from the hearts of the faithful in order to allow error to hold sway in its place, would it be a service to the Church or a betrayal to remain at peace in such circumstances? Would it amount to its defense or its ruin? And is it not clear that, just as it is a crime to disturb the peace if truth holds sway, it is also a crime to remain at peace when it is being destroyed? So there is a time when peace is just and another when it is unjust. And it is written that *there is a time for peace and a time for war,*[1] and it is the interests of truth that mark out such times. But there is not a time for truth and a time for error, and it is written, on the contrary, that *the truth of the Lord remaineth for ever;*[2] and that is why Jesus Christ, who says that he came to bring peace, also says that he came to bring war;[3] but he does not say that he came to bring both truth and falsehood.

So truth is both the first rule and the last purpose of everything.

---

1. Ecclesiastes 3:8: "*A time of war and a time of peace.*"

2. Psalm 117:2.

3. John 14:27: "Peace I leave with you, *my peace I give unto you*: not as the world giveth, do I give unto you"; and Matthew 10:34: "Do not think that I *came to send peace upon earth.*" See also fr. 753.

5. The Joly de Fleury Manuscript[1]

772

It is good to encourage people who have been renewed[2] internally by grace to undertake works of piety and of penitence proportionate to their capacity, because both grace and works are preserved by the proportion that exists between the goodness of the works and the spirit in which they are carried out. When you constrain someone who is not yet renewed internally to extraordinary works of piety and penitence, you spoil both, since the man corrupts the works by his malice, and the works overwhelm the weakness of the man, who is unable to bear them. It is a bad sign to see a person performing outwardly from the very instant of conversion. The order of charity must take root in the heart before performing good works outwardly.

773

I feel in myself a malicious streak that prevents me from agreeing with what Montaigne says, that vitality and firmness weaken with age.[3] I would not wish that to be the case. I envy myself. The me I was when I was twenty is no longer me.[4]

1. The fourteen fragments that follow were all omitted from the 1678 edition of the *Pensées*. Jean Mesnard discovered them in 1960 at the Bibliothèque Nationale, ms. 2466 ("Pensées à imprimer" [*Pensées* to print]) of the Joly de Fleury collection, and published them in *Blaise Pascal: Textes inédits* [Pascal: Unpublished texts] (Paris: Desclée de Brouwer, 1962).

2. Jean Mesnard points out that the use of this term links this fragment directly to the spirituality of Saint-Cyran.

3. Montaigne, *Essays*, I, 57, 289: "It is possible that in those who employ their time well, knowledge and experience grow with living; but vivacity, quickness, firmness, and other qualities much more our own, more important and essential, wither and languish."

4. Montaigne, *Essays*, III, 13, 1031: "I have portraits of myself at twenty-five and thirty-five. I compare them with one of the present: how irrevocably it is no longer myself! How much farther is my present picture from them than from that of my death!" See fr. 552.

774

Sleep is the image of death, you say;[5] and I say to you that it is rather the image of life.[6]

775

Aristotle, who wrote a treatise *Of the soul*, only speaks, according to Montaigne, of the effects of the soul, which are known to everyone; and he says nothing of its essence, nor of its origin, nor of its nature, and that is what we want to know.[7]

776

People withdraw and hide for eight months in the country, in order to live glitteringly at court for four.

777

No pleasure has any savor for me, said Montaigne, *without communication*,[8] a sign of the esteem in which man holds man.

778

Scripture sends man to look at the ants:[9] a great sign of the corruption of his nature. How splendid to see that the master of the world is sent to look at insects as if they were masters of wisdom!

---

5. Montaigne, *Essays*, II, 6, 325: "It is not without reason that we are taught to study even our sleep for the resemblance it has with death." The 1652 edition (Paris: Pierre Le Petit) carries in the margin: "Sleep, image of death."

6. In a sonnet published in 1658, the libertine poet Des Barreaux (see "The Contours of Disbelief," in the introduction of this edition), who was known to Pascal (fr. 29), returned to the Ovidian commonplace echoed by Montaigne (*Essays*, II, 6): "Great master of the art of loving, you deceive yourself cruelly / In naming sleep as the image of death: / Life and dreaming have more in common. / [...] Shall I say, mortals, what this life is? / It is a dream that lasts a little longer than a single night." On the philosophical front, the assimilation of life to dreaming, and thus of the state of waking to the state of sleeping, allowed the Pyrrhonists to throw into doubt the validity of all knowledge. See frs. 85 and 164.

7. Montaigne, *Essays*, II, 12, 492–93: "Now let us see what human reason has taught us of herself and the soul! [...]. Let us not forget Aristotle, what naturally makes the body move is something which he calls entelechy—by as frigid an invention as any other for he speaks of neither the essence, nor the origin, nor the nature of the soul, but merely notes its effect." See fr. 111.

8. Textual citation from Montaigne's *Essays* (see II, 9, 917) in the 1652 edition.

9. Proverbs 6:6: "Go to the ant, O sluggard, and consider her ways, and learn wisdom."

779

Whoever notices that he has said or done a foolish thing always believes that it will be for the last time. Far from concluding that he will do many more such things, he concludes that this one will prevent him from so doing.[10]

780

The philosophers of the Schools[11] speak of virtue and the rhetoricians of eloquence without knowing what they are. Offer to the former a truly virtuous man, but without panache, and to the latter a discourse full of beauty, but without conceits: they will understand nothing of them.

781

Sudden death alone is to be feared, and that is why confessors live with the great of this world.

782

He plays at being the disciple without ignorance, and the master without presumption. Annat.[12]

783

I find nothing easier than to dismiss all that as fiction.[13] But I find nothing harder than to reply to it.

784

Why does God not show himself? Are you all worthy of him?—Yes.— You are rather presumptuous, and unworthy because of that.—No.—Then you are unworthy of him.

785

God is hidden. But he lets himself be found by those who seek him.

There have always been visible signs of him in every age. Ours are the prophecies. Other times had other signs.

10. Montaigne, *Essays*, III, 13, 1002: "To learn that we have said or done a foolish thing, that is nothing; we must learn that we are nothing but fools, a far broader and more important lesson." See fr. 540.

11. See fr. 78.

12. Pere Annat, the Jesuit confessor to Louis XIV. See above, ch. XXXI, fr. 428, n. 36.

13. Mesnard sees this as an allusion to the chronologies of the Chinese, Greeks, Egyptians, Chaldeans, etc., which, by presenting the world as far older than Biblical chronologies, challenge the veracity of the Old Testament. Pascal dismisses them all in frs. 658, 688, 694, 716, etc.

All these proofs hold up together. If one is true, so is the other. So each age, having those that were appropriate to it, recognized the others as a result of this.

Those who saw the Flood believed in the Creation, and believed in the Messiah to come. Those who saw Moses believed in the Flood and in the accomplishment of prophecies.

And we, who see the accomplishment of prophecies, must believe in the Flood and the Creation.[14]

---

14. See fr. 327. On the Biblical chronologies, see above, fr. 370, n. 34, fr. 553, n. 5, and fr. 694, n. 7. The historicity of the Old Testament is proved by the accomplishment of its prophecies in the New Testament.

6. The Vallant Folders[1]

786

The most unreasonable things in the world become the most reasonable because of the disorderliness of men. What is less reasonable than to choose the firstborn son of a queen to govern a state? You do not choose the traveler who is from the best family to steer a ship. This law would be ridiculous and unjust; but because men are and always will be ridiculous and unjust themselves, it becomes reasonable and just, for who would you choose? The most virtuous and the cleverest? We are instantly at each others' throats, each claiming to be the most virtuous and the cleverest. So let us attach this status to something indisputable. He is the eldest son of the king: that is clear, there is no argument. Reason cannot do any better, since civil war is the greatest of all evils.

---

1. Dr. Vallant, close to the Périer family, frequented the group that prepared the *Pensées* for publication after Pascal's death. He recopied the text, already modified (probably by Nicole), of fragments 64 and 128, intended for the Port-Royal edition.

7. Fragments from the Original Collection[1]

787

That they[2] were treated as humanely as possible, so as to remain on the middle ground between the love of truth and the duty of charity.

That piety does not consist in never rising up against one's brothers. It would be rather easy, etc.

It is a false piety to preserve peace to the detriment of truth.

It is also a false zeal to preserve truth while harming charity.[3]

———

So they did not complain about it.

———

Their maxims have their time and their place.

———

Their vanity extends to promoting themselves on account of their errors.

In conformity with the Fathers by their mistakes,

And with the martyrs by their torture.[4]

———

Yet they still disown none of them.

———

All they had to do was to take the *Extract*[5] and disown it.

———

1. The fragments that follow belong to the album (in which the fragments were cut up to fit the cahier) compiled by the Abbé Périer and deposited in 1711 at the library of the abbey of Saint-Germain-des-Pres. They were not included in the first editions of the *Pensées* because they dealt principally with the anti-Jesuit polemic that is the subject of the *Provincial Letters*, and not with the projected Apology for the Christian religion that is the major concern of the *Pensées*.

2. The Jesuits.

3. Sellier notes that this recapitulates an important theme of the *Second écrit des cures de Paris* [Second brief of the Parisian clergy] (April 1658).

4. I.e., Jesuit martyrs. In his *Apologie pour les casuistes contre les calomnies des jansénistes* [Apology for the casuists against the Jansenists' Calumnies], which appeared anonymously in Paris in 1657, the Jesuit Pirot recognized that the casuist Vasquez had taught an erroneous doctrine concerning theft, but excused him by claiming that "if this Father has erred, the Fathers of the Church made just as many mistakes." He furthermore claimed that the "persecution" endured by the Jesuits as a result of the *Provincial Letters* was the equivalent of "the torture that the (Jesuit) martyrs were made to endure!" (Paris: Gaspar Maturas, 1657. The French National Library has a copy of a 1658 edition, published in Cologne, by P. de la Vallée).

5. An *Extrait de quelques-unes des plus dangereuses propositions de la morale de plusieurs nouveaux casuistes* [Extract from some of the most dangerous propositions concerning the morality of several new

They prepare war against him.[6]

Mr. Bourzeis:[7] at least they cannot deny the fact that he opposed the condemnation.

788

In his bull *By virtue of the Apostolic office*[8] by Paul IV, published in 1558:

We ordain, rule, decree, and define that each and every one among those who will be found to have been misled or to have fallen into heresy or schism, and of whatever quality and condition they may be, laypeople, ecclesiastics, priests, bishops, archbishops, patriarchs, primates, cardinals, counts, marquesses, dukes, kings, and emperors, as well as the aforementioned sentences and punishments, should be on simple account of that without any ministry of law or of fact, perpetually deprived in all respects and regards of their orders, bishoprics, benefices, offices, kingdom, empire, and be incapable of ever regaining them. We leave it to the discretion of the secular authorities to punish these same people, according grace only to those who by a true penitence should return from their errors, unless by the benignity and clemency of the Holy See they are judged worthy to be secluded in a monastery, there to do perpetual penance by bread and water. But they should remain deprived of all dignity, order, prelature, county, duchy, or kingdom. And those who conceal and defend them shall be considered on simple account of that to be judged excommunicate and infamous, deprived of any kingdom, duchy, wealth, and possession, which will belong by right and by propriety to those who will seize it the first.[9]

If they kill an excommunicated man, we do not consider them to be homicides in so far as it is their zeal for the Catholic Church their mother that will have driven them to eradicate him.

23 q. 5. of Urban II.[10]

---

casuists], accompanied the *Avis de Messieurs les Curés de Paris à Messieurs les autres Curés des autres dioceses de France* [Warning from the parish priests of Paris to parish priests of the other dioceses of France], September 13, 1656.

6. Micah 3:5: the false prophets. "Thus saith the Lord concerning the prophets that make my people err: that bite with their teeth, and preach peace: and if a man give not something into their mouth, they *prepare war against him.*"

7. The Abbé de Bourzeis, a member of the French Academy, was an Augustinian theologian close to Port-Royal. He stopped writing on disputed questions concerning grace after the bull *Cum occasione* of May 1653, which condemned the five propositions. He finally signed the *Formulary* in 1661.

8. *Cum ex apostolatus officio*, in *Roman Bullarium*, ed. Girolamo Mainard, 32 vols., 1733–1762, vol. 4., sec. 1, 354–357. To be compared with the bull *Unam sanctam* [One and holy] (see fr. 750). These two texts were considered by the Gallican party to be an intolerable trespass by the Church on the independence of the temporal power of states.

9. Pascal translated the papal bull of February 15, 1559 to use it in his other writings.

10. *Letter from Urban II*, incorporated in the *Corpus of canon law*, cause 23, qu. 5, chap. 47.

121. The pope forbids the king to marry off his children without his permission. 1294.

_____

We want you to know.[11] 124. 1302.
The childish one.

789

Do you have the right idea about our Society?

_____

The Church has survived for so long without these questions.

_____

Others do so, but not in the same way.

_____

What comparison do you think it is possible to make between twenty thousand who are separate and two hundred million who are joined together, all of whom are prepared to perish for each other? An immortal body.

_____

We uphold each other to the death. Lamy.[12]

_____

We give our enemies no rest. Mr Puys.[13]

_____

Everything depends on probability.

_____

The world naturally wants a religion, but an indulgent one.[14]

_____

I am struck by the desire to demonstrate it to you by means of a strange supposition. So I shall say: "Even were God not sustaining us by a special providence, for the good of the Church, I want to demonstrate that, even in human terms, we cannot perish."

If you grant me that principle, I will prove everything to you. Because the Society and the Church share a common fortune.

Without such principles you cannot prove anything.

_____

11. Pascal added in his margin references to these other abusive decrees of popes.

12. According to Pascal, it is a principle among Jesuits that they must all defend whatever one of their number has written in his books. Amico (Lamy), the author of a scandalous decision (that members of a religious community might kill to protect the reputation of their community) is cited as an illustration of this practice, since his fellow Jesuits, though they would have preferred he not proffer such an opinion, felt they nonetheless had to defend it as *probable*.

13. A parish priest in Lyon. The Jesuits, believing he was unfavorably disposed towards them, calumniated him in the person of Father Alby. When they were assured that this was not in fact the case, Father Alby withdrew his accusations of heresy and free-thinking. Pascal comments in the fifteenth *Provincial Letter* that "people were more scandalized by the reconciliation than by the quarrel."

14. These words are placed in the mouth of a Jesuit.

You do not live for long in open impiety, nor naturally in great austerity.

A religion that has adapted is likely to last.

The search for them is motivated by free-thinking.

With individuals who do not want to prevail by force of arms, I do not know whether they could do any better.

Kings, pope.

Third Petition; 246.[15]

---

6. Straightforward and in good faith with regard to devotion.

6, 452. Kings to foster them.[16]

4. Hated on account of their merit.

Apology for the University:[17] 159. Decree of the Sorbonne.[18]

(*To kill*) kings. 241, 228.

Jesuits hanged.[19] 112.

Religion. And the Society.

The Jesuit plays all the characters.[20]

Colleges, relatives, friends, children to choose.[21]

---

15. The page numbers 246, 241, 228, and 112 refer to the pages of the virulent *Historia jesuitica* [Jesuit History] by the Protestant Rodolphus Hospinianus, which appeared in Zurich in 1619. The substance of his argument is that the Jesuits are dispensed by the pope from obeying kings, and that they even teach regicide. The other references concern three texts published simultaneously by the Jansenist Godefroi Hermant in 1644: *Response de l'Université de Paris à l'Apologie pour les Jésuites, qu'ils ont mise au jour sous le nom du Père Caussin* [Reply of the University of Paris to the Apology for the Jesuits, which appeared under the name of Father Caussin]; several excerpts from the apologetic manifesto that the Jesuits published under the name of Father Pierre Le Moyne; and the *Troisième requête de l'université de Paris contre les libelles des Jésuites intitules l'Apologie par le Père Caussin, manifeste apologétique par le Père Le Moyne & autres: avec la Réplique de l'Université* [Third petition of the University of Paris against the Jesuits' tracts, the Apology of Father Caussin and the Apologetic Manifesto of Father Le Moyne, and others: With the university's reply].

16. In the *Imago primi sæculi Societatis Jesu* [Image of the first century of the Society of Jesus] (1640), V, 1, the Jesuits apply to themselves the verse from Isaiah 49:23: "You shall have kings to foster them."

17. Godefroi Hermant was author of an *Apologie pour l'Université de Paris* [Apology for the University] (1643) in which he defends the traditional privileges of the University of Paris against the Jesuits.

18. Hospinianus records the decree issued by the Sorbonne on June 4, 1610 against the book by the Venetian Jesuit Mariana entitled *De rege et regis institutione* [Of the king and the institution of the king] (1599), which contained a eulogy of the murder of Henri III.

19. Reference to Father Guignard, the former teacher of Jean Châtel (who attempted to assassinate Henri IV in 1594), and to Fathers Oldecorn and Garnet, who did not reveal the Gunpowder Plot hatched against King James I of England in 1605. In 1595, the Jesuit Guignard was hanged for inspiring one of his disciples to commit parricide.

20. Scottish Jesuit Alexander Haïus had taught publicly that it was necessary to dissimulate, and pretend to obey the king for a time, speaking regularly these words: *Jesuita est omnis homo*, in other words, a Jesuit can adapt to any circumstances and, like Proteus, can transform himself into all sorts of figures.

21. The Jesuits were accused of using their schools to recruit members for their congregation.

Constitutions[22]

253. Poverty, ambition.

257. Principally princes, great noblemen, who can be both harmful and useful.

12. Useless, rejected.

Healthy look.

Riches, nobility, etc. What? Were you afraid of failure by receiving them sooner?

27.

47. Give your possessions to the Society for the glory of God. DECLARATIONS.

51, 52. Unity of feelings. DECLARATIONS. Submit to the Society, and thereby keep uniformity. Now today that uniformity lies in diversity, for that is how the Society wants it to be.

117. CONSTITUTIONS: the Gospel and Saint Thomas. DECLARATIONS: Some more accommodating theology.[23]

65. Few pious scholars. Our seniors have changed their minds.

23, 74. Begging.

19. Not giving to relatives, and feeling comfortable because of the counsellors provided by the superior.

1. Not using the examination of conscience. DECLARATIONS.

2. Total poverty. Neither for saying masses, nor for sermons, nor by compensatory almsgiving.

4. *Declarations*, have the same authority as the *Constitutions*.[24] Aim, to read the *Constitutions* each month.

149. The *Declarations* spoil everything.

154. Neither incite to give perpetual alms, nor ask for them as of right, nor poor-box.

Declarations: "Not construed as almsgiving (but as compensation)."

---

22. Apart from the first two numerical indications (253, 257), which refer to the *Historia jesuitica*, Pascal refers here to the *Constitutiones Societatis Jesu cum earum Declarationibus*. [Constitutions of the Society of Jesus, with their Declarations]. His intention is to contrast the rigor of the *Constitutions* with the laxest implications he discerns in the *Declarations*.

23. The *Constitutions* stipulate: "In theology, the Old and New Testaments shall be taught, and the scholastic doctrine of Saint Thomas." *Constitutiones Societatis Jesu* (Rome: S. J., 1558). The *Declarations* add that it is legitimate to use "a *summa* or book of scholastic theology that seems more adapted to our times." *Declarationes et annotations in constitutionibus Societatis Jesu* (Rome: S. J., 1559).

24. Saint Ignatius writes in his prologue to the *Declarations*: "It has seemed fitting in Our Lord to draw up some *Declarations* and *Recommendations* which, having the same force as the remainder of the *Constitutions*, can clarify in more detail, for those who have responsibility over others, certain points that the brevity and universal character of the first *Constitutions* tended to make less clear."

200, 4. Warn us of everything.

190. CONSTITUTIONS: does not want troop. DECLARATIONS: troop, interpreted.

A universal, immortal body.

———

Great and unscrupulous affection for the community: DANGEROUS.

With religion we would all be rich, without our *Constitutions*. Therefore we are poor.

———

Both with the true religion and without it, we are strong.

Clemens Placentinus[25]

Our Generals feared failure because of external occupations: 208, 152, 150; because of the Court: 209, 203, 216, 218; because the most certain and the most authoritative opinions were not being followed, Saint Thomas, etc.: 215, 218.

"Retribution contrary to the Constitutions." 218.

Women: 225, 228.

Princes and politics: 227, 168, 177.—Politics: 181.

Probability, novelty: 279, 156. Novelty, truth.

To pass the time and amuse themselves more than to help souls: 158.

Laxist opinions: 160. Mortal to venial sin.

Contrition: 162.

Courtliness. (*164*) or 162.[26]

The Jesuits enjoy more of the good things in life: 166.

Father Le Moine, ten thousand *écus*, outside his province.

A show of false wealth that deceives them: 192 *ad*.

See how weak men's foresight is! Everything that led our first Generals to fear the ruin of our Society has led to its growth: the nobility, the contravention of our *Constitutions*, the multitude of religious, the diversity and novelty of opinions, etc.: 182, 157.

The first spirit of the Society, snuffed out: 170, 171 to 174, 184 to 187. *It is no longer the same.* Vittelescus.[27] 183.

Complaints of the Generals. None from Saint Ignatius, none from Laynez, some from Borgia and Aquaviva, endless ones from Mutius,[28] etc.

———

25. See fr. 750. Pseudonym of Giulio Scotti. A Jesuit who left the order and composed *The Pontifical Power*..., a veritable arsenal of anti-Jesuit polemics. The references that follow are to that text.

26. Pascal left the Latin *aulicismus* without translating Scotti.

27. Letter of Muzio Vitelleschi (Mutius Vitellescus), the new General of the Jesuits, to the Society: *Non e piu quella* (November, 1639).

28. The first Generals of the Society, after Saint Ignatius Loyola (who died in 1556), were J. Lainez (1558–65), Saint Francis Borgia (1565–72), Everard Mercurian (1573–80), Claudio Aquaviva (1581–1615),

790²⁹

Ep. 16 Aquavivae. *De formandis concionatoribus.*

p. 373. *Longe fallantur qui ad —irrigaturae.*

Reading the Fathers to bring them into line with his imagination, instead of shaping his thought in line with that of the Fathers.

Ep. 1 Mutii Vitellesci.

p. 389. *Quamvis enim probe norim—et absolutum.*

p. 390. *Dolet ac queritur —esse modestiam.*

modesty.

p. 392. *Lex ne dimidiata — reprehendit.*

The Mass. I do not know what he says.

408. *Ita feram illam —etiam irrumpat.*

Politics.

409. *Ad extremum pervelim —circumferatur.*

By a misfortune or rather by a singular good fortune for the Society, whatever one of them does is attributed to all.

410. *Querimoniae— deprehendetis,* p. 412.

Obeying the bishops exactly; so that it does not appear that we are trying to take them on, in imitation of Saint Francis Xavier.

412. *Ad haec si a litibus —aviditatis.*

Testaments. Law suits.

413. *Patris Borgiae— videbitur illam futuram.*

They add to, even invent untrue stories.

415. *Ita res domesticas —Nunc dimittis, etc. Ep. 2*

---

and Muzio Vitelleschi (1615–45). From their "complaints," Pascal considered assembling the material for a *Provincial Letter*, for which the notes in fragment 790 are a preparation. See the thirteenth *Provincial Letter*: "There is nothing more directly opposed to the explicit orders of Saint Ignatius and of your first Generals than this confused mixture of all sorts of opinions. I will speak to you about it one day perhaps, Fathers, and we shall be surprised to find how far you have fallen away from the first spirit of your Institute, and how your own Generals foresaw that the disorder of your doctrine with regard to morality could be fatal not just to your Society but to the universal Church."

29. Pascal annotates in French, in the right-hand column, excerpts from letters written by the Generals of the Society to remind its members of the early spirit of their institution. The Latin citations in the left-hand column (too fragmentary to be usefully translated), references to the *Epistolæ præpositorum generalium ad patres et fratres Societatis Jesu* [Letters from the Generals to the Fathers and Brothers of the Company of Jesus] (Antwerp: Johann van Meurs, 1635) are most likely in Arnaud's hand.

Mutii Vitellesci.

432. *Quarto nonnullorum— quam ardentissime possum urgere.*

433. *Quoniam vero de loquendi licentia—aut raro plectatur.*

Ep. 3 Mutii Vittelesci.

p. 437. *Nec sane dubium—nihil jam detrimenti acceperit.*

p. 440. *Ardentissime Deum exoremus—operari non est gravatus, et tu fili hominis,* etc.

Ezekiel, 37. p. 441. *Secundum caput—tanti facinus.*

p. 442. *Haec profecto una si deficiet—qui haec molitur,* etc.

p. 443. *Ex hoc namque vitio —importunum praebeas.*

p. 443. *Spectabit tertium caput—mutatus est color optimus.* 445. *De paupertate —non advertentur veritati.* 445. *Nobilis quidam Roma —collocabit.*

p. 446. *Faxit Deus—atque si praetermitterentur.*

Probability: *Tueri pius potest, probabilis est. Auctore non caret.*

Failure to punish those who speak ill.

That the Society should not be harmed.

Lack of obedience in search of *their reputation*

Lack of obedience, seeking the support of noblemen.

They do things that are indecent and out of keeping with the Society, and say that the great noblemen importune them to do so. But it is they who importune the noblemen. So that they either make enemies of them, if they refuse them, or they ruin the Society, if they consent to it. Chastity.

Poverty, laxity of opinions contrary to the truth.

Vines, etc.

791

Examine the motive for the censure[30] by the phenomena. Make a hypothesis that fits them all.

———

The habit makes the doctrine.[31]

———

I mistrust this doctrine, since it is too gentle with me, in view of the malice it is claimed I have in me.

In the year 1647, grace for all; in 1650, it was rarer, etc.

However modest the inconvenience, they make other (graces), since they dispose of them as if they were their own work.

———

In the end Mr. Chamillard[32] is so close to it that, if there are steps to descend into nothingness, (this sufficient grace[33]) is now the nearest.

———

There was no one who was not surprised by it, since it has never been found[34] in scripture or in the Fathers, etc.

———

For how long, Father, has it been an article of faith? It cannot be older than the expression "proximate power."[35] And I believe that it created this heresy in being born, and that it came into being solely for this purpose.

———

I mistrust their unity, in the light of their specific contradictions. I shall wait for them to agree, before taking sides: for the sake of one friend, I would make too many enemies. I am not learned enough to reply to them.

———

30. The condemnation of Arnauld, the principal theologian of Port-Royal, by the Faculty of Theology of Paris. The censure was pronounced on January 14, 1656, on the "point of fact": Arnauld was declared "foolhardy" to have doubted that the five propositions condemned by the bull *Cum occasione* were in fact in the *Augustinus*. On January 29, it turned to the "point of law": Arnauld had himself put forward a "heretical" proposition by maintaining "that grace, without which we can do nothing, was withheld from Saint Peter at the time of his denials." The first four *Provincial Letters*, from January 23 to February 25, 1656, take up the defense of Arnauld.

31. About forty religious, suspected of voting more out of discipline than out of conviction, had thrown their weight behind the condemnation of Arnauld (see the first *Provincial Letter*). The remark is a pun on the familiar adage: "The habit doth the monk not make."

32. Michel Chamillard, professor at the Sorbonne. This adversary of Arnauld nonetheless eventually recognized, in 1655, that Arnauld's defense was very orthodox and very catholic.

33. Sufficient grace is the subject of the second *Provincial Letter*. For its supporters, among whom the Jesuits took pride of place, it is the grace given by God, which men may accept or reject at their own volition. The theologians of Port-Royal, on the other hand, defend the idea of efficacious grace, which is not given to all, and which infallibly directs man's volition to act, although without prejudice to human freedom. The Dominicans held the middle ground.

34. The doctrine of "actual grace." See the fourth *Provincial Letter*.

35. The "proximate power" to fulfill the commandments that the adversaries of Arnauld explain in contradictory ways. It is the subject of the first *Provincial Letter*.

If there had not been similar occasions in the Church, but I believe my parish priest about that.

———

Luther: everything except what is true.[36]

———

Only one speaks truly.

———

Heretical member.

———

One and holy.[37]

———

We were harmed by the *Illuminations.*[38]

———

A proposition is good in one author, and wicked in another.[39]
Yes, but there are other bad propositions then.

———

There are people who defer to the censure, others to reasons, and all to reasons. So I am surprised that you have not taken the general way, instead of the particular one, or at least that you have not joined them together.[40]

———

Plurality of graces.
Jansenist translators.

———

(*Saint Augustine has the greatest number of them, because of the divisions between his enemies.*) Apart from something that can be considered to be an uninterrupted tradition for twelve [hundred years]: popes, councils, etc.

———

Mr. Arnauld must have a great many ill feelings, if he infects those he embraces![41]

———

36. Luther took the trappings of the faith without the essentials: papal communion, apostolic succession, the Real Presence, though he claimed to retain the last of these.

37. See fr. 750.

38. *Les Enluminures du fameux Almanach des PP. Jésuites intitule La Déroute et confusion des Jansénistes* [The Illuminations of the Jesuit Father's Notorious Almanac, entitled The Rout and Confusion of the Jansenists], a satirical poem in burlesque verse in which Le Maistre de Sacy replied in January 1654 to the mocking almanac from the Jesuits, mentioned in the *Enluminures'* title [*The Rout and Confusion of the Jansenists*]. Cf. the formula in the third *Provincial Letter* attributed to an adversary of Arnauld with regard to his censured proposition: "This proposition would be Catholic in the mouth of another; it is only when spoken by M. Arnauld that the Sorbonne condemns it."

40. Cf. the third *Provincial Letter.* The doctors of the Sorbonne "considered it more convenient and easier to censure than to reply [to the arguments of Arnauld], because it is easier for them to find monks than arguments."

41. Cf. the concluding irony of the third *Provincial Letter*: "The grace of Saint Augustine will never be the true one for as long as Arnauld defends it. It would become such, if ever he happened to oppose it. That would be a sure success, and is indeed the only way to establish it and to destroy Molinism, such is the misfortune communicated by Arnauld to any opinions he embraces."

The censure is good for them in this way that, when they are censured, they will fight it by saying that they are imitating the Jansenists.

___

What a relief! No Frenchman is a good Catholic.

___

The litanies.[42] Clement VIII. Paul V. Censure. God is visibly protecting us.[43]

___

Man is indeed senseless.
He cannot make a mite.[44]

___

Instead of gods, the grace to go there.

___

792

9.[45]

Everybody states that they are.[46] Mr. Arnauld and his friends protest that he condemns them in themselves, and wherever they may be found; that, if they are in Jansenius, he condemns them there; that even if they are not there, if the heretical sense of these propositions that the pope has condemned is present in Jansenius, then he condemns Jansenius.

But you are not satisfied with these protestations. You want him to affirm that these propositions are found word for word in Jansenius. He has replied that he cannot affirm this, since he does not know whether it is the case; that he has looked for them there, as have countless others, without ever being able to find them. You, and all those like you, have been urged to identify on what pages they occur. Nobody has ever done so. And yet you want him now to be cut off from the Church on the strength of this refusal, even though he condemns all that the Church condemns, for the sole reason that he will not affirm that certain words or a given sense are in a book in which he has never found them, and in which no one can show them to him. Indeed, Father, this pretext is so flimsy, that there has perhaps never been so strange, so unjust, and so tyrannical a process in the Church.

___

42. Father Adam, a Jesuit, had published in 1654 a book of *Hours*. He had "forgotten" to include Saint Augustine in the litanies of the saints. The publisher was obliged by the Augustinians to make good the omission.

43. As shown by the miracle of the holy thorn at Port-Royal in which Pascal's niece was healed. See fr. 753, n. 67.

44. Montaigne, *Essays*, II, 12, 480: "Man is certainly crazy. He could not make a mite, and he makes gods by the dozen." On the mite, see fr. 230.

45. Reference unknown.

46. Even Port-Royal recognizes as heretical these five propositions falsely attributed to Jansenius.

You do not have to be a theologian to see that their heresy consists only of their opposition to you. I have experienced it for myself, and you see the more general proof of it in all those who have attacked you.

The parish priests of Rouen, Jansenists.[47]

The Caen vow.[48]

You believe your projects are so blameless that you make them the subject of a vow.

Two years ago their heresy was the bull. Last year it was internal. Six months ago it was *word for word*.[49] At the moment it is the sense.[50] Can I not see clearly that your only wish is to make them into heretics? The Blessed Sacrament.[51]

I have taken issue with you on behalf of others.

———

You are thoroughly ridiculous to make such a fuss over the propositions. It is a lot of fuss about nothing, and that should be understood.

———

(*The Sorbonne doctors*) Without authors' names. But since your purpose was clear, seventy opposed it.[52]—Date the ruling.

———

So that the man you had not been able to make into a heretic out of his own mouth, etc.

———

For everything is out in the open.

———

47. The parish priests of Rouen were accused by the Jesuits of being Jansenists because they had addressed a petition to their archbishop in August 1656 to obtain the condemnation of laxist casuists.

48. The pupils of the Jesuit college in Caen had publicly addressed a solemn vow to the Virgin Mary, in June 1653, to the effect that Jansenists should be damned. Pascal alludes to this in the eleventh *Provincial Letter*.

49. The members of Port-Royal are to be considered as heretics, according to the Jesuits, because they will not recognize that the five propositions may be found "word for word" (*totidem verbis*) in the *Augustinus*.

50. The Jesuits, in particular Père Annat, in his *Chicanes des Jansenistes* [The Jansenists' subtleties] (1654), sought to force their adversaries to admit that the five propositions were to be found "word for word" in Jansenius' *Augustinius*. This fragment assembles notes for the writing of the seventeenth *Provincial Letter*.

51. Certain Jesuits went so far as to accuse the Jansenists of denying the Real Presence of Christ in the Eucharist. Father Meynier, a Jesuit, published in 1646 a pamphlet entitled *Le Port-Royal et Genève d'intelligence contre le Très-Saint Sacrement de l'Autel dans leurs Livres* [Port-Royal and Geneva of one mind against the Most Holy Sacrament of the Altar in their books]. It is treated in the fifteenth and sixteenth *Provincial Letters*.

52. The five propositions condemned by Innocent X had been "examined in their own right, without considering who might be their author" (eighteenth *Provincial Letter*). "Seventy doctors" of the Sorbonne refused to condemn Arnauld on account of the fact that he had expressed his doubt that they were in the *Augustinus*.

Either he knows, one way or the other, or he doubts; either he is a sinner or a heretic.

———

Preface.

Villeloin.[53]

Jansenius, Aurelius,[54] Arnauld, *Provincial Letters.*

What reason do you have for all this? You say that I am a Jansenist, that Port-Royal endorses the five propositions, and therefore that I endorse them: three lies.

If you do no more than consider the heathen.

That same light that reveals supernatural truths reveals them infallibly, whereas the light that, etc.

How can the sense of Jansenius exist in propositions that are not by him?

And I beseech you not to come and tell me that it is not you who are stirring all this up. Spare me the reply.

———

Either this is in Jansenius, or it is not. If it is, then he is condemned on account of it. If it is not, why do you want to have him condemned?

If just one of your propositions from Father Escobar is condemned, I will go and carry Escobar in one hand, and the censure in the other, and I will make a formal argument on that basis.

The pope has not condemned two things. He has only condemned the sense of the propositions.

Will you say that he has not condemned it? But the sense of Jansenius is contained in it, the pope says? I can see that the pope thought it, on account of your *totidems,*[55] but not that he said it on pain of excommunication.

———

How could he and the French bishops not have believed it? You said to them: *totidem,* and they did not know that you are capable of saying it, even though it was not the case. Impostors! They had not read my fifteenth *Letter.*

53. Michel de Marolles, abbé de Villeloin, had written as the preface to his translation of the New Testament (1653) a *Discourse on the Jansenist Cause.* His *Mémoires,* which appeared at the beginning of 1656, showed clearly that his sympathies were with Port-Royal.

54. Pseudonym of Saint-Cyran (1581–1643), friend of Jansenius and founding spiritual master of Port-Royal.

55. On *totidem,* "word for word," see above, n. 50.

793[56]
Diana[57]

11.

This is what Diana is used for.[58]

11. IT IS PERMITTED TO WITHHOLD BENEFICES WITH NO CURE OF SOULS FROM THE MOST WORTHY. The Council of Trent seems to say the opposite, but this is how he proves it: for if that were the case, all prelates would be in a state of damnation, since this is how they all behave in this respect.

11. THE KING AND THE POPE ARE NOT OBLIGED TO CHOOSE THE MOST WORTHY. IF THAT WERE THE CASE, THE POPE AND THE KINGS WOULD HAVE A DREADFUL RESPONSIBILITY.

21. And elsewhere: IF THAT OPINION WERE NOT TRUE, PENITENTS AND CONFESSORS WOULD HAVE A LOT TO THINK ABOUT. AND THAT IS WHY I CONSIDER THAT IT HAS TO BE FOLLOWED IN PRACTICE.

22. And in another place, where he gives the conditions necessary for a sin to be mortal, he provides so many conditions that you can hardly sin mortally at all; and once he has established that, he exclaims: HOW EASY AND LIGHT IS THE YOKE OF THE LORD![59]

11. And elsewhere: YOU ARE NOT OBLIGED TO GIVE ALMS FROM YOUR SURPLUS FOR THE ORDINARY NEEDS OF THE POOR. IF THE OPPOSITE WERE TRUE, THE MAJORITY OF THE RICH AND THEIR CONFESSORS WOULD HAVE TO BE CONDEMNED.

These reasons frustrated me, so I said to the Father: "But what is stopping them from being condemned?"—"That is what he has also taken into account at the same point" he replied, "where, after he has said: 22. IF THAT WERE TRUE, THE RICHEST MEN WOULD BE DAMNED, he adds: ARRAGONIUS'S REPLY TO THAT IS THAT INDEED THEY ARE. AND BAUNEZ, A JESUIT, FURTHER ADDS THAT THEIR CONFESSORS ARE DAMNED AS WELL. BUT I REPLY WITH VALENTIA, ANOTHER JESUIT, AND OTHER AUTHORS, THAT THERE ARE SEVERAL REASONS FOR EXCUSING THE RICH AND THEIR CONFESSORS."

I was thrilled with this argument, when he finished me off with this one:

---

56. Unused sketch for a *Provincial Letter*.

57. Diana was a Theatine religious (1586–1663) and author of the *Résolutions morales* [Moral resolutions]. He is pilloried in the fifth and sixth *Provinciales*.

58. Diana is useful to the Jesuits precisely because he is not a Jesuit. Thus, laxist propositions cannot be imputed exclusively to the Society.

59. Matthew 11:28–30: "Come unto me [proposes Jesus] for *my yoke is sweet and my burden light.*"

"IF THIS OPINION HELD TRUE FOR RESTITUTION, JUST HOW MANY RESTITUTIONS THERE WOULD HAVE TO BE!"

"Oh Father, I said to him, what a good reason!"—"Oh, the Father said to me, what an obliging man you are."—"Oh Father, I replied to him, without your casuists, what a lot of people would be damned! Oh Father, how wide you make the road that leads to heaven, and what a lot of people are able to find it![60] What a . . ."

794

It is, in its idiom, wholly the body of Jesus Christ, but it cannot be said to be the whole body of Jesus Christ.

The union of two things without change occurring does not mean that you can say that one thing becomes the other.

Thus the soul being united with the body,

fire with wood without change occurring.

But change must occur in order for the form of one thing to become the form of another.

Thus the union of the Word with humanity.

———

Because my body without my soul would not make up the body of a man, therefore my soul united to any matter whatsoever will make up my body.

He does not distinguish between necessary conditions and sufficient conditions. Union is necessary, but not sufficient.

The left arm is not the right.

———

Impenetrability is a property of bodies.[61]

———

Identity *de numero* with respect to the same time requires identity of matter.[62]

———

60. In distinction to Matthew 7:14. "How narrow is the gate, and strait is the way that leadeth to life: and few there are that find it!"

61. This fragment discusses Descartes's theology of the Eucharist, propounded in a letter to Father Mesland (February 9, 1645), a letter of which Pascal must have seen a copy, since it was not published until 1811, and the fragment makes specific references to Descartes's text. Descartes defines the identity of the human body by its union with the same soul, but this identity, for Pascal, equally presupposes the acknowledgment of the specific properties of matter, such as impenetrability.

62. Descartes rejects the criterion of the "identity of matter" in order to identify the identity of bodies, because he only considers their permanence through time; but this criterion becomes unavoidable, according to Pascal, when their existence is envisaged at the same time. Pascal takes up Descartes's opposition between *de numero* (in number/numerically) and *idem numerico* (the same in number).

Therefore, if God united my soul to a body in China, the same body *idem numero* would be in China.[63]

———

The same river that flows there is *idem numero* as the one that runs at the same time in China.[64]

795

Part 1. B. 2. C. 1. S. 4.[65]

What can be more absurd than to say that inanimate bodies have passions, fears, terrors? That insentient bodies, lifeless and indeed incapable of life, have passions, which presuppose at least a sensitive soul to receive them?[66] Furthermore, that the object of their terror should be the vacuum? What is there in the vacuum that could possibly frighten them? What could be more base and more ridiculous?

That is not all. [It is claimed] that they have within them a principle of movement for avoiding the vacuum. Have they got arms, legs, muscles, nerves?

If is not a sign of indifference.[67]

Malachi.[68]

Isaiah.

Isaiah: *If you be willing*, etc.[69]

In what day soever.[70]

---

63. Pascal pushes the consequence of the Cartesian thesis to the absurd.

64. Pascal draws on a comparison used by Descartes to support his dissociation of numerical identity from material identity. "The Loire is the same river that existed ten years ago, even though it is no longer the same water." Descartes confuses the conditions of identity, substituting spatial coexistence for temporal coexistence. See the "Lettre au Père Mesland [Letter to Father Mesland], 9 April 1645," in Descartes, *Œuvres*, ed. Charles Adam and Paul Tannery, vol. 4, *Correspondance* (Paris: Léopold Cerf, 1901), 165; translation here courtesy of the volume editors.

65. A reference relative to the *Treatise on the Vacuum*, on which Pascal worked during 1650–51 but never completed. There remains a prefatory project and two fragments published in 1663 after Pascal's death, along with the *Treatise on the Equilibrium of Liquids and on the Weight of the Mass of the Air.*

66. The sensitive soul, or the sensitive power of the soul, has as its function, in the scholastic classification, to perceive the totality of sentient bodies. It is situated between the vegetative soul, which enlivens the body to which it is joined, and the intellective soul, which accomplishes without any corporeal organ the operations bearing on the universal being. See Saint Thomas, *Summa theologiæ* I, q. 78.

67. A note for the *Writings on Grace*. In the following citations, the *if*, according to Pascal, does not presuppose a freedom of indifference in man, in other words the full and entire power to accomplish at his will the commandments of God.

68. Malachi 2:12: "*If* you will not hear, and *if* you will not lay it to heart [. . .]: I will send poverty upon you, and will curse your blessings [. . .]."

69. Isaiah 1:19–20: "*If you be willing*, and will hearken to me, you shall eat the good things of the land. But if you will not, and will provoke me to wrath: the sword shall devour you because the mouth of the Lord hath spoken it."

70. Genesis 2:16–17: "Of every tree of paradise thou shalt eat: But of the tree of knowledge of good and evil, thou shalt not eat. For *in what day soever* [= if] thou shalt eat of it, thou shalt die the death."

796[71]

You threaten me.

I am not a heretic, I did not endorse the five propositions. You say I did, but you cannot prove it. I say you have said this, and I can prove it.

I tell you that you are impostors, and I can prove it to you; and I say that you do not even hide it, in your insolence: d'Alby,[72] Brisacier,[73] Meynier:[74] and that you authorize it.

DESTROY.[75]

Since you have only dealt with this, you must approve of everything else. *From senatusconsults and plebiscites:*[76] ask for similar passages.

When you believed Mr. Puys[77] to be an enemy of the Society, he was an unworthy pastor of his church, ignorant, heretical, devoid of good faith and manners. Since then, he is a worthy pastor, full of good faith and manners.

To calumniate, *this is a great blindness of heart*. Not to see the ill of it, *this is a an even greater blindness of heart*. To defend it, rather than to confess it as a sin, *then the depth of iniquity envelopes men*, etc. 230, Prosper.[78]

To destroy.[79] Caramuel.[80]

Great noblemen are divided by civil wars.
And so are you by the civil war of mankind.

---

71. This fragment assembles a series of notes anticipating the eleventh through the sixteenth *Provincial Letters*, in which Pascal addresses the Jesuits directly and replies to their accusations of imposture.

72. On Father Alby see above, n. 13.

73. Jesuit author of *Jansenism confounded* (1651) a defamatory pamphlet condemned by the Archbishop of Paris. See the eleventh *Provincial Letter*.

74. Father Meynier, see above, n. 51.

75. ELIDERE ("cancel"). See fr. 750. Here Pascal alludes to a thesis proposed by the Jesuits of Louvain: "It is but a venial sin to attack the reputation of and to impute false crimes (falso crimine *elidere*) to those who speak ill of us." Antoine Arnauld takes up the same issue in the *avis au lecteur* [to the reader] of his *Reflexions sur un Decret de l'Inquisition de Rome portant defense de lire le Catechisme de la Grace et un autre catechisme contraire fait à Douay sous le mesme titre* [Reflections on a Decree by the Roman Inquisition forbidding to read the Catechism of Grace and another, contrary catechism professed in Douay with the same title] (Paris, 1651), and adds a note to specify his target: "Ces theses ont esté soustenües dans leur College de Louvain, sous le mesme Jesuite qui a fait les Theses contre M. d'Ipre" [These theses were defended in their Leuen college, under the same Jesuit who wrote Theses again M. of Ypres (Jansenius)]", in Pascal, *Œuvres*, ed. Léon Brunschwicg, Pierre Boutroux, and Félix Gazier, vol. 6 (Paris: Hachette, 1914), 170.

76. See fr. 94.

77. See above, fr. 789, n. 13.

78. Saint Prosper of Aquitaine, a disciple of Saint Augustine, is quoted several times in the *Writings on Grace*.

79. See above, n. 75.

80. A Spanish Cistercian, nicknamed "the prince of laxists." Pascal quotes him in the seventh *Provincial Letter*.

I am quite pleased that you should publish the same thing as me.
Contentious. Saint Paul.[81]
He has given me cause.

Saints engage in subtleties to make themselves appear criminal, and to make their best actions seem wrong, and these people engage in subtleties to excuse their worst actions.

————

Do not claim that this will be settled by argument.

Your entire works will be published, and in French: and everyone will become the judge of them.

————

The pagan sages erected a building equally beautiful on the outside, but upon an unsound foundation.[82] And the devil deceives men by this apparent resemblance, based on very different foundations.

————

No man has ever had a better cause than I have, and no men have ever laid themselves open to attack as you have.

————

Worldly people do not believe they are on the right track.

————

The more they draw attention to the weakness of my person, the more they legitimize my cause.

————

You say that I am a heretic. Is that allowed? And if you are not afraid that men will see justice done, are you not afraid that God will see it done in my case?

————

You will feel the force of the truth, and you will submit to it.

————

I appeal to be done the justice of their no longer being taken at their word.

You would have to force people to believe you on pain of mortal sin.—
Destroy.[83]

————

It is a sin to believe spiteful gossip lightly.

————

81. Romans 2:8: "But to *them that are contentious*, and who obey not the truth, but give credit to iniquity, wrath and indignation ..."

82. This is Pascal's response to La Mothe le Vayer's *De la vertu des payens* [On the virtue of pagans] (see "The Contours of Disbelief," in the introduction of this edition) and others who held that such virtuous pagans as Socrates were implicitly saved by Christ. See, also, fr. 715, n. 24. The Augustinian tradition, however, firmly insisted that only those having an explicit knowledge of Christ could be saved.

83. On the meaning and significance of this term, *elidere*, see above, nn. 75 and 79. The term recurs in this series of notes.

He did not easily trust a slanderer. Saint Augustine.[84]

———

And, by falling on all sides, he made me fall in turn in accordance with the maxim of the slanderers.

———

There is something supernatural about such blindness. *A necessity of which they were worthy.*[85]

———

I am alone against thirty thousand? Not at all. You keep the court, you keep imposture, I will keep the truth. Therein lies all my strength. If I lose it, I am lost. There will be no shortage of people to accuse and punish me. But I have the truth, and we shall see who will prevail.

I am not worthy to defend religion, but you are not worthy to defend error. And I hope that God in his mercy, without regard for the evil that is in me and with regard for the good that is in you, will grant grace to us all, so that truth does not falter in my hands and that falsehood does not...

———

You lie with an extreme impudence.[86]

———

230. The worst sin is to defend it. *Destroy.*

———

340, 23. The good fortune of the wicked.

———

A man shall be known by his learning.[87]

———

66. *Labor in order to speak lies.*[88]
80. Almsgiving.
False piety, double sin.

797[89]

B. You do not know about the prophecies, if you do not know that all this is bound to happen: princes, prophets, pope, and even priests; and nonetheless the Church must endure.

---

84. Saint Augustine, *Commentary on Psalm XIV*, 3, no. 14.

85. Wisdom 19:4: "For a *necessity, of which they were worthy,* brought them [the Egyptians] to this end."

86. Pascal seeks to transform this *riposte,* spoken by a Capuchin calumniated by the Jesuits, into a reflex formula, in order to counter all unfounded accusations uttered by any member of the Society. See the fifteenth *Provincial Letter.*

87. Proverbs 12:8.

88. Pascal contracts Jeremiah 9:5: "For they have taught their tongue to speak *lies:* they have *labored* to commit iniquity," echoing Saint Augustine's *Commentary on Psalm CXXXIX,* 10.

89. This fragment as well as fr. 800 are preparatory notes for the *Project for a Pastoral Letter Against the Apology for the Casuists* (1658).

By the grace of God, we have not yet reached that point. Woe to those priests! But we hope that God will be merciful to us, so that we are not of their number.

1 Saint Peter, c. 2: past false prophets, images of the ones to come.[90]

798

That cannot, said the Feuillant, be quite so certain, since argument is a mark of uncertainty.[91]

Saint Athanasius,[92] Saint Chrysostom.[93]

Morality. Unbelievers.

———

The Jesuits have not rendered truth uncertain, but they have rendered their impiety certain.

Contradictions have always remained in place to blind the wicked. For everything that harms truth or charity is evil. That is the true principle.

799

Man's heart is indifferent as to whether to believe that there are three or four persons in the Trinity, but not, etc.[94] And that is why they become heated in defense of one, and not the other.

It is good to do one thing, but not to abandon doing the other. The same God who has told us, etc.

And so, whoever believes one and not the other does not do so because God has told him to, but because his covetousness does not deny it and because he is pleased to give assent to it and so without difficulty have the witness of his conscience that . . .

But it is a false witness.

Letter about the Jesuits establishing themselves everywhere with violence.

———

Supernatural blindness.[95]

———

90. Actually 2 Peter 2:1: "But there were also false prophets among the people, even as there shall be among you lying teachers, who shall bring in sects of perdition."

91. See fr. 207.

92. See ch. XXXII, fr. 439, n. 15.

93. See ch. IV, n. 21.

94. *Factum pour les Curés d'Amiens* [Brief for the parish priests of Amiens] of July 27, 1658: "Is it not visible, by what Saint Bernard says, that he was just as powerfully touched by the novelties that Abelard wishes to introduce into Christian morality, as by his imaginings and errors on the mystery of the Holy Trinity?" In Pascal, *Œuvres complètes*, vol. 2. (Paris: Hachette, 1913), 273; translation by David Wetsel. This work is not, in fact, by Pascal.

95. See fr. 516.

This morality that is headed by a crucified God.

These are the people [who] took a vow of obedience *as if to Christ*!

The decadence of the Jesuits.

Our religion, which is wholly divine.

A casuist, mirror![96]

If you believe him to be good, it is a good sign.

It is a strange thing, that there is no means of giving them the right idea about religion.

A crucified God.

By detaching this punishable affair of the schism, they will be punished.

But what a reversal! Their children, by embracing it, love those who corrupt them. Their enemies abhor them.[97]

We are the witnesses.

For the mass of casuists, far from being something of which to accuse the Church, it is, on the contrary, something for the Church to bemoan.

And in order that we should not be open to suspicion.

Just as the Jews who parade their books are not open to suspicion from the Gentiles, so they parade their *Constitutions* for our benefit.

800

So that if it is true, on the one hand, that some lax religious and some corrupt casuists, who are not members of the hierarchy, have dabbled in these cases of corruption, it is indisputable, on the other hand, that the true pastors of the Church, who are the true depositories of the Divine Word, have kept it inviolate against the efforts of those who have undertaken to destroy it.

And so the faithful have no pretext for following this laxity, which are only offered to them by the alien hands of these casuists, in place of the sound doc-

---

96. In the *Imago primi sæculi* ... [Image of the first century ...] (1640), the Society of Jesus presented itself as *speculum Dei*, the mirror (image) of God. See above, n. 16.

97. On the aversion of the Calvinists to the casuists, see the fifth of the *Écrits des Curés de Paris* [Writings of the Paris priests] of June 11, 1658.

trine that is presented to them from the paternal hands of their own pastors. And the heretics and the impious have no reason to claim that such abuses are marks of the lack of God's providence for his Church, since as the Church is strictly speaking contained in the body of the hierarchy, far from concluding from the current state of affairs that God has abandoned it to corruption, it has never appeared more clearly than today that God is visibly defending it from corruption.

For if some of these men, who by an extraordinary vocation have professed to leave the world behind and don the habit of religion in order to live in a more perfect state than ordinary Christians, have fallen into errors that horrify ordinary Christians, and have become for us what the false prophets were among the Jews, that is a particular and personal misfortune that is indeed worthy of regret, but from which nothing may be concluded against the care that God takes of his Church, since all these things have been so clearly foretold, and since it was announced so long ago that such temptations would arise with regard to these sorts of people, that when one is properly instructed one sees in all this the signs of God's purpose rather than of his neglect with respect to us.

801

You must hear the two parties; that is what I was careful to do.

When you have only heard one party, you always come down on that side. But the opposing party makes you change your mind. Whereas in this case the Jesuit confirms you in your opinion.

———

Not what they do, but what they say.[98]

It is only against me that they are railing. I do not mind. I know to whom I have to answer.

———

Jesus Christ was a stumbling block.[99]

———

Worthy of condemnation, condemned.

———

Politics

We have found two obstacles to the plan of making things easier for men: one is the internal laws of the Gospel, the other the external laws of the state and of religion.

---

98. Matthew 23:3. Jesus, concerning the scribes and Pharisees: "All things therefore *whatsoever they shall say to you*, observe and do: but *according to their works do ye not*; for they say, and do not." The Jesuits, more corrupt than the Pharisees do not even say what needs to be done.

99. Isaiah 8:14, quoted in fragments 269, 734, and 735.

Of the one,[100] we are the masters; of the other, this is what we have done: *amplify, restrict, from the greater to the lesser.*
More recent.[101]

Probable.
They reason like people who prove that it is dark at midday.
If such bad reasons as these are probable, then everything will be probable:
First reason: *Master of conjugal acts.* Molina.
Second reason: *He cannot be compensated.* Lessius.[102]
Not countered with holy sayings, but with unspeakable ones.
Bauny burner of barns.[103]
Mascarenhas, the Council of Trent, for priests in a state of mortal sin, *as soon as possible.*[104]

802

Difference between dinner and supper.

_____

In God the word does not differ from the intention, since he is truthful; nor the word from the effect, since he is powerful; nor the means from the effect, since he is wise. Bernard, *Last Sermon on the "Missus."*[105]

_____

Augustine, V, *The City of God,* 10: This rule is general: God can do everything, except those things which, if he could do them, he would not be omnipotent, such as to die, TO BE DECEIVED, ETC., TO LIE, etc.

_____

Several evangelists for the confirmation of the truth. Their discrepancy useful.[106]

_____

100. The "internal laws of the Gospel" that the Jesuits interpret as they wish.

101. As far as the "external laws" are concerned, probability allows them to be avoided by "broadening them out," by "limiting" them, by moving "from the greatest to the least." And anything that a given probable opinion authorizes could not have been explicitly condemned by them, the Jesuits argue, because it is more recent than they are.

102. Molina: the husband is the "*master of the conjugal acts* of his wife." Lessius: "The offence of adultery *cannot be compensated for* with money." On this typical instance of casuistry, taken up by Escobar, see fragment 603.

103. In his *Somme des péchés* [*Sum of sins*], the Jesuit Bauny exempts from the obligation of repayment any man who asks a soldier "to burn the barn of a man who has offended him" since he has only asked and not done the deed himself. Cited in the eighth *Provincial Letter.*

104. See fr. 604. Pedro Mascarenhas, a Portuguese explorer and colonial administrator, had in 1656 defended a thesis contradicting a decree of the Council of Trent.

105. Saint Bernard, *Last Sermon* on Luke 1:26. "The angel Gabriel was sent (*missus*) by God to a city of Galilee called Nazareth."

106. See fr. 268. The discrepancies in the four Gospels attest to the fact that they were not written in concert as a fraudulent testimony.

Eucharist after the Last Supper: truth after figure.

Ruin of Jerusalem, figure of the ruin of the world.
Forty years after the death of Jesus.

Jesus does not know either as a man or as an emissary: Matthew 24:36.[107]

Jesus condemned by the Jews and Gentiles.

The Jews and Gentiles, prefigured by the two sons.[108]

Augustine, XX, *The City of God*, 29.[109]

803

With fear work out your salvation.[110]

The poor in grace.[111]

Ask and ye shall receive.[112] So is it in our power to ask? On the contrary, so it is not: because obtaining is in our power, asking is not. Now since salvation is not in our power and obtaining is, prayer is not in our power.

The just man should no longer hope in God then, for he must not hope, but rather strive to obtain what he asks.

So we may conclude that since man is incapable now of using this proximate power and since God does not wish this to be the means by which man avoids falling away from God, it is only by efficacious power that he may avoid doing so.

107. *Missus*: the emissary. "But of that day and hour no one knoweth, not the angels of heaven, but the Father alone." They are unknown therefore even to Christ either as "man" or as "emissary," that is to say as envoy of the Father.

108. Matthew 21:28–32: "A certain man had two sons; and coming to the first, he said: Son, go work today in my vineyard. And he answering, said: I will not. But afterwards, being moved with repentance, he went. And coming to the other, he said in like manner. And he answering, said: I go, Sir; and he went not. Which of the two did the father's will? They say to him: The first. Jesus saith to them: Amen I say to you, that the publicans and the harlots shall go into the kingdom of God before you. For John came to you in the way of justice, and you did not believe him. But the publicans and the harlots believed him: but you, seeing it, did not even afterwards repent, that you might believe him."

109. Saint Augustine interprets Malachi 4:5–6, as a prophecy of the conversion of the Jews to Christianity in the last days.

110. Philippians 2:12: "*With fear* and trembling *work out your salvation.*"

111. *Écrits sur la grâce* [*Writings on grace*]: "There is this difference between the poor in the order of nature and the poor in the order of grace, that the poor of the world have always the proximate power to ask, but are never certain of the power to obtain; whereas the poor in grace are always certain to obtain what they ask for, but are never certain of having the power to ask." Translation by David Wetsel. See Pascal, *Œuvres complètes*, ed. Jean Mesnard (Paris: Desclée De Brouwer, 1991), vol. 3, p. 715.

112. Matthew 7:7.

So those who fall away do not have this power without which you do not fall away yourself from God. And those who do not fall away from him have this efficacious power.

So those who, after persevering for a time in prayer by this efficacious power, stop praying, lack this efficacious power. And consequently, it is God who gives up first, in that sense.

8. The Guerrier Manuscripts[1]

804

M. de Roannez[2] would say: "The reasons come to me later, but first of all the thing itself pleases me, or shocks me, without knowing the reason, and yet it shocks me for the very reason that I only discover later."—But I do not think that it shocked for the reasons that one finds later, but rather that one only finds those reasons because it shocks.

805

Now probability is necessary for the other maxims, such as that of Lamy and the calumniator.[3]

By their fruits.[4] Judge their faith by their morals.

Probability is insignificant without corrupt means, and means are as nothing without probability.

There is a pleasure to be had in the certainty of being able to do good and of knowing how to do good. Grace: "*To know and to be able.*" Probability affords it, because you can give account to God with assurance on the strength of their authors.

806

The heretics who take advantage of the Jesuits' doctrine must be told that [it is not] that of the Church, [that this is not the] doctrine of the Church, and that our divisions do not keep us away from the altar.[5]

1. The following fragments appear in the *Second recueil* [Second collection] of Father Pierre Guerrier, consisting of copies made in 1733–34 of papers left to the Clermont Oratory by Marguerite Périer, niece and god-daughter of Pascal and the last of his direct legatees.

2. Duke and peer of France, Governor of Poitou and intimate of Pascal, whom he followed on the path to conversion. Pascal's *Lettres à Mlle de Roannez* [Letters to Mlle de Roannez] are addressed to his sister.

3. A proposition of the casuist Lamy, quoted in the eighteenth *Provincial Letter*: "That a religious can kill anyone who threatens to publish calumnies against him or against his community, when he cannot defend himself in any other way." On Lamy, see above, fr. 750, n. 51, and fr. 789, n. 12.

4. Matthew 7:16. Concerning false prophets: "By their fruits you shall know them. Do men gather grapes of thorns, or figs of thistles?"

5. Augustine, Letter 162, n. 24. "Schism is an intolerable evil since it opposes altar against altar." Quoted in French by Sellier in the 2010 edition of the *Pensées*, 652n1; translated from the French by the editors.

807

If in differing we condemned, you would be right. Uniformity without diversity, useless to the others; diversity without uniformity, ruinous for us. One harmful outside, the other inside.

808

... But it is impossible for God ever to be the end, if he is not the beginning. You train your gaze upwards, but you are supported by sand. And the earth will give way, and you will fall as you contemplate heaven.

809

The Jesuits have tried to link God with the world, and have gained only the scorn of God and of the world as a result. For on the side of conscience, that is obvious; and on the side of the world, they are no good at cabals. They have power, as I have often said, but I mean with respect to other religious. Their credit will allow them to have a chapel built or one of their churches declared a jubilee station,[6] but not to secure any appointment as a bishop or governor of a fortified town. Being a monk is a silly job in the world, as they are the first to admit (Father Brisacier, Benedictines). Meanwhile, you bend to the will of those more powerful than yourselves and you fully use the little credit you have to oppress those who are less artful than you in the world.

810

The Jesuits

By corrupting the bishops and the Sorbonne, they have not gained the advantage of rendering their judgement just, but rather of rendering their judges unjust. And therefore, when in future they are condemned for it, they will say *ad hominem*[7] that they are unjust, and so will refute their judgement. But that serves no purpose. For, since they cannot conclude that the Jansenists are rightly condemned by virtue of the simple fact that they are condemned, so likewise they will then not be able to conclude that they have been wrongly condemned themselves, because they will have been so condemned by corruptible judges. For their condemnation will be just, not because it will be given by judges who are always just, but by judges who are just in this matter; and that will be made clear by the other proofs.

---

6. I.e. a church designated, during a jubilee year, as a site where people could visit to receive indulgences.

7. That is to say, by disqualifying them on account of the decisions they have themselves taken in the past.

811[8]

As the two principal interests of the Church are the conservation of the piety of the faithful and the conversion of heretics, we are filled with sorrow to see the factions that are coming into being today in order to introduce such errors as are most capable of closing off entry into our communion to heretics forever, and of fatally corrupting those pious Catholics that are left. This enterprise that is being so openly undertaken today against those truths of religion that are most important for salvation does not just fill us with displeasure but also with fear and trembling; because, apart from the feeling that all Christians should have about these disorders, we also have the obligation to put them right and use the authority that God has given us to ensure that the people he has entrusted to us, etc.

812

All their casuists put together cannot confirm people's consciences in error, and that is why it is important to choose good guides.

So they will be doubly guilty, both of having followed ways they should not follow, and of having listened to doctors they should not have listened to.

8. The project of a *Requeste des Curez de Nevers* [Petition from the parish priests of Nevers] presented in July 1658 to their bishop against the *Apologie pour les Casuistes* [Apology for the casuists].

9. Annotation Discovered in 1952[1]

813

So either the Jesuits make people embrace error or they make them swear that they have embraced it and so drive them either into error or perjury, and corrupt either the mind or the heart.

1. This is a note discovered by Paule Jansen in 1952 in the margin of a copy of the *Response d'un ecclé-siastique de Louvain a l'advis qui luy a esté donné sur le sujet de la bulle pretendue du pape Urbain VIII contre le livre de M. Jansenius* [Reply from a Louvain ecclesiastic to the information given him about the supposed bull of Pope Urban VIII against the book of Mr. Jansenius], 3rd ed., by Dom Pierre de Saint-Joseph (Louvain, 1650), from Pascal's library, today part of the Bibliothèque Mazarine's collections (n. 61 298), which Pascal used for the eighteenth *Provincial Letter*.

EXCHANGE WITH
M. DE SACY ON
EPICTETUS AND
MONTAIGNE

INTRODUCTION

The *Exchange with M. de Sacy* constitutes the most celebrated of the over forty "conversations" reported by Nicolas Fontaine and set down between 1696 and 1700, some forty years after the events they purport to recount. Fontaine had been the secretary of Le Maistre de Sacy (1613–84), one of the principal theologians of Port-Royal.[1]

Fontaine's *Mémoires ou histoire des solitaires de Port-Royal* [Memoirs, or history of the solitaires of Port-Royal], and therefore the *Exchange with M. de Sacy*, were thought to be forever lost. Scholars had to make do with copies of copies, into which had crept many errors, deletions, and mutilated passages.[2] In 1992 Pascale Thouvenin discovered Fontaine's autograph in the library of the French Academy, a collection so well known that no one had ever thought to look for it there. The catalogue of this prestigious library listed the autograph under the original title and under Fontaine's own name. Jean Mesnard verified the handwriting of the entire manuscript as that of Fontaine. Pascale Thouvenin's discovery meant that an entirely new and original version of the *Memoirs* (and thus of the *Exchange*) had to be constituted.[3] Compared to the autograph, even the best of the copies of the Exchange contained over 140 textual errors, suppressed numerous citations, and summarized many passages.

Many scholars had thought that the Exchange was Pascal's actual transcript of a conversation with Sacy in January, 1655, when Pascal made a retreat at Port-Royal-des-Champs subsequent to the ecstatic religious experience recorded by the "Memorial" (fr. 742). In fact, what Fontaine found in Sacy's

1. On Sacy, see the introduction, n. 26.

2. See David Wetsel, *L'Écriture et le Reste: The Pensées of Pascal in the Exegetical Tradition of Port-Royal* (Columbus: Ohio State University Press, 1981), 9–15, for an idea of the complex genealogy of the manuscripts commentators had sought to establish.

3. Nicolas Fontaine, *Mémoires ou histoire des solitaires de Port-Royal*, Édition critique par Pascale Thouvenin [Memoirs, or history of the solitaires of Port-Royal, critical edition by Pascale Thouvenin] (Paris: Champion, 2001). This authentic text of the *Exchange* figures in Sellier's 2010 edition of the *Pensées*, pp. 721–44. The versions in the Lafuma and Mesnard *Collected Works* date from before Thouvenin's discovery and thus are not based on the original autograph. The *Exchange with M. de Sacy* that follows is the first English translation based upon Fontaine's original text.

papers after his death in 1684, some forty years later, was in all probability a "study" (as it is called in par. 44) sent by Pascal to Sacy three years afterward in 1658, when his writing of his Apology was rapidly progressing. It appears that Pascal was seeking Sacy's reaction to his quite radical idea that the Stoicism represented by Epictetus and the skepticism found in the *Essays* of Montaigne might be turned to the purposes of Christian apologetics. In fact, Philippe Sellier concludes, Pascal's intensely detailed study, particularly of Montaigne, must be taken to be a fragment belonging to the preparatory notes of Pascal's projected Apology itself.

Did an actual conversation between Pascal and Sacy ever take place? Probably not. Fontaine situates the fictitious conversation at the time of Pascal's retreat at Port-Royal in January of 1655. However, that precious but long-lost document Pascal sent to Sacy, and which Fontaine would discover forty years later, obviously dates from the spring of 1658. And what of Sacy's role in the *Entretien*? Is it entirely fictional?

It is highly significant that the passages attributed to Sacy take up only six paragraphs, whereas Pascal speaks in forty-six paragraphs. This disproportion, of course, is a function of the fact that Fontaine's principal written source was the study that Pascal had submitted to Sacy. Indeed, Fontaine forgets to erase an indication of his source. The phrase, "as I have tried to do in this study," (par. 44) subsists in a line attributed to Pascal.

It is easy enough to reconstruct the contours of Pascal's original fragment. Paragraphs 5–31 are linked to paragraphs 37–53 and then to paragraphs 55–57. Nowhere is this clearer than the way in which paragraphs 31 and 37 unfold. It was Fontaine who cut up Pascal's original "study" (the word, we have seen, is Pascal's own) in an attempt to create the movement of an actual conversation. Fontaine places in Sacy's mouth a series of extensive passages on the subject of profane reading drawn from Augustine's *Confessions*. He appears not to have realized that this avalanche of pedantry spoiled the spontaneity of his proposed dialogue and even rendered it somewhat unlikely as an actual conversation. For instance, paragraphs 53 through 55 form a perfectly coherent progression of an argument by Pascal. Fontaine breaks up this progression by inserting a comment by Sacy in paragraph 54. A thorough examination of how Fontaine uses his sources—Pascal's "study" and Sacy's annotations[4]—would constitute an extensive study in and of itself.

---

4. The existence of such a document, written by Pascal and annotated by Sacy, appears to Jean Mesnard to be the most plausible hypothesis concerning Fontaine's source. See Pascal, *Entretien avec M. de Sacy,* original inédit présenté par Pascale Mengotti et Jean Mesnard [*Exchange with M. de Sacy,* unpublished original, with a presentation by Pascale Mengotti and Jean Mesnard] (Paris: Les Carnets DDB, 1994), 37–41.

To recapitulate, Fontaine had two sources at his disposal. One was a long fragment on the uses of Stoic and skeptic philosophy in Christian apologetics, which Pascal had addressed to Sacy. The second was a list of citations on profane reading drawn from the *Confessions* of Saint Augustine—which serves almost exclusively as the basis for Sacy's interventions. However, it remains entirely possible that Sacy annotated the text sent to him by Pascal and that these annotations, principally Augustine's exposition on the futility of profane reading drawn from the *Confessions*, constituted the source of Fontaine's depiction of Sacy's interventions in the six paragraphs out of fifty-nine in which Fontaine allows him to speak.

In the twenty or so times Pascal's evokes Epictetus, his citations are precise, literal, and obviously borrowed directly from the *Enchiridion* (Manuel of Epictetus). They are cited in a form that is hardly conversational. In his sixty or so citations from Montaigne's *Essays*, Pascal manifests an almost unprecedented knowledge of Montaigne's text. He succeeds in harmoniously synthesizing diverse passages often a hundred pages apart. Pascal's magisterial synthesis of these key texts in the *Essays* would be used in the "Knowledge of Man" in the Apology to demonstrate the total wretchedness of man without God.

Pascal's borrowings hardly sound conversational. Yet one easily recognizes the force of his writing. How could Fontaine himself, writing forty years later, have reconstituted such a remarkable presentation from memory? He had to be working from a document composed by Pascal himself and submitted to Sacy. But it seems highly doubtful that the exchange (at least on this subject) actually took place in January of 1655. Fontaine insists, we might recall, that he was not present at the supposed conversation (par. 32).

Pascal's purpose in submitting his proposal to Sacy was to put forth the thesis that profane writing might be put to the uses of Christian apology, an unprecedented notion in the history of the genre and completely contravening Augustine's[5]—and Sacy's—beliefs about the profound dangers of profane literature. Pascal seeks to make the case for using the skepticism of Montaigne to clear the way for his presentation of divine history and the intervention of God into human history. Sacy could not be more horrified. Never had such a radical idea been advanced. But then, in the most memorable moment of the *Exchange,* Fontaine puts into Sacy's mouth a remarkable metaphor:

5. The collection of citations that Fontaine is using come from books one through five of the *Confessions* on the dangers of profane reading. Yet, in some of his other works we find the Doctor of Grace praising the great pagan writings, of Cicero and especially of Plato and the neo-Platonists. One might recall here Basil of Caesarea's *Address to Young Men on the Use of Greek Literature* (fourth century CE) where the risk of *seduction* is evoked through an allegory of Ulysses resisting the sirens' songs.

M. de Sacy could not prevent himself from telling M. Pascal at this point that he was surprised to see how well he was able to interpret things. He told him that he resembled those skillful doctors who, thanks to the clever way they have of mixing the most powerful poisons, are able to extract from them the most potent remedies. (par. 54)[6]

If doctors can use virulent poisons to heal diseases, then the poison of skepticism might be used to demolish the assumptions of Pascal's interlocutors about human nature, so they can see that it, along with everything that exists, had been corrupted by the Fall.

Epictetus

Pascal's discourse in the *Exchange with Monsieur de Sacy* includes twenty or so references to Epictetus. Epictetus (50–130 CE) came to Rome as a slave and there developed his theory of "Stoicism." Set free he was chased from Rome by the Emperor Domitian and went to live in the Greek port of Nilopolis. He opened a philosophical school and counted among his students his future biographer Arrian. Since Epictetus wrote nothing, we know his philosophy only thorugh Arrian's transcriptions. He left us four books of *Exchanges* and the celebrated *Manual* (or *Enchiridion*), a compendium of the most important teachings of the Master. The *Manual* was often praised by Christians as a preparation for conversion to Christianity. The Jesuits would use it in China to that end.[7]

In France a strong current of Stoic thought began in the sixteenth century and lasted for a century. Largely Christianized, and stripped of the materialist pantheism of Seneca and Marcus Aurelius, it came to represent the God of Providence to Christians. It was thought to coincide with the Christian examination of conscience and meditation on death. However, its ideal of auto-sufficiency came to be denounced by the neo-Augustinians. Jansenius himself had attacked it in the *Augustinus* (1649), as did Arnauld in the *Necessity of Faith in Jesus Christ* and Pascal in fragments 175, 177, and 180. However, in the *Exchange* Pascal praises Epictetus's ideas from the *Manual* (pars. 5–10). His critique of the philosopher is based on books 1 and 2 of Epictetus's *Exchanges*.

---

6. The metaphor, of course, could be Fontaine's. Whether it is based upon an annotation by Sacy in Pascal's "study" remains an open question.

7. On the quarrel of the Jansenists and the Jesuits on the matter of the Chinese Rites, see Wetsel, *Pascal and Disbelief*, 224–34.

Montaigne and Saint Augustine

Pascal borrows, rephrases, and refers to the *Essays* some sixty times in the course of the *Exchange*, forty of those times from the "Apology for Raymond Sebond." Pascal's use of the *Essays* attests to his unprecedented knowledge of the text, presented with masterful ease and leaping from one text to another some two hundred pages further on. This stunning synthesis, asserts Ph. Sellier, presents the *Essays* as the most remarkable "pagan" work in the history of culture, even if its author professes the Catholic faith. The *Essays* was the Bible of the *honnêtes gens*, the very interlocutors Pascal seeks to convert. What better strategy than to make the case for the wretchedness of man without God and the corruption of all men who ever lived than to use their own most beloved work?

Twenty references to Saint Augustine's works, of which seventeen are to the *Confessions*, emerge in the *Exchange with Monsieur de Sacy*. Like many at Port-Royal, Fontaine would have collected citations from Saint Augustine's *Confessions*, organizing them according to subject. One rubric would have certainly been Augustine's views on profane philosophy. Both Sacy and Pascal would have recalled that the young Augustine traversed a period of skepticism and doubt from 383 to 386 CE. Sacy would certainly have had in mind that, whereas Augustine succeeded in overcoming his doubts, Montaigne remained mired in a poisonous skepticism, the reading of which should be forbidden to Christians. Indeed, M. de Sacy only reticently, if at all, comes to understand why Pascal wanted to make use of Montaigne's skepticism in leading unbelievers to Christian belief. As the seventeenth century progressed, more and more theologians condemned the *Essays*, including the *Logic of Port-Royal* (1662). This work, so essential to the argument of the Apology, soon ended up on the Roman Index in 1676.

Note on the Text

The text that follows of the *Exchange with Monsieur de Sacy* is the first English translation of Fontaine's autograph discovered by Pascale Thouvenin and first published in 1994. The paragraphs of the text follow those of the autograph. They have been numbered for ease of reference. The translation of Richard H. Popkin and all other English translations not based on the autograph noted above are defective because they are translations of copies of copies.

Bibliography

Fontaine, Nicolas. *Mémoires ou histoire des solitaires de Port-Royal*. Edited by Pascale Thouvenin. Paris: Champion, 2001. (The "Exchange with Monsieur de Sacy" figures among the forty or so "exchanges" composed by Sacy's secretary between 1696 and 1700.)

Henri Gouhier. *Blaise Pascal: Commentaires*. Paris: Vrin, 1984.

———. *Blaise Pascal: Conversion et apologétique*. Paris: Vrin, 1986.

Thouvenin, Pascale, and Jean Mesnard, eds. *Pascal, Entretien avec M. de Sacy*. Paris: DDB, 1994.

Wetsel, David. *L'Ecriture et le Reste. The Pensées of Pascal in the Exegetical Tradition of Port-Royal*. Columbus: Ohio State University Press, 1981. Especially chapter 1: "Le Chemin aux Granges: Pascal's 'Entretiens' with Le Maistre de Sacy," 7–43.

EXCHANGE WITH M. DE SACY ON
EPICTETUS AND MONTAIGNE

[1] M. Pascal also came, around that time, to stay at Port-Royal-des-Champs. I shall not pause here to describe a man who was universally held in admiration not only in France, but in all Europe. His mind, which was always lively and active, had a breadth, elevation, firmness, penetration, and clarity beyond anything that could be believed. There was no one with a talent for mathematics, however great, who did not yield to him, as attested by the famous case of the cycloid, which all learned people were talking about at that time.[1] It is also well known that he seemed able to bring copper to life and to endow bronze with intelligence. He so contrived it that little wheels without the gift of reason, on each of which the ten digits figured, succeeded in proving the most rational people right in their calculations; and he made mute machines, in some sense, speak, in order to solve, by means of a game, the problems with numbers that were then baffling the most learned people. This cost him such mental effort and application that, in bringing his machine to the point where everyone admired it and which I saw with my own eyes, he had his own head all but taken to pieces by it for almost three years.[2]

[2] This admirable man, when at last touched by God, surrendered that elevated mind of his to the sweet yoke[3] of Jesus Christ; while his heart, so noble and great, embraced the humility of penitence. In Paris, he went and threw himself into the arms of Singlin,[4] determined to do anything the latter required of him. When Singlin saw this great genius, he thought it best to

---

1. Pascal worked on the properties of the cycloid in 1658, not before his stay at Port-Royal-des-Champs in January of 1655, as Fontaine implies. Jean Mesnard believes that Fontaine has confused the "cycloid" with the arithmetic machine discussed in the note below.

2. In 1642, Pascal started work on an arithmetic machine designed to help his father perform the long and tiresome calculations required of him in his work as a tax inspector. See Pascal's "Necessary Advice about the Adding Machine," in *Pascal: Selections*, ed. Richard H. Popkin (New York: Macmillan, 1989), 24–9.

3. Matthew 11:30.

4. Antoine Singlin (1607–64) undertook the spiritual direction of the nuns of Port-Royal in Paris upon the death of Saint-Cyran in 1643. As Pascal's spiritual director, it was he who sent Pascal to Port-Royal in January of 1655.

send him out to Port-Royal-des-Champs, where Arnauld would hold his own against him on the subject of his great learning and M. de Sacy would teach him to despise it.[5] M. Pascal came, therefore, to stay at Port-Royal-des-Champs. Out of courtesy and above all because Singlin had begged him to do so, M. de Sacy could not avoid seeing him. But the holy illumination that he found in the scriptures and the Church Fathers led him to hope that he would not be dazzled by all the brilliance of M. Pascal, who nonetheless charmed and captivated everyone. M. de Sacy found everything he said, indeed, to be entirely accurate. He observed with pleasure the strength of his mind and his way of talking; but he saw nothing new in either. Everything that was important in what M. Pascal told him he had already read in Saint Augustine; and so, doing justice to everybody, he said: "Monsieur Pascal is greatly to be esteemed for having discovered through the sheer penetration of his mind, and without ever having read the Church Fathers,[6] the same truths that they once discovered. He finds those truths surprising," he would say, "because he has never seen them anywhere else, whereas we are used to seeing them time and again in our books." So it was that this wise churchman, considering the ancients no less enlightened than the moderns, held firm, and valued M. Pascal highly for coming to the same view on all subjects as Saint Augustine.

[3] M. de Sacy's ordinary practice in his exchanges with people was to tailor his conversation to suit his interlocutor. If he were seeing Monsieur Champaigne, for example, he would talk to him about painting; if he were seeing Monsieur Hamon, he would discuss medicine; if he were seeing the local surgeon, he would question him about the best way of curing wounds.[7] Those who grew vines or trees or grain would tell him how to go about it. Everything served him as a means of moving straight to God—and of making others move in the same direction. He believed, therefore, that he ought to put M. Pascal on his mettle in the same way and talk to him about the readings of philosophers that took up most of his time.

[4] He led him to this topic in the very first discussions they had together. M. Pascal told him that the works of Epictetus and Montaigne had been his most frequent companions, and heaped praise upon these two thinkers.

5. Antoine ("le grand") Arnauld (1612–94), solitaire and principal theologian of Port-Royal, whose condemnation by the Sorbonne would provoke Pascal's *Provincial Letters.* His many works in defense of Port-Royal and Jansenist theology would earn him the title of "le grand." On *le grand Arnauld,* see also Introduction, n. 26.

6. Pascal had read the Church Fathers, as illustrated by Philippe Sellier in his *Pascal et saint Augustin* (Paris: Armand Colin, 1970).

7. Philippe de Champaigne (1602–74) was a court painter closely associated with Port-Royal, where his daughter was a nun. He painted many of the abbesses and "messieurs" (solitaires). His celebrated *Ex-voto* of 1662 now hangs in the Louvre. Jean Hamon (1617–87) was a doctor and solitaire at Port-Royal-des-Champs from 1650 onwards.

M. de Sacy, who had always believed that he ought, as much as possible, to avoid reading them both, asked M. Pascal to tell him about them in depth.

[5] "Epictetus," M. Pascal told him, "is one of the world's philosophers who has best understood the duties of man. He wants men above all to regard God as their primary object: to be persuaded that he governs all things justly, to submit to him gladly, and to follow him willingly in all things, with the idea that he does nothing that is not wholly wise. Such an attitude of mind will put a stop to all their complaints and murmurings and predispose their spirits to endure with composure the most grievous events.[8]

[6] "Never say, 'I have lost this or that,' declares Epictetus. Instead, say, 'I have given it back.' Is my son dead? 'I have given him back.' Is my wife dead? 'I have given her back.' The same goes for worldly goods and everything else. 'But he who took it from me,' you say, 'is a wicked man.' What concern is it of yours through whom he who lent you something chooses to ask for it back? While he allows you to make use of it, take care of it as you would any object belonging to someone else, as a traveler does in an inn. You should not, says Epictetus, wish that things should happen as you want them to, but rather you should wish that they should happen as they do.[9]

[7] "Remember, he says elsewhere, that you are here as though on a stage, playing whatever part the director chooses for you. If the part he gives you is a short one, play it short; if long, play it long. If he wants you to act the rogue, you should do so as naturally as you can. And so on. It is up to you to play well the part you have been given; choosing that part, however, is up to someone else.[10]

[8] "Keep death before your eyes, and the ills that seem most terrible, and you will never entertain base thoughts or desire anything to excess.[11]

[9] "He shows in this and a thousand other ways what man ought to do. He wants people to be humble, to hide their good resolutions—especially at the beginning—and to accomplish them in secret, since nothing is more likely to ruin them than displaying them.[12]

[10] "He never tires of repeating that all of man's study and desire ought to be to find out God's will and to follow it.[13]

8. Epictetus, *Manual*, 31. Pascal follows two texts, the *Manual* and the *Discourses*, in his account of Epictetus. See Epictetus, *The Discourses as reported by Arrian, the Manual, and Fragments*, 2 vols., with an English translation by W. A. Oldfather, Loeb Classical Library (Cambridge, Mass.: Harvard University Press, 1985–89).

9. Epictetus, *Manual*, 8.

10. Epictetus, *Manual*, 17.

11. Epictetus, *Manual*, 21.

12. Epictetus, *Manual*, 21.

13. Epictetus, *Manual*, 53.

[11] "Those, then, Monsieur," said M. Pascal to M. de Sacy, "are the truths glimpsed by a great mind who understood so well the duty of humankind.[14] If only he had recognized equally well its powerlessness, I should go so far as to say that he deserved to be adored, since you would have to be God to teach humans both lessons. However, since he was made of dust and ashes,[15] he had no sooner seen so clearly what we ought to do than he fell prey to the sin of presumption about what we are able to do.

[12] "God, he says, gave man the means of fulfilling all these obligations. These means are within our grasp. Happiness is to be sought through those things that are in our power,[16] since God gave them to us for that purpose.[17] It is important to see what, within us, is free. Wealth, life, and worldly esteem are not in our power and so do not lead to God;[18] but the mind cannot be forced to believe what it knows to be false, nor the will to love what it feels will make it unhappy. Those two powers are free,[19] therefore, and through them we can achieve perfection; and, by means of those powers, man can know God perfectly, love, obey, and please him, cure itself of all its vices, gain every virtue, and become holy, a friend and companion to God.[20]

[13] "These principles, born of a diabolical pride, lead him into further errors, such as the following: that the soul is a portion of the divine substance;[21] that pain and death are not evils;[22] that it is legitimate to kill yourself when you have been persecuted enough to make you believe that God is calling you; and more besides.[23]

[14] "As for Montaigne, whom you would also like me to tell you about, Monsieur, born as he was in a Christian country, he professes the Catholic religion, and in this respect there is nothing special about him. But, wanting to discover what kind of morality reason would be likely to dictate without the light of faith, he derived his principles from that very supposition; and, regarding humankind as deprived of all revelation, he proceeds in the following manner.

[15] "He calls all things into a universal doubt, which is so general that it carries itself along. In other words, he doubts that he doubts, and, doubt-

14. See *Pensées*, fr. 182.
15. Ecclesiastes 17:31.
16. Epictetus, *Discourses*, 1, 6.
17. Epictetus, *Discourses*, 1, 1 (17).
18. Epictetus, *Manual*, 1, 1–2.
19. Epictetus, *Discourses*, 1, 17 (21–28).
20. Epictetus, *Discourses*, 2, 8 (23 and 25).
21. Epictetus, *Discourses*, 1, 1 (12).
22. Epictetus, *Manual*, 5; *Discourses*, 1, 9 (2–13).
23. See *Pensées*, fr. 180.

ing even the truth of that last proposition, his uncertainty turns on itself in a perpetual and restless circle, offering equal opposition to those who assert that everything is uncertain and to those who assert that everything is not so, because he wants to assert nothing whatsoever.[24]

[16] "It is in this doubt that calls itself into doubt and this ignorance that is ignorant of itself, which he calls his ruling quality,[25] that the essence of his thinking is to be found. He was unable ever to express this by means of any positive term. For, if he says that he doubts, then he misrepresents himself by asserting, at the very least, that he does indeed doubt. This being strictly against his intention, he was able to express his thinking only interrogatively, so that, wanting to avoid saying, "I do not know," he says instead, "What do I know?" He makes this his motto[26] and places it beneath a pair of scales that weigh up contraries and find them to be perfectly balanced. In other words, he is a pure Pyrrhonian.

[17] "All his discourses and essays revolve around this principle, which is the only thing that he aims to establish, even though he does not always make his intentions obvious. Little by little, he destroys everything that is held to be most certain among humans, not in order to establish the contrary with a certainty that is his sole enemy, but merely in order to show that, since appearances are equal on either side, no one can know where to settle one's beliefs.[27]

[18] "In this spirit he pokes fun at all assertions. He attacks, for example, those who thought that they had created in France a major remedy against legal suits thanks to the large number and alleged precision of the country's laws—as if it were possible to cut off at their roots the doubts that give rise to these suits and there were dykes strong enough to stem the tide of uncertainty and halt conjecture. When he says one might just as well put one's case to the first person one meets as to judges armed with so vast an array of rulings, he is not claiming that the order of the state should be changed—he does not have such grand ambitions—nor that his own view is better: he believes that none is any good. It is merely to prove the vanity of the most commonly held opinions, by showing that the suspension of any law would be more likely to reduce the number of disagreements than does their current multitude, which serves only to increase them, because difficulties grow in the weighing of them, obscurities are only multiplied by the commentaries they receive, and the surest means of understanding the meaning of a discourse is to refrain

24. Montaigne, *Essays*, II, 12, 477 and 451.
25. Montaigne, *Essays* I, 50: "giving myself up to doubt and uncertainty and my ruling quality, which is ignorance" (266).
26. Montaigne, *Essays*, II, 12, 477.
27. Montaigne, *Essays*, II, 12, 452–54.

from examining it and take it at face value. One has only to look into it a little, and all clarity disappears.[28]

[19] "Consequently, he judges men's actions and historical events as the mood takes him, sometimes in one way and sometimes in another, following freely his initial view, never forcing his thinking to submit to the rules of reason, whose measurements are always wrong, and delighted to demonstrate through his own example the contradictions of a single mind.

[20] "So free is his spirit that it makes no difference to him whether he wins or loses arguments, since he invariably has, in either case, a means of revealing the weakness of any opinion whatsoever: he has stationed himself in universal doubt so advantageously that he draws equal strength from his triumphs and his defeats.[29]

[21] "It is from this position, shifting and irresolute as it is, that he fights with an invincible firmness the heretics of his day for insisting that they alone understand the true meaning of the scriptures.[30] It is from there, too, that he blasts still more vigorously the horrible impiety of those who dare to insist that there is no God.[31]

[22] "He particularly takes on such people in the 'Apology for Raymond Sebond.'[32] Finding them to be, of their own accord, stripped of all revelation and abandoned to their natural powers of understanding, with all faith set to one side, he inquires of them with what authority they set about judging a sovereign Being who is by his own definition infinite, when they do not truly know even the slightest thing in the natural world![33]

[23] "He asks them on what principles they rely. He presses them to show them. He examines all that they might produce and goes so deeply into each of them, thanks to the supreme talent he possesses, that he shows the vanity of all the principles that are thought most natural and solid.

[24] "He asks whether the soul knows anything; whether it knows itself; whether it is substance or accident, body or mind; what each of these things is, and whether anything exists that does not belong to one of these orders; whether it knows its own body; what matter is, and whether the soul can choose from among the innumerable variety of views that have been offered of it; how, if it is a material being, it can reason; and how, if it is a spiritual one, it may be joined to a particular body and experience its passions.

28. Pascal sums up the beginning of Montaigne's *Essay* III, 13 ("Of Experience"), 992–96.
29. Montaigne, *Essays,* III, 8, 855–56.
30. Montaigne, *Essays,* III, 13.
31. Montaigne, *Essays,* II, 12.
32. Montaigne, *Essays,* II, 12.
33. Montaigne, *Essays,* II, 12.

[25] "When did it come into being—at the same time as the body, or before? And whether it comes to an end with the body, or not; whether it never makes mistakes; whether it knows when it errs, given that the essence of being mistaken involves not being aware of it; and whether, in all this confusion, the soul does not believe that two plus three is six as firmly as it believes, a minute later, that it equals five.

[26] "Whether animals can reason, speak, and think; and who can decide that point. What time is, what space or extension is, what movement is, what unity is—all things that surround us and are entirely inexplicable.

[27] "What health, sickness, life, death, good, evil, justice, and sin are, which we are always talking about.[34]

[28] "Whether we have within us the principles of truth, and if those that we think we have, which we call 'axioms' or 'common notions' because they are identical in all humans, are identical to the essential truth; and—since the fact is that we know by faith alone that an entirely good Being gave them to us as truthful even as he created us to know the truth—who, without that light from faith, could tell whether they have not been formed by chance and are not uncertain; or whether they were not formed by a false and evil Being who gave them to us as false in order to trick us;[35] thus demonstrating that God and the truth are inseparable, and that if one of the two exists or does not exist and is certain or doubtful, then the other is necessarily the same. Who knows, then, whether or not common sense, which we assume is a good judge of truth, was given mandate by him who created it? Moreover, who knows what truth is, and how can one be sure of having it without knowing it? Who knows, indeed, what being is, which is impossible to define, since there is nothing more general, and since, in order to explain it, one must immediately use the selfsame word in saying, "It is," etc.?

[29] "And since we do not know what soul, body, time, space, movement, unity, truth, good, and even being are, nor can explain the ideas that we have of these things, how can we be sure that they are the same in all humans, given that the only indication we have of it is the uniformity of consequences, which is not always a sign of the uniformity of principles, for the latter may well be different and nevertheless lead to the same conclusions, since everybody knows that it is often possible to conclude truth from falsehood?[36]

34. Montaigne, *Essays*, II, 12.

35. Here, the account of Montaigne's questioning and specifically of his Pyrrhonian doubt seems to incorporate Descartes's own version of a radical doubt and his hypothesis of an evil genius, in his *Meditations*—a perspective foreign to Montaigne himself.

36. Despite containing various reminiscences of Montaigne, paragraphs 28 and 29 above develop distinctly Pascalian lines of thinking: for par. 28, see *Pensées*, fr. 164.

[30] "In the end, he examines all areas of knowledge in such depth—geometry, whose uncertainty he shows in its very axioms and in the terms that it uses but does not define, such as extension, movement, and so on; physics, in still more ways; medicine, in an infinite number of ways; history, politics, moral philosophy, jurisprudence, and all other kinds of knowledge—and in such a fashion, that we are left convinced that, were it not for revelation, we would go so far as to doubt whether we are awake (since we do not consider this to be the case at the present time with any more justification than we do in some dreams), and even whether life itself is not a dream from which we will awake only at death and in the course of which we possess the principles of truth as little as we do during natural sleep.

[31] "In this way he assails reason stripped of faith so strongly and savagely that, making reason doubt whether it is indeed reasonable, and whether animals are so or not, or whether more or less so, he brings it down from the exalted position that it awarded itself. He is kind enough to place it on a par with the beasts, but he will not allow it to leave that order of being until its Creator himself has told it what its proper station is, which it does not know; threatening, if it complains, to place it lower even than the beasts, which is just as easy as doing the opposite; and lending it meanwhile the power to act only so that it may recognize its weakness with sincere humility, instead of raising itself up with a foolish insolence."

[32] M. de Sacy, as he told me afterwards, listened quietly to M. Pascal, thinking that he was living in a new country and listening to a new language. He repeated to himself the words of Saint Augustine: "God of truth, are those who know these subtleties of reasoning any more pleasing to you for that? *Tell me, O Lord God of Truth, is whoever is skilful in these philosophical things thereby acceptable unto thee?*"[37] He felt sorry for this philosopher who pricked and tore himself all over on thorns of his own making: *They prick themselves with their own barbs.*[38] As Saint Augustine said of himself when he was in the same state: *I moved around as if on thorns. For thou hadst given forth the command, and so it came to pass in me, that my earth should bring forth briars and thorns in me.*[39]

[33] After showing a good deal of patience, therefore, he said to M. Pascal:

---

37. Saint Augustine, *Confessions*, 2 vols., with an English translation by W. Watts (Cambridge, Mass.: Harvard University Press, 1960–61), book V, 4, no. 7. Unless otherwise specified, all further quotations from the *Confessions* are taken from this edition. Sacy's comments are actually put together by Fontaine forty years later from his own list of citations from Saint Augustine on profane literature, particularly from the *Confessions.*

38. Cicero, *De oratore* [On the orator], 2 vols., with an English translation by E. W. Sutton, Loeb Classical Library (Cambridge, Mass.: Harvard University Press, 1967–68), II. 38. 158.

39. Fontaine here collates two passages from the *Confessions*: III. 7, no. 12, and IV. 16, no. 29.

"You have my thanks, Monsieur. I am sure that, even if I had spent a long time reading Montaigne, I would still not know him as well as I do in the light of the discussion I have just had with you. That man ought to want to be known only through the account that you give of his writings. He would then be able to say with Saint Augustine: *There it is that you should see me and know me.*[40] I firmly believe that this man had wit, but I wonder if you do not give him a little more than is properly his by making so coherent a chain of reasoning out of his principles. You will appreciate that I, having lived my life as I have done, was never encouraged to read this author, whose works do not contain what we ought principally to be looking for when we read according to the rule of Saint Augustine, which *is to lift our minds and hearts towards God,*[41] because his words do not seem to come from a particularly deep well of humility and piety: *There are no signs here of a very profound humility and an exceptional piety or wisdom.*[42]

[34] "The philosophers of the past known as the Academics could be excused for calling everything into doubt. But what need was there for Montaigne to amuse himself by renewing a doctrine that is viewed by Christians today as pure folly? *Such folly was held to be a higher and more fruitful form of study.*[43] *I fell among a sect of men,* says Saint Augustine, *proudly doting and always talking, in whose mouth were the very snares of the Devil.* That is Saint Augustine's judgment of such people. One might, echoing him, say of Montaigne in relation to the youth of today: *A great snare of the devil he was, and many were entangled by him in that gin of his smooth language.*[44] In everything he says, he sets faith aside; so we who have faith should likewise set everything he says aside. I have nothing against the mind of the author, which is a great gift from God, but he might have used it better and made a sacrifice of it to God rather than to the devil: *The quickness of mind and sharpness of disputing that I have is thy gift; and yet I did not sacrifice any part of it to thee,* says Saint Augustine.[45] *For by more ways than one is there sacrifice offered to the fallen angels.*[46] What is the point of having something good if one puts it to such bad use? *What good did it do to have good abilities, and not employ them to good uses?*[47] What was the use of

40. Augustine, Letter 231, §6 (to Darius, on the subject of the *Confessions*).

41. Augustine, *Retractations*, II. 6, no. 4. See Augustine, *Retractions*, trans. Sister Mary Inez Bogan, Fathers of the Church 60 (Washington, D.C.: The Catholic University of America Press, 1968).

42. The source for this quotation is probably Fontaine's own collection of citations of the *Confessions*.

43. Augustine, *Confessions*, I. 13 (in Augustine, the sentence is in the present tense; see Augustine, *Confessions*, trans. R. S. Pine-Coffin [Harmondsworth: Penguin, 1961], 34), and III. 6, no. 10.

44. Augustine, *Confessions*, V, 3, no. 3.

45. Augustine, *Confessions*, IV, 16, no. 30.

46. Augustine, *Confessions*, I, 17, no. 27.

47. Augustine, *Confessions*, IV, 16, nos. 30 and 31.

having a nimble wit able to run over all these sciences?[48] So says this holy doctor
of himself before his conversion.

[35] "You are lucky, Monsieur, to have raised yourself above those people who are called drunken doctors, *intoxicated teachers,* but whose hearts are
empty of truth: *Their heart was void of true meaning.*[49] God has poured into
your heart other delights and charms than the ones you found in Montaigne.
He has called you back from that dangerous pleasure, *that infectious sweetness,*[50]
says Saint Augustine, who gives thanks to God for pardoning the sins he had
committed by overindulging in these vanities: *In those vanities, thou forgavest
the sinfulness of my delight in them.*[51] Saint Augustine is all the more believable
in that he used to share these feelings; and, just as you say of Montaigne that
he fights the heretics of his day by invoking that universal doubt, so it was by
means of this very doubt, as practiced by the Academics, that Saint Augustine
abandoned the heresy of the Manicheans: *For there rose a conceit in me that
those philosophers that they call Academics should be wiser than the rest, for they
held men ought to make a doubt upon everything, and decreed that no truth can be
comprehended by man. After the manner therefore of the Academics, doubting now
of everything and wavering up and down between all, I absolutely resolved that the
Manicheans were to be abandoned.*[52]

[36] "Once he had come to God, he renounced these vanities, which he
calls sacrilegious, and did what he says of certain others: *Cast down and broken
in heart for their salvation, they killed in sacrifice to thee their own exalted imaginations, which are like the birds of the air, and their own curiosities, which are like
the fishes of the sea.*[53] He recognized Saint Paul's wisdom in warning us not to
let ourselves be seduced by such talk: *Beware lest any man cheat you through
philosophy and vain deceit.*[54] For he confesses that it has a certain charm that
could quite easily sweep you away: *His way of talking proved the more pleasing
and inveigling, being governed by a good wit, and set off with a kind of gracefulness
that was natural to him.*[55] We sometimes believe things to be true simply because they are said with eloquence. They are dangerous viands, he says, but are

48. Augustine, *Confessions,* IV, 16, no. 26.
49. Augustine, *Confessions,* I, 16, no. 26, and III, 6, no. 10.
50. Augustine, *Confessions,* I, 14, no. 23.
51. Augustine, *Confessions,* I, 15, no. 24.
52. Augustine, *Confessions,* V, 10, nos. 19 and 14, no. 25.
53. Augustine, *Confessions,* V, 3, no. 4, and IV, 1, no. 1.
54. Colossians 2:8: "Let no man seduce you, willing in humility, and religion of angels, walking in the
things which he hath not seen, in vain puffed up by the sense of his flesh." Cited in the *Confessions,* III. 4,
no. 8.
55. Augustine, *Confessions,* V, 6, no. 9. Augustine is referring to the Manichean Faustus.

served in beautiful dishes: *They are deliciously empty.*[56] Those viands, instead of nourishing the heart, only empty it: *Nor was I soundly nourished by them, but drawn dry rather.* At such moments, one resembles those people who think in their sleep that they are eating; those imaginary viands leave them as empty as before."[57] M. de Sacy told M. Pascal a number of such things. M. Pascal replied that, if M. de Sacy flattered him for knowing his Montaigne and being able to interpret him well, he could tell him without flattery that he knew his Augustine even better and was able to interpret him better too, although hardly to the benefit of poor Montaigne. He confessed to him that he had been extremely edified by the solidity of everything that M. de Sacy had just shown him. Still full of his author, however, he could not refrain from saying:

[37] "I must confess to you nonetheless, Monsieur, that I cannot help feeling overjoyed when I see in that author proud reason so invincibly crushed by its own weapons, and that all too bloody revolt of man against man, which removes him from the companionship with God to which he had raised himself through the maxims of the Stoics and, through those of the Pyrrhonians, reduces him to the level of the beasts. I would have loved the minister of so great a vengeance with all my heart if he had been a disciple of the Church through faith and had respected its moral teaching by persuading men, whom he had so usefully humbled, not to irritate with any further crimes him who alone can save them from those crimes that Montaigne has convinced them they are incapable even of knowing. But he behaves, on the contrary, like a heathen, and in the following manner.

[38] "Starting from the principle, as he puts it, that without faith everything is in a state of uncertainty, and considering how long we have been searching for the true and the good without making any progress towards peace of mind,[58] he concludes that we ought to leave the task to others—*Inquire, you who the laboring world survey*[59]—and remain all that time at rest, flitting over subjects so as not to become immersed in them by leaning too hard, and taking the true and the good at face value, without squeezing them, because they are so insubstantial that, however gently you close your hand around them, they escape between your fingers and leave you empty-handed.

[39] "This is why he follows the testimony of the senses and common notions, since he would have to force himself to contradict them and cannot be sure that he would succeed, not knowing where the truth is to be found. He

56. Augustine, *Confessions*, I, 14, in relation to the writings of Homer.
57. Augustine, *Confessions*, III, 6.
58. Montaigne, *Essays* III, 13, p. 995.
59. Lucan, *Pharsalia* [The civil war], I, 417; quoted by Montaigne, *Essays*, III, 13 ("On experience"), 1001.

flees pain and death in this same way, because his instinct urges him to and, for the reason already given, he does not want to resist it. But he never goes so far as to conclude that they are true evils: he puts little trust in natural movements of fear, given that we experience other movements of pleasure that are said to be bad, even though nature states the contrary.[60]

[40] "There is nothing, then, out of the ordinary in his behavior. He acts in the same way as others, and everything they do in the foolish belief that they are following the true good. He does in accordance with a different principle, which is that, since the likelihood is the same on either side, precedent and convenience are the counterweights that carry the day. He follows the morals of his country because he is driven by habit to do so. He mounts his horse, just as someone would who is not a philosopher, because the horse allows him to; but he never believes he has a right to do so and wonders whether the animal does not have the right, on the contrary, to make use of him.

[41] "He also makes strenuous efforts to avoid certain vices, and he even honored the fidelity required by marriage, on account of the trouble that irregular conduct can cause; but if the trouble this puts him to ever proves greater than that which he wants to avoid, he yields, the rule of all his actions being convenience and peace of mind.[61]

[42] "He thoroughly rejects that Stoic virtue which is portrayed with a severe expression, a wild look, its hair standing on end, its brow furrowed and running with sweat, in a tense and painful posture, far away from humans, in a mournful silence, and perched alone on the top of a rock: a ghost, as he calls it, liable to terrify children and doing nothing there but seek, through continuous effort, the peace of mind that it will never find. His kind of virtue is entirely natural, easygoing, amusing, playful, and, so to speak, frolicking. It follows only what it finds enchanting and pokes fun at good and bad events alike, reclining indolently in the midst of a peaceful idleness, and pointing out to other people, who take such pains to seek happiness, that it is to be found in that idleness alone, and that ignorance and incuriosity are two soft pillows for a well-made head, as he himself says.[62]

[43] "I shall not conceal from you, Monsieur, that, having read this author and compared him with Epictetus, I found them to be without doubt the two most illustrious defenders of the two most celebrated schools of thought in the world, and the only ones that conform to reason, since it is possible to follow only one of two routes: either that there is a God, and so the sovereign

60. See Montaigne, *Essays,* I, 14, "That the taste of good and evil depends in large part on the opinion we have of them."

61. See Montaigne, *Essays,* I, 43, and III, 10, 950.

62. See Montaigne, *Essays,* III, 13, 1001.

good is to be placed in him; or that this is uncertain, and so too is the true good, since the one cannot be separated from the other.

[44] "I took the greatest pleasure in discovering the ways in which these different kinds of reasoning reached some conformity with the true wisdom that they were trying to find. For if there is a certain pleasure to be had in observing nature's desire to portray God in all her works, where certain true features of the divine can be seen (since they are images of it) but which are nonetheless filled with numerous defects (since they are *only* images of it), then how much more fitting is it to consider the productions of minds and the efforts they make to represent essential virtue, even as they flee it, and in discovering where they succeed and fail, as I have tried to do in this study.

[45] "You have just shown me admirably well, Monsieur, it is true, of what little use these philosophical readings may be to Christians. I propose, nevertheless, with your permission, to tell you my thinking about them, while remaining ready at all times to renounce any enlightenment I have not received from you. In which case, I will have had the good fortune either to have chanced upon the truth or to have received it authoritatively from you.

[46] "It seems to me that the source of the errors committed by these two schools lies in their not knowing that the state in which man today finds himself is different from what it was at the moment of his creation. One school, observing various traces of humankind's original greatness and unaware of its corruption, treats nature as if it was healthy and in no need of a redeemer: this leads it to the height of arrogance. The other school, feeling the present wretchedness and unaware of the original dignity, treats nature as if it were necessarily weak and beyond remedy: this casts man into the despair of ever attaining any true good and, from there, into utter apathy.

[47] "So it is that these two states, which have to be known together if one is to see the whole truth, necessarily lead, when known separately, to one of those two vices, pride or sloth, in which all humans infallibly find themselves before the advent of grace. If they do not keep to their dissolute ways out of apathy, they abandon them out of vanity, so truthful is the saying of Saint Augustine that you have just told me and which I find to be of great import. *For by more ways than one is there sacrifice offered to the fallen angels.* People do indeed pay homage to them in many ways.

[48] "From this imperfect knowledge of theirs, then, it comes about that one school, knowing the duty of humankind but not its powerlessness, strays into presumption; while the other, knowing its powerlessness but not its duty, lapses into apathy.

[49] "It would seem to follow that, since each possesses the truth about

which the other is in error, one could unite them to make a perfect moral philosophy. Rather than peace, however, nothing short of war and general destruction would result from their being brought together: for with one establishing certainty and the other doubt, one the greatness of man and the other his weakness, each undermines the truths of the other as well as the falsehoods. This means that they cannot survive alone because of their defects, nor unite because of their differences, and, as a result, they shatter and destroy one another to give way to the truth of the Gospel.

[50] "The Gospel reconciles these contradictions by means of a wholly divine art: unifying everything in them that is true and dispelling everything that is false, it transforms them into a truly heavenly wisdom in which the differences that were incompatible in those human doctrines are reconciled. The reason for this is that those worldly sages placed the contraries in the same subject: one attributed greatness to nature, while the other attributed weakness to the selfsame nature, and this simply could not be sustained; whereas faith teaches us to put them in different subjects, since everything that is weak belongs to nature, and everything that is powerful to grace.

[51] "This is the astonishing new union that a God alone could have taught, and made, and which is nothing other than an image and effect of the ineffable union of two natures in the single person of the Man-God.

[52] "I beg your pardon, Monsieur," M. Pascal said to M. de Sacy, "for having allowed myself, in front of you, to get so carried away into the realm of theology, instead of remaining within philosophy, which was my sole subject; but the subject led me there imperceptibly, and it is difficult to avoid entering that realm, whatever truth one is dealing with, because it is the center of all truths—as is perfectly clear in the present instance, since it so visibly embraces all the truths that are to be found within these two doctrines.

[53] "For this reason I cannot see how any of these people could refuse to follow it. For if they are filled with a sense of man's greatness, what have they ever imagined that did not pale in the face of the promises of the Gospel, which nothing less than the death of a God could secure? And if they enjoy observing the infirmity of nature, their sense of it fails to match up to the true weakness of sin, for which that same death was the remedy. So it turns out that here all find more than they could have wished for; and the wonder of it is that they who were irreconcilable at an infinitely lower level find themselves united."

[54] M. de Sacy could not prevent himself from telling M. Pascal at this point that he was surprised to see how well he was able to interpret things. He pointed out to him at the same time that not everybody possessed the art,

as he did, of bringing to these readings such wise and elevated thoughts. He told him that he resembled those skillful doctors who, thanks to the clever way they have of mixing the most powerful poisons, are able to extract from them the most potent remedies.[63] He added that, while he could quite see from what M. Pascal had just told him that these readings were useful to him, he could not believe that they would be of equal benefit to the many people who were a little dull-witted and did not have the elevation of mind to read those authors with judgment and pick out pearls from the middle of the dunghill: *Gold from the dunghill of Tertullian*, as a Church Father used to say.[64] How much more fitting would it be to say this of these philosophers and their dunghill, whose black smoke could easily cloud the wavering faith of those who read them: *In much smoke there sparkled some little faith.*[65] He would, for that reason, always advise these people against exposing themselves lightly to such readings, for fear that they might lose their way with these philosophers and become, in the words of the scriptures,[66] the playthings of demons and fodder for the winds, as these philosophers were: *For, to feed the winds, what is it else but to feed them, that is, by our own errors to make ourselves the subjects of their pleasure and derision.*[67]

[55] "As for the usefulness of these readings," M. Pascal said, "I will tell you in the simplest terms what I think. I find in Epictetus an incomparable talent for unsettling those people who seek peace of mind in external things, and for forcing them to recognize that they are true slaves and blind wretches who cannot possibly find anything other than the error and pain from which they flee, if they do not give themselves unreservedly to God alone.[68]

[56] "Montaigne is incomparable when it comes to confounding the arrogance of those who, from outside the faith, pride themselves on a true system of justice; to disabusing those who cling to their opinions and are convinced that they find unshakeable truths in learning; and to convincing human reason of its lack of clarity and its many aberrations so effectively that, when good use is made of these principles, it becomes all but impossible to succumb to the

---

63. This telling metaphor hardly seems Fontaine's. Does he base it on an annotation made by Sacy on the document Pascal submitted to him? If it is Fontaine's, it shows he has understood Pascal's project better than he is usually thought to.

64. No precise source for this quotation has been found. The meaning is clear: Saint Cyprian (200–258CE), Bishop of Carthage, was able to find brilliant insights in the writings of his contemporary and fellow Carthaginian, the writer Tertullian (155–220 CE), despite the fact that the latter adopted the heresies of the Montanists after 207 CE.

65. Augustine, *Confessions*, IV, 2, no. 2.

66. 1 Peter 5:8–9; Proverbs 10,–5.

67. Augustine, *Confessions*, IV, 2, no. 3.

68. Epictetus, *Discours*, IV, 1 (173), etc.

temptation of looking for contradictions in the mysteries of the faith. For the mind is so battered by them that it finds itself in no position to judge whether the Incarnation and the mystery of the Eucharist are possible—issues that ordinary minds stir up all too often.

[57] "But if Epictetus fights sloth, he fosters pride, and this means that he can be very harmful to those who are not persuaded of the corruption of even the most perfect righteousness that is not based on faith. And Montaigne is absolutely pernicious to those with any kind of tendency towards impiety and vice. That is why the readings of these authors need to be conducted with a great deal of care, discretion, and consideration for the condition and morals of those to whom they are recommended. It seems to me simply that they might not work too badly, if joined together, because each counters the harm caused by the other. Not that they could ever inspire virtue in people, but merely unsettle them in their vices; since the soul, assailed by these contraries, one of which dispels pride and the other sloth, finds itself equally unable to take refuge in either of these vices, thanks to these arguments, or for that matter to escape them."

[58] This is how two minds as fine as these finally reached agreement[69] on the issue of reading these philosophers. They came to the same conclusion, although by rather different means: M. de Sacy had gone straight to it through his clear-sighted view of the principles of Christianity, whereas M. Pascal reached it only after many twists and turns, having attended closely to the principles of these philosophers.

[59] M. de Sacy and everyone else at Port-Royal-des-Champs were still full of the joy that the conversion and sight of M. Pascal had brought them—and in awe at the all-powerful might of grace that had, in an act of divine mercy for which there are few precedents, so humbled a mind that had raised itself so high through its own efforts—when we were a great deal more taken, at around the same time, by the almost miraculous transformation of another person,[70] which filled that wilderness with joy. I still feel, even now, entirely transported outside of myself by the memory of the infinite consolation that God gave us all through that conversion.

---

69. Sellier points out that Fontaine's editorial conclusion demonstrates how little he has understood the degree to which Sacy views Pascal's project as a dangerous one. Sacy's annotations written on what Pascal calls his "study" are in essence serious reservations. The "pagan" and Augustinian perspectives are in fact not reconciled at all in paragraph 57, which curiously lacks any further annotations on the part of Sacy.

70. Nicolas Richer's (1612–59) "conversion" took place in July of 1657, not during Pascal's stay at Port-Royal-des-Champs in January of 1655. Once again we are reminded that Fontaine is recalling events forty years after they took place.

TABLE OF CORRESPONDENCES

For each numbered *pensée* in this translation ("Sellier"), the following table provides the number of the corresponding fragment in the other two traditions: "Krailsheimer" refers to the translation following the Lafuma edition, and "Trotter" to the translation of an early Brunschvicg edition. There is no exact correspondence among the fragments in the various editions, nor, as a result, among the translations. A single number in Sellier may correspond to several fragments in the other translations, and the other way around. There are some discrepancies between the tables of correspondences among the French editions and between the translations. The Trotter edition, in particular, lacks some fragments added by Brunschvicg in his later editions. We hope that this table will prove useful to readers interested in the history of both the editions and the translations of Pascal's *Pensées*.

Sellier	Krailsheimer	Trotter	Sellier	Krailsheimer	Trotter	Sellier	Krailsheimer	Trotter
1			18	399	438	35	416	546
2	383	197	19	400	327	36	417	547
3	384	629	20	401	437	37	1	595
4	385	706	21	402	290	38	2	227
5	386	203	22	403	174	39	5	247
6	387	241	23	404	424	40	6	60
7	388	739	24	405	421	41	7	248
8	389	793	25	406	395	42	8	601
9	390	616	26	407	465	43	9	291
10	391	748	27	408	74	44	10	167
11	392	643	28	409	220	45	11	246
12	393	442	29	410	413	46	12	187
13	394	288	30	411	400	47	13	133
14	395	478	31	412	414	48	14	338
15	396	471	32	413	162	49	15	410
16	397	426	33	414	171	50	16	161
17	398	524	34	415	130	51	17	113

Sellier	Krailsheimer	Trotter	Sellier	Krailsheimer	Trotter	Sellier	Krailsheimer	Trotter
52	18	–	89	56	181	126	92	335
53	19	318	90	57	379	127	93	328
54	20	292	91	58	332	128	94	313
55	21	381	92	"	332	129	95	316
56	22	367	93	59	296	130	96	329
57	23	67	94	60	294	131	97	334
58	24	127	95	61	309	132	98	80
59	25	308	96	62	177	132	99	80
60	26	330	97	63	151	132	99	535
61	27	354	98	64	295	133	100	467
62	28	436	99	65	115	134	101	324
63	29	156	100	66	326	135	103	298
64	30	320	101	67	878	136	104	322
65	31	149	102	68	205	137	105	342
66	32	317	103	69	–	138	106	403
67	33	374	104	70	165	139	107	343
68	34	376	105	71	405	140	108	–
69	35	117	106	72	66	141	209	392
70	36	164	107	73	110	142	110	181
71	37	158	108	74	454	143	111	339
72	38	71	109	"	–	144	112	344
73	39	141	110	75	389	145	113	348
74	40	134	111	76	73	146	114	397
75	41	69	112	77	152	147	115	349
76	42	207	113	78	126	148	116	398
77	43	136	114	79	128	149	117	409
78	44	82	115	80	317	150	118	402
78	45	83	116	81	299	151	119	423
79	46	163	116	82	271	152	120	148
80	47	172	117	83	327	153	121	418
81	48	366	118	84	79	154	121	418
82	49	132	119	85	877	155	122	416
83	50	305	120	86	297	156	123	157
84	51	293	121	87	307	157	124	125
85	52	305	122	88	302	158	125	92
86	53	429	123	89	315	159	126	93
87	54	112	124	90	337	160	127	415
88	55	111	125	91	336	161	128	396

Sellier	Krailsheimer	Trotter	Sellier	Krailsheimer	Trotter	Sellier	Krailsheimer	Trotter
162	129	116	198	166	183	234	202	516
163	130	42	199	168	224	235	203	594
164	131	434	200	169	811	236	204	591
165	132	170	201	170	268	237	205	489
166	134	169	202	171	695	238	206	235
166	133	168	203	172	185	239	207	596
167	135	469	204	173	273	240	208	435
168	136	139	205	174	270	241	209	598
169	137	142	206	175	562	242	242	242
170	138	166	207	176	261	243	210	451
171	139	143	208	177	384	244	211	453
172	140	466	209	178	–	245	212	527
173	140	466	210	179	256	246	213	551
174	141	509	211	180	837	247	214	491
175	142	463	212	181	255	248	215	433
176	143	464	213	182	272	249	216	493
177	144	360	214	183	253	250	217	649
178	145	461	215	184	810	251	218	597
179	146	350	216	184	–	252	219	251
180	147	361	217	185	265	253	220	468
181	148	415	218	186	–	254	221	773
182	149	430	219	187	254	255	222	746
183	150	226	220	188	267	256	223	569
184	151	211	221	189	546	257	224	815
185	152	213	222	190	542	258	225	788
186	153	238	223	190	542	258	226	522
187	154	237	224	191	548	259	227	223
187	155	281	225	192	526	260	228	750
188	156	190	226	193	98	261	229	444
189	157	225	227	194	208	262	230	–
190	158	236	228	195	37	263	321	511
191	159	204	228	196	86	264	232	565
192	160	257	228	197	–	265	233	795
193	161	221	229	198	692	266	234	580
194	162	189	230	199	72	267	235	770
195	163	200	231	200	347	268	236	577
196	164	218	232	200	347	269	237	794
197	165	210	233	201	206	270	238	644

Sellier	Krailsheimer	Trotter	Sellier	Krailsheimer	Trotter	Sellier	Krailsheimer	Trotter
271	239	810	309	278	446	347	316	799
273	241	764	310	278	446	348	317	700
274	149	430	311	279	689	349	318	754
275	242	584	312	280	613	350	319	698
276	243	600	313	281	612	351	320	178
277	244	228	314	282	615	352	321	599
278	246	656	315	283	654	353	322	801
279	247	673	316	284	604	354	323	772
280	248	652	317	285	866	355	324	729
281	249	680	318	286	608	356	325	732
282	250	666	319	287	606	357	324	729
283	251	899	320	288	688	358	326	693
284	252	647	321	289	607	359	327	769
285	253	678	322	290	625	360	328	731
286	254	648	323	291	586	361	329	733
287	255	757	324	292	623	362	330	724
288	256	661	325	294	702	363	331	747
289	257	683	326	295	628	364	332	709
290	258	727	327	296	624	365	333	707
290	259	684	328	297	701	366	334	715
291	260	677	329	298	283	367	336	708
292	261	756	330	299	741	368	335	705
293	262	761	331	300	785	369	337	752
294	263	685	332	301	771	370	338	723
295	264	745	333	302	808	371	339	737
296	265	676	334	303	798	372	340	719
297	266	718	335	304	742	373	341	722
298	267	679	336	305	637	374	342	636
299	268	682	337	306	762	375	343	697
300	269	691	338	307	763	376	344	755
301	270	669	339	308	792	377	345	–
302	271	544	340	309	796	378	346	728
303	272	686	341	310	800	379	346	734
304	273	744	342	311	639	380	348	717
305	274	641	343	312	696	381	349	651
306	275	642	344	313	568	382	350	622
307	276	690	345	314	638	383	351	536
308	277	345	346	315	751	393	361	209

Sellier	Krailsheimer	Trotter	Sellier	Krailsheimer	Trotter	Sellier	Krailsheimer	Trotter
394	362	472	427	842	587	445	885	–
395	363	913	427	843	835	445	886	51
396	364	249	427	844	836	445	887	78
397	365	496	427	845	860	445	888	52
398	366	–	428	840	842	445	889	165
399	366	–	429	846	807	445	890	436
400	367	671	430	847	892	445	891	803
401	368	474	430	848	805	446	892	821
"	369	610	430	849	664	447	893	572
402	370	480	431	850	820	448	894	843
403	371	473	436	856	827	448	895	285
404	372	483	437	857	818	448	896	390
405	373	476	437	858	839	448	897	532
406	374	475	438	859	851	448	899	843
407	375	503	439	860	806	448	900	886
408	376	384	439	861	804	448	898	–
409	377	280	439	862	882	449	901	840
410	378	470	439	863	813	449	902	840
411	379	824	439	864	883	450	904	–
412	380	284	439	865	831	450	905	385
413	381	286	440	866	–	450	903	850
414	382	287	440	867	874	451	906	915
415	971	632	440	868	889	451	907	55
416	972	633	440	869	508	451	908	262
417	970	631	440	870	844	451	909	923
418	970	631	440	871	–	451	912	780
419	830	–	440	872	812	451	909	923
420	831	809	440	873	823	451	910	780
421	832	802	440	874	880	451	911	780
421	833	487	440	875	819	452	515	48
422	834	825	440	876	300	452	516	879
423	835	563	441	877	848	452	517	868
423	836	854	442	878	845	452	518	378
424	837	822	442	879	138	453	519	70
424	838	670	443	881	849	453	520	375
424	839	826	444	882	222	453	521	387
425	840	842	444	883	–	453	522	140
426	841	828	444	884	859	453	523	145

Sellier	Krailsheimer	Trotter	Sellier	Krailsheimer	Trotter	Sellier	Krailsheimer	Trotter
453	524	852	471	564	485	500	602	884
454	525	325	471	565	590	500	603	502
454	526	408	472	566	574	501	604	870
454	527	40	473	567	873	502	605	36
454	528	57	473	568	814	502	606	155
454	529	105	473	569	871	503	610	30
455	530	274	474	570	767	503	611	30
456	531	85	474	571	774	504	607	765
457	532	373	475	572	54	504	608	765
457	533	331	465	573	645	504	609	735
457	534	5	477	574	263	505	612	219
457	535	102	478	575	650	506	613	443
458	536	578	479	576	566	507	614	443
458	537	407	480	577	234	508	615	662
458	538	531	481	578	26	509	616	659
458	539	99	482	579	53	510	617	492
458	540	380	482	580	28	511	618	479
459	541	120	483	581	12	512	619	394
459	542	370	484	582	668	513	620	146
460	544	777	485	583	56	514	621	412
460	545	458	485	584	15	515	622	131
460	546	514	486	585	32	516	623	495
460	547	783	486	586	33	517	624	731
460	548	778	486	587	34	518	625	214
460	549	779	487	588	279	519	626	462
461	550	743	488	589	703	520	627	150
461	551	84	490	591	186	521	625	153
461	552	107	491	594	575	522	629	417
462	553	76	491	595	450	523	630	94
463	554	303	492	592	749	524	631	422
464	555	47	493	593	759	525	632	198
465	557	45	493	596	202	526	633	411
465	558	114	494	597	455	527	634	97
466	559	27	495	598	867	528	635	13
467	450	551	496	599	907	528	636	42
468	561	173	497	600	440	529	637	59
469	562	533	498	601	906	529	638	109
470	563	885	499	–	–	529	639	109

Sellier	Krailsheimer	Trotter	Sellier	Krailsheimer	Trotter	Sellier	Krailsheimer	Trotter
529b	640	182	657	678	358	595	717	17
529b	641	129	558	679	893	596	880	830
529b	642	448	559	680	63	597	719	787
529b	643	159	560	681	353	598	720	911
529b	644	909	561	682	232	598	721	916
530	645	312	562	683	20	599	967	895
531	646	95	563	684	21	600	722	921
532	647	35	564	685	401	601	723	69
533	648	832	567	588	323	602	722	–
534	649	65	568	689	64	603	722	–
535	650	333	568	689	64	604	722	–
536	651	369	569	690	506	605	724	352
536	652	14	570	691	432	606	725	884
537	653	912	571	692	914	607	726	875
538	654	–	572	693	905	608	727	903
539	655	377	573	694	61	609	728	–
540	656	372	574	695	445	610	728	31
541	657	452	575	696	22	611	729	–
542	658	391	576	697	383	612	730	753
543	589	910	577	698	119	613	731	196
544	660	91	577	699	119	613	732	38
544	661	81	633	700	–	614	733	861
544	662	521	579	701	9	615	734	816
544	663	121	580	702	507	616	735	817
545	664	94	581	703	515	617	736	96
546	665	311	582	704	–	617	737	10
547	666	–	583	705	180	617	738	341
547	667	25	584	706	869	617	739	863
547	668	456	585	707	897	617	740	582
548	669	188	586	708	876	617	741	340
549	670	46	587	609	175	617	742	108
550	671	44	588	710	24	617	743	858
551	672	124	589	711	301	618	744	18
552	673	123	590	712	529	618	745	18
553	674	359	591	713	922	619	746	7786
554	675	29	592	714	–	620	747	588
555	676	–	593	715	118	621	748	239
556	677	872	594	716	215	622	749	456

Sellier	Krailsheimer	Trotter	Sellier	Krailsheimer	Trotter	Sellier	Krailsheimer	Trotter
622	750	176	645	786	864	662	432[71]	–
622	751	3	645	787	–	663	822	592
622	752	865	645	788	486	664	823	217
623	653	179	645	789	50	665	824	522
624	754	501	645	790	626	666	825	900
625	755	258	645	785	775	667	826	672
626	756	365	645	791	776	667	827	672
626	757	212	646	792	101	668	828	304
627	758	856	646	793	736	668	829	351
628	759	346	647	794	393	669	509	49
629	760	567	648	795	160	669	510	7
629	761	–	649	796	314	669	511	2
629	762	–	650	797	310	670	512	1
629	763	568	650	798	41	671	513	4
630	764	11	651	799	611	671	514	356
631	765	39	652	800	531	672	504	250
631	766	8	653	801	665	672	505	250
632	767	306	653	802	122	673	506	90
633	768	345	653	803	386	674	506	87
634	679	902	653	804	447	675	507	363
635	770	103	653	805	106	676	508	364
636	771	355	653	806	147	677	508	364
636	772	58	654	807	518	678	508	364
637	773	135	655	808	245	679	508	364
638	774	497	656	809	230	680	418	233
639	775	898	657	810	193	680	422	534
640	775	898	658	811	740	680	419	89
641	776	857	658	812	797	680	420	231
642	777	846	658	813	894	680	421	477
643	778	68	658	814	6	680	421	605
643	779	88	659	815	259	680	426	541
644	780	62	659	816	240	680	424	278
644	781	242	659	817	614	680	423	277
645	782	266"	660	818	781	680	425	603
645	783	357	660	819	711	681	427	194
645	784	23	660	820	560	682	428	195
645	785	775	661	821	252	682	429	229

71. This section of fr. 432 is filed after 821.

Sellier	Krailsheimer	Trotter	Sellier	Krailsheimer	Trotter	Sellier	Krailsheimer	Trotter
683	430	341	703	465	321	736	491	439
683	431	559	703	466	428	736	490	720
684	432	–	704	467	449	736	494	713
685	433	783	705	468	561	736	495	640
686	434	199	706	469	576	736	496	713
687	435	620	707	470	404	736	492	629
688	436	627	708	471	441	736	497	713
689	437	399	709	472	573	736	493	713
690	438	847	710	473	500	736	498	714
690	439	564	711	474	621	736	499	791
690	440	–	711	475	675	737	501	658
690	441	201	711	476	687	737	500	699
690	442	–	712	477	406	738	502	570
690	443	862	713	478	137	738	503	674
690	444	556	714	479	74	739	975	275
690	445	557	715	480	589	740	976	19
690	446	585	716	481	593	741	–	–
690	447	768	717	482	289	742	913	–
690	448	558	718	483	725	743	978	100
690	449	555	719	484	710	744	914	881
690	450	493	720	485	721	745	915	–
691	451	619	721	486[72]	681	746	916	919
692	452	630	722	486	681	746	917	539
693	453	609	723	486	681	747	979	–
694	454	618	724	486	681	748	918	459
695	455	716	725	486	681	749	919	552
696	456	617	726	486	681	750	920	–
696	457	571	727	486	681	751	919	697
697	458	–	728	486	681	751	919	790
697	459	–	729	486	681	751	936	697
698	973	918	730	486	681	752	921	517
699	460	543	731	486	681	753	924	498
700	461	583	732	486	681	753	922	855
701	462	738	733	486	681	753	923	904
702	463	243	734	487	726	754	925	519
703	464	419	735	489	712	755	926	581

72. In fr. 486, Krailsheimer lists only the biblical references, without giving the text of the passages quoted by Pascal.

Sellier	Krailsheimer	Trotter	Sellier	Krailsheimer	Trotter	Sellier	Krailsheimer	Trotter
756	927	505	771	974	–	794	957	512
756	928	499	772	Addl. 3[73]	–	795	958	75
756	929	554	773	Addl. 4	–	795	959	635
757	930	513	774	Addl. 5	–	796	960	920
758	932	191	775	Addl. 6	–	796	960	362
759	931	549	776	Addl. 7	–	797	961	887
760	980	–	777	Addl. 8	–	798	962	901
761	933	460	778	Addl. 9	–	799	963	–
762	934	579	779	Addl.10	–	799	964	–
762	935	490	780	Addl. 11	–	800	965	888
763	938	657	781	984	216	801	966	–
763	937	104	782	992	–	802	968	653
764	939	896	783	Addl. 12	–	803	969	514
765	940	789	784	Addl. 13	–	804	983	276
766	941	264	785	Addl. 14	–	805	985	–
766	942	–	786	977	320	806	986	809
767	943	554	787	949	–	807	987	891
767	944	250	788	950	–	808	988	488
767	945	660	788	951	–	809	989	–
768	946	784	789	952	–	810	990	–
768	947	504	790	953	–	811	991	–
769	948	667	791	954	–	812	993	908
770	981	917	792	955	–	813	–	–
770	982	–	793	956	–			

73. "Addl." refers to the section titled "Additional Pensées" in Krailsheimer.

WORKS CITED

Antiquity and Early Modern

Arnauld, Antoine, and Pierre Nicole. *The Logic or the Art of Thinking: Being the Port-Royal Logic.* Translated by Th. Spencer Baynes. Edinburgh: Sutherland and Knox, 1850.

Augustine. *The City of God.* Translated by Marcus Dods. From Nicene and Post-Nicene Fathers, 1st ser., vol. 2. Edited by Philip Schaff. Buffalo, N.Y.: Christian Literature Publishing Co., 1887.) Revised and edited for New Advent by Kevin Knight. https://www.newadvent.org/fathers/1201.htm.

———. *Confessions.* 2 vols. With an English translation by W. Watts. Cambridge, Mass.: Harvard University Press, 1960–61.

———. *Confessions.* Translated by R. S. Pine-Coffin. Harmondsworth: Penguin, 1961.

———. *On the Grace of Christ and on Original Sin.* Translated by Peter Holmes and Robert Ernest Wallis, and revised by Benjamin B. Warfield. From Nicene and Post-Nicene Fathers, 1st ser., vol. 5. Edited by Philip Schaff. Buffalo, N.Y.: Christian Literature Publishing Co., 1887. Revised and edited for New Advent by Kevin Knight. http://www.newadvent.org/fathers/1506.htm.

Boileau, Nicolas. *Œuvres.* Edited by Sylvain Menant. Vol. 2, *Épîtres, art poétique, œuvres diverses.* Paris: Garnier-Flammarion, 1969.

Charron, Pierre. *De la sagesse . . ., plus . . . quelques discours chrestiens, trouvez apres le deceds de l'Autheur.* Rouen: Vve Durant, 1623. Published in English as *Of Wisdom,* trans. George Stanhope. 3rd ed. London, 1729.

Cicero. *De oratore* [On the orator]. 2 vols. With an English translation by E. W. Sutton. Cambridge, Mass.: Harvard University Press, 1967–68.

Clemens Placentinus [Giulio Scotti]. *De potestate pontificia in Societatem Jesu* [*The Pontifical power in the Society of Jesus*]. Paris: Barthélemiy Macé, 1646.

Constitutiones Societatis Jesu. Rome: S. J., 1558.

Corneille, Pierre. *Œuvres complètes.* Edited by André Stegmann. Paris, Seuil, 1961.

Cotgrave, Randle. *A Dictionarie of the French and English Tongues.* London: Adam Islip, 1611.

Cum ex apostolatus officio. In *Roman Bullarium,* edited by Girolamo Mainar. 32 vols. (n.p.: 1733–1762), vol. 4, sec. 1, pp. 354–57.

Declarationes et annotations in constitutionibus Societatis Jesu. Rome: S. J., 1559.

Descartes, René. *Discourse on Method and Meditations.* Translated by Laurence J. Lafleur. Indianapolis: Bobbs-Merrill, 1960.

———. *Œuvres de Descartes.* Edited by Charles Adam and Paul Tannery. Vol. 4, *Correspondance.* Paris: Cerf, 1901. Vol. 7, *Meditationes de prima philosophia* [Meditations on first philosophy]. Paris: Cerf, 1904.

———. *Principes de la philosophie.* Textes philosophiques. Paris: Vrin, 1993.

Du Ryer, Pierre, trans. *L'Alcoran de Mahomet.* Paris: A. de Sommaville, 1647.

Epictetus. *The Discourses as reported by Arrian, the Manual, and Fragments*. 2 vols. With an English translation by W. A. Oldfather. Cambridge, Mass.: Harvard University Press, 1985–89.

Epistolæ præpositorum generalium ad patres et fratres Societatis Jesu [Letters from the Generals to the fathers and brothers of the Company of Jesus]. Antwerp: Johann van Meurs, 1635.

Escobar de Mendoza, Antonio. *Liber theologiæ moralis*. Brussels: Franciscus Vivienus, 1651.

Fontaine, Nicolas. *Mémoires ou Histoire des solitaires de Port-Royal* [Memoirs, or History of the solitaires of Port-Royal]. Edited by Pascale Thouvenin. Paris: Champion, 2001.

Furetière, Antoine. *Dictionnaire universel, contenant généralement tous les mots françois tant vieux que modernes, et les termes de toutes les sciences et des arts....* La Haye, A. et R. Leers, 1690.

Gournay, Marie Le Jars de. Preface to *Les Essais de Michel, Seigneur de Montaigne, édition nouvelle*. Paris, Pierre Rocolet, 1635.

Grotius. *The Truth of the Christian Religion*. Edited by Le Clerc, translated by John Clarke. Oxford: Baxter, 1818.

Jansenius, *Oratio de interioris hominis reformation* [Discourse on the reformation of the inner man]. 1628. Translated as *Discours de la reformation de l'homme intérieur*, by Arnaud d'Andilly, 1642.

―――. *Augustinus seu doctrina Sancti Augustini de humanæ naturæ sanitate, ægritudine, medicinâ adversùs Pelagianos et Massilienses*. Louvain: Jacob Zeger, 1640.

La Rochefoucauld, François de. *Maximes et réflexions diverses*. Edited by Jacques Truchet. Paris: Garnier-Flammarion, 1977.

Lafayette, Marie-Madeleine de. *The Princess of Clèves*. Edited and translated by John D. Lyons. New York: W. W. Norton, 1994.

Le Maistre de Sacy, Isaac-Louis. *L'Histoire du Vieux et du Nouveau Testament, représentée avec des figures et des explications ... par le Sieur de Royaumont, prieur de Sombreval* [Le Maistre de Sacy]. 3rd ed. Paris: Le Petit, 1671.

Martin, Raymond. *Pugio Fidei adversus Mauros et Judaeos* [The dagger of faither against the Muslims and the Jews]. Edited by Joseph de Voisin. Paris: M. Henault, 1651.

Méré, Antoine Gombaud, chevalier de. *Œuvres posthumes de M. le Chevalier de Méré*. Paris: Jean and Michel Guignard, 1700.

Montaigne, Michel de. *Les Essais*. Édition Villey-Saulnier (Paris: PUF, 1924; new edition, 1965).

―――. *The Complete Works. Essays, Travel Journals, Letters*. Translated by Donald M. Frame, introduction by Stuart Hampshire. London: Everyman's Library, 1948.

―――. *Essais*. With an Epistle and a preface by Mademoiselle de Gournay. Paris: Pierre Le Petit, 1652.

Nicole, Pierre. *La Vraie Beauté et son fantôme* [*Dissertatio de vera pulchritudine et adumbrata*]. Edited and translated by B. Guion. Paris: Champion, 1996.

Pascal, Blaise. *Entretien avec M. de Sacy*. Unpublished original presented by Pascale Mentgotti and Jean Mesnard. Paris: Les Carnets DDB, 1994.

―――. *Œuvres completes*. Paris: Hachette, 1913 [1871].

―――. *The Provincial Letters, Pensées. Scientific Treatises by Blaise Pascal*. In Great Books of the Western World 33, *Pascal*. New York: Encyclopedia Britannica, 1952.

―――. *The Provincial Letters*. Translated by A. J. Krailsheimer. London: Penguin, 1967.

Périer, Gilberte. *La Vie de M. Pascal, escrite par Mme Perier, sa sœur, femme de M. Perier, conseiller de la Cour des aydes de Clermont*. Amsterdam: Abraham Wolfgang, 1684.

Petronius. *The Satyricon of Petronius Arbiter*. Translated by W. C. Firebaugh. https://www.gutenberg.org/files/5225/5225-h/5225-h.htm#linkVOLUME_III.

Philo. *Volume VI: On Abraham, on Joseph, on Moses*. Translated by F. H. Colson. Loeb Classical Library. Cambridge: Harvard University Press, 1935.

Pierre de Saint-Joseph, Dom. *Response d'un ecclésiastique de Louvain a l'advis qui luy a esté donné sur le sujet de la bulle pretendue du pape Urbain VIII contre le livre de M. Jansenius*. [Reply from a Louvain ecclesiastic to the information given him about the supposed bull of Pope Urban VIII against the book of Mr. Jansenius]. 3rd ed. Louvain, 1650.

Pirot, Georges. *Apologie pour les casuistes contre les calomnies des jansénistes* [Apology for the casuists against the Jansenists' calumnies]. Paris: Gaspar Maturas, 1657.

Tallemant des Réaux, Gédéon. *Historiettes*. Edited by Louis Monmerqué. Paris: Mercure de France, 1906.

The Vatable Bible: Biblia sacra hebraice, græce & latine, cum annotation Francisci Vatabli. Ex officina Sanctandreana, 1686.

Voltaire. "Sur les pensées de M. Pascal." In *Lettres philosophiques*, 289–387. Amsterdam: E. Lucas, 1734.

Voltaire. *Candide*. Paris: Larousse, 2002.

Nineteenth to Twenty-First Centuries

Armour, Leslie. *"Infini Rien": Pascal's Wager and the Human Paradox*. Carbondale: Southern Illinois Press, 1993.

Benjamin, Walter. "The Task of the Translator." In *Selected Writings*, vol. 1, *1913–1926*, edited by Marcus Bullock and Michael W. Jennings, 253–63. Cambridge, Mass.: Harvard University Press, 1996.

Blaise Pascal: L'Homme et l'Œuvre. Cahiers de Royaumont 1. Paris: Editions de Minuit, 1956.

Blocher, Henri. *Original Sin: Illuminating the Riddle*. Grand Rapids, Mich.: Eerdmans, 1999.

Cenkner, William, ed. *Evil and the Response of World Religion*. St. Paul, Minn.: Paragon House, 1997.

Couton, Georges, ed. *L'Édition de Port-Royal*. Saint-Étienne: Université de la région Rhône-Alpes, 1971.

Farrell, John. *Paranoia and Modernity: Cervantes to Rousseau*. Ithaca, N.Y.: Cornell University Press, 2006.

Goldmann, Lucien. *Le Dieu caché: Étude sur la vision tragique dans les "Pensées" de Pascal et le théâtre de Racine*. Paris: Gallimard, 1955. Translated by Philip Thody as *The Hidden God: A Study of Tragic Vision in the Pensées of Pascal and the Tragedies of Racine*. London: Routledge, 1964.

Gouhier, Henri. *Biaise Pascal: Commentaires*. Bibliothèque d'Histoire de la Philosophie. Paris, J. Vrin, 1966.

Grubbs, Henry A. *Damien Miton (1618–1690) "Bourgeois honnête homme"*. Princeton, N.J.: Princeton University Press, 1932.

Hammond, Nicholas. *Playing with Truth: Language and the Human Condition in Pascal's Pensées*. Oxford: Oxford University Press, 1994.

Hammond, Nicholas, and Michael Moriarty. *Evocations of Eloquence: Rhetoric, Literature and Religion in Early Modern France; Essays in Honour of Peter Bayley*. Oxford: Peter Lang, 2012.

Howells, Bernard. "The Interpretation of Pascal's '*Pari*.'" *The Modern Language Review* 79 (1984): 35–63.

Jaouën, Françoise, ed. *Seventeenth-Century French Writers*. Dictionary of Literary Biography 268. Detroit, Mich.: Gale Group, 2002.

Jordan, Jeff. *Pascal's Wager: Pragmatic Arguments and Belief in God*. Oxford: Oxford University Press, 2006.

Kohler, Kauffman. *Jewish Theology: Systematically and Historically Considered*. New York: Ktav, 1968.

Kolakowski, Leszek. *God Owes Us Nothing: A Brief Remark on Pascal's Religion and on the Spirit of Jansenism*. Chicago: University of Chicago Press, 1995.

Lafond, Jean, ed. *Moralistes du XVIIᵉ Siecle. De Pibrac à Dufresny*. Paris: Laffont, 1992.

Larkosh, Christopher, ed. *Re-engendering Translation: Transcultural Practice, Gender/Sexuality and the Politics of Alterity*. Manchester: St Jerome Publishing, 2011.

Lataste, Joseph. "Port-Royal." In vol. 12 of *The Catholic Encyclopedia*. New York: Robert Appleton Company, 1911.

Margolis, Max, and Alexander Marx. *A History of the Jewish People*. Philadelphia: Jewish Publication Society, 1967.

McKenna, Antony. "L'histoire du brochet et de la grenouille: Pascal et Izaac Walton" [The story of the pike and the frog: Pascal and Isaac Walton]. *Courrier du Centre International Blaise Pascal*, December 1990, 18–19. doi: 10.4000/ccibp.637.

———. *Dictionnaire de Port-Royal*. With an introduction by Jean Mesnard and Philippe Sellier. Paris: Honoré Champion, 2001.

———. *Pascal et son libertin*. Littérature, libertinage et spiritualité 6. Paris: Classiques Garnier, 2017.

Melzer, Sara E. *Discourses of the Fall: A Study of Pascal's "Pensées"*. Berkeley: University of California Press, 1986.

Mesnard, Jean, ed. *Blaise Pascal: Textes inédits* [Pascal: Unpublished texts]. Paris: Desclée de Brouwer, 1962.

———. *La Culture du XVIIe siècle: Enquêtes et synthèses*. Paris: PUF, 1991.

Miller, Robert J. *The Jesus Seminar and Its Critics*. Santa Rosa, Calif.: Polebridge Press, 1999.

Pascal, Blaise. *The Provincial Letters, Pensées. Scientific Treatises by Blaise Pascal*. In Great Books of the Western World 33, *Pascal*. New York: Encyclopedia Britannica, 1952.

Pintard, René. *Le Libertinage érudit dans la première moitie du 17e siècle* [Scholarly disbelief in the first half of the 17th century]. Geneva: Slatkin Reprints, 1983.

Pugh, Anthony. *The Composition of Pascal's Apologia*. Toronto: University of Toronto Press, 1984.

Ratzinger, Joseph. *"In the Beginning. . ." A Catholic Understanding of the Story of Creation and Fall*. Translated by Boniface Ramsey, OP. Grand Rapids, Mich.: Eerdmans, 1990.

Sachar, Howard M. *The Course of Modern Jewish History*. Cleveland, Ohio: World Publishing, 1958.

Scholar, Richard. *The "je ne sais quoi" in Early Modern Europe: Encounters with a Certain Something*. Oxford: Oxford University Press, 2005.

Sellier, Philippe. *Port-Royal et la littérature. Vol. 1, Pascal. 2nd ed. Paris: Champion, 2010.

Steinmann, Jean. *Richard Simon et les origines de l'exégèse biblique*. Paris: Desclée de Brouwer, 1959.

Strack, Hermann L. *Introduction to the Talmud and Midrash*. Minneapolis: Fortress Press, 1996.

Thirouin, Laurent. *Le Hasard et les Règles: Le modèle du jeu dans la pensée de Pascal* [Chance and rules: The model of game theory in the thought of Pascal]. Paris: Vrin, 1991.

Wittig, Monique. "Mark of Gender." In *The Straight Mind, and Other Essays*, 76–89. Boston: Beacon Press, 1992.

Zoberman, Pierre. "'*Homme*' peut-il vouloir dire '*femme*'? Gender and Translation in Seventeenth-Century French Moral Literature." In *The Gender and Queer Politics of Translation: Literary, Historical and Cultural Approaches*, edited by William Spurlin, 231–52. Comparative Literature Studies 51. University Park, Pa.: Penn State Press, 2014.

BIOGRAPHY OF PHILIPPE SELLIER

Philippe Sellier (1931–), Professor Emeritus of the University of Paris—Sorbonne, is universally respected as the preeminent specialist on the *Pensées* of Blaise Pascal and the literature emanating from Port-Royal. When I came under his tutelage in 1976, the second edition of his groundbreaking edition of *Pensées*, based upon the largely ignored but most accurate Second Copy, had just been published. It remained untranslated into English in a scholarly edition until the present volume, which is based upon Sellier's 2010 edition of the text.

Professor Sellier received the doctorate in History of Religions in 1965 and the Doctorat d'État ès lettres, under the direction of the venerable René Pintard, in 1970. His exhaustive study of *Pascal and St. Augustine* (1970) remains the authoritative text on the subject, as does his *Pascal and the Liturgy* (1966).

Sellier's work was closely allied with that of Jean Mesnard, dean of Pascal studies until his death in 2016. Together, they rehabilitated and vastly expanded the primordial religious and theological dimensions of the *Pensées*, which had fallen into neglect in the wave of modernist literary criticism that swept France in the 1960s. Named Professor at the Sorbonne in 1988, Sellier inherited Mesnard's seminar on Pascal and Port-Royal, which inspired generations of young Pascal scholars from many countries. He was, and continues to be known as a generous mentor and adviser of students from a great many countries from as far away as Japan who come to France to study under his tutelage.

Of greatest interest to our readers will be Sellier's exhaustive, three volume *Port-Royal and Literature* (1999–2019). The first of the volumes is devoted to Pascal; the second to the other writers of the Classical period in France who gravitated around or were influenced by Port-Royal: Racine, La Rochefoucauld, Mme de Lafayette and Fenelon; the third, *From Cassian to Pascal*. Of equal interest will be his *Essays on the Classical Imagination: Pascal and Racine* (2005).

Always approaching his work on Pascal, the *Pensées*, and Port-Royal from the perspective of his training as a religious scholar, a background rare among professors of literature, Sellier was long interested in the history of the Bible in pre-modern France. The closest translation into Classical French comparable to the Authorized Version in English, the monumental Bible of Le Maître de Sacy (1672–93) was long unavailable to readers. To Philippe Sellier we owe the first modern edition of the Sacy Bible (1990), with his own brilliant preface.

In his *The Bible: Toward the Sources of Western Culture* (2016), Sellier explores how episodes in scripture have inspired painters, philosophers, writers, sculptors, and cineastes. And in his *The Bible Explained to Those Who Have Not Read It* (2007) he had returned to exercise himself that apologetic discourse which he spent a lifetime exploring in the *Pensées*. He is presently working on a new book on Pascal and original sin.

Our translation of the *Pensées* into English, some twenty years in the making, has been eclipsed by translations into seven other languages. Nonetheless, and with our apologies, we present this translation to Professor Sellier in the year after his ninetieth birthday.

David Wetsel

ABOUT THE GENERAL EDITOR

Pierre Zoberman, Professor Emeritus at Université Sorbonne-Paris-Nord, has published extensively on the literature and the social history of the Ancien Régime. He is the author of two award-winning books on ceremonial oratory during Louis XIV's reign, *Les Panégyriques du Roi prononcés dans l'Académie française (1671-1689)* (Paris: Presses de l'Université Paris-Sorbonne, 1991)— which won the Prix de littérature Générale from the Académie française, 1992—and *Les Cérémonies de la parole* (Paris: Champion, 1998)—winner of the Prix Thiers from the Académie française, 1999. He has edited or co-edited ten volumes, including *Interpretation in/of the Seventeenth Century* (Cambridge: Cambridge Scholars Publishing, 2015). His recent work has centered on questions of gender and sexual identities in early modern culture—"Genre et littérature au XVIIᵉ siècle: *La Princesse de Clèves* et ses enjeux politiques," *Lublin Studies in Languages and Literature* 43, no. 1 (March 2019)—and specifically moral literature—"No Place for (a) Woman: the Generic Use of *l'homme/ les hommes* as a Gendered Discursive and Cultural Topos," in W. Brooks, Chr. Probes, and R. Zaiser, eds., *Les Lieux de culture dans la France de la première modernité*, 2012. In a comparative perspective, he has explored the contrasting ways in which scholars view issues of gender and sexuality in the French and Anglo-Saxon cultural contexts—"Gender, Identity, Sexuality: French and American Approaches," in B. Bolduc and H. Goldwyn, eds., *Concordia Discors* (Tübingen: Narr, 2011)—and addressed issues of translation in "'Homme' peut-il vouloir dire 'femme'? Gender and Translation in Seventeenth-Century French Moral Literature," *Comparative Literature Studies* 51, no. 2 (May 2014): 231–52; and "Scarron's Taming of the Shrew," *Seventeenth-Century French Studies* 36, no. 2 (December 2014): 156–71. He is currently preparing a book on Proust's intertextual dialogue with early modern writers (Pascal, Racine, La Bruyère, and Saint-Simon).

THE TRANSLATORS

PIERRE FORCE, Professor of French and History at Columbia University, received his academic training in France, where he was a fellow of the École normale supérieure. He took his BA in Classics (1979), doctorate in French (1987), and habilitation (1994) at the Sorbonne. He works at the interface between the humanities and the social sciences and has published in the fields of early modern French literature, intellectual history, and social history. He is the author of *Le Problème herméneutique chez Pascal* (Paris: Vrin, 1989), *Molière ou Le Prix des choses* (Paris: Nathan, 1994), *Self-Interest before Adam Smith* (Cambridge: Cambridge University Press, 2003), and *Wealth and Disaster* (Baltimore: Johns Hopkins University Press, 2016).

JOHN A. GALLUCCI is Professor of French at Colgate University, Hamilton, N.Y. He has published articles on Pascal, La Fontaine, and Boileau; and, more recently, on the images of Native Americans in the Latin writings of the Jesuit missionaries to Canada in the seventeenth century. He has translated and edited the book *Castorland Journal: An Account of the Exploration and Settlement of Northern New York State by French Emigrés in the Years 1793 to 1797* (Ithaca: Cornell University Press, 2010).

NICHOLAS HAMMOND specializes in seventeenth-century French thought, drama, poetry, and culture. He is the author of *Playing with Truth: Language and the Human Condition in Pascal's Pensées* (Oxford: Oxford University Press, 1994); *Creative Tensions: An Introduction to Seventeenth-Century French Literature* (London: Duckworth, 1997); *Fragmentary Voices: Memory and Education at Port-Royal*, Biblio 17 (Tübingen: Narr, 2004); *Gossip, Sexuality and Scandal in France (1610–1715)* (Oxford: Peter Lang, 2011); *The Powers of Sound and Song in Early Modern Paris* (University Park, Penn.: Penn State University Press, 2020). He is also the editor of the *Cambridge Companion to Pascal* (2003). He is the editor of a special issue of the journal *Early Modern French Studies* devoted to soundscapes (vol. 41, no. 1, 2019); and co-editor, with Bill Burgwinkle and Emma Wilson, of *The Cambridge History of French Literature* (2011); and, with Michael Moriarty, of *Evocations of Eloquence: Rhetoric, Literature and Re-*

ligion in early modern France (Oxford: Peter Lang, 2012); and, with Joseph Harris, *Racine's "Andromaque": Absences and Displacements* (Leiden: Brill, 2019).

EREC R. KOCH is Dean of the Division of the Humanities and the Arts at the City College of New York, CUNY, and he is Professor of French at Hunter College, CUNY, and the CUNY Graduate Center. He has published extensively on Pascal and Jansenism, seventeenth-century French theatre, the moralists, and early modern philosophy and history of medicine. His most recent book, *The Aesthetic Body: Passion, Sensibility, and Corporeality in Seventeenth-Century France* (2008), examines, in that century, the transformation of models of the passions and of how emotions were produced and controlled. He is currently working on a study, tentatively titled "Before Aesthetics," that explores taste as a faculty associated with sociability in early modern France and accounts for its shift to a faculty associated with aesthetics in the late eighteenth century.

FRANK MARINER is Associate Professor of French Emeritus in the Department of World Languages and Cultures at Iowa State University. He has published a wide range of articles in Pascal studies and on life-writing genres and practices in the early modern period, including a book on Jansenist memoir writing, *Histoires et autobographies spirituelles: les Mémoires de Fontaine, Lancelot et Du Fossé* (Tübingen: Gunter Narr Verlag, 1998).

MICHAEL MORIARTY is Drapers Professor of French at the University of Cambridge, and a Fellow of Peterhouse. He was formerly Centenary Professor of French Literature and Thought at Queen Mary, University of London. He works chiefly on the literature and thought of the early modern period. His publications include *Early Modern French Thought: The Age of Suspicion* (Oxford: Oxford University Press, 2003); *Fallen Nature, Fallen Selves: Early Modern French Thought II* (Oxford: Oxford University Press, 2006); and *Disguised Vices: Theories of Virtue in Early Modern French Thought* (Oxford: Oxford University Press, 2011). He has published various articles on Pascal. He is a Fellow of the British Academy and a Chevalier dans l'Ordre des Palmes Académiques.

RICHARD PARISH, (d. 2022), was an emeritus professor of French at the University of Oxford and a fellow of St. Catherine's College. He published extensively on Pascal as well as on other writers of the French Catholic reformation and on neo-classical theater. His *Catholic Particularity in Seventeenth-Century French Writing: "Christianity is Strange"* was published in 2011. He was appointed Commandeur dans l'Ordre des Palmes Académiques in 2012.

RICHARD SCHOLAR is Professor of French at Durham University. He moved to Durham in 2019, having spent thirteen years as Fellow and Tutor in French at Oriel College, University of Oxford, where from 2015 he was also Professor of French and Comparative Literature. He has published widely on early modern French literature and thought, comparative literature, and critical method. Among his publications are several journal articles on Pascal and an edition of Pascal's *Entretien avec Sacy sur la philosophie* (Arles: Actes Sud, 2003) based on the original autograph. Other publications include *The "Je-Ne-Sais-Quoi" in Early Modern Europe: Encounters with a Certain Something* (Oxford: Oxford University Press, 2005); and *Montaigne and the Art of Free-Thinking* (Oxford: Peter Lang, 2010). Both books have been translated into French. He is also the author of *Émigrés: French Words that Turned English* (Princeton University Press, 2020). He is currently continuing his work on the European afterlives of Thomas More's *Utopia*

PAUL SCOTT is associate professor of French at the University of Kansas and specializes in early modern subversion and has published widely on theater, liturgy, and fashion. He is a fellow of the Royal Society of Arts and of the Royal Historical Society.

DAVID WETSEL, Professor Emeritus at Arizona State University, is the author of *L'Ecriture et le reste: The Pensées of Pascal and the Exegetical Tradition of Port-Royal* and *Pascal and Disbelief: Catechesis and Conversion in the Pensées*, and numerous articles, book chapters and encyclopedia entries on Pascal, Port-Royal, and anti-Christian thought in the Classical period. His other writings include the literature of the AIDS crisis in France and papers on the French language in Louisiana. He received a doctorate from Brandeis University and a masters in divinity from the Divinity School of the University of Chicago. Organizer of an International Colloquium in honor of the eightieth birthday of Jean Mesnard, he edited the five volumes of papers presented at that conference. He was president of the North American Society for Seventeenth-Century Literature and a Visiting Professor at the University of Stuttgart. He was awarded the Palmes Academiques by the French Republic for his efforts to preserve the native French of Louisiana. He became a pupil and disciple of Philippe Sellier in 1977 when writing his doctoral dissertation and later lectured in Professor Sellier's Pascal Seminar at the Sorbonne. Wetsel authored the introduction and notes for the present volume, assisted in the translation and editing of the text, and wrote the introduction to Richard Scholar's translation of *The Exchange with M. de Sacy*.

INDEX

N. B. Some terms (such as *Christ, reason, thought, time, truth, world*), which play an important role in Pascal's writing, have nonetheless not been included in this index, as the sheer number of occurrences would make the entries, not only unwieldy, but practically useless.

1. The term *Authority* gives its title to Chapter XLIV (340–42).

2. When *certain* is used as an indefinite adjective (as in *certain facts*), it is not recorded in the index. The term *certainly* has also been ignored, because of its loose relationship to the notion of certainty.

3. The term *Church* here refers to *the Church* as an institution (as in *Fathers of the Church*), or a division thereof, not to a specific building (*a church*).

4. Chapter XIII (89–96) bears the title, "Contradictions."

5. The term *corrupt* and its cognates are taken in their moral sense.

6. Chapter XVII (135–41) bears the title, "Nature Is Corrupt and Falsity of Other Religions."

7. Chapter XLVII (363–71) bears the title, "Discourse on Corruption;" Chapter LIII (383–89) bears the title, "Around Corruption;" and Chapter LX (417–19) bears the title, "Prophecies, Jews, Corruption."

8. The verb, *to create*, as well as *Creation* here will refer to *the Creation* or such occurrences as *the creation man* or *of the world*.

9. Except for Pascal's death, the term refers here to death in general, not to the death of specific individuals.

10. Truth in general, and the truth of the Christian religion (i.e. that the Christian religion be true).

11. *Diversion* is the title of Chapter IX (99–103).

12. This entry does not include occurrences of *doubtless*, *undoubtedly*, which do not have the same metaphysical and religious implications.

13. Chapter VI (77–84) bears the title, "Reasons for Effects."

14. The short Chapter V (76) bears the title, "*Ennui* and the Essential Qualities of Man."

---

15. Chapter XVII (135–41) bears the title, "Nature Is Corrupt and Falsity of Other Religions."

---

16. Chapter XX (150–72) bears the title, "That the Law Was Figurative" and chapter LVI (420–23) bears the title, "Law Was Figurative."

17. The term *figure* here refers to figurative representation.

18. The very short Chapter XXVI bears the title, "Particular Figures" (194)

19. Chapter XIX (144–49) bears the title, "Foundations of Religion and Reply to Objections."

20. Chapters XLII (336) and XLIII (337–39) bear the title, "Geometry/Intuition" [1] and [2].

21. Chapter VII (85–88) bears the title, "Greatness."

23. The entry does not include references in the footnotes to the chapters titled "Miracles."
24. Chapters XXX, XXXI, and XXXII (211–44) bear are titled "Miracle" 1, 2, and 3.

25. The "Exchange with M. de Sacy on Epictetus and Montaigne" covers 497–512, with an Introduction (491–96).

26. Pascal's *nom de plume* when he published the *Provincial Letters*.

27. Chapter XXIII (173–75) bears the title, "Proofs of Moses."

28. *Mystery* here does not refer to trivially puzzling attitudes, as when Pascal's sister does not understand her brother's behavior (see *The Life…*, 29), but religious and/or metaphysical elements hard to fathom for the human mind.

29. Chapter XXVII (135–41) bears the title, "Nature is Corrupt and Falsity of Other Religions".

30. The term refers to the *notion* of order, not to a command or religious orders, nor to phrases such as *in order to.*

31. Chapter II (52–54) bears the title, "Order."

32. Only occurrences of the term *perfectly* that could be interpreted as referring to perfection (no matter how remotely) have been recorded. Occurrences of the term used only as an equivalent of *completely* have been omitted.

33. Chapter X (104–5) bears the title, "Philosophers."

34. The *Exchange with M. de Sacy...* (497–512, preceded by an introduction, 491–96) is explicitly devoted to Epictetus and Montaigne, hence the heightened frequency of occurrences of cognates of *philosopher*.

35. Chapter XXIII (173–75) bears the title, "Proofs of Moses."

36. Chapter XXIV (176–84) bears the title, "Proofs of Jesus Christ."

37. Chapter XXV (185–93) bears the title, "Prophecies."

38. Chapters LIV-LIX (390–416) bear the title, "Prophecies" (1, 2 … 6), and Chapter LX (417–19) bears the title, "Prophecies, Jews, Corruption."

39. Chapter VI (77–84) bears the title "Reasons for Effects."

---

40. References to the "Exchange with M. de Sacy," included in this volume, are too numerous to be usefully included here.

41. Chapter XLVI (355–65) bears the title, "Letter Urging the Search for God."

42. The entry refers to the *self* as an entity. In most cases, occurrences with compound words (such as *self-portrait, self-satisfied*) have been ignored.

---

43. *Sense*, here, refers to a kind of understanding, as in the following phrases: *common sense, good sense, natural sense.*

44. Chapter XI (106–7) bears the title, "The Sovereign Good."

45. Chapter XIV (118–22) bears the title, "Submission and Use of Reason."

46. Chapter III (55–66) bears the title, "Vanity."

47. Chapter XLV, "Discourse on the Machine" (345–53) is more commonly known as "The Wager."

48. Chapter IV (67–75) bears the title, "Wretchedness."

Pensées was designed in Arno Pro and composed by
Kachergis Book Design of Pittsboro, North Carolina.
It was printed on 55-pound Natural Offset and bound
by Maple Press of York, Pennsylvania.